PennyPress®

PUZZLER'S GIANT BOOK OF CROSSWORDS 11

Penny Press is the publisher of a fine family of puzzle magazines and books renowned for their editorial excellence.

This delightful collection has been carefully selected by the editors of Penny Press for your special enjoyment and entertainment.

PENNY PRESS, INC.
6 Prowitt Street, Norwalk, Connecticut 06855-1220

Printed in Canada

PENNY PRESS PUZZLE PUBLICATIONS

◆ PUZZLE MAGAZINES ◆

All-Star Variety Puzzles
All-Star Word Seek Puzzles
Approved Variety Puzzles
  Plus Crosswords
Classic Variety Puzzles
  Plus Crosswords
Easy & Fun Variety Puzzles and Games
Easy Crossword Express
England's Best Logic Problems
Family Variety Puzzles & Crosswords Plus
Family Variety Puzzles & Games
Fast & Easy Crosswords
Favorite Easy Crosswords
Favorite Fill-In Puzzles
Favorite Variety Puzzles & Games
Favorite Word Seek Puzzles
Fill-In Puzzles
Garfield's Easy Crosswords
Garfield's Word Seeks

Good Time Crossword Puzzles
Good Time Variety Puzzles
Good Time Word Seek Puzzles
Large-Print Crossword Puzzles
Master's Variety Puzzles Plus
Merit Variety Puzzles & Games
Movie & TV Crosswords
Nice & Easy Crosswords
Original Logic Problems
Penny's Famous Fill-In Puzzles
Quick & Easy Crosswords
Recipe Word Seek Puzzles
Super Word Seek Puzzles
Tournament Variety Puzzles Plus
Variety Puzzles & Games
Variety Puzzles Special Issue Plus
Word Seek Puzzles
World-Class Logic Problems Special
World's Finest Variety Puzzles

◆ SPECIAL COLLECTIONS ◆

Selected Anagram
  Magic Square
Selected Brick by Brick
Selected Codewords
Selected Crostics
Selected Crypto-Families
Selected Cryptograms
Selected Diagramless
Selected Double Trouble

Selected Flower Power
Selected Frameworks
Selected Jigsaw
  Squares
Selected Letterboxes
Selected Masterwords
Selected Missing List
  Word Seeks
Selected Missing Vowels

Selected Places, Please
Selected Quotagrams
Selected Quotefalls
Selected Scoremaster
Selected Syllacrostics
Selected Word Games
  Puzzles
Selected Word Math

◆ PUZZLER'S GIANT BOOKS ◆

Crosswords   Word Games   Word Seeks

Puzzler's Giant Book of Crosswords, June 2004, No. 11. Puzzler's Giant Books are published quarterly (March, June, September, December) by Penny Press, Inc., 6 Prowitt Street, Norwalk, CT 06855-1220. On the web at www.pennypress.com.

Penny Press is a trademark registered in the U.S. Patent Office.

ISBN: 1-55956-872-0   Printed in Canada

ACROSS

1. Caviar
4. Little devil
7. Spanish cheer
10. Mama sheep
13. Anger
14. Sketched
16. Posy
18. Speak bluntly
21. Otherwise
22. For
23. One, in Bonn
24. Stare at
27. Shower
30. Funny guy
33. Household god
34. Bustle
35. Space
38. Pie ____ mode
39. Curvy letter
40. Sign up
42. ____ firma
44. Nudge
46. Consumed
48. Newsman Rather
49. Crazy
50. Existed
52. Evergreen
53. Make do
54. Copy
55. Actress Merkel
56. Actor Danson
57. Actor Beatty
58. Actor Olin
59. Unused
60. Oarsman
62. Made a mistake
64. Go downhill
67. Exclamation of disgust
69. Mineral source
70. Numerals: abbr.
71. Limb
73. ____ Khan
74. Patriotic org.
75. Blackthorn
76. Rogers and Scheider
78. RBI, e.g.
81. Commercials
83. Floundering
87. Make a fresh start
92. At a loss
93. Low joint
94. Ms. Gabor
95. Recipe abbr.
96. Little Woman
97. Favorite
98. Each

DOWN

1. Oriental staple
2. Aloud
3. Snakelike fishes
4. Actress Lupino
5. "____ Miniver"
6. Green and red veggies
7. Singleton
8. Mauna ____
9. Ruhr Valley city
10. Actor Richard
11. Walk through water
12. Orb
15. Armed conflict
17. Finial
19. Zodiac sign
20. Copperfield's wife
25. Gathered painfully
26. ____ Vegas
28. Summer drink
29. Particle
30. Hose
31. Pub brew
32. Flower growers
35. Yellow weed
36. Priest's vestment
37. Turn beneath the soil
41. Harvester
43. Autumn lawn workers
45. Wax and ____
46. Toward the stern
47. Stadium layer
49. Seize an opportunity
51. Adage
61. Pitch ____
63. Historical time
65. House wing
66. New: pref.
67. Root veggie
68. Past
72. Equipment
75. Hurricane
77. "My Gal ____"
78. Has a bite at night
79. Snare
80. Pismire
82. Poppa
84. Ooze
85. Roof overhang
86. Distant
87. Egyptian king, for short
88. Victory sign
89. Brain scan: abbr.
90. Holiday night
91. Sopping

PUZZLE 2

ACROSS
1. Moist
5. Canine
8. Query
11. Perfect
13. Inspire respect
14. Foot digit
15. Saying
16. Acceptable
18. City
20. Ready for business
21. Movie house
24. Lad
26. Fragrance
27. Spare
29. Beret or tam
32. Cow call
33. Solitary
34. Conceit
35. Moose
36. Lease
37. King of the beasts
38. Emote
39. Emanate
41. Pokey
44. Boast
45. See
48. Summarize
52. Sick
53. Lubricate
54. Scoundrel
55. Wedding-announcement word
56. Cave dweller
57. Sketched

DOWN
1. Faded
2. Fuss
3. Convened
4. Talk
5. Daybreak
6. Be in debt
7. Set
8. Above
9. Any
10. Sharp
12. Weaver's need
17. Demure
19. Billfold
21. Arrive
22. Fan's favorite
23. Alcove
24. Teasing talk
25. Three Dog Night hit
28. Time period
29. Beneficiary
30. Expectant
31. Pitch
33. Curve
37. Saga
38. Lager
40. Denote
41. Connect
42. Fit
43. Wight or Man
44. Pants support
46. Pilfer
47. By way of
49. Sedan
50. Hail!
51. Church seat

PUZZLE 3

ACROSS
1. Stockings
5. Marsh
8. Water-blockers
12. Competent
13. Hatchet
14. Spoken
15. Las Vegas game
17. Nil
18. For each
19. Standard
20. Leaven
21. Tell
23. Worth
26. Not in
27. Taste
30. Revise
31. Sphere
32. Soft drink
33. Child
34. Baby goat
35. Convivial
36. Extract
38. Finicky
42. Catch
43. Embrace
46. Paradise
47. Sport for Dodgers
49. Chromosomal part
50. Craft
51. Sea bird
52. Fill fully
53. Stain
54. School official

DOWN
1. String instrument
2. Woodwind
3. Smear
4. Snakelike fish
5. Deadly
6. Exceptional
7. Formerly called
8. Nod off
9. Region
10. Red planet
11. Place for a coin
16. Rapier's kin
20. Still
21. Groove
22. Vat
23. Dog doc
24. Commotion
25. Blazing
27. Sun
28. Sick
29. Remit
31. Lubricate
32. Bunk
34. Francis Scott ____
35. Agree
37. Social system
38. Dowels
39. Thought
40. Penny
41. Leg joint
43. Rabbit
44. Arm bone
45. Valley
47. Naughty
48. Cradle

6

PUZZLE 4

ACROSS
1. Purse
4. Singer Johnny
8. Lake makers
12. ____ Le Gallienne
13. Miami of ____
14. Western state
15. Summit
16. Sounded
17. Quite a few
18. Show disdain
20. Express shock
22. Baby's seat
24. Required
28. Breakfast fare
32. Old saying
33. Bitter brew
34. Took the cake
36. Jogged
37. Regulating device
40. Moments
43. Complete
45. Lambaste
46. Preservative
48. Savage one
52. "The King ____": 2 wds.
55. Barbie or Ken
57. Cote call
58. Sore big-toe cause
59. Great Lake
60. Sn
61. Has bills

62. Slender as a ____
63. Crafty

DOWN
1. Track transactions
2. Shakespeare's river
3. Yawn
4. Ranch pen
5. Eureka!
6. Play the canary
7. Golfer Ben
8. Discarded
9. One ____ time: 2 wds.
10. Homo sapiens
11. Timid
19. Leprechaun
21. Black or Red
23. Church seat
25. Mend socks
26. Mild oath
27. Cozy places
28. Sea feature
29. Comic King
30. Hat material
31. Distress signal
35. Tennis court divider
38. Pays a call
39. Roman or Tudor
41. Wired
42. Billfold item
44. Church officer
47. Wrenched

49. Drama units
50. Earth
51. Actor Danza
52. Past
53. This minute

54. Expected
56. Prevaricate

PUZZLE 5

ACROSS
1. Pitcher spout
4. The pair of them
8. Remote
12. Pub drink
13. Magnet
14. Arrived
15. Valuable metal
17. Elm, for one
18. Previously
19. Demon
20. Encroach upon
23. Storage drawer
24. "____ Men Don't Wear Plaid"
25. Suitcases
29. Building parcel
30. Lager and Pilsner
32. Pekoe or oolong
33. Put in bondage
35. Home VIPs
36. Fine-wine trait
37. Go by
39. Baby beds
42. Empty the boat
43. Give a job
44. With drawing power
48. Matinee ____
49. Skillful
50. Court in love
51. Puts to paper
52. Number suffix

53. Ump's call

DOWN
1. ____ of luxury
2. Sickly
3. Soup or jacket
4. "Three ____ Mice"
5. Small weight
6. Make level
7. Sewn edge
8. Olivier's forte
9. Get along
10. Sound from a church corner
11. Oliver or Rex
16. Loathsome one
19. Pear-shaped fruits
20. At rest
21. Broadway light
22. Tubs
23. Lawyers' group
25. Bonnet buzzer
26. At the peak of
27. Muffins
28. Soothe
30. Hunts successfully
31. Ms. Merriam
34. Tabs
35. He
37. American bird
38. Flax cloth
39. Golf shot

40. Astronaut Sally
41. Do laundry work
42. Baseballer Ruth
44. Pad at the gym
45. Company, proverbially

46. Debt letters
47. Camp bed

PUZZLE 6

Theme Words

There are eight Theme Words in this puzzle which are related to one another.

ACROSS

1. Successful show
4. Pig's digs
7. From ____ Z
8. Refrain syllable
9. Ribbed fabric
10. Active person
11. Three in Italy
12. Mountain ash
13. Counterfeit
15. Entered a pool, in a way
16. Eared seal
18. Comedian Johnson
19. Dudgeon
20. Vermilion
22. Listened
24. Ampersand
25. Scull
26. TV spots
27. Butterfingers' word
29. Wed
31. Theme Word
33. Theme Word
36. Pick over
37. Auditor: abbr.
40. Night before a holiday
41. Pennies: abbr.
42. Puritan work ____
44. Four-in-hand
45. Government medical agency: abbr.
46. Execrate
47. Frighten
49. Importune
51. Politician Long
52. Theme Word
53. Opposite of NNW
54. Queue
55. Beige
56. Double curve
57. Car starter: abbr.
58. Tiny
59. Society-page word

DOWN

1. Theme Word
2. Repeat
3. Theme Word
4. "Uncle Tom's Cabin" author
5. Tire pattern
6. Skein substance
10. Theme Word
12. Actress Gam et al.
14. Baseball misplay
15. Slave Scott
17. Fifty-two weeks
18. Exclamation of surprise
19. Bugs
21. Arid
23. Dunce
24. GI's address: abbr.
28. Unit of resistance
29. Wire measure
30. Wheel rod
32. Greek letters
33. Matched group
34. Rara ____
35. Parasite
37. Pursue
38. Coal mines
39. One-spot
41. Theme Word
43. The ones here
45. Forecast
48. Theme Word
49. Equilibrium
50. Wash lightly
52. Puffed

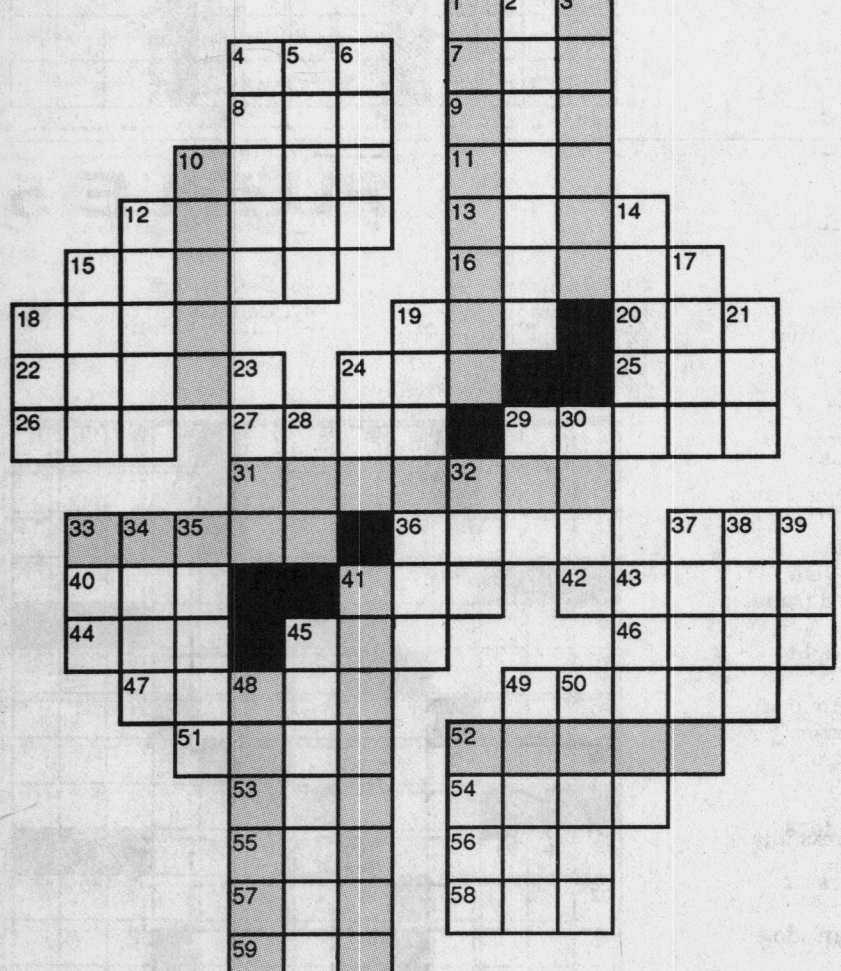

8

PUZZLE 7

ACROSS
1. Ms. Teasdale
5. Tennis stroke
8. Examine
12. Paradise
13. Telephone ____
15. Recurring tap
16. Plane curve
17. Coral island
19. Table support
20. Negative
21. Meat
23. Spread hay
25. Gosh!
27. Card game
29. Auto
33. Blunders
35. Exclamation of disgust
37. Broad
38. City officer
40. Except
42. Plant
43. Crony
45. Disorder
47. Batter
50. Encore
52. Blossom
55. Hostile
58. Stew pot
59. Harden
60. Done
61. Finales
62. Shirt type
63. Mountaintop

DOWN
1. Bristle
2. Mine entrance
3. Act of getting well
4. Body joint
5. Cut off
6. Semiprecious stone
7. Flat cap
8. Flap
9. English school
10. Indian shrub
11. Serving platter
14. Storms
18. Fall behind
22. Edge
24. Light moisture
25. Jewel
26. Age
28. Seize suddenly
30. Melt
31. Fuss
32. Modern
34. Soak up
36. Sing wordlessly
39. Mad
41. Vat
44. Lawful
46. Sailing vessel
47. Go up
48. Presently
49. Gentle
51. Out of danger
53. Olive genus
54. Goodson of game shows
56. Wrong: pref.
57. Harsh alkaline

PUZZLE 8

ACROSS
1. Mr. Namath
4. Gloomy
8. Part of GBS
12. Gershwin
13. California town
14. Evergreen
15. 1969 Indy 500 champ
18. Hockey star
19. Surname of the only brothers to win the Indy 500
20. Mechanics' needs
23. Skidded
25. Thomas ____ Edison
26. Backers
30. Peleg's son
31. Sources
32. Large snake
33. 1957 Indy 500 winner
35. Tableland
36. French river
37. Oscar ____
38. Scottish county
41. Race-car part
42. 1963 Indy 500 winner
48. Oklahoma city
49. Car
50. Constellation
51. Knocks
52. Hebrew measure
53. Dab

DOWN
1. Singer Croce
2. ____ pro nobis
3. Auricle
4. Gates
5. Slightly open
6. Sped
7. Young goat
8. Disburses
9. Top songs
10. Poker stake
11. Dam
16. Kansas town
17. Wrecks
20. Sailors
21. Olive genus
22. Egg
23. Talked
24. Land parcels
26. Offspring
27. Heed
28. Flower
29. German district
31. Pay increase
34. Hunting dogs
35. Note
37. Military rank
38. Mimicker
39. "Peter Pan" dog
40. Hold
41. Summon
43. ____-tse
44. "____ and Abner"
45. Short sleep
46. Historic period
47. Used a chair

PUZZLE 9

ACROSS
1. Twenty-four hours
4. Dog's foot
7. Favorite
10. "___ Got a Secret"
11. Single unit
12. Sailor's response
13. Nurse's concern
15. Ocean
16. California and Alaska
18. Of an epoch
21. Make happy
24. Competitor
26. Throws a fit
27. Backbone
28. Writing tools
29. Vipers
32. Take a chair
34. Welcomed
38. Fuss
39. Aquatic eagle
40. Miner's quest
41. Armed conflict
42. Fast flier
43. Fresh

DOWN
1. Brief swim
2. Actress Gardner
3. However
4. Verse maker
5. "___ Karenina"
6. Damper
7. Corridor
8. Ogle
9. Steeped beverage
14. "Treasure ___"
17. Pass, as time
18. Stammering sounds
19. Tear
20. Flier
22. Finger count
23. Curvy letter
25. Shelves
30. Makes mistakes
31. Tenant's payment
32. Witnessed
33. Journalist Wells
35. Heavy weight
36. Before
37. Morning moisture

PUZZLE 10

ACROSS
1. Info
5. Actor Baldwin
9. Singer Jerry ___ Lewis
12. Eve's mate
13. Fleetwood Mac hit
14. Caviar
15. Exercise system
16. Small bouquets
18. Menageries
20. Piano-key material
21. Declare
24. Unit
25. Shut
26. The Sunshine State
30. Coal scuttle
31. Inflate dishonestly
32. Demand payment from
33. Longed
36. Revise
38. Craving
39. Underhanded
40. Gambler's destination
43. Cloy
44. Individuality
46. "Kiss Me ___"
50. Ripen
51. Historic times
52. Type of jacket or collar
53. Bandleader Brown
54. City on the Truckee
55. Pull apart

DOWN
1. Doris or Dennis
2. Commotion
3. Label
4. Flabbergasts
5. Neck wear
6. Asian land
7. Blunder
8. Monte Carlo establishment
9. Corporate symbol
10. At all times
11. Trouble-free
17. State positively
19. Mine output
21. Sore
22. Blackthorn fruit
23. Pop
24. Ancient
26. Craze
27. Brainstorm
28. Immerse
29. Griffith or Devine
31. Sty
34. Baseball's Nolan
35. Homesteader
36. Picnic intruder
37. More submissive
39. Authority
40. Small bottle
41. Rim
42. Turns to the right
43. Saxophonist Getz
45. Wrath
47. Broke bread
48. 2,000 pounds
49. Finish

ACROSS

1. Gab
5. Foxy
8. Mimics
12. Toil
14. Certain gem cut
16. Succotash bean
17. Blue
18. Wife of a rajah
19. Yoked animals
20. Biblical fisherman
21. Pen fluids
22. Baseball team
23. Prod
25. Rimmed
27. Call
30. Agile
32. Feeble
33. Feed the kitty
35. Gladden
40. Straddling
42. Extreme
44. Vapor
45. Pound down
47. Photographer's need
48. Gone
50. Man from Stockholm
52. Explode
55. Gardener, at times
57. Path
58. High
60. Bid
65. Related
66. Incensed
67. Business
68. Allot
69. Quote
70. Equipped to hear
71. Make tea
72. Cave
73. Decades

DOWN

1. Applaud
2. Smog
3. Touch on
4. Sped
5. Small branch
6. Having the least fat
7. Jerk
8. Beside
9. Fairy
10. Revise
11. Rational
13. Summer TV feature
15. Stair part
24. Peruse
26. Tinted
27. Nuisance
28. Detest
29. Gumbo ingredient
31. Hair wave
32. Existed
34. Gains
36. Biography theme
37. Tart
38. Story
39. Shade tree
41. Demons
43. Church recess
46. Michael Jordan, e.g.
49. Garret
51. Authored
52. Pastry chef
53. Merge
54. Update
56. Ancient
57. Mary had one
59. Parched
61. College social gp.
62. Charge
63. Paradise
64. Beatty flick

Linkwords

Add a Linkword to the end of the word on the left and the beginning of the word on the right to form two compound words or phrases. The dashes indicate the number of letters in the Linkword. For example, if the words were PEANUT _ _ _ _ _ _ FLY, the Linkword would be BUTTER (Peanut butter, Butterfly).

1. BUBBLE _BATH_ TUB
2. COW _BOY_ SCOUT
3. FIRE _PLACE_ MAT
4. GUM _DROP_ OFF
5. CAR _HOP_ SCOTCH
6. BROWN _Sugar_ CANE
7. HIGH _WAY_ STATION
8. SEA _Shell_ FISH
9. SKY _BLUE_ JEANS
10. PIG _SKIN_ FLINT

PUZZLE 13

Cryptic

British-style or cryptic crosswords are a great challenge for crossword fans. Each clue contains either a definition or direct reference to the answer, as well as a play on words. The numbers in parentheses indicate the number of letters in the answer word or words.

ACROSS

1. Salad ingredient is hard to get sliced up (6)
4. He has two partners in crime? (8)
9. Lowest kind of bathroom furnishings (6)
10. Dish out or do without (8)
12. Imparts no skill for the scalawags (4)
13. Ambitious to turn up bashful (5)
14. Poke Peter initially with a stick (4)
17. Queen's entire materials used for a female rider (12)
20. Implacably trust holding fast time to a smaller degree (12)
23. Holds title to township holding (4)
24. Hero's confused between land and water (5)
25. Wise men get mother fixed up with a soldier (4)
28. They put on coats to hurt the rest perhaps (8)
29. Warmed some drink and thought it over (6)
30. Memo about someone who cares (8)
31. Webster spied her, it is said (6)

DOWN

1. Enter air pump for a fee (8)
2. Storm that could make Rod own up (8)
3. Lose out at the bottom (4)
5. Resists their sort of dogs (5,7)
6. Snakes like an afterthought (4)
7. Disregard and get one rig upset (6)
8. Cares about the capital of Russia's inclinations (6)
11. Courter hoarse-voiced to go two furlongs (7,5)
15. Property like a collection (5)
16. Part of a dangerous mood (5)
18. Attacked animal felt sick (8)
19. Small doctor nicely upset part of the engine (8)
21. One who spins a hat (6)
22. Unsteady in business (6)
26. The rise of bananas causes shock (4)
27. Inflate the quiet official (4)

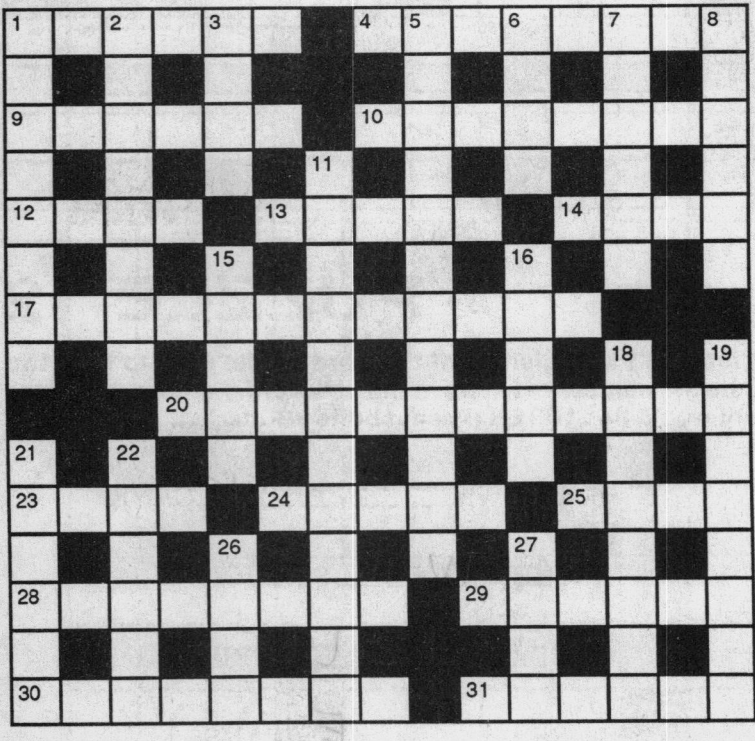

12

ACROSS

1. Plead
4. Fellow
8. "___ Girl"
12. Before, in poems
13. Went on horseback
14. Angel's headgear
15. Wrath
16. Beatles hit
18. Beaks
20. Self-esteem
21. Nobler
24. Merrily
28. "M*A*S*H" character
30. Oak or maple
31. Dowel
34. Was fond of
36. Baseball's Griffey, Jr.
37. Ellipse
39. Rips
41. Mexican coins
43. Rained ice
47. Mr. Calloway
49. Market
50. Naval Academy site
55. Outdo
56. Vessel
57. Singing cowboy Autry
58. Fuss
59. Rim
60. "My Three ___"
61. Allow

DOWN

1. Human ___
2. Mistake
3. Waterfowl
4. Comedian Billy ___
5. Weed
6. Consumer lures
7. Tennis's Sampras
8. Tonsils' site
9. Owned
10. Chicken ___ king
11. Child's treasure
17. Quiche ingredient
19. Corn serving
22. Revise
23. Gathers leaves
25. Annoy
26. Politician Atwater
27. Desire
29. Genuine
31. Burst
32. Actress Arden
33. Pump purchase
35. Puts on clothing
38. Find
40. Tennis unit
42. Drain
44. Add up
45. Wear away
46. Bus station
48. Swamps
50. Lincoln's nickname
51. Incline the head
52. Pester
53. MGM lion
54. Hostel

PUZZLE 14

PUZZLE 15

ACROSS
1. Crush
5. Thanksgiving dish
9. Pigpen
12. Mountain's melody
13. A Baldwin brother
14. The Gay Nineties, e.g.
15. Youth
16. Not as wide
18. Acorn bearer
20. Finished
21. Rough
24. Certainly!
25. Blockhead
26. Do a tailor's job
28. Chilly
32. Try
34. Somber
36. Flounder
37. Cast
39. Smidgen
41. Statute
42. Sailor
44. Carts
46. Horrify
49. Color
50. Showers
52. Hearing organs
56. Toolbox
57. Cleveland's lake
58. Fastener
59. Foxy
60. Act
61. Fidgety

DOWN
1. "When Harry ____ Sally . . ."
2. High card
3. Her
4. Respect
5. New Englanders
6. Pie ____ mode
7. Compassion
8. Silver ____
9. Stitches
10. Aspen, e.g.
11. Three feet
17. Refuge
19. Cigar residue
21. Charge
22. Pledge
23. At a distance
27. Enraged
29. Horseback sport
30. Blueprint
31. Evergreens
33. Started
35. Lingered
38. Gobbled
40. Harbor
43. Bellow
45. Water birds
46. Clumsy boats
47. Bucket
48. Sympathy
51. Deceive
53. Also
54. Cleaning cloth
55. Mata Hari, e.g.

ACROSS
1. Short, explosive sound
4. Lackaday!
8. Daring
12. Ostrich's relative
13. Went by car
14. Suspicion
15. Hot ____ balloon
16. Straight-forward
17. Require
18. Vapor
20. Male deer
22. Truck component
24. Hooded snake
28. Terror
31. Unemployed
34. Closet bar
35. Pivot
36. Sorrow
37. Chilly
38. "____ Hard" (Willis movie)
39. Bustles
40. Astonishes
41. Iron alloy
43. Sucker
45. "The Sun ____ Rises"
48. Obligations
52. Wanes in intensity
55. Type of clarinet
57. Decorative vase
58. Dueling tool
59. Look slyly
60. Pasture
61. Narrate
62. Sound quality
63. Ask for, as a favor

DOWN
1. Snow and chick
2. Delete
3. Chaste
4. Fragrance
5. Sever
6. Lemon and orange drinks
7. Transmitted
8. Church game
9. Poem
10. Pinky or Peggy
11. "Major ____"
19. Land unit
21. Top pilot
23. Flying vertebrate
25. Forehead
26. Function
27. Sums
28. Short-term fashions
29. Freeway sign
30. Away from the wind
32. Pair
33. Smaller amount
37. Cod or Ann
39. "____ About Eve"
42. Art stand
44. Idolize
46. Sailor
47. Butterlike product
49. Light component
50. Elm or maple
51. Hindrance
52. Decide upon
53. Primate
54. Solidify
56. Finger count

PUZZLE 16

PUZZLE 17

ACROSS
1. Gusted
5. Gape
9. "Ain't ____ Sweet?"
12. Great review
13. Amiss
14. Lock opener
15. Frozen
16. Dinner hour
18. Repairs
20. "The Raven" author
21. Engrave
24. "The ____ Ape"
28. Reduced to dust
32. Rescue
33. Actor Vigoda
34. Ethical
36. Can metal
37. Viewed
39. Courteously
41. Uses a keyboard
43. Close by
44. Beat walker
46. Step part
50. Avid reader
55. Lima's country
56. Actress Lupino
57. Cleveland's lake
58. Cooking fat
59. Wager
60. Mortgage, e.g.
61. What ____ is new?

DOWN
1. Hat part
2. Doily material
3. Level
4. Married
5. Sweet potato
6. Respectful wonder
7. Enclose
8. Man-made fabric
9. Schuss, e.g.
10. Dress edge
11. Ocular orb
17. Herbal drinks
19. Flower stalk
22. Farmer's yield
23. Wading bird
25. "____ & Allie"
26. Wicked
27. Refuse
28. Gone by
29. Follow orders
30. Cry
31. Broad valley
35. False witness
38. Collar site
40. Three-bag hit
42. Planted
45. Skin opening
47. Close tightly
48. Goes wrong
49. Boorish
50. Highchair wear
51. "____ to the West Wind"
52. Stable morsel
53. Torso bone
54. Encountered

ACROSS

1. Gamble
5. Tantrums
9. Be in hock
12. Actor Arkin
13. Mideast nation
14. Triumphed
15. Exam
16. Remembered
18. Tomato jelly
20. Pay dirt
21. Boast
23. Taste, e.g.
26. Genuflected
29. Defrost
31. Attention
32. Worries
35. Consume
36. Damsel
38. Gave in
40. Fibbing
43. Happy
44. Likewise not
45. Sassy
48. Boring
53. Ohio Indian
54. Tennis point
55. Arden et al.
56. Luncher's haunt
57. Bunk or canopy
58. Evergreens
59. Fragrance

DOWN

1. Statistics
2. Porter and stout
3. Archie Bunker's noise
4. Complete
5. Christmas tree
6. Wrath
7. Mexican sandwiches
8. Pitfall
9. Hooter
10. ___ is me!
11. Conclude
17. Loaned
19. Cow's offspring
22. ___ whiz!
24. Trembled
25. Allay
26. Barrel
27. Hammer's target
28. Singer Doris ___
30. Joined
33. Outfit
34. Ego
37. Queue
39. Town in Texas
41. Curious
42. Orchard
46. Missile housing
47. Descendant
48. Check
49. Hockey surface
50. ___ herring
51. Kitten sound
52. Double curve

PUZZLE 18

PUZZLE 19

ACROSS
1. Pelt
4. Narrow strip
8. Potter's material
12. Orangutan, e.g.
13. Apiece
14. Go by bus
15. Shredded paper
17. Bettor's numbers
18. Plenty
19. Pigeon's sound
21. Observe
22. Topeka's state
26. Postpone
29. That woman
30. Rage
31. Mine finds
32. Pot's partner
33. Run away
34. Olive or canola
35. Used a bench
36. Cape
37. System
39. Shoe tip
40. Ancient
41. Pester
45. "Less ____ Zero"
48. Type of tennis smash
50. Limo, e.g.
51. Train units
52. Top pilot
53. Bambi, e.g.
54. Leg joint
55. Decade number

DOWN
1. Visage
2. "Once ____ a Time"
3. Nevada city
4. Folk singer Pete ____
5. Wood turning machine
6. Play a part
7. Become denser
8. Sing like Bing
9. Jar top
10. Increase
11. Affirmative word
16. Melds
20. Rower's need
23. Farm tower
24. Vicinity
25. Look for
26. Condemn
27. New York canal
28. Touched
29. Fedora, e.g.
32. Horse enclosure
33. Meat
35. Fa follower
36. Roughly textured
38. Integrity
39. In that place
42. Chair, e.g.
43. Doily fabric
44. Biblical garden
45. Little bit
46. Tint
47. Consumed food
49. Rip ____ Winkle

PUZZLE 20

ACROSS

1. Table support
4. Paid athlete
7. Competent
11. Footed vase
12. Implement
13. Gather a harvest
14. Repugnant
16. Arrived
17. Windstorm
18. Trio
19. Thespians
22. Have obligations
23. Play prompts
24. Decorated
28. Fury
29. Financial assets
31. Trailing vine
32. Tooth doctor
34. Open happiness
35. Pub quaff
36. "A ____ in need . . ."
38. Geometric corner
41. Hitchcock's "____ Window"
42. Statute distance
43. Confuse
47. Religious image
48. Paradise
49. Lode's load
50. Unpaid bill
51. Neither's partner
52. Flit about

DOWN

1. Haul
2. Goof
3. African antelope
4. Puddles
5. Italian capital
6. Cheer, in Madrid
7. Bowman
8. Polar or grizzly
9. Crippled
10. Dueling sword
12. Russian emperor
15. Self-images
18. Pairs
19. Corrosive stuff
20. Remedy
21. Adolescent
22. "The ____ Couple"
24. Hill dweller
25. Cairo's river
26. Level
27. Tinted
29. Emery board
30. Purpose
33. Natural ability
34. Young female
36. Not as many
37. Shower
38. Surrounded by
39. Pleasant
40. Rounded lump
41. Make over
43. Actor Gazzara
44. Canine
45. Baseball stat: abbr.
46. Comedian Buttons

19

PUZZLE 21

• FOR THE BIRDS •

ACROSS

1. Douglas tree
4. Pickup section
7. Drawing room
9. Relish
11. Loony
12. Hoisting devices
14. Smash
15. London drink
17. Witch's pet
18. Mountain ____
19. Have capacity for
20. Solder
21. Shortly
23. Not near
25. Varnish resin
26. According to
27. Little rascal
29. Capture
31. Maui memento
33. Short sock
35. Roman loan
36. Kitchen gadget
38. Overpriced
39. Game bird
41. "I Never Promised You ____ Garden"
42. As well as
43. Australian bird
45. ____ de France
48. She sheep
49. Caviar
50. Anthem poet
51. Switch position
54. Gorilla
55. Opposite of WSW
56. Period
59. Actress Burstyn
61. Williams of "Mrs. Doubtfire"
65. Italian actress
67. Straightened
69. Workout room
70. Tame
71. Twitch
72. Humor
74. Grazing land
75. Noise
76. Not young
77. Make do
79. Extra
81. Fine
83. Like a fox
84. Actress Plumb
86. Seeing red
87. Marine bird
88. Date
89. Porter
91. "Hotel California" group
93. Uprisings
94. Tolerated
95. ____ close for comfort
96. Subside

DOWN

1. Truth
2. Kind
3. Cheerleader
4. Package
5. Gardner of films
6. Goldfinger's foe
7. Tuxedo
8. Christmas carol
9. Thumb through
10. Coral shelf
11. Coward
13. Gulp
16. French farewell
17. Blue Grotto isle
19. Sleigh jockey
20. Soggy
22. Siesta
24. Songstress Della ____
25. Spanish article
26. Energy
28. Pasture sound
30. Arthur of "Maude"
32. Dander
34. Escorted
37. Before of yore
39. Peculiar
40. Compare
43. Generation

44. Floor cleaner
46. Author Deighton
47. Needle center
51. Kukla's pal
52. Twinkle
53. Marsh
56. Sleepy's roommate
57. Baltimore team
58. Actor Savalas
59. Have a muffin
60. Never used
62. Leered
63. Toodle-oo!
64. Likeness
65. Actor Chaney
66. Buntline or Beatty
68. Poorly lit
70. Accomplished
73. Salad ingredient
75. Contribute
78. At any time
80. Sings like Hammer
82. Tin and copper
83. Canary food
85. Revise copy
88. Messy fellow
90. Dove call
92. Sailor

PUZZLE 21

21

PUZZLE 22

ACROSS

1. Cribbage piece
4. Italian mountains
8. Demonstrate
12. Memorable time
13. Follow
14. ___ the last laugh
15. According to
16. Prized
18. Stretched the truth
20. Gauges
21. Find out
23. Iowa city
24. Acknowledged
25. Ballpoint, e.g.
26. Bullring shout
29. Eric the ___
30. Fashion
31. Pea's home
32. Double curve
33. Foul up
34. Deluge
36. Conspire
37. Dangerous
38. Entertainer Mel ___
41. Young goats
42. Sedimentary rock
44. Coffee vessel
47. Rewrite
48. Address for Adam
49. Cow's comment
50. Dampens
51. Accomplishment
52. Clique

DOWN

1. Vigor
2. Sooner than, to Keats
3. Wreaths
4. Minister to
5. Rendered fat
6. Easy as ___
7. Banged
8. Closes
9. ___ and hounds
10. Again
11. Ties the knot
17. Detected
19. Infuriate
21. Traditional knowledge
22. Woolly females
23. Separate
26. Animals that play dead
27. Glance
28. Religious leader Mary Baker ___
30. Covered with ice
33. Part of B.P.O.E.
34. Comrade
35. Flip one's ___
36. Verse writers
38. Squandered
39. Amusement park attraction
40. Leave out
41. Reflex site
43. "___ to Billy Joe"
45. Beluga eggs
46. "She's ___ There"

PUZZLE 23

ACROSS
1. Snoop
4. Spring peeper
8. Platter
12. Ogle
13. Des Moines's state
14. Function
15. Military leaders
17. Minute amount
18. Join
19. Thespian
20. Pilot's realm
23. Peddle
25. Goals
26. Petted
30. Actor Majors
31. Istanbul natives
32. Corrida cheer
33. Comforter's stuffing
35. Nuzzle
36. "The Big ___"
37. ___ Cottontail
38. Thin-shelled nut
41. Polish
42. Uproars
43. Carved
48. Resting
49. TV's Helen ___
50. Wrath
51. Colored
52. Comply
53. Sty

DOWN
1. Small spike
2. Deli loaf
3. Desire
4. Dismisses
5. Highway
6. Night bird
7. Fuel
8. Bamboozles
9. Tooth part
10. Choir voice
11. Fifty-two weeks
16. Woolly ones
19. Overwhelms
20. Me
21. Leg joint
22. Thought
23. "When ___ Met Sally . . ."
24. Clumsy boats
26. Billiards sticks
27. Grime
28. Otherwise
29. Stag
31. Comparative word
34. Ridiculed
35. Succeeding
37. Peppermint ___
38. Reimbursed
39. Whirlpool
40. Nat King ___
41. Port
43. Which person?
44. Center
45. Sass
46. Bard's before
47. Lion's lair

23

PUZZLE 24

ACROSS
1. Sack
4. ___ Na Na
7. Party
11. Large vase
12. Tendency
13. Actress Markey
14. Apprentices
16. Suit to ___
17. Fashion
18. Small birds
19. Well-known
22. Robert E. ___
23. Upon
24. Father goose
27. Neither's partner
28. Seashore
30. Poodle
32. Casabas
34. Yield
35. Monkey
36. Person with dark hair
38. Black card
41. Excursion
42. Desert condition
43. Bounded
47. Obscure
48. Actress Bancroft
49. Amaze
50. Gaper
51. Poor grade
52. Animal enclosure

DOWN
1. School vehicle
2. Picasso's specialty
3. Wildebeest
4. Makes like Sinatra
5. Strong dislike
6. Beast of burden
7. Fortified
8. Poker term
9. Debtor's burden
10. Orange and lemon drinks
12. Actor Bridges
15. Fall
18. Left
19. Devotee
20. Power source
21. Additional
22. ___ Vegas
24. Car fuel
25. Adam's home
26. Traveled by car
28. Deal with
29. Dollar bill
31. Understand
33. Hook-and- ___
34. Remedy
36. Carried
37. Disrespect-ful
38. Secure
39. Implore
40. Camp helper
41. Mood
43. Not good
44. Chat
45. Flock mama
46. Cozy room

PUZZLE 25

ACROSS

1. Neon, e.g.
4. Blustered
8. Absent
12. Drink cube
13. Carry on
14. Trademark
15. Fresh
16. Impression
17. Juvenile
18. Elitist
20. Fish gametes
22. Anxiety
25. Fare
29. Watercraft
32. Merchandise
34. Sugar ____ Leonard
35. Bireme's need
36. Activated
37. Impersonate
38. Nibbled
39. Caesar's last day
40. Wallet stuffers
41. Elevator ____
43. Bouilla- baisse, e.g.
45. Comic Skelton
47. Pork or beef
50. Appraise
53. Regal steed
56. Repent
58. Hautboy
59. Went by car
60. Tavern
61. Look after
62. Water vessel
63. Pa

DOWN

1. Rummy
2. "____ High"
3. Sutured
4. Buy off
5. Boy
6. Seth's mother
7. Don
8. Transform
9. Anguish
10. ____ of Aquarius
11. Hither and ____
19. Frequently
21. Untie
23. Frightened
24. Furies
26. Persia today
27. Mantle
28. Potato buds
29. Feathered scarves
30. Pledge
31. Locale
33. Oxidize
36. Mouthful
40. Have IOUs
42. Released
44. Fire remnant
46. Chance
48. Moistureless
49. Sandwich fish
50. Putrefy
51. Mr. Lincoln
52. Heavy weight
54. Fray
55. Summer refresher
57. Stop

PUZZLE 26

ACROSS
1. Peat ____
5. Child's summer destination
9. Knight's title
12. Discharge
13. Opera highlight
14. Highest card
15. Ceramic piece
16. Heard
18. Rock
20. Plant
21. Petroleum transporter
23. Average
27. Health resort
30. Cozy room
31. Satan
32. Rug
34. Taste
35. Change
36. Auto
37. Astrological lion
38. Require
39. Actor Fonda
41. Small particle
43. Hinder
47. Roared
51. Drill
52. ____ Baba
53. Actor Wilder
54. Great Lake
55. Gratuity
56. Table scraps
57. Loan

DOWN
1. New York baseball team
2. Leave out
3. Farm structure
4. Office worker
5. Coolidge's nickname
6. Got up
7. Penny pincher
8. Liver spread
9. ____ Francisco
10. Frozen water
11. Crimson
17. A Ford
19. Downy duck
22. Allow
24. Racetrack shape
25. Location
26. Butter substitute
27. Look over quickly
28. Wan
29. Comic Johnson
31. Challenged
33. Foot lever
34. Mrs. Nixon
36. Mortar
39. Force
40. "____ Without a Cause"
42. African republic
44. Ripped
45. Miss Moran
46. Singer Lou ____
47. Cave dweller
48. Actor Wallach
49. Edge
50. ____ Moines

ACROSS
1. Type of session
4. Crop
7. British streetcar
11. Brainstorm
13. In the manner of
14. Des Moines's state
15. Partner of old, new, and blue
17. Copied
18. Trot
19. Risked
21. Eternally
23. Governor Grasso
24. Periods in history
25. Type of club
26. Levin or Gershwin
29. Shopper's memory jogger
30. Rowing blade
31. Platter
32. Permit
33. Kitchen containers
34. Meander
35. Impertinent
36. Left
37. ___ the town red
39. Track circuit
40. Ornamental vases
41. Dublin native
46. Of sound mind
47. Grown male
48. New Haven university
49. Organs of sight
50. Mother sheep
51. Peach seed

DOWN
1. Chest bone
2. Tumult
3. Part of MPH
4. Grassy area
5. Cheer at a bullfight
6. Canoeists
7. Crown
8. Lasso
9. Overwhelmed
10. Ticked off
12. Stop
16. "___ Town"
20. Pub brew
21. Famous canal
22. Big beyond belief
23. Fill with joy
24. House wing
25. "___ Charlie's Got the Blues"
26. Press
27. Speak wildly
28. Nautical response
31. Winner's award
33. Play on words
35. "The Sun Also ___"
36. Petrol
37. Implore
38. Actress Baxter
39. Sales pitch
40. Manipulate
42. Uncooked
43. Motorist's guide
44. Potent pugilist
45. Seine

PUZZLE 28

ACROSS
1. Treaty
5. Minimum ____
9. Lincoln, to friends
12. Reed instrument
13. Bakery worker
14. Hang loosely
15. Opposite of push
16. Blue Hen State
18. Delayed
20. Polish
21. Corn portion
22. "____ Jude"
23. Pointy
26. Massachusetts cape
27. Lawn droplets
30. Hurl
31. Hound
32. Stuffing herb
33. Certainly!
34. Carpenter's blade
35. Cliff shelf
36. James Bond, e.g.
37. Feather scarf
38. Lance
41. Colonized
45. Veteran
47. Grow weary
48. Low cloud
49. "____ That Tune"
50. Actress Olin
51. Overwhelm
52. Pluck
53. Paradise

DOWN
1. Boston orchestra
2. Be adjacent to
3. Soft drink
4. Bank employees
5. More expansive
6. Made a hole in one
7. Mousse alternative
8. Deleted
9. Jai ____
10. "____ Free"
11. Fencing weapon
17. Child's question
19. Track circuit
22. Swine
23. Filthy place
24. Weeding tool
25. Fool
26. Calf's mom
27. June VIP
28. Easter basket item
29. Tiny
31. Judgment ____
32. Supersonics' city
34. Bed coil
35. Destiny
36. Perched
37. French cap
38. Couch
39. Snow remover
40. Advantage
41. Half: pref.
42. Told a falsehood
43. Marine bird
44. "Giant" actor
46. Ruin

ACROSS

1. Moolah
5. Chair
9. Bar Harbor's state
10. Zodiac sign
12. Reverend Luther King, Jr.
13. Remove
15. Morsel
16. Urge
18. Pack away
19. Wharf
21. Ivy League school
23. First lady
24. Antitoxin
26. Goes to bed
28. Caspian or Red
30. Turf
31. _____ up (gathers)
35. At no time
39. "A Chorus Line" song
40. Journey
42. Assistant
43. Evils
45. List extender: abbr.
47. Lubricate
48. Postage
50. Certain jury verdict
52. Rotund
53. Coastal fliers
54. Omelet needs
55. Dispatched

DOWN

1. Reagan's predecessor
2. Small island
3. Trim
4. Statesman Kissinger
5. Equestrians' needs
6. Before, to Keats
7. Suffers
8. Waver
9. Singer Osmond
11. Kitchen appliance
12. Swabs
14. Fleecy females
17. Paddle
20. Reddish brown
22. English prep school
25. Encounter
27. Notion
29. Takes into custody
31. Peat _____
32. Divisions
33. Legislative body
34. Perch
36. "Peanuts" character
37. Prepares for publication
38. Depend
41. Messengers
44. Air pollutant
46. Entice
49. Wrinkly faced dog
51. Tavern

PUZZLE 30

ACROSS
1. Deceive
4. Flutter
8. Long time
12. "___ to a Nightingale"
13. Nevada gambling city
14. Slothful
15. Deep in pitch
16. Spoke to
18. Pyromaniac's crime
20. Holler
21. Speed
23. Rains ice
27. Slip-on shoes
30. Valuable item
31. Little devil
32. Scrap of cloth
34. English brew
35. Touches
38. Asleep
41. Register
43. Smile radiantly
44. Prompts
46. Sleepy or Happy
49. Not together
53. Roofing material
54. Military group
55. Window ledge
56. Sooner than, in poetry
57. Brink
58. Pennsylvania port
59. Witness

DOWN
1. Carbonated drink
2. Scent
3. "The Daily Pianet," e.g.
4. Paris's country
5. Conducted
6. A Rooney
7. Ponders intently
8. Theater walkways
9. Koch and Begley
10. "Grand ___ Opry"
11. Actor Beatty
17. "___ Cinders"
19. Lout
22. Bungle
24. Calculates approximately
25. Adolescent
26. For men only
27. Existence
28. Harbinger
29. ___ Diego
33. Chat
36. Find
37. Insult
39. Sell
40. Dog's foot
42. Rental contract
45. Mix
47. Barely cooked
48. Turn loose
49. Pamela ___ Martin
50. Conclusion
51. Glutton
52. Yalie

30

PUZZLE 31

ACROSS
1. Chart
4. Health clubs
8. "___ to Morocco"
12. Large bird
13. Hair line
14. Maui dance
15. Trousseau item
17. Mideastern country
18. Doubtful
19. Play on words
21. Free
22. Roves stealthily
26. Banana ___
29. Tokyo currency
30. Work in the garden
31. Crave
32. Awful
33. Emulate a model
34. Mine output
35. Moose
36. Group of students
37. Government agency
39. "Runaround ___"
40. Indignation
41. Yemen's peninsula
45. Boast
48. Custodians
50. Cry of pain
51. Certain female singer
52. Tear
53. Sugar root
54. Affirmative votes
55. It comes before tee

DOWN
1. Bill of fare
2. Revival shout
3. Small dogs
4. Ghost
5. Summoned
6. "Diamonds ___ Forever"
7. Walked
8. Thick-skinned animal, for short
9. ___ Father
10. In the manner of
11. Mr. Aykroyd
16. Gruesome
20. Coffee maker
23. Stop!
24. Destruction
25. Goes out with
26. Stuck-up person
27. Brazil's neighbor
28. Ogler's look
29. Shaggy ox
32. Toronto athlete
33. Skirt fold
35. Corn serving
36. Knickknacks
38. Skating figure
39. ___ Monica
42. Drill
43. Bearded bloom
44. Vipers
45. Comedian Hope
46. Be repentant
47. High card
49. Lager's kin

31

PUZZLE 32

ACROSS

1. Aries symbol
4. Baths
8. Armed conflict
11. Milo's film pal
13. Bit
14. Generation
15. Barbie or Ken
16. Horse's gait
17. Actor Beatty
18. Soil amender
20. Rectifies
22. Society page word
24. Sargasso, e.g.
25. Suitcases
29. Synthetic textile
33. Have debts
34. Rap
36. Dander
37. Glitter
40. Gabriel's instrument
43. Blue
45. Metric land measure
46. Leg joints
49. Takes a siesta
52. High card
53. Third day of the wk.
55. Boat-builder's lumber
57. In favor of
58. Light brown
59. Store event
60. Sawbuck
61. Judge
62. Shoat's home

DOWN

1. Staff
2. On
3. Race distance
4. Command to Fido
5. Skin opening
6. Particles
7. Lustrous fabric
8. Baton
9. "Rock of ___"
10. Primary color
12. Argot
19. "___ and Sympathy"
21. No
23. Hen product
25. Swamp
26. Boring tool
27. Turn right
28. Have a bite
30. Glass edge
31. Native metal
32. Tennis necessity
35. Lingerie item
38. Invite
39. ___ milk
41. Ceremonial vessel
42. Lamb and veal
44. Playing card
46. Land measure
47. Bright sign
48. Withered
50. Pod dwellers
51. Seasoning
52. Liable
54. Total
56. West or Largo

ACROSS

1. Sound quality
5. Hardwood tree
8. Choir voice
12. Declare frankly
13. ___ the Lion
14. Watch face
15. Talk irrationally
16. Car fuel
17. Only
18. Big
20. Contaminate
22. Weep
23. Formal address
24. Small cask
27. Bikini part
29. Cantaloupe
33. Asian republic
35. "You ___ My Sunshine"
37. Eat
38. Neck parts
40. April follower
42. Domesticated animal
43. Slash
45. Attach by stitches
47. Make different
49. Strong thread
52. Melody
53. Female sheep
55. Fly upward
57. Observer
58. Negative conjunction
59. Money, in Chile
60. Tablets
61. Johnson of "Miami Vice"
62. Winter vehicle

DOWN

1. ___ and feather
2. Egg-shaped
3. PBS series
4. Pitchers
5. Branch of mathematics
6. Ocean
7. Emcees
8. Respected
9. Legal claim
10. Small pie
11. Spanish cheer
19. Lump or mass
21. Direct toward a target
24. Relatives
25. Distinctive time
26. Breach
28. Upper limb
30. Mouth part
31. Single unit
32. Mesh
34. Juices from plants
36. Oriental
39. Bring action against
41. Evergreen shrub
44. Style
46. Slender traces
47. Vicinity
48. Spoke falsely
50. Christmas song
51. Relaxation
52. Venomous snake
54. Seek the affection of
56. Stick

PUZZLE 34

ACROSS
1. Jeer
6. Petticoats
11. Hi-fi
12. Buccaneer
14. Oil transporter
15. Bellowed
16. Hill insect
17. Is able to
18. Table support
19. Cake froster
21. "None ____ the Brave"
22. Fishing stick
23. Mocked
25. Peeled
26. Horseback seats
28. Gloss
31. Renters
35. Heavy weights
36. Collection
37. Give off
38. Make a mistake
39. "Mary ____ a little lamb"
40. Opposite of WSW
41. Rubs out
43. Price
46. Cowboy Roy ____
47. Pestered
48. Prepared
49. Smile scornfully

DOWN
1. Point of view
2. Middle
3. Mork's planet
4. Lawyer's payment
5. "____ the Boys"
6. Jack who ate no fat
7. Pride cat
8. Lyricist Gershwin
9. Ice-cream shop
10. "Remington ____"
11. Solemn
13. Moved sideways
17. Snuggled
20. Gets up
21. ____ of roses
22. Outdated
24. Newsman Rather
25. Pod vegetable
27. Allow
28. Ranch animal
29. Shuddering fear
30. Infuriate
32. Appear
33. Feat in horseshoes
34. Spirited mount
36. Pert
39. Group of sheep
42. Ocean
43. TV network
44. Attila, e.g.
45. Grow older

ACROSS

1. Alcott's "Little ___"
6. Ciphers
11. Entertained
13. Holy place
14. ___ Antilles
15. Memorial Day march
16. Overhead trains
17. Evil spirit
19. Cap
20. Prophet
22. Armed conflict
23. Guns the engine
24. Russian ruler
26. Make fun of
28. Foot digit
30. Tennis match division
31. Coat arm
34. Feat
37. Lean-to
38. TV alien
40. Obstacle
42. Pie pan
43. Loafed
45. Wildebeest
46. Withstand
48. Comfort
50. Della and Pee Wee
51. Theater platforms
52. Sinned
53. Put forth

DOWN

1. United Kingdom region
2. Egg dish
3. Rumples
4. Road curve
5. Want
6. Detective Charlie ___
7. Hockey great
8. Used a rotary phone
9. Chicory plant
10. Apple pips
12. Ms. Barrymore
13. Germ cells
18. Insane
21. Given a PG or G
23. Ceremonies
25. Caviar
27. Stoplight color
29. Avoids
31. Black eye
32. Bank, at times
33. House extension
35. Hire
36. Ballerina, e.g.
37. Cordwood measure
39. ___ up (admit)
41. Visitor
43. Outraged
44. Love to excess
47. Utilize
49. Negligent

PUZZLE 35

35

PUZZLE 36

ACROSS
1. Spider's snare
4. Throb
8. Prickly ____
12. Commotion
13. Traveled
14. Homely
15. Precious gems
17. Burrowing mammal
18. Expedition
19. Discontinue
21. Unused
23. Rice wines
26. Sweltering
29. Presently
31. "The Prince of ____"
33. Object of devotion
35. Drenched
37. Sleek
38. Potpourri component
40. Fawn
42. Actress Irving
43. Car style
45. Golf instructor
47. Shades
49. Metal corrosion
52. Restaurant
55. Furlough
58. Consumer
59. Enthusiasm
60. "Tea for ____"
61. Lengthens
62. Tear
63. Terminate

DOWN
1. Lump
2. Prepare for publication
3. Wild pig
4. Busted
5. A billion years
6. Appends
7. Orals
8. Halloween item
9. Id's counterpart
10. Whole
11. Ham on ____
16. Husbands
20. Type of meal
22. Exclamation
24. Suggestion
25. Union
26. Joint
27. Ballads
28. Haul
30. Unite
32. Pen
34. Firemen's needs
36. Cover
39. Amateur
41. Chore
44. No way!
46. Umpire's cry
48. Bargain event
50. Locale
51. Suburb
52. Pool stick
53. Interrogate
54. Payment
56. Dismiss
57. Bow the head

PUZZLE 37

ACROSS
1. Mast
5. Small drink
8. ___ Aviv
11. Sharpen
12. Expert pilot
13. Clinton's vice president
14. Jot
15. Neckline shape
16. Boundary
17. Magician's word
19. Merchant
21. Paddle
22. Inventor Whitney
23. Revolving lure
27. Deserve
31. Baseball stat
32. "L.A. Law" actress
34. Exist
35. Musical sounds
38. Hotel employees
41. "___ Miserables"
43. Owing
44. Boulevard
47. Blackboard cleaner
51. Singer Clapton
52. Dipstick coating
54. Wander
55. Mother's sister
56. Hawaiian guitar, for short
57. Part of HOMES
58. Shake a ___
59. Mr. Danson
60. Small valley

DOWN
1. Ocean liner
2. Penniless
3. Poker payment
4. Logic
5. Relished
6. Glacier material
7. Annoyance
8. Mary ___ Lincoln
9. Therefore
10. Sly glance
13. Magic-lamp spirit
18. Light brown
20. Shade tree
23. Filming site
24. In favor of
25. Writer Fleming
26. Blushing
28. Lamb's dad
29. Ill temper
30. Sawbuck
33. Sang a Swiss song
36. Choose
37. View
39. "___ Town"
40. Raised
42. Portly
44. Stamplike label
45. Genuine
46. Wedding band
48. Bruised
49. Immoral
50. Virginia dance
53. "I Like ___"

PUZZLE 38

ACROSS
1. Headland
5. Auction offers
9. Carbine
14. Asian river
15. African lily
16. Mr. Flynn
17. Joy- ——
18. Luxor's river
19. Labors
20. Atlantic mystery: 2 wds.
23. Rained ice
24. Kind of antenna
25. Writer Buntline
26. Valley
28. Explosive: abbr.
31. Sharpens
34. Exists
35. Pt. of EEC
36. Skater Brinker
37. Wanderer
38. Within: prefix
39. Days of yore
40. Lear's daughter
41. Map feature
42. "—— Go to My Head"
43. Black
44. Actor Carney
45. Kentucky Derby, e.g.
47. Made anxious
51. London's tribute to Nelson: 2 wds.
55. Clues
56. Seaweed
57. Give the once-over
58. Broad necktie
59. Voting unit
60. Turn's companion
61. Adolescents
62. Of sound mind
63. Snick and ——

DOWN
1. Restrains
2. "Tempest" sprite
3. Chaplain
4. Factors
5. Striped
6. Greek epic
7. Stupid fellow
8. Prophet
9. Sells
10. Mangles
11. Startles
12. Lounge
13. Otherwise
21. Shoshoneans
22. Loafer
26. Sofa
27. Plumb
29. Artist's model
30. Horse's gait
31. Watery part of milk
32. Nimbus
33. Staying power
34. Identifying symbol
37. Mutineer
38. Confides
40. Forms again
41. Mideast country
44. French region
46. "Flow Gently, Sweet ——"
47. Inert gas
48. Georgia city
49. Rub out
50. Crowded
51. "—— Old Black Magic"
52. Go up
53. Shoots the breeze
54. —— breve

ACROSS

1. Ultimate
5. Nothing: Latin
10. Luminary
14. Eastern nurse
15. Make into law
16. Under: prefix
17. Lost Dutchman, e.g.
18. Land measures
19. Amor's counterpart
20. Ms. Davis
22. Spring mo.
23. Dwelling
24. Stain
26. Supped
27. Loom part
28. Ill. city
32. Male singer
35. Ruler: abbr.
36. Crystalline mineral
37. Skip
38. Roly-poly
40. Kin of etc.
41. Swims
44. Floral wreath
46. Small rodent
47. On an even keel
48. Shop equipment
50. "The —— Drum"
51. Ralph Waldo ——
54. Wife of Amphion
57. Cobb and Hardin
58. Employer
60. Wine city
61. Egyptian Christians
63. Number of Muses
64. Drudge
65. Chips in
66. Track event
67. Plant
68. Draws close
69. Or ——!

DOWN

1. Meek one
2. Fifi's girl friends
3. —— Domingo
4. Country Western hit: 4 wds.
5. Teachers' gp.
6. Envelope words: 3 wds.
7. See 4 Down: 3 wds.
8. Cake topper
9. Mil. offs.
10. See 4 Down: 4 wds.
11. Novice
12. Like two peas in ——: 2 wds.
13. Type of wine
21. Guidonian note: 2 wds.
23. At the pinnacle
25. Ship's letters
26. Morning hours: abbr.
29. "—— each life . . ."
30. Patricia of film fame
31. She, in Paree
32. Cuts short
33. Latin I word
34. Spot
39. Wagon driver
42. Ms. Adams
43. Antonym's ant.
45. Resident: suffix
49. Regal inits.
52. Bay window
53. Hawaiian geese
54. Has a siesta
55. Fortune-teller's phrase: 2 wds.
56. Certain Amerind
57. —— of voice
59. Anatomical network
61. Throw out
62. Draft agcy.

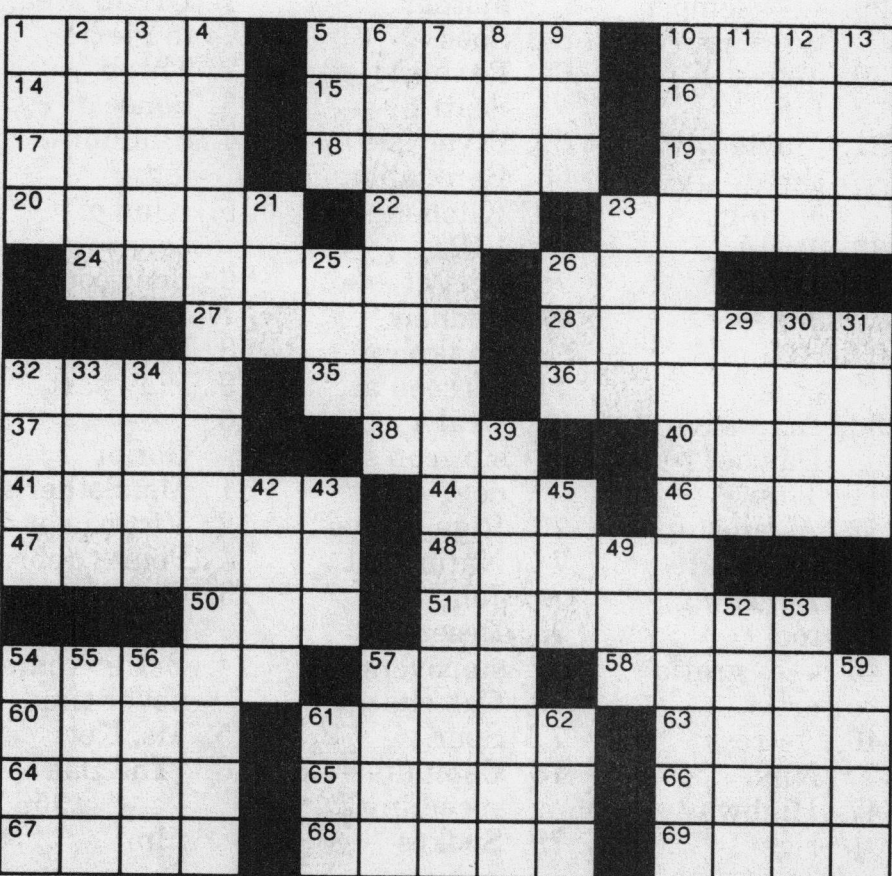

PUZZLE 40

ACROSS

1. —— society
5. Go by yawl
9. Health resorts
13. French land masses
17. Chills
18. Stewpot
19. Penny
20. Cloy
21. Jennifer Jones film: 4 wds.
25. Wriggly one
26. By way of
27. Bulwer-Lytton heroine
28. Mountain nymph
29. —— semper tyrannis
30. To be, to Fifi
31. Movie with three endings
33. Tasty
36. Actor Jacques
37. Arthur et al.
38. Actress Dawber
41. Thin
42. Asian staple
43. By's mate
44. Punching tool
45. —— gratia artis
46. Actress Nina
47. Highway rigs
48. Singer Jacques
49. French mountain range
51. Goes over like a lead balloon
52. Take for —— (con): 2 wds.
53. Party spreads: 4 wds.
57. Love, Italian-style
59. Name of eight popes
60. Certain sculptures
63. Reims mother
64. Sobs
65. Racing's Seattle ——
67. River isle
68. Bank abbr.
69. Kitchen VIPs
70. Feet of —— (hidden weakness)
71. As soon as
72. Oral surgeon's deg.
73. Riga native
74. Naturalist John
75. Desert stopovers
76. Cab charge
77. Spar
78. Computer-speed inits.
79. Spokes
82. Muralist Jose
83. Hearty brew
84. Containing nitrogen: prefix
87. Gene Hackman film: 3 wds.
92. Republic of Ireland
93. Rhythm
94. TV's "—— McCluskey"
95. Singer Guthrie
96. Agent: suffix
97. Gamma's predecessor
98. Rouse
99. Munich's river

DOWN

1. Urban area, to Pierre
2. Throb
3. Sense
4. Sibilant letter
5. Kind of boom
6. Seaweed
7. UN body
8. Pirate Jean
9. Play part
10. "—— Goriot"
11. Ms. Sothern
12. Victoria or Penn.: abbr.
13. Grenoble's department
14. Better-than-never time
15. Ms. Kett
16. "The Bad ——" (1956 film)
22. Latin poet
23. Soprano Lucrezia ——
24. Soak
29. Moral transgression
30. Per
31. Red hue
32. Falls behind
33. Croat, e.g.
34. Aviation prefix
35. International travel musts
36. Obsession
37. Disney deer
38. Left Bank natives
39. Thunderstruck
40. Young lady in Arles: abbr.
42. Broadway's Billy
43. Mechanical headache
46. Gala affair
47. Couches
48. Thin nail
50. Stop for le train
51. Mamans' treasures
52. Lined up
54. Certainty, in Caen
55. General meaning
56. Lady Jane ——
57. Surrounded by
58. Repair
61. Fr. resort city

62. Jeanne
d'Arc et al.:
abbr.
64. "Moonstruck"
star
65. Skirt
feature
66. Tutelary
god
69. "—— de
Lune"
70. Mores
71. New World
gp.
74. Painter

Chagall
75. Oil cartel
76. Drummer's
cohort
77. Maestro
Zubin
78. Net
79. Numbered
ways: abbr.
80. Make ——
(be success-
ful): 2 wds.
81. "——
Mable"
82. Ella

Fitzgerald's
forte
83. Caesar's
years
84. Broadcasts
85. Author
Emile
86. —— about
(roughly):
2 wds.
88. Wane

89. Society-page
word
90. "But ——
for Me"
91. Skater
Babilonia

PUZZLE 40

PUZZLE 41

ACROSS
1. Invites
5. Occurs
10. Be bold
14. Indiscretion
15. Texas shrine
16. Surrounded by
17. Marco ——
18. Second showing
19. King, of films
20. Wrestling personality: 2 wds.
23. Golf mounds
24. Posed
25. Sight
28. Takes away
33. Chemical compound
34. Unfailing
35. Back talk
36. European Recovery Program author: 3 wds.
40. Coach Parseghian
41. Pool measures
42. Ms. Lavin
43. Pioneers
46. Chunk
47. Sweet potato
48. Big blowout
49. "Rhapsody in Blue" composer: 2 wds.
56. Pumice source
57. Olympic gymnast Comaneci
58. Expert pilots
60. Terrible tsar
61. Court proceeding
62. Days of old
63. Karate award
64. Crystal gazers
65. Cover for Rainier

DOWN
1. Cleopatra's last resource
2. Walk heavily
3. Metric weight unit
4. More flashy
5. Lurch
6. Table spreads
7. Japanese ship
8. Ratite birds
9. Johnny Cash, e.g.
10. Sioux Indian
11. Cupid
12. Writer Lardner
13. Advantage
21. German composer Telemann
22. Attention
25. Robert Urich TV series
26. French river
27. Ermine, in summer
28. Dilapidated houses
29. Time periods
30. Metallic sound
31. Diacritical mark
32. Slapping sound
34. Cicatrix
37. Atmospheric forces
38. Kind of fund
39. Truck routes
44. Despot
45. Fall behind
46. Speech sounds
48. Fine pipe
49. Smooth-talking
50. Roof overhang
51. Running track
52. Station, in Cannes
53. Actress McClurg
54. Sacred image
55. Sleuth Wolfe
59. Hemstitch

ACROSS

1. Ship parts
6. Partner of tear
10. Grouch
14. Houston athlete
15. "Where —— All the Flowers Gone"
16. Breath sound
17. H.G. Wells novel: 3 wds.
20. Aquatic bird
21. Singer James
22. Fermentation agent
23. Suit to ——: 2 wds.
25. Coarse file
27. German city
30. "—— in the Attic"
32. Greek letter
36. TV actress Meyers
37. More: Scot.
39. Rin ——: 2 wds.
41. Magician's forte: 2 wds.
44. Stable worker
45. Area: abbr.
46. "Norma ——"
47. Starling's sanctuary
48. Enraged
50. Jewish months
52. Writer Gardner
54. —— duck
56. Chicago airport
59. Retreat
61. Mardi ——
65. Magic lotions?: 2 wds.
68. Cross or curtain
69. Measure
70. Still soft
71. Bell sound
72. Run into
73. Utopias

DOWN

1. Helm or Houston
2. Tennis notable
3. Eng. money
4. Threefold
5. Heir
6. Formal attire: 2 wds.
7. Orient
8. Dovecote
9. Johnny ——
10. Kind of juniper
11. Vishnu incarnation
12. Word of dismay
13. Crooked
18. Victory sign
19. European river
24. Phoenix's neighbor
26. Out of bed
27. Wore: 2 wds.
28. Get up
29. Shopping reminders
31. Preach
33. Japanese port
34. Old Thai coin
35. Pays up
38. Good time to see Paris?
40. Type of legal action: 2 wds.
42. Changing
43. Traffic signal: 2 wds.
49. Mark again
51. Tradition
53. Legal matter
55. Rainbow
56. Roman poet
57. Mata ——
58. Soon
60. Noun suffix
62. Destroy, to a Brit
63. Prayer ending
64. Concordes
66. That man
67. Herb

PUZZLE 43

ACROSS

1. Hive denizens
5. Concordes
9. Affectation
13. Egad, e.g.
14. Dutch flower
15. Iridescent gem
16. Pisa's river
17. Spyri heroine
18. Healthy
19. Like some fire companies?: 2 wds.
22. Actress Diana
23. Melody
24. Foam prefix
26. Actress Carter's bio?: 2 wds.
31. AFL-——
32. "——, I'm Adam"
34. Director Sidney
35. Insects
37. Jeans fabric
39. Comedian Jay
40. Does an usher's job
42. Brilliance
44. Ms. Sheridan
45. Like the prepared cobbler?: 2 wds.
47. Nursemaid
49. Hall-of-Famer Mel
50. Before: prefix
51. Bette Davis roofing manual?: 3 wds.
57. Wicked
58. Blunder
59. Fast steed
61. Tokay, e.g.
62. Gives the once-over
63. Terrible
64. Town in Judah
65. Fable
66. Etching fluid

DOWN

1. Constrictor
2. Warren or Holliman
3. Lab burner
4. Thrown together
5. Litigants
6. Gaffe
7. Ocean rise
8. Helix
9. Mighty
10. Oil cartel
11. Mariner
12. Building addition
14. "On ——" (Kerouac): 2 wds.
20. College residence, for short
21. Occupy
24. Tendon
25. Complete
26. McKeon or Walker
27. Actor Jannings
28. You know what ——?: 2 wds.
29. Comedian Bruce
30. School on the Thames
31. Juan's house
33. Legal document
36. Toddler's conveyance
38. Etiquette
41. —— good example: 2 wds.
43. Good-by: hyph.
46. Optimally: 2 wds.
48. "—— Smith" (McQueen film)
50. Expiate
51. Ardent
52. "Rock Island ——"
53. Killer whale
54. Caspian Sea feeder
55. Actor Blore
56. Indian wear
57. Ma that baas
60. Four-poster

ACROSS

1. Canine mothers
5. Sailors
9. Food plan
13. Power source
14. African lily
15. Greek enchantress
16. Ripped
17. Tribe
18. Bellows
19. Greek gods: 3 wds.
22. Conway
23. Convened
24. Soul: Fr.
27. Arrests
30. Greek island
34. Saltpetre
36. Garden bloom
38. Winglike
40. Greek goddesses: 3 wds.
43. Waste allowance
44. Mother of Castor
45. Loot
46. Fragrant resin
48. Supple- ments
50. Distress call
51. Kimono sash
53. Lair
55. Greek festival sites: 3 wds.
64. Warning flare
65. Roman 1102
66. French department
67. Released
68. Nota ——
69. Geraint's wife
70. Spanish painter
71. Greek god
72. Back talk

DOWN

1. Facts
2. Upon
3. Philippine Muslim
4. Refine ore
5. Washington city
6. —— breve
7. Speckled horse
8. Dispatches
9. Couturier
10. "Dies ——"
11. Beige
12. Hardy girl
15. Greek island
20. Flax fabric
21. Titles
24. Premed subject: abbr.
25. English bishop's cap
26. RFK's widow
28. Scottish hillside
29. Weather balloon
31. French composer
32. Bread spreads
33. —— Domingo
35. Nerve network
37. Coyote State: abbr.
39. Alejandro and Fernando
41. Excuse
42. Actor Buddy
47. Sulked
49. Whirlpools
52. Demeter's racy raconteur
54. Hawaiian birds
55. Switch positions
56. Attract
57. Belgian river
58. Convene
59. Maple genus
60. Boy: Sp.
61. "—— Lisa"
62. Greek goddess
63. Totals

PUZZLE 44

45

PUZZLE 45

ACROSS

1. Buddy
4. Brown
9. Gremlin
12. Epic
13. Spy
14. Entrance
16. Clan symbol
17. Campfire treat
20. Chemical-compound suffix
21. Trudge
23. Pod dweller
24. Small coin
25. Spiced wine
27. Quart components
29. Brimless hat
30. Guided
31. Train units
32. Concerning
34. Hose
37. Frilly fabric
38. Asset
39. Pack the car
40. Fishing spot
41. Aircraft carrier
44. Swiss mountain
45. Dove shelter
46. TV's "—— Times"
47. Hail!
48. Telegram
50. Night call
51. Nova
52. Heal
53. Farm worker
54. Snail
55. Disgrace
57. Labyrinth
58. Halloween word
59. Silent Coolidge
60. In that place
62. Use
66. Safflower and sunflower
68. Say further
69. Twilight
70. Heart, in prescriptions
71. Legal specialist: 2 wds.
74. Engine
76. A few
77. Soil deposit
78. First garden
79. Formerly named
80. —— in the grass
81. Clear profit

DOWN

1. Eucharistic plate
2. Mature
3. Eel
4. Mead's islands
5. Old oath
6. Each
7. Embolden
8. Georgia city
9. Actress Lupino
10. Shape
11. Repressed nation: 2 wds.
12. Fizzy drink
15. Numeral type
16. "—— the season . . ."
18. Grass rug
19. Blubbered
22. Topper
26. Happy
27. Gait
28. Dinner course
31. Dessert choice
33. Betel or hazel
34. Shut noisily
35. Fishing rod
36. Scamp
37. Tardy
38. Scheme
40. Theater section
41. Nourish-ment
42. Ellipse
43. Extra
45. Proofread-er's mark

46. Auction word
49. Final amount
50. Smog
51. Market
53. Not easily achieved: hyph.
54. Laborers
55. Highlander
56. Threads
57. Decorations
58. City vehicle
61. "2001" computer
62. Bag
63. Singing group
64. Anon
65. Misdo
67. Ditto
69. Writing table
72. Actor Majors
73. Affirmative vote
75. Pindaric

PUZZLE 46

ACROSS
1. Formal affair
5. Persian sprites
10. Pillow ——
14. Yvette's friend
15. Vast, to poets
16. Stance
17. Famed musical theme
18. They make things fast?
20. Traffic problem
22. Arrow poisons
23. Crossed d
24. Triptych parts
26. Yacht basin
30. Ledger entry
31. Grand Canyon's st.
32. Fan or prop
33. Expert
36. Secured: 4 wds.
40. Trevino of golf
41. Bridge positions
42. Deputy
43. Results of a tumble
44. French housemaids
46. Take heed
48. —— of averages
49. Wild water buffalos
50. Horse's leg projections
55. Place for a pep talk: 2 wds.
58. Expedition
59. Filly
60. Grass genus
61. Mal de ——
62. Biblical garden
63. City on the Ruhr
64. Was obligated

DOWN
1. Big —— theory
2. Cupid
3. Caron role
4. Graphite
5. Jai alai
6. Methuselah's father
7. "—— around the Clock"
8. Annoy
9. Slipper sizes: abbr.
10. Small piano
11. "The —— New Hampshire"
12. Campfire residue
13. Confusion
19. Underling
21. Quarterback Dawson
24. Bonuses, for short
25. Biblical title for God
26. Sledge-hammer
27. English composer
28. Merry-go-round
29. Verb suffix
30. Conduits
32. "—— a fine lady upon . . .": 2 wds.
33. Related
34. Relinquish
35. "—— of Laura Mars"
37. Crate again
38. Cowardly Lion
39. Entertainer Aykroyd
43. Get up
44. Caped crusader
45. Pussycat's friend
46. Extensive
47. Ink: Fr.
48. Sierra ——
49. Egyptian dancer
50. Antagonists
51. Director Preminger
52. Work gang
53. Flying toy
54. Hastened
56. Actress Charlotte
57. Beach buggies, e.g.: abbr.

PUZZLE 47

ACROSS
1. Apron
4. Elf
7. Dole out
11. Dry
13. Dear: It.
15. Expiate
17. Ulna
18. Hero
19. Measures
20. "—— in those days . . ." (I Sam. 28:1): 5 wds.
23. Shade tree
24. Native metal
25. Lake between Texas and Louisiana
29. Verbal reaction to a mouse
31. Mister's wife: abbr.
34. Got up
35. Pier
36. Fish-snake
37. "For _____ . . ." (Ps. 86:13): 4 wds.
41. Sound receiver
42. Espies
43. Cream
44. Federal draft agency: abbr.
45. Paving substance
46. Star in Gemini
47. Salt, to Pierre
49. Adult boys
50. "—— angel . . ." (Rev. 10:9): 5 wds.
59. Indian corn
60. Take pause
61. Nourishment
62. Clock
63. Before: prefix
64. Jumper
65. Smaller amount
66. Mideast nation: abbr.
67. Supplement

DOWN
1. Ali ——
2. Press
3. Tie
4. Winter sight
5. Female title of respect
6. School event
7. City official
8. Day's march
9. Pentateuch
10. Finishes
12. Gods, to Cato
14. Tavern brew
16. Curved letter
21. Belief
22. Grape
25. Wise ones
26. Tapestry
27. S.Africans of Dutch extraction
28. Bible book: abbr.
29. Come in
30. Old English letters
31. Earn
32. Right hand page of a manuscript
33. More cunning
35. On the briny
38. Agave fiber
39. Signified
40. Above-ground trains
46. Core
47. Smalls
48. Jugs
49. Having a moldy odor
50. Measurement: abbr.
51. Brad
52. Coin
53. New Deal initials
54. Sawbucks
55. Awry
56. Ripped
57. Ladder's companion
58. Rim

PUZZLE 48

ACROSS

1. Stocking mishap
5. Make cookies
9. Pretext
13. Perforation
14. Turn inside out
16. Ocean movement
17. Biblical mate
18. Type of race
19. Bookie's quote
20. That woman
21. Distort
22. Fondle
24. Stings
26. Flat fish
27. Pinocchio's bane
28. Of the shore
32. Call upon
35. Deserves
37. Beer's kin
38. Adjoin
39. Pseudonym
40. Stain
41. Understand
42. Sacred song
43. Releases
44. Pull out
46. Congou or cha
47. Dueling necessity
48. Bookworm
51. Mixologist
54. Scorch
55. Goal
57. Zone
58. Takes out
60. Gawk
61. Bound
62. Barrel part
63. Supplication
64. Clearance event
65. Potato buds
66. Examination

DOWN

1. Persian king
2. Swellings
3. Terror
4. Kind of muffin
5. Upbraid
6. Maintains
7. Brown algae
8. Memorable period
9. Emporiums
10. Pelt
11. Sums up
12. Jumble
15. Magnates
21. Decree
23. Word of sorrow
25. Came down
26. Beat it!
29. Anecdote
30. Lotion additive
31. Tolerates
32. Urn
33. Mountain goat
34. Hard fat
35. Gladden
36. Be unwell
39. Arises
40. Small nail
42. Hemingway's nickname
43. Apprehension
45. Transformed
46. Heckles
48. Superman portrayer
49. National bird
50. Provokes
51. Twilight swoopers
52. Opera highlight
53. Bobbin
54. Linger
56. Essence
59. Dined
60. Make a choice

ACROSS

1. Amo, ____, amat
5. Eva or Zsa Zsa
10. Fence prong
14. Golly!
15. By yourself
16. Opera tune
17. General Robert ____
18. Browned bread
19. Depend
20. Sweet Bambi?
22. Standards
24. Short wooden rods
25. Smooth-talking
26. Melon variety
29. Writer Duke?
33. Very warm
34. Book name
36. Newscaster Shriver
37. Of a certain period
39. More gentle
41. Actor Hudson
42. " . . . a poem lovely as ____"
44. Gives way
46. Diocese
47. Peel two?
49. Makes furious
51. Remainder
52. Dressing cheese
53. Shoulder garments
56. Weight drop?
60. Wan
61. Jagged
63. "Gone with the Wind" place
64. Man from "M*A*S*H"
65. French aunt
66. Same length
67. Wise one
68. "____ Magnolias"
69. Student's need

DOWN

1. Got older
2. Lawn tunneler
3. On a voyage
4. Himalayan
5. Opening pace?
6. Lotion ingredients
7. Wild pig
8. Switch positions
9. Plow again
10. Naked Teddy?
11. Scope
12. Little stream
13. Howls
21. Obligation
23. Per ____
25. Avarice
26. Inexpensive
27. Main artery
28. Belle or Bart
29. Fudd of cartoons
30. "____ by any other name . . ."
31. Kitchen gadget
32. Titicaca and Tanganyika, e.g.
35. Unspoken
38. Ogle King?
40. Genuine spool?
43. Zorro's blade
45. Snick-and- ____
48. Holdings
50. Removed the insides
52. Sew loosely
53. Healthy places
54. Tall or fairy
55. Shoppe adjective
56. Actor Franchot ____
57. House part
58. Greek god of war
59. Position
62. Mouse relative

PUZZLE 49

REVELATION

Solve this puzzle as you would a regular crossword. Then read the circled letters from left to right, and they will reveal a quotation.

ACROSS

1. Zest
6. Liable
11. Guitar features
16. Permit
17. Fanatical
18. Synthetic fabric
19. Aver
20. Excuse
21. Last of a series
22. Butt in
23. Jutland native
25. Freight barge
27. Soft touch
28. Back talk
30. Omit
32. Dancer Tommy
34. Make use of
36. Son of Jacob
38. Negligent
42. Prayer ender
44. Termagant
46. Likewise
47. In cipher
49. Bowline, e.g.
51. Melt
52. Past
53. Urban pall
55. ___ of heaven
57. Hail, to Caesar
58. It might be pica
60. Fortified wine
62. Lessened
64. Kind of peach
66. Short-winded
68. Roman and Victorian
69. Led
71. Tack item
72. Caravansary
73. Uppish one
75. Flour source
77. Tar
81. Jokester
84. Zounds!
86. Do autumn work
88. Meadow
89. Straightedge
91. Flies high
93. Inexpensive
95. Sports site
96. Computer fare
97. "A Man Called ___"
98. Jury
99. Oozes
100. Aquatic mammal

DOWN

1. Betrays astonishment
2. Super
3. Smites romantically
4. Wee one
5. Had IOUs out
6. Practical joke
7. Sir Walter ___
8. Osaka sash
9. Pen points
10. Decree
11. Scowled
12. Zodiac beast
13. Watches
14. Forum wear
15. Cinch
24. Cleo's snake
26. "___ Town" (Wilder)
29. Staircase unit
31. Yellowstone, e.g.
33. Radiate
35. Picnic pests
37. Fender bend
39. Home of Odysseus
40. Barrel slats
41. Planted
42. Kind of socks
43. Nearsightedness
44. Reporter's coup
45. Cause concern
47. Nab
48. Little devil
50. Football prop
54. C rations, to a GI
56. Sir Anthony ___
59. Goals
61. Prune
63. Samovars
65. Wholesale
67. Rider's support
70. Follow
72. Kind
74. Foundation
76. Endures
78. On the qui vive
79. Rent
80. Thin gradually
81. Swaddle
82. Nimbus
83. Singer Campbell
85. Finished
87. Reverberate
90. Chemical ending
92. Orangutan, e.g.
94. On a roll

ACROSS

1. Graceful steed
5. Proportion
10. Squabble
14. Seethe
15. African antelope
16. Singing group
17. Beige
18. Make amends for
19. Heckled
20. Perfume
22. Canters
23. Haphazardly
27. Tethers
31. Debatable
32. Tennis call
35. Felony
36. Yield
37. Tolerate
38. Rant
39. Trims
40. Fury
41. High cards
42. Author Leon ____
43. Plunges
44. Each
45. Saga
46. Track officials
47. Montgomery native
49. Inclines
52. Conduct
57. African lily
58. Incite
61. Oklahoma city
62. Young salmon
63. Diner
64. Picking-up implement
65. Very: Fr.
66. Apparel
67. Snick's mate

DOWN

1. Busy as ____
2. Mythical birds
3. Affectations
4. "____ Monday"
5. Responds
6. Change
7. Confucian concept
8. Lodge
9. Song of praise
10. Senator Thurmond
11. Stage article
12. ____-de-camp
13. Digits
21. Scruff
22. Building site
24. "Lost in ____"
25. Knots
26. Female deer
27. Discard
28. Smidgen
29. Monongahela, e.g.
30. Iowa college city
32. Exit
33. Enthusiastic
34. Ringlet
36. South American Indian
37. Lip
39. Cocoon denizen
43. Enjoy a repast
45. Chicago trains
46. Becomes narrower
47. Mimics
48. Track star Edwin ____
49. Absorbed
50. Having wings
51. Extra
53. Soaks to remove fiber
54. Shortly
55. Fork part
56. Advantage
58. "The ____ Pony"
59. Sculler's need
60. Colorado Indian

Common Combos

Listed below are groups of four unrelated words. Can you find a word that can either precede or follow each of the words in each group?

1. PREP	HIGH	BOOK	HOUSE	_____
2. PIPE	SPIN	COTTON	CAT	_____
3. COUNTRY	SANDWICH	SODA	SERVICE	_____
4. END	MARK	PASS	DATE	_____
5. TREE	HORSE	HORN	SOFT	_____
6. SNAP	GUN	JUMP	PUT	_____
7. SPY	JAW	STAINED	SNAKE	_____
8. FLAG	CAT	NORTH	STAR	_____

PUZZLE 53

ACROSS

1. Lavender
5. Faux pas
10. Bill's partner
13. Topnotch
14. Woody ____
15. Burn
16. Rotate
17. Fight unit
18. Lie down
19. Fixed
20. Flag
21. WWII vehicles
23. Summon
24. Lose liquidity
25. Go back on a pledge
28. "Jeepers, ____, where'd you get . . ."
31. White poplar
32. South Africans
33. ____ a chance!
34. Tidy
35. Fountain treats
36. Flintstones' pet
37. Go wrong
38. Adjusted in color
39. Zoo favorite
40. Bric-a-brac stands
42. Ship ladings
43. Belief
44. Allergy response, often
45. Greek city
47. Mardi ____
48. Hail, to Caesar
51. Tops for bikinis
52. Sticks
54. Riled
55. Mother Hubbard's quest
56. Very fat
57. Chinese dynasty
58. Total up
59. Shadings
60. Goose liver

DOWN

1. Let go by
2. Canter
3. One
4. Guys
5. Car spot
6. Unaccompanied
7. Chimney need
8. Swamp
9. Those who last
10. Lessening in value
11. Kiln
12. Food scraps
15. Respiratory illness
20. Carry on
22. Farewells
23. Stone
24. Deep fear
25. Rajah's spouse
26. Film critic
27. Very close
28. Morse and zip
29. Musical composition
30. Greek porches
32. "A Different World" former star
35. Vulnerable site
36. Pub missile
38. Ga. neighbor
39. Buddies
41. Ganders
42. Halts
44. Take forcibly
45. Scandinavian rock group
46. Walk heavily
47. Singer Campbell
48. Opera piece
49. Air
50. Lip
53. Sash
54. Sprite

PUZZLE 54   Three to One

Starting with each word in Column A, add a word from Column B and then one from Column C to build eight longer words. For example, CORN plus ERST plus ONE is CORNERSTONE. Each small word will be used only once.

	A	B	C		
1.	IN	HE	DON	1.	_____
2.	CON	FOR	TIC	2.	_____
3.	A	TIN	ION	3.	_____
4.	UP	READ	ATE	4.	_____
5.	TO	BAN	GENT	5.	_____
6.	PER	FLAT	CUT	6.	_____
7.	BULK	IS	AD	7.	_____
8.	ART	PER	OR	8.	_____

ACROSS

1. Tiff
5. Religious pictures
10. Gusted
14. Comfort
15. Concerning ships
16. Aged
17. Decorate
18. Follow the history of
19. Candid
20. Metal fasteners
22. Edited
24. Always, in poems
25. Carouse
26. Twaddle
30. Vitality
34. Leave out
35. Exclamation of regret
37. Male bee
38. Chess pieces
39. Porch swings
41. Tennessee footballer
42. Greek marketplace
44. Nothing more than
45. Strong fiber
46. Breakfast treat
48. Brings back
50. Bosc and Anjou
52. Chum
53. Subtlety
56. Dressmaker
60. Soon
61. Seville's location
63. Daybreak
64. Descend
65. Inclines
66. In the center of
67. Headliner
68. Delight
69. Cravings

DOWN

1. Backdrops
2. Segment
3. Largest continent
4. Squall
5. "____ Affairs"
6. Autos
7. Eggs
8. Mother-of-pearl
9. Record envelope
10. Stove compartment
11. Rims
12. Fencing blade
13. Travel forward
21. Singer Greenwood
23. Sells
25. Bookworms
26. Wanderer
27. Last Greek letter
28. Sheer fabric
29. Svelte
31. Rambler
32. Dwarflike being
33. Dogs' cries
36. Parched
39. Vapors
40. Answer
43. Aging agent
45. Fete
47. Nuisance
49. Young boy
51. Ward off
53. Trends
54. First letter: abbr.
55. TV science series
56. Coin
57. Corresponding
58. Double
59. Ceases
62. Motor club letters

Circle Sums

Each circle, lettered A through I, has its own number value from 1 to 9. No two circles have the same value. The numbers shown in the diagram are the sums of the circles which overlap at those points. For example, 8 is the sum of circles C and G. Can you find the value of each circle?

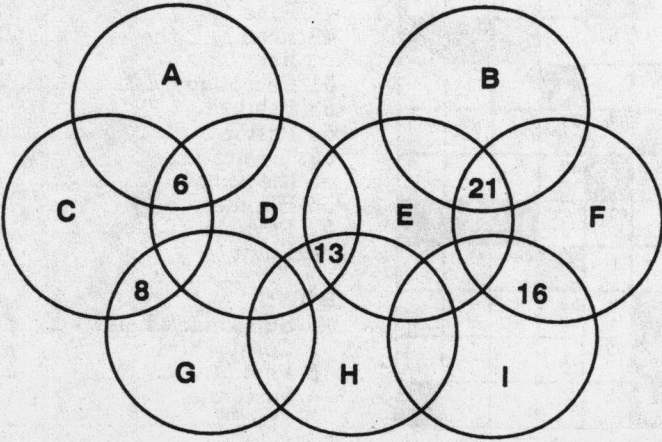

PUZZLE 57

ACROSS
1. Hurried
5. ____ mode
8. Russian ruler
12. Fuss
13. Fabulous bird
14. Architect Saarinen
15. River to the Caspian
16. Hearing organ
17. Observed
18. Belittle
20. Chooses
22. Pretentious
26. Horrible
29. Horse's flake
30. Sorrow
31. Christmas carol
32. Umpire's cry
33. Greek cheese
34. ____-la-la
35. No ____, ands, or buts
36. Passenger
37. Meddled
40. Provo's locale
41. Knitted blanket
45. South American country
47. Fitting
49. Roof edge
50. Ripened
51. Insect egg
52. Canter
53. Win by a ____
54. Doris or Dennis
55. Cravings

DOWN
1. Fastener
2. Tiny opening
3. Dutch cheese
4. Melancholy
5. Stadium
6. Mauna ____
7. Gymnast
8. Irritable
9. Played on the teeter-totter
10. Exist
11. Director Howard
19. "____ in the Family"
21. Cooking utensil
23. Cat's toy?
24. Memo
25. Weeping sign
26. Opposed
27. Corroded
28. Highlights
32. Informal
33. Jittery
35. Gershwin of song
36. Game official, for short
38. Musical composition
39. Shabby
42. Tortoise's rival
43. Bard's river
44. Meshes
45. Unfavorable review
46. Conceit
48. Actress Zadora

PUZZLE 58

ACROSS
1. Branch appendage
5. Stitch
8. Wail
11. Freight
12. Beer's kin
13. Epoch
14. Irritate
15. Progressive
17. Honey producer
18. Saga
20. Glen
21. Furnish
23. Lion's sound
26. Appointment
27. Forget-me-____
30. Saying
32. Innocent
34. Mattress
35. Woodwind instrument
39. Scheme
40. "The Red Badge of ____"
42. Too
45. Appraise
46. Dine
49. Read ____ the lines
51. Cacophony
53. Pasture
54. Pester
55. "Desire ____ the Elms"
56. Blunder
57. Payable
58. Plant

DOWN
1. Superman's Lois
2. Coastal bird
3. Past
4. Vestibule
5. Spittle
6. Trigger
7. "Charlotte's ____"
8. "Buona ____, Mrs. Campbell"
9. Spoken
10. Bundle
11. Taxi
16. Night before
19. Pea home
21. Paid athlete
22. Lair
23. Chest bone
24. "____ on a Grecian Urn"
25. Help
27. Nothing
28. Eggs
29. Decade number
31. Bovine bellow
33. Imitate
36. Part of FBI
37. Citrus fruit
38. Devour
40. Milk producer
41. Category
42. Fit
43. Ogle
44. Night light
46. Step or show starter
47. Secondhand
48. Each
50. Finish
52. Single

PUZZLE 59

ACROSS
1. Duelist's memento
5. E.T.'s transport
8. Applaud
12. Step
13. Unfavorable review
14. Favorable review
15. Broadcasts
16. Hollywood bigwig
18. One who pries
20. Dormant
21. Luge
22. Singer Davis
23. Change
25. Burrowing rodents
29. Skater Babilonia
30. Pancake
32. By way of
33. Cry out
35. Having regrets
37. Up in years
38. Parry
39. Subsequently
42. Most neat
45. Buried booty
47. Skier's joy
48. Radiate
49. Rummy-player's shout
50. Eight: pref.
51. Lion's pride
52. Coal scuttle
53. Capone's nemesis

DOWN
1. Health resorts
2. Third person
3. Word puzzle
4. Repair a shoe
5. Raised
6. Klinger's portrayer
7. Lennon's widow
8. Cereal-eater's sound
9. "Arsenic and Old ____"
10. Declare
11. Saucy
17. Changed, as a baby
19. Cotton fabrics
22. Swab
23. Had lunch
24. Careless
25. Jewel
26. Proof
27. ____ Tin Tin
28. Droop
31. Disencumber
34. Find
36. Harmony
38. Wicked one
39. Plant supporter
40. "My Friend ____"
41. No, in Vienna
42. Musical group
43. Drunkards
44. Deuces
46. Yuck

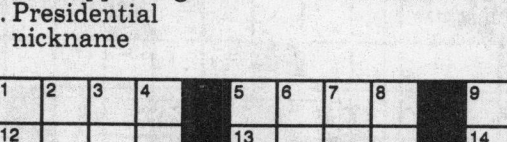

PUZZLE 60

ACROSS
1. Secular
5. Deal
9. Coal scuttle
12. "Betsy's Wedding" director
13. Pinnacle
14. Gardner
15. Wall Street pessimist
16. Wrist wear
18. Sacred
20. Special edition
21. Where the Alps rise
24. The Greatest
25. Dice game
26. Nightclubs
30. Gear
31. Boy king
32. Part of a GI's address
33. Futile
36. Aviator
38. Pro
39. Lawyer's customer
40. Eddy
43. Honest
44. Parrot
46. Woman
50. Mine yield
51. Atom
52. Orchestral instrument
53. Unite
54. Stench
55. Dampens

DOWN
1. Scientist's place
2. Tavern treat
3. Ms. Lupino
4. Drive-in waiter
5. Pay television
6. Grand Ole ____
7. Pod particle
8. Outdoes
9. Sentry's shout
10. Above
11. Info
17. Sign above a door
19. Goddess of plenty
21. Beige
22. Author Leon ____
23. Storm
24. River islet
26. Kramden's vehicle
27. Martha ____
28. Ajar
29. Ilk
31. Mao ____-tung
34. Spree
35. Bakery purchase
36. Winter malady
37. Bide one's time
39. Emulate a frog
40. Flat-bottomed vessel
41. Lasted
42. Frozen
43. Luggage item
45. Foot appendage
47. Presidential nickname
48. I topper
49. Affirmative

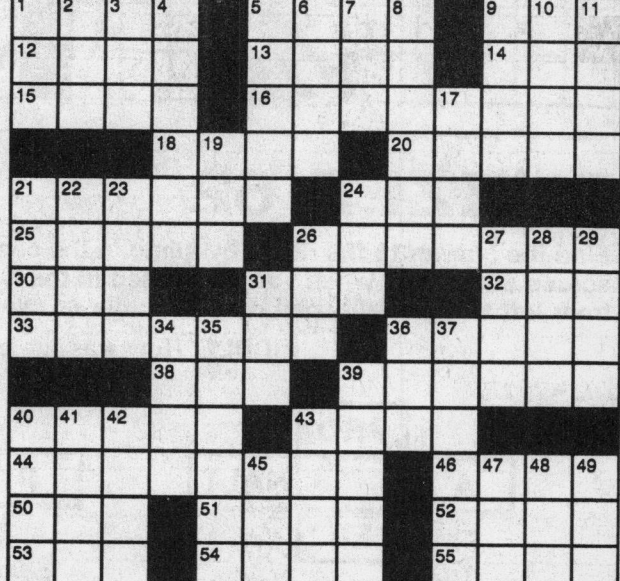

PUZZLE 61

ACROSS

1. Pointed end
4. Quick to learn
7. Blaze
12. "Much ___ About Nothing"
13. College yells
15. Three-leaf forage plant
16. Baby's cradle
18. Spin
19. Defeats a bridge contract
20. Commands
22. Snakelike fish
24. Territory
25. Immerse
28. Burst
30. Had title to
32. Ruled mark
33. "My Gal ___"
34. British noblemen
35. Untrue
36. Enliven
38. Steadier
40. Enters a swimming pool
41. Gloss
43. Sounds of hesitation
44. Frosted
45. Fixed gaze
46. Actor Carney
47. Curvy letter
48. Swiss archer
49. Arrest
51. Metal fasteners
53. Communists
56. Mechanic's shop
59. Letter packet
62. Arouse
63. Destroy
64. Bitterly amusing
65. Actor O'Toole
66. Actress Arthur
67. Comedian Louis ___

DOWN

1. Dinner check
2. Actress Lupino et al.
3. Assumed attitude
4. Get up
5. Skillet
6. Lieutenant Kojak
7. Actress Robson
8. Building sites
9. Actress Gardner
10. Ran into
11. Sooner than, to a poet
14. String of pearls
15. Statement of faith
17. Footfall
21. Chest of drawers
23. Booty
25. Comedienne Phyllis ___
26. Letter enclosure
27. A jury of his ___
28. Becomes alarmed suddenly
29. Martini garnishes
31. Grapple
32. Science workroom
33. Miss Thompson of "Rain"
34. ___ Vegas
35. Cooling device
37. Club ___
39. Adolescent
42. Horse restraint
45. Lucky number
46. Cain's brother
48. Saber-toothed ___
50. Scene of action
51. Gather leaves
52. Ignore socially
54. Toward the ground
55. Agile
56. Space
57. Reverent fear
58. Large rodent
60. Contend
61. Organ of sight

PUZZLE 62   CRACKERJACKS

Find the answer to the riddle by filling in the center boxes with the letters needed to complete the words across and down. When you have filled in the Crackerjacks, the letters reading across the center boxes from left to right will spell out the riddle answer.

RIDDLE: How was the pool party of Mr. and Mrs. Rich?

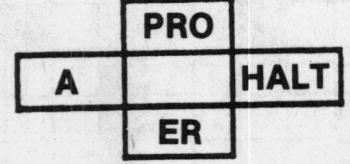
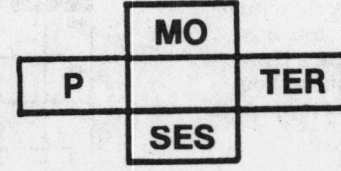
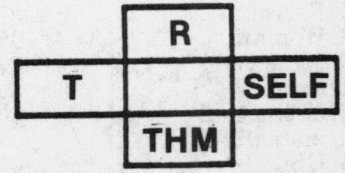

ANSWER: _____

58

ACROSS

1. Lid
6. Carry
10. Comes up to the plate
14. Similar
15. Summit
16. Reed instrument
17. Thin marks
18. Harvest
19. Certain
20. Enemy
21. Tall cereal plant
23. Endured
25. Rage
26. Cordlike
27. Academic title
30. Long-eared animal
31. Damage
34. Less cooked
35. Stores away
36. Baseball stat
37. Chills and fever
38. Glowing cinder
39. Delay
40. Males
41. Be of use to
42. Minister's home
43. Singer Garfunkel
44. Denomination
45. Cared for
46. Special privilege
47. Physique
48. Double-cross
51. Group of animals
52. Lump
55. Amount of land
56. Above
58. Sizable
60. "____ Masquerade"
61. Diamond squad
62. Banish
63. Jumps
64. Orient
65. Prevent

DOWN

1. Young cow
2. Miscellany
3. Creeper
4. ____ out a living
5. Deliverer
6. Linger
7. Forthright
8. Oolong, e.g.
9. Magellan, for one
10. Domineering
11. Touch on
12. Ripped
13. Kernel
22. Mine product
24. Gibbons, e.g.
25. Unattached
26. "Bolero" composer
27. Stage play
28. Avid
29. Hog's sound
30. Custom
31. Signifies
32. Get up
33. Graded
35. Slap
38. All people
39. Suspicious
41. On the ocean
42. Confused
45. Neither's mate
46. Printing machine
47. Tam
48. Immersion
49. Resound
50. Stumble
51. Barnyard fowls
52. "True ____"
53. Gape at
54. Tavern order
57. By way of
59. Hatchet

Bubbles

In each of the circles is the name of a sport minus one letter! Find that missing letter to complete the sport's name. Then arrange the missing letters to spell the bonus sport.

1.
2.
3.
4.
5.
6.

1. _____
2. _____
3. _____
4. _____
5. _____
6. _____

Bonus: _____

PUZZLE 65

The answers to the clues can be found in the diagram, but they have been camouflaged. Their letters are in correct order, but sometimes they are separated by extra letters which have been inserted throughout the diagram. You must black out all the extra Camouflage letters. The remaining letters will be used in words reading across and down. Solve Across and Down together to determine the correct letters where there is a choice. The number of answer words in a row or column is indicated by the number of clues.

	1	2	3	4	5	6	7	8	9	10	11	12	13	14	15
1	B	T	E	G	I	E	S	N	A	N	C	M	A	S	E
2	R	A	H	V	N	D	O	B	M	D	R	F	E	I	P
3	W	P	A	R	T	Y	N	E	N	R	H	I	R	E	Y
4	O	P	M	E	R	A	D	C	O	I	A	G	R	S	E
5	W	S	R	K	I	N	G	K	L	E	W	A	O	L	E
6	I	L	O	A	C	Q	E	T	U	A	F	R	D	Y	T
7	S	A	L	P	A	D	R	V	E	M	T	O	Z	T	E
8	E	U	Y	L	S	E	O	I	E	R	L	C	W	A	N
9	M	U	N	T	T	U	W	E	R	S	E	N	H	D	K
10	A	D	C	D	E	R	U	N	I	T	L	I	T	I	N
11	R	O	B	A	U	I	S	E	T	A	D	C	E	M	D
12	T	N	S	E	L	T	A	I	H	C	S	L	K	E	E
13	H	M	A	B	S	O	L	F	G	V	E	E	R	S	R
14	S	T	R	I	C	P	J	C	E	A	M	A	S	E	V
15	H	O	U	T	E	B	L	K	F	E	X	T	E	N	L

ACROSS

1. Initiate • Legal matter
2. Occurring by chance • Leaky faucet's output
3. Associate • Wrath
4. Musical drama • Grating
5. Innovation • Affliction
6. Fasten • Caustic
7. Vegetable mix • Unlikely
8. Center • Bribe • Lacking forcefulness
9. Grumble • Propel
10. Viper • Apparatus • Ignited
11. Full-bodied • Made a hole in one
12. Ensnare • Theater walkway
13. Excuse • Blunder
14. Runway • Discontinue
15. Lodging place • Sharp

DOWN

1. Graze • Wetland area
2. Praise • In the know about
3. Premature • Counter
4. Numerous • Bookkeeping entry
5. Involved • Exploit
6. Temper • Certain toy
7. Oppressive • Entirely
8. Cravat • Notch
9. Infiltrator • Religious practice
10. Goal • ____ off (forestall)
11. Swimming stroke • Otherwise
12. Sardonic • Meadow
13. Pointed shaft • Brusque
14. Nap • Study
15. Certain rapier • Offer as payment

ACROSS
1. Skewer
7. Pleasure ship
12. Environs
16. Kinsman
17. Bellowing
18. Cincinnati players
19. Wandering
20. Heavenly fare
21. Snip
22. Spot
23. 100 yrs.
25. Pass over
27. Blind ambition
28. Timberland
31. Abe's Secretary of War
33. ____ metabolism
36. Sprig
38. Lecherous looks
39. Pliny's language
40. Anecdotal collection
41. Small child
42. Asian sea
43. Weatherman's visual aid
45. Fired a gun
47. Play part
50. "Dombey and ____" (Dickens)
51. Pea capsule
52. Keats poem
53. Rod
54. Terminal
55. Throw for a ____
57. Unite
58. Judicial wear
59. Father
60. ____ before beauty
62. CSA president
63. Wooden shoe
66. Bob Hope's "____ to Rio"
68. Range parts
69. Voted into office
72. Irish lilt
74. WWII lady
75. Epochs
77. Energy unit
78. Elusive one
81. Fast horse
83. Improper
86. Graduates
88. Miff
89. ____ Bush Johnston (Abe's stepmother)
90. Country
91. ____ Edith Evans
92. Adversary
93. Sleeping sickness fly

DOWN
1. Cold desserts
2. Additional
3. Unadulterated
4. "Not ____ Stranger": 2 wds.
5. Abe
6. Come in
7. Sweet potato
8. Coach Parseghian
9. Pros and ____
10. Nancy ____ (Abe's mother)
11. Quality
12. ____ de Triomphe
13. Link
14. Magazine head
15. Quaking poplars
24. New Jersey cager
26. Sense of taste
28. Get an F
29. Exchange
30. Soft metal
32. Mr. Rorem
33. Jaded
34. Baseball great
35. Put up with
37. Kind of fuel
41. Mary ____ (Abe's wife)
43. Mental state
44. "Much ____ About Nothing"
46. Chop out weeds
47. Upstairs
48. Lodge
49. Lock of hair
51. Nebraska river
56. Average
57. Sport
58. Kind of review
59. Mr. Severinsen
61. Seaman
62. Abe's rival
63. Abe's secretary of state
64. Seaweed genus
65. Bring to a standstill
67. Anonymous John or Jane
70. Clean, as a blackboard
71. Rodentlike, rock-dwelling animal
73. Abe's general
76. Paddock parent
78. Discharge
79. Space monkey
80. Genealogy
82. Hive insect
84. Golfer Snead
85. Bashful
87. Certain Shoshonean

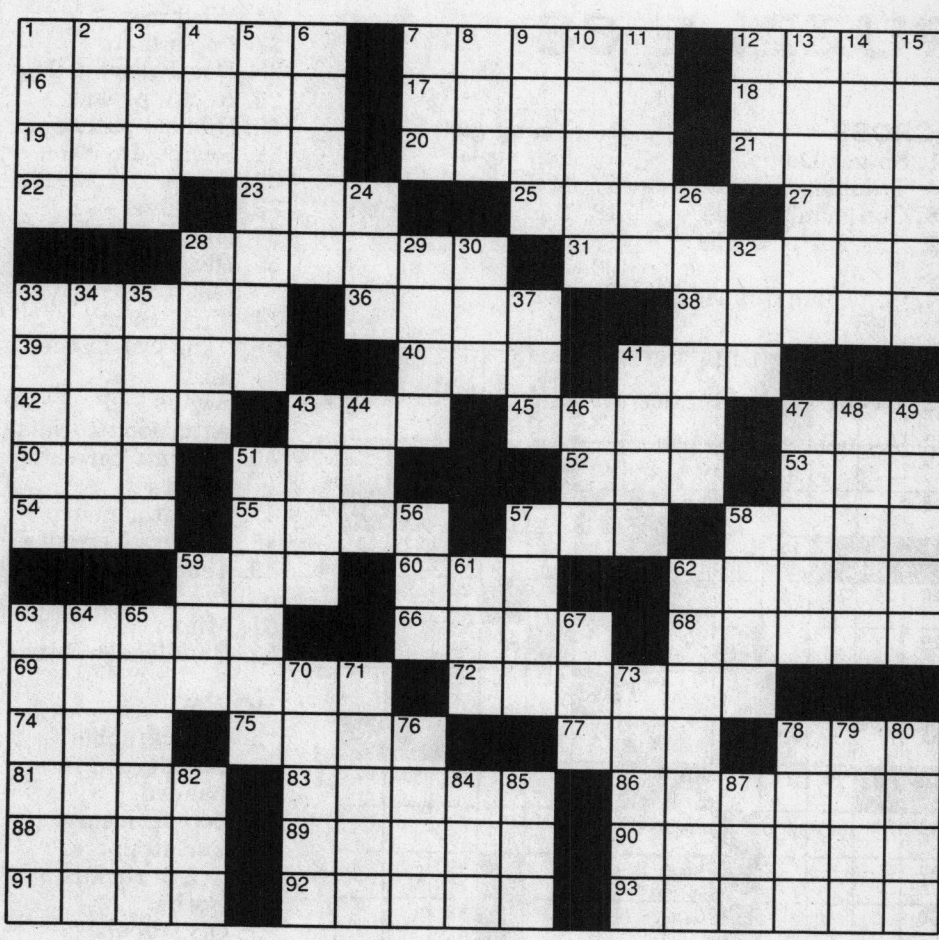

PUZZLE 67

ACROSS
1. Football, e.g.
6. Knight's attendant
10. Prohibition
11. Claw
12. Foe
13. Distribute
14. Flat-topped hill
15. Rental document
16. Legislative body
19. That girl
20. Storage container
21. Statute
24. Hunting dog
28. Mr. Carroll's heroine
30. Mine products
32. Temptress
33. Coral structure
34. Happening
35. Fred Allen's medium
36. Take five
37. Vote in

DOWN
1. Plant stalk
2. Window segments
3. Overweight
4. Cato was one
5. Plaything
6. Ashen
7. Islamic supreme being
8. Gander's mate
9. Join in a contest
11. Natural ability
17. Off the scene
18. Knot
21. Compact-disc player
22. Animated
23. Cables
25. Sum
26. Wear down
27. Old souvenir
29. Penny
31. Vegas machine
33. "You ____ There"

PUZZLE 68

ACROSS
1. Singer Davis
4. Troublesome tot
8. Con man's game
12. ____ carte: 2 wds.
13. Foray
14. Comedian Johnson
15. Young girls' hair-style
17. Malicious look
18. Barbecue favorites
19. Chat
20. Actress Grant
21. Zany
24. Wise men
27. Pop's mate
28. Dos Passos trilogy
29. Rocky peaks
30. Biblical patriarch
31. Recipe direction
32. Santa ____, Calif.
33. Pushover
34. Houses in Madrid
35. Old Faithful, for one
37. "____ Sack"
38. "The Cat in the ____"
39. Swaps
43. Afternoon socials
45. Aircraft carriers, to tars
47. Elevator man
48. Actress Veronica
49. Tennis call
50. "____ Poppins"
51. Mimic
52. Bandleader Brown

DOWN
1. Cartographers' output
2. Landed
3. Zoo enclosure
4. Car stoppers
5. ____ a ruckus
6. Bother
7. QB's goals
8. Menu item
9. Boot camp coifs: 2 wds.
10. Had a bite
11. Sea: Fr.
16. Yarns
19. Bread spread
21. Angry crowd
22. Land east of the Urals
23. Golf scores
24. Men-only party
25. Top-notch: hyph.
26. Worry's yield: 2 wds.
27. Swab
30. Jolt
31. Egypt's Anwar
33. Theatrical construction
34. 39th President
36. Pert
37. Tent peg
40. Barbie or Ken
41. Fencing weapon
42. Concordes
43. "____ Brown's School Days"
44. Airport info: abbr.
45. Tampa's state: abbr.
46. ____ of luxury

62

CIRCULAR CROSSWORD

PUZZLE 69

Fill in the answers to the Around clues in a clockwise direction; to the Radial clues, from the outside to the inside.

AROUND (Clockwise)
1. Utilities customers
6. Wall St. pessimist
10. Well I ____!
15. Portal
19. Fine mash
20. Ointment
21. Tasty tidbit
22. Puts by
23. American author and novel
27. ____ for the ride
28. Wireless
29. Composer Franz
30. Impressionist painter
32. British change
33. Kilmer poem

34. Took an oath
35. Aver
36. Actor Oliver
37. Patriotic org.
38. Kind
39. Printers' measures

RADIALLY (Out to in)
1. Bothers
2. Musical piece
3. White-tailed eagle
4. Born-again tire
5. Vendor
6. Burst (in)
7. Building wing
8. Prevent

9. Wanted-poster figure
10. More of a buttinsky
11. Saint ____ fire
12. By way of
13. Sins
14. Freshens
15. Attic
16. Hail, to Caesar
17. Pours
18. The press, for one
20. Thereafter
22. Drummer Ringo
24. Top-notch
25. Brainstorm
26. Scat!
31. A Bobbsey Twin

Note to Solvers: This Crossword does not have aids such as "2 wds." and "hyph."

PUZZLE 70

• O'NEILL'S PRIZEWINNERS •

ACROSS
1. Politician Gingrich
5. Youngster
8. Dance step
11. Toboggan
15. Colorful fish
16. Wander
17. Play personnel
18. Poi source
19. Actress Anderson
20. Historic periods of time
21. In addition
22. Way out
23. Straddling
25. Under the weather
27. Buffalo's waterfront
29. 1928 Pulitzer play
35. San ____, California
37. Chilled
38. Vaudeville's Blossom ____
39. ____-relief
40. Helper: abbr.
42. Melody
44. Philosopher Descartes
45. Seed coat
47. Jug
49. Actor Idle
52. Norm: abbr.
53. Wings
54. "The Sheik of ____"
57. Like a grandparent
59. 1957 play "____ Night"
66. Indian garb
67. Equipped
68. Space
69. Favoring
72. Cherry variety
74. On the briny
76. Initial bet
77. Earring position
79. Hockey net
82. Celsius number: abbr.
84. German article
85. Appear
88. Hint
90. Sharp crest
92. 1920 Pulitzer play
95. Guy
96. Mouths
97. Ally
101. "La Boheme" heroine
104. Adored person
106. Duplicate
108. Roman writer
109. Gulf of ____
110. Writer Ferber
111. Long spans of time
112. Affection
113. Sharp flavor
114. Change color
115. Schnauzer, e.g.
116. Former ugly duckling

DOWN
1. Lopez's theme tune
2. Group of poems
3. Desire
4. Need for water
5. Seoul's location
6. Yellow bugle
7. Pattern
8. Friend
9. Piece of property
10. Supplies
11. Pittsburgh athlete
12. Loose
13. Silkworm
14. Point
16. House of Lancaster's symbol
17. Cotton fabric
24. Virginia willow
26. Garlands
28. Rage
30. Memo makers
31. Hawaiian goose
32. Rubber trees
33. Fender damage
34. Looked at
35. "That Girl" star
36. Far East native
39. False god
41. Moving back and forth
43. Spanish nobleman
46. Table supports
48. Indian prince
50. "____ Got a Secret"
51. Small island
55. City division: abbr.
56. Arizona city
58. Money in Florence, once
60. Smear
61. Actress Meyers of "Kate and Allie"
62. Person who reposes
63. Composition for nine
64. Comedian Fields
65. Forewarning
69. Commoner
70. Colosseum's location
71. Conform to
73. Member of a Germanic people
75. Mythical female warriors
78. Wearing down
80. Ring of color
81. Cowardly Lion actor
83. School dance
86. Antelope
87. Swirled
89. Plated
91. Registers
93. Stuffed animal
94. Cake decoration
98. Declare firmly
99. Prima donna
100. Ideal place
101. Small rug
102. Actress Lupino
103. Males
105. Small bill
107. Court

ACROSS

1. Preserve
4. Imp
8. Sweet singer
12. Earlier
13. Part
14. Comedian Young
15. Awful
17. Singer Seeger
18. Conform
19. Outlaw James
20. Stitch loosely
23. Sniggler's quarry
24. Footed vases
25. Rustic rug
30. Zodiac sign
31. "____ Beauty"
32. Author Levin
33. Baseball great
35. Nature's building block
36. Entertainer Pinky ____
37. Landscape
38. Fling
41. Vatican City dweller
43. Stack
44. Lingerie item
48. Buffalo's lake
49. Baker's need
50. Put on
51. Sculpt
52. Actor Hackman
53. Bomb

DOWN

1. Cougar, e.g.
2. Ripen, as cheese
3. Negative word
4. Payoff
5. Housecoat
6. Associate
7. Pullover
8. Jacket features
9. Ginger drinks
10. Squealers
11. Reflex site
16. Decays
19. Steve Martin film with "The"
20. Holland export
21. Sector
22. Snooty one
23. Every
25. "____ Lagoon"
26. Nibble
27. High flyer
28. Steamy appliance
29. Epithet
31. Make coffee
34. Ran off to marry
35. Fighter pilots
37. Cactus's defense
38. Those people
39. Villain's foe
40. Banister
41. Blacktop
42. Sign
44. Wheel tooth
45. Peculiar
46. Actor Gossett, Jr.
47. Outcome

PUZZLE 71

65

ACROSS

1. "The Subject Was ___"
6. "Family Ties" actor
11. "Franken-stein ___ the Wolf Man"
16. Popeye's girlfriend Oyl
17. Lease an apartment again
18. "Kate & ___"
19. Refashion
20. Lend ___
21. "___ Syndrome"
22. Farrow of films
23. "Two Years Before the ___"
25. "Celebration at Big ___"
27. Court divider
28. Mistakes
30. Dorothy's dog
31. "Presenting Lily ___"
32. "___, Two, Three" (Cagney film)
33. Long, long time
34. Professional figurer: abbr.
36. "Death Becomes Her" actress
39. "___ Heard the Mermaids Singing"
40. Roger Corman film

44. Director Kazan
45. "Pair of ___" (Willie Nelson film)
46. "___ New-man, M.D." (Peck film)
48. "___ and Bill"
49. Jennifer Jones film, with "The"
50. Silent star Negri
51. Wedding words
52. Willis role on "Moon-lighting"
54. Dunn of "Saturday Night Live"
55. "They ___ What They Wanted" (Lombard film)
56. Twangy tone
57. "Holiday ___"
58. Stack character
59. TV's "___ a Life"
61. Stallone nickname
62. Andy's aunt
64. Gambling game
67. Johnson of "Laugh-In"
69. Actress Carter of "A Room With a View"

72. "___ to Pieces"
73. "Apple ___" (Rue McClanahan series)
74. "___ Lisa"
75. Globe
77. Actor Novarro
80. "___ Give a Sucker an Even Break"
82. Actress Massey
84. Storehouse
85. "The ___ Menagerie"
86. "___, don't mean maybe . . ."
87. Ms. Berger of "Cross of Iron"
88. "A ___ of Loss"
89. Islamic ruler

DOWN

1. Ramble
2. Kukla and Fran's friend
3. Shankar's instrument
4. "All About ___"
5. Homily
6. "The ___ Is Singing" (Karen Black film)
7. Tear
8. Comedian Olsen
9. Actress Hubley

10. Swagger
11. Town in Chad
12. Nightmare street
13. Ms. Verdugo
14. "Save the ___"
15. Chairs
24. "Butterflies ___ Free"
26. Dutton TV series
29. Columnist Barrett
30. "On Your ___" (Eddie Albert film)
31. TV detective Houston
33. "___ Knievel"
35. "___, Mama, the Maid and I"
36. Strong guy
37. Actress Valli of "The Cassandra Crossing"
38. "The ___ of Kitty Hawk"
39. Religious image
41. Singer Frankie ___
42. Assistants
43. "The ___ of Kilimanjaro"
45. "Much ___ About Nothing"
46. "The ___ Is Green" (Bette Davis film)

47. Chicken ____ king
49. "____ of Fury" (Bogart film)
50. "There Must Be a ____"
53. Shakespearean villain
54. "Queen of the ____" (Jeanne Crain film)
55. "Banjo on My ____"
60. "____ Roots"
61. "Remington ____"
62. "____ Casey"
63. Julia Louis-Dreyfus role on "Seinfeld"
64. "____ on the Plain"
65. Marble
66. "____ Holiday"
68. "____ on Her Fingers"
69. "A Man Called ____"
70. "The ____ Hangs High"
71. Paymer's role on "The Commish"
74. "A Fine ____" (Danson film)
76. "Designing Women" actor
78. Choose
79. Teachers' org.
81. "The Dick ____ Dyke Show"
83. Actor Herbert ____ (Pink Panther series)

PUZZLE 73

ACROSS

1. Golf ball prop
4. Inspires with fear
8. To another place
12. Large vase
13. Angry fury
14. Ponder intently
15. Free of something unpleasant
16. Scent
17. Colony insects
18. Bird homes
20. Burn
22. Primary color
24. Fodder
28. Satisfy fully
31. Male sheep
34. Put into service
35. Employ
36. Gone by
37. Malt beverages
38. Busy activity
39. Was obligated to
40. In an orderly condition
41. Unit of length
43. Break a fast
45. Sleeveless garment
48. Depressions
52. Land measure
55. Deceived
57. Cereal grass
58. Loud outburst
59. Not working
60. Fasten
61. Reproduction
62. Merge
63. Freddy's street

DOWN

1. Rotate
2. Pennsylvania port
3. Terminates
4. Got up
5. Small mass
6. Selves
7. Dry
8. Into pieces
9. Finished first
10. Decorative piece
11. Positive response
19. Forest growth
21. Donkey
23. Sketch
25. Regulation
26. On the water
27. East's opposite
28. Hoax
29. Assistant
30. Horse's gait
32. Length of life
33. Method
37. Poker stake
39. Native metal
42. Each
44. Included
46. Slender
47. Motion of the ocean
49. Short letter
50. Dog appendage
51. Flower stalk
52. Curved line
53. Talk fondly
54. Knock
56. Building extension

ACROSS

1. Bill
4. Outdated
7. Bigwig
9. Path
11. Medieval
12. Tattered
14. Tack on
15. Inn
17. Vote against
18. Actor Arnaz
20. Have being
21. Penalty
22. Responsibility
24. Linkletter and Carney
25. Distant
26. Nursery item
27. Poet Keats
28. Sorrows
30. Deli sandwich
31. Cushion
32. Comparative word
36. Female sheep
37. Hackett or Holly
39. In the past
40. Dues payer
42. Smirked
44. Tier
45. Football measures
46. Butterfly catcher
47. Sugar ____ Leonard

DOWN

1. Dull sounds
2. Assist
3. Grin
4. Verbal
5. Jet ____
6. Self-respect
7. Grant
8. Be buoyant
9. Ginkgo, e.g.
10. Tilts
11. Craze
13. Hair coloring
16. Sample
19. Boise's state
21. Ice
23. Coffee server
24. Dined
25. Supervisor
27. Gem
28. Roll of bills
29. Strangely
30. Edge
31. Feline sound
33. Author Thomas ____
34. Rock of ____
35. Land of ____
37. Root vegetable
38. Fifty-two weeks
41. Ciao
43. Feminists' goal

PUZZLE 75

ACROSS

1. ____ Vegas
4. Long way off
8. Radiance
12. Interrogate
13. Adorable
14. Abate
15. Blew through puckered lips
17. African river
18. Lemon skin
19. Fast car
21. Recorded
23. Emblem
24. Tints
25. Mom and dad
29. Prove human
30. Language units
32. Metallic rock
33. Makeup kit item
35. Sooty matter
36. Gibb or Williams
37. Secret agents
38. Extremely small
41. Graceful bird
42. Uproars
43. Musical programs
47. Mrs. Kennedy
48. Ages
49. Chamomile drink
50. Snow toy
51. Studies
52. Hen output

DOWN

1. Statute
2. Bat wood
3. Captains
4. Played the part
5. Maximum load
6. Had a pizza
7. Carrot-top
8. Docile
9. Lion's home
10. Norway's capital
11. Garden intruder
16. Witnesses
20. Propels
21. The other guys
22. Emanation
23. Mist
26. Put up for office
27. Not false
28. Tennis units
30. Desire
31. Commanded
34. Brought to pass
35. Tiff
37. Kind of cheese
38. Red planet
39. Icon
40. Snout
41. Scrutinize
44. Before, in verse
45. Break a ____!
46. Droop

ACROSS

1. Bit
4. Green gem
8. To's mate
11. Poem
12. Theater sign
13. Spanish custard
14. Gaming cube
15. Gambling town
16. Soothe
17. Weasellike mammal
19. ____ Pole
21. Deli bread
23. Social insect
24. Copycat
27. "The ____ of the Mohicans"
30. Self
33. Transgress
34. Songbirds
35. Sunburned
36. Caress
37. Against
38. Colored
39. Tattle
41. For each
43. Fast car
45. Considerably
49. "The Twilight ____"
50. Hawaiian island
53. Immerse
54. Noshes
55. Jai ____
56. Bullring cry
57. Being: Lat.
58. Incline
59. "Do the Right Thing" director

DOWN

1. Flightless bird
2. Mine entrance
3. Sugar source
4. Ben's ice cream partner
5. Lumberjack's tool
6. Noise
7. Jacket or collar
8. Soft soap
9. Impulsive
10. Washington bill
13. Flowerless plant
18. Stray
20. Horse food
22. Pep
24. Horned viper
25. Easy as ____
26. Contestants
28. Mr. Linkletter
29. Pass over
31. Horse command
32. Strange
34. Overdue
38. Actress Joanne ____
40. Point-winning serves
42. Rig
43. Type of horse
44. Lion's cry
46. Baal
47. Mosaic piece
48. Rapier
49. Final letter
51. ____ carte
52. Prosciutto

PUZZLE 77

ACROSS
1. Mist
4. Boutique
8. Secret agent
11. Infrequent
13. Chapter unit
14. Foot digit
15. Spoken
16. Feels poorly
17. Museum display
18. Urban problem
20. Comeback
22. Father
24. Rec room
25. School subject
29. Enjoy
33. Bambi's mom
34. Peculiar
36. "...violets ___ blue..."
37. Not tart
40. Wipes out
43. Take it on the ___
45. Tail movement
46. List of candidates
49. Crow
52. Shoot the breeze
53. Offense
55. At all
57. Actor Vigoda
58. African river
59. Musical sound
60. Of course!
61. ___ off (angry)
62. Marry

DOWN
1. To and ___
2. Rowing items
3. Metric weight
4. Health resort
5. Moustache
6. Stared
7. Bother
8. Celebrity
9. Harbor
10. Neverthe-less
12. Flee, romantically
19. Sailor
21. Three minus two
23. ___ and con
25. Newspaper items
26. Not loud
27. Horse command
28. Tack on
30. Large tub
31. Before, in poems
32. Guitarist Paul
35. Moisture
38. Building wing
39. Special aptitude
41. Scientist's room
42. Long-plumed heron
44. Picture
46. Baseball's Ruth
47. Primates
48. Floor square
50. Affirm
51. Film critic Shalit
52. Sunbeam
54. Conducted
56. Stop-sign color

CODEWORD

Codeword is a special crossword puzzle in which conventional clues are omitted. Instead, answer words in the diagram are represented by numbers. Each number represents a different letter of the alphabet, and all the letters of the alphabet are used. When you are sure of a letter, put it in the code key chart and cross it off in the alphabet box. A group of letters has been inserted to start you off.

Code key chart:

1	2	3	4	5	6	7	8	9	10	11	12	13

14	15	16	17	18	19	20	21	22	23	24	25	26
		N	U			R						

Grid (selected entries):

Row: 12 11 20 4 | 11 15 8 | 3 20 11 13
Row: 11 20 10 11 | 20 11 20 10 | 6 17 2 20 10
Row: 1 10 11 22 | 15 20 2 13 | 17 16 3 2 3
Row: 10 16 3 | 10 21 13 20 11 15 10 3
Row: 11 5 4 2 20 10 | 11 20 10
Row: 22 23 2 16 | 11 16 8 | 25 10 7
Row: 5 4 20 17 16 19 | 7 12 2 1 | 11 26 10 (R U N)
Row: 8 10 11 21 | 9 2 11 | 6 17 2 3
Row: 23 20 8 | 5 22 11 19 | 18 11 17 16 8 5
Row: 11 8 10 | 12 23 8 | 21 11 19 2
Row: 15 11 4 | 10 21 23 8 | 10 5
Row: 8 20 11 9 10 22 10 3 | 20 2 21
Row: 22 10 11 9 10 | 10 3 3 14 | 19 23 16 10
Row: 10 22 9 10 5 | 19 11 22 10 | 11 5 24 5
Row: 11 22 10 5 | 21 10 8 | 22 10 5 5

ALPHABET BOX

A B C D E F G H I J K L M N O P Q R S T U V W X Y Z

PUZZLE 79

ACROSS

1. Little Joe's brother
5. Has a burger
9. Chore
13. Lion's locks
17. Esau's wife
18. Close loudly
19. Mountain's melody
20. Mt. Olympus god
21. Nil, to Newcombe
22. ___ Alto
23. Outsmart
24. Musical symbol
25. "Brigadoon" composer
28. Amphora
29. Noise
30. Drama by Euripides
31. Floral garland
33. Device
37. Hill insect
38. Farmer
42. Sigourney Weaver film
43. Jazz job
44. That girl
46. French wine valley
47. Gambler's city
48. Cookie grain
49. Start of a Sousa march
51. Elvis ___ Presley
52. Seeks penance
54. Washstand pitcher
55. More or less
57. Earned
58. Goody
59. "___ Abner"
60. Photographer's word
63. Word-of-mouth
64. Combat chow
68. Dangle
69. Severity
71. Youngster
72. Purple plum
73. Grant portrayer
75. Baseball's Bando
76. Female bear
77. Outburst
78. Pyramid builder
80. SMU's rival
81. Academy
82. Sauna site
83. Spy gp.
84. Ostrichlike bird
85. Clockmaker Thomas
88. "Oklahoma!" composer
96. Brag
97. Key
98. White House car
99. Sky juice
100. ___ spumante
101. Critic Gabler
102. He was: Lat.
103. "The Thin Man" dog
104. Broadway sign
105. Actress Rowlands
106. "Entertainment Tonight" host, once
107. Bottomless

DOWN

1. Moiety
2. Redolence
3. Except for
4. Outbuilding
5. ___ de corps
6. Actor Delon
7. After-bath sprinkle
8. Type of jacket
9. Montana river
10. Realtor's measure
11. "Pygmalion" playwright
12. Actor Bernie ___
13. "A Chorus Line" composer
14. Precinct
15. Promontory
16. Italian family
26. Adam's address
27. Parcel of land
32. Otologist's concern
33. "Tootsie" actress
34. Windward's opposite
35. Dent
36. "Girl Crazy" composer
37. River island
38. Part of MPH
39. Pamplona bull
40. Space chimp
41. Apartment fee
43. Highway sign
44. Plagiarize
45. Male deer
48. Loki's victim
49. Curse
50. Coleslaw, e.g.
53. Goddess of dawn
54. Actor Flynn
56. Ignited
58. Galba's garb
60. Book segment: abbr.

61. Brunch food
62. Sicilian resort
64. Inexperienced
65. Toast topper
66. Double negative
67. Blind, as hawks
70. Comedian Kabibble
71. Actor Gossett, Jr.
74. Hip-hopper's music
76. Tanager's color
77. Skim along easily
79. Rowing
80. Actress Carrere ("Wayne's World")
81. Glossy
83. Crab claw
84. Columnist Bombeck et al.
85. Eye
86. Gael
87. Canine star
89. Words of understanding
90. Tribe
91. Dreadful
92. Alumnus
93. Soothe
94. Communion, e.g.
95. Crack

PUZZLE 80

ACROSS

1. Green vegetable
5. French clergyman
9. Indonesian island
13. Food fish
17. Stagger
18. Mysterious
19. Mr. Shepard
20. Earthenware pot
21. Rocky ledge
22. Spanish painter
23. Cleave
24. Wotan's counterpart
25. Pianist Claudio ____
27. Chocolate base
29. Give orders
31. Delegate
33. Conclude
35. Young female
36. Game official
39. Skillet
40. Diva's song
41. City in Missouri
45. Arrive
47. Chinese, e.g.
48. Objective
49. Determine
50. Critical
51. Lump
54. Friar's title
55. Dutch export
56. Christmas song
57. French satirist
59. Fast-food offering
61. Dessert shop
62. Bed framework
65. Military student
66. Schooner need
70. Lincoln or Fortas
71. Lamprey
72. Mr. Burr
73. Mild cheese
74. Misplace
76. "Peer Gynt" author
77. Phone user
78. Mystery
81. Despot
82. Island food
83. Parent
84. Chatter
85. Bro or sis
86. Imperfectly
88. City on the Tigris
92. Orange type
94. Sailboat
98. American author
99. Soap members
101. Fast steed
103. Frost type
104. Sandwich filler
105. Provo's state
106. Early Peruvian
107. Heraldic wreath
108. Origin
109. Prudent
110. ____ -do-well
111. Russian city

DOWN

1. Whale
2. Actress Deborah ____
3. In the back
4. Seaweeds
5. Include
6. Guiding light
7. Make fast
8. Heroic story
9. Like some castles
10. Malted beverage
11. Country
12. Dark blue
13. Make moonshine
14. "The Four Seasons" actor
15. Crack
16. Sensible
26. Loosen
28. Lofty
30. Bad guy
32. Movers' vehicle
34. Actor Duryea
36. Cajole
37. Fungal growth
38. Request
40. American fur trader
42. Divan
43. Eastern dress
44. Expression of distress
46. Baby sheep
47. Discussed
50. Of a cranial nerve
51. Arouse
52. Drive the getaway car
53. The: Ger.
56. Canadian Indian

76

57. Dangerous gas
58. Bathroom cleaner
60. Shoshonean
61. Less ornamented
62. Bundle
63. Poet's black
64. Mr. Arnaz
65. Melon
67. "____ Lang Syne"
68. Hunch
69. Fat
72. Liqueur
73. In a festive way
75. Highbrow
76. Part of TGIF
77. Grand Banks catch
79. Cross
80. Old calculating device
82. Mansion
86. Swiss city
87. Boorish person
88. Belfry dwellers
89. Winter ill
90. Hereditary unit
91. Info

93. Futile
95. Underground stem
96. Dutch painter
97. Expedition
100. Slump
102. Exclude

PUZZLE 81

ACROSS

1. Out of
5. Cleanse
9. Egyptian bird
13. Furnace food
17. Volcanic output
18. Garden worker
19. Apportion
20. Ballet dancer Spessivtzeva
21. Cracked
22. Exercise system
23. Hammer part
24. Around
25. Of apples
27. Ultimate
29. Connecticut city
31. French city
33. Facilitate
35. Chou En-____
36. Remark of discovery
39. Thing to bend or lend
40. Behold: Lat.
41. Spain's continent
45. North Carolina city
47. Sir, in India
48. Actor Martin ____
49. Imagine
50. Hanker for
51. Butter serving
54. Resembling: abbr.
55. Czech
56. She's Reddy to sing
57. Greek philosopher
59. Egyptian god
61. Like some highways
62. Expressed amusement
65. Button
66. Coin of South Africa
70. "____ the ramparts ..."
71. ____ in the bag!
72. Grimy
73. Leg bone
74. Tide phase
76. Capital of Morocco
77. Take away
78. Actor Gould
81. Goldie ____ of films
82. Beach acquisition
83. Golfer's mound
84. Turmoil
85. Miner's quest
86. Large estate house
88. Substitute
92. Norwegian dramatist
94. Young mayfly
98. Places
99. Long, long time
101. Actor Alan ____
103. Out of use
104. Music and painting
105. Disbursed
106. Wild goat
107. Harbor mammal
108. Pesky fly
109. Algerian port
110. Gold fabric
111. Medieval peasant

DOWN

1. Falsehood
2. Indian prince
3. President's office
4. "West Side Story" song
5. Bashful
6. Sound system unit
7. Protection
8. Cereal ingredient
9. Unspoken
10. Good grade
11. It's on the agenda
12. Doddering
13. Authenticate
14. Bread spread
15. Culture medium
16. Meat by-product
26. ____ of the crop
28. German city
30. Baseball's Charlie ____
32. Take it on the ____
34. Society girl
36. Supplements
37. Toss
38. Region
40. Overhanging structures
42. Remove
43. Dance position
44. New Haven trees
46. Chaos
47. Compact
50. Large asteroid
51. Verses
52. Complexion woe
53. Three: pref.
56. Dagger handle
57. Actor Baio
58. Bitter
60. Hit the slopes

61. American painter
62. Frozen-yogurt holder
63. Shoe feature
64. Russian range
65. Spider construction
67. End at
68. Agreeable
69. Appointment
72. Architect Eero ___
73. Mortise's partner
75. Hamlisch, e.g.
76. Greek letter
77. "Roseanne" character
79. Peculiar
80. Trinidad and ___
82. Trailer type
86. Singer Moore
87. Elevate
88. Metal residue
89. Ripped
90. Court minutes
91. Time interval
93. Boat cloth
95. March 15th
96. Actor Ladd
97. Remove
100. Pliny's breakfast
102. Chopping tool

PUZZLE 82

ACROSS

1. Rebuff
5. Important vessel
10. Original
13. Regrettably
17. Albright of films
18. Severe
19. Caesar's breakfast
20. Insect sense organ
21. Face shape
22. Chart again
23. Apple dessert
25. Japanese cheer
27. TV's Vigoda
29. Arm bone
30. Increase
31. Whale of a movie
33. Spool of film
35. Bowling, Italian style
38. Expansive
39. Performers
42. Expression of discovery
43. Tulip beginning
44. American publisher
45. Sleeve lurker
47. Bird's bill
48. Required
49. Small part
51. Russian ruler
52. Face hair
54. Pointer
55. Plants
56. Austrian city
57. Rare gas
58. Overshadow
59. Propelled a raft
61. Dim
62. Carpenter's groove
65. Looked at
66. Pipe
67. Mecca man
69. A few
70. German article
71. Accomplishment
72. Border
73. Policeman
74. Astrology chart
76. Norwegian dramatist
78. Leg joint
80. Was carried
81. Arlene ____ of Hollywood
82. Passing through
83. Wild hog
85. Clod
86. City on the Hudson
90. Wild party
93. Thrash about
97. French cheese
98. Sarge's dog
99. Sedan
100. French river
101. Italian volcano
102. English college
103. Hot time in Paris
104. Heron
105. Fabric worker

DOWN

1. Messy one
2. PBS series
3. ____ Bator
4. French novelist
5. Pungent
6. Colliery find
7. Island drink
8. Social gathering
9. Peruvian mammal
10. Not yup
11. Gabor or Peron
12. Ashen
13. NASA spacecraft
14. Chair or mower
15. "M*A*S*H" star
16. Catch a glimpse of
24. Compositions for two
26. Cool drink
28. Ugly
31. Heraldic feature
32. Burglarize
33. Indy 500 entrant
34. Canyon sound
35. Sudden noise
36. Dayton's state
37. Southwestern horseman
38. Baby rose
40. Wild pig
41. Blemish
43. Singer Joan ____
44. Harbinger
46. Historic period
48. Flex
49. Close but no ____
50. God of love
51. Golf or social
53. All even
54. Size
55. Excess fat
57. Glowing

58. Stubborn child
59. Footed: suff.
60. Courtroom sound
61. Ortho-dontist's item
63. Chemical compound
64. Prepare a letter
66. Draw a ____ on (aim at)
67. Adam's son
68. Flow
71. Bay, in Norway
72. Bonfire residue
75. Puff, for one
76. Crete mountain
77. Confound
78. Disturb
79. Captured
82. Personal servant
83. Cable fastener
84. Aware of
85. Brute
87. Bohemian
88. Prime-time time
89. Time span
90. Misery
91. Freeze
92. Styron's Turner
94. Kind of cabin
95. Broadcast
96. Dander

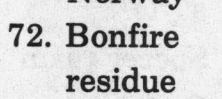

PUZZLE 83

ACROSS

1. Dogie
5. Syrup source
10. ____ of Gilead
14. Zodiac sign
16. Willow shoots
18. Coined money
20. Heeded, as advice
22. Eager
23. Till bill
24. French department
25. City of slots
27. Get the drift
28. Symbols of royalty
29. Movie villain's word
31. Pub quaff
33. Needles
34. Bundle
39. Transporter
40. Poet Marianne ____
41. Water growth
42. Before bellum or chamber
43. Diamond wear
44. Frozen dessert
47. Asian land
48. French legislative body
49. Record player
50. Sprite
51. Snowed under
53. What Horton hears
56. Bigots
58. Wrongdoings
59. Lacking rain
60. Flow forth
62. " . . . fetch her poor dog ____ "
63. Muscle fitness
64. Volunteer St.
65. Filmmaker Lee
66. Distributes
68. Mighty mountains
70. Strong thread
71. Strays
72. Tooth covering
74. Ship sections
76. Large container
79. Part of Caesar's boast
80. English river
81. 1101, Roman style
84. Soccer team
86. Go cuckoo
91. Briny
92. Camelot lady
93. Trunk
94. Roofing material
95. Heating vessels
96. Husk

DOWN

1. Stoic philosopher
2. Irish islands
3. Much the same
4. Retainer
5. Bullwinkle, e.g.
6. Ruins
7. Large tart
8. Grassy area
9. Guess wrong
10. River bottom
11. Fearless fliers
12. Don Juan's patter
13. Dispense
15. Catnap
17. Walk purposefully
18. In control
19. Urges on
21. Roman waterway
26. Raised railways
28. Actors' parts
29. Treat
30. Sculls
31. Commonplace
32. Beyond control
33. Assaulted
35. Lepus
36. Space to operate
37. Biographical datum
38. Hefty
39. In the pink
40. King of Crete
43. British length
44. Lacking vitality
45. Towel pronoun
46. Stammering sounds
48. Small barracuda
49. Fishing net

PUZZLE 83

51. Hagen of the stage
52. Call forth
54. Innuendos
55. Horatian output
57. Designer Klein
59. Earth holder
60. Airport info: abbr.
61. Fellows
62. Church section
65. Figure of speech
66. Sprang up
67. Cheapest
69. "Itch" year
70. Shaver
73. Baseball team
74. City in India
75. Norse writings
76. Suit part
77. Jai ___
78. Archer from Uri
81. Lake
82. Bar challenge
83. Object of worship
85. Engage in rivalry
87. Cadiz cheer
88. Convened
89. One, in Vienna
90. Skip and jump's partner

PUZZLE 84

MOVIES & TELEVISION

ACROSS

1. "The Prodigal" actress
4. "____ Appeal"
8. "Good ____" (Cooper film)
11. TV's "____ Smart"
14. "To ____ With Love"
15. Mine access
16. Irene Cara film
17. "Star Trek: The Next Generation" role
18. "Cliffhanger" actor
20. John ____ (Temple's ex)
21. Greek letter
22. ____ de mer
23. "Beau ____" (Milland film)
25. Burt Lancaster film
27. "The Revolt of ____ Stover"
29. "The ____ Picture Show"
30. ____ Khan (Rita Hayworth's ex)
31. "____ 21" (Dunne film)
32. "East of ____"

34. Actor Prine of "The Wide Country"
37. Women's gp.
38. "Cheers" brew
39. "Jurassic Park" actress
42. Eggs: Lat.
43. Hemsley series
44. Writer Deighton
45. Jacob's child
46. Dirk Bogarde film
49. "Inherit the Wind" actor
51. British film magnate J. Arthur ____
52. New Deal initials
53. Coup d'____
54. Table crumb
55. Mrs. Chaplin
57. Lawyer: abbr.
58. "The ____ and the Beautiful"
61. "Colleen" actress
64. "Love at First ____"
66. Ms. Gilbert of "Roseanne"
67. Howard or Ely
68. Actress Adams
70. "Tap" actor
71. ZaSu ____ ("The Gale Storm Show")

73. TV's "The Addams Family" actor
75. Quick ____ wink
76. Actress Thurman
77. Hungarian politician Nagy
79. "____ Have Tender Grapes"
83. Caesar's 1,002
84. Sumptuous ball
85. Cricket term
86. "Mr. ____" (Raft film)
87. Sothern or Jillian
88. Modern: pref.
89. Ollie's partner
90. TV's "Island ____"

DOWN

1. Curved letter
2. Set fire to
3. "Frasier" actor
4. French director Louis ____
5. "Much ____ About Nothing"
6. "____, You Sinners"
7. "Remington ____"
8. Bob ____ of "Full House"

9. "I ____ Camera"
10. Ethel ____
11. Stripper Lee
12. "At ____" (Jimmie Walker TV series)
13. Baseball's Speaker
16. Minnesota ____ (Gleason role)
19. Den
24. "Blood and ____"
26. "The ____ Maid" (Bette Davis film)
27. "The ____ Squad"
28. Henner role on "Evening Shade"
32. Ella Joyce's "Roc" role
33. "Goodfellas" actor
34. Actress Bening
35. "____ in My Heart" (Stanwyck film)
36. "The ____ Lover" (McQueen film)
38. Electrical unit
40. Overhead railways

41. "___ Performance"
43. "___ Any Girl" (David Niven film)
45. "___ of Love" (Bardot film)
46. "Truth or ___"
47. "Let Me ___ You"
48. "He ___ All the Way"
50. ___ King Cole
51. Korean soldier
56. Touch upon
58. Allen film
59. TV's "People ___ Funny"
60. "___ Boot"
62. "Salem's ___"
63. "___ Pulver"
65. "___ Delight" (Norma Shearer film)
66. Spanish agreement words
68. "That Girl" girl
69. Confused
70. Safe harbor
71. Jungle cat
72. "___ the Mood for Love"
74. Night, in Paree
78. West or Busch
80. Communications comp.
81. Italian writer Umberto ___
82. Actor Victor ___ Yung ("Bonanza")

PUZZLE 85

ACROSS
1. Strong beers
5. ____ Hawkins Day
10. Bristle
14. Shock
19. Fuzz
20. Improve
21. Privy to
22. Paul Anka hit
23. What makes Henri a girl
24. Aunt: Fr.
25. Edible seaweed
26. Prank
27. Seafood treat
30. Migratory birds
31. Cataloguers
32. Footlike part
33. Allonyms
35. Wynn and Asner
36. Little one
39. Knock for ____ (astonish)
40. Sideslips
43. Baseball great
46. Poplars
50. Small river island
51. Australian tree dweller
52. Small measure
54. Pork cut
55. Fats Domino song
59. Core
62. Got on a jet
63. Author Talese
64. Sale record: abbr.
65. View
66. Canine star and namesakes
67. Japanese coin
68. Goatee
70. Church vestment
73. Impressario Hurok
74. Appropriate
75. Land areas
79. Italian dessert
81. Steinbeck classic
84. Mixture
85. Night, in Milan
87. Tests
88. Meadow
89. Cater to
92. Herb plant
94. Rubbish
96. Small nails
98. Arguable
99. Nectar collector
100. Fitness guru
103. Confucian way
105. Abate
109. Pay the penalty
110. Burgess novel, with "A"
115. La Douce et al.
116. Of flying
117. Immigrant
118. Mr. Wolfe
119. Laughing
120. Den
121. Ranted
122. Adolescent
123. Wynter and Andrews
124. Epidermis
125. Tizzies
126. Concordes

DOWN
1. Herrings
2. Stone: pref.
3. Submit a contest solution
4. Began
5. Mythical man-goats
6. Collect
7. Nick
8. Division word
9. First place
10. Inasmuch as
11. Organic compounds
12. African antelope
13. Menagerie denizen
14. Showy dances
15. Pina colada fruit
16. Head tops
17. Flavorful seed
18. Spikes the punch
28. Beatty film
29. Foil's kin
34. Mauna ____
36. Planks
37. In a capable way
38. Boring
39. Some history: abbr.
40. Kemo ____
41. Oast
42. Keep ____!
43. Aurora ____
44. Lombardy city
45. Solely
47. Eternities
48. Riviera city
49. Cut, of yore
51. Bandleader Stan ____
53. "____ the Girls"
56. Top of Guido's scale
57. Deep voice
58. "____ Kick out of You"

60. Carpentry joints
61. Toss around
67. Fine mist
68. Volcanic rock
69. Exclusive org.
70. Above
71. Ms. Falana
72. Lip
74. Taj Mahal site
76. Big bash
77. Parisian summers
78. Persian king
80. Star
82. Gourd fruit
83. World's Fair, for short
86. German spa
90. Borgnine et al.
91. Operated
93. Wild
94. Rip
95. Rescinds
97. Stick-ons
99. Fair-haired lads
100. Scottish squire
101. Open courtyards
102. Literary salesman
103. Shinto temple portal
104. Oak nut
105. Shooting sport
106. Cap and hole
107. White heron
108. Ad signs
111. Seep
112. Conflicts
113. "The Good Earth" name
114. Swiss peak

PUZZLE 86

ACROSS

1. Warbled
5. Period
8. Michael Jackson album
11. Stink
12. Ages in history
14. ____ League
15. Cleanser
17. Ascot
18. Where equilibrium resides
19. Pierced
21. Luck
24. Countdown ending
25. Gam
26. Anthem poet
28. Cruising vessel
32. Sector
34. Baste
36. "Rich Man, ____ Man"
37. Roost
39. Bar check
41. Edgar Allan ____
42. '60s-style
44. Withdraw
46. Javelin
48. Deface
49. Scraping tool
50. Character witness
55. Pindaric poem
56. Podium
57. Anon
58. Guy's mate
59. Encountered
60. Stepped

DOWN

1. Peat
2. Citrus drink
3. Forget-me-____
4. Envy color
5. Temperature units
6. Raw metal
7. Latin-American dance
8. Snack
9. Raring to go
10. Change the color of
13. Unyielding
16. Store frame
20. Harvest
21. Applaud
22. Roll call response
23. Antiquing apparatus
27. Still
29. Manage
30. "Boyz N the ____"
31. "A ____ Grows in Brooklyn"
33. Apex
35. Most tepid
38. Hidden supply
40. Smokey the ____
43. Fantasy
45. Peak
46. Soft drink
47. Fruit skin
49. Pig
51. For shame!
52. Neither hide ____ hair
53. Pigeon sound
54. Finish

ACROSS
1. Lackaday!
5. Brag
10. Ace
14. Ruse
18. Part
19. Corbin's TV character
20. Shearer or Kelly
21. Pack animal
22. North African port
24. Danish port
26. Outstanding
27. Sherbets
28. ____ in on (pointed at)
29. Pairs
30. Ruffian
31. Earth
32. ____ and Charybdis
35. Hard-hearted
37. Wane
38. Ooh's partner
41. Kilmer poem
42. Defrosts
43. Parts of comet heads
45. Field
46. Sense of direction
47. Companion to her
48. Smell
49. Delves
50. Ruff's mate
51. German port
56. Tarry
57. Noisy sleepers
59. Abodes
60. Elegant
62. Leafy vegetable
63. Type of energy
64. Chilly
65. Gypsy language
68. Melodies
69. Councils
72. Deuterium discoverer
73. Tanzanian port
75. Bill
77. Wire measures
78. Expectation
79. Poetic contraction
80. Color
81. Track's Mathias
82. Gauge
83. Thin pancake
85. Broker
87. Miscellany
88. Bullfight cheer
89. Leg parts
90. Soprano Maria ____
91. Defeat
92. Lather
93. Mood
94. East African republic
97. Carry through the air
98. Revealed
101. Mediterranean port
103. New Zealand port
106. Uncommon
107. Coal barges
108. Supplied
109. "____ in a Blue Moon"
110. Declare positively
111. Hotels
112. Residue
113. Rouse

DOWN
1. Curve
2. Mortgage
3. Additionally
4. North Pacific port
5. Spanish explorer
6. Some vaccines
7. Actress Archer
8. Incite to attack
9. Souchong, e.g.
10. Courted
11. Rose fruits
12. Choler
13. East African port
14. Astute
15. Author Victor ____
16. Toward shelter
17. Heal
20. The real ____
23. Bellows
25. Basil and chervil
27. Charged atoms
30. "____ About You"
31. Fiend
32. Sirius, e.g.
33. Shouts
34. Arabian country
35. Carpenters' wedges
36. Gentle
38. Assumed name
39. Sponsorship
40. Rash
42. "____ Goes My Baby"
43. Conceal
44. Poems
49. Lived
51. Wheat husk
52. Depend confidently
53. Avignon's river
54. Openings
55. Pile up
58. Approves
60. Spanish lady
61. Meander
63. More certain
64. Stop
65. Cuban dance
66. Sky hunter
67. ____ toast
68. Cellophane
69. Errors
70. Blues singer Waters
71. Finnish bath
73. Loves to excess
74. Egyptian sun god
76. Antes
78. Baltic port
82. Dough
83. Talk
84. Rend
85. Composer Copland
86. Scottish port
89. Settees
90. Symbols of love
91. Less strict
92. Jibs, for example
93. Spindles
94. Actress Gilbert
95. King of Norway
96. Pond
97. Brown-gray songbird
98. Seamen's saint
99. Sicilian volcano
100. Pier
102. Shelter
103. Roll of bills
104. Blunder
105. Formerly named

PUZZLE 88

ACROSS
1. Engrave
5. Embroider
8. Forward
12. Miss Storm
13. Gershwin
14. Famous canal
15. Utah attraction
18. Says
19. Money handler
20. Depend (on)
21. Yoko ____
22. Twist
24. Weave together
28. Tailor's need
29. Letter afterthoughts
30. Educator's group: abbr.
31. Fishermen
34. Appraiser
36. Night before
37. Dressing gown
38. Kind of paint
41. Merited
44. Virginia tourist attraction
46. At an end
47. Make a knot
48. John ____
49. Views
50. Conger
51. Singer Nelson

DOWN
1. Breakfast food
2. Pastry
3. Becoming unclouded
4. Slangy gun
5. Cowardly one
6. Age
7. TV family
8. Author Saul
9. Vocal
10. Similar to
11. Stag
16. William ____
17. Camper's home
22. Resort
23. Triumph
24. Kind of curve
25. Meant
26. Born
27. Lobed feature
29. Bishop
32. Madagascar mammals
33. Always
34. Jungle noise
35. Always a bridesmaid, never ____
37. One who resists authority
38. Biblical name
39. Wheel part
40. To ____
42. Mild oath
43. Contradict
45. Fabrication

PUZZLE 89

ACROSS
1. Relax
5. Terhune's pup
8. Vehicles
12. Bert ____
13. S. state: abbr.
14. Woodwind
15. Means to ascend
17. M. Coty
18. Map abbr.
19. Biased
21. Yawned
23. Frozen water
24. Feel remorse
25. Betting
30. River in Italy
32. Cigar residue
33. Asterisk
34. Nursery item
36. Adam's rib
37. Seedcase
38. "The Taming of the ____"
40. Student
44. Split ____ soup
45. At one time
46. Repudiated
50. Small boat
51. Cup handle
52. Bird's home
53. Rams' mates
54. Arid
55. Cooling drinks

DOWN
1. Literary monogram
2. Dine
3. Hones
4. Banal
5. Statute
6. Woe is me!
7. Sunshine
8. Places for naughty kids
9. Aid and ____
10. Jaw or wish
11. Kernel
16. Scarlet
20. High card
21. Seize
22. Atmosphere
25. Roamed
26. Peer Gynt's mother
27. Repeated
28. Church part
29. Flourished
31. Fish hawks
35. Charged atom
38. Health resort
39. Salon substance
40. Ore vein
41. Plenty to a poet
42. Mideast port
43. Back
47. Sob
48. Compass pt.
49. Sot's ailment

PUZZLE 90

• SIMPLY SIMON •

ACROSS

1. Phonograph inventor
7. Hill
12. Highway division
16. Lawn game
17. Italy's locale
19. Sea nymph
20. Simon's Jerome play
22. Strange
23. Posted
24. German resort
25. Nigerian city
27. Uno, ____, tres . . .
28. Stage decorations
30. Sacred book
32. Descendant
36. Too much: Fr.
37. Bay
38. Payable
41. Brilliance
43. Claire or Balin
44. Cheap seats
46. Coarse food
48. Green vegetables
49. Custom
50. Switch positions
51. Self
52. Devout
53. Social insects
54. Enemy
55. Money, in Tijuana
56. Water vessel
57. Among
59. Remainder
60. Color or angle starter
61. Scandinavian rug
64. Obie, e.g.
65. Nasty
66. Tiniest
68. Columbo, e.g.
70. Once around
71. Alpine singing
72. Botanist Gray
73. Wayne flick
74. Ambulance crews: abbr.
76. Plant spore masses
77. Ones
78. "____ the Roof"
79. Deuce
82. Links group: abbr.
83. Chinese-American architect
84. Yorkshire waterway
88. Fend off
90. Simon's Writer play
96. Make proud
97. Artists' stands
98. Commands
99. Jazz singer Fitzgerald
100. Broad piece of wood
101. Burning

DOWN

1. Recedes
2. Golden
3. Symbol
4. Sing like Crothers
5. Resembling: suff.
6. Freshest
7. Foundation
8. Gist
9. Mexican gold
10. Ed Asner role
11. Hosp. worker
12. Falsity
13. Dry
14. Famous pianist
15. Football positions
18. Food
19. Simon's Valentine play
21. Explorer Vespucci
26. Circus or collar
29. Resort
30. Object of beauty
31. Applies in the surface
32. Favorite
33. Univ. course
34. Founder of Troy
35. Scrap
38. Obligation
39. "Mila 18" author
40. N.Y. clock zone
42. Simon's Madison and Unger play
45. Slugger Aaron
47. Period
48. Band
52. Cobblers
54. Conflagration
55. Hedge shrub
56. Vocation
57. Amazes
58. ____ Hari
60. Walked quietly
61. Make over
62. French river
63. Hun king
64. Nabokov heroine
65. Spoil
66. Light column
67. ____ Angeles
69. Spice
70. Romanian coin
75. Duke of baseball
79. Conifer, e.g.
80. Water source
81. Iridescent gem
84. Amino or lactic
85. Hankering
86. Printing process
87. Once, once
89. Greek H
91. Possesses
92. Seer's letters
93. Clot
94. Palm leaf
95. "____ on Melancholy"

PUZZLE 91

Diagramless crosswords are solved by using the clues and their numbers to fill in the answer words and the arrangement of black squares. Insert the number of each clue with the first letter of its answer, across and down. Fill in a black square at the end of each word. Every black square must have a corresponding black square on the opposite side of the diagram to form a diagonally symmetrical pattern.

ACROSS

1. Frequently
4. Solving aid
8. Foreigner

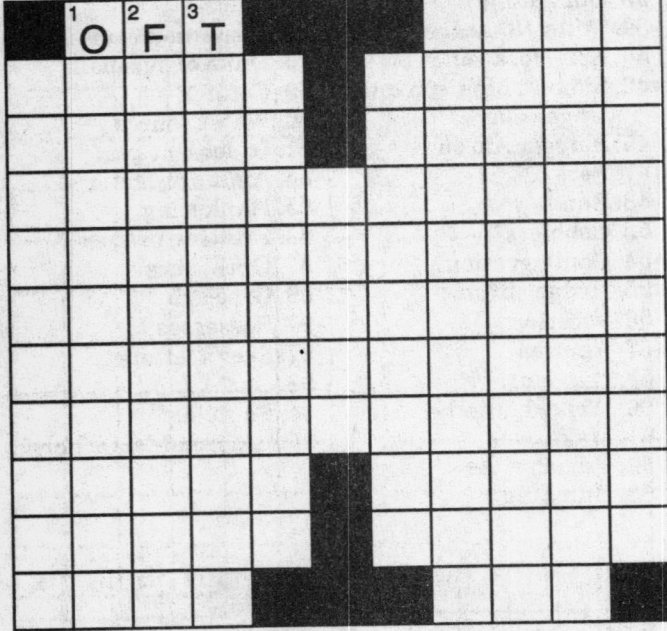

10. Large deer
11. Pooh's creator
12. Deduce
13. First lady
14. Hairpiece
16. Attempt
17. Wynn and Sullivan
19. Fischer's game
21. Choice group
23. Giant
25. Fall behind
28. Comedian DeLuise
29. Cry of disgust
31. Ocean
33. Oscar or Tony
35. Say
37. Las ____, Nevada
38. Slightly wet
39. Paradise
40. ____-Columbian

DOWN

1. Relish dish offering
2. Used a rasp
3. Decade number
4. Against
5. Garrets
6. On-line workers
7. Strange
8. French soul
9. Recent
10. Strength
15. Frosting
18. Clique
20. Slippery one
22. Praises
23. Pulled behind
24. Reflection
26. In motion
27. Web-footed fliers
28. TV host Garroway
30. Continuous murmur
32. Host Linkletter
34. Sprinted
36. Spinning toy

PUZZLE 92

ACROSS

1. Acorn provider
4. Small meal
8. Unadulterated

9. Region
10. Humorous
11. Constrictors
12. Conger
13. Crowded
14. Boast
16. Possesses
17. Existed
19. Metal container
20. Scrape
23. Hit lightly
24. Hearing organ
26. Large liquid container
27. Imprint
30. Type of heat
33. Hint
34. Fossil fuel
35. Entity
37. Poker stake
38. Is the proprietor of
39. Take ten
40. Plead

DOWN

1. Fugitive
2. Mr. Carney
3. Lock opener
4. "____ in Toyland"
5. Strong metal
6. Pekoe and Darjeeling
7. Leisure
8. Wharf
10. Spider's construction
13. Reel or polka
15. Motor fuel
16. Chapeau
18. Beat it!
19. Tam
21. Rodent
22. Sandwich meat
25. Speeding
26. Manservant
28. Operates
29. Beer container
30. Permanent blemish
31. Musical sound
32. Corrodes
35. Hope or Newhart
36. Flock mother

PUZZLE 93

ACROSS
1. Shed feathers
5. Dialect phrase
7. Street or side follower
10. Words of encouragement
12. Pulsate
14. Period in history
15. Be abusive verbally
18. Tout
19. Prince, formerly?
21. ____ de deux
23. CPA, often
24. New Haven university
26. "Gorillas in the ____"
27. Doll
28. Insipid
29. Remedy
30. Chicago transports
31. Judging panel
32. Two together
34. Short sleep
37. Ornamental vase
38. Deficiency
40. Eastern
42. Postponement of an invitation

44. Social insect
47. Suspicious
48. Bank employee
50. Football holder
51. Flavor
52. Prescribed amount

DOWN
1. "Of ____ and Men"
2. Scent
3. Capital of Peru
4. Type of dancing
6. Unassuming
7. Minor
8. Objet d'____
9. Fiddler's spot?
11. Cancel
12. "____ shalt not ..."
13. Hide underground
16. RR depot
17. Perfectly
20. Splendor
21. Peso, formerly
22. Invite
25. Observe
26. Casaba or cantaloupe
28. Spider's work
29. Mongrel
31. Trip
33. Mend
34. Oyster lining

35. Pale
36. Baked dessert
39. Count calories
41. Drama division
43. Formerly called
44. Too
45. Realizes
46. Oak or elm
49. Boy

Starting box on page 525

Word Math

PUZZLE 94

In these long-division problems letters are substituted for numbers. Determine the value of each letter. Then arrange the letters in order from 0 to 9, and they will spell a word or phrase.

1

0	1	2	3	4	5	6	7	8	9

```
            O N E
TOTE | G O T T E N
       R H I S
       O I R T E
       O E N N S
       M I E E N
       M R M I E
       M T N T
```

2

0	1	2	3	4	5	6	7	8	9

```
           T O T
OUT | S P O K E
      L U T
      C F K
      O U T
      L L E
      L U T
        S
```

3

0	1	2	3	4	5	6	7	8	9

```
              S H E
SUET | A S S E T S
       J H K E
       E A B T
       C A C K
       U T J S S
       U K A U S
       U T U B
```

93

PUZZLE 95

ACROSS
1. Escorted journey
5. Russian river
6. South American rodent
10. Leaning
11. Eastern European
12. Turkey embellishment
13. Singer Frankie ___
14. Doddering
15. Leg parts
16. Greek goddesses of the seasons
18. Resound
19. Go too far
21. Forest dweller
22. Old calculating device
25. Ledge
27. Muslim woman of nobility
28. Incredible bargain
29. Preserves' kin
32. Marvin and Van Cleef
33. Piercing tool
34. Tibetan monk
35. Finale
36. Earth's figure
37. Disorder
38. Mont ___
39. Indicate the periphery of
40. Japanese parliament
41. Exodus
44. Eastern
46. Entertainer Josephine ___
47. Universe
49. Holy book
51. Amend
52. Mideast nation
53. Entreaty
54. Costa Rican monetary unit
55. Queen Catherine's family name
56. Ape
57. Wet with morning moisture

DOWN
1. Entire
2. Kind of oil
3. Unattractive
4. Tattle
5. Diverse
6. Sacred poem
7. Dynamic
8. Sugar source
9. Prayers
12. Growl
13. Lion's abode
14. Martial god
15. Head cook
16. ___ pocus
17. Egg
18. Biological unit
20. Long-necked bird
21. Letter opener
22. Skillful
23. Existed
24. Advanced in years
26. Take notice of
28. Before long
29. Coffee
30. Spanish affection
31. ___ the Knife
33. Cadence
34. Colorado city on the Arkansas River
36. Valley
37. In this place
38. Favoritism
39. Water container
40. Fashion celebrity
42. Flowing out
43. Festive affair
44. Showy flower
45. Tarnish
47. Andy ___ (cartoon character)
48. Widemouthed jug
49. Court baron's ordinance
50. Sarcasm
52. Tender
54. Food fish

Starting box on page 525

PUZZLE 96

Deduction Problem

Four Corners

Four friends (Diane, Gus, Joe, and Terry) are all working at different places which happen to be located at the four corners of a city block. Two parallel streets of the block run east-west, and the other two north-south. The workplaces are a bookstore, a dental office, a gas station, and a grocery. From the clues that follow can you determine in which workplace each of the four works and in which corner of the block each of the workplaces is located?

1. The gas station is located further north than Joe's workplace.
2. Gus's workplace is further east than the bookstore.
3. Diane works at a workplace southwest of the dental office.

PUZZLE 97

ACROSS

1. Greek letter
4. Eggs
7. Piece of timber
8. Flipper
9. Female horse
10. Make lace
11. Venomous snake
12. Overhead trains
15. Pleasingly pretty
16. Bad-luck gem
19. Enthusiastic
20. Bowling target
23. Back of the neck
24. Provide furnishings
26. White heron
27. Arms storage building
30. Acute
34. Dainty
39. Luau dance
40. Ocean
41. High cards
42. Twelvemonth
43. Outlaws
44. Matched group
46. Find the sum
47. Notable period
50. Unrefined minerals
51. Jog
52. Garment border
53. Faced
54. Messy place

DOWN

1. Resilient
2. Ocean missile
3. Mature
4. Many a time
5. By way of
6. Before: pref.
9. Pale purple
13. Yearn
14. Box
15. Scoundrel
17. Gorilla
18. Permit
20. Golfer's goal
21. ___ a boy!
22. Urgent wants
25. Knock
26. Biblical judge
28. Maiden name word
29. ___ carte
30. Timid
31. Tint
32. Woeful word
33. Out of the ordinary
35. Liza Minnelli film
36. Private high school
37. Looks after
38. Double curve
45. Semester
48. Feel remorse
49. Picnic pest
50. Surprised sounds

Starting box on page 525

Escalator

PUZZLE 98

Place the answer to clue 1 in the first space, drop a letter, and arrange the remaining letters to answer clue 2. Drop another letter and arrange the remaining letters to answer clue 3. The first dropped letter goes into the box to the left of space 1, and the second dropped letter goes into the box to the right of space 3. Follow this pattern for each row in the diagram. When completed, the letters on the left and right, reading down, will spell related words or a phrase.

1. Nun
2. Becomes weary
3. Relax
4. Tarantula
5. Midway treats
6. Dreadful
7. Card game
8. Rapidity
9. Chair
10. Theater paths
11. Circus performers
12. Miss
13. Matures
14. Steeple
15. Tarts
16. Concords, e.g.
17. Boscs, e.g.
18. Grate

	1		2		3	
	4		5		6	
	7		8		9	
	10		11		12	
	13		14		15	
	16		17		18	

95

PUZZLE 99

ACROSS
1. Actor Sharif
5. Repute
6. Chicken ____ king
9. Swindle
13. Columnist Barrett
15. Volcano's output
16. Russian ruler
18. Ballet skirt
19. Muscat's land
20. Hitch
22. RBI and ERA
24. Animal enclosure
25. Pull behind
27. Wood sorrel
29. Goofs
31. Shortly
32. Mythical bird
33. Solo
34. Roe provider
38. Music timer
40. Legal authorization
43. Certain variable
44. Theaters
45. Painter Edouard ____
46. Had dinner
47. Tiny particle
48. Ego
50. Knight's title
51. Reckon
53. ____ Alamos
56. Tobacco ovens
60. Paper quantity
62. Plaster backing
63. Theoretical
64. Jog
66. Nick and Nora's dog
67. Singing voice
68. Touring troupe
70. ____ Jones Average
71. Heraldic border
72. Water hole

DOWN
1. Switch word
2. Beer ingredient
3. Accumulate
4. Send back
6. Wiles
7. Oaf
8. Rectangular pilaster
9. Failure
10. Crippled
11. ____ the Terrible
12. Grown boy
14. Independence
17. Scarce
21. Cramped attic
23. Teatime pastry
26. Cave
28. Actress Sue ____ Langdon
30. Food fish
31. Soothing plant
33. "____ Karenina"
34. Whack
35. Skirt edge
36. Zones
37. Speckled
38. Deface
39. Miner's find
40. Wide view
41. Utah city
42. Bug's antenna
43. Terrace's kin
45. More, in Spain
49. Yard parts
52. Bone contents
53. Whip
54. Director Preminger
55. George Bernard ____
57. ____-out (with no tickets left)
58. Dorothy's pooch
59. Stash
61. Actress Demi ____
62. ____ Vegas
65. Towering
69. Dolores ____ Rio

Starting box on page 525

PUZZLE 100   Mind Tickler

Gepetto made Pinocchio's nose one inch long. Whenever Pinocchio told a lie his nose doubled in size. How long was his nose after he told his tenth lie?

ACROSS

1. Flower spot
4. Falling-off place
7. Exist
8. Law ____ order
9. Brand ____
10. Commuters' carriers
13. Mail
16. Undo
17. Past
18. Small-town street name
19. Old card game
20. Spot
21. Stinger
23. Neither's pal
26. Apex
28. Through
29. Cat's batter
31. Nest egg: abbr.
32. Good person
34. Holiday night
35. ____ excellence
36. Ply
37. ____ in the face
38. Grassland
40. Guitar adjunct, for short
41. Jasmine, e.g.
43. British title
45. Ascot
46. Small drink
47. Tress
48. Rooters
49. Clans
51. Zilch
53. Humor
54. Metallic rock
55. Keats's output
56. From ____ to green

DOWN

1. Glenn Miller had one
2. Rather than, poetically
3. Morning wetness
4. Narcissus's need
5. Country hotel
6. Docs
10. Family ____
11. Bylaw
12. Intention
13. Bargain event
14. Pride
15. "High ____"
20. Lean
21. Potato holder
22. Dine
24. "Faust," e.g.
25. Carry on wildly
26. Pourboire
27. Spoken
28. Fight
30. Marry
32. Total
33. Small snake
39. North's dog
40. ____ and sciences
41. Recap
42. Lampreys
44. Charged particle
45. Vat
47. Quote
48. Get away fast
49. Duo
50. Free
51. "____ As a Stranger"
52. Fury

Starting box on page 525

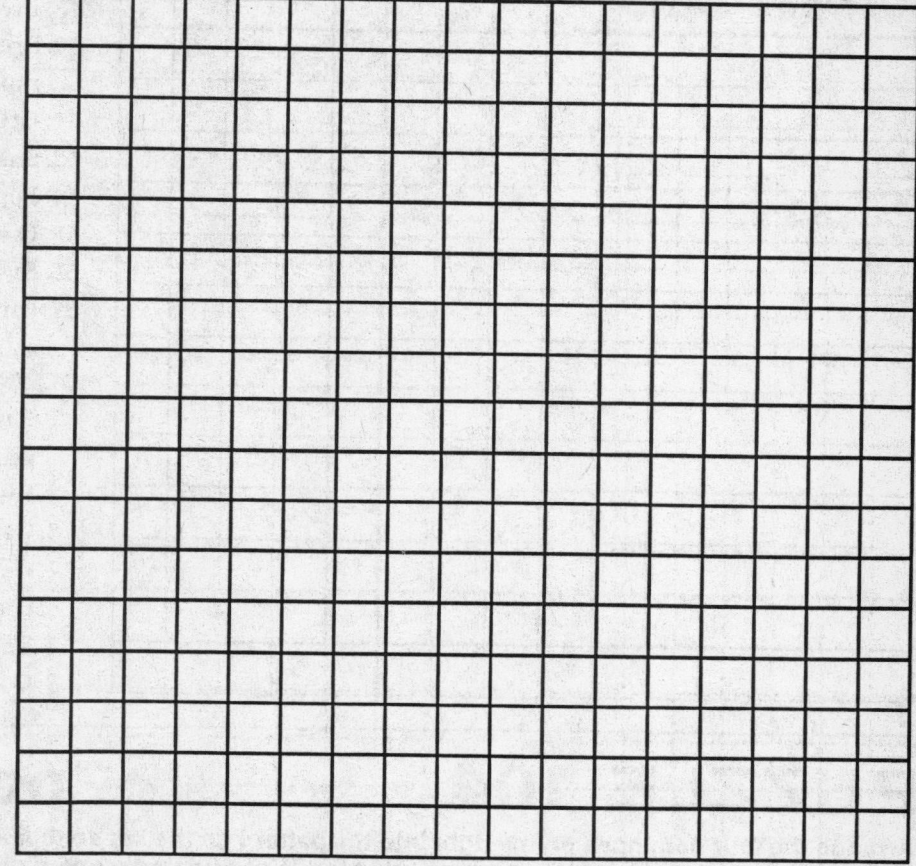

Changaword

Can you change the top word into the bottom word in each column in the number of steps indicated in parentheses? Change only one letter at a time and do not change the order of the letters. Proper names, slang, and obsolete words are not allowed.

1. BACK (3 steps) 2. POST (3 steps) 3. PEAT (4 steps) 4. LAND (5 steps)

YARD HOLE MOSS FILL

PUZZLE 103

ACROSS

1. Pesters
5. Fairy tale monster
6. Downhearted
9. Nourished
12. Expensive
13. Attempt
14. ____ in the hole
15. Plunge downward
17. Blaze
18. Incensed
21. Novel
22. From the moon
23. Measuring stick
24. Vigor
26. In the past
28. Former tadpole
29. "Beauty and the ____"
31. Bullion metal
32. Lamprey
35. Consented
38. Firearm
42. Sweeping tool
43. Sprite
46. Pass along
47. Parliament member
48. Invasion
50. Preholiday night
51. Utilize
52. Sassy
54. Pop
55. Crimson
56. Swerve
57. Cutting side

DOWN

1. Positive gesture
2. Ripened
3. Cereal
4. Cater to
6. Bite
7. Layout
8. Color changer
9. Carnival
10. Beige
11. Bargain
16. Widemouthed jars
17. Pelt
19. Afternoon beverage
20. Unit of work
22. Table support
25. Written comment
27. Woodwind
28. Craze
30. Church officer
31. Opal, e.g.
33. Make a mistake
34. Fib
35. Got up
36. Pierced
37. Staff
39. Escaped
40. Molten flow
41. Watched closely
42. Indistinct sight
44. Slip-up
45. Meadow
49. Medicine
53. Golfer's mound

Starting box on page 525

PUZZLE 104   DOMINO THEORY

Arrange the four dominoes on the right into the pattern on the left so that a correct multiplication problem is formed. The number of dots on each half-domino is considered a one-digit number; for example, a half with six dots represents the number 6.

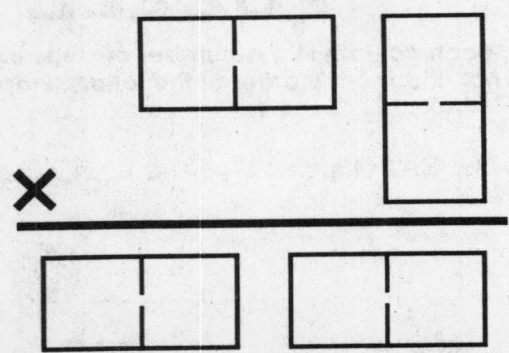
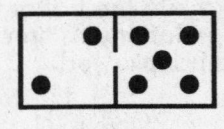

WORDBENDERS

The answers for this crossword puzzle might be just around the bend! Solve the puzzle as you would a regular crossword. The clues for the words which bend in the diagram are listed under the heading BENDERS.

BENDERS

1. Sorcerer
2. Soft, greenish mineral
8. Bend
9. Repair a wall
17. Dwelling
18. Continues
28. Dissociates
29. Working ship
30. Newsman
32. Suitable
43. Cape ____
49. ____ au rhum

ACROSS

1. Prevent
6. Force
10. Indigent
13. Wood eater
14. In what way?
19. Calico wearer
21. Mickey's ex
22. A Gershwin
23. Time period
24. Country
25. Infantrymen
26. Crack pilot
33. Actor Carey
34. Land fit for
    cultivation
36. Irish county
38. Rive
39. Prosecute

40. Cereal grain
41. Politician Beame
42. Vast amount
44. Accept as truth
50. One who corrects
51. Ships off
52. Try to find

DOWN

3. Select
4. "The Gold Bug"
    author

5. Limb
6. Singer Benatar
7. Unity
11. Expressing
    succession
12. Optical
    phenomena
15. Roe
16. Ocean painting
19. Electricity makers
20. Football's Donovan
27. Food fish

29. Railroad bridge
    support
31. Came in
35. Tease
37. Comedian Louis ____
44. Spoiled
45. Typesetting measures
46. Squid squirt
47. Animal doc
48. Goof

99

PUZZLE 106

ACROSS
1. Party-giver Maxwell
5. Purple Heart, e.g.
10. Word in a "Perry Mason" title
14. Speaker's platform
15. Idolize
16. Admit frankly
17. When rescue arrives, in a melodrama
20. Golf gadget
21. Cover snugly
22. "____ My Thumb" (Stones hit)
23. Friendly talk
24. Gumbo
26. Four pecks
29. Emulate a greyhound
30. Summon by name
34. Sacrifice locale
35. Leonine feature
36. Triumphed
37. ____ lively!
38. Alvin Ailey's domain
39. Portion
40. Wrath
41. Continuing impulse
42. Freight boat
43. Find fault unfairly
45. Have being
46. Meditate
47. Sole
49. Black dust
50. Craft at summer camp
53. For fear that
54. Fuss
57. Shirk one's obligations
61. Spoken
62. Kind of mother or fly
63. Fortune's partner
64. Blood-group term
65. Command
66. Deuce topper

DOWN
1. Prepare for printing
2. Attorney-author Mark
3. Whereabouts
4. Gray shade
5. Guide to a new car
6. Decree
7. Wharf
8. Noah's boat
9. Count Tolstoy
10. Short sleep
11. Greedy
12. Indefinite number
13. Water pitcher
18. Anesthetic
19. Make the ____ fly (cause a scene)
23. Fellow
24. Unit of weight
25. What a proposer bends
26. Programming language
27. Extreme
28. Ox, e.g.
29. Vary within limits
31. Bestow
32. Eat gluttonously
33. March into
35. Espouse
38. Twofold
39. Gasp
42. Cafe compartment
44. French ____
46. Placard
48. Modern: prefix
49. Intelligence
50. Coagulate
51. Breezy
52. ____ tide
53. Noisy
54. Partly open
55. Rounded roof
56. Follow orders
58. Which person?
59. And not
60. Small lizard

PUZZLE 107   MINI-CROSSWORDS

Fill in the diagrams below with eight different 4-letter words to construct your own crossword puzzles. Only common English words are allowed. You may repeat letters as often as you wish.

1.

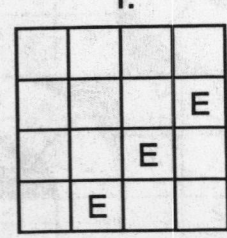

2.

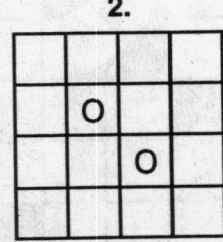

3.

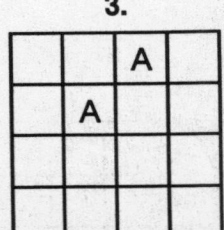

ACROSS

1. Go marketing
5. Islamic god
10. Entrance barrier
14. Architect Saarinen
15. Measuring device
16. Eastern bigwig
17. Encoded message
19. Bring home the bacon
20. Levier
21. Ready, _____, go
22. Cosmetician Lauder
23. Comedian Caesar
25. Love seat
27. City transport
30. Label
32. Attack term
33. Exploit
36. Stimulated
39. Tasks
41. Infrequent
42. Mantle
44. Force
45. Diamond pattern
47. Deep fissure
49. British custom
50. Circle segment
52. Refrain starter
53. "And I Love _____"
54. Blue flags
57. Hoagie
59. Law
61. Pen point
63. Bottle parts
67. Enthusiastic
68. Repetitions
70. Actor Wilder
71. Fit for a king
72. Sand
73. Cogito, _____ sum
74. Competition scene
75. Diner sign

DOWN

1. Religious group
2. Zeus's wife
3. African antelope
4. Vatican officials
5. In the past
6. Hangs back
7. Attracts
8. Playing marbles
9. Skirt edge
10. Birds of a flock
11. Unprofessional
12. Wheel covering
13. Coastal flier
18. Hackneyed
22. Inscribe
24. Ballerinas
26. Hearts, slangily
27. Gem weight
28. Conscious
29. Negotiating
31. Toothpaste type
34. Insight
35. Chemical compound
37. Door opener
38. "What's up, _____?"
40. Harem room
43. Knack
46. Reclined
48. Boast
51. Core
55. Cowboy's contest
56. Blockade
58. Light tan
59. Enclosure
60. Avouch
62. Type of muffin
64. Mrs. Dithers
65. Grow together, as bone
66. Swift jets
68. Author Levin
69. Chicken _____ king

Quotagram

Fill in the answers to the clues. Then transfer the letters to the correspondingly numbered squares in the diagram. The completed diagram will contain a quotation.

1. Crudites
   $\overline{9}\ \overline{54}\ \overline{46}\ \overline{49}\ \overline{32}\ \overline{28}\ \overline{5}$

2. Branch
   $\overline{18}\ \overline{43}\ \overline{21}\ \overline{50}\ \overline{7}\ \overline{30}\ \overline{20}\ \overline{2}$

3. Godot's creator
   $\overline{57}\ \overline{10}\ \overline{34}\ \overline{13}\ \overline{48}\ \overline{6}\ \overline{39}$

4. Diploma holder
   $\overline{27}\ \overline{44}\ \overline{51}\ \overline{31}\ \overline{24}\ \overline{41}\ \overline{11}\ \overline{37}$

5. Actor Gould
   $\overline{14}\ \overline{58}\ \overline{17}\ \overline{1}\ \overline{35}\ \overline{42}\ \overline{29}$

6. Amtrak, e.g.
   $\overline{38}\ \overline{26}\ \overline{56}\ \overline{47}\ \overline{52}\ \overline{23}\ \overline{12}\ \overline{55}$

7. 4-base hit
   $\overline{40}\ \overline{45}\ \overline{3}\ \overline{59}\ \overline{25}\ \overline{4}\ \overline{15}$

8. Warnings
   $\overline{22}\ \overline{16}\ \overline{36}\ \overline{53}\ \overline{8}\ \overline{19}\ \overline{33}$

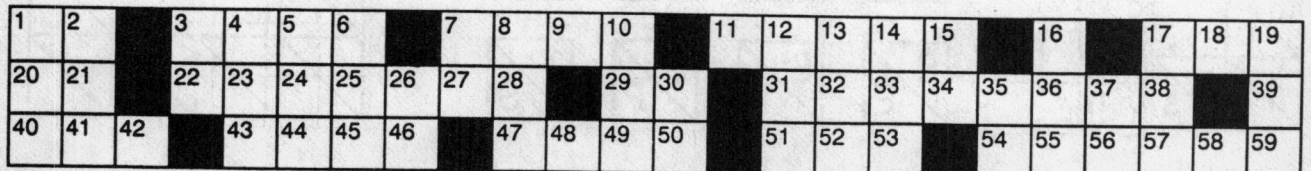

PUZZLE 110

ACROSS
1. Reef material
6. Uttered
10. Former Iranian ruler
14. Love a lot
15. Song
16. Tramp
17. Cowboy contest
18. Actress Bancroft
19. Tavern drinks
20. Before, to Keats
21. Aspect
23. Oar
25. Naked
26. In this place
27. Classify
30. Sharpen
31. Take a chair
34. In advance
35. Fills completely
36. Paid athlete
37. Propels, as a canoe
38. Put away for use later
39. Skinny
40. Mined matter
41. Slander
42. Like the ocean
43. Actor Beatty
44. Paradise
45. Delicious, e.g.
46. Forest creature
47. Total failure
48. Shaving necessities
51. "True ____"
52. Evil
55. Singer Burl ____
56. Ring of light
58. The ones there
60. Parisian papa
61. Store sign
62. Strange
63. God of love
64. Departed
65. Great fear

DOWN
1. Worry
2. Smell
3. Took a taxi
4. "You ____ My Sunshine"
5. Panther's kin
6. Look fixedly
7. Uncle's mate
8. Roadside motel
9. Thickened
10. What elms provide
11. Contain
12. Eve's son
13. Stockings
22. Museum piece
24. God of war
25. Snakes
26. Inn
27. Baseballer Hank ____
28. Coastline
29. Basted
30. Refuge
31. Incantation
32. Angry
33. Theater awards
35. Sword
38. Circus attraction
39. Reindeer herder
41. Sly look
42. Saw
45. Actress MacGraw
46. Medicinal amounts
47. ____ and center
48. Ready to eat, as fruit
49. Affirm
50. Nothing
51. Secluded valley
52. Drill, as a hole
53. Continent
54. Feat
57. Imitate
59. That woman's

PUZZLE 111   MOSAIC

Place the twelve boxes, each containing two letters, into the empty diagram to form four 8-letter words reading across and down, as shown with 6-letter words in the example on the left.

Example:

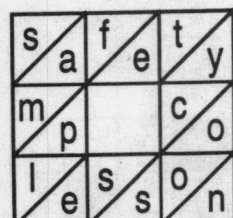

ACROSS

1. "____ and Circumstance"
5. Thick glue
10. Soft lump
14. Diva's forte
15. Theater aide
16. Emerald Isle
17. Package wrap
19. RBI, e.g.
20. Poe's middle name
21. Freudian word
22. Tuscan city
23. Beat walker
25. Staircase part
27. Perform surgery
31. Invalidate
34. Orangutans, e.g.
35. Divides
37. Bibliog. term
38. Disencumber
39. Heeling, at sea
40. Danube city
41. Washington bills
43. River mouth deposit
44. Angers
45. Snuggle
47. Legislative bodies
49. Lock of hair
51. Southern power company: abbr.
52. Eagle's nest
54. Bill and ____
57. Classic song
61. Turn over
62. Comrades
64. Wings, to Ovid
65. Actor Ryan ____
66. Author Kingsley ____
67. Rip
68. Comedian Milton ____
69. Brief missive

DOWN

1. South American rodent
2. Pitcher Hershiser
3. Factory
4. Royal residences
5. Young dog
6. Tennis great Arthur ____
7. Kind of rug
8. Pavarotti, e.g.
9. Before, poetically
10. Attack and surround
11. Body of writings
12. Algerian port
13. Alpha follower
18. ____ about (approximately)
22. Opposite of NNW
24. Processions
26. Moment
27. Express a belief
28. Foot traveler
29. Mosaic piece
30. Misfortunes
32. Stories
33. Shade givers
34. Elvis ____ Presley
36. Punta del ____
42. Like a zebra
44. Native of Rome
46. Golfer Trevino
48. Stratford's river
50. Teatime pastry
52. Distantly
53. She, to Pierre
55. Hebrew measure
56. Milky gem
58. Major-____
59. What's ____ for me?
60. To be, to Pliny
62. Male swan
63. Beer's kin

PUZZLE 112

Escalator

PUZZLE 113

Write the answer to clue 1 in the first space. Drop one letter and rearrange the remaining letters to answer clue 2. Put the dropped letter into Column A. Drop another letter and rearrange the remaining letters to answer clue 3. Put the dropped letter into Column B. Follow this pattern for each row in the diagram. When completed, the letters in Column A and Column B, reading down, will spell related words or a phrase.

1. Rarely
2. Mock-up
3. Merge
4. Traveler's vehicle
5. Dairy product
6. Marathon, e.g.
7. Good sense
8. Saw wood
9. Cey and Ely
10. Taper
11. Stick-on design
12. Served for a point
13. More active
14. Picture puzzle
15. Chafes
16. Pure
17. Hoodwink
18. Yearning
19. Group of words
20. Lance
21. Gather

PUZZLE 114

ACROSS
1. Alphabet trio
4. Commercials
7. Hat
10. Make a mistake
11. Scale note
12. Gorilla, e.g.
13. Stout
14. Pekoe
15. Make leather
16. Fight with swords
18. Russian rulers of old
20. Make points
22. Explosive letters
23. Took care of
25. Liquid measures: abbr.
26. Appears
28. Las Vegas openings
30. Sag
32. Mauna ____
33. Child's game
35. One: Sp.
36. Cries of pain
37. Fruit drink
38. York's rank: abbr.
39. Superlative suffix
40. Neither's cohort
41. Letter before tee

DOWN
1. Fall on ____ ears
2. Writer Gardner and others
3. Breakfast item: 2 wds.
4. Aft
5. Bambi's mom, e.g.
6. Trellis board
7. Child's game: 3 wds.
8. Separated
9. Writes
17. Seashore
19. Pilot
21. Asner and Sullivan
24. Accountant's book
25. Makes furrows
27. Carols
28. Kind of gin
29. Mr. Musial
31. Kitchenware
34. Fuss

PUZZLE 115

ACROSS
1. Minus
5. Mata Hari, e.g.
8. Rock-star Turner
12. Spoken
13. Pedal digit
14. Small songbird
15. Story
16. Certain TV fare
17. Orient
18. Direct
20. Imparted
21. Brewing tub
22. Poker kitty
23. Do gardening work
26. Instructive sessions
30. Actor Wallach
31. Lair
32. Actor Marvin
33. Voted in
36. West Point student
38. Use an adz
39. Melancholy
40. Towards shelter
42. Jogs
45. Without restraint
46. Saratoga, e.g.
48. TV's "____ People"
50. Bring up
51. Bobby of hockey
52. Singer Fitzgerald
53. Barks
54. ____ is me!
55. Winter vehicle

DOWN
1. Building site
2. Epochs
3. ____ of the earth
4. Arm covering
5. Begin
6. Pea case
7. Oui or si
8. Chirps
9. Tehran's land
10. Bird's home
11. Picnic pest
19. Corn unit
20. ____ Angeles
22. Writing utensil
23. Itsy-bitsy
24. "That's ____, folks!"
25. Gift for dad
26. Guided
27. On in years
28. Wedding-announcement word
29. Establish
31. Morning moisture
34. TV bar
35. Golf peg
36. "____ 54, Where Are You?"
37. Worships
39. Long look
40. Vicinity
41. Jump
43. Archer William
44. Fire or tag
45. Saute
46. Plant
47. In favor of
49. Young boy

PUZZLE 116

ACROSS
1. Duffer's device
4. Generation ____
7. Colorado Indian
10. Deputy
11. Mrs. Roosevelt
12. Espy
13. Separates
15. Subdued
16. Actress Berger
17. Grand ____ National Park
19. Baseball's Mel ____
21. Respond
23. Suffer an unexpected defeat
27. Fire remnants
29. Elec. unit
30. Weir
32. Lennon's wife
33. Actor Schroder
36. Above
39. Copying machine need
41. Director Peckinpah
42. Pouts
44. Amphibians
48. Stand in line
50. Robs, in a way
52. Coastal eagles
53. To ____ his own
54. Kaminska or Lupino
55. Entreat
56. Prefix for three
57. Hair holder

DOWN
1. Typewriter settings
2. Paddy's land
3. Xanadu
4. Vapor
5. In ____ (stagnant)
6. Tiger or doll
7. Nautical order
8. Male turkey
9. Summer, on the Somme
11. Three-handed card games
12. Porticos
14. On the acme of
18. Bohea or souchong
20. Spread hay
22. Incline
23. Prohibit
24. Give out
25. About to take place
26. Greek letter
28. Distress letters
31. AWOL chasers
34. Shoelace problems
35. Affirmative for Cooper
37. Timepiece
38. Berserk
40. Alley button
43. Vega, e.g.
45. A ____ apple
46. Tenderfoot
47. Petty quarrel
48. Arachnid's trap
49. Metric land measure
51. Here, to Jacques

PUZZLE 117

ACROSS
1. Yak
4. Stripling
7. Ponder
11. Go astray
12. Arrive
13. English rock group
14. Plaything
15. Actress MacGraw and others
16. Tyne or Timothy
17. "Q" actor David ____
20. Do a purl stitch
21. Articles
25. "M" star
29. Columnist Buchwald
32. Trouble
33. Sampled the smorgasbord
34. "V" actor
39. "Butterfield 8" author
40. Rumple
43. Taylor of "X, Y and Zee"
47. Draft brews
50. Stare open-mouthed
51. Aries
53. Oven glove
54. Lollapalooza
55. Rage
56. "Z" actor Montand
57. Rubicund
58. Porky or Petunia

DOWN
1. Receive
2. "I Am ____" (Simon & Garfunkel hit)
3. "F/X" star Brown
4. Montez or Falana
5. In the thick of
6. Lucie Arnaz's dad
7. ____ order
8. "Born in the ____"
9. Diamond gal
10. Type of preacher
12. ____ blanche
18. Tombstone initials
19. Zip
22. The Roaring Twenties, e.g.
23. Star of "The A-Team"
24. Fathom
26. Dialect in Ghana
27. Ages and ages
28. TV producer Grundy
29. Part of a Latin trio
30. Stadium shout
31. La la lead-in
35. Hilltops
36. Actor Mineo
37. Smoldering coal
38. "Golden Girl" McClanahan
41. Uncover
42. Lamb Chop's lady
44. Composer Stravinsky
45. Actor Buxby
46. Parroted
47. Carter or Irving
48. "Changing" author Ullmann
49. Savoy season
52. Eldest of the "Little Women"

105

PUZZLE 118

ACROSS
1. Profit and ____
5. Cager Larry
9. Reverence
12. Fairy-tale start
13. Melange
14. "L.A. ____"
15. Equipment
16. Laggard
18. Profuse
20. Great!
21. Censure
23. Row
25. Moo
26. Voucher
28. Mary's follower
32. Turkish official
33. Stopwatch
35. Charge
36. Pleads
38. Small coin
39. Treat leather
40. Mimicked
42. Correct
44. Phase
47. Goad
48. Showy pianist
51. Praise
54. Summer cooler
55. Mangle
56. Otherwise
57. Tie the knot
58. Pre-Easter season
59. Did away with

DOWN
1. Yule feature
2. "A Chorus Line" song
3. Rascal
4. Blood fluid
5. Nonsense!
6. "____ Get By"
7. Rita's river
8. Search for water
9. Askew
10. Rout out of bed
11. Washstand piece
17. Knitting stitch
19. Religious group
21. Tell all
22. Theater section
23. Shy
24. Thing
27. Stash away
29. Nevertheless: 2 wds.
30. Nasty
31. Stoop
34. Harvest
37. Western growth
41. Danger
43. Slippers
44. Cabbage dish
45. Ocean current
46. Sleeping
47. Transmitted
49. Exist
50. Against
52. Operate
53. A.M. moisture

PUZZLE 119

ACROSS
1. Blunders
5. Atlas entry
8. Wipe lightly
11. Reducing plan
12. Singer Fitzgerald
14. Barcelona cheer
15. Soft drink
16. Word of woe
17. Tin
18. Henry McCarty's nickname: 3 wds.
21. Divvies up
23. Agent's percentage
24. Race track prize
25. Oft dented items
29. Self
30. "Cheers," for one
31. Understand
32. Indicated
35. Implied
37. Retainer
38. Kidney and larynx
39. William Cody's nickname: 2 wds.
43. Dollar bill
44. Viewpoint
45. Cup handles
48. Humor
49. Hazzard County deputy
50. Take ____ from me: 2 wds.
51. Depot: abbr.
52. Before
53. Large: prefix

DOWN
1. Begley and Murrow
2. ____ Bravo
3. Snoopy's foe, with "The": 2 wds.
4. Flight features
5. Spreads
6. Confederate
7. Disk
8. Pier
9. Jai-____
10. Curve
13. Pale
19. Marvin or Majors
20. Lineman
21. Hurried
22. Enormous
25. Short-lived style
26. Increase
27. Harness part
28. Pairs
30. Direct course
33. Away
34. Tantalize
35. Three: prefix
36. Glowing
38. Fat
39. "Buttons and ____"
40. Cohesive group
41. Greek cheese
42. Smell
46. Manipulate
47. Vacation spot

106

PUZZLE 120

ACROSS

1. Ready to pick
5. Work out
10. Tattle
14. Etching liquid
15. Connection
16. Tibetan priest
17. Saucer-shaped bell
18. Snug retreats
19. All through
20. Starts
22. Large-billed seabirds
24. Electric _____
26. Torah closet
27. Nabbed
32. Dream
36. Remorse
37. Vapors
39. The Dynamic _____
40. Area for skating
41. Objet d'_____
42. Coops
43. Terminate
44. Measuring device
46. Tranquillity
47. Compositions
49. News broadcasts
51. Teamster's command
52. Came in first
53. Cabbage salad
58. Approaches stealthily
63. Similar
64. Marry on the run
66. Pine fruit
67. Gasp
68. Cut off
69. Forest plant
70. Organs of sight
71. Clairvoyants
72. Sutured

DOWN

1. Boil
2. Holy picture
3. Eighth of a gallon
4. Rim
5. Nightfall
6. Single unit
7. Speech impediment
8. Ballot
9. Subjugate
10. City units
11. Molten rock
12. So be it!
13. Saloons
21. Repose
23. Blue flag
25. Within the law
27. Be of the same opinion
28. Destroys
29. Skins
30. Antlered animal
31. Gauntlet thrower
33. Notions
34. An _____ of prevention
35. Pries
38. Disperse
42. Pod dweller
44. Cereal grasses
45. Futile
46. Confined
48. Real estate sellers
50. Also-rans
53. Promontory
54. Give a nod of assent
55. Spiel
56. Opposite of aweather
57. Used a loom
59. Pretends
60. Folk knowledge
61. Comprehended
62. Witnessed
65. Part of MPH

Accordion Words   PUZZLE 121

Reduce each word one letter at a time until it is as short as possible. Each deletion must leave a new word. Do not change the order of the letters.

Example: *OLIVE: Live, Lie.*

1. SPRINT: _____

2. SCARCE: _____

3. TRAPPING: _____

4. BREAST: _____

5. STINGER: _____

6. STATUTE: _____

7. TAPPER: _____

8. BRAMBLE: _____

9. ARROW: _____

10. MANSE: _____

107

PUZZLE 122

ACROSS

1. Fall short
5. Wine-growing region of France
10. Unites
14. Correct
15. Ring site
16. Yoked animals
17. Painful
18. Adornment
19. Weathercock
20. On guard
22. Deadly snake
23. You are something ___!
24. Chatty
27. Stage direction
28. Handle roughly
31. Munch
32. Baste
34. Canyon sound
36. Jalopy
42. Bone dry
43. Fear
44. Judge's attire
45. Create again
47. Ivy League college
48. "Have you ___ wool?"
49. Mind power: abbr.
51. ___ of iniquity
52. Sleep-producing jumpers
56. Michaelmas daisy
58. Eye drop
59. Calico-wearer
61. Cringe
65. Moreover
66. Overhead
69. Unspoiled
70. Luge
71. Bottled spirit
72. Run in place
73. Cavity
74. Unbelievable bargain
75. Sportscaster Dizzy ___

DOWN

1. Flatland
2. Graven image
3. Father
4. Strict
5. Incensed
6. Middle of a palindrome
7. Rot
8. Yoko and namesakes
9. Goldfish
10. Interlaced
11. Praise
12. Thick
13. Grimace
21. Football holder
25. Keeper
26. Stellar
27. Lamb's dam
28. Pome
29. Israeli city
30. Tory's counterpart
32. Declares
33. Firstborn
35. Poem
37. Pekoe
38. Judge
39. Path
40. Fit
41. Hammer head
46. Catch forty winks
50. Bench
52. Cache
53. Greeting
54. Canvas-holder
55. Wear away
56. Solitary
57. Stiff
59. Chokes
60. Help
62. Lump
63. Soda
64. Paradise
67. By the route of
68. Moray

PUZZLE 123   ODDS AND EVENS

Every other letter (all the odds OR all the evens) of each answer to a clue in Column A can be rearranged to form the answer to the corresponding clue in Column B. When completed, the first letters of the answers, reading down, will spell the names of card games.

COLUMN A

1. Boaster _____ _____ _____ _____ _____ _____ _____
2. Handgun _____ _____ _____ _____ _____ _____ _____
3. Devilish _____ _____ _____ _____ _____ _____ _____
4. Infirm _____ _____ _____ _____ _____ _____
5. Lexicon _____ _____ _____ _____ _____ _____ _____
6. Heavenly _____ _____ _____ _____ _____ _____ _____

COLUMN B

1. Snatch _____ _____ _____ _____
2. Completed _____ _____ _____ _____
3. Equitable _____ _____ _____ _____
4. ___ tea _____ _____ _____ _____
5. Destroy _____ _____ _____ _____
6. Lagomorph _____ _____ _____ _____

CODEWORD

Codeword is a special crossword puzzle in which conventional clues are omitted. Instead, answer words in the diagram are represented by numbers. Each number represents a different letter of the alphabet, and all of the letters of the alphabet are used. When you are sure of a letter, put it in the code key chart for easy reference. A group of letters has been inserted to start you off.

Code key chart:

1	14
2	15
3	16
4	17
5	18
6	19
7	20
8	21
9	22
10	23
11	24
12	25
13	26

(15 = I, 17 = N, 21 = W)

Codeword grid (■ = shaded square):

1	18	15	12	■	■	1	25	14	25	1	■	8	21	8	3
16	15	23	8	■	19	21(W)	15(I)	4	8	■	4	25	23	8	
11	14	8	4	■	8	14	23	8	3	■	26	25	11	1	
1	19	16	4	17	16	1	■	■	10	15	25	14	8	19	
■	■	8	8	14	■	8	4	8	22	5	■	■			
6	8	16	23	1	■	15	3	8	■	12	8	14	19	1	
14	16	11	■	19	25	22	16	19	25	■	23	16	3	8	
8	3	3	■	5	16	12	■	19	21	25	■	19	8	8	
1	19	8	12	■	3	8	20	8	4	19	■	8	4	23	
1	2	8	14	24	■	23	16	23	■	2	8	3	23	1	
■	■	16	14	19	8	3	■	10	8	13	■	■			
1	16	20	7	9	8	■	24	16	3	19	2	8	3		
8	20	3	9	■	4	25	19	8	1	■	3	25	14	8	
19	3	8	8	■	23	3	25	4	8	■	16	12	1	8	
1	8	21	1	■	1	8	4	23	1	■	1	8	8	18	

FAN WORDS

Place the 5-letter answers to the clues into the fan to discover an 8-letter word reading across the shaded area. As an added help, pairs of answers are anagrams (1 is an anagram of 2, 3 is an anagram of 4, etc.)

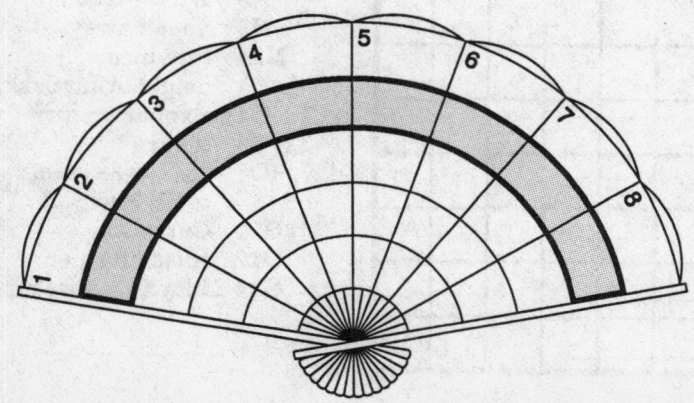

1. Kitchen range

2. Ballots

3. Confidence

4. Swagger

5. Pottery furnaces

6. Slither

7. Lamb's cry

8. Dining board

PUZZLE 126

The diagram represents the sea which contains a crossword puzzle; the answer words are Battleships. The letter-number combination to the left of each clue indicates the location in the diagram where a Battleship has been hit (for example, A4 is in the first row, fourth column). A hit is any one of the letters in the answer word. Using this clue, you must determine the exact location of each answer and whether it is an across or a down word. Fill in black squares to separate words as in a regular crossword. We have filled in the answers to clues A4 and B1.

A2	Polynesian porch	
A4	Sharp smack	
A7	Ireland	
A10	Fable writer	
A15	Hazard	
B1	Entourage	
B2	Mellow	
B6	King Arthur's resting place	
B8	Stringed instrument	
B12	Comedienne Phyllis ____	
B14	Inventor Sikorsky	
C1	Straightaway	
C4	Write	
C7	City near Marseilles	
C9	Cheer, in Cadiz	
C13	Prevaricator	
C15	Sins	
D1	Devotee	
D7	Elation	

D10	Claws
D13	Exchange premium
D14	Dappled horse
E1	Rossini's hero
E3	In the middle of
E8	Bottoms of shoes
E11	Heisted
F5	Network
F7	____ and needles
F9	Knack
F11	Charity
F13	Verve
F15	Recliner part
G2	Lassoed
G4	Emulated
G7	Research cells
G10	Beethoven symphony
G13	Author Tolstoy
G15	"On Your ____"

H1	Fury
H3	Dedicated
H6	Coat part
H8	Outer: pref.
H12	Whittle
H14	Withered
I2	Elliptical
I3	Interval
I7	Washbowl
I12	"The Waste Land," e.g.
I14	Dr. McCoy's nickname
J1	Titanium, e.g.
J3	Tube
J4	Complained
J7	Type of daisy
J9	Split
J11	Swimsuit tops
K4	Jazz's Peterson
K5	Optimum
K8	Refurbished
K10	Meddle
K15	Location device
L1	Chief
L4	Goddess of sorcery
L8	Newts
L13	Combines together
L15	Egg cells
M2	Singer Brickell
M4	Blissful place
M7	Large spoon
M10	Web-footed mammals
M12	Large tub
M15	Nullify
N3	Congressional assistant
N6	Round Table knight
N8	Willow tree
N9	Sneak away
N14	Province neighboring Sask.
O1	Exploit
O3	Yield
O7	"____ was going to St. Ives . . ."
O10	Currents
O12	Russian ruler
O14	Lloyd Webber musical

	1	2	3	4	5	6	7	8	9	10	11	12	13	14	15
A	S	L	A	P	■										
B	T														
C	A														
D	F														
E	F														
F	■														
G															
H															
I															
J															
K															
L															
M															
N															
O															

PUZZLE 127

• HUE-MAN PARTS •

ACROSS

1. White House dog
5. Kind of steak
9. Wedding-cake layer
13. Yearning
17. Singer Redding
18. Swiss flower
19. Piedmont province
20. Roe provider
21. In the act
23. Secret criminal group
25. Demolish
26. Markdown event
28. Power
29. ____ Bareli, India
30. Port
31. Grocery checkout machine
32. Blind as ____
34. Hullabaloo
35. Type of opera
36. Lingerie buy
39. Herman Munster's wife
40. Legal-tender notes
42. Watch display acronym
43. Queen ant in "B.C."
44. Petitions
45. Comparable
46. Ditty
47. Since
49. Ranges
51. "Dead ____ Society"
52. Do a cable stitch
53. Haberdashery item
54. Mary's pet
55. Not suitable
57. Persistent attack
58. Analyze
61. Office group
62. French father
63. Peckinpah and Wanamaker
64. Macaw genus
65. Prefix for equal
66. Nursery skill
69. Witch's concoction
70. Badminton need
71. Belonging to us
72. Street portrayer
73. Constructed
74. Mobsters' guns
75. File's companion
76. Incarcerated one, for short
77. "... stirring, not even ____"
80. Cleave
81. Delicate
85. Diving duck
87. Aristocrat
89. Film director Kenton
90. So-so grades
91. Is unwell
92. Major ending
93. Letter beginning
94. Gaelic
95. Solidifies
96. Bless

DOWN

1. Henry or Harrison
2. Fit to ____
3. Covers
4. Smoker's need
5. Birchbark
6. Tramp's love
7. Singer Midge ____ of Ultravox
8. Type of manner
9. Part of a dinette set
10. Man, for one
11. Seventh Greek letter
12. Snack food
13. Blanched
14. Cleaning woman, in Soho
15. Suspend
16. Pianist Duchin
22. Smell ____
24. Summits, to a Brit
27. Soon
30. Sorrows
31. Clintons' cat
32. Helper
33. Plains Indian
34. Shoe-shape maintainer
35. Canonized one
36. Folklore name
37. Budget item
38. Summer coolers
39. Freedom, for short
40. Puff
41. Loud, strident noise
44. Tuxedo, for one
46. Jones and Sawyer
48. Blue dye
49. Fulton or Martin
50. Overeat, with out
51. Free admittance slip
53. Fathers
54. Appendage
55. ____ arms
56. On the ____ (accurate)
57. Visionaries
58. Titled woman
59. Algonquian speaker
60. Shooter
62. Wariness
63. Pout
66. Cook someone's ____
67. Word of comparison
68. Woman's accessory
69. Bracelets
73. Grandson of Lot
74. Cheekier
75. Poet Lizette ____
76. Mustard family plant
77. Ancient
78. Theme from "Mondo Cane"
79. Widemouthed jar
80. Certain liquors
81. ____ house (poker hand)
82. Smidgen
83. French novelist Pierre ____
84. Paradise
86. Poetic contraction
88. Be recumbent

111

PUZZLE 128

ACROSS

1. Former time
5. Anecdote
9. Slight
13. Bridge
17. Woodwind
18. Yemen seaport
19. Nylons
20. Genuine
21. Sinbad the Sailor's burden
24. Bygone time
25. Vaulted
26. Deck wood
27. Abrade
29. Scoundrel
30. Congers
33. Some whiskeys
35. Identical
37. More difficult
41. Gambling machine
43. "M*A*S*H" character
46. Alley Oop's girl
47. Pennsylvania Indian
49. Female pigs
51. Desert feature
52. Competition
53. Pickle marts
55. Gratuity
56. Torah closets
57. Road curves
59. Self-conceits
61. Kernel
63. Professional job recruiters
67. Cayennes and jalapenos
71. It got a gift horse
72. Actor Costner
77. Territory
78. Russian aircraft
80. More confident
83. Ivy League member
84. Segment
85. Eliot's Bede
87. Uproar
88. Cinders of cartoons
89. English horse race site
91. Oklahoma city
93. Most minute
95. Singles
97. Pesky insect
99. O'Hara's fictional plantation
100. Actor Brynner
102. Newscaster Rather
104. Brainchild
106. Distribute
110. Omani, e.g.
112. Police dog, often
116. "Klondike ____"
117. Biblical hunter
118. Knotted
119. Joy Adamson's subject
120. Toboggan
121. Stern's opposite
122. Carpenters' tools
123. Shut with force

DOWN

1. Place for crawling
2. Qualified
3. Ice-cream treat
4. Moderate
5. Neutral color
6. Tumult
7. Departed
8. Enroll
9. Hebrew coins
10. Refusals
11. Manipulator
12. Admirers
13. Pigpen
14. Course of action
15. Emanation
16. Want
22. Egyptian sun god
23. Feeds the horses
28. Saloon
31. Misrepresented
32. Withered
34. Chimney sweep's problem
36. "Call Me ____"
37. Volume
38. Cultivates
39. Bullfight cheers
40. Upset
42. Strong thread
44. Singer Paul ____
45. Take it easy
48. Piece of ____ (peso)
50. Prod
54. Curdles
58. Haggard heroine
60. Muzzle
62. Exclamation of disapproval
64. Columnist Bombeck
65. Comment to the audience
66. Innsbruck's province
67. "____ Was a Rollin' Stone"
68. Epochs
69. Ooze
70. "Cry, the Beloved Country" author
73. Flirt's flutterers
74. Jerry or Vicki
75. Maladies
76. Orderly
79. Rowdy bunch
81. Emend
82. Church tribunal
86. Least possible
90. Actor Knight
92. Early 20th-century art form
94. Excursion
96. Wise men
98. Canvas shelters
100. Tibetan oxen
101. River to the Caspian
103. Snake's home
105. English rock group
107. Convince
108. Sky bear
109. Waxed cheese
111. Flower plot
113. Actress Dawn Chong
114. Chop
115. Wynn and Koch

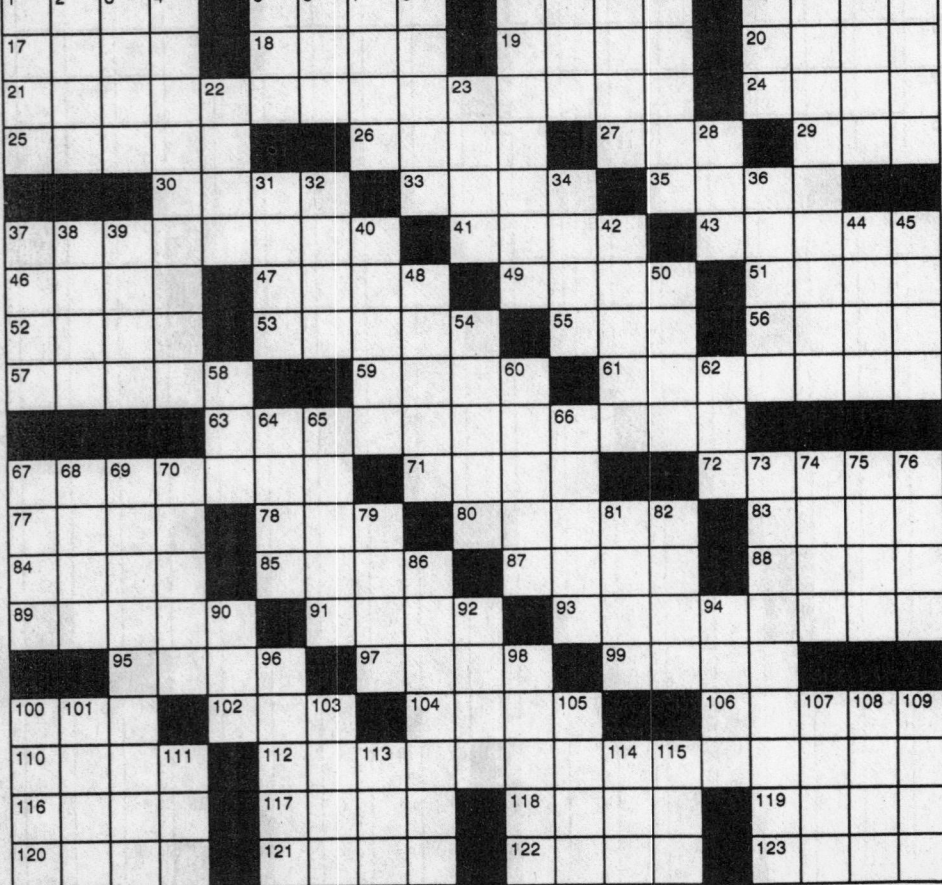

ACROSS

1. Amusing
4. Spoils
8. Caustic remark
12. Style
16. Ever and ____ (occasionally)
18. All: pref.
19. Salmon
20. Currier and ____
21. Craze
22. Levitate
23. Aloud
24. Groupies
25. Brawn
27. Tipsy reef?
30. Skier's tow
32. Cravat
33. Whiskey
34. African range
37. Glacial ridges
39. Galleries
43. Approach
44. Competitors
45. Painter John ____
46. Likely
48. Pattern
50. Walk clumsily
51. ____ Luis
52. Disrespectful
53. Paris river
54. Depleted
56. Heavy weight
57. Playwright Oscar ____
58. Yalie
59. Rendezvous
62. Glass bead
63. Outstanding
67. Baseballer Durocher
68. Campus buildings
69. Feature
70. Raucous cry
71. Oklahoma town
72. Dory
73. Skip
74. Dive
76. Marshal Dillon
77. Low-lying land
78. Catch
79. "Native ____"
80. Expressed admiration
82. Colorful accessory?
86. Shangri-la
90. Witticisms
91. Islamic prince
92. Just
95. African gully
96. Mountain's melody
97. Apollo's mother
98. Reverse
99. Empty, in math
100. Slim
101. Speech defect
102. City on the Rhone
103. Bandleader Brown

DOWN

1. Till
2. Two-toed sloth
3. Holiday potions
4. Peloponnesus
5. Friend, to Chantal
6. Hosp. employees
7. Naps
8. Teacake
9. Parliament member
10. King of Israel
11. Earth's "hat"
12. Vexed
13. Racetrack
14. Reject
15. Road turn
17. Asphalt ade?
26. Units of wt.
28. Melody
29. Baseball's Nolan ____
31. Haley work
34. Against
35. Pour
36. Tiffany product
38. Cathedral town
39. Isolated
40. Eternal City
41. Comfort
42. Bridge part
44. Mythological figure
45. Playground item
47. Small fry
49. Plunder
50. Prison pads
53. Greek letter
54. Rosebud, e.g.
55. Gossip's pad?
57. Sausage
58. French state
59. What nurses give
60. Gain
61. Caterwaul
62. Trunk
63. Military alliance
64. Bean
65. Blue dye
66. Nerve network
68. Oaf
69. Sultry
71. Govt. agent
72. Pernicious
75. In ____ (together)
76. Me, to Miss Piggy
77. Solidify
79. Razor sharpener
81. Large lake
82. Contest
83. Muslim leader
84. Sacred mountain
85. At ____ end
87. Artist Cezanne
88. Slothful
89. Feels poorly
90. Hairstylist's goo
93. Some
94. Altar words

PUZZLE 129

• BEFORE AND AFTER •

113

PUZZLE 130

• ARE YOU GAME? •

ACROSS
1. Fling
5. Garden green
9. Pungent bulb
15. Once more
19. Hawaiian port
20. MP's concern
21. Handsome youth
22. 320 rods
23. Economist Smith
24. Barks
25. Disk game
27. Hand game
29. Leaders
30. That is, to Livy
31. Earnings
32. Bride's portion
33. Some army women
35. Fiery crime
38. Reef denizen
39. Legend
43. Trunks
44. Singer Loggins
45. Liquefy
46. Glass part
47. Singing brothers
48. Aspects
49. String game
51. Bishopric
52. Against
53. Trevino's gouge
54. Hold up
55. Jumping game
58. Solar disk
59. Bureau
61. Boggy
62. Voice
64. Touched down
65. March
68. Algonquian language
69. Game of quick reflexes
74. October's stone
75. Clad with hoof-plates
76. Cheers
77. "I'm ___ Rappaport"
78. Jackstraws
81. Actress Scacchi
83. Hare's kin
84. Home addition
85. Mine entrances
86. Singer Lopez
87. "___ California"
88. Leavings
90. Low tract
91. Make blank
92. Rackets
93. Vex
94. Diamond cover
96. Manipulate
99. Mitigate
100. Calling game
104. Hunting game
107. Retina cell
108. Jot
109. Is obliged to
110. Lighter fluid
111. Over
112. Wade
113. Brand-new
114. Put up with
115. Sassy
116. Italian mount

DOWN
1. Rub raw
2. Verdi opera
3. Louver
4. Salad fruits
5. Inuit vessel
6. Vigilant
7. Run easily
8. Some trains
9. Portal
10. Bee farm
11. Actor McDowall
12. Attorneys' degs.
13. Neighbor of Wis.
14. Coquettish
15. Surrounded by
16. Lineup number
17. Wapitis
18. "Go ___, young man"
26. Basket material
28. Preserves
29. Fanfare instruments
32. Fully cooked
33. Most awful
34. Sir Guinness
35. Shame
36. Master Montague
37. "The Big ___"
38. Doc
39. Japanese mattress
40. Shakespearean forest
41. Fragrant shrub
42. Course corundum
44. Money pool
45. Some bricks
48. Saw wood
49. Refer to
50. Supports
52. Having a low pH
53. Outmoded
56. Picayune
57. Canadian Indians
59. Maui farewell
60. Game traps
63. Some shirts
64. Rare violin
65. Stumper
66. Winesap, e.g.
67. Complains bitterly
68. Vouchers
70. Peace goddess
71. Author Loos
72. Garment pieces
73. Fusty
75. Heavens
79. Pretentious
80. Norse goddess
81. Boat or train
82. Incite
83. Marine mammal
86. Pinched
87. Frau's fellow
89. Most inactive
90. Sister of Helios
93. Implore
94. Choir voice
95. Proficient
96. To ___ it may . . .
97. Hawaiian honeycreeper
98. Sir Anthony ___
99. Wine region city
100. Sound of surf
101. Electrical unit
102. Harrow's rival
103. Indian melody
105. Cagers' org.
106. Name
107. Cover

PUZZLE 131

• AND THE WINNER IS . . . •

ACROSS
1. Swiftly
6. Recorded
11. Terra ____
16. Nitpicks
18. Brutal persons
20. Certain female fowl
21. Film listing
22. 1945 Oscar film
24. One: Ger.
25. "____ on the inarticulate" (Eliot)
27. Waste allowance
28. Limo
29. Emulate Xanthippe
30. Relish
31. "The Sheik" extras
32. Franchot of film
33. 1975 George Burns Oscar film
37. Looks sullen
38. Namesakes of Gardner
39. Voice votes
40. Grassy area
41. Monastics
44. Lawyers: abbr.
45. "Mr. ____ Holiday"
47. Sea thief
48. "____ Grows in Brooklyn"
50. Behaves
52. Heads you win, tails ____
53. Besmirch
54. Greater
55. Truly
56. High-flown thing
57. 1939 Oscar-winning actor
59. Liquid measures: abbr.
60. ____ Buttons
61. Chinese money
62. "____ to Live"
63. Salutes
65. Sharp-toothed sedge
68. Rigg or Ross
69. ____ Beach, Fla.
70. Hall of Fame Tiger
71. Diamond strategy
72. Bijou weeklies
74. Aches
75. Arrived
76. Frees
77. Disabled
79. 1968 Oscar lady
86. Mine finds
87. Andrea del ____
88. Dries
89. Buck's mate
90. Orig. state
91. Hautboy
92. Listens to
93. School letters
94. 1939 Oscar film
99. Kay Thompson heroine
102. Church officers
103. Tranquilizes
104. Of greater propinquity
105. Authority
106. Having a cupola
107. Attire

DOWN
1. Stress
2. Outcast
3. Exact punishment for
4. Spanish hero
5. Wallach the actor
6. "Mutiny on the Bounty" location
7. Photographer Richard ____
8. Crony
9. Self
10. Totals
11. Middling mark
12. Sturdy tree
13. Grace Kelly's 1954 Oscar film
14. Lessee
15. Guitarist Segovia
17. Become motionless
18. Hoard
19. Is errant
20. Lassie and Asta
23. Entanglements
26. Ballet or charlotte
31. Lessen
32. "____ is a pleasure . . ."
34. Rooms in casas
35. Grape conserve
36. One who amuses
37. Feeler
40. "Pawnbroker" director
41. Problem for 28 Across?
42. 1928-29 Oscar film
43. Dances for Carmen Miranda
44. Sandarac tree
45. Greek goddesses
46. Adler and Kowalski
47. Breakwaters
49. Youthful suffix
50. Serpentine dances
51. Impertinent
53. Milland's role in 22 Across
54. Sound of pain
57. Irene and Robert of films
58. Mild oath
63. Temple flick
64. "A glass is good, and ____ is good"
66. Unaccompanied songs
67. Fruit cover
68. 1941 Disney film
69. Dan of baseball
71. Smetana's "The ____ Bride"
73. Flubbed
75. "The Hustler" shots
77. Rude shelters
78. Interstice
79. Infant
80. Radiant
81. Oozed
82. Hair lock
83. Hold in high esteem
84. Sound effects
85. Dissuades
87. Bean sauces
95. ____ Plaines
96. Sib
97. ____-Magnon
98. Skirt bottom
100. Was ahead of
101. Rower

115

PUZZLE 132

• USE YOUR NOGGIN •

ACROSS

1. Arthur of tennis
5. Baby's affliction
9. Cotton unit
13. "____ are the times . . ."
18. Hockey's Mikita
19. Pennsylvania port
20. Paul's co-worker
21. Slogged
22. Philosopher Immanuel ____
23. Beverly Sills, e.g.
24. Bonnie or John
25. Incensed
26. Ova
27. Irving's equestrian
30. Van Owen of "L.A. Law"
31. Styling stuff
32. Coracle and punt
33. New Jersey hoopsters
34. Scottish resort
36. Spurs
37. Two points connector
38. Certain vote
41. Caster
43. Some cereals
44. Tribal bonnet
46. Masters
47. Etruscan Porsena
48. Beethoven's birthplace
49. Musical clef
50. Hurt
51. Loving
52. Pitcher Blue
53. Composer Gustav ____
55. "____ Devil"
56. Remain undecided
57. Celebratory
58. Tropical nuts
59. Much better than
65. "La ____ Vita"
66. Poorly
67. Malicious smile
68. Zero
69. Detroit suburb
71. Mild oath
72. Cultivates
73. Saint Philip ____
74. Sitarist Shankar
75. Bearing
76. Obscure
77. Minor Prophet
78. Lead
81. Tips
82. One of Dumas's three
83. Byron's always
84. Certain paints
85. Firewood measures
86. Gratis
87. Sonja Henie's birthplace
88. Motets, e.g.
89. Abraham's nephew
90. Deity of recklessness
93. Brainstorm
98. Month after Shebat
99. Have ____ (invitation to sit)
100. "If ____ the wings . . ."
101. Top-notch
102. Italia's capital
103. Core
104. Trencherman
105. Deep grooves
106. ____ first you don't . . .
107. Street show
108. Brit. cur.
109. Easy gait
110. Hairstyle

DOWN

1. Invited
2. Thespian's milieu
3. Be ashamed of
4. Tolkien beings
5. "The Little ____"
6. Prospero's ally
7. Hindu god
8. Bed part
9. Critters
10. Off kilter
11. Plaster backing
12. Talinn native
13. Warped
14. Lagomorphs
15. Cheese town
16. Bristle
17. Blissful place
20. Fears
28. Bank transactions
29. Sunder
31. Heaters
35. Venerable one
36. Some pianos
37. Capp's hyena
38. Complain loudly
39. Punta del ____
40. Hebrew zither
41. Collide
42. Mazo de la ____
43. Fair-haired lady
44. Surfing groupie
45. Biblical spy concealer
48. Actor Mumy
51. Parry and thrust
52. Hurdle
53. Exodus hero
54. Wing-shaped
56. Cronies
57. City of refuge
58. Angler's baskets
60. Andrea ____
61. Employed
62. Removes by law
63. Greenfinch, e.g.
64. Walter ____ Disney
69. Gaelic
70. Headland
71. Explorer Bartholomeu ____
72. Preschool program
73. Symbol of music
75. Airs
76. Brink
77. Robert Wagner role
79. Flowerlike ornament
80. Seed scars
81. More protracted
85. Kitchen appliance
86. Black or Sherwood
87. Midwest airport
88. Condition
89. Slow, musically
91. Absalom's sister
92. Shelley's Muse
93. A Garland costar
94. Confused
95. "____ of the Dragon"
96. ASAP, medically
97. Watch cycle
98. ____ di bravura

TOPSY-TURVY
PUZZLE 133

Better check your sense of direction before starting this puzzle. All the answers in a Topsy-Turvy read back and up, just the opposite from a regular crossword.

BACK

1. Sustain
2. Tantalize
3. Timber tree
4. Isolated
5. Small bay
6. "Can You Top ___?"
7. Dismounted
8. Coin-flipper's call
10. Natural color
11. "Hardhearted ___"
14. Well said: 2 wds.
18. Horseshoe shape
19. Stylish
20. Attack: 2 wds.
22. Supplies meals
24. Ladder part
25. Fleur-de-lis
26. Sweetsop
27. Assert
28. Stacks
29. Own
30. Villain's antagonist
31. Lichen
32. At all times
33. Sly
36. Climber's support
40. Has a snack
41. Mild oath

42. Pause and wait: 2 wds.
44. Small wolf-like animal
46. Open surface
47. Famous
48. Paper measure
49. Count calories
51. Make amends
52. Arm bone
53. Wholly
56. Enjoy fully
61. Swamplands

UP

9. Compass dir.
11. 50%
12. Medicinal plant
13. Baseball team
14. Pacific island pine
15. Yodeler's reply
16. Opera high spot
17. Toasted biscuit
19. Surrenders
21. A Gershwin
22. Pure
23. Atmosphere
28. Bat for another: hyph.
31. Glee
33. Map
34. Musical show
35. Circus ring

36. Book page
37. Egg-shaped
38. Crowbar
39. Clothe
41. Gives medicine
43. Make lace
45. Cereal
50. Assume: 3 wds.

53. Eden resident
54. Money in Roma, once
55. Sinister look
56. Mental health
57. Potent particles
58. Cast a ballot

59. United
60. Relief society: 2 wds.
61. Make peace: 3 wds.
62. Margarine
63. Small fly
64. Ditto

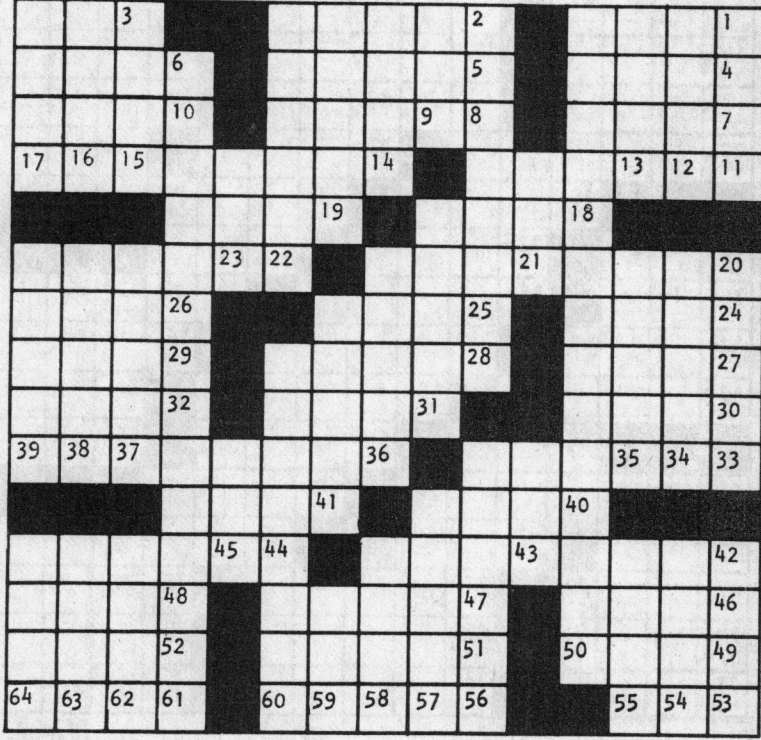

CRYPTIC GEOGRAPHY
PUZZLE 134

A country is pictured below. The name of the country and some interesting information about it are given in a substitution code (different letters are substituted for the correct ones).

NZEAMWN
(country)

NZEAMWN WE PXGQX OGM WAE TWSXXSES

DGOOSS BGZESE, DZUAZMNU OWRZMSE

EZDB NE KGCNMA, NXF ABS FNXZIS

MWTSM. NDAZNUUJ, EAMNZEE'E

"ISNZAWOZU IUZS FNXZIS" QNE NXF

WE KZMPJ IMGQX!

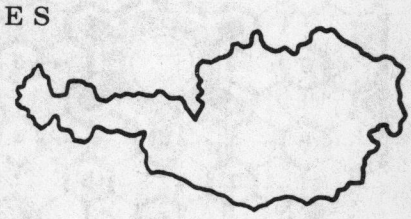

PUZZLE 135

ACROSS
1. Shove
5. Snares
10. Bridge
14. Person against
15. "Bolero" composer
16. Military assistant
17. Fibber
18. Overact
19. Turn the soil
20. Scatters
22. Require
24. Raw mineral
25. Takes a chair
27. Splash
29. Scarlet
32. Thick slice
34. Knight's title
35. Actress Gardner
36. Actress Hayes
38. Flanks
42. Butterfly snares
44. Business transactions
46. Stallion's mate
47. "The ___ Gatsby"
49. Birds of peace
51. Make a knot
52. Male
54. Departed
55. Ampersand
56. Esteems
60. Train track
62. Period in history
63. Mama's mate
65. Hobos
69. Quite a few
71. Beatle Starr
73. Storm wind
74. Phrase of understanding: 2 wds.
75. Penetrate
76. Adam and Eve's home
77. "___ of the D'Urbervilles"
78. Adjudges
79. Enjoy a book

DOWN
1. Buddies
2. Component part
3. Night twinkler
4. Employs
5. Railroad bridges
6. Ewe's mate
7. Bard of ___
8. For ___ sake!
9. Slumbers
10. Tree juice
11. Aviator
12. Worship
13. More modern
21. Desire
23. Podium
26. Dish of mixed greens
28. Decorate a tree
29. Pealed
30. Always
31. Social appointment
33. Underneath
37. At no time
39. Facts
40. ___ go bragh
41. Kernel
43. Identical
45. Upper House members
48. Canvas cover, for short
50. Mix
53. Approached
56. Forward payment
57. Clean a slate
58. Weathercocks
59. Backbone
61. Aged beer
64. Poker kitty
66. Constructed
67. Entreaty
68. Dispatch
70. Word of agreement
72. Jewel

PUZZLE 136

Honeycomb

The small arrows indicate the beginning of each 6-letter answer word. Each answer will circle its number in either a clockwise or counterclockwise direction.

1. Song verse
2. South American river
3. Tepee
4. Having great talent
5. Wily
6. Prom flower
7. Prom outfit
8. Extravagance
9. Quite attractive
10. Siesta locale
11. Alibi
12. Hamburger condiment

PUZZLE 137

ACROSS
1. TV's Donahue
5. Laundry-day need
9. Sizzling
12. Calhoun et al.
14. Wicked
15. Rescue
16. Want a lot
17. "The Way We ___"
18. Alder or aspen
19. Canvas shoe
21. Noncitizens
23. Free (of)
24. Bible songs
25. Dodged
29. Map marking
30. Lemons' kin
31. ___ Haute
32. Literary collection
35. Killed
36. "___ You Went Away"
37. Let fall
38. Poetic close of day
39. "The ___ of a Nation"
40. Self-assurance
41. Morse and area
42. Roam
43. 747s
45. Mineo or soda
46. Sparkles
47. Pompous shows
51. Lily pad's home
52. Cure
54. Large box
56. Amos's buddy
57. Sooner State: abbr.
58. Artist's stand
59. Boston ___ Party
60. Actress Tuesday ___
61. Precious stones

DOWN
1. Use a lever
2. Works the garden
3. Boxer Barkley
4. Apollo's instrument
5. Stitched
6. Finished
7. Make public
8. Enjoyment
9. Moslem women's quarters
10. Stove parts
11. Golf gadgets
13. Hidden traps
15. Fence steps
20. Billy the ___
22. Not on time
24. Veranda
25. What ___ is new?
26. Loathsome
27. Prayer ending
28. Small drops of moisture
29. Leases
31. Flat and spare
32. Dry
33. A ___ for news
34. Copycat
36. Circus feature: 2 wds.
37. Comedian Knotts
39. Mother Hubbard's lack
40. Home for royalty
41. Sugary treat
42. Armed conflict
43. Dial
44. Actress Lavin
45. Meal course
46. Lover's quarrel
47. Become boring
48. Pull along
49. Comfort
50. From ___ to stern
53. Piece (out)
55. Overhead trains, for short

MISSING LINKS   PUZZLE 138

The answers to the clues on the left end at the first heavy line. The answers to the clues on the right start after the second heavy line. Fill in the Missing Link between each pair of words to make a single word reading across. For example: NIGH and CAP become NIGHTCAP when you add the letter T. The Missing Links spell a word reading down the center column.

In favor of

Footwear

Sail beam

At all times

Nobleman

Punctuation mark and cons

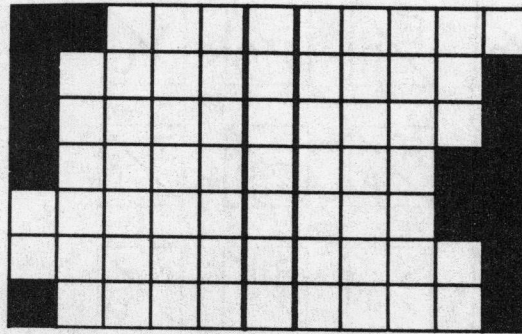

Stable division

High cards

Mr. Lardner

Raw metal

Cardinal color

Forest denizen

Fixed charge

119

PUZZLE 139

• ALL-AMERICAN •

ACROSS
1. Tool house
5. Anthracite
9. Fitting
12. Roof parts
14. ___ facto
15. Cupid
16. All-American date: 4 wds.
19. Possesses
20. Resinous substances
21. Steak order
22. Inca's land
23. Cloudless
25. Bell sounds
28. Barrel part
30. Skill
33. Florence's river
34. Jacket or collar
35. High hill
36. All-American hues: 4 wds.
41. King's better
42. Same: Latin
43. Shucks!
44. Mo. and Ark.
45. Stop
47. Diamond facets?
48. Frozen desserts
49. British gun
51. Japanese aborigine
53. Solar disk
54. Anger
57. See 16 Across: 2 wds.
61. French holy women: abbr.
62. Prophet
63. Cut in two
64. French possessive
65. Tracy's Trueheart
66. Golf mounds

DOWN
1. Adam's third son
2. Laughter sounds: hyph.
3. Holiday nights
4. Lexicon yield: abbr.
5. ___ Maximus
6. Chooses
7. Cigar residue
8. Old card game
9. Asian river
10. Krakow native
11. Attempt
13. What cobblers try to save
15. Slightly open
17. Inits. for Nasser
18. Pal
22. John Deere's tool
23. ___ Morgana
24. The Bard's river
25. Montenegro coins
26. Build
27. Aconcagua's range
29. Swarms
30. Map book
31. Course
32. Lock
37. Sot's sound
38. ___ fixe
39. Aromatic beverages
40. Grain husk
46. Fruit-essence compounds
47. Dugout seat
48. ___ de Castro
50. Decade
51. Poker stake
52. ___ of March
53. Summer drinks
54. Unemployed
55. Rant
56. "The ___ of Laura Mars"
57. Creed
58. Winter hrs. in Boston
59. Born
60. Have brunch

PUZZLE 140

MOSAIC

Place the twelve boxes, each containing two letters, into the empty diagram to form four 8-letter words reading across and down, as shown in the small example on the left.

Example:

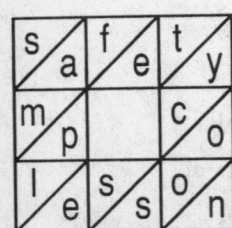

120

DOUBLE TROUBLE

PUZZLE 141

Not really double trouble, but double fun! Solve this puzzle as you would a regular crossword, EXCEPT place one, two, or three letters in each box. The number of letters in each answer is shown in parentheses after its clue.

ACROSS

1. Whirlybird (10)
5. Old sailing vessel (7)
9. Hesitate (6)
10. Jousting spears (6)
11. Conflict (6)
12. Presses clothes (5)
14. Young child (3)
15. Restless (5)
16. Alaskan sea (6)
17. Beanies (4)
18. Warble (4)
19. Small amounts (4)
20. Twin of Romulus (5)
21. ____ firma (5)
22. Harvesting machine (6)
23. Rich milk (5)
24. Coconut trees (5)
25. Forehead (4)
27. Synagogue singer (6)
28. Young boys (4)
29. Wood finish (5)
30. Confederate general (3)
31. Gestures (7)
32. 29th President (7)
33. Battery terminal (5)
35. Frightens (8)
37. Scraps of food (7)
38. Representatives (6)

DOWN

1. Of sound body (7)
2. Small (6)
3. Deal (with) (4)
4. Scottish dogs (8)
5. Quantities of gasoline (7)
6. Not fatty (4)
7. Cuttlefish (7)
8. Birds' homes (5)
9. Looking in the eye (6)
11. Boring tools (4)
13. Wedding band (4)
16. ____ au rhum (4)
17. Recreational vehicle (6)
19. Reverie (5)
20. Empires (6)
21. Extreme fright (6)
22. Peruses (5)
23. USO centers (8)
24. Corridor (7)
25. Restrains a horse (7)
26. Possessing (6)
27. Loud noise (6)
28. King of beasts (4)
29. Begins (6)
31. Roadside inns (6)
32. Male deer (4)
34. Lyric poem (3)
36. Light brown (3)

KEYWORD

PUZZLE 142

To find the KEYWORD fill in the blanks in words 1 through 10 with the correct missing letters. Transfer those letters to the correspondingly numbered squares in the diagram. Approach with care—this puzzle is not as simple as it first appears.

1	2	3	4	5	6	7	8	9	10

1. S _ A C E
2. B L _ N D
3. P A _ T S
4. _ E W E R
5. S H O R _

6. _ R O W N
7. R E A C _
8. S T _ L E
9. D R _ V E
10. _ E V E R

PUZZLE 143

OVERLAPS

Place the answer to each clue into the diagram beginning at the corresponding number. Words will overlap with other words.

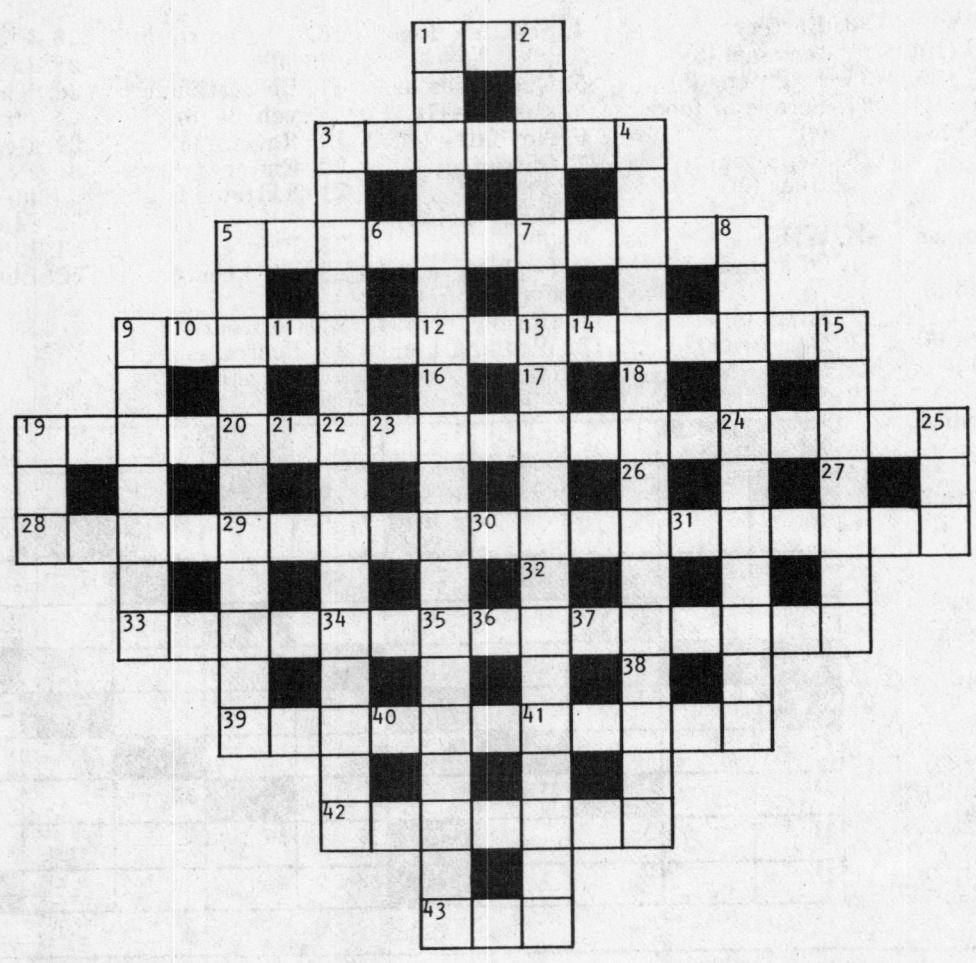

ACROSS

1. Cleverness
3. Supplied with new weapons
5. Nab
6. Elate
7. Slipped up
9. "____ of Eden"
10. Actress Mary
11. Baseball-manager Joe
12. Peruse
13. Yemen port
14. Mile-High City
19. Cost
21. French legislative body
23. Of course!
24. Melodious
28. Ploy for Becker
29. Rod for thread
30. Host
31. Ahead
33. Popeye or Sinbad
34. Hunter in the sky
36. "____ upon a midnight dreary"
37. Cherry red
39. Actress Betty
40. Cloud, as with tears
41. Bedouins, e.g.
42. Foes
43. Droop

DOWN

1. Forecaster
2. Concern of 1 Down
3. Meted out
4. Kind of window
5. Trig functions
8. Fiend
9. Awaits
15. Unusual
16. West African baboon
17. Soup dish
18. French dramatist
19. Flow's partner
20. Building an aerie
22. Magazine worker
24. Certain soup ingredients
25. Massachusetts cape
26. Movie houses
27. Life of Riley
29. Smart
32. Genial
34. Emulate Bryan
35. Malady
38. Church service

At 6's and 7's

Clues to all the 6- and 7-letter words in this crossword puzzle are listed first, and they are in scrambled order. Use the numbered clues as solving aids to help you determine where each one goes in the diagram.

6-Letter Words
Oozed
Garment arm
Contemporary
Commands

7-Letter Words
Vengeance
Clothed
Beauty contest
Downpour
Were alike
Trenches
Piled up
Moral
Built
Give courage to

ACROSS
1. Cathedral roof
5. Necklace fastener
10. Edges
14. ____ Khayyam
15. Hindu queen
16. Songstress Adams
17. ____ is of the essence
18. Finished
19. Shift direction
24. Gratuity
25. Cantaloupe
26. Poe's bird
29. Wicked
30. Actress Moorehead
34. Had debts
35. Strike
37. Prohibit
40. Tiny
43. In what manner
44. Look after
45. Irritable
46. Encountered
47. Harbors
48. Salome's stepfather
50. ____ diem
58. Secular
59. "The ____ Year Itch"
61. Great Lake
62. Songstress Fitzgerald
63. Attempted
64. Famous fiddler
65. Vend
66. Breaks suddenly
67. "Harold ____"

DOWN
1. Ellipses
2. Leave out
3. "I Remember ____"
5. Crawl
6. Acreage
7. "Night ____ Day"
9. Foot treadle
11. Brainstorm
12. Bearing
13. Spanish painter
21. Kith and ____
23. Targets
26. Mechanical man
27. Conscious (of)
28. Sells
29. Nipped
31. More up-to-date
32. Occurrence
33. Kernels
35. ____ Honor
(Mayor)
36. Stitch
38. Laundry machine
39. Torrid
47. "The Princess and the ____"
49. Relaxes
50. Remains undecided
51. Pub orders
52. Story
53. Money drawer
54. Uriah ____
55. Genealogy diagram
56. Irish republic
57. Sign gas
60. By way of

(crossword grid diagram with numbered cells 1–67)

QUOTAGRAM

Fill in the answers to the clues below. Then transfer the letters to the correspondingly numbered squares in the diagram. The completed diagram will contain a quotation.

1. Launch
   37 8 30 13 34 24 7 31 19

2. Pamper
   9 32 14 21 26 3

3. Flabbergasts
   15 33 10 25 35 2

4. Dinah ____
   6 4 23 29 39

5. Niagara or Angel
   38 1 16 36 27

6. Scorch
   22 5 28 20

7. Steel ____
   18 12 17 11

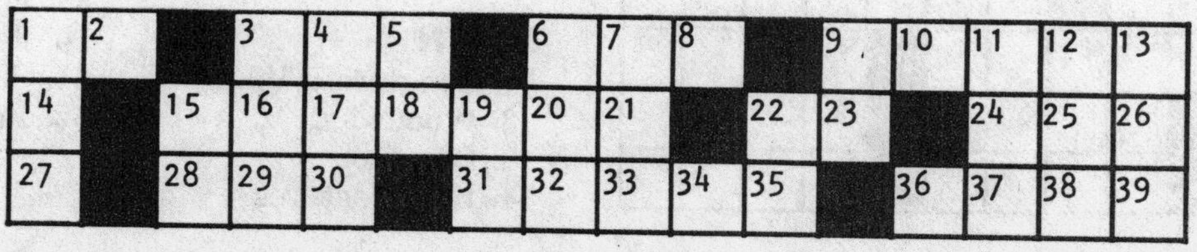

(quotagram grid diagram with numbered cells 1–39)

PUZZLE 146

ACROSS
1. Burst
4. Pant
8. Lions' homes
10. Musical drama
12. Distribute
13. Smooth
14. Victory symbol
15. Not on
17. Snakelike fish
18. Come
20. ____-Margret
21. Pennies
23. That woman
25. Antics
29. Fib
30. Skirt edge
31. Actress West
32. Texas shrine
34. Establish guilt
36. Actress Day
37. Locations
38. Photocopy, for short
39. Cozy room

DOWN
1. More ashen
2. Tank ship
3. Paid athlete
4. Palmer's game
5. Monkey
6. Lucky number
7. Clean feathers
8. Molten rock
9. Kitchen item
11. Everything
16. Property divider
19. Frozen water
20. Egyptian snake
22. Packs down tobacco
23. Fodder towers
24. Vital organ
26. Overact
27. Black bird
28. Uses the eyes
29. Young boy
30. Party giver
33. Actress Farrow
35. Disencumber

PUZZLE 147

ACROSS
1. Policemen
5. Snatch
9. Ripen
12. Aid in crime
13. First-rate: hyph.
14. Light brown
15. Lion's cry
16. Ferretlike animal
18. Goes to bed
20. Total
21. Birds' homes
23. Fissure
26. Ballads
29. Golfer Snead
31. Menagerie
32. Stages of growth
34. Discourages
36. Point a gun
37. Paving liquid
39. Merry pranks
40. Foot digits
42. Sooner or ____
44. Family member, for short
46. Gazing narrowly
50. ____ Delano Roosevelt
53. False god
54. Acorn tree
55. Military assistant
56. Singer Fitzgerald
57. Needle opening
58. Exam
59. Before Sea or end

DOWN
1. Songstress Vikki
2. Woodwind
3. Bog fuel
4. Harp features
5. Pastimes
6. Perches
7. Dancer Miller
8. Pleads
9. Spray can
10. Car fuel
11. Opposite of WSW
17. "____ Town"
19. Change, as an alarm
22. Unhappy
24. Utensil
25. Flip
26. Petty quarrel
27. Reds' state
28. Junior, to senior
30. Confused fight
33. Actor Mineo
35. Lingered
38. Cedar ____
41. Transgression
43. Article of faith
45. Card game
47. Unemployed
48. Piano novelty
49. Happy
50. Enemy
51. Sunbeam
52. Falsehood

PUZZLE 148

ACROSS
1. Fish appendage
4. The city of the Seven Hills
8. Tease
12. Have being
13. Off yonder
14. Opera solo
15. Crow's cry
16. Mix
17. Escapade
18. Lured
20. Sheriff's men
21. Is able to
22. Energy
23. ____ band
26. Baby's enclosure
30. Aspire
31. Purchase
32. Pub specialty
33. Atomic particle
36. Washer cycle
38. "____ Jude"
39. Ewe's mate
40. Sculled
43. Joked
47. Native metals
48. Deli offerings
49. Bard's before
50. Indonesian island
51. Hearty
52. Corduroy feature
53. Additions
54. Ogled
55. Encountered

DOWN
1. Visage
2. Modern Persia
3. Salamander
4. Mischief-maker
5. Frequently
6. Housekeeper
7. Blunder
8. Rattletrap
9. Epochs
10. Knights
11. Swipe
19. Frost
20. Podded vegetable
22. Layer
23. ____ Francisco
24. Cravat
25. Flightless bird
26. Witticism
27. Cooking vessel
28. Chicago trains
29. Born, to Brigitte
31. Lad
34. Dissertation
35. Ruby
36. Hoisted
37. Elf
39. Russian monetary unit
40. Judge's garment
41. Kind of exam
42. Wishing ____
43. Wharf
44. Beauty salon treatment
45. Cleveland's lake
46. Mortgage
48. Feminine pronoun

PUZZLE 149

ACROSS
1. Went by helicopter
5. ____ California
9. Lower digit
12. Slat
13. Tiptop
14. Addition
15. Soprano Moffo
16. Flowered wreaths
18. Oyster stone
20. Ginkgo, e.g.
21. Suspicious
23. Moccasin or clog
27. Owns
30. Harbor
31. Loud
32. Up and about
34. Collapse
35. Authorized
36. Acquire
37. Turf
38. Honolulu's island
39. Respond
41. Faculty figure
43. A Great Lake
47. Bustle
51. Air
52. Oath
53. Small land mass
54. Pindar poems
55. Self
56. Singers Brenda and Peggy
57. Repose

DOWN
1. Flutter
2. Byway
3. Lab burner
4. Dock
5. Purse
6. Indifference
7. Ben's ice cream partner
8. Wheel part
9. Decade
10. Ancient
11. Overhead trains
17. Fable writer
19. Written defamation
22. ____ Diego
24. Hula-Hoop's locale
25. Norwegian capital
26. Stared at
27. Angel's headgear
28. Zone
29. Express regret
31. Groove
33. ____ Arabia
34. Afternoon social
36. Mild
39. Grow
40. Mentor
42. Bad
44. Coarse
45. Units
46. Cozy abode
47. Blvd.
48. Tooth
49. Duet number
50. Affirmative

125

PUZZLE 150

ACROSS
1. Off the ___ (weird)
5. Space
8. Used
11. Sills's specialty
12. Farm structure
13. Court
14. Pace
15. False appearance
17. Voyage
19. Exams
20. Humble
23. Singer Torme
24. Covered with water
25. Individuals
29. Certainly!
30. Rug
31. Denial word
32. Stuck
35. Sports site
37. Sprinted
38. More intimate
39. Bulgur
42. Equine sport
43. Burrowing rodents
45. Charts
49. "The Greatest"
50. Swag
51. Sinful
52. Child
53. Tip
54. Refuse

DOWN
1. Existed
2. Mr. Linkletter
3. Deceive
4. Slips
5. "That ___"
6. Saloon order
7. Author Beatrix ___
8. Has
9. "___ in Yonkers"
10. Performs
12. ___ curl
16. Morays
18. Bat wood
20. Poet Angelou
21. Was obligated to pay
22. Smidgen
23. Joined
25. Apartment
26. Wallet fillers
27. Zilch
28. Altair or Deneb
30. "A Few Good ___"
33. Epochs
34. Baby's toy
35. Everything
36. Lodged
38. Expense
39. Reporter's question
40. Angel's headgear
41. Discharge
42. Encourage
44. Eternity
46. Blvd.
47. Tailor's tool
48. Drummer Dunbar

PUZZLE 151

ACROSS
1. Labels
5. Mama's mate
9. To's partner
12. Brainstorm
13. Flock members
14. Canon
15. Closet items
17. Sorbet
18. Thesis
19. Knocked
21. Peruse
24. Bark
25. Roman garment
28. Witch
30. Information
33. Greek peak
34. Bauxite, e.g.
35. And not
36. Congers
38. ___, team!
39. Plant support
40. Scientist's milieu
42. Trickle
44. Fumbled
47. Actor Phoenix
51. Back talk
52. Gibberish
55. Flamenco bravo
56. Dryad's dwelling
57. Donations
58. Unite
59. Shoe part
60. For fear that

DOWN
1. Tempo
2. Hubbubs
3. Stakes
4. African desert
5. Pod dweller
6. Boring tool
7. Hide
8. Evaluate
9. Disrespectful
10. Marathon
11. Was in the red
16. Ciao!
20. Cushion
22. Nautical greeting
23. Chanced
25. Dead heat
26. Poem
27. Ran
29. Paraphernalia
31. Piggy
32. Appendage
37. Maple syrup base
39. Helix
41. Bunk
43. Author Wolfert
44. Incandescence
45. Incense
46. Extreme
48. Mouse's kin
49. Graceful trees
50. Relax
53. Command to Dobbin
54. Actor Gibson

126

PUZZLE 152

ACROSS
1. Pung
5. Jazz pianist Garland
8. Hairdo
12. Crown of light
13. Pinna
14. Jack rabbit
15. Forewarning
16. Ready
18. Stamina
19. More crowded
20. Sleet's relative
22. Prototype
26. Expunge
28. Word before diem
29. Free-for-all
30. Official standing
31. Needlefish
32. Aspiration
33. Skill
34. Harden
35. Race official
36. School assignment
38. Promontory
39. Favor
41. Head gesture
44. Came into sight
47. Bundle
48. Transportation charge
49. Devoured
50. Unoccupied
51. Walked on
52. Steered
53. Close by

DOWN
1. Boutique
2. Lacking substance
3. Pachyderms
4. Boxing promoter King
5. Disgust
6. Bring home the bacon
7. Bedroom furniture
8. Amulet
9. Bireme's need
10. Choler
11. Nourished
17. Pulpy fruit
19. Mold
21. Interrogate
23. Boardwalk
24. Easy gait
25. Vaselike jug
26. Of an age
27. Steak order
28. Butter serving
31. Not specific
32. Femur-innominate bone joint
34. Marsh bird
35. Pitch
37. Go beyond the limit
38. Yielded
40. Banquet
42. Clay pot
43. Range player
44. Toward the stern
45. Golfing goal
46. In favor of
47. Storage box

PUZZLE 153

ACROSS
1. City on the Adda
5. Bubbling ____ (1926 Derby winner)
9. Brokers ____ (1933 winner)
12. Egyptian god: var.
13. Read: Fr.
14. Cultivate
15. Enormous
16. Mild oath
17. Cut a ____ (dance)
18. Workers' collective
20. Comfort
22. Apex
25. Be unmoving, as a ship
28. 1883 winner
31. Pair
32. Branch
33. Seacoast sights
35. Summer, to Jacques
36. Doll's cry
38. Lucky ____ (1965 winner)
40. ____ Gold (1924 winner)
42. "M*A*S*H" clerk
43. Undiluted
45. Valued property
48. Contained
50. Eurasian mountain range
53. Cobbler's concern
54. ____ de France
55. Excellent
56. Others: Lat.
57. ____ Barton (1919 winner)
58. Concept
59. Land tenure system

DOWN
1. Krakatau outpouring
2. ____ Khayyam (1917 winner)
3. 1970 winner
4. Student teacher
5. ____ Rosebud (1914 winner)
6. By the route of
7. Marine bird
8. Stately
9. Derby entrant's usual age
10. Chit
11. Cribbage pin
19. Be in front
21. Imogene's costar
23. Horse for breeding
24. TV part
26. Comic Jacques ____
27. German river
28. Young sheep
29. Epochal
30. Eldest son of Cush
34. Sodium carbonate
37. Maven
39. Bahamian capital
41. ____ King (1966 winner)
44. Stomped on
46. Kazan of films
47. River duck
48. ____ Eminence (1901 winner)
49. Ben ____ (1886 winner)
51. Chemical suffix
52. Grazing area

PUZZLE 154

• WOODY'S WORKS •

ACROSS
1. Casino game
5. Final
9. Seasons
14. Blue-pencil
15. Diminutive suffix
16. "Let's Make ____"
17. Woody Allen, 1979
19. Serenity
20. Hair-grooming aid, at times
21. Tide type
23. Kin of hwy.
24. Opposed
27. Attempt
28. Small bite
29. Roman god of war
30. Taut
33. Prefix with phone or photo
34. Holy ones: abbr.
35. Defense gp. formed in 1949
36. Kind of duck
37. Woody Allen, 1978
40. Carried
43. Withered
44. Craze
47. 29 Across, to Greeks
48. "La Boheme," e.g.
50. Antares or Betelgeuse
51. Court divider
52. "Exodus" hero
53. Woolly South Americans
55. In the past
56. Drill
58. Native of: suffix
59. Smartly dressed
61. Woody Allen, 1977
66. French diarist, with 62 Down
67. Weekend enjoyer's abbr.
68. Songstress Adams
69. Shoe parts
70. Sea eagles
71. Germ

DOWN
1. Gender abbr.
2. 1961 Dean Martin film
3. Doorbell users
4. Different ones
5. Rent
6. Lawyer: abbr.
7. Comedian Freberg
8. Beliefs
9. Sentimental
10. Humorist George
11. Erudite
12. Of touch
13. Woody Allen, 1973
18. Green and Unser
22. Exist
24. Morns: abbr.
25. Wine container
26. Coup d'____
31. Summer on the Seine
32. Scandinavian
33. "____ better to have loved . . ."
35. Dir.
36. Byron's before
37. Election winners
38. Comparative ending
39. Like some vaccines
40. Woody Allen, 1971
41. Spice in tomato sauce
42. Add up again
44. S. Dak. milit. base
45. Motorists' org.
46. Members of the AMA
48. Gold, in Granada
49. Freebooter
50. Door frames
52. Bottomless pit
54. Grant's foe
57. Train driver: abbr.
60. ____-dye
62. See 66 Across
63. Partner of ands and buts
64. Recline
65. Guided

PUZZLE 155

Say That Again?

Five well-known quotations or phrases have been reworded below—but the original meanings have been kept. Can you identify the originals?

Example: Unnoisy, like a small rodent (Answer: Quiet as a mouse)

1. A period of preeminence is passed through by all canines.

2. Prodigality is manufactured by precipitancy.

3. Tenants of vitreous abodes ought not to hurl lithoidal fragments.

4. Every article which coruscates is not compounded from aureate material.

5. Domestic fowl ought not be enumerated before nascency.

PUZZLE 156

ACROSS
1. Waist accessory
5. "You ____ There"
8. Cease
12. Medley
13. Each
14. Furniture wood
15. Choir voice
16. Refinement
18. Shade tree
20. Frozen water
21. Moray
22. Blemish
24. Spring holiday
27. Eggs
28. Fire residue
29. Snake
32. Flower parts
34. Hubbub
37. Scarlet
38. Feel unwell
39. Princess poker
40. Make numb
43. Corn unit
44. Also
47. "... and a barrel of ____"
48. Melody
50. Curtain fabric
53. Channel changer
56. Audacity
57. Vex
58. Mine find
59. Out of the wind
60. Peg for Palmer
61. Formerly

DOWN
1. Constrictor
2. Building addition
3. Able to read
4. Implement
5. Simian
6. Savor
7. Upright
8. Resort of sorts
9. Prong
10. Fairy tale starter
11. Pare
17. Golly
19. Repast
22. Swab
23. Profess
25. Beast of burden
26. Batter
30. Of better quality
31. Appeal
33. Do sums
34. Bind
35. Arm bone
36. Roofing material
38. Esteem
41. Marine bird
42. Examine accounts
44. Forum wear
45. Spoken
46. Leer
49. Loaf
51. Pub libation
52. Supplement
54. Newspaper items
55. Permit

PUZZLE 157

ACROSS
1. Road guide
4. Fabric with metallic threads
8. Nip
12. Anger
13. Ready for business
14. Throb
15. Put in curlers
16. Bellow
17. Spiritual being
18. Steam bath
20. News
22. Respite
24. Firearm
25. Frog's relative
27. Reverberation
29. Used a chair
32. Marine eagle
33. "I ____ Rhythm"
34. Impolite
35. Seine
36. Location
37. ____-de-camp
38. Public transport
39. Aerie
41. Belfry
45. Stage
48. Molten rock
49. African lily
51. Bunk
52. Eye part
53. Story
54. Gam
55. Skin
56. Odds and ____
57. Augment

DOWN
1. Overlook
2. Region
3. Irritable
4. Faithful
5. Orang
6. Thaw
7. Inform
8. Sink
9. Sacred picture
10. Ruffian
11. Snigglers' prey
19. In the buff
21. Twosome
23. Enact
25. Gymnast's goal
26. Raw mineral
28. Rollaway's kin
29. Fitting
30. Tot up
31. Links stand
34. Foolhardy
36. Dine
38. Beauty's love
40. Fencing swords
41. Undergarment
42. Weight allowance
43. Malicious
44. Spirit
46. Search for
47. Rim
50. Ancient

PUZZLE 158

ACROSS

1. Swiss mountains
5. Change the decor
9. Crisp cookie
13. Bore
14. Eat away
16. The T of TV
17. Leave out
18. Cornered
19. Diva's solo
20. Chess pieces
21. Prophet
22. "____ Delight"
24. Was able to
26. Asterisk
27. Whine
29. TV advertisers
33. November birthstone
34. Gaze intently
35. By way of
36. Bun
37. Bards
38. Pre-Easter period
39. Unit
40. Dramatic parts
41. Concise
42. Annoyed
44. Takes a dip
45. Piper followers
46. Inferior
47. Take long steps
50. Cures leather
51. Fuss
54. Baby's bed
55. Cheek cosmetic
57. On
58. Military assistant
59. More rational
60. Folksinger Seeger
61. Little piggies
62. Scarlet hues
63. First garden

DOWN

1. Small particle
2. Rickey ingredient
3. Basic doctrines
4. Matched group
5. Narrate again
6. Made a mistake
7. Active person
8. "____ on a Grecian Urn"
9. Flight of steps
10. Famous fiddler
11. Dismounted
12. ____ and carrots
15. Newspaper executives
21. ____ Canal
23. Copenhagen resident
25. Egg-shaped
26. Gaiters
27. Sharpen a razor
28. Not a soul
29. Charger
30. Too hot
31. Wash lightly
32. Gluts
34. Shoe bottoms
37. Redcaps
38. Rents
40. Study a text
41. Sailors
43. Indian clans
44. Goofs, slangily
46. Carried on
47. Shoo!
48. Three musicians
49. Go by bus
50. Melody
52. Be overly fond
53. Frank
56. Paddle
57. Monkey

PUZZLE 159   Cryptic Trivia

An interesting bit of trivia is in a substitution code (different letters are substituted for the correct ones).

OYCOCBDWKU SPB SWWDVSLCYU KSL ULCPKU,

SPB LTK ULCPKU YKHSDP DPUDBK LTKDY

ULCHSOTU. UODKPLDULU LTDPN LTKM HDVTL

BC LTDU LC TKWZ LTKH BDAK, CY LC TKWZ

VYDPB QZ LTKDY ICCB, CY LC NKKZ LTKH IYCH

IKKWDPV TQPVYM.

ACROSS
1. Close
5. "Major ____"
8. Crush
12. Vehicle
13. Alter ____
14. Yearn
15. Lakers or Bulls, e.g.
16. Provided dinner
17. Advertising sign
18. Embarrassment
20. Move smoothly
22. Refrain syllable
23. Snakelike fish
24. Greatest
27. President Ronald ____
31. Glimpse
32. Citrus cooler
33. Joins
37. Associate
40. Tank
41. Ginger ____
42. Essay
44. Knife
47. Persia, today
48. "____ for one and one for ..."
50. Fool
52. Bits of thread
53. Add color
54. Immoral
55. Fireplace wood
56. "____ Giorgio" (Pavarotti film)
57. ____ of the woods (neighborhood)

DOWN
1. Occupied
2. Shades
3. State west of Colorado
4. Ketchup ingredient
5. Loss
6. Mellow, as wine
7. Los Angeles baseball player
8. Philippine city
9. Mastered
10. Sandal or loafer
11. Mad as a wet ____
19. Title for Robinson or Muir
21. Actress Jamie ____ Curtis
24. Function
25. "The ____ Commandments"
26. Congregated
28. Guy's date
29. Excitement
30. Innovative
34. Occurrences
35. Aries
36. Constant
37. Allegories
38. Plumbing joint
39. Heavy
42. Singing group
43. Suspend
45. Peaceful bird
46. Heroic
47. Unsound
49. Caustic substance
51. Lodge member

PUZZLE 161

ACROSS
1. Wander
5. Shoo!
9. "We ____ the World"
12. Enthusiastic
13. Horseback game
14. "My ____ Sal"
15. Crooned
16. Forsakes
18. Clothing fold
20. Baltic or Black
21. Polishes
24. Theatrical piece
28. Flowers
32. Was aware of
33. Drink like a cat
34. String tangles
36. Golf ball stand
37. Arden and Plumb
39. Conceited people
41. Subsides
43. Hurried
44. Hearing organ
46. Seven-day periods
50. Judge's office
55. Length times width
56. "No Way ____"
57. Onion's kin
58. Legal claim
59. Like Willie Winkie
60. Whirling current
61. Mail

DOWN
1. Rough file
2. Racetrack shape
3. Grape plant
4. Allan Poe and Rice Burroughs
5. Mineral spring
6. Corn core
7. Cry of dismay
8. ____ down (moderated)
9. Gone by
10. Stood for election
11. Chicago loop trains
17. Unlit
19. Elephant's tooth
22. Skeleton material
23. Smoke and fog mixtures
25. Picnic pests
26. Encounter
27. Inspires with wonder
28. Gusted
29. Fluid rock
30. Ready for business
31. Cease
35. Goulash
38. Appear
40. High standards
42. Expensive fur
45. Critic Rex ____
47. Toledo's lake
48. Sharp
49. Beach granules
50. Female bovine
51. Color
52. Had a meal
53. Comedian Buttons
54. Firmament

PUZZLE 162

ACROSS
1. Bulk
5. Have a friendly talk
9. Not processed
12. Unfold
13. ____-and-seek
14. Lode load
15. Splitsville
16. Catch up with and pass
18. Excessive
20. "The ____ Badge of Courage"
21. Use the resources of
22. Flaunts
25. Bart Simpson's dad
28. ____ richer or poorer
29. Tyke
30. Agog
31. Baby apron
32. Scorched
33. ____ Lizzie
34. ____ excellence
35. Throw about
36. Magazine worker
38. Actor's signal
39. Posed for a portrait
40. Wondrous occurrence
44. Scattered trash
47. Secure, as a ship
48. King topper
49. Square root of 81
50. Therefore
51. ____ diem
52. Excursion
53. Poor grades

DOWN
1. Extra
2. Zenith
3. Dispatched
4. Grunted
5. Munch
6. Bees' home
7. Humorist George ____
8. Great fright
9. Auto
10. Floating menagerie
11. Minuscule
17. Social gathering
19. Pitcher handle
22. Comedian Goldthwait
23. Sped
24. Ragout
25. Loathe
26. Roman poet
27. Ambassador
28. Evergreen tree
31. Saloon
32. Cooked with water vapor
34. Robust
35. Big ____, California
37. Tit for ____
38. Fall drink
40. Bill of fare
41. Apple center
42. Theater box
43. Son of Aphrodite
44. Swimmer's division
45. "____ Station Zebra" (Hudson film)
46. Brazilian resort

PUZZLE 163

ACROSS

1. Having a high temperature
4. Crowd
7. Banana treat
12. Heart of Dixie
14. "Remember the ____!"
15. Discounts
16. Diamond weight unit
17. Shed feathers
18. Mouth part
20. Pester
21. Opposite of NNW
22. Buttes
24. Russian plane
26. Took a chair
27. Plunder
29. Flies alone
32. Welcome
33. Singer Frankie ____
35. "Night and ____"
36. Dripping
37. Comes closer
39. Comedian Knotts
42. Confederate soldier, for short
44. Distress
45. Accurate
46. The Red ____ (Snoopy's foe)
48. Give forth
50. Conscious
51. Stumbled
52. Leased again
53. Yes vote
54. Bitter vetch

DOWN

1. Injures
2. Butter substitutes
3. ____ of contents
4. Doorway rug
5. Egg dish
6. Foundation
7. Baglike structure
8. Blueprint
9. Wyoming city
10. Picture mentally
11. Toddler
13. Hitter's stick
19. Golfer's standard
22. ____-Dixon line
23. Heroic stories
25. Acquire
26. Fa follower
28. Move by leverage
29. Witnessed
30. Intimidate
31. Sidelong
34. Modern
35. Cheerless
38. Main artery
39. Heavy curtain
40. External
41. Requires
43. Tiresome person
45. Bellboy's reward
46. Saloon
47. Butterfly snare
49. Gaming cube

PUZZLE 164

ACROSS
1. Poke
4. Atlas inclusion
7. Turn into leather
10. Dismounted
12. Bucket
13. Mined matter
14. Create
15. Orchestrated
17. Military guard
19. Foot digit
20. Fish snare
21. Good, ____, best
24. Epidermis
26. Possesses
27. Baled commodity
28. "____ the night before . . ."
29. Fall behind
30. This place
31. Author Fleming
32. Point a gun
33. Bull's weapon
34. Hire
36. Earth's star
37. Ginger ____
38. Wall or Easy
41. Lemon ____ pie
44. Snow slider
46. In the past
47. Students' residence
48. Former Russian ruler
49. Self-image
50. Consumed food
51. Actress Irving

DOWN
1. Jelly's cousin
2. Word of woe
3. Two-wheeled vehicle
4. She had a little lamb
5. Ventilate
6. Dishes
7. In unison
8. "Roses ____ red . . ."
9. Actor Beatty
11. Jimmy Connors's sport
12. Piece
16. That's ____ funny!
18. Decimal unit
21. Sack
22. Receive a wage
23. Sandwich bread
24. Graceful water bird
25. Australian hopper
26. Bad actor
28. Bind
29. Fib
30. Truthful
32. List of things to do
33. "Ben ____"
35. Actress MacGraw
36. Flower stalk
38. Certain
39. "Born Free" lioness
40. Sports group
41. ____ West (life jacket)
42. Breakfast fare
43. Received
45. Remove moisture from

135

PUZZLE 165

ACROSS
1. Chewing or bubble
4. Sculpture
8. Ran away
12. "Long, long ___ . . ."
13. "___ the Woods"
14. Volcanic flow
15. Faster way
17. Leave out
18. Gripped
19. ___ of contents
20. Compassion
23. Octet number
25. Fragrance
27. Rower's tool
28. Likely
31. Matures
33. Hockey's net-minder
35. Curve shape
36. Catch
38. Make broader
39. Planted
41. Thrown missile
42. Sticky
45. Merchandise
47. Singer Fitzgerald
48. Chemise
52. Strip of wood
53. Mine products
54. Ventilate
55. Kind
56. Office item
57. Golfer's peg

DOWN
1. Helium, e.g.
2. Cry of disgust
3. Cow's call
4. Sting
5. Dad's brother
6. Artist's place
7. Young child
8. Parade vehicle
9. Baby sheep
10. Malevolent
11. Social engagement
16. Verse
19. Hurl
20. Peel
21. Eye part
22. Exceeds
24. Joke
26. Irritate
28. Actor Alan ___
29. Wharf
30. Camping shelter
32. Carpenter's cutter
34. Assistants
37. Look out!
39. Glide on ice
40. British noblewomen
42. Exam, e.g.
43. Friendly nation
44. Applaud
46. Gamble
48. New England cape
49. Stable morsel
50. Untruth
51. Sooner than, in poems

PUZZLE 166

ACROSS

1. Pep
4. Excavates
8. Signal
12. Lemon beverage
13. Actor West
14. Minnesota's neighbor
15. Relay partner
17. Swig
18. Red tag events
19. Every
21. To a ____
23. Classification
27. Absolutely
30. Scientist's workshop
32. Ride a bike
33. Expert pilots
35. Basin
37. Stray
38. Sparks
40. Pat lightly
42. Corrosive liquid
43. More inquisitive
45. Seize
47. Brad
49. Salts away
53. Dateless
56. Prognosticate
58. Pit
59. Den
60. Grant's foe
61. "It Was a Very Good ____"
62. Singer Arnold
63. Morose

DOWN

1. Industrial cauldrons
2. Thought
3. Repast
4. Gentlewoman
5. Asian peak
6. Fence opening
7. Smudge
8. Boxer
9. Mrs. Herbert Hoover
10. Drill
11. Hiatus
16. Had a session
20. Bottle top
22. Take nourishment
24. Revered one
25. Fleet
26. Exultation
27. Gape
28. Mountain refrain
29. Gets the point
31. Actor Abbott
34. Creme de menthe and brandy
36. Outlaw
39. Diver's milieu
41. Pastry shop
44. Winchester, for one
46. "You ____ Your Life"
48. Onus
50. Snakelike fish
51. Entreaty
52. Musher's conveyance
53. Demure
54. Shoe tip
55. Chicken ____ king
57. Purge

PUZZLE 167

ACROSS

1. Family companions
5. Fruit skin
9. ____ Speedwagon
12. Leave out
13. American lake
14. Cup handle
15. Dock
16. ____ the men from the boys
18. Band of color
20. Hog chow
21. Gentle
23. Records
26. Regretted
30. Defrost
31. Slip up
32. Detach
34. Southern st.
35. Over again
37. Confusion
39. Flower part
41. Jeans maker Strauss
42. Work on copy
44. More scarlet
48. City dwelling
51. City slicker
52. Past one's prime
53. Opposite of aweather
54. Frog or year
55. "____ the season . . ."
56. Kernel
57. Shade trees

DOWN

1. ____ the question
2. Radiate
3. Stadium level
4. Hit
5. Begrudged
6. Anger
7. Small bites
8. Handed out a hand
9. Show up again
10. Nibble
11. Mine yield
17. Wander
19. On ____ and needles
22. "____ or Angel"
24. Singer Fitzgerald
25. Linger
26. Harvest
27. Marine bird
28. Makes believe
29. Abandoned
33. Rant
36. Walk in water
38. Puzzling question
40. Green beans
43. Prefix with vision or graph
45. Sword fight
46. Soft cheese
47. Corded fabrics
48. Small child
49. Actor Wallach
50. Born

ACROSS

1. Yosemite ____
4. "Green Eggs and ____"
7. Elsie's offspring
11. Scheme
13. Female sheep
14. Medicinal plant
15. Came into view
17. Window ache?
18. Self-image
19. "Good Night" girl
21. Current
23. Night twinkler
24. Swimming place
25. Stick around
26. Possesses
29. Contribute a share
30. Kindergartner
31. Remove from print
32. Term of agreement
33. Valid
34. Governor Grasso
35. "____ the Clock"
36. Spot
37. Change for the better
39. Mine find
40. Opera solo
41. Left
46. More or ____
47. Actress Thompson
48. Story
49. Quick
50. Building addition
51. Wrestling coup

DOWN

1. Mineral spring
2. Swiss peak
3. Glove compartment item
4. Brave man
5. Amazement
6. Ponder
7. Antic
8. Actor Arkin
9. The ____ Ranger
10. Rate
12. "The Panic in ____ Park" (Pacino film)
16. Allow to ripen
20. Sunbeam
21. Dial sound
22. Smallest Greek letter
23. Portly
24. Compensate
25. Sit astride
26. Lend a hand
27. Booster
28. Ocean
31. Abandon
33. Toe count
35. "Beauty and the ____"
36. Distinctive time
37. Neighborhood
38. Fail to hit
39. October birthstone
40. TV nonhuman character
42. Snakelike fish
43. Spigot
44. Inventor Whitney
45. Room for relaxation

PUZZLE 169

• DARK AND DANGEROUS •

ACROSS

1. Explosion sound
5. Flee
8. Purchase
11. Charles Lamb's pen name
12. Nuptial phrase
13. Goods
15. Fidgety
16. Fond du ____
17. Disappeared
20. Stadium cheer
21. Nasty dreams
24. Shaped like an egg
26. In addition
28. Effortlessly
29. Treasure
30. Set aside
32. Actress MacGraw
33. Genuflected
35. Work toward a goal
37. Cerise
38. Crackpot
39. Spring month, in Paris
40. Dismiss
41. "____ on a Grecian Urn"
42. Mosses' kin
44. Expression
46. Actress Chase
47. Bet
51. Chatters
55. Motivate
58. English lavatory
59. Murmur sweetly
60. Lass
61. Charged atom
62. Ampersand
65. Unrefined
67. Arranges
71. Mr. Bolger
72. Pressure
73. TV host Funt
74. Cuban capital
77. Eva, to Zsa Zsa
78. Entreaty
79. Disreputable
82. Amateur
85. Blurts out
87. Major-leaguer
88. Vicky Lawrence role
89. Wading bird
90. By means of
91. What the nose detects
92. High fashion
93. Longing
94. Fringe benefit

DOWN

1. "99 bottles of ____ on the wall"
2. "M*A*S*H" actor
3. Billy club
4. Cheery
5. Leslie Caron film
6. Proverb
7. Coffee flavored chocolate
8. Scourge
9. "Topaz" author
10. Okay!
13. Circumspect
14. Coast
17. Bona fide
18. Morally wrong
19. Stupor
21. Apprentice
22. King
23. Missed by a ____
25. Blazed the trail
27. Kayak blade
29. Pumpkin eater
31. Writer Hunter
33. Granny, for one
34. Uncovered
35. Spinnaker
36. Naval officer: abbr.
39. Caesar's 1,051
43. Crone
45. Atlas feature
48. Potentially poisonous plant

49. Waiter's aid
50. Finless fish
52. Foreigner
53. Windfall
54. Male children
55. ____ cube
56. Ancient mariner
57. Most indignant
62. Swift horses
63. Dark blue
64. Actress Cannon
66. Skater Babilonia
67. Doze off
68. Fashion magazine
69. "Family Ties" role
70. Instruct
74. Sunday song
75. Chilly
76. Come to terms
79. Gambling game
80. Maned male
81. Trumpet
83. Cupid
84. "The ____ of Zorro"
86. Permit
88. Swab

PUZZLE 170

ACROSS
1. Roll
4. Cowgirl Evans
8. Farm worker
12. Before, to poets
13. Thought
14. Huron's neighbor
15. "Long, long ____ . . ."
16. Fly high
17. Shoestring
18. Copenhagen's locale
20. Fossil resin
21. "Butterflies ____ Free"
22. Hearty bread
23. Warning signal
26. Slimming down
30. Turf
31. Baby's napkin
32. Shad delicacy
33. Pushed and shoved
36. Cupid's target
38. Chew and swallow
39. Underwater boat
40. Strangely
43. Muttered
47. Bucket
48. One of the three bears
49. Climbing vine
50. "____ of Green Gables"
51. Portent
52. Professional charge
53. Lascivious look
54. Take a chance
55. Finish

DOWN
1. Rosary element
2. Encourage
3. Gas for signs
4. Deprive of weapons
5. Worship
6. Drip
7. Corn unit
8. Biker's headgear
9. Graceful steed
10. Pleasant
11. Venison animal
19. Damage
20. Sailor's yes
22. Chest bone
23. Fire residue
24. "Iron Horse" Gehrig
25. Commercials
26. Performed
27. Self-made pension
28. Neither's partner
29. Obtain
31. Wager
34. Bank clerk
35. Deposit, as eggs
36. Compassionate
37. Recede
39. Terrific
40. Milky gem
41. Person from Copenhagen
42. Have supper
43. Doll's cry
44. Not on your ____!
45. Level
46. ____-in-the-wool
48. Pea container

142

ACROSS

1. Vat
4. ____ of the line
7. "The Purple ____ of Cairo"
11. Miner's yield
12. Stolen goods
14. Bad
15. Carver
17. Camera part
18. Smidgen
19. Morning juice
21. Poker pot
22. Zoot ____
23. Have supper
24. Dotted
28. Lyric poem
29. Noah's birds
30. Grow up
31. Wood-eating insects
33. King of the beasts
34. Peck film, with "The"
35. Skillets
36. Vegetable plot
39. Lend a ____
40. Slender woodwind
41. Young ones
45. Dull
46. Old times
47. Have bills
48. Witnessed
49. Join together
50. Favorite

DOWN

1. Water tester
2. Coffee pot
3. Tenderfoot
4. Make happy
5. ____ Scotia
6. Female deer
7. Narrate
8. Kiln
9. Vocalize
10. Additional
13. Companies
16. Footballer Kyle ____
20. Tears
21. Helper
22. Lucky number
23. Spot
24. Strength
25. Downpour beginning
26. Easily bruised items
27. Lair
29. Piggy-bank filler
32. Recent
33. Property
35. Faded
36. Scads
37. Up to it
38. Man about town
39. Employ
42. In what way
43. Female sheep
44. Fisherman's tool

PUZZLE 171

PUZZLE 172

ACROSS
1. Slams
6. Poet's before
9. Grass
12. Wide-eyed
13. Spar
14. Edgar Allan ___
15. Proportion
16. Christen
18. ___ and con
20. Branded
21. Quandary
25. Requires
26. Chilled
27. Tolerate
29. Change the color of
30. Inoculations
31. "The Old Man and the ___"
34. Drudge
35. Ajar
36. Postpone
39. ___ City (Oz locale)
41. Sum
43. Weaken
44. Domain
46. Vertical passage
50. Omelet ingredient
51. Historic time
52. Keen
53. Negative votes
54. Actor Buttons
55. Kind of egret or owl

DOWN
1. Saloon
2. ___ carte
3. Butterfly catcher
4. Complained
5. Hurricane
6. Wane
7. Wander
8. Distends
9. Volleyball shot
10. Seeped
11. Property documents
17. Oak, e.g.
19. Nebraska city
21. Accomplished
22. Frozen
23. Gypsy Rose ___
24. Superior to
28. Things
30. Willowy
31. Health resort
32. Long fish
33. Also
34. Belt
35. Little ___ Annie
36. Occupied
37. Pedro's pal
38. Tolls
40. Relaxes
42. Ripped
45. Demented
47. In the past
48. "A ___ Good Men"
49. Have a go at

PUZZLE 173

ACROSS
1. Groove
4. Mast
8. Grub
12. "Long, Long ____"
13. Moolah
14. Be wildly enthusiastic
15. Detective story
17. Unrefined minerals
18. Singleton
19. Brogue
21. Solve
24. Defraud
25. Jitney
26. Soda
27. Edible root
30. "____ You Lonesome Tonight?"
31. Designated for residential or business use
32. Kimono sash
33. Crimson or scarlet
34. Perpetually
35. Ruminate
36. Raised dogs
37. Ventured
38. The modern kind of plumbing
41. Garment edge
42. Rancid
43. Secluded
48. The ____ Ranger
49. Salamander
50. Savings plan: abbr.
51. Supplemented
52. Grand celebration
53. Incensed

DOWN
1. Green
2. Grunting sound
3. Likewise
4. Pepe Le Pew
5. Window section
6. Muhammad ____
7. Merchant
8. Earthenware pot
9. Jack rabbit
10. Baker's need
11. "Go ____, young man"
16. Pier
20. Garbed
21. Scorch
22. Seldom seen
23. Did exceedingly well on
24. Removed the skeleton from
26. Coating
27. "____ Cheatin' Heart"
28. Equal to the task
29. Not spicy
31. Naught
35. ____ Cass
36. Wearied
37. Actress Burke
38. ____ of Man
39. Cranny
40. Kind of buggy
41. Canine sound
44. Caribbean or Coral
45. Actor Allen of "Home Improvement"
46. Anagram for ear
47. Papa

145

PUZZLE 174

ACROSS
1. Portend
5. Veteran mariner
8. Kind of rug
12. Banister
13. Fish beginning
14. Boob-____
15. Purple flower
18. Fast flier
19. Keats poem
20. Phooey's kin
21. 16th president's nickname
22. Go by air
23. Cook in water
26. Exist
27. Master
30. Avocado
34. Summer drink
35. Creek
36. Frenzy
37. Gangster's gun
38. Wield
40. Radiate
42. Murmur
43. Comedian Paulsen
46. Twin bills
49. "____ the Night"
50. Anagram for arm
51. On a cruise
52. "____ Me in St. Louis"
53. Hesitation sounds
54. Wild hog

DOWN
1. Bikini parts
2. Blockheads
3. Gossip
4. Yalie
5. Profession
6. Tiptop
7. Accelerate sharply
8. Anecdote
9. Honolulu bowl
10. Help in crime
11. Understand
16. Cygnet's pop
17. Ne'er-do-well
21. Muhammad ____
22. To and ____
23. Bleat
24. Stale
25. ____-de-France
26. ____ glance
27. Pod dweller
28. Provoke
29. Raw mineral
31. Dog's warning
32. Help
33. Use a crowbar
37. R2D2, e.g.
38. Sonnets
39. Mauna ____
40. Departed
41. Minstrel's instrument
42. Scorch
43. Acapulco coin
44. Section
45. Tyrant
46. Faint
47. Sooner than
48. Small amount

ACROSS

1. Cuts off
5. Do sums
8. Thick slice
12. Declare openly
13. Court
14. Mine deposit
15. Only
16. Time gone by
17. Seep
18. Deer's horn
20. It attracts iron
22. Guided
23. Health resort
24. Children's illness
28. Go in
32. Escort's offering
33. Pat gently
35. Misfortune
36. Downward measure
39. Extremely hard gem
42. Musical sense
44. Without water
45. Morally pure
48. Dreary
52. Multitude
53. Hive insect
55. Enameled metalware
56. Toward shelter
57. Make a mistake
58. ____ the Terrible
59. Peruse
60. ____ Vegas
61. Penny

DOWN

1. Dalai ____
2. Baker's need
3. Harbor
4. Expands
5. Bestowed on
6. Man's best friend
7. Condemns to death
8. Motto
9. Crazy as a ____
10. Wood-shaping tool
11. Borscht vegetable
19. Conger or moray
21. Imitate
24. The ____ Hatter
25. Sooner than, poetically
26. Electrical unit
27. Sorrowful
29. Duo number
30. Very long time
31. Ruby-colored
34. Possible buyers at an auction
37. Tried out
38. Fedora or fez
40. Jackie O's second
41. Connecticut seaport
43. Insurgent
45. Scorch
46. Opening
47. On the briny
49. Shift
50. Actor Arkin
51. Period before Easter
54. Historic age

PUZZLE 176

ACROSS
1. "Duke of ___"
5. Sign up
9. Workroom, for short
12. Authentic
13. Wrong
14. Before
15. Snares
16. Noon, for instance
18. Vast chasm
20. Fairy tale's White
21. Violinist Bull
23. Peace prize
27. Whirlwinds
32. Long tale
33. Manipulate
34. Cliched
36. Destiny
37. Modeling compound
39. Broadcast
41. "M*A*S*H" setting
43. Actress Meriwether
44. Permits
47. Bows
51. Parachutist's garb
55. Hop, ___, and jump
56. In the past
57. Aware of
58. Facility
59. The ___ (Roger Daltrey's band)
60. Annoyance
61. Colored

DOWN
1. Alcohol lamp
2. Omani, for one
3. Color of Dorothy's slippers
4. Lecture
5. Traffic tie-up
6. Has IOUs
7. OPEC country
8. Clothing material
9. Garland
10. Provide with weapons
11. Spelling or quilting
17. Noah's ark pairings
19. Bed board
22. Revise copy
24. Indonesian island
25. Conceited people
26. Overdue
27. Fold
28. Norway's capital
29. Admiral or guard
30. Unrefined mineral
31. Hawk
35. Nolte film, with "The"
38. Howl
40. Proficient
42. Greek fabulist
45. Melody
46. Holds a session
48. Approve
49. Sagacious
50. Raced
51. Mandible
52. Cry of disgust
53. Barnyard sound
54. Youngster

148

PUZZLE 177

ACROSS
1. Tory's foe
5. Charlie Brown's cry
9. Norman Vincent ___
10. Ocean eagles
12. Irritate
13. ___ Miss Muffet
15. Consume
16. Caribbean, e.g.
18. Tariff
19. High card
20. Butchers' offerings
22. Opposite of WSW
23. Concise
25. Detailed accounts
27. Reply: abbr.
29. Moral lapse
30. Places of learning
34. Comedienne Burnett
38. Air safety agency: abbr.
39. Taunt
41. Actor Vigoda
42. Showery month: abbr.
43. Sgt., e.g.
44. "Ode ___ Nightingale"
45. Captured
48. Trash
51. Singer Della ___
52. Certain exams
53. Prophet
54. Wise one

DOWN
1. More damp
2. Top or bowler
3. Sick
4. Waterfowl
5. Tells
6. Mr. Onassis
7. Explosive letters
8. Irish or English dog
9. Serenity
11. Perspective
12. Tidy
14. Former spouses
17. Cock an ___ (listen)
20. Forget-___ (flower)
21. Nutmeg or ginger
24. ___ Paulo
26. Stop ___ dime
28. Lean
30. Read quickly
31. Prank
32. Author Bret and kin
33. Baglike structure
35. Baby's toy
36. Woodwind instruments
37. Shake-spearean king
40. Flies alone
46. Casual shirt
47. Language suffix
49. Lyricist Gershwin
50. Child's game

PUZZLE 178

ACROSS
1. Misplaced
5. October birthstone
9. Accede
12. Prima donna's song
13. Advocate
14. Lincoln nickname
15. Spotted dog
17. Tease
18. Spills
19. Stopover
21. Pilgrim settler John ____
23. Plateau
26. Onyx, e.g.
29. Dine
30. Cook's attire
31. Roused
33. Most knowing
34. Sum up
35. Vermilion
36. Buck's mate
37. Spoiled child
38. Financial investigation
40. Shoals
42. Audacity
46. Scary greeting
48. Differed
50. Possess
51. Colored eye part
52. Warbled
53. Actress MacGraw
54. East Indian wood
55. Whirlpool

DOWN
1. Young fellows
2. Unwritten
3. Storage place
4. Florida city
5. Not at home
6. Hedge shrub
7. Once more
8. Telescope part
9. Traded
10. Japanese sash
11. Arachnid's creation
16. Gone to bed
20. Mischief makers
22. Pop
24. Middling
25. Poker stake
26. Outfit
27. Pitcher
28. Pasta
30. Helping
32. Actress Jackson
33. United
35. Slavic land
38. Burning
39. Laconic
41. Revise
43. Peruse
44. Sell
45. Tense
46. Scarf
47. Nocturnal bird
49. Inquire

150

ACROSS

1. Served for a point
5. Angelic instrument
9. Tearful moan
12. Type of ranch
13. Butter substitute
14. Spanish gold
15. Bongo or snare
16. Shade of purple
18. Center
20. Taunt
21. Hoisting device
23. Medicinal amount
25. Allow
26. Stain
28. GOP's foes: abbr.
32. Commotions
34. Picnic intruder
35. Break suddenly
36. Nick Charles's wife
37. Horn sound
39. Contend
40. ____ Rabbit (Harris character)
42. Modify
44. Blue or finback
47. Spoken
48. Clergyman's title
51. Jotted message
54. Before, poetically
55. Grew older
56. Forthright
57. "Neither snow, ____ rain . . ."
58. Drowses
59. Army surgeon Walter ____

DOWN

1. Do sums
2. Mongrel
3. Teacher
4. Fiendish creature
5. Cavity
6. Pie ____ mode
7. Gun in neutral
8. Bards
9. Bicarbonate of ____
10. Mine finds
11. Drill
17. Requires
19. Confederate soldier, for short
21. Family group
22. Change over
23. Generous one
24. German statesman Von Bismarck
27. Tardy
29. Letter container
30. Principal
31. Hurried
33. Expensive fur
38. Roofing liquid
41. Showed again, as a film
43. Estate house
44. Small bird
45. Savior
46. State positively
47. Gamblers' concerns
49. Psyche part
50. Actor Beatty
52. Golfer's ball support
53. Final word

PUZZLE 179

151

PUZZLE 180

ACROSS
1. Cook in oil
4. Noble horse
8. Curved doorway
12. Caviar
13. Zoo enclosure
14. Sandwich shop
15. Watched
17. Smell
18. Has-____ (former star)
19. Residence
20. Fiddler or hermit
23. Robbed
25. Lubricated
27. USS "Nautilus," e.g.
28. "____ on a Grecian Urn"
31. Dug
33. Underground passage
35. X, to Caesar
36. Vote in favor
38. Tiny things
39. Sleeper's illusion
41. Zip ____
42. Forgeries
45. Actor Hackman
47. Motels of yore
48. Changing
52. Stench
53. Transmission part
54. Buck's mate
55. Sheep mothers
56. Norway's capital
57. Fruit cooler

DOWN
1. To and ____
2. Actor/director Reiner
3. Word of consent
4. Land measure
5. Talks deliriously
6. Representatives
7. Fourposter, e.g.
8. Sun-dried brick
9. Make over
10. Lump of soil
11. Engage
16. Subsided
19. Snapshot book
20. Expense
21. Ready to pick
22. Astronaut Shepard
24. Away from home
26. Precious ones
28. Aware of
29. Exploit
30. What ____ is new?
32. Pigment
34. More congenial
37. Birds of prey
39. Classroom items
40. Ore's yield
42. Conflagration
43. Once again
44. Leg joint
46. Roman emperor
48. In the past
49. Mountain overlooking Troy
50. Assenting head motion
51. Command to a horse

PUZZLE 181

ACROSS
1. Recorded
6. Short snooze
9. Male sheep
12. ____ and beyond
13. High card
14. Pub drink
15. Adjust, as a clock
16. Little devil
17. Unite
18. ____ clef
20. Air opening
21. Split ____ soup
23. Fish eggs
24. Military assistants
25. Hankering
27. Accept, as a plan
29. Move unsteadily
31. Goober
35. Shrubbery fence
37. Learning
38. Fray
41. Exist
43. ____ of a kind
44. Smell
45. Ignited
47. Arrow's partner
48. Buddy
49. Cotton bundles
52. Metallic rock
53. Fuss
54. Turn inside out
55. Actor Knight
56. Decade number
57. State again

DOWN
1. ____ and feather
2. Lincoln's nickname
3. ____ due
4. Always
5. Hinder
6. Used a hammer on
7. Highest point
8. Vigor
9. Graded
10. Straighten
11. Encounters
19. Piece of lumber
20. Essential
21. Place
22. Before, to a poet
24. Mimic
26. Anesthetic
28. "Carmen," e.g.
30. Electric ____
32. Soup pasta
33. Vase
34. Golf peg
36. Ten-____ hat
38. R2D2, e.g.
39. Cherish
40. Promised
42. Fiery spark
45. Grow dim
46. Roof overhang
48. Square of butter
50. Important age
51. Pig's place

PUZZLE 182

ACROSS

1. Donations to the poor
5. Beast of burden
8. First-rate
12. Plunder
13. Snooze
14. Actor Donahue
15. Genuine
17. In this place
18. Musical drama
19. Gone by
21. Shout
23. Negligent
27. Science workshop, for short
29. Back talk
31. Fracas
32. A Gershwin
33. ___ and feather
35. Grassland
36. Point of view
39. Pilfer
41. Supply with weapons
42. Vacation spot
44. Diplomacy
46. Roadster
47. "Falcon ___"
50. Living room item
53. Up ___ (unsettled)
56. Malicious
57. Dove's call
58. Medieval serf
59. Decline
60. Fleecy one
61. For fear that

DOWN

1. White: pref.
2. Section of Chicago
3. Wealthy person's nickname
4. Gape
5. Black cuckoo
6. Sorrowful
7. Asparagus unit
8. In
9. Unrefined metal
10. And not
11. "___ of the Needle"
16. Autumn
20. Precious stone
22. Ignited
24. Uncomfortable
25. Psychic
26. Line of stitches
27. Fibber
28. British composer
30. Median
34. Perish
37. Site
38. Important period
40. German composer
43. Instant
45. Fisherman's basket
48. Transgressions
49. Waste allowance
50. Use needle and thread
51. Fish eggs
52. Fiver
54. At this time
55. Sock end

PUZZLE 183

ACROSS
1. Pop
5. Crop
8. Extract
12. Unwritten
13. Paddle
14. Song
15. Devote
17. Readies a printing press
18. Mischievous
19. Twilight
21. Wing it
24. Litter littlest
25. Opposing forces
26. Starved
30. Pie ____ mode
31. Side
32. Hebrew priest
33. Redirected
35. Bargain event
36. Property title
37. Gem weight
38. Critic's output
41. Swine
42. Periods
43. Ecstatically
48. Barn's neighbor
49. Give permission to
50. Hawaiian feast
51. "Harold ____"
52. Speak falsely
53. Caterwaul

DOWN
1. Cape ____, Massachusetts
2. Natural resource
3. Young boy
4. Excuses
5. Freight
6. Kind of meal
7. "____ Innocent" (novel)
8. Sketches
9. Large vases
10. Be fond of
11. "____ of the Red Hot Lovers"
16. Hailed vehicle
20. Military group
21. From a distance
22. Disburse in small amounts
23. Page
24. Competed
26. So long!
27. Listen to
28. Songstress Fitzgerald
29. Food plan
31. Gratis
34. Light bulb inventor
35. Prudently
37. Portable bed
38. Take ten
39. Canal between Albany and Buffalo
40. Jerry ____
41. Abhor
44. Hawaiian wreath
45. The Dynamic ____ (Batman and Robin)
46. Attorney's field
47. Actor Brynner

155

PUZZLE 184

ACROSS
1. Grain husk
5. Chocolate source
10. Church recess
14. Routine
15. Admits
16. Multitude
17. Low female voice
18. Metal fasteners
19. Phone prefix
20. Haw's opposite
21. Malicious
22. Models
24. Of warships
26. To a distance
27. Females
29. Quality of being tart
33. Actor West et al.
34. Formal procedures
35. Ingested
36. Freight units
37. Shabby
38. Orchard sight
39. TV set component
40. Wept
41. Restrained
42. Hirelings
44. Luxuriously
45. Food containers
46. City on the Volga
47. Disconnect
50. Amphibian
51. Old horse
54. Travel
55. Blunder
57. Very dry
58. Rim
59. Utilize again
60. Largest continent
61. Prophet
62. Quickness
63. Russian ruler

DOWN
1. Boast
2. Function
3. Escorts
4. Recent: pref.
5. Tent material
6. Benefit
7. Spiral
8. Shoemaker's tool
9. Became rigid
10. In a backward direction
11. Appeal
12. Retail
13. Meadow moms
21. Arden and Plumb
23. Pops
25. Objectives
26. Performed
27. Fasten, in a way
28. Worship
29. Helpers
30. Quality of being realistic
31. Band or wool
32. Run-down
34. Pours
37. Those who send mail for free
38. Course of action
40. So long, in Sicily
41. Basketball's Larry ____
43. Game official
44. Bellowed
46. Simpleton
47. Colorado Indians
48. Knot
49. Massive
50. Faithful
52. Solo for Sills
53. Equipment
56. Corded fabric
57. Calendar abbr.

PUZZLE 185   Domino Theory

Arrange the four dominoes on top into the pattern below so that a correct multiplication problem is formed. The number of dots on each half-domino is considered a one-digit number; for example, a half with six dots represents the number 6.

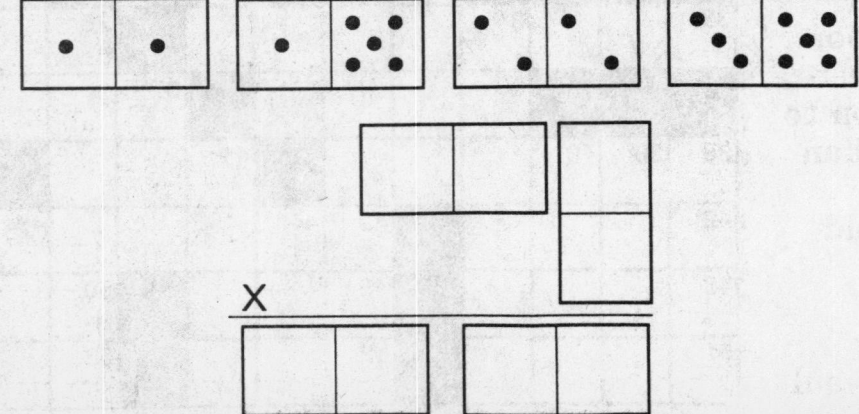

156

PUZZLE 186

ACROSS
1. Increment
5. Abrade
9. Ovum
12. Dad
13. Jai ____
14. Top
15. Actress Moran
16. Design consultants
18. Leave hastily
20. Arrange
21. Heavy hammer
23. Crown
26. Column
30. Notable
31. Gilbert and Sullivan princess
32. Insect colonies
34. Business abbr.
35. Smoke-cured salmon
37. Overlooks
39. Hits
41. Phony
42. Garish
44. "All by ____"
48. Legitimate target
51. Vicinity
52. Be in debt to
53. Actor Hale
54. Small monkey
55. ____ annum
56. Fissure
57. Fervor

DOWN
1. Raced
2. Weight without cargo
3. Legendary
4. Central American republic
5. Russian mystic
6. Model Carol ____
7. States
8. Guide
9. Thrilled
10. Heater
11. Docs
17. Rainbow
19. Squash
22. Even
24. Vehement speech
25. Moves in a curve
26. Fasteners
27. Rock's Billy ____
28. Pendant
29. Army unit
33. Overwhelm with humor
36. Cupid
38. Artificial
40. Cane product
43. Actor Robertson
45. Pennsylvania port
46. "I ____ Song Go Out of My Heart"
47. Bomb
48. Dandy
49. Wonder
50. "____ of Iron"

PUZZLE 187

ACROSS
1. Unite
4. Desert robe
7. Babble
12. Female rabbit
13. Bother
14. Varnish ingredient
15. Understanding
17. Havens
18. Equal
19. Last
21. ____ firma
23. Pop
24. Split
27. Lead to the ____
29. To be, in Nice
30. "____ Nikita"
33. Jester
35. Invention
36. Behaves unnaturally
38. Standard
39. Offense
40. Feudal lord
44. Occupations
47. At any time
48. Bay window
50. Exhausting
52. Lariat
53. Equip
54. Murmur softly
55. Bundled
56. Still
57. Make lace

DOWN
1. Capable
2. Recipient
3. Bar
4. Politician Richards
5. Restrain
6. Plan
7. Stately
8. "____ Window"
9. Claims
10. Hitch
11. Naval off.
16. Mistakes
20. Pub game
22. "____ I Know"
25. Fury
26. For each
28. Unenthusiastic
29. More lenient
30. Back talk
31. Apple-cider girl
32. Wing feather
34. Elongated fish
37. Traffic sign
39. Caesar, for one
41. Throw out
42. Italian seaport
43. Rye disease
45. Nerve network
46. Dry
48. Heavenly body
49. Narrow inlet
51. Qty.

PUZZLE 188

ACROSS

1. Warning sound
5. Service branch: abbr.
9. Taj ____
14. Speed
15. Biblical captain
16. Smell
17. Official records
18. Indian princess
19. Marry again
20. Battle mount
22. Troops on horseback
24. Whip
26. Singer Torme
27. Of the mind
31. Cain's brother
33. Nabokov heroine
36. Audibly
37. Concerning
38. Skating feat
39. Marching formation
42. Gamble
43. Broadway musical
44. Ham it up
45. Simple sugar: suff.
46. Ebb
47. Nonprofessional
48. Paddle
49. Banister
51. Forays
55. Combat strikes
60. Encourages
61. Fictional plantation
63. Fossil fuel
64. Belief
65. Atop
66. Poet Millay
67. Oglers
68. Refute
69. Judge

DOWN

1. Bric-a-____
2. Apiece
3. Kett of comics
4. Juicy fruit
5. Imaginary
6. Flies high
7. Chess piece
8. Stylish
9. Wonder
10. Of a region
11. Wolf call
12. Part of USA: abbr.
13. "____ Luck"
21. Forest opening
23. Arabian chief
25. More accessible
27. Very large in scale
28. New York island
29. Rope loop
30. Ivory source
32. ____ Rabbit
33. Saying
34. Actress Burke
35. Ludden or Funt
37. Mideast nation
38. Salvation ____
40. Chicago airport
41. Distributed
46. Middle body parts
47. Prayer
48. Playful swimmer
50. Brother of Moses
51. Glut
52. Pay heed to
53. Mathematician Descartes
54. Kind of poker
56. Served a winner
57. Zip or Morse
58. "Citizen ____"
59. Bridge coup
62. Imitate

PUZZLE 189   COMPLETE-A-WORD

Fill in the dashes with the 4-letter answers to the clues to complete 7-letter words.

1. Wagon   __ H __ __ I O __
2. Flunk   __ R __ G __ __ E
3. Precinct   A __ K W __ __ __
4. Undiluted   __ A S T __ __ __
5. Peal   W A __ N __ __ __

6. Otherwise   __ C __ I P __ __
7. Watch face   A __ M __ R __ __
8. Hollow grass   F __ __ __ __ O M
9. Associate   W __ __ __ A B __
10. Quick look   __ R __ C __ __ T

ACROSS

1. Component
5. Flared up
10. Discharge
14. Indian garb
15. Make amends
16. Forfeit
17. Arab chieftain
18. Connections
19. Fishing or telephone
20. Look like
22. Jets
24. Soar
25. Bent
26. Thespians
29. Wind instruments
33. Barrels
34. Establish again
35. Gypsy boy
36. Finished
37. Accomplishments
38. Provided
39. Cincinnati to New York direction: abbr.
40. Shriek
41. "Full _____ Jacket"
42. Sequoias
44. Most rational
45. Fusses
46. Personal history
47. Put on
50. "_____ People" (Midler film)
54. Therefore
55. Piano-key material
57. Corrupt
58. Slender
59. Saltpeter
60. Evening: It.
61. Smaller amount
62. _____ up (fills the tank)
63. Playing card

DOWN

1. Computer nut
2. Title
3. Purple flower
4. Tedious
5. Jewish religious officials
6. Reef
7. Departed
8. At the _____ of one's rope
9. Abhors
10. Texas city
11. "Blue _____" (Marcels song)
12. _____ of Man
13. Football props
21. Red planet
23. "_____ Tango in Paris"
25. Moisten with drippings
26. Poisonous snake
27. Hag
28. Adjusted
29. "The Bad News _____"
30. Make a speech
31. Bright stars
32. Small food fish
34. Peruses
37. Deluging
38. Least rough
40. Foreshadow
41. Alan Alda series
43. Carts
44. Greek woodland deities
46. Thick liquid
47. Vend
48. "A _____ Grows in Brooklyn"
49. Turkish rulers
50. Deteriorates
51. Always
52. King's title
53. Destroy
56. By way of

SCRAMBLED ART

Match up each pair of letters in column A with pairs from columns B and C to form ten words about art. Each letter pair will be used once. Do not switch the order of a pair of letters.

A	B	C	
CA	UD	CO	_____
ST	SI	IC	_____
SK	AD	IL	_____
MO	NV	EL	_____
CR	ES	CH	_____
SH	AY	AS	_____
PA	ET	OW	_____
FR	NC	GN	_____
PE	SA	IO	_____
DE	ST	ON	_____

PUZZLE 192

ACROSS

1. Victor's opponent
6. Baby carriage
10. Realize
14. On top of
15. Bait
16. Baseball side
17. Prototype
18. Invites
19. Chills
20. Green vegetable
21. For every
23. Most secure
25. Long-eared mammal
26. Restaurant
27. Meal
30. Epic story
31. Signal for help
34. ____ Oyl
35. Afterward
36. Friend
37. Fade
38. Enclosures
39. Elevate
40. Noshed
41. Caster of a ballot
42. Challenged
43. Actor Beatty
44. Eye part
45. Intermission
46. Religious image
47. Guitarlike instrument
48. Actor James ____
51. Enjoy a meal
52. Land parcel
55. Margarine
56. Jeannie portrayer
58. Onion's kin
60. Trim
61. Interval
62. Heavy volumes
63. Shackelford and Danson
64. Revolve
65. Commencement

DOWN

1. Lantern
2. Woodwind instrument
3. Fizzy drink
4. Adam's mate
5. Let go
6. Site
7. Hurry
8. Clumsy boat
9. Notes
10. Carving tool
11. Pleasant
12. "The Defiant ____"
13. "____ Side Story"
22. Pianist Tatum
24. At a remove
25. Hold
26. Supply food for
27. Martin's partner
28. Gladden
29. Hankered
30. Wise persons
31. Tower
32. Desert refuges
33. Sleighs
35. Caesar's language
38. Tiaras
39. Competition
41. Moral weakness
42. Discovers
45. Sprint
46. Shackles
47. Cloth
48. Dunce
49. Away from the wind
50. Scan
51. Actress Moore
52. Peruvian capital
53. Wrapped up
54. Trial
57. Plunge
59. Fiery

PUZZLE 193   BITS AND PIECES

Can you identify these jazz musicians from the Bits and Pieces shown in the boxes? The first names are always on the top and the last names on the bottom.

1.
```
O U I
S T R
```

2.
```
L E N
I L L
```

3.
```
A V E
R U B
```

4.
```
U N T
A S I
```

5.
```
E N N
D M A
```

6.
```
Y N T
R S A
```

ACROSS

1. Octopus's cousin
6. Ragout
10. Not closed completely
14. An ____ of prevention
15. Mitchell's plantation
16. Nevada city
17. Sees socially
18. Flat
20. Fuss
21. Wise man
23. Buenos ____
24. Musical Fountain
25. Type of excuse
27. Hope
30. Store clerk
34. Bias
35. Gamble
36. Spanish cheer
37. Story
38. Exists
39. Blackthorn
40. First lady
41. Apply a wall covering
42. Get up
43. Kept aside
45. Pep
46. Char
47. Coagulate
48. Dalmatian's markings
51. Buckeye State
52. Spade's kin
55. Astronomer's tool
58. Poet Ezra ____
60. Words of understanding
61. Summer drinks
62. Proved human
63. Space
64. Flexed
65. Postpone

DOWN

1. Soft drink
2. College courtyard
3. "Do ____ others . . ."
4. Drink cube
5. Baked Alaska, e.g.
6. Phase
7. Ticker-____ parade
8. Notable period
9. Child's card game
10. Troops
11. Taunt
12. Actress Bancroft
13. Decays
19. Circus employee
22. Had dinner
24. Conifer
25. Tavern staple
26. Ginger drinks
27. Daisylike flower
28. Bondservant
29. Becomes ashen
30. Delivered
31. Grinding tooth
32. "Take Me ____"
33. Poor
35. Windshield blade
38. Molten rock
39. Opposite of dele
41. Iron
42. Acted like a busybody
44. Hold in high regard
45. Actor Wallach
47. Thorax
48. Mix
49. Mexican coin
50. Margarine
51. Not closed
52. Fling
53. Draft classification
54. Whirlpool
56. Hired vehicle
57. "____ to the West Wind"
59. Mined matter

MYSTERY WORD

There is a six-letter Mystery Word hidden in the diagram. Can you find it in four minutes or less?

My first letter occurs in the diagram only once.

My second is the only consonant which is in a corner.

My third stands at the beginning in one line and at the end of another one.

My fourth is a vowel that occurs twice in a column.

My fifth occurs more than four times in the diagram.

My last letter occurs twice in one line.

Mystery Word: ___ ___ ___ ___ ___ ___

A	W	Y	N	L	R
O	N	E	D	D	C
L	H	M	H	O	S
I	R	E	N	F	Y
C	N	S	E	A	M
E	W	O	N	L	I

PUZZLE 196

ACROSS
1. Black and Red
5. Trims
10. Fools
14. Rhythmic swing
15. Type of squash
16. Liveliness
17. Vicinity
18. Alan Ladd film
19. Bark cloth
20. Occident
21. High-strung
22. Stratagem
23. Chill
25. Ms. Caldwell
27. Groups of fish
31. Sky streakers
35. Corrupt
36. Divided
38. Sitter's creation
39. Hi-fi parts
40. Linda or Dale
41. Fill
42. Ribbed fabric
43. Former Ohio State coach
44. Actress Braga
45. Made a groove in
47. Quito's country
49. Indian mulberry
50. With-it
51. Cupid's weapon
54. Incensed
58. Load
62. Wild disorder
63. Observes
64. Encourage
65. Useless
66. Occurrence
67. Awful
68. "____ Gynt"
69. Marsh plants
70. Hurried

DOWN
1. Picnic salad
2. Ireland
3. Tavern drinks
4. Train stops
5. Soft shade
6. Throb
7. Certain horse
8. Marine fliers
9. Hay fever sufferers
10. Couch
11. Having wings
12. Hungarian city
13. Cinch
24. Folding bed
26. Baseball great
27. Celebrities
28. Dromedary
29. Large mammal, for short
30. Kept
31. Stately home
32. Swedish island
33. Proportion
34. Javelin
37. Score for Faldo
40. Cosmetic pencil
41. Lather
43. ____ glance
44. "Runaround ____"
46. Scrap
48. Bureaus
51. Trickle
52. Right-hand man
53. Purpose
55. Meander
56. Fit to ____
57. Minister to
59. Stumble
60. Monster
61. Garden pest

PUZZLE 197   SYLLABILITY

Choose one syllable from each column to form eight words of different lengths: one 8-syllable word, one 7-syllable word, etc., down to a 1-syllable word. Use each syllable once. Do not change the order of the syllables; if the syllable appears in column 3, it will be the third syllable of a word.

1	2	3	4	5	6	7	8
Mor	si	de	o	la	na	ty	al
Re	di	tank	ac	tiv	i	tion	
Su	al	ble	nom	i	tion		
Den	tar	pit	u	gram			
Ra	ca	o	er				
Par	ter	lel					
In	per						
Fea							

162

PUZZLE 198

ACROSS

1. Lower California
5. Craze
8. Pie ___ mode
11. Raise one's spirits
13. Gossip-column bit
15. Cowboy-boot adjunct
16. Certain train
17. Reign
18. Biblical weed
19. Albanian coin
20. Log makers
23. Soho rental
25. Downhill racers
26. Shade of 38 Across
28. Money to stay out of the slammer
30. Scent
31. Hospital's brine
33. Foreman's forte
36. Stingy one
38. Crimson
39. Blackboard material
41. Mel of baseball
42. Just ___ (for emergencies)
45. Chilled
46. Tilt, as a ship
47. Wagon-wheel parts
49. Valuable item
52. Makes leather
53. Former heavyweight champion
57. Arrest
60. Zone
61. ___ avis
62. Roman magistrate
64. "___ Be Cruel"
65. Pay-telephone feature
66. Mature
67. Compass pt.
68. Flock member
69. Require

DOWN

1. Tinkler
2. Medicinal plant
3. Nose nipper of song
4. ___ loss for words
5. Company
6. ". . . three men in ___"
7. Take out, in printing
8. Quickly
9. Skulks
10. God of war
12. Raines and Fitzgerald
14. Arthur's magician
15. Men's party
21. Shoshones
22. Mr. Verne
24. Italian coins, once
26. Italian lake
27. Blue-pencil
28. Cry from 68 Across
29. Assists
32. Rainbows
33. Sandpiper
34. Suit to ___
35. Fourposters
37. Angered
40. Lahr role
43. Saltpeters
44. Ancient Italian city
48. Check writer
49. Baseball's Hank ___
50. Vista
51. Card game
53. Gemstone
54. Boy
55. Head of a ship
56. Fill completely
58. Windward's opposite
59. Curve
63. Racket

DISCO

PUZZLE 199

Each numbered circle has a 5-letter answer (Clue A) and a 4-letter answer (Clue B) reading in a clockwise direction. Enter the first letter of each 5-letter answer in the circle in the preceding disc. For example, in disc 1: L + EAST = LEAST.

A.

1. Minimal amount
2. Swell
3. Veneer
4. Brushed
5. Exaggerated self-esteem
6. Wander
7. Songbird
8. Wire

B.

1. Bridge position
2. Impel
3. Defeat
4. Mourned
5. Carousel, e.g.
6. Split
7. Creep slowly
8. Competent

163

PUZZLE 200

ACROSS
1. Soapstone
5. Counterfeit
9. Alone
13. Cushions
17. Director Kazan
18. Arizona Indian
19. Eager
20. African lily
21. Lantern
22. Pub potables
23. February missive
25. Bookworm's hangout
27. Nitwit
29. Fall flower
30. Cooler contents
31. Fibber
32. Infant
34. Vote in
37. Mixed-breed canine
38. Rattles
39. Crusty dessert
42. Marathon, for one
43. Malone of "Cheers" et al.
44. Make coffee
45. Liquid measure
46. Timber tree
47. Petticoat
48. Seize
49. Spanish dance
50. Halted
52. Salty solution
53. German steel city
54. Astronaut Sally
55. Dawdle
56. Rave
58. Fundamental
61. Lacks
63. Cardigan, for one
67. Foe
68. Socks
69. Talk
70. Cutting tool
71. Sound
72. Outlaws
73. Actor Donahue
74. Simmer
75. Plus
76. Speaker's platform
77. Let fall
78. Out of practice
79. Cherished
80. Deckhands
81. Press for payment
82. Virile gents
85. Coves
86. Circus performer
90. Galoshes
93. Chowder
95. Zhivago's lover
96. Belgrade native
97. Encourage
98. Otherwise
99. Give forth
100. Playing card
101. Become weary
102. Gels
103. Copenhagen native

DOWN
1. Tattle
2. Jai ____
3. Bough
4. Whim
5. Percentage
6. Sacred
7. Gibbon
8. Outsiders
9. Relish
10. Ellipse
11. "____ Abner"
12. Pindar poem
13. Singer Cline
14. Dismounted
15. Finished
16. Prophet
24. Collars
26. Behave
28. Cereal grain
31. Chunk
32. Kind of quartet
33. Biblical zoo
34. Generations
35. Final
36. Reverberate
37. Certain fern
38. Actress Stapleton
39. Brooches
40. "Bus Stop" playwright
41. Short jacket
43. Luge
44. Stuffed shirts
45. Macaroni
47. Zesty
48. Report-card mark
49. Belief
51. Top-drawer
52. Consecrate
57. Apart
58. Greek letter
59. Shortly
60. Transmit
62. Eternities
64. New Mexico town
65. Freeway ramp
66. Depend
69. Brag
72. Ewe said it!
73. Locks
74. Botched
76. TV rooms
77. Arid
78. Floor mat
79. Churchill Downs event
80. Social class
81. Fools
82. Emcee
83. At all times
84. Simple
85. On-tap drink
86. Fair
87. Tibetan monk
88. Ireland
89. Charge
91. Stetson, for one
92. Kimono sash
94. Bravo!

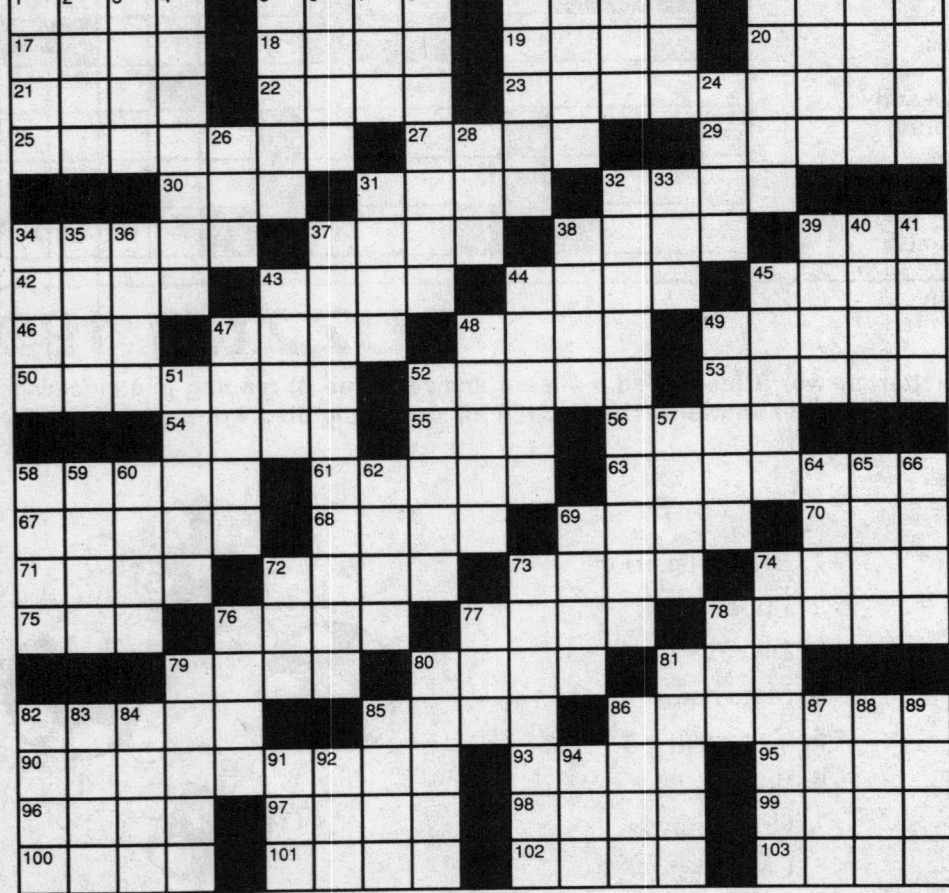

ACROSS

1. Spry
6. Chicken ____ king
9. Jeweler's weight
10. Pronoun
13. Hunting dog
16. Ripped
17. Ven.'s locale
18. Canine comment
21. Writing tool
22. Johnny ____
25. Actor Lugosi
26. ____ Grande
27. "____ at Sea"
29. Petty quarrel
33. Bagel's partner
34. Small Mexican dog
38. Be in the red
39. Baseball's Mel ____
40. Assist
41. Liable (to)
42. Males
43. Gladden
46. Feeling
49. Free (of)
50. Corn unit
51. Della or Pee Wee
54. Actress Garbo
56. Mr. Baba
58. Carney or Buchwald
60. Pastry item
61. Singer King Cole
64. Observe
65. Large, square-muzzled dog
69. Sorbet
70. Chervil or sage
72. Of birds
73. Landers or Miller
74. Grew older
78. Terminate
79. Actress Lupino
82. Beatty or Buntline
83. Cherish
84. Aggravate
86. Burly mountain dogs
92. Everything
93. Riveter of WWII
94. Spinning toy
95. Realtor

DOWN

1. High card
2. Needlefish
3. Tax org.
4. Track circuit
5. Greek letter
6. Play division
7. Noose
8. Farm unit
10. Location
11. Cure
12. Fitzgerald and Raines
14. Entertainer Olin
15. Penpoint
18. Woody's son
19. Civil disturbance
20. Small hunting dog
22. Stadium cheer
23. Ratite bird
24. Comedienne Lillie
27. Performed
28. ____ Na Na
30. Small, long-haired dog
31. Reverential fear
32. Sawbuck
34. Puma, e.g.
35. Hasten
36. ____ and downs
37. Dined
44. Fib
45. Fruit drink
47. Born, in Paris
48. Took a chair
52. Wilt
53. Go astray
54. Type of rummy
55. Ruff's mate
56. Fire residue
57. Director Spike ____
59. Steeped beverage
60. "Peter ____"
62. Skin problem
63. Minister to
66. Rd.
67. Can
68. Pop
71. Light wood
75. Type of post
76. Devilish
77. Lair
79. A Gershwin
80. Soil
81. Actor Ray
85. Psychic power, for short
87. ____ la la
88. Fen
89. Compass pt.
90. Movie dog's first name
91. Seine

• MAN'S BEST FRIEND •

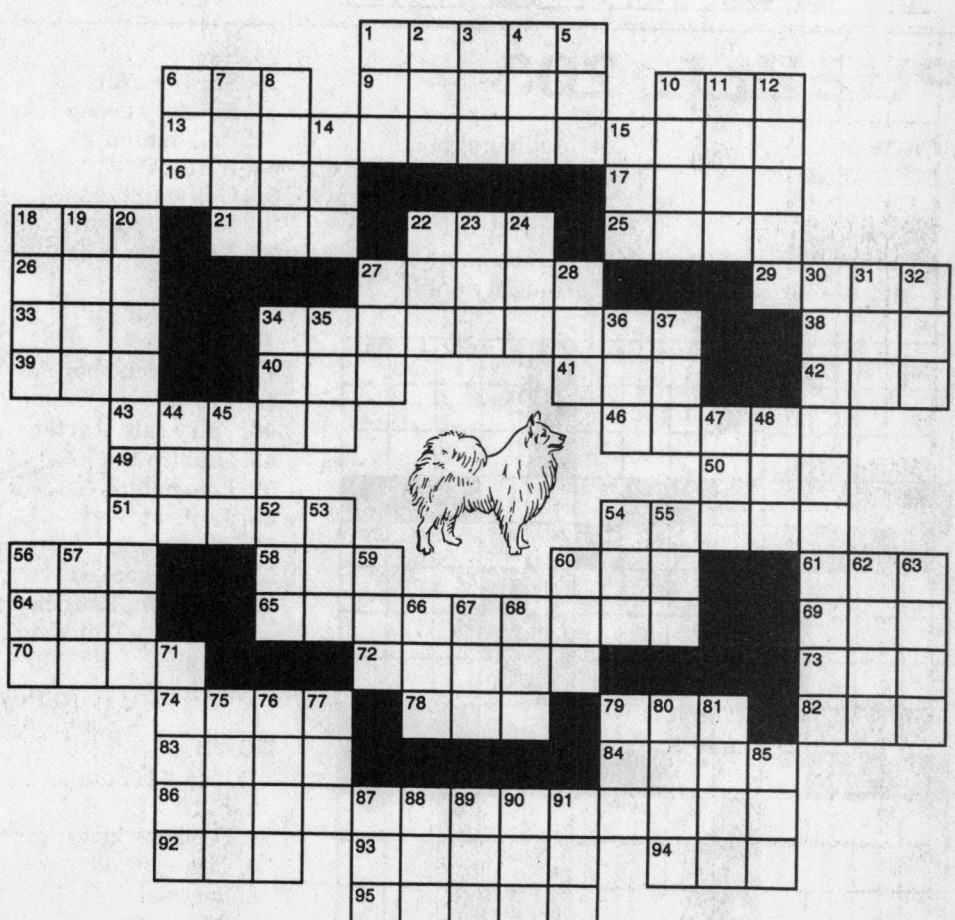

PUZZLE 202

ACROSS
1. Use needle and thread
4. In the center of
8. Lobster appendage
12. Grow older
13. Lucid
14. Capital of Italy
15. Miami team
17. High cards
18. Prompted
19. Elbow grease
21. Aromas
23. Worry
24. Apple or pear
25. Ocean swell
26. Spigot
29. Gorilla
30. Insertion mark
31. Regret
32. Guided
33. Goals
34. Abrupt
35. Carney and James
36. Semiconscious states
37. Respond
40. Twist
41. South American weapon
42. Wickedness
46. At any time
47. Window part
48. Bind
49. Cheryl or Alan
50. Television units
51. Mineral springs

DOWN
1. Unhappy
2. Self-image
3. Received gladly
4. Fire remnants
5. Young unmarried woman
6. Tavern
7. Merits
8. Vessel
9. Crazy
10. Part of USA
11. Sunset direction
16. Unmixed
20. Twelve-inch lengths
21. Iridescent gem
22. Simpleton
23. Cultivates
25. Restaurant employee
26. Wind instruments
27. Atmosphere
28. Caresses
30. Caution
34. Maize
35. Medal
36. Telephones
37. Eve's son
38. Variable star
39. Snow vehicle
40. Droop
43. Compete
44. Small drink
45. Neptune's kingdom

PUZZLE 203

ACROSS
1. ____ mode
4. Curvy letter
7. Sweet red wine
11. Prong
13. Mouse's kin
14. Medicinal plant
15. Plea
17. Split
18. Briny drop
19. Lamb's mother
21. Haughty one
24. Smell
28. Study hard
31. Military group
33. Fall behind
34. Imitate
35. Golf ball holder
36. Frozen water
37. Cooking utensil
38. Singe
39. Go-getter
40. Solo
42. Sandwich shop
44. Pro vote
46. Fairy tale starter
49. Dial up
52. Learned
56. Table spread
57. First mate
58. Barely cooked
59. "Reuben, Reuben, I've ____ Thinking"
60. Profit
61. So long

DOWN
1. Had a tamale
2. Fluff
3. Feed the kitty
4. Time period
5. Perched
6. Eyesore?
7. Kitchen gadget
8. Bullring cheer
9. Ely or Moody
10. Senator Kennedy
12. Wipe out
16. Sea eagle
20. Road
22. Vow
23. Moola
25. Hodgepodge
26. Heavy club
27. Golden ____ (retiree)
28. Mama's partner
29. October's birthstone
30. Gambler's paradise
32. Only
38. Bee follower
39. Greasy spoon
41. Clothing material
43. Fate
45. Prayer ending
47. Grouch
48. Spooky
49. Corn holder
50. Pub drink
51. Pinky or Brenda
53. "____ Maria"
54. Harden
55. Actress Ruby ____

ACROSS
1. Afternoon party
4. Health resort
7. Buddy
11. ___ de Triomphe
12. Cod or Hatteras
14. Gardener's tube
15. Meant
17. Help a criminal
18. Single
19. Pass over
21. Small pie
23. Doe's mate
24. Home plate, e.g.
25. Hung in the air
29. Scamp
30. Make a basket
32. ___ of Reason
33. Dinner follower
35. Symbol
36. Paid athletes
37. Pistols
38. Movie theater feature
41. Needlefish
42. Pressing need
43. Fundamentals
48. Related
49. Rational
50. Hole-making tool
51. Female sheep
52. Of course!
53. Lad

DOWN
1. Scottish cap
2. Historic period
3. Perform
4. Smell
5. Peel
6. Primate
7. Alter
8. Vagabond
9. Customer
10. Allot
13. Publishing position
16. Ripped
20. Donated
21. Domesticated
22. Venomous snakes
23. Attempts
24. Offer
26. Downpour
27. Omelet ingredients
28. Lair
30. Very dry
31. Hags
34. Pays out
35. Certain
37. Party pastimes
38. Location
39. Black bird
40. Character
41. Unit of heredity
44. Set down
45. Arrest
46. Pair
47. Nickname for Stallone

PUZZLE 204

ACROSS
1. Fiery particle
6. Puff up
11. Passionate
13. Polite word
14. Drowsy one
15. Spring festival
16. Roof edges
18. Reporter Donaldson
19. Wall painting
23. Masterpiece
24. Levin and Gershwin
25. Golf mound
26. TV commercials
29. Rowdiness
32. Nonsense
34. Overhead railroads
35. Immediately
37. Annoy
38. In addition
39. Made over
40. Existed
43. Wear away
45. Shout from the audience
47. Ethically neutral
52. Gazed fixedly
53. Make larger
54. Having prongs
55. Plains Indian tent

DOWN
1. ___ Francisco
2. In favor of
3. Find a sum
4. Stoplight shade
5. Take a prayerful position
6. Chargeman
7. Bandleader Brown
8. Dinner for Dobbin
9. On the ocean
10. Semester
12. ___ la la
13. Looked searchingly
17. Wine tank
19. Speechless actor
20. Asian river
21. Beams
22. Fireplace residue
26. Enthusiastic
27. Sandwich shop
28. Snow toy
30. Went in
31. Secured, as a boat
33. Fury
36. Court
39. Send payment
40. Actress Mae ___
41. Opposed to: pref.
42. Scrutinize
44. Mom's partner
46. Mine output
48. Spanish cheer
49. Knock lightly
50. Devoured
51. Golfer Trevino

PUZZLE 205

167

PUZZLE 206

ACROSS
1. Love excessively
5. Actress Lupino
8. Pulverize
12. Cain's brother
13. Comedian Skelton
14. "The Diary of ___ Frank"
15. Marinate
16. Creator
18. Skirt edge
19. Daisylike flower
20. Wane
21. Fabricated
23. Umbrella part
25. Emergency tires
27. Small hound
31. "Kiss Me, ___"
32. Dirt
33. Perfect examples
36. Martinis' fruit
38. Used a chair
39. Tempo
40. "___ on a Grecian Urn"
43. Bouquet jugs
45. Cloth scrap
48. Five-sided shape
50. ___ 500 (car race)
51. Alan ___ of "M*A*S*H"
52. Building addition
53. Wander
54. Roster
55. ___ sauce (condiment)
56. Upper limbs

DOWN
1. Sprint
2. Reed instrument
3. Co-player
4. Large deer
5. Eye parts
6. Ding
7. Action-word modifier
8. Grown boy
9. Poker opener
10. Snooty one
11. Dill or thyme
17. Buffalo's lake
19. Citrus cooler
22. Regions
24. Fundamental
25. Snow runner
26. Tablet of paper
28. State's chief executive
29. Fib
30. Overhead trains
34. Volcano's output
35. Theater platforms
36. Forthrightly
37. ___ Vegas
40. October's gem
41. Sandwich shop
42. Terminates
44. Alone
46. Eve's husband
47. Exercise buildings
49. Tit for ___
50. Savings plan

PUZZLE 207

ACROSS
1. Dog's foot
4. Shoo!
8. Hat edge
12. Self
13. Old King ___
14. Ore vein
15. Ink writer
16. Opera song
17. Wise birds
18. Mend socks
20. Shuts
22. Stage setting
24. Those people
25. Caution
26. Ship's jail
27. Caribbean, e.g.
30. Zone
31. Battle of Bull ___
32. Baseball's Musial
33. Newsman Koppel
34. Crooner Crosby
35. Gone by
36. Pale red
37. Chablis and Cabernet
38. Powerful
41. Beach material
42. By word of mouth
43. Chair, e.g.
45. Do sums
48. "A Chorus ___"
49. Powerful desire
50. ___ de Janeiro
51. Specks
52. Look searchingly
53. Lion's lair

DOWN
1. Vigor
2. Years of life
3. Speculated
4. Frighten
5. Maize
6. Boxer Muhammad ___
7. Instructing
8. Blossom
9. Uses oars
10. Out of work
11. Untidy situation
19. "___ Karenina"
21. Table support
22. Whack
23. Be concerned
24. Elephant's nose
26. Raises, as a child
27. Norm
28. Relaxation
29. Social insects
32. Whirl
34. Storage box
36. Gdansk natives
37. Common liquid
38. Peddled
39. Group of three
40. Speak violently
41. Wise
44. Before, poetically
46. Do-or-___
47. Actor Ameche

PUZZLE 208

ACROSS
1. Bashful
4. Opponent
7. Ultimate
11. House of Lords member
13. Tell a falsehood
14. Knowledgeable about
15. Against
16. Without exclusion
17. Chew
18. Cunning one
20. Swerve
21. Short letter
23. Lamb's mother
25. Operated
26. Ease up
28. Punch
31. Be under the weather
32. ____ diem
33. Baba of legend
34. Work at
35. Omens
37. Pop
38. Frigid
39. Concurring word
41. Shoelace mishap
44. Wonderment
45. Matched set
46. Carton
48. Light gas
52. Singer Fitzgerald
53. Pussycat's shipmate
54. Take apart
55. Rind
56. Diminutive
57. Morning condensation

DOWN
1. Evian or Vichy
2. Barnyard mother
3. As of this time
4. Linen plant
5. Petroleum
6. Slithery creature
7. Theater section
8. Actress Meara
9. Marquee name
10. Pull behind
12. Separation
19. "____ the ramparts . . ."
20. Torment
21. Hammer's target
22. Just
23. Mournful poem
24. Alert
25. Knock smartly
27. Saga
28. Stone for carving
29. Comedy's King
30. Bridge declaration
35. Make a lap
36. Adage
40. Bill of fare
41. Cabbagelike plant
42. African river
43. Spoken
44. Wheel holder
45. Energy
46. ____ out (leave)
47. Part of IOU
49. Culmination
50. Poetic form
51. At this time

PUZZLE 209

ACROSS
1. Level
5. Eden dweller
9. Flower-to-be
12. Croquet or Ping-Pong
13. Byway
14. Id's companion
15. Tyrolean peaks
16. Vision
18. Silt deposit
20. Crumple
21. Author Wilde
24. Divans
28. Sunbeam
30. Demeanor
32. Laze
33. Scratch a living, with out
34. Implant
36. Purpose
37. Severe
39. Bone dry
40. Author Serling
41. Start
43. Cargoes
45. Hunting dog, for short
47. More congenial
50. Asks advice
55. Novelist Vidal
56. President Lincoln
57. Brad
58. Turkey's neighbor
59. Offer
60. "____ Came to Cordura"
61. Experiment

DOWN
1. Mild epithet
2. Glen
3. Bosses
4. Cozy dwellings
5. Malt beverage
6. "Night and ____"
7. Again
8. Plateaus
9. Beseech
10. Word of disgust
11. Speck
17. One on a pedestal
19. Summit
22. Goals
23. Revolutionary
25. "____ and seven . . ."
26. Moreover
27. Luge or toboggan
28. Remodel
29. Similar
31. Sleuth Wolfe
35. Jan's singing partner
38. Congers
42. Ridicule
44. Number from one to nine
46. Dull
48. Historic times
49. Lease
50. Bandleader Calloway
51. Japanese sash
52. Actor Beatty
53. Ascot
54. Foxy

169

PUZZLE 210

ACROSS
1. Louisville sluggers
5. Mr. Carney
8. Wagon
12. Toward the sheltered side
13. Billiards stick
14. Vicinity
15. Found's counterpart
16. Single
17. Chain segment
18. A or B
20. Dish
21. Cavalry soldier
24. Rhythm
27. Sunbeam
28. Cove
31. In excess
32. Derby
33. Skin opening
34. Skillet
35. Prohibit
36. Scent
37. Develop
39. Theater platform
43. Leaped
47. Therefore
48. Bustle
50. Edison's middle name
51. Legal claim
52. Give silent consent
53. Bamboo shoot
54. Ore vein
55. Poor grade
56. Luxury

DOWN
1. Zany comedienne
2. Medicinal plant
3. Try out
4. Pioneer
5. Tidbit for a squirrel
6. Trot
7. Wooden peg
8. Shout
9. Formal solo
10. Apartment fee
11. Swipe
19. Pitcher handle
20. Interfere
22. Derrick
23. Have a pizza
24. Wash the floor
25. Argentine Peron
26. Sawbuck
28. Sound of disapproval
29. Branch
30. Type of vote
32. Radio operator
33. Get ready
35. Spelling contest
36. Past
38. _____ Island
39. Peddle
40. The Kingston _____
41. Like some cheese
42. Departed
44. Entreaty
45. Nights before
46. Miami's county
48. Ampersand
49. Bambi's mom

PUZZLE 211

ACROSS
1. Deed
4. Bloke
8. Restrain
12. Batman and Robin, e.g.
13. Great affection
14. Dorothy's dog
15. Banner
17. False god
18. Kind of berry
19. By oneself
20. Of the mouth
22. One of fifty
24. Burdened
26. Female sib
27. London's Big _____
30. One who makes amends
32. Secondhand
34. Distant
35. Turf
37. Map book
38. Precipitous
40. Charity
41. Capital of France
44. Texas shrine
46. OPEC country
47. Pennant bearer
50. Metallic sound
51. Artist Magritte
52. Neither's partner
53. Wise man
54. War god
55. Energy source

DOWN
1. TV spots
2. Sever
3. Bullfighter
4. Dressed
5. Residences
6. Turns aside
7. According to
8. Fence steps
9. Fuss
10. English school
11. Spy
16. Barkin of "The Big Easy"
19. On the ocean
20. King of Norway
21. Pro _____
23. Ventilate
25. Birds' dwellings
27. Party decorations
28. Shem's son
29. Headland
31. Fish eggs
33. Postage item
36. Casino worker
38. Scorch
39. Aircraft
41. Domino spots
42. Opera solo
43. Pealed
45. Grows older
47. Monk's title
48. Baseballer Gehrig
49. Sea eagle

ACROSS

1. High, musically
4. British field marshal
8. Stage items
13. Lett
17. Biblical book: abbr.
18. Statesman Eban
19. Examine accounts
20. Beehive State
21. Louisiana
24. Muse of history
25. Isolated
26. Whip part
27. Furnace laborers
29. All possible
30. English ponds
31. Heraldic band
32. Mouthward
33. Twelve o'clock
34. Woman's undergarment
37. Dry, as wine
38. Long, long time
39. Brave man
40. Greek resistance force: abbr.
44. Safe port
46. Part of Missouri's nickname
48. First number
49. Assembled
51. Hi-fis
52. Dill
53. Choir section
54. Paint additive
55. City on the Adige
56. Equipment
57. Sunshine State products
58. Magical word
59. Tenth month: abbr.
60. Part of Wisconsin's nickname
61. Fob off
62. Approval
64. March date
65. Actress Celeste
66. 100 square meters
69. Author Joyce Carol
71. Parrot membrane
72. Thrive
73. Potpourris
76. Brilliance
78. Fake jewelry
79. Own
82. Capricorn
83. River mouth
84. S. American monkey
85. Minnesota
89. ____ Stanley Gardner
90. Thesaurus author
91. Part of QED
92. British beverage
93. Whitetail
94. Building level
95. Tatters
96. N.Y. summer zone: abbr.

DOWN

1. Pismire
2. French port
3. Georgia
4. Singer Belafonte
5. Aid in wrongdoing
6. Niger tribesman
7. Sailing ship
8. Old hat
9. Babe and family
10. Harem room
11. Holes
12. Let it stand
13. Ohio state tree
14. Tamarisks
15. Dens
16. "____ Were the Days"
22. Funny guy
23. Work for
28. Frequently, poetically
29. Dawn goddess
30. Earth's satellite
33. Requirement
34. Flycatchers
35. Knight's protection
36. Negative votes
38. Prayers
39. "Little Jack ____"
41. Texas
42. Concerning
43. Fight
45. Hebrew lyre
46. Smarts
47. Bronze Age structure
49. Nearsighted cartoon character
50. Smart ____
51. Tints
52. Son of Zeus
54. Profession
55. Light haircut
57. News item, for short
58. Native of Warsaw
61. Garrison
63. Part of Indiana's nickname
65. Scottish shrub
67. Spun
68. Lamb's mother
70. Peer Gynt's mother
71. Applaud
72. Sir Alexander Tilloch ____
73. Chose
74. Longest river in France
75. Bagging fiber
76. Tent caterpillar
77. Louse
78. Annoying insects
80. Ships: abbr.
81. Fired a gun
83. Tow behind
86. Self
87. Historical age
88. Take nourishment

PUZZLE 212

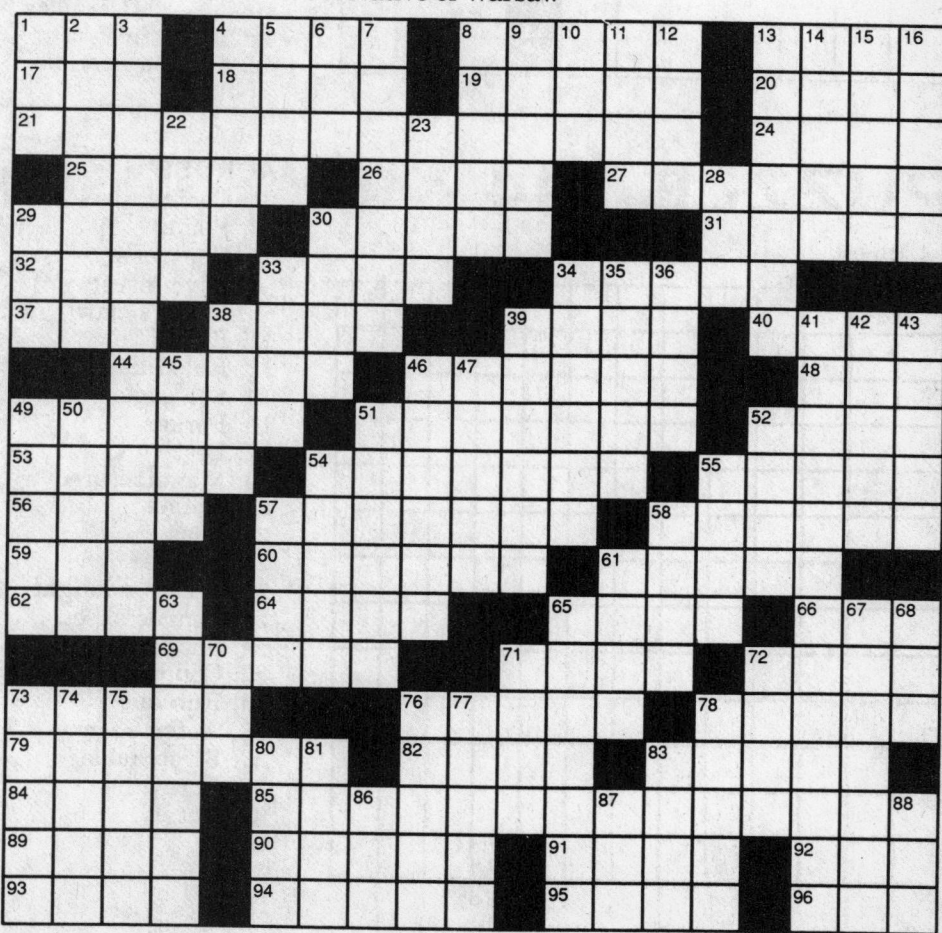

PUZZLE 213

Diagramless crosswords are solved by using the clues and their numbers to fill in the answer words and the arrangement of black squares. Insert the number of each clue with the first letter of its answer, across and down. Fill in a black square at the end of each word. Every black square must have a corresponding black square on the opposite side of the diagram to form a symmetrical pattern.

ACROSS
1. ____ code
4. Not many
7. Peach seed
10. Low number
11. Become older
12. Lyric poem
13. ____ King Cole
14. Corn center
15. Knight's title
16. Pass a law
18. American buffalo
20. Vend
21. Articles of faith
22. Residence
24. American fir
27. Take a break
31. In error
32. Condition
33. Male child
34. Soak up
36. Army commander: abbr.
37. Annoy
38. Historical period
39. Zodiac lion
40. "____ Miserables"
41. Twice five
42. Make a mistake

DOWN
1. Town districts
2. Silly
3. Flower part
4. Truth
5. Conceit
6. Like duck's feet
7. Sheriff's group
8. Foolish person
9. Sea birds
17. Group of students
19. Inactive
21. Male turkey
23. Long-eared hound
24. Actor Rathbone
25. Love, Italian-style
26. Chain segments
28. National bird
29. Guide a car
30. Male singer
32. Stretch across
35. Crude metal

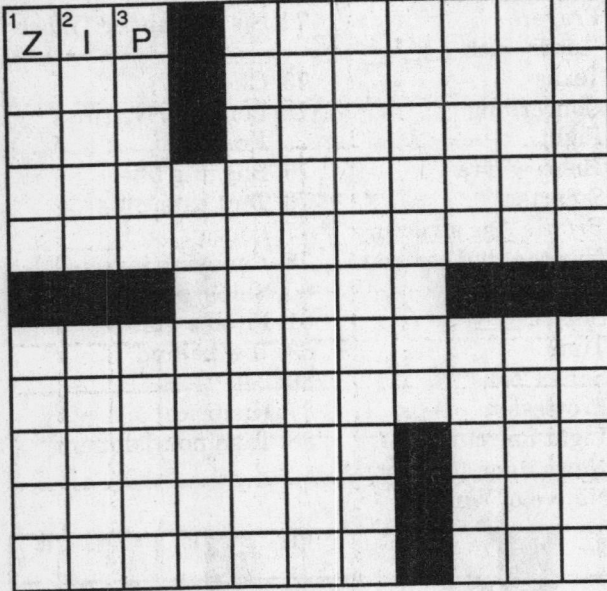

PUZZLE 214

ACROSS
1. Cooling device
4. Flank
5. Chevrons
8. Hive insect
9. Eagle's claw
11. Ebbed
13. Ruled mark
14. Sea eagle
15. Porker
17. Festive
20. Manufactured
22. Deface
24. Cease
25. Bridge
26. Create a knight
28. Female sheep
29. Sudden breeze
32. Copper-zinc alloy
34. Rub out
36. Actor Carney
37. Stretchable
39. Foray
40. Total

DOWN
1. Evergreen
2. Mine entrance
3. Himalayan kingdom
4. Brew tea
5. Japanese coin
6. Actor Wallach
7. Ballads
8. Wound covering
10. Tidiest
11. Enclose in paper
12. Faint
14. Type measures
16. Flit (about)
18. Depressions
19. Monkey
21. Accustom
23. Massage
27. Plait
30. Actor Mineo
31. Russian kings
33. Circle segment
35. Jacob's twin
38. Actor Conway

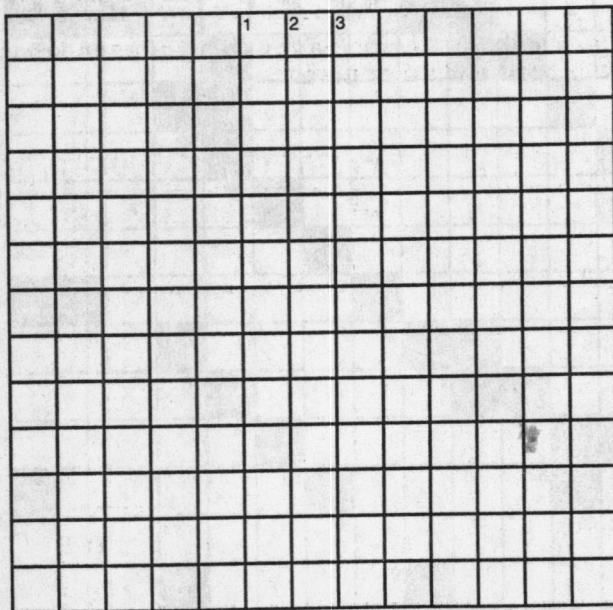

ACROSS

1. Teases
5. Field
6. Arno city
10. Abounds
12. Seed appendage
13. Spanish hero
16. Off-smelling
18. Quote
19. Odor
22. Takes for one's own
24. Lettuce dishes
26. Accomplishes
27. Main course
28. Aerie
29. European river
31. Satanic
32. Aborigine
38. Cloudless
39. Climbs
40. Posted package
42. Sign
43. Beige color
45. Buffalo's lake
47. Exist
48. Writer Anita
49. Kind of energy
52. Maintained
53. Christen
54. Bit

DOWN

1. Desert or pack
2. Dander
3. Gripe
4. Pacific island group
6. Covenants
7. Blue bloom
8. Hold session
9. Dark brew
11. Abrupt
13. Court action
14. Formerly Persia
15. Ninny
17. Eases
20. Calendar abbr.
21. Fruit drink
23. Dog or cat
25. Assistance
28. Zero
30. Employers
31. Bend one's ____
33. Behave
34. Chinese principle
35. Actress Chase
36. Change course
37. Ancient serf
38. Gounod opera
40. Brace
41. Celebrities
43. Wapiti
44. Runner Sebastian
46. Dash
50. French boyfriend
51. Corded fabric

PUZZLE 215

Starting box on page 525

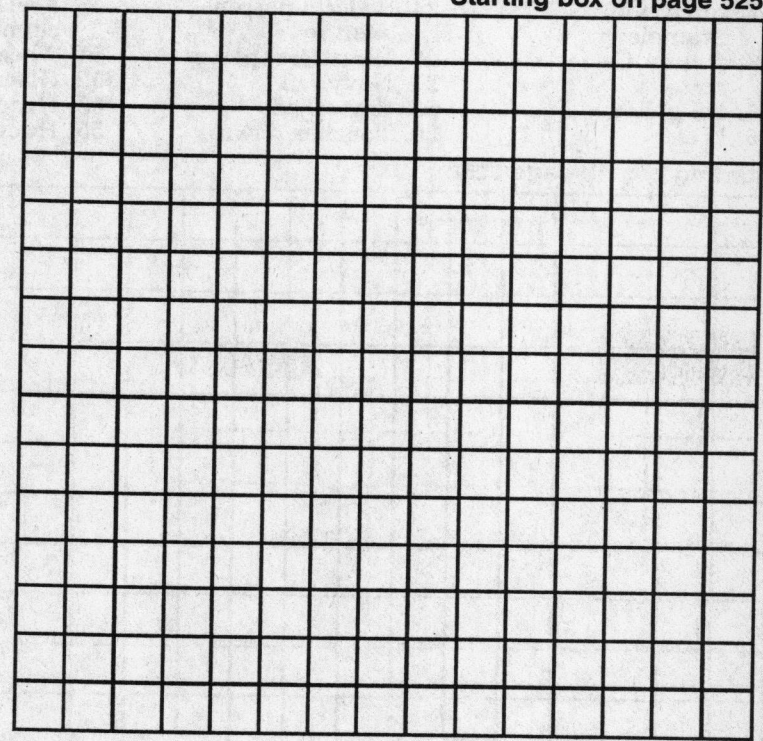

WORD MATH

PUZZLE 216

In these long-division problems, letters are substituted for numbers. Determine the value of each letter. Then arrange the letters in order from 0 to 9, and they will spell a word or phrase.

1

0	1	2	3	4	5	6	7	8	9

```
              S U N
  CURL | C O L L A R S
          C I N A C
          N O S O R
          N N S O B
            I B B R S
            S I A N
              S I A
```

2

0	1	2	3	4	5	6	7	8	9

```
                L E I
  REED | H O B B L E
          R E E D
          U B C L L
          L C B L H
            O R D O E
            O U H L U
              E U E L
```

3

0	1	2	3	4	5	6	7	8	9

```
                S E A
  TON | T A L O N S
        T A D C
          L H N
          T O N
          E N D S
          E T A T
            A O H
```

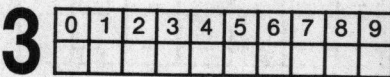

PUZZLE 217

ACROSS

1. Humble pie
5. Comedian Bob
6. Distant
9. Perused the joint
10. Tiresome types
12. Circe, for example
13. Jimmy Carter's state
15. 1/8 gallon
16. Fret
18. ____ of the situation: 2 wds.
21. Corrida cheer
22. To
23. Yam of the Philippines
24. Sailor's patron saint
26. Wrestlers' ploys
27. Navy jail
28. Smoothed
30. Touches down
31. Input
32. Pelt
33. Liberated
36. Rough-edged
39. Budget item
40. Ale type
43. Equitable
45. Galley powerer
46. Ways up
47. ____ de la Cite
48. Feel about clumsily
51. Ahead of time
52. Glacier maker
53. Heads of state
55. Homeric works
57. High-tech acronym
58. Wrap
59. Johnny ____
60. Dice toss
61. Sole

DOWN

1. Mariner's map
2. Abie's Irish friend
3. Frank
4. Married
6. In favor of
7. Jason's ship
8. Curb
9. ____ verite
10. Actor Stephen
11. 6th planet
12. Window ledges
13. Alum
14. Blunders
15. "The Raven" writer
16. Xylophone material
17. Sage bird
19. Roman poet
20. Diamond throws
22. Oft-cited source
25. Beginning
27. Flat-bottomed boat
29. Mom's mate
30. Haul
32. Musician Domino
33. Kermit, for one
34. Kind of admiral
35. Register
36. Courtroom panel
37. Show plainly
38. Apollo's island
40. Stand out
41. Sailors
42. Upton Sinclair novel
44. Recent
46. Crystal gazer
49. Anjou, e.g.
50. Slacken
52. Nonsensical
54. Society girl, for short
55. Short jacket
56. Roper's output
58. Full-house letters

Starting box on page 525

PUZZLE 218   CHANGAWORD

Can you change the top word into the bottom word (in each column) in the number of steps indicated in parentheses? Do not change the order of the letters, and change only one letter at a time. Proper names, slang, and obsolete words are not allowed.

1. HALF (4 steps)   2. HARD (4 steps)   3. WIND (5 steps)   4. FISH (6 steps)

TIME   SELL   GUST   TANK

PUZZLE 219

ACROSS
1. Center of activity
4. Kind of meat
8. Western Indians
10. Salve plant
11. Feted satirically
13. Tiny bit
14. Tart
15. Recipe amount
17. Sear
18. Vend
19. Attention-getter
20. Quite
21. Sphere
23. ___ Aviv
24. Actor Penn
25. Use a besom
27. Silents' successors
29. Type of cheese
31. Oasis trees
32. Wild hog
33. Recline
34. ___ a plea
35. Provide financing
36. Glazier's unit
37. Cancel out
39. Thin coin
40. Staircase adjunct
?. Bonnet intruders
4. Kirghiz range

45. Derisive one
47. Danger
48. Walk
49. Park flyer
50. Like a fox

DOWN
1. Rime
2. High times
3. Swamp bird
4. Cosseted
5. Hodgepodge
6. Newspaper section, for short
7. Sharp
8. Time
9. Worse for wear
11. Gad
12. Mom's mate
14. Wood finish
16. More snaillike
17. Not costly
18. Pod dwellers
19. Envelope abbr.
20. Victory letters
22. Chaotic scenes
24. Silly smile
25. Spring fish
26. Revolutionary Thomas
28. Yukon region
29. Geometric solid
30. Ruff's mate
32. Hudson and Rhett
35. Swoon

36. Wharf
38. Vapor
39. Legal document
40. Listen!
41. Et ___ (and others)
42. Cartoonist Thomas
43. Burro's cry
46. Conger

Starting box on page 525

WORD MATH

PUZZLE 220

[In] these long-division problems, letters are substituted for numbers. Determine the value of each letter. [T]hen arrange the letters in order from 0 to 9, and they will spell a word or phrase.

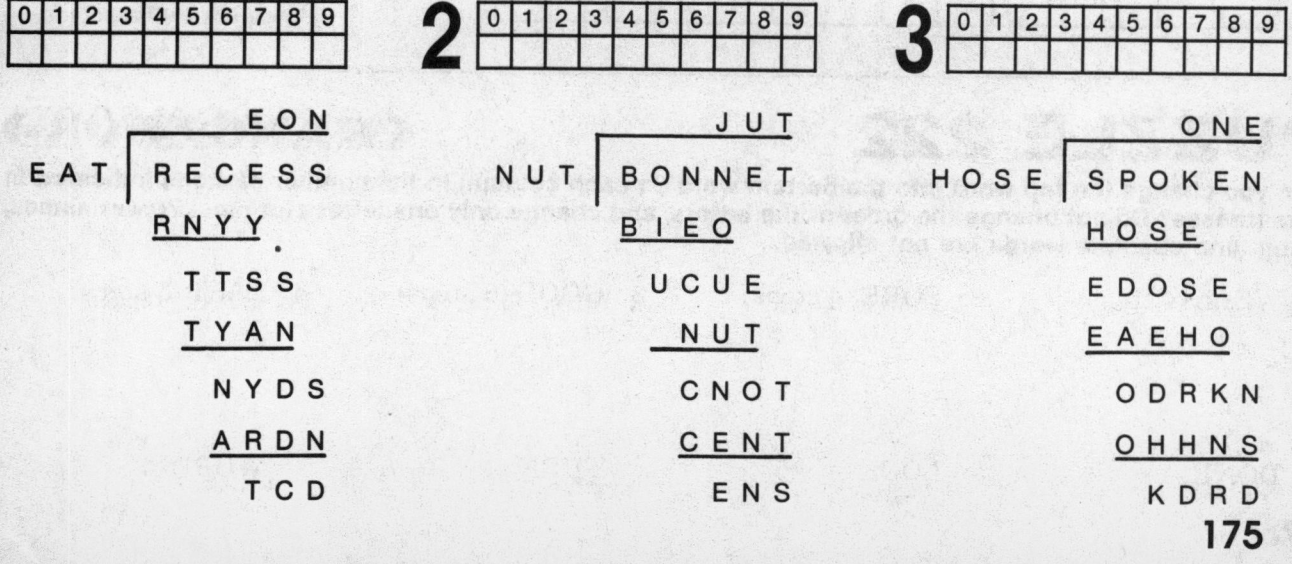

1

0	1	2	3	4	5	6	7	8	9

```
            E O N
EAT | R E C E S S
        R N Y Y .
          T T S S
          T Y A N
            N Y D S
            A R D N
              T C D
```

2

0	1	2	3	4	5	6	7	8	9

```
                J U T
NUT | B O N N E T
          B I E O
          U C U E
            N U T
          C N O T
          C E N T
            E N S
```

3

0	1	2	3	4	5	6	7	8	9

```
                O N E
HOSE | S P O K E N
         H O S E
         E D O S E
         E A E H O
           O D R K N
           O H H N S
             K D R D
```

175

PUZZLE 221

ACROSS
1. Center
4. On one's way
7. Fable ending
9. Muhammad ____
10. Ridicule: 2 wds.
12. Buss
14. Choice word
15. Tam or beret, e.g.
17. TV's "____ Girl"

19. Gosh!
20. Handle
22. Stallone's nickname
23. Fitted case
25. Suggestion
26. Snooze
29. Leave be: 2 wds.
31. Honeycomb segment
32. Deface

33. Regal title
34. Betrayal
36. West or Largo
37. Broke a fast
38. Badger
39. Knight's title
40. Fruit skin
43. The long ____ of the law
46. Rope fiber
48. Coupe, e.g.
49. Double-reed instrument
50. Ledge

52. VIP: 2 wds.
54. Certain vote
55. Helmsman
56. Coloring
57. Neither's pal

DOWN
1. Dwelling
2. Yen
3. Rubbish!
4. Table wood
5. Gad
6. Tall tale: 2 wds.
7. Tom or buck, e.g.
8. Deficiency
10. Gam
11. Beach color
13. Briny
16. Kind of face
18. Sort
21. Took the bait
24. Stint
26. Skip it: 2 wds.
27. Porter or stout
28. Scheme
29. Secular
30. Stretch out
31. Municipalities
32. Sleight of hand
34. Deep cut
35. Armed conflict
41. Arrest
42. Nerd
43. Detest
44. Cheer
45. Was in session
47. Stage drama
49. Baltic capital
51. Caustic substance
53. Card game

Starting box on page 525

PUZZLE 222   CHANGAWORD

Can you change the top word into the bottom word (in each column) in the number of steps indicated in parentheses? Do not change the order of the letters, and change only one letter at a time. Proper names, slang, and obsolete words are not allowed.

1. WELL (4 steps)   2. FORE (4 steps)   3. GOOD (5 steps)   4. LAST (5 steps)

DONE   LOCK   TURN   WORD

176

ACROSS

1. High mountain
4. Likely
7. Small arrow
9. Let fall
11. Fear greatly
13. Scent
14. Nimble
15. Generous
18. Consumed
19. Gorilla
20. "____ Miserables"
22. Train parts
24. Upper storage area
25. Style
26. Provisional
28. Get up
29. ____ and dandy
30. Scoops of ice cream
31. To and ____
32. Historical period
35. Thousands of years
36. Inconsistent
39. Vincent van ____
41. Avoid artfully
42. Synthetic fiber
44. Easterner on a ranch
45. Half: prefix
46. Mal de ____
47. Spinning toy

28. Curl
30. Entranceways
32. Musical study
33. Horseman
34. High card
35. Self
37. Crimson
38. Astringent substance
40. ____ sapiens
43. Pinch

DOWN

1. Do sums
2. ____ Porsena
3. Make ready
4. Soaking wet
5. Investigate
6. Heavy book
8. Small pies
10. Golf norm
12. Hair coloring
13. ____ carte
16. Unaccompanied
17. Went
21. Personnel
22. Sheltered bay
23. Citrus beverage
24. Minus
25. Asia ____
26. Waiter's bonus
27. Exhaust

PUZZLE 223

Starting box on page 525

WORD MATH

PUZZLE 224

In these long-division problems, letters are substituted for numbers. Determine the value of each letter. Then arrange the letters in order from 0 to 9, and they will spell a word or phrase.

1

0	1	2	3	4	5	6	7	8	9

```
                BUN
MOLE | WOOLEN
       WMBE
       EBNE
       MOLE
       MDETN
       MLOTE
        UWTL
```

2

0	1	2	3	4	5	6	7	8	9

```
                 SIN
EAST | NEAREST
       NADIT
       FAFES
       SDSST
       NRSST
       ASXAT
        IXAT
```

3

0	1	2	3	4	5	6	7	8	9

```
               ZIP
PEP | PYTHON
      YSZO
      YZIO
      YISP
       ZPN
       TIO
       YTS
```

177

PUZZLE 225

ACROSS
1. Quaker's your
4. Linen-closet item
6. Earth's midriff
8. Outspoken
9. Sup
11. Dinner course
12. Uproar
14. Sedan
15. Garden spot
17. ___ transit
19. Loot
21. Allude
23. Entreat
25. Hide
27. Pea-souper
28. Swab
30. Poker stake
31. Feldspar, e.g.
34. Apple's kin
35. "___ any drop to drink"
36. Hot cross ___
37. Freedom
39. Mr. Reiner
41. Uptight
43. Fashion capital
44. Carpenter's tool
46. Finale
48. Pose
49. Summer color
50. Fiend
52. Uppermost
54. Invigorating quaff
55. Opposite
57. Wash cycle
58. Summer cooler

DOWN
1. Thor's domain
2. Warm up
3. Heretofore
4. Young pigeon
5. Pedal digit
6. Building section
7. O'Reilly of "M*A*S*H"
8. Freight craft
10. Speaker O'Neill
11. Hollandaise, e.g.
13. Beak
14. Manage
16. Legal argument
17. Kingly
18. Dishonorable mention
19. Endowment source
20. Eggs' accompaniment
22. Pro
24. Nanny and billy
25. Half a French dance
26. Slander's kin
29. Be nosy
32. Sister
33. Sass
34. Pauline's woe
38. Elementary
40. "You ___ Your Life"
41. Choir voice
42. Back
45. Dyeing vessel
47. Thick
51. Contend
53. ___ capita
54. Care for
56. By way of

Starting box on page 525

PUZZLE 226

CHANGAWORD

Can you change the top word into the bottom word (in each column) in the number of steps indicated in parentheses? Do not change the order of the letters, and change only one letter at a time. Proper names, slang, and obsolete words are not allowed.

1. CARD (3 steps)   2. HALF (4 steps)   3. FOOT (4 steps)   4. BLUE (6 steps)

GAME   TIME   BALL   CHIP

178

PUZZLE 227

ACROSS
1. Quick blow
4. Ring out
8. Musical work
10. "God's Little ___"
11. Tall palm
13. ___ in Rome, do as . . .
14. Follow secretly
16. Solemn vow
18. Clown
20. Oklahoman
22. ___ Marie Saint
23. Set afire
24. Equip
25. Holds firmly
27. Superlative ending
30. Relief
31. Grassy meadow
32. Caesar and friends
35. Seed
37. Show weariness
39. Fate
40. Watery castle-ditch
42. ___ by jury
45. New York canal
46. Amos's partner
47. Peddle
48. Legal John or Jane

32. Awake memories
33. Appoints
34. Took an oath
36. Ibsen's doll-wife
38. Brad
41. AT&T part: abbr.
43. Bustle
44. Caustic substance

DOWN
1. 9-5 activity
2. Mimic
3. Dairy product
4. Rabbit's foot
5. Repeat
6. Regions
7. Slow, in music
9. Seven or high
12. Metric measure
15. Jacob's son
17. Vacation time
18. Blue Angels' craft
19. Tattered cloth
21. Quick drink
25. London prison
26. Edge
27. Wapiti
28. Beginning
29. Occult cards

Starting box on page 525

WORD MATH

PUZZLE 228

In these long-division problems, letters are substituted for numbers. Determine the value of each letter. Then arrange the letters in order from 0 to 9, and they will spell a word or phrase.

1. 0 1 2 3 4 5 6 7 8 9

```
              SEE
    ELF [ EFFIGY
          CYSF
          CLIG
          ANEF
          AGGY
          ANEF
           CY
```

2. 0 1 2 3 4 5 6 7 8 9

```
               I RE
KICKER [ ETCETERA
         KICKER
         IEAIICR
         IRPIPOO
         OKSTATA
         OPASEAO
          PTTPEK
```

3. 0 1 2 3 4 5 6 7 8 9

```
               REO
   EWES [ FLOWERS
          FGEGL
          FRTOR
          FFGFO
          TOGOS
          TLWOE
           OAL
```

179

PUZZLE 229

ACROSS

1. Entranced
5. Sass
8. Fragrance
9. Wag's stock in trade
10. Station
12. Crow's kin
13. Kitchen VIP
15. Labyrinth
16. Bronze element
18. Wow
20. Mongrel
21. Actress Balin
22. Fateful phrase: 2 wds.
23. Sweet potato
25. At that time
26. Camp bed
27. Via
28. Chocolate source
30. Keep at bay: 2 wds.
33. Prop for Dali
34. Small lizard
37. Emmet
40. Mast support
42. Very pale
44. Ocean
45. Old Fr. coin
46. Clucker
47. Even match
49. "____ Sloopy" ('60s song): 2 wds.
51. Prod
52. Deli offering
53. Floor
55. Beelzebub
58. Owl sound
59. Vendition
60. Conclusion
61. Ragout

DOWN

1. Actor Steiger
2. Fruit drink
3. Cinema snack
4. Boy Scout unit
5. Beautiful
6. I Like ____
7. Mighty weapon
9. "All That ____"
11. Theme
12. Stropped item
14. Game of chance
15. Fabricated
16. Signal
17. Squeal
18. Pickpocket
19. To ____ his own
20. Complete disorder
24. Low
25. Pauley's show
29. Polish
31. Chosen quantity
32. Leeds apartment
34. Lamb work
35. Ongoing dispute
36. Faucet
37. Bat wood
38. Mr. Webster
39. Makes harmonious
40. Make a goal of: 2 wds.
41. Lacrosse number
43. Up to ____: 2 wds.
48. Classify
50. Shade of green
53. Andress film
54. Heavy weight
56. Stout, e.g.
57. Freshly coined

Starting box on page 525

PUZZLE 230   CHANGAWORD

Can you change the top word into the bottom word (in each column) in the number of steps indicated in parentheses? Do not change the order of the letters, and change only one letter at a time. Proper names, slang, and obsolete words are not allowed.

1. **BACK** (4 steps)

2. **JUNK** (5 steps)

3. **HEAD** (5 steps)

4. **LIFE** (5 steps)

SEAT   YARD   LINE   BOAT

ACROSS

1. Villain's word
4. "My Gal ____"
7. Musical conclusion
11. June VIP
12. Pindaric work
13. Gone over the hill: abbr.
14. Robin Hood's home
19. Cuckoo
20. ____-do-well
21. Women's org.
24. Spider's "parlor"
25. Gave food to
27. Sheep's cry
30. Mark ____
33. Elec. measures
35. British princess and others
37. Roman waters
44. Ovum
45. Mire
46. Requires
47. English title
51. Heel-and-____
52. Outfit
53. Female deer
56. Duty
57. Constellation
59. Horse food
60. ____ de la Cite
61. U.S. waterway
67. Gravy
68. Tend
69. Laborers
71. Armed conflict
72. Recent: prefix
73. Child's food
76. Path: abbr.
78. Put on ____
80. Fish eggs
83. Western heights
90. Large lake
91. Vive this man
92. Mauna ____
93. School official
94. Printers' letters
95. Wind dir.

DOWN

1. Newspaper notices
2. Laughter sound
3. Seaport in South Yemen
4. Plant seeds
5. Trouble
6. One of the Spinkses
7. Auto
8. Present a chit
9. John ____ Passos
10. High, in music
15. Dispose
16. Moisture
17. Charge
18. Sphere
22. Astern
23. "Thank-you" money
26. ____ Andrews
27. Token of achievement
28. French friend
29. Suitable
31. Hostelry
32. Maiden name indicator
34. Arabic, e.g.
36. ____ Remo

37. Encountered
38. Self
39. Cut a ____
40. Seine
41. Red in the Mideast
42. Newspaper workers: abbr.
43. Inquire
47. On the ____
48. Onassis
49. Negative prefix
50. Of course
52. Blame, mob style
53. Underwater worker
54. Spanish cheer
55. Always, to Keats
58. Family member, for short
59. Cork remover
62. Tree product

63. Take to court
64. Religious image
65. Crude
66. ____ Gershwin
70. Drunkard
73. Remit money
74. Point a gun
75. In favor of
77. Epoch
79. Certain
81. Lubricates
82. Adam's grandson
83. Primary color
84. Mine product
85. Govt. agency
86. Knowledge
87. Sine qua ____
88. "____ the season . . ."
89. Cutting tool

Starting box on page 525

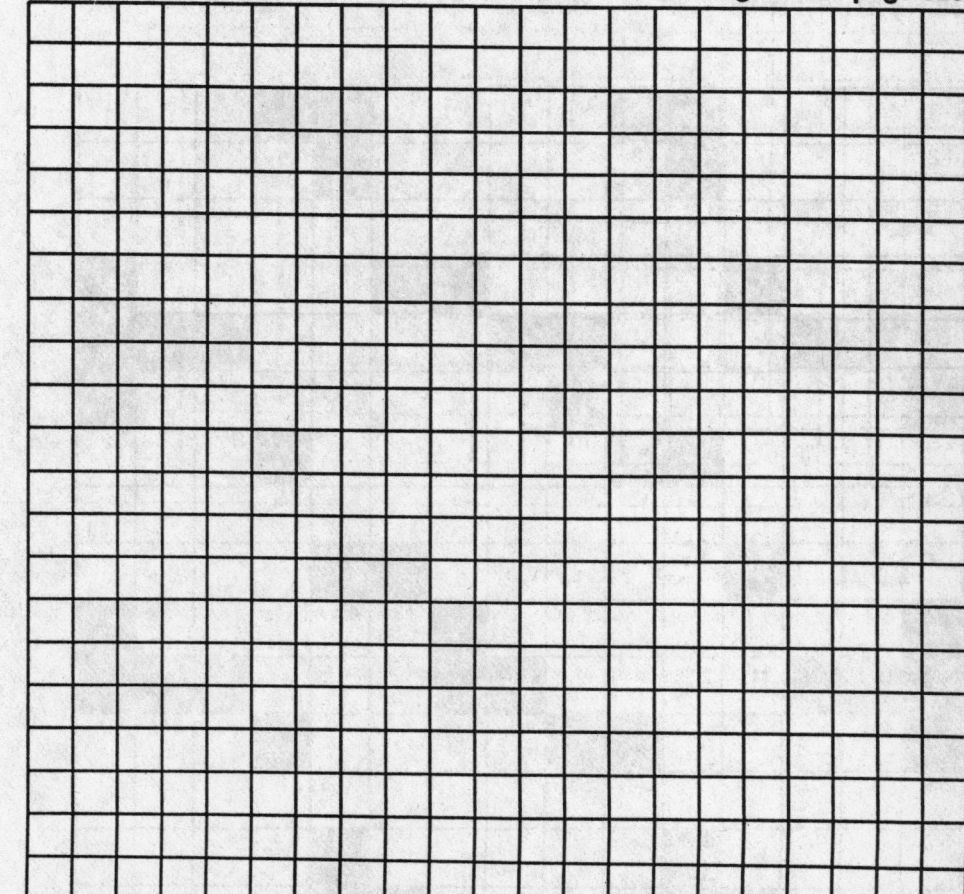

Note to Solvers: This Diagramless does not have aids such as "2 wds." and "hyph."

PUZZLE 232

ACROSS
1. Time gone by
5. Scientific suffix
9. Chum
12. Play part: 2 wds.
13. —— acid
14. Lucid
15. "All —— which I . . ." (Deut. 8:1): 2 wds.
18. Dress edge
19. Art resort
20. Prayers
21. Distress signal
22. Make cookies
24. Palm fruits
26. Mothers and fathers
29. Cross a ford
30. Tobacco pipe
31. Kind of race
33. "—— unto Moses . . ." (Lev. 8:1): 4 wds.
37. Set
38. New York city
39. Verily
40. Colonizes
42. Rapture
44. Hollow stalk
45. Exterminate
46. Mil. truant
48. Fly with the eagles
50. Biddy
53. "—— enter . . ." (Matt. 12:29): 5 wds.
57. Healthy
58. Carried
59. Biblical book
60. Consume
61. Partner of pieces
62. Supervisor

DOWN
1. Trail
2. Yearn
3. Pipe part
4. Nervous twitch
5. Bullets
6. Creeks
7. Hostel
8. Turf
9. Plate glass
10. Hill builders
11. Them: Fr.
13. Stockpile
14. Lucky number
16. Sioux
17. Producers
21. Editor's word
22. Child, in Edinburgh
23. Romanian city
24. Copenhagen residents
25. Confuse
26. Malayan outriggers
27. Mine carts
28. Interests
29. Witty person
30. Run, as dye
32. Half a score
34. Commercial lodgings
35. She, in Cannes
36. Compensated
41. Mythical cave-dweller
42. Tauten
43. Money in Milan, once
46. Neighborhood
47. Whip mark
48. Ilk
49. Possesses
50. —— sapiens
51. Adam's grandson
52. Headland
53. Be in debt
54. Kind of tide
55. —— polloi
56. Capture

ACROSS

1. Chose
6. Andy's radio partner
10. Facilitate
14. Task
15. Tender to touch
16. Addresses for GIs
17. "Praise ye ——..." (Psalm 148:2): 4 wds.
20. Sugar suffix
21. Bind
22. Ye —— Tea Shoppe
23. Lion's den
24. French friend
26. Methods
29. Menacing
33. Type of collar or jacket
34. **Ice-cream** holder
35. Scottish "no"
37. "—— the winterhouse ..." (Jer. 36:22): 5 wds.
42. —— Moines
43. Kiln
44. Middle: prefix
45. Locales
48. Concerns
49. Kinfolk: abbr.
50. Breach of legal duty
52. Go by boat
54. Common verb
55. Professionals cost
58. "—— according-, ing ..." (Gal. 6:16): 5 wds.
63. The New ——
64. Away from the wind
65. Name
66. Political party members: abbr.
67. —— off (angry)
68. Horse

DOWN

1. Eight, to Pedro
2. Greek letters
3. Heavy book
4. Baseball statistic: abbr.
5. **Greek Ds**
6. Namesakes of Jacob's eighth son
7. French pronoun
8. Choice words
9. Caribbean ——
10. Aerie fledgling
11. Mimed
12. Only
13. Curved letter
18. 52, to Brutus
19. Discordant sounds
23. Pre-Easter period
24. Later
25. Chinese dynasty
26. Repair
27. Siouan-speaking **Indians**
28. Use a divining rod
30. Frosting
31. Come in
32. Lift
36. Son of Seth
38. **Waldorf-**Astoria and The Plaza, e.g.
39. Morally wrong
40. Under-stands
41. **Amo, amas, ——**
46. Court events
47. Remained
48. Tops of waves
51. Money of account
52. Snicker ——
53. Genesis name
55. Destiny
56. French female
57. Squeezed through, with "out"
58. Total
59. Word after welcome or door
60. Ginger ——
61. Wedding announce-ment word
62. Clever one

PUZZLE 233

183

PUZZLE 234

ACROSS

1. Secular
5. Ms. Bovary
9. Soft cheese
13. Thick slice
17. Aviation prefix
18. Military assistant
19. Pay or jelly
20. Pear, for one
21. Captain, e.g.: 2 wds.
25. Empowers
26. Don Juan's patter
27. Glaze
28. Under the weather
29. 1/8 gallon
30. Make out
32. By oneself
35. Wings
36. Lose luster
37. Before
40. Complete: prefix
41. Arabian Sea gulf
42. Confronted
43. With it
44. Printemps follower
45. On the briny
46. Southern staple
47. Identical
48. Seed covering
49. Hilarious one
50. Ms. Dinsmore
51. U.S. Navy VIP: 4 wds.
56. Ponder
57. Reluctant: var.
58. Pb
59. Lean and ___
60. Inverness natives
62. Scheme
63. Wellfleet's cape
66. Turku, to a Swede
67. Aids to navigation
68. Prophet
69. Cipher
70. Norse god of strife
71. Obscene
72. British carbine
73. Spondulicks
74. Walls: Fr.
75. Espied
76. Provide crew
77. Alarm
80. Harlequin gem
81. Serious
85. Harbor protectors: 3 wds.
89. Singer Redding
90. Muslim weight
91. Exchange premium
92. ___ avis
93. Diminished in part
94. Deserter's status
95. Bellow
96. Ukrainian river

DOWN

1. Tatting's yield
2. Endless span
3. "___ la Douce"
4. Mix
5. Studio stand
6. Mile's equal
7. 1501
8. Wind-blown
9. Actor George
10. Went on horseback
11. Workers' gp.
12. Leprechaun
13. Cumin, e.g.
14. Sites
15. Seconding word
16. Ice mass
22. That: Latin
23. Nonet number
24. Pulled the trigger
29. Cop a ___
30. Jury's quest
31. Humorist George and kin
32. Blind impulse
33. Forest Hills call
34. Bravo
35. ___ Rogers St. Johns
36. Trust
37. Stage
38. Send payment
39. Saber's kin
41. Saudi Arabian district
42. Foam
45. Desertlike
46. Freebies
47. Pung
48. In a frenzy
49. Pulls for a team
50. Spirit
51. James Joyce story
52. Philan-thropist
53. Frank ___ Wright
54. Actress Terry
55. Find intimidating
56. Sheep's cry
60. Litigant

184

61. Herd members
62. Hammer part
63. Opposed
64. Wordsworth work
65. Tunisian ruler, of yore
67. To the point
68. Outstanding
69. Netman

Jimmy
72. Barking juggler
73. Kind of brandy
74. Disheveled
75. Fall
76. City VIP
77. Flat-bottomed boat
78. Jot
79. Joan

Crawford film
80. Football-great Graham
81. Assam silkworm
82. Part of QED
83. Nimble

84. Winter Palace resident
86. Macaw genus
87. Argument
88. I, to Caesar

PUZZLE 234

185

PUZZLE 235

ACROSS
1. Twofold
5. Binge
10. Auditors: abbr.
14. Capital of Norway
15. —— Oyl
16. Bind with rope
17. Lazy butcher?: 2 wds.
19. —— en point
20. Trains
21. Brazilian state
22. Dollar bills
23. O'Hara home
24. Carpet pile
27. Neat
29. Chan actor
31. Pilewort fiber
33. Lawyer?
36. Grade
37. Bitter medicine
38. History Muse
39. Sculptors?
41. Med. tests
42. Dividing membranes
43. "—— Wonderful Life": 2 wds.
46. Genetic inits.
47. Seines
48. Seaweed
50. Your: Fr.
52. Rodgers and Hammerstein show
56. "—— La Douce"
57. Referee?: 2 wds.
59. Tidy
60. Of a space
61. Taro root
62. Old laborer
63. Officious
64. Couple

DOWN
1. Portuguese title
2. Customer
3. Wings
4. Bingo's kin
5. Oklahoma native
6. Believable
7. Prevalent
8. Holiday nights
9. Always, in poetry
10. Headroom
11. Chef?
12. —— spumante
13. Mets' stadium
18. Fuzz
21. Cotton bundle
23. Tykes
24. T-man
25. Esau's wife et al.
26. Doctor?: 2 wds.
28. New Zealand native
30. Condescend
32. Urgently reckless
34. Turnpike stops: 2 wds.
35. Diva Ponselle
37. Alack!
40. Diminutive suffix
44. Gradually
45. Water: Sp.
49. —— as a beet: 2 wds.
50. Climbing plant
51. Native metals
52. Dear: Ital.
53. Iowa city
54. Vortex
55. Helen's mother
57. Chat
58. Drowse

PUZZLE 236

ACROSS

1. Visit
5. Unified: 2 wds.
10. Lenient
14. Neighbor-hood
15. Fairylike
16. Cleo's river
17. Civil War struggle: 4 wds.
20. Laws
21. Brings up
22. Freezes
23. Dame Myra
24. Motes
27. Mattress support
31. Formal mall
32. Thin strip
33. 2nd-year student
34. Formal dance: Fr.
35. Peruvian silver coins
38. Place for swells
39. And others: abbr.
41. Fit one within another
42. Eskimo craft
44. Holds back
46. Paddles
47. One on the move
48. Dock
49. T-bone and chuck
52. Frantic scrambles: 2 wds.
56. NYSE optimists: 3 wds.
58. Asian sea
59. Heavy
60. —— of
Worms
61. Equine
62. Equestrian
63. American admiral

DOWN

1. Taxis
2. Smell ——: 2 wds.
3. "I —— Song Go . . .": 2 wds.
4. Trellis
5. Medea's father
6. Wild plums
7. Dial settings
8. Penpoint
9. Toughened by: 2 wds.
10. Signs up
11. Publicizes
12. Turn on an axis
13. Yearnings
18. —— out (prospered)
19. Damsel
23. Courage
24. Cavalry sword
25. Silver or gold
26. Fitzgerald et al.
27. Consecrate
28. Red dye
29. Vertical
30. East Indian trees
32. Villain's expression
36. Stock purchaser
37. Majestic
40. By law
43. Plunders
45. Korean soldiers
46. Baby-——
48. Country: Ital.
49. Exchange
50. Starchy root
51. Verve
52. Willis or Rex
53. 152, in Calpurnia's day
54. Basic: abbr.
55. Fast planes
57. Baseball stat

187

PUZZLE 237

ACROSS

1. Actress Tilly
4. More drafty
10. ____ to say
14. Eggs
15. "Robinson ____"
16. Skirt panel
17. ____ Perce
18. Deep North American gorge
20. Semite
22. Born
23. Article of food
24. Was beholden to
26. Iowa college
28. Loyalists
31. Cerise
32. Biblical king
36. Hawaiian crow
37. Missile industry
39. Wilderness area
41. Boots
42. Rolling Stones hit
43. D'Urbervilles heroine
44. Choler
45. Cupidities
46. Misery
47. Lip
48. Brazilian dance
52. Go schussing
53. Scowl
57. Lake, mountains, river, or town
61. Deck or dial
62. King of the comedians
63. Smoothed out
64. Easily bruised item
65. TV's Foxx
66. Cranes and herons
67. Studio decor

DOWN

1. "____ Lisa"
2. At any time
3. Israeli strip
4. Alas: Ger.
5. Castle and Dunne
6. Headed
7. ____ of Man
8. Goddess of the dawn
9. Cooking instruction: abbr.
10. Hindu god of fire
11. Kind of bean
12. Anemia antidote
13. Parry
19. Hail
21. Water heaters
25. Puts on
26. Mackerel
27. Redolence
28. Fortuneteller's card
29. Martini garnish
30. Gushes
31. Comedy-writer Taylor
32. Suitability
33. Value
34. Biting
35. Heredity units
37. In front of
38. Burns
40. Columbus's state
45. Half or full dive
46. Armed conflict
47. Part of a Greek theater
48. Cicatrix
49. Hawaiian refusal
50. Boulder Dam lake
51. Political society
52. Vehicle for Nanook
54. Exploits
55. Winter Olympic event
56. Shoelace hazard
58. Mountain ____
59. Mickey's ex
60. Wynn et al.

188

PUZZLE 238

ACROSS
1. Queen's address
5. ___ God
10. Gather
14. Concerning
15. French river
16. Verbal
17. Leroy Anderson song, with "The"
20. Without a belt
21. Greek fury
22. Swiss river
23. Ruler: suff.
24. Actress Woodward
27. Hung around
31. High: pref.
32. Numskull
33. Commotion
34. Burgess book, with "A"
38. OPEC's asset
39. Marine birds
40. Bridge support
41. Church towers
43. Uses money
45. Actress Jackson
46. Winglike
47. Captain Ahab, for one
50. Being indignant
54. Line from "Hickory Dickory Dock"
56. Italian river
57. ___ Heep
58. Wander
59. Observed
60. Large books
61. Finales

DOWN
1. "Little ___ Marker"
2. Writer Seton
3. Scottish alders
4. Grease monkey
5. Current unit
6. Stop
7. Expresses disapproval
8. Sugar suffix
9. Director Fellini
10. Mannerly
11. Do a laundry chore
12. Frilly
13. BPOE members
18. Buck heroine
19. Volcano hole
23. Hits on the head
24. John ___ Astor
25. Stan's friend
26. Coral reef
27. Baits
28. Arrested
29. Added trim
30. Go-getters
32. Recipient
35. Corn seed
36. Twist to dry
37. Small hole
42. "The Maltese ___"
43. Lazy animals
44. Young salmon
46. Vase handles
47. School gps.
48. Honor: Ger.
49. Actor Hackman
50. ___ milk
51. Religious image
52. OGPU's successor
53. Bestows, in Scotland
55. ___ -Magnon

PUZZLE 239

ACROSS
1. —— Benedict
5. Chancel table
10. Icicle holder
14. "—— Back in Anger"
15. Free
16. Surrounded by
17. Chauncey Olcott song: 4 wds.
20. Jose or Juan
21. Atmosphere: prefix
22. Ratings man
23. Padded
25. Sandra —— O'Connor
26. Subjects
29. At any time
31. Operated
34. Declare
35. Outlaws
36. U.N. gp.
37. Puccini opera: 2 wds.
42. Sch. org.
43. French articles
44. Salve ingredient
45. Fr. seasoning
46. Hwys.
47. Thins gradually
49. O'Hare inits.
50. Time units
52. Brawls
56. "O Sole ——"
57. Baseball's Traynor
60. Lehar classic: 3 wds.
63. Shrub genus
64. Loos or O'Day
65. Equal
66. Visits
67. Mideast land
68. Tabula ——

DOWN
1. "Desire Under the ——"
2. Spanish artist
3. Ball attire
4. Slalom
5. Mayflower family members
6. Longest French river
7. Craggy hill
8. Z —— zebra: 2 wds.
9. Occupant
10. Ahead of time
11. Andy's partner
12. Shop clamp
13. Garden spot
18. Secular
19. Kind of candelabrum
23. Milan money, once
24. "La Mer" composer
26. Packs down
27. Egg-shaped
28. Bike feature
30. Large tank
31. Ransack
32. —— nothing: 2 wds.
33. "Highwayman" poet
38. Arthur or Bill
39. Ingress
40. Bonnet intruder
41. Seance sounds
47. Formosa
48. In a line
49. Wall tapestry
51. Ham it up
52. French friends
53. Celebration
54. Rid
55. Trig ratio
57. Cop a ——
58. Natives: suffix
59. Hebrew prophet
61. Obscured
62. Shower mo.

FOUR-MOST

All of the four-letter entries in this crossword puzzle are listed separately and are in alphabetical order. Use the numbered clues as solving aids to help you determine where each four-letter entry goes in the diagram.

4-LETTER ENTRIES

ALAN
ALEE
ALIT
ALTO
AMEN
AMON
ATOM
ATOP
AUTO
DART
DELI
DOVE
ETNA
ETON
IRON
LADS
LAIR
LAMA
LASS
LURE
MAID
MOVE
NATO
ODIN
PALE
PATE
PAWN
REAM
RENE
SONS
STAR
TINS
TONE
UNIT
URAL
WELD

ACROSS

14. Salutation
17. Belted constellation
20. River island
21. Change
26. Vermin
28. Lettering device
31. Legal profession
32. Weird
38. Burghoff role
42. Juicy fruit
44. Spread out to dry
45. Pekoe vessels
48. Grave
52. Mr. Kramden
54. Certain poem
60. Tribal leader
64. Actor Claude _____

DOWN

4. Uses
5. Earn
7. UN agcy.
8. Give
9. Water cooler item
12. Born
14. More raspy
22. Take one's place at
24. Goddess of rashness
25. Filch
26. Emulate O'Keeffe
27. Bert's pal
28. Factions
29. Fuming
30. Subsequently
31. Cal.'s kin
33. Inclines
35. _____ Zeppelin
37. "The Black _____"
39. Personnel lists
43. Tours negative
46. Ceiling
47. Theater workers
49. "Sleeping Beauty"
51. Paradises
59. Genetic abbr.
61. Thai language

PUZZLE 241

• MOVIE GREATS •

ACROSS

1. Waist cincher
5. "Mermaids" star
9. Extinct bird
12. Tree exudation
15. Operatic highlight
16. "Gilligan's Island" star
17. Give weapons to
18. Window parts
20. Art Carney film
23. Queues
24. Spuds
25. Rds.
26. Certain tooth
27. Pismire
28. DDE et al.
29. Midler
30. Blueprints
33. ___ Rabbit
34. Preserve
35. Food fish
38. Fleming et al.
39. Time spans
40. Delta deposit
41. "The ___ of Reason"
42. French friend
43. Rotate
44. Mine finds
45. Hint
46. Typewriter roller
48. Flank
49. Became ashen
50. "Peggy ___" (Kathleen Turner film)
54. Southern nut
57. Binds
58. Pencil end
61. Hit for the Beatles
62. Abhors
64. Tibetan beasts
65. Vied for office
67. Choler
68. Iowa town
69. Parts of wheels
70. Choir voice
71. Weaver's device
73. Pro
74. Bottom lines for Dior
75. Derisive smile
76. Some wines
78. Towel word
79. Tom Hanks film
80. Sword parts
82. Remove from a job
83. Mexican titles
86. Gnawed
87. Quinn film
90. Actor Peter ___
91. Spanish cheer
92. Booty
93. Nick and Nora's pooch
94. ___ Francisco
95. Strange
96. Comprehends
97. Remain

DOWN

1. Humbug
2. Part of QED
3. Italian money, once
4. Scottish fabrics
5. Map
6. ___ Christian Andersen
7. Ancient times
8. Captures again
9. Prides of lions
10. Table scraps
11. I love, in Italian
12. Angels
13. Woody Allen film
14. Hammerhead
18. Town map
19. Compass pt.
21. Desires
22. Atop
26. Pennies
28. Neighbor of Iraq
29. Straw unit
30. Actress Zadora
31. Light giver
32. Indigo plant
33. "April showers ___ ..."
34. Apple drink
36. Malarial fever
37. Legal document
39. Fencing weapon
40. Soft drinks
43. Daze
44. Citrus fruits
45. Bounders
47. Kin of PDQ
48. Swine homes
49. Pod fillers
51. Playful mammal
52. Paper quantities
53. Pesters
54. Singer Collins
55. Architect Saarinen
56. Taylor role
59. Writer Gardner
60. Grade
62. Sword handles
63. "___ and Andy"
64. Sweet potatoes
66. Neither's correlative
69. Breakfast foods
70. Silky-haired cats
72. Up-to-date
74. Musician Alpert
75. Trill
77. Coty
78. Employed
79. Chards
80. Actress Barbara ___ Geddes
81. Asian country
82. Sheep enclosure
83. Sabot or brogan
84. Musical pause
85. Bristle
87. San Diego tourist attraction
88. Foot part
89. Singer Starr

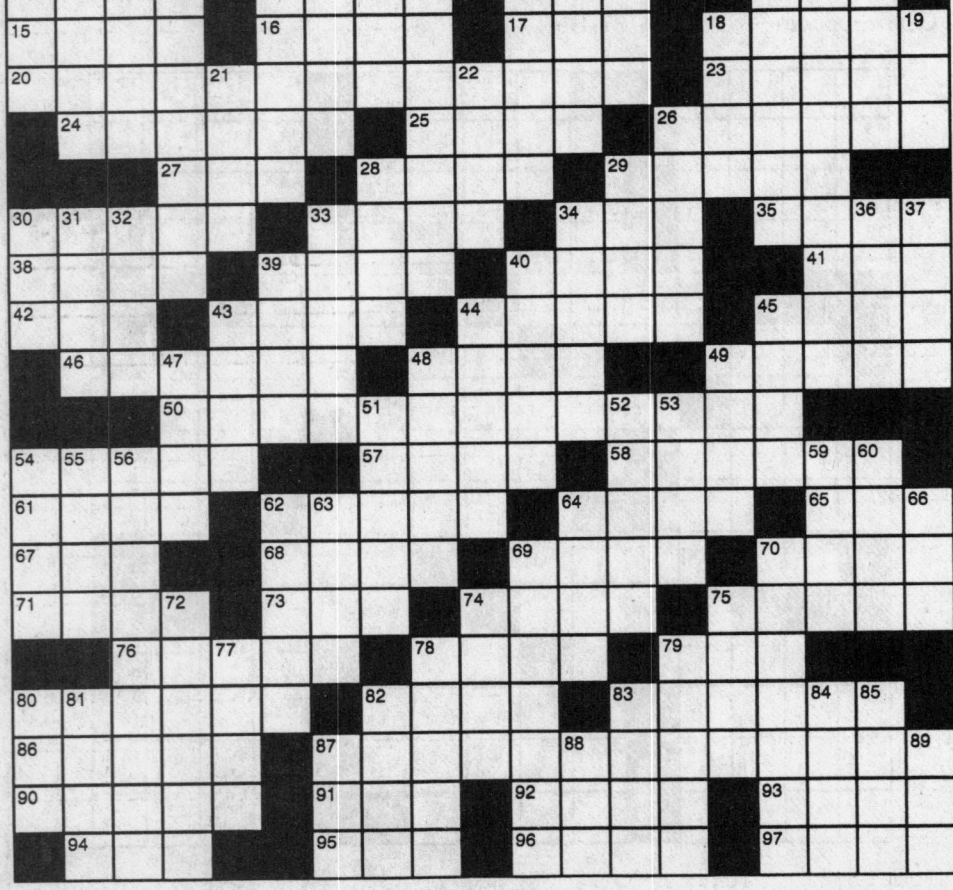

192

ACROSS

1. Emcee
5. Map
9. Liquor amount
13. Large quantity
17. Declare positively
18. Italian capital
19. Track-and-field contest
20. Commotion
21. Infrequent
22. Town on the Thames
23. Send forth
24. Storm
25. Entreats
27. Spoils
29. Ridicules
31. Stumble
33. Place for a lark
35. Ribbed fabric
36. Contemplate
40. Letter beginning
42. Corporate transactions
46. 18 or 30
47. Daisy feature
49. Like molasses in January
51. ____ gin fizz
52. Arbor Day gift
54. Lucky number
56. Chicken's home
58. Anger
59. Enclosed car
61. Make merry
63. Kitchen appliance
65. Perry Mason's thing
67. Imp
69. Use a straw
70. Shield
74. Crowbar
76. Written defamation
80. Sass
81. Cruise
83. Stiff
85. Sliced
86. Goddess of the rainbow
88. Pilot's stunt
90. Appointments
92. "B.C." insect
93. Kind of pie
95. Civil wrong
97. Parental speeches
99. Polka follower
101. Dabbling duck
103. Bed support
104. Pushed
108. Asterisk
110. Purpose
114. Actual
115. Crown of the head
117. Midday
119. Actress Sedgwick
120. Concerning
121. Do a laundry task
122. Wine and ____
123. Paddy plant
124. Stone covering
125. Bucky ____ of baseball
126. Snow toy
127. Dam up

DOWN

1. Angel's instrument
2. Elliptical
3. Very dry
4. Foots the bill
5. Acts as chairperson
6. Parking spot
7. Cupid
8. Mortise and ____ joint
9. Gowns
10. Ewe's mate
11. Lab liquid
12. Poetic measure
13. Army uniform decorations
14. Burden
15. Advantage
16. Sorrows
26. Faucet problem
28. Mr. Danson
30. Alert color
32. Author Benchley
34. Powder mineral
36. Felines
37. Monster
38. Poverty
39. Talked wildly
41. Origin
43. Touched down
44. Traditional knowledge
45. Prophet
48. Horizontal
50. Courts
53. Nobleman
55. At no time
57. Bucket
60. New Jersey team
62. Furious
64. Sputter
66. Aquatic mammal
68. Pad or tender
70. Petticoat
71. Employ
72. Legend
73. Melee
75. Ceremonies
77. Male swine
78. Irish lake
79. "____ Twist Again"
82. Pillage
84. Refused
87. Bicycle seats
89. Introduce
91. Musician Kenton
94. Doze
96. Tit for ____
98. Voices
100. Lukewarm
102. Countries
104. Prissy
105. Divorce center
106. Paddles
107. Challenge
109. Disturb
111. Revise
112. Agreeable
113. Swarm
116. 2,000 pounds
118. Washington bill

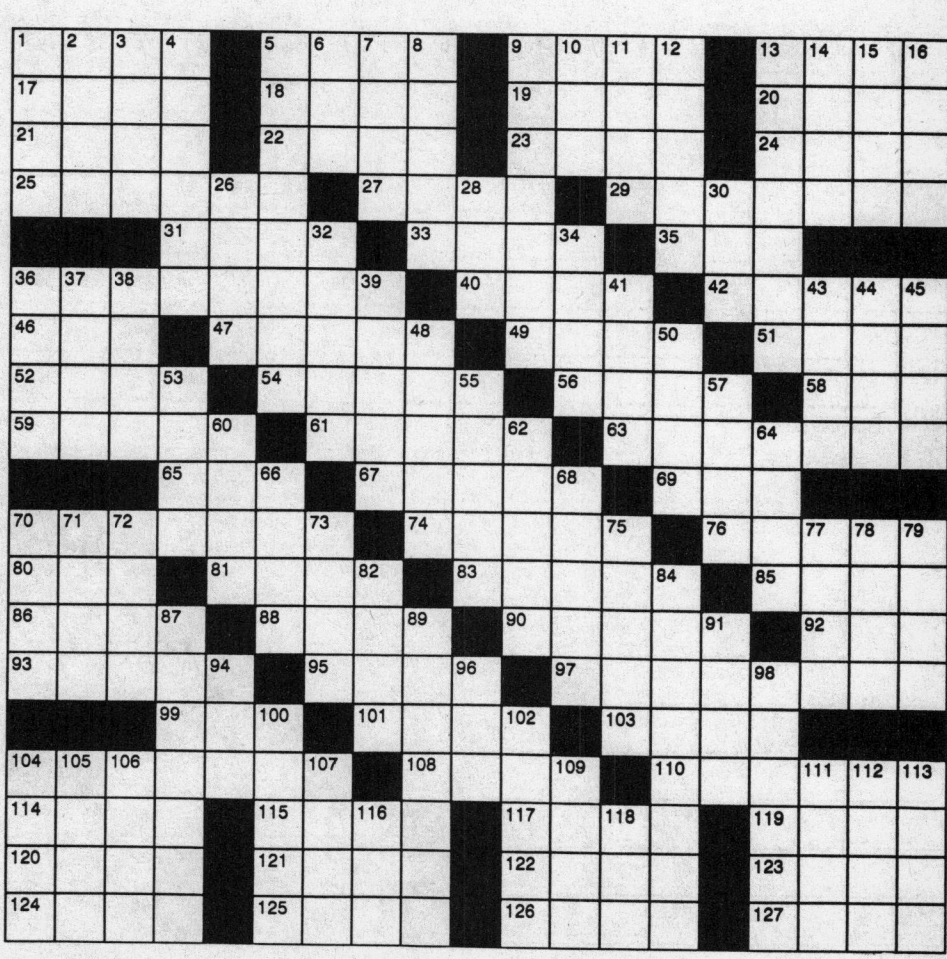

PUZZLE 243

• LEGAL TENDER •

ACROSS
1. Zodiac cat
4. Raindrop sound
8. Aesop's lesson
13. Oscar Madison, e.g.
17. Parabola
18. Goneril's father
19. Florida city
20. The Moor's nemesis
21. Carioca's coin
23. Chef Julia ___
24. Arizona river
25. Some retrievers
26. Enjoyed
28. Over there
30. Strong thread
32. Abelard, to Heloise
33. Eastern bishop
34. Sapient
35. Leafed
36. Dutch coin, once
40. Sternward
41. Diners' lists
42. Carols
44. Quenching suffix
45. Livy's coin
47. "Green ___"
48. Radar spot
49. Welfare
50. Garments of India
51. Scacchi of "The Player"
52. Perspiring
55. Geologic samples
56. Shoddy
57. Truck, in Dover
58. Look out ___!
59. "Pygmalion" playwright
60. Huge time periods
61. Obey the dentist
62. Former Spanish Main coin
66. Samuel's mentor
67. Tunney's namesakes
68. Minds
69. Ms. Zadora
70. Beethoven's coin
72. Pilot's pin
73. Fruit part
74. Otic appendages
75. Wish listings
76. Oklahoma city
77. Foxy
80. Actress LuPone
81. Fictional Jane
82. Misrepresented
83. Deteriorate
85. Former cockney coin
89. Eurasian range
90. More rational
91. Farm or frog
92. Guernsey, e.g.
93. Richard ___ of "King David"
94. Harmless bear
95. Impudent reply
96. Potato bud

DOWN
1. Varnish ingredient
2. Bungle
3. Vision specialists
4. West Point freshman
5. Fragrant necklaces
6. Sculler's necessity
7. Introduction
8. Derided
9. Dark yellow
10. Plunder
11. "___ in the Family"
12. Gardener's friends
13. Indication
14. Placed
15. Gawk
16. Wild pig
22. Writer Grey
27. Currier's partner
29. Sashes
30. "___ the night . . ."
31. Chaucer's ___ of Bath
32. Marine ___ corporal
33. Choreographer de Mille
35. Jaunty
37. Valleys
38. Chanteuse Piaf
39. Recompense
41. Substantial
42. Fastener
43. "Stanley & ___"
46. Nicholas and Ivan
47. Brother of Moses
48. Fracas
50. Cobbler's concerns
51. Seizes
52. Saw logs
53. Novelist Virginia ___
54. Journalist Pyle
55. Grant
56. Dull sounds
58. Sweet cherries
59. Ditties
61. Most peculiar
62. Fang fixers
63. Riches
64. Corn and peanut
65. Wine valley
67. Chew on
68. Cast
71. Heckle
72. Diluted
73. Unadulterated
75. Forded
76. Sorts
77. Snail's kin
78. Engage
79. "___ Window"
80. Walden, e.g.
81. Spouses of yore
84. Arctic explorer John ___
86. Babylonian war god
87. Coquettish
88. Meadow mower

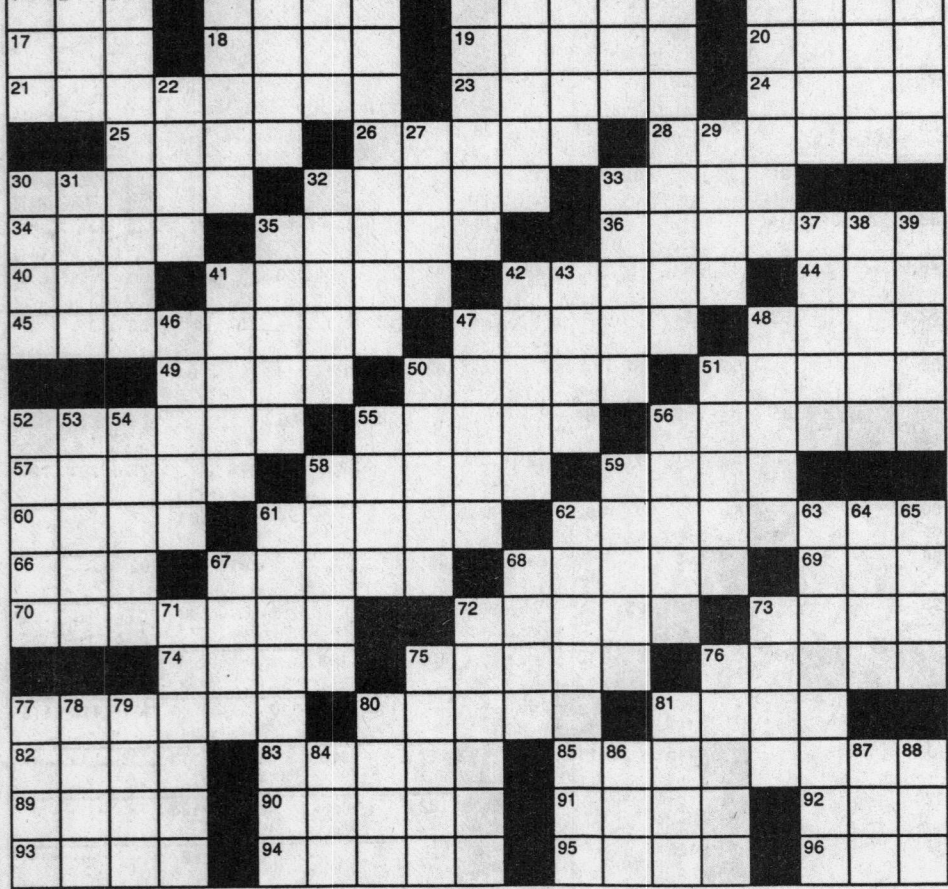

194

ACROSS

1. Trail mix
5. Poisonous snakes
9. Implied
14. Stir-fry need
17. "Waiting for the Robert ____"
18. Sound of thunder
19. Individually
20. Scurry
21. Berlin hit, with "I"
24. Road haven
25. "____! perchance to dream:"
26. ____ Speedwagon
27. Used a rocker
28. Ref's decision
29. Begleys
30. Palindromic credo
32. Hawaii state bird
34. Houston player
37. Sleeveless garment
38. Pulls back
42. Ebenezer's words
43. Time gone by
44. Used to be
45. Road sign word
46. Previous to, to a poet
47. Disarray
48. Grocery greens
50. Debtor's ink
51. One in the know
53. Scads
54. Ballet movements
56. Tabriz's locale
57. Throws a fit
58. Covers
59. Zipped
61. Gives way
62. Inspirations
65. Canadian prov.
66. Brought out
68. Bean or noodle
69. ____ tai
70. Flabbergast
72. Allen and Levin
73. Mobsters' pieces
74. Summon aloud
75. Everglades craft
77. Nimbus
78. Dogie catcher
79. James ____ Carter
80. Indian tribal symbol
82. Palindromic child
83. "Whether ____ nobler . . ."
85. Saint of Ireland
87. Bandleader Brown
88. Gulf area
92. Hooray!
93. Berlin hit
96. "Long ____ in Alcala"
97. Kind of ink
98. Ameliorate
99. Waxed cheese
100. Do a lawn job
101. Fits one upon another
102. Bed down
103. Titled lady

DOWN

1. Chap
2. Bread topper
3. Guns, as an engine
4. Potato skinners
5. Dull pains
6. Hit openhanded
7. Tablet
8. Most lean
9. Sierra Nevada lake
10. In the manner of
11. Hoodwinks
12. Recited
13. Wobble
14. Berlin hit
15. Pig talk
16. Casino game
22. Accomplish again
23. 1/100 of a dollar
30. D'Urberville lass
31. Tire grooves
33. Styron's Turner
34. Fortas and Ribicoff
35. Actress Gilbert
36. Berlin hit, with "At"
37. Immense
39. Commits a faux pas
40. Acorn's adulthood
41. Foam
43. Robert ____ Warren
44. "____ up, Doc?"
47. Union general
48. With a pointed shape
49. Haste
52. Choler
53. Puts on cargo
55. Actress Massari
57. Fashioned anew
58. Angelico and Filippo Lippi
59. Dickens character Dartle
60. Not pro
61. Sportscaster Gowdy
62. Key letter
63. Roach and March
64. Sail single-handed
67. Telephone noise
68. Injure
71. Roundball gp.
73. Conjectured
74. Provided lunch
76. "____ of Species"
77. To ____ (exactly)
78. Ore find
81. Wide-mouthed jars
82. Officiates at a swim meet
83. Mine wagon
84. Shakespearean villain
86. Totals
88. Blob
89. Radames's love
90. Con game
91. Broken to the saddle
94. Drill attachment
95. ____ Paolo

PUZZLE 244

• SING WITH IRVING •

195

PUZZLE 245

ACROSS

1. Macadamize
5. Warsaw native
9. Fisherman's hook
13. Cylinder
17. Oriental sashes
18. Yemen's seaport
19. Vex
20. Singer Fitzgerald
21. Search
22. Latest word
23. Arab chieftain
24. Son of Seth
25. Swirled around
27. Music for two
29. Ape
31. Woman's title
33. Iran's neighbor
35. Sooner than, in poems
36. "___ Barbara"
39. Poet St. Vincent Millay
41. Current
46. Companions of ids
47. Rocky projection
48. Bridge expert
49. Daybook
50. Diving bird
51. Deposited
52. Wielded
53. Actor Carvey
54. Most profound
56. Grimy
57. Flinched
58. Have a snack
59. Restrains
60. Halloween greeting
61. Kent or Gable
64. Director Edwards
65. Tractor attachment
69. Deficiency
70. Meat juices
71. Tree of India
72. Logger's tool
73. Singleton
74. Adult goslings
75. Sword's grip
76. Celebration
77. Meal closers
79. Unfailing
80. Minty cocktail
81. Vientiane native
82. Thine
84. Train track
86. Stalactite sites
90. Takes a spouse
92. Show hosts
96. Took advantage of
97. Sacred figure
99. Licks
101. ___ and hearty
102. Warble
103. Lawn pest
104. Reverberation
105. Sinister
106. Liver spread
107. Was in the red
108. Pass over
109. Easter stamp

DOWN

1. Sit for a picture
2. Still snoozing
3. Fought
4. Arctic natives
5. Black and white "bear"
6. "___ to Joy"
7. Indecent
8. Following
9. Actress Garbo
10. Shoot (for)
11. Gymnast's feat
12. Searched about
13. Was rife
14. Arm bone
15. Smudge
16. Relaxation
26. Jug handle
28. Baseball stat
30. Wrought ___
32. Deserve
34. Game like horseshoes
36. Honey wine
37. Malarial fever
38. Gag
40. Mom's mate
42. Quarry
43. Jai ___
44. Musical pitch
45. Good heavens!
47. Play's personnel
48. Sphere
51. Security problem
52. Cartoon pig
53. Arabian ship
55. Cheer
56. Debonair
57. Steep
59. Elegant
60. Spoiled child
61. Lump of dirt
62. Rural road
63. Flying pros
64. Author Harte
65. Postpone
66. Ancient deity
67. Wheel rod
68. Glean
70. Apache chief
71. Feather adhesive
74. Equipment
75. Runner's barriers
76. Ravines
78. Heavy hammer
79. Pamela ___ Martin
80. Actor Belushi
83. Had title to
85. Fable man
86. Pointed end
87. Largest continent
88. Air opening
89. Barge, e.g.
91. Large bag
93. Roof overhang
94. Kazan of films
95. Peddle
98. Corrida cry
100. ___ Beta Kappa

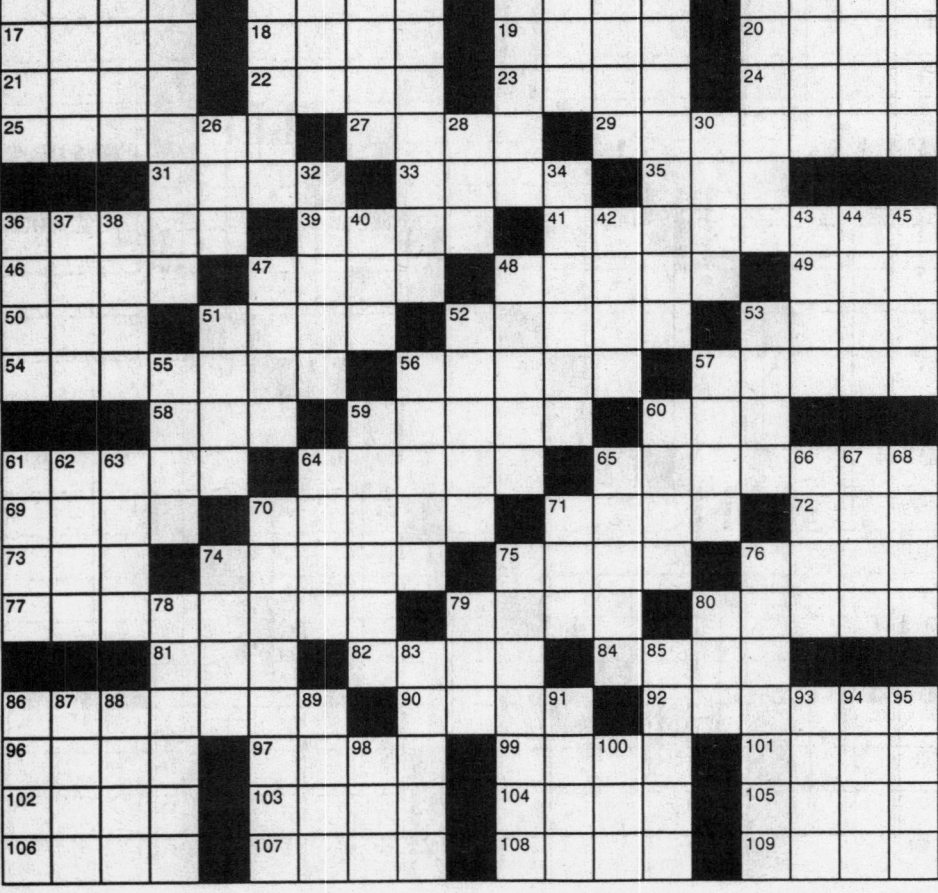

ACROSS

1. Ego
5. Speed-ratio unit
9. Commotion
15. Divider
19. General Bradley
20. Singer Brickell
21. Come forth
22. Away from the wind
23. Capital of Peru
24. Much
25. Emergency water source
27. Hothouse
29. Delay
30. Mine entrances
31. Painter Paul ____
32. Director Lee
33. Feign
35. Stone pillar
38. Abrasions
39. Fits in
42. Conductor Maazel
43. Hamelin musician
44. Alaskan language
45. Cry of triumph
47. Algerian port
48. Israeli Dayan
49. Station-house dog
51. Fast plane: abbr.
52. Island veranda
53. Egyptians, for example
55. Pursuit
56. Pumper's companion truck
59. Emergencies
61. Old World ruminants
62. One billion years
63. Pouting grimace
64. Confront boldly
67. Unburnable clothing
73. Itinerary
74. Eagle's nest
76. Scots
77. Contemporary
78. Lifesaving device
81. Medieval tales
82. High point
83. Poet's before
84. Goes to sea
85. Tilts
86. Hang loosely
87. Climbs
89. Meat pie
90. Plus
91. Bering Sea island
92. Routes
93. London district
95. Second president
98. Plateaus
99. Tedium
103. Smoke-eater's footgear
106. Humerus, e.g.
107. ____ of Man
108. Not in use
109. Wasp
110. Part of AD
111. Mast
112. Forest animal
113. Black Sea port
114. "Radio ____"
115. Sort

DOWN

1. On one's own
2. Kuwaiti leader
3. Tibetan monk
4. Volunteer brigade founder
5. Ruckus
6. Worship
7. Metropolis
8. "____ So Shy"
9. Weightier
10. Eskimo boats
11. "Mr. Television"
12. Songwriter Jacques ____
13. Exclamation of disgust
14. Ottoman governor
15. Guardian
16. Asian mountain range
17. Mardi Gras's follower
18. "____ Stay Together"
26. Plains Indian
28. Narrow valley
29. Binge
32. Actress Loren
33. Senses
34. Grad
35. Spill over
36. Trunk
37. Muse of lyric poetry
38. Rope fiber
39. Yak
40. ____ Julius Caesar
41. Classic Western
43. Swimming holes
44. Jewish month
46. Colony insects
48. Painter Edouard ____
50. South Vietnamese leader
52. Thailand's neighbor
53. Sun-dried brick
54. Philosopher Descartes
57. Danish currency
58. Lucy's costar
59. Prices
60. Actor Tamblyn
63. Casts off
64. Cathedral part
65. Actress Bow
66. Lunchrooms
67. Skills
68. Fragrances
69. Cranky
70. Ancient Peruvians
71. Arizona university site
72. Bonbon
74. Singer O'Day
75. Elongated fish
79. African fly
80. Tug
81. Argon and neon
82. Blaze starter
85. Rummy variety
86. Author Roald ____
88. Arch slightly
89. Adhesives
92. Redbone and Spinks
93. Fair
94. Butter substitutes
95. Like a desert
96. Tenderfoot
97. Qualified
98. Further
99. Spanish noblewoman
100. See at a distance
101. Critical remark
102. Dried up
104. Greek letter
105. Physique, for short
106. Unfavorable

PUZZLE 247

• SPORTING BIRDS •

ACROSS

1. Wood strip
5. Truth
9. Piano practice
14. Seasoning
18. Epithet for Athena
19. Off yonder
20. Swashbuckler Flynn
21. Characteristic
23. Motor City birds
26. French river
27. Planter
28. Piece (out)
29. City in southeast Serbia
30. Traveled
31. Bitterly amusing
32. Stuffing herb
34. Old French coins
35. "I Married ___"
38. Elf
41. Smallest
44. Mimics
46. Singer Bailey
47. Conceals
48. Dawn goddess
50. Fracas
51. Puzzled
52. Shoshonean
53. Tale
55. Sooner than, poetically
56. Concur
58. Cozy homes
60. Mr. Kravitz (neighbor on "Bewitched")
61. Positioned
62. Toddler
63. Youngster
64. Tramples
65. Meat order
67. Fanny ___
68. Prepared
70. Grave risks
73. Ingenuous
75. 61
76. Emulate Hammer
79. Cream of the crop
80. Shinbone
81. ___ in the neck (bothersome person)
83. Depression-era agency initials
84. Sibilant sounds
85. Roe
86. K to Q connection
88. Earth holder
90. Pizza ___
91. Colorado's ___ Park
93. Mentions
94. Ogles
95. Manors
97. Ester of any acid with boron
98. Mrs. Kennedy
99. Throat-clearer
100. Type of skirt
101. Swiss river
103. Singer Baker et al.
106. O'Brien or Sajak
107. Museum display
110. Coronets
114. Reestablish
115. Maryland bird
118. Salesperson
119. Aquatic mammal
120. Cash register
121. "High ___"
122. Minus
123. Chicago airport
124. Iridescent gem
125. Let it stand

DOWN

1. Young boys
2. Out of the weather
3. Place for a beret
4. Kind of store
5. Godmother or tale
6. Astern
7. Concern
8. Arduous journey
9. Baste
10. Wince
11. TV attorney Becker
12. Lumberjacks' concerns
13. Chicago trains
14. Missouri bird
15. Stimulate
16. Lion's place
17. Grow weary
22. Danson or Koppel
24. "___ the ramparts . . ."
25. Crave
30. Muscle condition
33. Georgia bird
34. Teams
35. Feminine titles
36. Met offering
37. Rent again
38. Ancient Greek city
39. Singer Seeger
40. Demolish
41. Giggle
42. Medicinal plant
43. Backpacked
45. Washington birds
47. Rind
49. Indian weight units
54. Comply
57. Departs
59. Needle hole
64. Move down the runway
65. Location
66. Forks' companions
67. 1002
69. Slip by
70. Quick look
71. Famous dairy cow
72. "The Sun Also ___"
74. Desert robes
76. Birling contest
77. Armadillos
78. Outmoded
80. Indian tribal symbol
81. Rectangular pilaster
82. Bard
87. Sister of Moses
89. Land tracts
92. Fr. canonized women
96. Tubers
97. Acrid
100. Valletta's country
101. Coral island
102. Cushion or pocket
103. Rainbow
104. Actress Carter
105. Arrow poison
106. Walkway
108. Printing process
109. Stumble
111. Plant part
112. African lily
113. Transmitted
115. Sound of derision
116. Choler
117. Guido's high note

198

PUZZLE 248

• GBS PLAYS •

ACROSS

1. Down source
6. Cleopatra's snake
9. Time's dir.
12. GBS play
14. Attractiveness
17. Bridge maven Omar
20. Giant star
21. Collection of Hindu legends
22. Charge with gas
23. Salinger's grain
24. Sniggler's prey
26. Bible book
27. Ask
28. GBS play, with "The"
34. Arrest
35. Comic Phillips
36. Greek letter
37. GBS play
43. "The ____ Quartet"
44. RBI, e.g.
48. Omani, e.g.
49. Diamond Head garland
50. Indolent
52. Actor Lee J.
53. "El ____"
55. Beverages
58. Aviator
59. Xiamen
60. Ms. Sumac
61. Time to do
63. Merlin's name for Arthur
64. In the style of
66. Beefwood
67. Hawaiian legend
70. Oft potted flower
75. Painter Jean
77. Ages and ages
78. Like some wreaths
81. Corrida animals
83. Road sign
84. Sorry mounts
85. Capture back
86. Convened
87. Popular ballad
89. Eager
90. Tidbit for Dobbin
93. Don't upset ____
96. Barker's line
98. Before, to Browning
99. Conglomerate inits.
100. GBS play
109. Like Papa Bear's porridge
110. Bacchanal cry
111. Upward: prefix
112. Mountain: prefix
113. Not alfresco
114. Ligament
116. Certain Amerinds
120. Earth pigment
121. Debtor's writ
122. Fate
123. Cedar Rapids college
124. Fr. seasoning
125. Glacial ice

DOWN

1. Ingress
2. Crete mount
3. Pakistan town
4. Dutch commune
5. Incised
6. Hawaiian cup
7. Herring
8. Atlanta bowl
9. Do Thanksgiving work
10. Asian snake
11. Skater Katarina and kin
12. Jokester
13. Author Seton
14. Cool
15. Fed the kitty
16. Actress Louise
17. GBS play
18. Hair dye
19. Charge
25. Looker
29. Like some knees
30. Maldives coin
31. Religious jurisdiction
32. Paddock young
33. Palm leaf
37. Brightly hued parrot
38. Fragrance
39. Ruffled bib
40. "____ House"
41. Vintage cars
42. Assistant
44. Regal title
45. Actor Hanks
46. Bible king
47. Decade
51. Muscle spasm
54. Town in Vietnam
56. Pismire
57. Gk. porticoes
62. Hat feature
65. I love, to Catullus
67. Arboreal marsupial
68. Indignation
69. Good quality
70. Rocky height
71. Tibetan ox
72. "Caesar and ____"
73. Formerly
74. Actor Beery
76. Part of a Fr. hoist
77. Legislates
78. Brother's title
79. Gam
80. Ear: prefix
82. Expensive
88. Soaks
91. Aura
92. Slender and smooth
94. Notorious
95. Laborer
96. Faint
97. Carpenter's tool
100. Like some polynomials
101. Cowboy entertainment
102. Beamed
103. Canonical hour
104. Coarse grass
105. Nutriments
106. Type of acid
107. Algeria port
108. Intrusive
109. "____ the season . . ."
115. Black gold
117. Born a she
118. Blood test inits.
119. Give ____ go

Note to Solvers: This Crossword does not have hints such as "2 wds." and "hyph."

PUZZLE 249

• OUT AND ABOUT •

ACROSS
1. Chow
5. Roughen
9. Cold cuts store
13. Quip
17. Capture
18. Hitch
19. Light measure
20. Voice range
21. "The ___ in Red"
22. Medicinal shrub
23. Computer symbols
24. Resorts to
25. Stroll
26. Alley denizens
28. Nibbles
29. Sportscaster Allen
30. Bother
32. Apartment
33. Perched
34. Unemotionally
36. Wheelbarrows
37. Basins
41. Franklin bill
42. Smallest of the litter
43. Bits of paper
44. Emblems

45. Sassy
46. Shred
48. Wedding party member
49. Bronte character
50. Watch chains
51. Singer Eartha ___
52. Dynamite initials
53. Hearth's fuel source
55. Chromosome spot
56. In good shape
57. Check
60. "___ Your Move"
61. Kitchen appliance
64. Baseball stat
65. Behold
66. Author Buntline
67. Spouse
68. Valiant
70. Tablet
71. Short race
72. Tarts
73. Flightless birds
74. Sea jewel
77. Ages
78. Alack!
79. Cheerful

80. Comment upon
82. Verve
83. Russian distance measure
84. Claret, e.g.
85. Brindisi's location
87. Extravagant meal
88. Tract of land
89. Sleeping sound
90. Hurried
91. Psychic ability
94. Undercover cops
97. Flirt's attribute
99. Spud state
101. Muslim leader
102. Mountain call
103. Unlocked
104. Dubs
105. Equal
106. Gather
107. Tear
108. Immense
109. The Seven ___
110. Bother
111. Favorable votes
112. Feudal farmer

DOWN
1. Garden figure
2. Laura Dern film
3. River to the Caspian
4. Charity events
5. Elegant
6. Stops

7. Hebrew lyre
8. Game bird
9. Tickets
10. Express feeling
11. Camera part
12. Influential people
13. Most sporty
14. Actress Lanchester
15. Brood
16. Fling
17. Dog-paddled
19. Legitimate
27. Mongolian dwelling
28. Simon's partner
31. Caucho
33. Japanese title of respect
35. Murmured
36. Mongrel dogs
37. Swab the deck
38. Utmost
39. Had lunch
40. Geraint, for one
41. Prairie predator
42. Renaissance fiddle
43. Hour, in Chicago
44. Track's Carl ___
45. Steered a raft
46. Recoil
47. Roman road
50. Put away in order
51. One of Mick's fellow Stones
52. Forum garments
54. Fines
55. Turf
56. Feeds the pot
57. Freight vessel
58. Unexpected
59. Itsy-___
62. Federal agent
63. Oriental
69. Puts on
70. Police vehicles
71. Fawn's mother
72. Frolic
74. Standard
75. Hydrocarbon suffix
76. Connecting word
77. Summer, in Nice
78. Fable
79. Captions
81. Miscellany
82. Attain
83. Flying formation
85. Devote
86. Works hard
87. Demons
89. Soft drinks
90. African scavenger
92. Bundle
93. Job
94. Siestas
95. "A Death in the Family" author
96. Bird like an ostrich
97. Italian city
98. Fencer's weapon
100. Take a risk
102. Jabber

200

ACROSS

1. Ardor
8. Magic healer
14. Table protectors
18. Goddess of fertility
19. Heat unit
21. Pains' mates
23. Jack Carson film
25. Lobster claw
26. Ms. Hayes
27. Stranger
28. Token of challenge
30. Set
31. Vega and Deneb
32. Fish glands
33. Croc's kin
34. Eight: prefix
35. St.-John ____
36. Red-eyed ____
37. Heaps
38. Mr. Landon
41. Disposition
42. Ms. Turner
43. Gest
45. Angelic one
49. Enhanced
52. Wandering ones
53. 100-santimi pieces
54. Dundee hill
55. Author Fleming
56. Certain fruits
57. Cummerbund
58. Whip
59. Henri's mother
60. Cricket sides
61. "____ Old
    Summertime"
63. Tarzan's son
64. Selves
66. Poet Thomas
67. Toff
68. Certain salamis
71. Showed the way
72. Dowel
73. Shape
74. Otoconia
75. Bring up
77. Abundant
79. Okla. city
80. Actor Bond
81. Author James
82. Guy's mate
83. Superlative
85. Blaze suddenly
87. Heavy works
89. ____ Cruces
90. Frustrates
91. N.Y. college and
    Hebrides isle
92. Aspen incline
97. ____ longa, vita brevis
98. "O, my Luve's like
    ____ . . ."
99. Late minister's
    executors' stipend:
    Scot.
100. Muslim magistrates
101. Tangle
103. Song at evening's end
107. Part of the writing on
     the wall
108. Learned
109. Atom's combining
     capacity
110. Society tyros
111. Kind of fir
112. Accumulated

DOWN

1. Routes
2. Platter, in Inverness
3. Monument
4. More wise
5. Chains
6. Siouan Indian
7. Mr. Sparks
8. Rows
9. Descendent of
   Noah's son
10. "A Lesson from
    ____" (Fugard)
11. Poetic time
12. Branch
13. Marilyn Monroe film
14. Staff bearer
15. Alas, in Ulm
16. "Only ____" (Billy
    Joel)
17. Choose
20. Growing out
22. Seasons
24. Coiffure
29. Greeting
32. Catty remarks
33. Juniper liquors
35. Surgeon Percival
    and kin
36. Contends
37. Actor Marvin
38. Time mimic
39. Knowledge
40. Well I'll be!
41. Talking birds
42. In the black
44. Dutch commune
46. Condemns
47. Dark gray
48. Beanery fare
49. City in Romania
50. Gob
51. As ____ (united)
54. Stain
57. Hangup
58. Peter, Henry, or Jane
59. Henri's world
61. Qom's land
62. Anglo-Saxon tax
63. TV's Milton
64. Shade tree
65. Command to Dobbin
66. ____ what ails you
68. Stares wide-eyed
69. "The Thin Man" dog
70. Pillar: prefix
72. 102, to Cato
73. Additional
74. Rims
76. Powerful inits.
77. Needlefish
78. Broadway Joe
80. Kind of salad
83. Dynamite time
84. Worked for
86. Faithful
87. Explosive
88. Ancient catapult
90. Cataracts
91. Ireland's ____ Fail
92. Milan's La ____
93. Takes on cargo
94. Aesir rulers
95. Segment
96. Roman chariot
99. Egyptian skink
102. Johnny ____
104. Your and my
105. Powerful inits.
106. ____ out (flee)

PUZZLE 250

• NOT BAD •

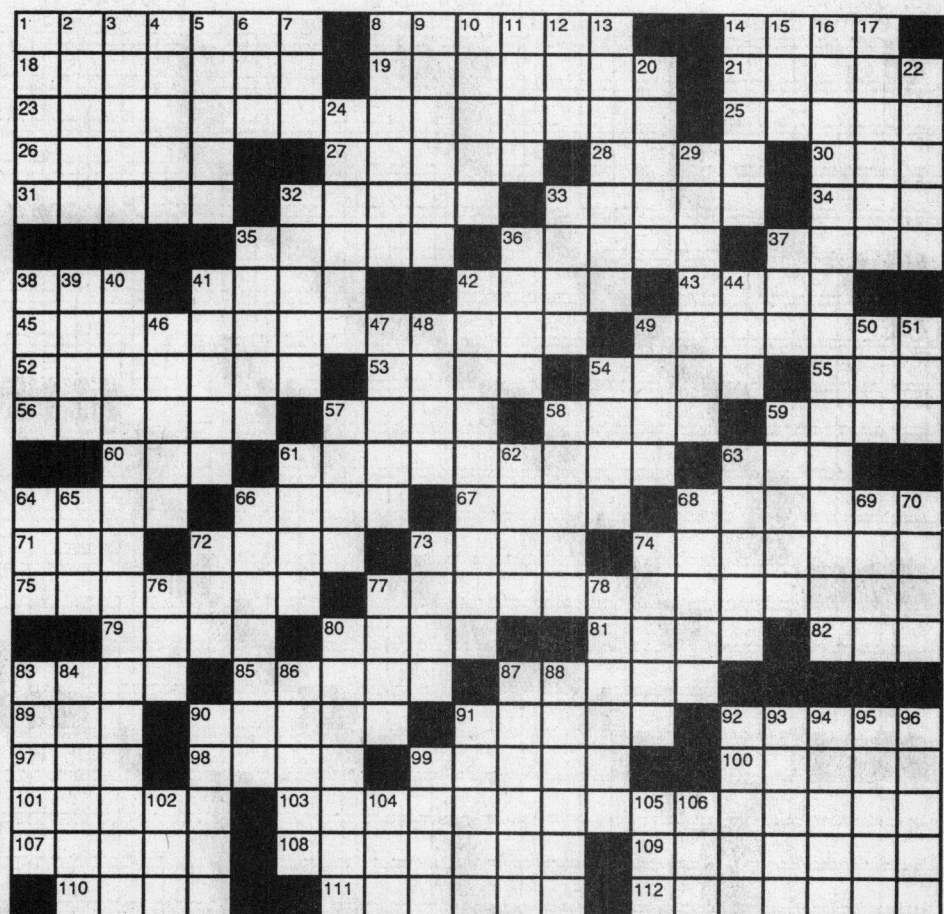

Note to Solvers: This Crossword does not have hints such as "2 wds." and "hyph."

201

PUZZLE 251

ACROSS

1. Flexes
6. Cheshire Cat's expression
10. Crow
14. Rope fiber
18. Vidalia, e.g.
19. Helen of Troy's mother
20. Fry
21. Composer Stravinsky
22. Playwright Edward ____
23. Polish river
24. Minnesota village
25. Roy's partner
26. Native Israeli
27. Just barely
29. Swirl
30. Sesame
31. Painter Paul ____
33. Compels
34. "The ____ Divorcee"
36. Revises
38. Middle part
39. Accidents
43. Bellowed
45. Writer Heinrich ____
46. Handel work
47. Statesman Sadat
48. Stitches
49. Kaboodles' partners
51. Weaver film
52. Festoon
53. Goes down a slope
54. Electrical unit
55. For shame!
56. Remunerates
57. Violin part
58. Take on
59. Rattle
60. Array
63. Stat for Ryan
64. Very reticent
67. As being
68. Pesticide initials
69. Coffee server
70. Urge on
71. Morse code signal
72. Osso ____
73. Japanese monetary unit
74. American naturalist
75. Mythical birds
76. Site of Samson's victory
77. Feather
80. Sheet of matted cotton
81. Bog
82. Flies
83. Abandoned
85. Roses' fruits
86. Croquet hoop
87. Put down
88. View
90. Cheerful
91. Soap ingredient
92. Wild hogs
93. Tumult
94. Hour in St. Louis
97. Tibetan priest
100. Pregame picnickers
103. Ma's instrument
105. Seaweed
106. Comedian Kovacs
107. Whiskeys
108. Baseball shoe
109. Tawny cat
110. Bulrushes
111. Gaelic
112. Giraffe's kin
113. Marsh matter
114. Brashness
115. Minus
116. Perceive

DOWN

1. Speak vainly
2. Premier Zhou ____
3. Diminish slowly
4. Mover and shaker
5. More sly
6. Balls
7. Change color again
8. Brainstorm
9. Tusked whales
10. Hound variety
11. Zwiebacks
12. To ____ (perfectly)
13. Athens's state
14. Concealed nook
15. Yikes!
16. Sculpt
17. Quarry
20. Loams
28. Praise
32. British Inc.
35. "Top Hat" star
37. Hauls
38. Stuns
39. Sra., in English
40. Jackie's second
41. Pastry dish
42. "____ of Flubber"
43. Spoke hoarsely
44. Ahead
45. Tan color
46. Giant Hall of Famer
48. String
49. Purity measure
50. Element
53. Reject
54. More prudent
55. Observes Lent
58. Routine
59. Fruit product
60. Spotless
61. 32-card game
62. Lao-tzu follower
64. Oddly
65. Tight
66. Smells
72. Prevent
73. Be suspicious
74. Cross
75. Mellow
77. Comedic composer Bach
78. Romanian coin
79. Spend
80. Garden plot
81. Medieval singer
82. Hot winds
84. Wobbles
85. Wife of Zeus
86. Joined
88. Three-dimensional objects
89. Pens
90. Search parties
92. Twining plant stems
93. Lock
95. Hits
96. Comic Fields
97. Finland native
98. Fever and chills
99. Papa's mate
101. Locality
102. Fictional governess
104. Actress Sommer

ACROSS
1. Bride
5. Beret
8. Male cat
11. Run in neutral
12. Lyric poem
13. Wait
14. Scorch
15. Fish snare
16. Commotions
17. Terraces
19. European vipers
21. Sooner than, poetically
22. Fireplace item
23. Messy dwelling
26. Terminate
28. Canadian flyers
32. Work on the garden
33. Personal quirk
35. Merry
36. Bread ingredient
39. Lobster _____
41. Part of IOU
42. Purpose
44. Disfigure
46. Canyon
49. Prim and _____
53. Downwind
54. British beverage
56. Folk knowledge
57. Heavy weights
58. Chicken
59. Pork cut
60. Matched group
61. Foxy
62. Winter vehicle

DOWN
1. Lock of hair
2. Concept
3. Car trouble
4. Mysterious
5. Approval
6. Lemon beverage
7. Flower leaf
8. Ocean movement
9. Fragrance
10. Disorder
13. "The Red _____ of Courage"
18. Norwegian coin
20. Man's best friend
23. Bashful
24. Tip of Italy
25. Affirmative vote
27. Ice-cream scoop
29. Id's kin
30. Adage
31. Aesthetic sense
34. Part of a battalion
37. Comedian Soupy _____
38. _____ the knot
40. Sailor
43. Fables
45. _____ Royce
46. Industrial cauldrons
47. African lily
48. Period after Mardi Gras
50. Common fund
51. New York canal
52. Tear to bits
55. Sniggler's quarry

PUZZLE 253

ACROSS
1. Keen
6. Tennis unit
9. Actor Holbrook
12. Drying cloth
13. Guacamole ingredient
15. "____ of Two Cities"
16. Women
17. Neighbor of Belgium: abbr.
18. At a distance
20. Nothing
21. Thin
23. Baby's dinner attire
25. Bizarre
27. Dancer Tommy ____
28. Toronto's locale
31. Subsided
33. Stink
34. Lawful
36. Filbert, e.g.
37. Flaws
41. Top
43. Ride the waves
44. Chapeau
45. "South ____"
47. Rental agreement
49. List
50. Creme de la creme
51. "Cheers" actor Danson
52. Crossed out
53. Greasy spoon

DOWN
1. Male deer
2. "Grand ____"
3. Cognizant
4. Family mem.
5. Implored
6. African expedition
7. Always
8. Actor Berenger
9. Food fish
10. "Sweet ____"
11. ____ Alamos
14. Tin
19. Wild
22. Close by
24. Flower plot
26. Anxious
27. Narrative
28. Pro's opposite
29. Praise excessively
30. Observed
32. Puzzled
35. Evoked
38. Network
39. Sample
40. Guide
42. ____ sum
43. Dimensions
45. Peach seed
46. Repair
48. Actor Wallach

PUZZLE 254

ACROSS

1. Asterisk
5. Ewe's mate
8. Not us
12. Actor Alan ___, Jr. ("Gilligan's Island" skipper)
13. Yale nickname
14. Uncommon
15. Yaks
16. Fish appendage
17. Genesis garden
18. Allot
21. Wed
22. Leather worker's tool
25. Courteous
29. Withstand
31. Scent
32. Scope
33. Mend
36. Order
38. Curvy letter
39. Wooden moth repellant
41. Adornment
46. Fail-safe
49. Squid's camouflage
50. Domicile
51. Orient
52. "The Raven" writer
53. Impresses greatly
54. Store sign
55. Goof
56. Crave

DOWN

1. Not barefoot
2. Hack
3. Tavern stock
4. Rift
5. Clarify
6. Proof of absence
7. Minuscule
8. House or frog
9. Possessed
10. Sooner than, in poems
11. "Three ___ and a Baby"
19. Groove
20. Half a score
22. Atmosphere
23. Architect Christopher ___
24. Evidence
25. Study hard
26. Poetic works
27. Cuts off
28. Author Levin
30. Water barrier
34. Diamonds
35. Cook's formula
36. Gloomier
37. Age
40. Patron
41. Actor Harry ___ Stanton
42. Dissolve
43. Des Moines's state
44. Peck film, with "The"
45. "Empty ___" (TV sitcom)
46. Japanese term of respect
47. Function
48. ___ Grande

PUZZLE 255

ACROSS
1. Dude
5. Catered to
8. Capture
12. "Annie ___"
13. Mine product
14. Unusual
15. Zone
16. Type of doll
17. Performs
18. "___ 911" (TV series)
20. NASA vehicle
22. Double curve
23. Palindromic female
24. ___ hound (hunting dog)
27. Make esteemed
31. Gaze
32. Have unpaid bills
33. Kitchen whistler
37. Mended socks
40. Bemoan
41. Eden-dweller
42. Elf
45. Knocked lightly
49. Reimbursed
50. A Stooge
52. Cleveland's lake
53. Pot builder
54. Printers' measures
55. Traditional knowledge
56. Casual shirts
57. Period
58. Sprinted

DOWN
1. Singe
2. Jack rabbit
3. Tavern drinks
4. Sets
5. Sherwood ___
6. Distinctive period
7. Graduate's reward
8. Copied
9. ___ and pinion
10. Comedian Johnson
11. Irksome one
19. Consume
21. Possess
24. Gamble
25. Sailor's affirmative
26. Yellow or Black
28. Long time period
29. Dread
30. A primary color
34. Groups of lions
35. Umpire's call
36. Abounded
37. Abhor
38. Actress Gardner
39. Disgusts
42. Petty quarrel
43. Window unit
44. Liturgy
46. Stage item
47. Republic of Ireland, once
48. Achievement
51. Singer Yoko ___

PUZZLE 256

ACROSS

1. Flower stalk
5. Peddle
9. Snoop
12. Molten rock
13. Actor Alda
14. Feel sorry about
15. Beasts of burden
16. Neighbor
18. Pittsburgh player
20. Knock
21. Monopoly and Ping-Pong
24. Prepare potatoes, perhaps
27. Garden tools
30. Have a taco
32. Fish eggs
33. Polar abundance
34. Late
36. Mess up
37. Short-sleeved shirt
38. Yale grad
39. Glue
41. Serpents
43. Crowbar
45. Underwater boat, for short
47. Sneak away
51. Red suit
55. Parched
56. Annoy
57. Support
58. Feat
59. Daisy ____
60. Members of the flock
61. Simple

DOWN

1. Pig's dinner
2. Cab
3. Always
4. Cope
5. Sultan's wives
6. Beer's kin
7. "I ____ a Teen-age Werewolf"
8. Purl's opposite
9. Fixes
10. Skedaddle
11. Still
17. Block
19. Sample
22. Ghostly
23. Down in the dumps
25. Kind
26. Present
27. Actress Hayworth
28. High cards
29. Remembrance
31. Uses a keyboard
35. The whole shebang
40. Gallery
42. Total
44. Waistcoats
46. Drill
48. District
49. Tarts
50. Singer Arnold
51. Faint
52. Retirement plan: abbr.
53. At this moment
54. Forest creature

207

PUZZLE 257

ACROSS
1. Pout
5. Acorn producer
8. Book leaf
12. Japan's location
13. Brooch
14. Actress Meara
15. Nasty look
16. Kind of rug
18. Prose works
20. Peep
21. Throw
23. Building addition
24. Slugger's goal
27. Soft drink
30. Supposed sky sight
31. Poet Dickinson
34. Pea holder
35. Engrave
37. Taps
39. Corn holder
41. Packed
42. Caesar's language
44. Boxer Foreman
48. Flowering shrub
50. Aquatic mammal
51. Malicious
52. Female rabbit
53. Chows down
54. Lairs
55. Conclusion
56. Orchard component

DOWN
1. Bargain
2. Utilizes
3. Reclines
4. Self-defense method
5. Animal with a pouch
6. Ventilate
7. Weave together
8. Juries
9. Pronghorn
10. Tiny insect
11. Moray
17. Flock member
19. Long ago
22. Smell
24. Tint
25. Frequently
26. Soft leather shoe
28. Speck
29. TV commercials
32. Chuckled
33. Christmas
36. Inns
38. Storage place
40. Apron front
42. Adore
43. Bare
45. "____ Window"
46. Turnstile
47. Otherwise
48. Crimson or cerise
49. Male descendant

ACROSS

1. Witticism
4. Chicken ____ king
7. Gear
10. Singleton
11. Large truck
12. Purpose
13. Vague
14. High flyer
15. Sensed
16. Ranges
18. Mexican coins
19. Facial fringe
22. Wagons
25. Humble
26. Place
29. Horatian specialties
30. Shoe tip
31. Medicinal portion
32. Drift off
33. Succeeded
34. Octet
35. Certain geese
37. Seethes
40. Bends
44. Piece of news
45. Boxers, e.g.
47. Pay dirt
48. Popeye, e.g.
49. Plumbing joint
50. Rickey or rummy
51. Her, subjectively
52. Tiny
53. Hardened

DOWN

1. Seed vessels
2. Component
3. Verne captain
4. Stand up
5. Illuminated
6. The ____ of Aquarius
7. Billiard sticks
8. Norway's capital
9. Fetches
14. Locks' companions
15. "A ____ Good Men"
17. Animal drs.
18. Whack!
20. Towhead
21. Caviar
22. Against
23. Commotion
24. Comedian Buttons
26. Journal
27. Pale gray
28. Nevertheless
30. Heavy weight
31. Type of jockey
33. Had being
34. Bungles
35. Ruby, e.g.
36. Bird of prey
37. Tantrums
38. Beehive State
39. Nothing more than
41. Gluttons
42. Cleveland's lake
43. Shipped
45. Condensation
46. Bullfight cheer

PUZZLE 259

• OLDIES BUT GOODIES •

ACROSS

1. Genesis man
5. Vega or Deneb
9. Indian garb
10. Solo for Sills
11. Metal-worker
14. Gumbo ingredient
15. Viper
16. Embrace
19. ___ Altos
22. Ms. MacGraw
23. Forty winks
25. Song from "A Chorus Line"
28. Application
29. Nest egg letters
30. Soaps
32. "My Life as a ___"
33. Perched
34. Book leaves
36. Bleater
37. Honk
39. Portable light
42. Toward shelter
45. Capitol feature
46. Certain pendants
49. Picnic pest
52. Big wheel
53. Fool's mo.
54. Yak
55. Girdles
57. Lode
59. Sycamore, e.g.
60. Etiquette
63. Thunder-struck
66. Luau treat
68. English horns
70. Annex
72. Still
74. Umbrella
77. Baby food
78. Set
79. Hebrew priest
80. ___ deco
81. "___ Blue"
82. Historic age
83. Be in the red
84. Singer Torme
86. Spirit
87. Paving piece
91. Toast topper
92. Florence's river
93. Sea swallow
94. Sheepskin leather

DOWN

1. ___ de corps
2. Wine valley
3. Iron source
4. Knight
5. Snead and Shepard
6. Camera stand
7. River islet
8. Stadium cry
11. Heating apparatus
12. Neighbor of Kan.
13. Weakens
16. Bamboozler
17. "Born in the ___"
18. Procure
19. Edge
20. Verbal
21. Epic
23. Modern
24. "People ___ Funny"
26. Negative
27. Kind of trip
31. Egg source
35. Purpose
38. Acorn producer
40. Radiate
41. Corded fabrics
43. Greek H
44. Clairvoy-ance initials
46. Fluid rock
47. Earnest
48. Garment shaper
49. Drama part

210

50. Neither
51. Foot lever
56. Do embroidery
58. Bird's bill
60. Ms. Farrow
61. Lasso
62. Singe
64. Needle feature
65. Neighbor of N.J.
66. Standard
67. Table scrap
69. Resort
70. Past
71. Dawn drops
73. Wood
74. Bore
75. Watering hole
76. Muscat's country
85. Black, poetically
86. Sicilian mount
87. Bed
88. Cry for the matador
89. Pitcher handle
90. Theater sign

PUZZLE 259

PUZZLE 260

ACROSS

1. Exclamation of triumph
4. Broadway hit
8. Gab
12. Twilled fabric
13. Aweather's opposite
14. Jacob's son
15. Strong anger
16. Cruel
17. Chopping tools
18. Evade
20. Leading actor
22. Pacino and Gore
24. Squander
28. Fired a gun
31. Possess
34. Long fish
35. Female sailor
36. Keats work
37. Ball holders
38. ____ de France
39. Ready for business
40. Stage actress Case
41. Fable message
43. Veteran mariner
45. Animal hide
48. Weathercocks
52. Robert or Alan
55. Great Lake
57. Break bread
58. Stare rudely
59. Close to
60. Role on "Evening Shade"
61. Confined
62. Camp shelter
63. Journey section

DOWN

1. Very dry
2. Man of the hour
3. Emulated Rich Little
4. Dromedary
5. Porter
6. Social affairs
7. Posted
8. Nurse Barton
9. Jinx
10. "____ Maria"
11. "____ the season . . ."
19. Fence opening
21. Fearful admiration
23. Store
25. Watched
26. High school student
27. Heroine of "Born Free"
28. Do the backstroke
29. Angel's headdress
30. Completed
32. Lemon refresher
33. Air outlet
37. Scarlett's home
39. Bullfight cheer
42. Detached
44. Ward off
46. Period after Mardi Gras
47. Maple, e.g.
49. Actress Patricia ____
50. Roof projection
51. Male deer
52. European mountain
53. Actress Remick
54. Lair
56. Writer Fleming

PUZZLE 261

ACROSS
1. Tie securely
5. Bambi's mom
8. Gait
12. She, in Barcelona
13. Actress Kaminska
14. Press
15. Paradise
16. Fido's doc
17. Guide
18. Equestrian's need
20. Stools
21. Beer container
24. Tossed dish
27. Attention-getting word
28. "___ of the Roses"
31. Branch
32. "Lorenzo's ___"
33. Texas city
34. Thus far
35. Sped
36. Assisted
37. Close by
39. Gorilla's cousin
43. Hi-fi
47. Air
48. Fire residue
50. Not far
51. Blueprint
52. Fib
53. Or ___!
54. Lucid
55. Foul up
56. Colors

DOWN
1. Brenda and Bruce
2. TV's Hawkeye
3. Santa's chariot
4. Purse
5. Scuba ___
6. Poem
7. Dine
8. Heap
9. ___ code
10. Joseph's was multi-colored
11. Terminates
19. Aberdeen boy
20. Cunning
22. Thick-skinned one, for short
23. Conger
24. Shoat's home
25. Respect
26. Inebriated
28. Small mass
29. Perfect serve
30. Singer Stewart
32. Paddle's cousin
33. Broadened
35. Knock
36. Aardvark's prey
38. Escort
39. Tams
40. Hawaiian dance
41. Modern Persia
42. Lion's ruff
44. Count (on)
45. Comfort
46. Bauxite and cinnabar
48. Tavern fare
49. Title of respect

PUZZLE 262

ACROSS
1. Cowgirl Evans
5. Split
10. Stalk
14. Household appliance
15. Ghostly
16. Overhang
17. Brand-new
18. Pluck
19. "The Planet of the ___"
20. Lawn tools
22. Home-steaders
24. Housetop
26. That female
27. Wanted
30. Task
35. Vast amount
36. Tart fruit
38. Fracas
39. Hotel employee
41. Sand hills
43. Depressed
44. Diminish
46. Boat crew member
48. Fisherman's aid
49. Hi-fi
51. Update
53. "Sister ___"
55. Raise
56. Endless
61. Catches
65. Wild duck
66. Quick-witted
68. Vogue
69. Cleveland's lake
70. Scene of an event
71. Opposed to aweather
72. Notation
73. Chemical compound
74. Forward

DOWN
1. A ___ a dozen
2. Waterless
3. Drawn-out
4. Joins
5. Inhibited
6. Marvin or Majors
7. Strays
8. Lincolns
9. Grow choppers
10. Playful mammal
11. Record
12. At any time
13. Disorder
21. Muddle
23. Time span
25. Leg bone
27. Distributed
28. National bird
29. Contributor
31. Vermilion
32. Isolated
33. Stairway support
34. Nick
35. Saratoga Springs, et al.
37. More modern
40. Auricle
42. Academic period
45. "___ of the Dragon"
47. Horse color
50. Group of eight, musically
52. Plays
54. "___ from the Crypt"
56. Ingredient
57. Simple
58. Injure
59. Dairy-case purchase
60. Advanced
62. Function
63. First home
64. Sow
67. Lament

PUZZLE 263

ACROSS

1. Small nail
5. Caesar, perhaps
10. Deed of derring-do
14. Ms. Falana
15. Rare violin
16. Encourage
17. At any time
18. Climbing plants
19. King of beasts
20. Crew member
22. Aptitude
24. Fury
25. Visage
26. Combat
29. Toadstool
33. TV's "F ___"
34. Goudy and Bodoni
35. Creek
36. Injure
37. Eat away
38. Indonesian island
39. NY zone in June
40. Alleges
41. Doomed
42. Felix, to Oscar
44. Distance runners
45. Geologic time periods
46. Poker term
47. Meager
50. Put up with
54. Sword handle
55. Motionless
57. Newspaper item, for short
58. Division word
59. Kayak
60. Spanish pot
61. Lowly worker
62. Use
63. Tournament

DOWN

1. Ran, as colors
2. Wander
3. Writer Waugh
4. Photo lab
5. Brutal
6. Organic compound
7. End a flight
8. Had a snack
9. Repugnance
10. More sated
11. Cleveland's lake
12. Greek competition
13. Pup ___
21. Hinged fastener
23. German exclamations
25. Resources
26. Alternate
27. Madrid museum
28. ___ Alegre
29. Mary Tyler ___
30. Speechify
31. Type of tanker
32. Domestics
34. Fusses
37. Dissipate
38. Style of dancing
40. Andy's partner
41. Manicurist's tool
43. Greater London borough
44. Hammer
46. "The ___ of Money"
47. Liner
48. Languish
49. Singing part
50. Prong
51. Skillful
52. Scrabble piece
53. Coup d'___
56. Levy

215

PUZZLE 264

ACROSS

1. Wits
5. Map collection
10. Dude
14. Hymn ending
15. Hangman's loop
16. Protagonist
17. Have lunch
18. Probe
19. Popular cookie
20. Most profound
22. Expel
24. Nil
25. Locale
26. CIA operatives
28. "____ Mutant Ninja Turtles"
32. Show gratitude to
33. Convulsion
35. Author Talese
36. Tolled
37. Graph
38. Overdue
39. St. or rd.
40. Raps
41. Lariats
42. Biked
44. Quarries
45. "The ____ Vanishes"
46. Drink to excess
47. Insist
50. Flattener
53. On top of
54. Skirt style
56. Statue
58. Thailand, formerly
59. More unusual
60. Ohio Indian
61. House wings
62. Disputes
63. Govern

DOWN

1. Clump
2. Surrounded by
3. Simmons of Kiss
4. Sniffling's partner
5. Provokes
6. Girdle's place
7. Treasure
8. Cleopatra's viper
9. Dingiest
10. Selected
11. Rosemary or thyme
12. Realm
13. Inadequate
21. Steal a look
23. Detail
25. Night lights
26. Use a razor
27. Sheeted with glass
29. Wide open
30. Fence openings
31. "For Your ____ Only"
32. Snare
33. Deceitful
34. Butter portion
37. Certain cheeses
38. More solitary
40. Tribe
41. Ready to pick
43. Startles
44. Shakers' partners
46. Canon
47. Medicine measure
48. Bad
49. Repast
50. Venetian money, once
51. Off-white
52. Irritate
55. Once around a track
57. Previously named

216

ACROSS

1. Huck's transport
5. Rever-beration
9. Word of woe
13. Unit of land
14. Hideout
15. Run off to marry
16. Wharf
17. Region
18. Mature
19. Downgrade
21. Biggest
23. Mislead
24. Barnyard mother
25. Big ____ (London landmark)
28. Charitably given
31. Pump purchase
34. Breathing requirement
36. Vigor
37. Cuddly
38. Type of tanker
39. Energy
40. Travel course
41. Las Vegas machine
42. Respectful title
43. Barbra Streisand, e.g.
44. Command-ments number
45. Session
47. Coastal bird
48. Gardener's tool
49. Cow's sound
50. Spring back
54. Door
58. Warn
59. On the peak
61. Like some cars
63. Slit
64. Astute
65. Grizzly, e.g.
66. Despise
67. Lack
68. Simple

DOWN

1. Emulate Hammer
2. Sour
3. At no cost
4. Cycle
5. Happiness
6. Lurch
7. Scurry
8. Spoken
9. Adjust
10. Steady gait
11. Mimics
12. Mailed
15. Strayed
20. More aged
22. Throat-clearer
25. Push up
26. Banish
27. Clothing material
29. Ward off
30. Point
31. Chisel out
32. Subsequent to
33. Severe
35. Obtain
37. Dennis, to Mr. Mitchell
39. Apple or pecan
40. Inflexibility
42. Witnessed
43. Pried
45. Tooth locale
46. Force
48. Secretariat, e.g.
50. Impulsive
51. Governor Grasso
52. Defeat
53. Daybreak
55. Toothpaste container
56. Totally confused
57. Grasslands
60. Even-steven
62. Towel off

PUZZLE 266

ACROSS

1. Current measure, for short
4. Ginger cookie
8. Thick slice
12. Singer Peggy ____
13. Ripped
14. Strong cotton
15. Curved letter
16. Stagger
17. Andy's partner
18. Devil's food, for one
21. Authorizes
22. Dander
23. Glitter
26. ____ nut- shell (briefly)
27. Humor
30. Undiluted
31. Haze
32. Crazy
33. Noah's vessel
34. Whitney's invention
35. Currency
36. Golf score
37. ____ Diego
38. Popular barbecue items
45. Hold up
46. Tree covering
47. Female deer
48. What ____ is new?
49. Egg on
50. Chicken ____ king
51. Have on
52. Turned right
53. "When Harry ____ Sally . . ."

DOWN

1. Actor Baldwin
2. Network
3. Mexican moolah
4. Tennis shot
5. Coward and Harrison
6. Vicinity
7. Striking
8. Room
9. Type of bean
10. Frenzied
11. Foundation
19. Pine ____
20. Time period
23. Belgian resort
24. Ben ____
25. Bother
26. Tiny particle
27. Were the victors
28. Frost
29. Plaything
31. Arsonist
32. Hanker
34. Fuel
35. Striking
36. "____ Pan"
37. Swell
38. Masticate
39. Patriot Nathan ____
40. Actress Lanchester
41. Expose
42. Dutch cheese
43. Actor's part
44. Chair

PUZZLE 267

ACROSS
1. Lose color
5. ____ Angeles
8. ____ up (explode)
12. Steel ingredient
13. Picnic intruder
14. Dressing gown
15. Melee
16. Split ____ soup
17. Succulent plant
18. Wed
20. Hammered down
22. Farewells
24. Accomplished
25. Opponent
27. Bashful
29. Allude
33. Boring tools
35. Ages and ages
37. Gamble
38. Put off
40. Up-to-date
42. Juice from a maple
43. Morning moisture
45. Try out
47. Ice cream creation
50. The ones here
53. Lineage chart
54. Obscure
57. Poker stake
58. Conceits
59. African antelope
60. Bargain
61. Attended
62. Conclusion
63. Mis-calculates

DOWN
1. Solid
2. Opera solo
3. Entrance chime
4. Admission
5. Race circuit
6. Individual
7. Rise from a seat
8. Plaited
9. Recline loosely
10. Woodwind instrument
11. Garden pest
19. Certainly!
21. Ventilate
23. "Ain't ____ Sweet?"
25. Current fashion
26. Be in debt
28. Over there
30. Staple or paper clip
31. Paleozoic, e.g.
32. Capitol Hill regular: abbr.
34. Unhappiest
36. Seine
39. Pro vote
41. Soaked
44. Pie piece
46. Hue
47. Soupy meat dish
48. Strong impulse
49. Sign gas
51. Heavenly light
52. Conger and moray
55. Wayside lodging
56. Damp dirt

219

PUZZLE 268

ACROSS
1. Mischievous
4. Emanation
8. Acquire
11. George Washington
12. Actor's aid
13. Space or station start
14. Bumpkin
15. "____ each life . . . "
16. Seethe
17. Harsh
19. Appeared
21. Sorry mount
22. Aver
23. "Father Knows ____"
25. Lash wound
26. Father's Day gift
29. Shoe width
30. Recoils
31. Disagreeably damp
32. Completely
33. On ____ and needles
34. Long
35. Clear the tape
37. Curve part
38. Pitch in
40. Slightest
43. Writer Macdonald
44. Behindhand
47. Yarn measure
48. Useless
49. Constantly
50. On the ____
51. Singer Dennis
52. Take a flat
53. Time periods: abbr.

DOWN
1. Sounds of disapproval
2. Med. subj.
3. Without protection
4. Imitating
5. Samovar
6. Corrupt
7. Peter and Paul, e.g.
8. In Euclidean fashion
9. Toledo's lake
10. Narrated
13. Aid a criminal
18. Squeal
20. Beanery offerings
22. Left Bank's river
23. Ms. Arthur
24. Moray or conger
25. American painter
27. Mr. Fleming
28. She-sheep
30. Resorts
34. Ante
36. Ascend
37. On the ball
38. Saharalike
39. Pop
41. Char
42. Highland headwear
45. Hail, to Pliny
46. Hamilton bill

PUZZLE 269

ACROSS
1. A son of Noah
4. Establish
7. Soothe
12. Southern state
14. Primp's pal
15. Upper House member
16. Helped
17. Giggling sounds
19. Bis!
22. Saturates
26. Gave for a time
27. Snarl
28. Sprite
29. Uncooked
30. Levy
34. Reproductive cell
37. Blue-pencil wielder
38. Soapboxer
39. Indiana native
41. ____ Abdel Nasser
44. Toughens
48. Quickly
49. Hides
50. Prized violin, for short
51. Mayday!
52. Blind impulse

DOWN
1. Possesses
2. House or wife
3. British isle
4. Literary caricature
5. Acted ineptly
6. Piquant
7. Athens's foe
8. Come up
9. Was in the van
10. Victory sign
11. Finis
13. Wand
18. Some NYC hrs.
19. Cream of the crop
20. Bedouin, e.g.
21. Blue Grotto site
23. White heron
24. Academy founder
25. Stitcher
31. Home of Ulysses
32. Duped
33. To and ____
34. Investigate: 2 wds.
35. Stadiums
36. Grown-up fillies
40. Back talk
41. Fuel
42. Quick to learn
43. Disfigure
45. Triumphant cry
46. Permit
47. Wind pt.

PUZZLE 270

ACROSS
1. Overzealous actor
4. Rose or Fountain
8. Like a fast-talker
12. Brewer's product
13. Ladd or King
14. Crazy
15. Environs
17. Mine products
18. Takes a chair
19. Comedienne Joan ____
21. Schemes
23. Diamond feature
24. "____ of Angels"
25. Glass unit
26. Tin
29. Single
30. Tango, e.g.
31. Fruit drink
32. ____ Moines
33. Helper
34. Do hedge work
35. Taverns
36. Brief fight
37. Droopy-eared hound
40. Role for Liz
41. By mouth
42. Neighbor of Kentucky
46. Cairo's river
47. Tidy
48. Negatives
49. Lyric poems
50. Precious stones
51. Take to court

DOWN
1. Owned
2. Actress MacGraw
3. Notes
4. Sections
5. Whitney and Wallach
6. Tic-____-toe
7. Portal
8. Hand cover
9. Folk knowledge
10. Cake finisher
11. Chief
16. Fork prong
20. Palmist's words
21. Spur
22. Rural road
23. Musical groups
25. Artistic endeavor
26. Animations
27. Mine entrance
28. Verne captain
30. Native of Copenhagen
34. Adolescent
35. Small bodies of land
36. Narrow openings
37. Mayor Sonny ____
38. Like the Gobi
39. Mall event
40. Tight-lipped one
43. Actress Grant
44. Chit
45. Wind dir.

PUZZLE 271

ACROSS
1. Prohibit
4. Scarlett's home
8. Cloak
12. Feel regret
13. Revise
14. Military hooky: abbr.
15. Curved line
16. Active at night
18. Los ____
20. Facilitate
21. Inspired
23. Made a mistake
27. Additional
29. Eager
32. Ms. Gabor
33. Among
34. "____ Pan Alley"
35. Unwrap
36. Jogged
37. Walkers
38. Completed
39. ____ de menthe
41. Above
43. Actress Moran
46. Fall bloom
49. Necessary
53. Flightless bird
54. Sugar source
55. Beige
56. Disencumber
57. Baseball-players' needs
58. Allot
59. Fr. holy woman

DOWN
1. Boast
2. Halo
3. Peach kin
4. Stiff
5. Stir
6. Food staple
7. Tropical ant
8. More scarce
9. Possess
10. Constrictor
11. Right angle
17. Utilized
19. Was in debt
22. Appointment
24. Newspaper employees
25. Level
26. Hamlet, e.g.
27. Mr. Antony
28. Actor Sharif
30. Contend
31. "____ the Woods"
35. Poems
37. Spore plant
40. Encounters
42. Worth
44. Article
45. Pleasant
47. Radiate
48. Uncouth
49. Recede
50. Ocean
51. Tennis match
52. Actor Carney

221

PUZZLE 272

ACROSS

1. Singer Crosby
5. Play part
8. Sear
12. Territory
13. Sadness
14. Car
15. Young woman
16. Gorilla, e.g.
17. Narrow opening
18. Of the sun
20. Sacred hymn
22. Ancient
23. Snakelike fish
24. Pictures
27. Without trouble
31. Hearing organ
32. Born: Fr.
33. Sign up
37. Easter headgear
40. Crusty dessert
41. "Where the Boys ____"
42. Bean color
44. Summer vacation spot
47. Lend
48. Sticky stuff
50. House covering
52. Poker payment
53. Couple
54. Azure
55. Forest creature
56. Rooster's mate
57. Three feet

DOWN

1. Lunch holder
2. Spring flower
3. Famous fiddler
4. Gasoline measure
5. Trophies
6. Robber's foe
7. Indian dwelling
8. Spanish cellist Pablo ____
9. Seed husk
10. Tiny particle
11. Decay
19. Pub brew
21. Ocean
24. Observe
25. Is able to
26. Goof
28. Country hotel
29. Jamie ____ Curtis
30. However
34. Kitchen gadget
35. Recline
36. Linear extent
37. Large monkey
38. Native mineral
39. Close at hand
42. Departed
43. Speed
45. Carbonated drink
46. Time span
47. Youth
49. Have unpaid bills
51. Nourished

PUZZLE 273

ACROSS

1. Baseball stadium
5. Press
9. Use a straw
12. Draft animals
13. Belonging to me
14. Historic period
15. Sandwich shop
16. Model
17. Male
18. At a distance
20. Border
22. Prom rental
24. British brew
25. Inventor Whitney
26. Adam's mate
28. Bus station
32. "____ Karenina"
34. It came first?
36. Volcano output
37. Basketball's Johnson
39. Over the hill
41. Lip
42. Director Reiner
44. Penny or video
46. Attorney
49. Colored
50. Malt beverage
51. Use a book
53. ____-a-ling
56. Ruin
57. Zoo enclosure
58. On the Caspian
59. Baker's creation
60. Biblical garden
61. Lively dance

DOWN

1. School of whales
2. Lumberjack's tool
3. Like a bubble bath
4. Kitchen utensil
5. Make better
6. ____ Grande
7. Start
8. Necessary
9. Half: pref.
10. Mideastern nation
11. Spasm
19. Fruit drink
21. Celt
22. Buffalo Bills, e.g.
23. Forearm bone
27. Personality
29. Utopia
30. Roman poet
31. Docile
33. Light
35. Delight
38. Compel by force
40. Parched
43. Sandwich requisite
45. Fragrant wood
46. Genie's home
47. Jai ____
48. Existed
52. Ripen
54. Formerly named
55. Guy's date

PUZZLE 274

ACROSS
1. Cease
5. Divan
9. Appointment
13. Out of the wind
14. Bridge fees
15. Mild oath
16. Actor Hackman
17. Zones
18. Earth's center
19. Transport for pioneers
22. "____ My Turn"
23. Coffee server
24. Bowling term
27. Connection
32. Author Walker
33. Simple song
34. "Norma ____"
35. Create
36. Waits
37. Garfield and Odie, to Jon
38. Small bill
39. Buenos ____
40. French painter
41. Alien
43. Provide service
44. Expression of contempt
45. Law exam
46. Diner worker
54. Volcano output
55. Prepare marshmallows
56. Silvery
58. Keen
59. Brief letters
60. Infrequent
61. Ancient Iranian
62. Card game for three
63. Mother Bloor

DOWN
1. Witch
2. Actor Baldwin
3. Comic Jay ____
4. Adolescent
5. Kinds
6. Toast spread
7. Pennant
8. Attacks
9. Pour
10. Excited
11. Tropical tuber
12. Paradise
14. Sample
20. Irish republic
21. Actress Fay ____
24. Tilt
25. Cheapskate
26. King beater
27. Equestrienne
28. Summers, on the Seine
29. Ryan or Dunne
30. Western
31. Egg holder
32. Andy's partner
33. Dreadful
36. Rocky Mountain sheep
37. Lobster trap
39. Med student's course
40. Artist Chagall
42. Scrape
43. Small vehicles
45. Surround
46. Bang
47. Own
48. Roman poet
49. Chess piece
50. Information
51. Hideous beast
52. Spoken
53. Socialist Marx
57. Affirmative vote

Cryptic Geography

PUZZLE 275

One of the United States is pictured with a question mark showing the location of one of its cities. Some interesting information about the city is in a substitution code.

UDTTFXKYTQ, BAJJXVENDJFD
    (city)   (state)

UDTTFXKYTQ FX IUA RDBFIDE MZ

BAJJXVENDJFD. IUA RFIV EFAX MJ IUA XYXHYAUDJJD

TFNAT DJC KAQDJ DX D ITDCFJQ BMXI AXIDKEFXUAC KV

OMUJ UDTTFX. BTMCYRIX MZ UDTTFXKYTQ FJREYCA

KYFECFJQ SDIATFDEX DJC DFTBEDJA BDTIX.

223

PUZZLE 276

ACROSS

1. Cob vegetable
5. Heat-giver
8. Other name

DOWN

1. Be concerned

10. Having a twangy sound
12. Raised strip
13. Humor
14. First woman
15. Flow out
17. Dined
18. Wear away
20. Soar
21. In reserve
23. Rested
25. Requires
28. Nocturnal bird
29. Grow old
30. Steal
32. Item from the past
34. Bore
36. Vote into office
37. Strainer
38. Corrosive liquid
39. Prepare by steeping

2. Tropical fruit
3. One carried
4. Pester
5. Sleuth Spade
6. Ordinary
7. Mean
9. Garden plantings
10. Arrest
11. Grant or Majors
16. Essence
19. Cereal grain
20. Commission
22. Acts
23. Puff up
24. Bowling lane
26. Less moist
27. Find the answer to
28. Metal source
29. Play division
31. Got windy
33. Skater's surface
35. Tease

PUZZLE 277

ACROSS

1. Eve's spouse
5. Rant
9. Smash
12. Binding material
13. Equal
14. Mine find
15. Foretoken
16. Undertook
18. Interfere

20. Examination
21. Merit
23. Tall grasses
26. Daybreak
29. Snick and ____
30. Consumed
31. Salamanders
34. Adage
35. Tree growth
37. Pencil parts
39. Mr. Kefauver
41. Hire
42. Tide type
44. Marbles
48. Moon-shaped
51. Sinful
52. Possesses
53. "Citizen ____"
54. "Born Free" lion
55. Those holding office
56. Snow toy
57. Prophet

DOWN

1. Minute particle
2. Titled lady
3. Mocked
4. Repairer
5. Opposite
6. Hail!
7. Air duct
8. Go in
9. Empress Josephine's daughter
10. Anger
11. Actor Danson
17. Employs
19. Reclined
22. More modern
24. Precious
25. Uses a needle
26. Bargain event
27. American Indians
28. State of being tidy
32. Handled
33. Chanted
36. Charges
38. Barrel slats
40. Bags
43. Resound
45. Roof unit
46. Otherwise
47. Scorch
48. Greek letter
49. Hastened
50. Mariner's direction: abbr.

FOUR-MOST

All of the four-letter words in this crossword puzzle are listed separately and are in alphabetical order. Use the numbered clues as solving aids to help you determine where each four-letter word goes in the diagram.

4-LETTER WORDS

ADAM
AIDE
ALAI
ALIA
ANNA
ARIA
AVES
CALM
DAMP
DARE
EDGE
EDIT
ERIE
EVES
LEDA
LIED
LIND
MIRE
OLIO
OMAR
PAGE
PENT
PIER
RAMS
RANT
REED
RIND
SALA
SAVE
SPAN
STAR
STEN
TALL
VIAL

ACROSS

5. Belgian town
13. Decorative vessels
17. Of sound
19. Commotion
20. Tyke
21. Fleet of warships
26. Tremendous
28. Colonists
32. Expire
33. Send payment
35. Article of faith
38. Tendon
41. Tablelands
43. Deserve
45. Jalopy
46. Church dignitaries
48. Unpleasant

52. Waters parted by Moses
55. Comedian Olsen
56. Track circuit
60. Hearsay
65. Musial and Javier, of baseball
68. Sooner than, in poems

DOWN

1. Policeman
4. Sad
5. Faint
7. Hero of "Exodus"
8. Wood insects
13. Plantations
14. Milan's La ____

24. Face value
25. Modify
26. Donor
27. Songstress Della ____
28. Evergreen trees
29. Pass a law
30. Team race
34. Silent actors
37. Store clerks
39. Victors
44. Beige
47. Signs of weeping
49. Serving tray
51. Solitary
61. Shoshonean
63. Conducted

225

PUZZLE 279

Clues in Twos

ACROSS

1.] Head
5.] Head
8. Decide
11. ____ nothing
12. ____ out (add to)
13. Actress Arthur
14.] Word with
15.] tongue
17. Pronto, to a doctor
18. Roster, in Dijon
19.] Cast
21.] Cast
25. Sault ____ Marie
28. MCAT's relative
29. Craze
30.] Mule, e.g.
32.] Mule, e.g.
33. Fragrant root
34. Shorten
35. Before, in verse
36.] Fleece
37.] Fleece
39. Inventor Howe
41. Divorce city
45.] Sellers
48.] Sellers
49. Ms. Gardner
50. Fall month: abbr.
51. ____-garde
52. Decade number
53.] Spot
54.] Spot

DOWN

1. City map
2. Seaweed
3. Fang
4. Aquatic bird
5. Experience again
6. Czar's edict
7. Robin's creation
8. Kimono accessory
9. Drawing tool
10. Playground game
11. Shouts of protest
16. Macho guy
18. Cooking fat
20. Sponsorship
22. Wave, in Paris
23. Deceiver
24. Cowgirl Evans
25. Exhibition
26. Amateur
27. Spanish river
29. ____ Hari
31. Bothered
32. Takes to court
34. Innocent
37. Greek enchantress
38. Roman fountain
40. Author Anita ____
42. State, to Pierre
43. Hawaiian goose
44. Food scrap
45. Large container
46. Abel's mother
47. A Bobbsey twin
48. Dance step

PUZZLE 280

Throwbacks

You have to throw your mental gears into reverse to play this game. Reading backward there are at least three 4-letter words to be found in each of the longer words. You can skip over letters, but don't change the order of the letters. For example, in the word DECLARE you can find the word RACE reading backward by starting with the next-to-last letter and skipping over the L, but you can't find the word READ without changing the order of the letters.

1. MERMAID _____ _____ _____
2. PREACHER _____ _____ _____
3. STRAIGHT _____ _____ _____
4. TREASURE _____ _____ _____
5. PENTAGON _____ _____ _____
6. CELEBRATE _____ _____ _____

ACROSS

1. Cassoulet
5. Stole
9. Startle
14. Knotty mass
15. Zeus's wife
16. Shy
17. Curved arch
18. Milky stone
19. Doing very well
20. Provide funds for
22. Feather an arrow
23. Chair or street
24. Equal
25. Statue's base
28. Clear soup
32. Harts
33. Pick
34. Kind of meal
35. Designer Saint-Laurent
36. Hold responsible
37. Closet nuisance
38. Celtic god of the sea
39. Oafs
40. Strong point
41. Pronghorn
43. Tighter
44. Lug
45. Polish cavalryman
46. Musical note
49. Accelerate
53. Actor Robert ___
54. Like some lingerie
55. Ohio Indian
56. Absurd
57. Atoll
58. Turkish titles
59. Organic compound
60. Molt
61. Oliver's request

DOWN

1. Snooty one
2. Nero's garb
3. Utopia
4. Leisure times
5. Rushing sound
6. Answer
7. Kazakhstan sea
8. Buddy
9. Most tiresome
10. Roman statesman
11. In the middle of
12. Band
13. Trim
21. Phooey!
22. Parry
24. Works by Keats
25. Zoological divisions
26. Pep up
27. Stagnant
28. Irish county
29. Anchors
30. Dull
31. Anesthetic
33. Wed secretly
36. Kiosk
37. Night light
39. Desk item
40. Defect
42. Flammable gas
43. More than satisfied
45. Sam or Remus
46. Singer Brickell
47. Particles
48. Mosquito's cousin
49. Obi
50. Jason's craft
51. Fabricator
52. ___ majesty
54. Fleur-de-___

Anagram Quote

Unscramble each set of letters below the dashes to complete the humorous quotations.

1. _____ _____ the _____ of _____ more than _____
   NTINGOH   OSWRLE   ELLVE   OENRVAICOSNT   IRGNASI
   the _____.
       COEVI

2. A _____ who does not _____ ___ in ten _____ _____ stop _____
      PSREKEA   ETKRSI LOI   USINEMT LHOUSD   RGBOIN

PUZZLE 283

• LAUGHING MATTERS •

ACROSS

1. Animal's stomach
5. Flyer
9. Worth: abbr.
12. "____ Is Born"
17. French novelist
18. Standout
19. Effervescent drink
20. Look over casually
21. Amo, amas, ____
22. "Beetle Bailey" dog
23. Kind of sch.
24. Unusual thing
25. Soften
26. Appendage
27. Comic's Andy
28. Valuable violin
29. Thomas Nast, for one
33. Huntley
34. Not a single unit
35. Reo man
36. Bitter vetch
39. French composer Milhaud
42. For fear that
43. Ceases
44. Get ready, for short
45. Wrong
46. "Bei Mir ____ Du Schon"
47. Joy
48. Cold-cut unit
49. Ruin
50. Lackaday!
51. Nail
52. Position
53. Emmet
54. Musial
55. One-armed-bandit part
56. Pinched
57. Work of Shakespeare
60. Arouse to passion
63. Bone: pref.
64. Head appendages
65. Jokester
68. Back teeth
69. Writes down quickly
70. Make like a top
71. Use a stopwatch on
72. Salty water
73. Swindles
74. Shortly
75. Small western evergreen
76. Rulers: abbr.
77. Tree trunk
78. Legal paper
79. Supplies food to
80. Bounce
81. Straight man, to a comedian
82. Rough-napped cloth
83. Shed feathers
84. "____ on the Way to the Forum"
91. Plant used for flavoring
92. Weight measure
93. Wyatt
94. Tease
95. Horse groomer
96. Lubricates
97. Ceremony
98. Part of a list
99. Moon valleys
100. ____-dokey
101. Hand-to-mouth-er
102. Jules Verne hero
103. "The Green Room" actress Nathalie and family
104. ____ Moines
105. Demands payment from
106. Take suddenly

DOWN

1. Fastener
2. Lover
3. In any way
4. Product of 65 Across
5. Baby shoes
6. Whole
7. Networks
8. Humorous quaintness
9. 1958 Modugno song
10. Skillful
11. Satirized
12. Dumas character
13. Rail birds
14. Giggling
15. Italian wine district
16. Spanish king
19. Geometric line
20. Makes of merchandise
30. In such a manner
31. Price
32. Ye ____ Shoppe
37. British reconnaissance
38. Velocity
39. Baby's word
40. Chief Egyptian god
41. Storm
42. Climbing vine
43. Make happy
44. Architect's products
46. Accusation
47. U.S. composer Ferde
48. Moves
50. Very small particles
51. Stains
52. Avowed
54. Frighten
55. Methods: abbr.
56. Freight hauler
57. Bates and Thicke
58. Lorna ____
59. Transfer, as a plant
60. Fix in the mind
61. "____ Rae"
62. Frivolously
65. Burgundy
66. Roman version of Eros
67. Grant and Lee: abbr.
69. Excellent, in London
70. Laughed slyly
71. Giggling
73. Peso
74. Galway Bay island group
75. Feeler
77. Mistakes
78. Fanciful humor
79. Pennies, colloquially
81. Flares
82. Easily split rocks
83. Small mammal
85. French girl
86. Child's wheels, for short
87. Japanese poem
88. Saltpeter
89. Swelling with fluid
90. Discharge from the armed forces, to a Brit
91. Land mass
95. Sphere

228

ACROSS

1. Fellow
5. Nora's pet et al.
10. Norse tale
14. Memory, for one
15. On _____ (active): 2 wds.
16. Simple Simon's desire
17. Palo _____
18. Excessive
19. Claire et al.
20. Commitment borderline: 4 wds.
23. Q-U connection
24. Time period
25. Mouser
29. Stoic philosopher
31. Consumed
34. Poppy product
35. Food store
36. Pod cover
37. Future officers: 3 wds.
40. Gaelic
41. Ex-GIs
42. Biblical mount
43. Sunbeam
44. Dampens
45. Gasoline word
46. Women's gp.
47. Mineral spring
48. Gets down to brass tacks: 4 wds.
57. Destroy
58. Bloc
59. Opinion
60. Aide: abbr.
61. French income
62. King of woe
63. Puts money on
64. Organic compound
65. Old times

DOWN

1. Applaud
2. Nimbus
3. Naysayer
4. Unskilled worker
5. Optimally: 2 wds.
6. Roundtree role
7. Part of TVA
8. Commission
9. Of a Greek philosopher
10. Malice
11. Japanese primitive
12. Equipment
13. Org.
21. "My Three Sons" dog
22. Self
25. Watch or ivory
26. Musical drama
27. Gold of "Benson"
28. Pretty
29. Piggybank fillers
30. Heights: abbr.
31. Football stadium
32. Giant
33. Miss Dinsmore
35. Try to lose
36. Mine entrance
38. Introductory part
39. Writers' org.
44. Existed
45. Church key
46. Car mishaps
47. Pig
48. Type of apple
49. English river
50. Wet fog
51. Singles
52. Hue
53. Viscous
54. Thought: prefix
55. Close by
56. Import term

PUZZLE 284

229

PUZZLE 285

ACROSS
1. Cowboy's rope
6. Con game
10. Insect stage
14. Lessen
15. Young boys
16. Chalcedony
17. Beatles' Rita et al.: 2 wds.
19. Egyptian river
20. Entreaty
21. Melody
22. Thespian
23. Byron poem: 3 wds.
27. Large cave
30. Pollster Roper
31. Forestall
32. Metric weight
34. Bridge
38. Marsh
39. More piquant
42. Gold: Sp.
43. Goddess of discord
45. God of war
46. Dark
48. Exchange premium
50. Cold symptom
51. Vessel's debut: 2 wds.
56. Got up
57. Canine
58. Haul
62. Actress Foch
63. Spinster: 2 wds.
66. Lyrical
67. Fashion magazine
68. Started
69. Take heed
70. Celt
71. Resource

DOWN
1. Lantern
2. First victim
3. Glut
4. Soft-shell clam
5. Bard's above
6. Sedate
7. Capital of Egypt
8. Annex
9. Authors' submissions: abbr.
10. Spanish cloaks
11. Merge
12. Marking post
13. Firers
18. Principal
22. Isotope weight: abbr.
24. —— and sciences
25. Cat genus
26. Century plant
27. Bistro
28. Allege
29. I came: Latin
32. Leningrad ballet
33. Rink surface
35. Staff
36. Grand Canyon State: abbr.
37. Memo
40. Charley horse
41. Ladder step
44. Inept GI: 2 wds.
47. Goads
49. Golly!
50. Sausage herb
51. Estate house
52. Take for ——: 2 wds.
53. Column style
54. "Swan Lake" impostor
55. Swiss song
59. Tatters
60. Together, in music: 2 wds.
61. "Peer ——"
63. A March sister
64. —— carte: 2 wds.
65. Cagers' group: abbr.

ACROSS

1. Bulk
5. Social group
10. Heavy hammer
14. Silkworm
15. Of birds
16. Unemployed
17. Is suspicious: 3 wds.
19. 1492 ship
20. Decade
21. French river
22. Lease income
24. Unyielding
26. Italian city
27. Japanese statesman
28. Diminish
32. Third month
35. Mild oath
36. 5,280 feet
37. Neighbor of Turkey
38. Ascended
39. Gen. Bradley
40. Ruled mark
41. Force
42. Stale
43. Sweetheart
45. Cattle genus
46. Female horse
47. Ruined: 2 wds.
51. Silky wool
54. Stone ax
55. —— pro nobis
56. Inca country
57. Court danger: 3 wds.
60. Cupid
61. Depart
62. Behind time
63. Venetian ruler
64. Concluded
65. Ran away

DOWN

1. Famed hostess
2. Provided weapons
3. Italian city
4. Actor Mineo
5. Gambling room
6. Stop!, at sea
7. Horse father
8. Chinese pagoda
9. Intermission
10. Disney character: 2 wds.
11. Mine entrance
12. Arm bone
13. True, in Scotland
18. Averse
23. Be human
25. Disney character: 2 wds.
26. Brute
28. Male bee
29. Goals
30. Lath
31. Weird
32. Factory
33. Diva's song
34. Writer Ayn
35. Tee off
38. Cute
42. Thirty days
44. Malay gibbon
45. Escaped
47. Do research
48. Central
49. Speechify
50. Graded
51. Imitated
52. Fiddling emperor
53. Sailor's drink
54. Clothed
58. Still, in poems
59. Sprite

PUZZLE 286

231

PUZZLE 287

ACROSS
1. English furniture designer
5. Make a touchdown
10. "How sweet ___!"
14. Trig function
15. Kind of kitchen
16. Bedouin dwelling
17. Greenhorn
19. "___ partridge in . . ."
20. "For want of ___ . . ."
21. Sophia's she
22. Hitch, e.g.
23. Hollywood offering
25. ___ fixe
27. Vine parts
31. Ems, for one
34. Famed censor
37. Russian city
38. Gobi refuge
40. Tenth of an ephah
41. Beauty shop
43. Membrane
44. Parsonage
46. Grape juice
47. "___ Angel"
48. Alfonso's queen
49. Squid limb
52. Hod or tar
54. Children: Ger.
58. Zoology suffix
60. Church nook
64. Expiate
65. Owl calls
66. Made less tough
68. Touch
69. Chopin piece
70. Green, of old
71. Actress Armstrong
72. Actor George ___
73. Amor

DOWN
1. "___ Is Born"
2. Chemical compound
3. Former Asian state
4. Peacemakers
5. Sunday talk: abbr.
6. ___ au lait
7. Amerinds
8. Spanish rivers
9. Involve
10. "___ This Woman"
11. Volunteer State
12. Subcontinental prefix
13. RBI, e.g.
18. Actress Sommer
24. Son of Seth
26. Brit. medal
28. Attracted
29. Kindled anew
30. Actress Massey
32. Heap
33. Strong ___ ox
34. Reach
35. "___ Called Horse"
36. Obstinate
39. Heedful
42. Nape site
45. Greek letter
50. Thrills
51. Prevaricator
53. Malt ovens
55. Nap taker
56. Madrid's first month
57. Foxx et al.
58. Husband of Jezebel
59. Earring site
61. Musician Fountain
62. Nestled
63. Norse anthology
67. Moray, e.g.

ACROSS

1. English carriage
5. Actor O'Toole
10. Small arrow
14. Humdinger
15. Straighten
16. German river
17. Upon
18. Income: Fr.
19. National flower
20. TV show: 4 wds.
23. Orient
24. Woodwind
25. Roles
28. Sault —— Marie
30. Flower leaf
34. Rubbed out
36. House wing
38. Feast
39. Do sums
40. Postponed
43. Actress Arthur
44. Mariner Ericson
46. Existed
47. Sky paths
49. Muzzle
51. Actor Vereen
53. Leavening
54. Sniffer
56. And others: abbr.
58. TV show: 3 wds.
65. Hindu queen
66. Gladden
67. Angers
68. Siouan
69. Actor Alain
70. Shoshoneans
71. Hardy heroine
72. Paradises
73. Allot

DOWN

1. Town map
2. Actress Buzzi
3. African lily
4. TV performers
5. "I Love ——"
6. Chooses by vote
7. Prong
8. Totally
9. Baseballer Pee Wee
10. Ridiculed
11. Excited
12. Hebrew letter
13. Waste allowance
21. Demolished, in England
22. Corded fabric
25. Rings
26. "As You Like It" forest
27. Wireless set
29. Twit
31. Shinbone
32. Dills
33. Slightest
35. Morning moisture
37. Writer Tolstoy
41. Tagged
42. Wood nymph
45. Comic strips
48. Neighbor of France
50. Shoe tip
52. Gravity theorist
55. Stockholm native
57. Adolescent years
58. Jog
59. Detest
60. Son of Seth
61. New Haven school
62. Commedia dell'——
63. Encounter
64. Being: Latin

PUZZLE 288

233

PUZZLE 289

ACROSS
1. Close
5. Foundation
10. Detective Spade
13. Sumptuous
14. Dress size
15. Gobbled up
16. Towards shelter
17. Depth charge
18. Tyke
19. Artist Chagall
20. Overly
21. Think
23. Have debts
25. Overgrown, like foliage
28. Discernment
31. ____ goose
32. Poet Brooke
33. Some
34. Work gang
38. Dwelling
39. Donkey: Fr.
40. Reproach
41. "The ____ Love": 2 wds.
42. Plus
43. Supporting pipe rim
44. Jellied salad
46. Came down
47. Meeting place: 2 wds.
50. Terminate
51. Obliterate
52. Queer
54. Actress Harlow
58. Fishwife
59. VIP
62. Advocate strongly
63. Summer: Fr.
64. Immediately: 2 wds.
65. Terrible
66. Emcee Mack
67. Tantalize
68. Twelvemonth

DOWN
1. Shut loudly
2. Hawaiian dance
3. Consumer
4. Graham Greene book: 2 wds.
5. Spanish kiss
6. 1962 Jason Robards play: 3 wds.
7. Thus: Latin
8. Call ____ day: 2 wds.
9. Spanish housewife
10. Shiny fabric
11. Expiate
12. ____ out (apportioned)
14. Kind of leather
22. Puppet show: 3 wds.
24. "____ in the Money"
26. Not a bit
27. Layer
28. Ancient Syria
29. Castro's land
30. Atop
35. Edam's exterior
36. Brink
37. Worthless plant
39. Dye plant
40. Highland tribe
42. Psychiatrists' org.
43. Rear, as a bird
45. Jewish month
47. Principle
48. Speechify
49. Conducted
53. Cubes
55. Pa. port
56. Taj Mahal city
57. ____ -do-well
60. Adherent: suffix
61. Tibetan gazelle

234

PUZZLE 290

ACROSS

1. Quarrel
5. Squabble
9. Aid
13. Mine: 2 wds., Fr.
14. Ark dimension
16. "It's a Sin to Tell ——": 2 wds.
17. Nutmeg spice
18. Sports palace
19. Cloy
20. "Coal ——": 2 wds.
23. Idiot
24. Ogles
25. CSA president
28. Without face value: hyph.
31. Wellaway!
32. Stocked a trap
34. —— Alamos
37. Young series: 3 wds.
40. "—— the season . . ."
41. Frankie and Cleo
42. Scold
43. Cheerful
44. IQ name
45. Surveyed
48. Melodies
50. Stowe book: 3 wds.
56. Iranian coin
57. Egg-shaped
58. Mine entrance
60. Fashion magazine
61. Cheap person
62. Not any
63. Char
64. Actress Diana
65. Robert ——: 2 wds.

DOWN

1. Scottish cap
2. Mosque priest
3. Central points
4. Diabolical
5. Line of cliffs
6. Handbag
7. Sleeping
8. Songstress Turner
9. Diner waiter
10. Make happy
11. Metric quart
12. A jury of his ——
15. Greek cross
21. Dawn goddess
22. Showy flowers, for short
25. Silly
26. Jai ——
27. Cauldrons
28. Simpleton
29. Nebraska Indian
30. Church seats
32. Grain husk
33. Related
34. Tilt
35. Bone: prefix
36. Let it stand
38. Get away from
39. Capital of Queensland
43. Vendor
44. Bikini top
45. Heals
46. Old-womanish
47. La ——
48. Fall flower
49. Cake decorators
51. Lid
52. Roman poet
53. Shark
54. False god
55. Baseball team
59. Ball holder

235

PUZZLE 291

ACROSS

1. Macaroni
6. Upon
10. ____ one's head
14. Kind of squash
15. Latvia's capital
16. Liana
17. Wanderer
18. Sea bird
19. Writer Wiesel
20. Healed
22. ____ Foxx
23. Miss Gabor
24. Cummerbund
26. Doctrine
29. "Born Free" heroine
32. Violinist Isaac et al.
36. WWII agcy.
37. Empire
39. Gazelle
40. Novice
42. Artist John
44. "____ Cinders"
45. Extant
47. Caruso, for one
49. Deer
50. Brews tea
52. Bristle
53. Opposite NNW
54. Puerto ____
56. ____ glance: 2 wds.
58. Main part
61. 1917 Cohan song: 2 wds.
66. Alaskan isle
67. Glacial snow
68. Rust
70. ____ about: 2 wds.
71. Actress Moran
72. Moreno et al.
73. Easy gait
74. French city: 2 wds.
75. Appears

DOWN

1. Seek gold
2. Acidity
3. Portion
4. Outline
5. Massachusetts town
6. Comic Johnson
7. Row
8. Monsters
9. Ling-Ling et al.
10. This way!: 2 wds.
11. Loathsome
12. Arthurian lady
13. Oboe, e.g.
21. Glens
25. Subway stop: abbr.
26. Particles
27. " . . .crying over ____ milk"
28. ____ Antoinette
30. Pepper's mate
31. Lilies
33. Irks
34. Carter and Gwyn
35. Refresh
38. Lion's locks
41. Prelude
43. ____ home (away): 2 wds.
46. Finial
48. Newsman Dan and kin
51. Tea biscuits
55. Manifest
57. Penthouse
58. British prison
59. Pay ____ mind: 2 wds.
60. Call it quits
62. Satanic
63. Splitsville
64. Learning method
65. Yellow cheese
69. Curvy letter

ACROSS

1. "____ and Jeff"
5. So longs: hyph.
10. Be prominent
14. Pa. port
15. Sphere of conflict
16. ____ Alto
17. Alamo site: 3 wds.
20. Cunning
21. Orient
22. Aromatic herb
23. Reduce
24. Animal hide
26. Expects
29. Honeycomb part
30. Doleful
33. Droops
34. King of the road
35. Jacket or soup
36. China-manu-facturing site: 3 wds.
41. Compass pt.
42. Picnic pests
43. Sills solo
44. Links mound
45. Bakery products
46. Kind of snake
48. Riga native
49. Songbird
50. Eastern prince
53. Poker holding
54. Gratuity
57. Circus winter home: 2 wds.
61. Pagan god
62. Discussion group
63. Troubles
64. Lease
65. Rows
66. Sugar source

DOWN

1. Untidy heap
2. Russian range
3. Dickens's Tim
4. Social event
5. Asian tribesmen
6. Popped up
7. Omar's output
8. Blackbird
9. ____ Paulo
10. Exhausted
11. Public vehicle
12. Woeful word
13. Gypsy ____ Lee
18. In good order
19. Animal fat
23. City on the Arno
24. Laborer
25. German river
26. Anything of value
27. The "Duke"
28. Harmonize
29. Fischer's game
30. Good egg
31. Eagle's abode
32. Senegal city
37. Escapades
38. Military group
39. Printing directive
40. Tale
46. Gives the third degree
47. Aviation prefix
48. Inclined
49. Thin cracker
50. Hebrew lyre
51. Manufactured
52. Actress Moran
53. Window part
54. Mah-jongg piece
55. Unemployed
56. History's milieu
58. Make a choice
59. Bangkok native
60. Kid

PUZZLE 292

237

PUZZLE 293

ACROSS
1. Alphabetic trio
4. Hit hard
8. Demure
12. Tra ____: 2 wds.
14. Inlet
15. Electron tube
16. Strong ____ ox: 2 wds.
17. Rare bird
18. Map addition
19. " ...thy elect ____" (II John 13): 3 wds.
22. Glow
23. Harden
24. Snare
27. Tot's garb
32. Night sight
35. Cranial nerves
37. Handle
38. "____ his father's ..." (Prov. 13:1): 4 wds.
41. Poses
42. Arrow poison
43. Bonus
44. Injures
46. Bristle
48. ____ Vegas
50. Land measures
54. "____ of Judah ..." (II Kings 14:21): 4 wds.
61. Go
62. Wander
63. Bosc, e.g.
64. Ties
65. Mime
66. Abominable Snowman
67. War god
68. Enclosures
69. Observe

DOWN
1. Woe!
2. Foundation
3. Collide
4. Timekeeper
5. Tall
6. State
7. Fathers: Fr.
8. Liquid measure
9. ____ Hashanah
10. ____ fixe
11. Allot
13. Against
15. Likewise
20. ____ nous
21. Creepy
25. Bard's river
26. Glass sections
28. Fertilizer type
29. Of air: abbr.
30. Superlative suffixes
31. Stadium cheer
32. Do the backstroke
33. Small monkey
34. Helper: abbr.
36. Indies butter
38. Fool
39. Hemp
40. With speed
45. Females: Fr.
47. Candles
49. Thong
51. Threadlike
52. Swords
53. Blackboard
54. ____ breve
55. At hand
56. Fish
57. Prayers
58. Wish
59. Steady
60. N.Y. canal

ACROSS

1. Gaiter
5. Fish basket
10. Repeat
14. Tops: hyph.
15. Tidal bore
16. Region
17. Needs no explanation: 3 wds.
20. Suture
21. Corrodes
22. Woodwinds
23. Listeners
24. Two-____ sloth
26. Granular
29. Musician Alpert
30. "____ of La Mancha"
33. All: pref.
34. Board
35. Spanish gold
36. Wrapped up: 3 wds.
40. Lubbock campus: abbr.
41. Aromatic plants
42. Overdue
43. Idiot
44. French islands
45. Bowling scores
47. Mellows
48. Noun suffix
49. Fact
52. Land division
53. Nincompoop
56. Sure thing: 4 wds.
60. Confront
61. Revoke
62. Swiss landmarks
63. Tout's offering
64. Wampum
65. Big Bird's retreat

DOWN

1. Lip
2. Church leader
3. Once more
4. Bag or caddy
5. One of the Borgias
6. Floats
7. Vanities
8. Transgress
9. Garland
10. Gave comfort
11. Indian
12. Kept back
13. Clumsy ones
18. Parrots
19. One of the clefs
23. Paddy's land
24. Ministers to
25. Minerals
26. ____ Rica
27. Forgets
28. Breed of cattle
29. Crew
30. Dentist's concern
31. Ridge
32. Protuberances
34. Skins
37. Puzzle
38. Valley
39. Winged
45. Plucks a guitar
46. Idyllist
47. Kinfolk
48. Hurt
49. Major-____
50. Burlesqued
51. ____ off (sore)
52. Bewildered
53. Fire or white event
54. Serpents
55. Nuisance
57. Catch
58. Ike's monogram
59. Preserve

PUZZLE 294

PUZZLE 295

ACROSS
1. "A ____ for Adano"
5. Fragrant wood
10. Medicinal pellet
14. Thine, in Toulouse: 2 wds.
15. Having wings
16. Wild ox
17. Jacket style
18. Governed
19. Gael
20. Outlaw
22. Turn
24. Bistro
25. Skin
26. Vaquero's blanket
29. Colt
33. ____ de cacao
34. Lighter
35. Somebody
36. Harvest
37. Type of clam
38. Ore locale
39. Lt.'s school
40. Sign of omission
41. Northeasters
42. Removed cattle weapons
44. ____ emptor
45. Senate employee
46. Legends
47. Err in bridge
50. Vaquero's topper
54. River of England
55. Interlace
57. Mideast hot spot
58. Wall word
59. Kind of conflict
60. Round: abbr.
61. Cattle stick
62. Thin, as a voice
63. Place for a patch

DOWN
1. Max or Buddy
2. Feminine ending
3. Crazy bird
4. Ranch extension: 2 wds.
5. Decanter
6. Give the slip
7. Small valley
8. Had a taco
9. Southwest stream: 2 wds.
10. Delicate tint
11. Peruvian
12. Plunder
13. Tardy
21. Yawn
23. Reputation
25. Spartan slave
26. Young haddock
27. Mountain ridge
28. Attain
29. Destroyed
30. Sheer fabric
31. Nine: prefix
32. Smoke-dry
34. "Gay ____"
37. Basis of many Westerns: 2 wds.
38. Bret or Bart
40. Projecting rock
41. Getup
43. Started a hand
44. Farce
46. Adored
47. Highway entrance
48. Always
49. Definite taboo: hyph.
50. Identical
51. Ireland
52. Unusual
53. Formerly
56. Bard's before

PUZZLE 296

ACROSS

1. Miami's county
5. Depiction
10. Verbal
14. Stove chamber
15. More pleasant
16. Cotton bundle
17. Actor Foxx
18. Ornament
20. Greek letter
21. Transmitted
22. Acting team
23. Quote
25. Podium
27. Sought
29. Music programs
33. Grades
34. Italian poet
35. Historic time
36. Geraint's wife
37. Rotates
38. Photographer Nykvist
39. Past
40. Actor Wallace
41. Lieu
42. Gently
44. "A —— Garden of Verses"
45. Weapons
46. Zhivago's love
47. Fr. river
50. Thrash
52. Pocket flap
55. Annoyance
58. Pepper grinder
59. Read quickly
60. Telegraph inventor
61. Fixed routine
62. Sharp taste
63. Iron
64. Winter white

DOWN

1. Village
2. Prayers
3. Devotion
4. Terminus
5. Truly
6. Demeanor
7. Ledger item: abbr.
8. Part of Washington's signature
9. Be human
10. Insensitive
11. Shower
12. Thanks ——!: 2 wds.
13. Camera eye
19. Wonderland girl
21. Fr. holy women: abbr.
24. Frosted
25. Singer Osmond
26. Colony insects
27. Pick up the check
28. Cookstove
29. Tote
30. Disclosure
31. Tire pattern
32. The —— of time
34. Single combats
37. Semester
38. Use a spoon
40. French cap
41. Matted wool
43. Adventurous
44. Duplicates
47. Catalog
48. Killer whale
49. Persia
50. Blaze
51. Deprivation
53. Choir member
54. Puffed
56. Electric unit
57. Rocky hill
58. "—— Miniver"

PUZZLE 297

ACROSS

1. Oration
7. Enamels
13. Random try: 2 wds.
15. Blamed
17. Angrily
18. Smokey ——: 2 wds.
19. Hen fruit
20. —— -de-lance
21. Employment suffix
22. Deuce
23. Fibbed
25. Capital of Delaware
27. Undo
28. Antitoxin
30. Actor Cariou
31. Uptight
32. Family car
34. Misers
36. Indicate
38. Ms. MacDonald
42. Lone Star State
46. Cherub
47. Train systems: abbr.
49. Graceful maiden
51. Strike-breaker
52. Defeats
54. Naught
55. Hawaiian food
56. Neighbor of Ger.
57. Spike of corn
59. Molasses liquor
60. Borgnine et al.
62. Greed
64. Say again
65. Threatener
66. Pelted
67. Places

DOWN

1. Barkers' pitches
2. Scups
3. Bric-a-brac stand
4. Superlative suffix
5. Head cook
6. Sank a putt
7. Forbearance
8. Complainer
9. Bakery worker
10. Gist
11. Mao ——: hyph.
12. Able, as a sailor
14. Alpine region
16. Male bees
24. Defective bomb
26. Evensong
27. Old car
29. Actress Normand
31. Bus fare
33. Clear profit
35. Hair pad
37. Emphasized
38. Green quartz
39. Added songs
40. Opposed to
41. Bird's beak
43. —— Affair
44. Land of the free
45. Preened
48. Water vapor
50. Baseball scores
52. Isolated hill
53. Rescues
56. Wise —— owl: 2 wds.
58. Talk wildly
61. Ike's area: abbr.
63. "Norma ——"

242

ACROSS

1. Disney
5. Reflection
10. NBC rival
13. Epithet of Athena
14. Calif. county
15. Circle of light
17. Coward play: 2 wds.
19. Austrian river
20. "So —— My Heart": 2 wds.
21. Parcel out
23. Hops kiln
25. Lotion ingredient
26. Transplanted
30. Scenes
33. Things
34. Local deity
36. How: Ger.
37. Hiatuses
38. Studied carefully
39. Sport
40. Antonym: abbr.
41. More rational
42. Fathered
43. Della and Pee Wee
45. C.F. and Karl
47. Wash out suds
49. Civil wrong
50. Pet rodents
53. —— Zee
57. Came to earth
58. Moving by leaping
60. Grape juice
61. Ordinary
62. Wiesel
63. Liner: abbr.
64. Singer Como
65. Act

DOWN

1. Hospital room
2. To shelter
3. "—— and the Swan"
4. Pubs
5. Customs duty
6. Atlas chart
7. Scope
8. Lasses
9. Held in bondage
10. Greasewoods
11. Unglazed Wedgwood
12. Lath
16. Metallic dirt
18. Les —— - Unis
22. Actor Howland
24. Mortise and ——
26. Harshness
27. Day's march
28. Gum flavor
29. German engraver
31. Bombsight operator
32. Germs
35. Deserve
38. Forgoes: 2 wds.
39. "Lazy fokes stummucks don't ——" (J.C. Harris): 2 wds.
41. Mailed
42. Shoulder gesture
44. Nun
46. Snugly
48. Rub out
50. Hem and ——
51. Actress MacGraw et al.
52. Disparage
54. Cowgirl Evans
55. Songstress Adams
56. Hollow stalk
59. Paving liquid

PUZZLE 298

PUZZLE 299

ACROSS

1. Kermit, for one
5. Danger
10. Rebuke
14. "Saturday Night ___"
15. Wonderland girl
16. Lacquered metalware
17. Not closed
18. Ranted
19. Lamb's pen name
20. Create
22. Servant
23. Lyric poem
24. Surety
26. Aloof
30. Assimilated
34. Wear away
35. Quoted
36. Actor Wallach
37. Jack or trey, e.g.
38. Raise dogs
39. Nuisance
40. Ninny
41. Exploits
42. Sew loosely
43. Incomparable
45. Vocation
46. Ventilates
47. Devotee
48. "77 Sunset ___"
51. Stayed
56. Mine products
57. Palm leaf
59. Appointment
60. Ceremony
61. Competitor
62. Religious image
63. Tootsies
64. Miss Astaire
65. Camper's home

DOWN

1. Horsewhip
2. Mature
3. Stove part
4. Hereditary factor
5. Procession
6. Fill with joy
7. Split
8. Sherbet
9. Guided
10. Is a thief
11. Lounge
12. "I cannot tell ___": 2 wds.
13. Bog fuel
21. Fixed routine
22. Contended
24. Nips
25. Mellowed
26. Retreaded tire
27. Obliterate
28. Telegraph code
29. Strange
30. Counts calories
31. Make fun of
32. Choice group
33. Roadside eatery
35. Vulgar
38. Stein contents
39. Golfer's goal
41. Comic Wilson
42. Slam noisily
44. Lifts
45. Taper
47. Last
48. Type
49. Threesome
50. Nerve network
51. Adore
52. Revise copy
53. Speed
54. English school
55. Baseball's Bucky
57. Monk's title
58. Evict

PUZZLE 300

ACROSS
1. Off-the-cuff: hyph.
6. Highlander
10. Narrow opening
14. Penniless
15. Defrost
16. Shetland, e.g.
17. Place for a posy
18. Unfortunate: 3 wds.
20. Needle hole
21. Weaver's need
23. Machine tool
24. "____ of Fools"
25. In addition to
27. PTA's concern
30. Secure position
34. Holding device
35. Baseball ploy
36. Menagerie
37. Leak out
38. Comic Chevy
39. Orange or Cotton
40. Take advantage of
41. Disgrace
42. Jury
43. Informer
45. Dip vegetable
46. Nobleman
47. 007
48. Top of a wave
51. Crazy bird
52. Naughty
55. Eve tried to do this: 2 wds.
58. Diminish
60. Monster
61. Highest point
62. Actor James
63. Equal
64. Partridge fruit
65. Foe

DOWN
1. Competent
2. Heavy wagon
3. Gallop easily
4. "I Like ____"
5. Hotel worker
6. Doorstep
7. Buddy
8. Dobbin's grain
9. Number for Noah
10. 1984 Tom Hanks film
11. Clumsy fellow
12. Small measure
13. Small child
19. Wind instrument
22. OPEC's concern
24. "____ Like it Hot"
25. Aplomb
26. Vein of ore
27. Troop member
28. Near
29. Witch ____
30. Lover
31. Upper air
32. Bring down
33. Songstress Parton
35. "I ____ return"
38. Scorch
39. Like Telly
41. Maine or Idaho, e.g.
42. Writer's alias: 2 wds.
44. The ____ of two evils
45. Murmur lovingly
47. Goof
48. Farm output
49. Storm
50. Irish republic
51. Capital of Peru
52. Foundation
53. Mighty mite
54. Refuse
56. Beanie
57. Top flier
59. Outlaw

PUZZLE 301

ACROSS
1. Kind of sandwich
5. Injury mark
9. British streetcar
13. Traditional knowledge
14. Concern
15. Tsar, for one
17. White House office
18. Leave out
19. Join
20. Bank person
22. Time belt
24. Prohibit
25. "A Chorus Line" song
26. Lode load
27. River deposit
28. Three, so they say
31. Snare
33. Nonsense!
34. Neptune's domain
35. Johnny-jump-up
39. Lady's maid
42. "____ for Bonzo"
43. Leave windless
44. Owns
45. ____ and games
46. Popeye, for one
48. Flood height
50. Inclined walkway
53. Tennis call
54. Opponent
55. Stir
56. Pod vegetables
57. Start a war
61. Rule of thumb
63. Stink
65. Stern
66. Go bad
67. Church part
68. Ready to pluck
69. Banyan, for one
70. Leading actor
71. Luxury

DOWN
1. Lump
2. "____ at First Bite"
3. River in Russia
4. Author Saul
5. Hit a homer
6. Machine part
7. Grand Canyon locale
8. Sharp reply
9. Quiz answer
10. Scamper
11. Excuse
12. Copper, for one
16. Landlord's due
21. Football position
23. Jitters
27. Hit the ____
28. Crosspatch
29. Dressing gown
30. Of the ear
31. Conger, e.g.
32. Assistance
34. Figure of speech
36. Biography
37. Flightless birds
38. Camp must
40. Pant
41. Chicken ____ king: 2 wds.
42. Cocktail lounge
44. Embarrassing situation: 2 wds.
47. Finds out
48. Folding bed
49. Hit the sack
50. Butters
51. Make one's own
52. Engine
54. Fraud
56. Walesa, for one
58. Opera melody
59. Policemen
60. Leg joint
62. Bind
64. Topsy's playmate

ACROSS

1. Khyber ____
5. ____ touch
10. ____ the Stilt
14. Mine entrance
15. Change to fit
16. Huron's neighbor
17. Baseball in the U.S.: 2 wds.
20. Build
21. Director Kazan
22. Japanese coin
23. Sort
26. Oklahoma city
28. "High ____"
31. Ooze
33. Tangle
36. Between
38. Small particle
40. TV's "F ____"
42. Prima donna
43. Track race
45. Bacchanal's cry
46. Arrests
48. Network
49. Dispatched
50. Kind of bath
52. React to a bear market
54. "Catcher in the ____"
55. Untidy one
57. Mineral springs
59. Immerse
62. Toward shelter
64. Suit or age
68. Antiquated: 5 wds.
72. Wild plum
73. Take up again
74. Civil disturbance
75. Detained
76. Prolonged look
77. Diminutive suffix

DOWN

1. Window glass
2. Hebrew month
3. Plot
4. Twig
5. ____ about town
6. Actress Lupino
7. Miss Evans
8. An ____ a day . . .
9. Discolors
10. Rainy
11. Bearded flower
12. Citrus fruit
13. Adolescent
18. Elevator man
19. Holy person
24. Close at hand
25. Hinder
27. Challenges
28. Young boys
29. Leaves out
30. Metal bolt
32. Tent supports
34. Wanderer
35. Mad as a hatter
37. Fonteyn and Whitty
39. Spouses
41. Jazzman Fountain
44. Bark
47. Tossed greens
51. Grinders
53. Whip
56. Harass
58. Steeple
59. Short race
60. Ait
61. Minnesota Fats's forte
63. Sicilian volcano
65. Landed
66. Coagulate
67. Italian family
69. Wielded the baton
70. That woman
71. Lambkin's ma

PUZZLE 303

ACROSS
1. Essential
6. ___ in point
10. Kiwanis, e.g.
14. Dispatch boat
15. Actor Montand
16. Whetstone
17. Mediocre: hyph.
19. Fence
20. Alaskan inhabitant: abbr.
21. Frenchmen
22. Same here
23. Rockfish
24. Nut type
25. Backwater
28. Dizzy
30. Lone Ranger's pal
31. Citadel
32. Verbal
36. Adjoin
37. Beef grade
38. Slow
39. Got up
40. Effortless
41. Church singers
42. Mr. Butler
44. ___ Green
45. Having vices
48. Lion sound
49. Young turkey
50. Baseball's hot corner
52. Forelimb
55. Opposed to
56. Tour lecture
58. Location
59. Hawaiian dance
60. ___ Cologne: 2 wds.
61. Baseballer Willie
62. Scream
63. Trapshooting

DOWN
1. Urn
2. Singer Burl
3. Tock's partner
4. Japanese volcano
5. In time past: 2 wds.
6. Inventor McCormick
7. Grandparental
8. Adjusts
9. Wind dir.
10. Actor Reeve
11. Reluctant
12. Consolidate
13. Underneath
18. Sprint
22. Cupid's title
23. "___ Are Free"
24. Mention
25. Headliner
26. Timber wolf
27. Responsibility
28. Impose (upon)
29. Multitude
31. College gp.
33. Implant firmly
34. Resembling
35. Northern constellation
37. Pare
41. Babies' beds
43. Shack
44. Author Vidal
45. Muscle cramp
46. Coastal strip of Asia
47. Zany
48. Adversary
50. Quiz answer
51. TV host Monty
52. Malarial fever
53. Discourteous
54. Swimming event
56. "Honor ___ Father"
57. Acorn grown mighty

248

PUZZLE 304

ACROSS
1. SOS!
5. Confronts
10. Conceited
14. L x W
15. Fragrant seed
16. Actress Lanchester
17. Layer
18. Express
19. Kind of party
20. Mix up
22. Cap brims
24. Medicinal portion
25. Hibernia
26. Frozen
29. Snakelike
34. Entertains
36. God: Latin
37. Actress McClanahan
38. Parasites
39. Attempted
41. Coop
42. The Greatest
43. Vocalized
44. Joyful
46. Tranquilizers
49. Mimics
50. Highway
51. Scottish caps
53. Laud
56. Dracula et al.
60. Toga
61. "Tosca," for one
63. Bantu tribesman
64. Mr. Guinness
65. Persuades
66. Being: Latin
67. Parcel out
68. Fly catchers
69. Property document

DOWN
1. Milliners' products
2. Writer Ambler
3. Sly look
4. Eden
5. Smears
6. Deer's hatrack
7. Ceremony
8. Oppposite WNW
9. Bondage
10. Ship
11. Choir voice
12. Austrian river
13. Whiners
21. Fashion
23. Fleur-de-lis
25. Fencing weapon
26. Parties
27. Author Zola
28. Clear
30. Roman official
31. Wrathful
32. Boring tool
33. Wants
35. Delete: 2 wds.
40. Praise highly
41. Overturned
43. Cornelia ____ Skinner
45. Aladdin's treasure
47. For each
48. Gazed
52. Pile up
53. Baby buggy
54. Guise
55. Aid and ____
56. Star in Lyra
57. Trick
58. Otherwise
59. Prosecuted
62. Expert

249

PUZZLE 305

ACROSS
1. Grouch
5. —— waist
9. Scandinavian
13. Trompe l'——
14. Knock for ——: 2 wds.
16. Matured
17. Bill of fare
18. Respect
19. Roast: Fr.
20. 1941 song: 4 wds.
23. On cloud ——
24. Wernher —— Braun
25. Piranha
28. Eucalyptuses: 2 wds.
33. Actor Walter et al.
34. Arabian gazelle
35. Born
36. Director Clair
37. Goblet
38. Soprano Sayao
39. Hoary
40. Knight's helmet
41. Wild plums
42. Calm waters: 2 wds.
44. Finnish baths
45. Religious assoc.
46. Walking stick
47. U.S. flag: 4 wds.
55. Persian poet
56. High nest
57. Modicum
58. Prima donna
59. German refusals
60. Highways: abbr.
61. Footfall
62. Encounter
63. Region: abbr.

DOWN
1. Cock's crest
2. Lively dance
3. Japanese native
4. River from Lake Tana: 2 wds.
5. Hawaiian woman
6. Unaccompanied
7. Are: Fr.
8. "Winnie-the-——"
9. Venturesome
10. Excited
11. Holland: abbr.
12. Revise copy
15. Film teasers
21. Brothers, e.g.
22. Actor Harrison
25. St. John's-bread
26. "—— for Adano": 2 wds.
27. All in: Fr.
28. Scottish hillsides
29. Roster
30. Labor group
31. Wife of Jason
32. Dr. ——
34. —— mater
37. From Athens
38. "The —— of Happiness": 2 wds.
40. Writer Sholom
41. Beach material
43. Bundle up
44. Most lucid
46. "The —— Mutiny"
47. Curtain fixtures
48. Radiate
49. Emcee Garroway
50. Abound
51. N.Y. canal
52. French novelist
53. Colorado Indians
54. Orient

PUZZLE 306

ACROSS

1. "—— Lisa"
5. Bartlett
9. Esprit de ——
14. Organic compound
15. Volcanic flow
16. Woodwinds
17. Beach material
18. Irish island
19. Pie piece
20. "Guys and Dolls" character: 2 wds.
23. Previously, of old
24. Meadow
25. Ascot
28. Actor Young
30. See 63 Across
33. Gossip bit
37. Factual
40. "—— Doone"
41. "Guys and Dolls" character: 3 wds.
44. Hopscotch
45. Legume
46. Wings
47. Click beetle
49. Insane
51. Honorary deg.
52. Cobra
55. Ark measurements
60. "Guys and Dolls" character: 2 wds.
63. "Guys and Dolls" creator, with 30 Across
66. —— spumante
67. Diminutive suffix
68. Aviator Balbo
69. Avoid
70. Sheltered
71. French novelist
72. Suspend
73. Confusion

DOWN

1. Middle, in law
2. Very happy: 2 wds.
3. Time being
4. Pilgrim John
5. Be a team member to: 2 wds.
6. Merit
7. Be of use
8. Belgian marble
9. Monk's hood
10. Mind
11. Pole
12. Wooden nail
13. Compass pt.
21. Ship's diary
22. Cup handle
25. Alpine region
26. Old Greek region
27. Growing out
29. Snatch
31. Last month: abbr.
32. Mrs. Charles
33. Push along
34. Cave dwarf
35. Inward
36. Spar
38. One: Fr.
39. Dutch cheese
42. Ship's chain
43. Passing a law
48. Mr. Bolger
50. Payable
53. Shatter
54. Turkish VIP
56. Porgy
57. Carpet fiber
58. Lugs
59. Dirks
60. Foot part
61. Gordian ——
62. Daze
63. Excavate
64. Devoured
65. Grown boy

251

PUZZLE 307

ACROSS
1. Young lions
5. Phi —— Kappa
9. Identical
13. Highly spiced stew
14. Paddled
15. Selves
16. Chew
17. Horned animal
19. Animal pouch
20. First murderer
21. Delete
22. Tree marsupial
24. Jack rabbit
26. Lodges
28. Large terrier
32. Miss Astaire
33. Stubborn animals
34. Varangians
35. Inlets
36. —— Clara
37. Writer Kingsley
38. "—— the ram- parts . . ."
39. Animal skins
40. Fixed gaze
41. Furry rodents
43. Battery terminals
44. Eternities
45. Giraffe's cousin
46. Blackbird
49. Sprig
50. Baby's seat
53. Borneo apes
56. German river
57. Eye amorously
58. Skirt panels
59. Burrowing animal
60. Activist
61. Engine cover
62. Consumer

DOWN
1. Gear teeth
2. Arm bone
3. Grizzlies' cousins: 2 wds.
4. Cutting tool
5. Brazilian state
6. Ireland
7. Decade
8. Confusion
9. Become angry: 2 wds.
10. Taj Mahal site
11. Cow sounds
12. —— est percipi
14. Verbal exams
18. Goddess of agriculture
20. Sugar source
23. Lubricates
24. Dagger handles
25. Region
26. Billiards shot
27. Good-by: Fr.
28. Relatives
29. Armored animals
30. French river
31. Curvy letters
33. Thick drinks
36. Actor Connery
37. Upon
39. Tine
40. Obstacle
42. Sharper
43. "—— for Corliss": 2 wds.
45. Had title to
46. Crucifix
47. Jason's ship
48. —— of Kashmir
49. Poi source
51. Skillful
52. Nobleman
54. Cry of disgust
55. Also
56. Ratite bird

ACROSS

1. Extorted money from
5. Secret agent
8. Ringlet
12. Church court
13. Meadow
14. Length x width
15. Sacred image
16. Shade tree
17. Explosive noise
18. Cur
20. Tall stories
21. Football pass
23. Jabbed
26. Heavy weight
27. Knight's title
30. Oatmeal-cookie fruit
32. Cows
34. Frequently, in poems
35. Murmur softly
37. Merrily: var.
38. Poisonous snake
40. _____ wave
43. Horse's gear
47. Military group
48. Dancer Shawn
49. Netman Lendl
50. Withered
51. Before, in poems
52. Rail bird
53. Ship's spine
54. Donkey
55. Pile

DOWN

1. Lip
2. Crazy
3. English school
4. Hangs
5. Snow and rain
6. Pill
7. Sweet potato
8. Conspiracy
9. Russian mountains
10. Descartes
11. Falls behind
19. Extreme
20. Scarlet bird
22. Fabulous bird
23. Paid athlete
24. Lout
25. Toolbox
27. Pigpen
28. _____-at-ease
29. King: Sp.
31. Forget-me- _____
33. Lose luster
36. Different ones
38. Badgerlike animal
39. Puts on cargo
40. Elephant tooth
41. Arrow poison
42. Dreadful
44. Bacchanalian cry
45. Franklin's mother
46. Crisp cookie
48. Iced beverage

PUZZLE 308

PUZZLE 309

ACROSS
1. Kitty
5. Oil source
10. Singsong
14. Medley
15. Weighty volumes
16. Whistling swan genus
17. Countess's title
18. "Reversal of Fortune" actor
19. Zinfandel, e.g.
20. United
21. Advantageous position
23. Spree
25. Sounds
26. Make a sudden assault
28. Peace goddess
30. Singular
31. Fight back
33. "Alice" character
36. Actor Ed ____
38. Basketball official, for short
39. Acrylic fiber
41. Peaks: abbr.
42. Card game for two
45. Irish republic
46. Ecclesiastical vestment
47. Small boy
49. Arthurian paradise
52. Organ features
53. Certain rattlesnakes
56. Likable guy?
59. Rainbow: pref.
60. Strong point
61. River to the Baltic
62. Eager
63. Overjoy
64. Split apart
65. News finder?
66. Paper sections
67. Bones

DOWN
1. Equine game
2. ____ Bator
3. Presley trademark
4. Kind of sauce
5. Wasp, sometimes
6. Revere's transport
7. Mine, in Nice
8. Give temporarily
9. Palestinian ascetics
10. Colorful shell
11. Assumed name
12. Particular occasion
13. Travels by ox wagon
21. Business abbreviation
22. Scout's rider
24. Strophanthus product
26. Baby carriage
27. Drying kiln
28. Grenoble's river
29. Fissure
32. Of a historic time
33. Opposite aspects
34. Folk knowledge
35. Humdinger
37. Pull a trailer again
40. Ribbed fabric
43. Pine
44. Menu listings
46. Heavy hammer
48. Hawaiian hawks
49. Oriental
50. September sign
51. Farewell, in Mexico City
52. Fight
54. Refuse: Lat.
55. Mild expletive
57. Murray and Howard
58. Earth goddess
61. ____ y plata

PUZZLE 310

ACROSS

1. Glacial pinnacle
6. Toward the mouth
10. Facts and figures
14. Island off Venezuela
15. Strike an attitude
16. Of an age
17. Go over with a ____ (search thoroughly)
20. Native of: suff.
21. Phoenician seaport
22. Balances
23. Artist Mondrian
24. Unified
25. Fields-Kern song
29. Part of AFL
30. Helm position
31. Actor Hoskins
34. List extender
35. Stinging
37. No-no
38. Cowboy's nickname
39. Police acronym
40. Type of energy
41. Unsuspected details
44. Roman religious buildings
46. Snakelike fish
47. Syllabic sound
48. Body fluids
49. Damage
52. An alarming situation
55. Gator's kin
56. Fencing tool
57. Inventor Howe
58. Descartes
59. Foxx of TV
60. Skin layer

DOWN

1. Secure
2. Sister of Ares
3. Old alphabet character
4. Lincoln or Fortas
5. More spiteful
6. City on the Douro
7. Manner of learning
8. Residue
9. Became more profound
10. Choose
11. "____ by any other name . . ."
12. Like Kate, ultimately
13. Priestly garments
18. Court document
19. ____ far niente
23. ____ Penh
24. Bamako's locale
25. Came to earth
26. Destiny
27. Wild goat
28. Cuban patriot
31. Indonesian island
32. Scottish resort town
33. ____ Lancaster
35. Opposite of 30 Across
36. Small restaurant
37. Rocky crags
39. Glow
40. Like a duck's feet
41. Medium's state
42. Required
43. Architect Saarinen
44. ____ de Perote
45. Alliance
47. Holy: pref.
48. Native of Stockholm: abbr.
49. Naturalist John ____
50. Actor West
51. French painter Bonheur
53. Unclose, poetically
54. Cheer from the corrida

255

PUZZLE 311

ACROSS
1. Side of a doorway
5. Country south of Libya
9. Family car
14. Notion
15. Singer Horne
16. Clan
17. Priests' garments
19. Some Middle Easterners
20. Printer's measures
21. In listening distance
23. Building site
24. "___ and Ivory"
26. Explodes
28. Chews
29. "___ Dreams" (Heart hit)
31. Posters
32. Wear out, as clothing
33. At no cost
37. Appeal
38. Stickers
39. Make over
40. Knitting thread
41. Give up
42. Lustrous fabric
43. Home
45. Blouse
46. Maiden
49. Make amends
50. Cheer for a toreador
51. Fan
54. Turkish high official
57. Flooring squares
59. Police detective
61. Occurrence
62. Eight-sided sign
63. Warmth
64. Acts
65. Shade of color
66. Inactive

DOWN
1. Slangy talk
2. Seaport in Yemen
3. Courier
4. Baseball stick
5. Washes
6. Statesman Kissinger
7. Picnic visitors
8. Smidgen
9. Prestige
10. Miscalculate
11. Watch faces
12. Head monk
13. Birds' homes
18. Makes a cat's noise
22. Heeds
25. "Yes! We Have No ___"
27. Chorus
28. ___ monster (lizard)
29. Swap
30. Patriot Nathan ___
31. Secret agent
32. Give a meal to
34. Turned back
35. Revise copy
36. One billion years
38. Reprimand
42. Beach
44. Animals
45. Treeless plain
46. Was overly fond
47. Active
48. Brawl
49. Firebug's crime
52. Fog
53. Toward the center of
55. Aim
56. Johnson of "Laugh-In"
58. Finale
60. Ho ___ Minh City

256

ACROSS

1. Give the once-over
5. Shopper's paradise
9. Color fabric
12. Writer Bombeck
13. Of birds
15. River duck
16. Frog's kin
17. Skin prefix
18. Signs
19. Dish depositories
22. ____ de plume
23. His wife turned salty
24. Trotter's cousin
27. Cooler cooler
30. It all comes out in the ____
33. German exclamation
34. Calm with drugs
37. Gab
39. Marble game
42. " . . . a ____'clock scholar"
43. Aged bronze surface
44. Airport abbr.
45. Kennel occupants
47. Command to Fido
48. Potter's rabbit
50. Large amount
52. Sniggler's quarry
53. Jack Lemmon film, with "The"
60. Secluded valley
61. Cobblers' concerns
62. Fleshy fruit
64. The walls have ____
65. "Stormy Weather" singer
66. Wicked
67. Needle hole
68. Grapefruit skin
69. Certain farmer's valley

DOWN

1. Collection
2. Gator's kin
3. Asian nursemaid
4. Kim Basinger film
5. Woman's title
6. With: Fr.
7. Money in Milan, once
8. Mary's pet
9. Inside-out bump
10. Chatty beasts?
11. Urban trains
14. Place for polish
15. Cravat holder
20. Scandinavian
21. Presently
24. Treaty
25. Needed liniment
26. Twilled cotton cloth
27. Notions
28. Desert plants
29. Moral precept
31. Mattress covering
32. Short-story author
35. Psi power
36. Poetic dusk
38. Autocrat
40. Heads
41. Gambol
46. Junior
49. Skipped the wedding march
51. Wild party
52. One of the Fords
53. Modeling medium
54. Roll call response
55. "Little ____ of Horrors"
56. In days of ____
57. Hawaiian goose
58. Change address
59. German chemist Fischer
60. Command to an ox
63. Museum extension

PUZZLE 313

ACROSS

1. Stylish
5. Peace symbol
9. Bar or cake substance
13. Student cheers
17. Italian coin, once
18. Arab prince
19. Center of activity
20. Charles Lamb
21. Sandarac tree
22. Women's dressing jackets
24. Saucy talk
25. Cite
27. In the present
28. Playfully mischievous
30. Antiquity
31. "____ Girls"
33. Aggregate
34. Zero
37. Knowledge
39. Esprit de ____
41. Dogs' yowls
45. Poetic works
47. Drawing room
49. Paint ingredient
51. Ratify
52. Allude
54. Forefront, for short
55. Deep, audible breaths
57. Monk
58. Signified
60. Polka ____
61. Foot part
63. Jeers
64. Speak
65. Muse of love poetry
66. Dried plums
68. Machine part
69. Expression of rebuke
72. Creek
73. Lawful
75. ____ favor
76. Mournful poem
77. Site of Taj Mahal
79. Man-o'-____ bird
80. Pertaining to hydrophobia
82. Canadian-border lake
83. Wildly
85. Interior design
87. Unit of energy
89. Cry-for-aid letters
90. ____ Alamos
92. Label
93. Charged particle
95. Pours
99. Variety of lettuce
101. Chants
105. Off
106. Conservative: 2 wds.
109. Indian canoe material
110. Portion out
111. To shelter
112. Israeli seaport
113. Ancient instrument
114. Goad
115. Sonneteer
116. Greens gadgets
117. To be, to Pliny

DOWN

1. Bivalve
2. Take on
3. Iraq's neighbor
4. ____ blanche
5. Solves
6. Arabian gulf
7. Pep
8. ____ go bragh
9. Give in abundance
10. Black gold
11. Affirm
12. Mexican coins
13. Summaries
14. Jai ____
15. Snake's sound
16. Door frame
23. Wise legislator
26. Genre
29. Fellow
32. Banana sundae
34. Character on "Cheers"
35. Whim
36. Football player: 2 wds.
38. Areas of churches
39. Opposed
40. Temporary economic decline
42. Meal scraps
43. Whittle
44. Word with happy or stick
46. Imbed firmly: 2 wds.
48. Young boy
50. Bird's sound
53. One who resists authority
55. Bean for Chinese sauce
56. Entangle
59. Stitch over
60. Equine mother
62. Shawl
64. Actor Mineo
65. Unearthly

66. Baby carriage, in London
67. Capital of Latvia
68. Proofreader's mark
69. Purloin
70. Premium on money in exchange
71. Caustics used in soapmaking
74. Flit about socially
75. Duffer's aim
78. Put at rest
80. Automaton
81. Draws back in fear
84. Over there
86. Prestige
88. Procured
91. Belt
94. Gallant
95. Slightly wet
96. Creamer
97. Ancient Roman statesman
98. Farm building
100. Swing at
101. Concerning: 2 wds.
102. Certain votes
103. Commits a faux pas
104. ____-Ball
107. Mild expletive
108. Freeze

1	2	3	4		5	6	7	8		9	10	11	12		13	14	15	16
17					18					19					20			
21					22			23							24			
25			26				27				28		29					
		30					31		32		33							
34	35	36		37		38		39			40		41		42	43	44
45			46		47		48			49		50		51			
52				53		54				55			56		57		
58				59				60				61		62			
		63					64			65							
66	67				68				69					70	71	
72			73		74			75			76					
77		78		79			80			81		82				
83			84		85		86			87		88		89		
		90		91		92					93		94			
95	96	97			98		99		100		101				102	103	104
105				106		107			108				109			
110				111				112				113				
114				115				116				117				

259

PUZZLE 314

ACROSS

1. Amo, amas, ——
5. Comic-book response to a punch
8. Box
12. Garment stiffeners
17. Foal's mom
18. Numero ——
19. Sped
20. "Serpico" director
21. "Beauty —— the eye of the beholder" (Hungerford): 2 wds.
22. —— Buddhism
23. That hurts!
24. "Watership Down" author
25. T.H. White work: 5 wds.
29. Ukraine seaport
30. Fills up
31. Sioux, e.g.
33. Canad. prov.
35. Modernist
36. Speaker of baseball
37. Bond
38. Most meager
42. "A Witness Tree" poet
44. Canape spread
45. First name in mysteries
46. Loch ——
48. Vote in favor
49. Gave medicine to
50. Island welcoming gift
51. Susan Hayward film
52. Mexican treat
54. Actor Jack
55. Did everything possible: 4 wds.
62. Country hotel
63. Sumac tree
64. Paddle
65. Ginger ——
66. "There Is Nothin' Like ——": 2 wds.
69. Cry of disapproval
70. Biblical land
72. Place for corn
73. Tardy
74. Actor or actress in "On Golden Pond"
76. "—— a Time": 3 wds.
78. Unsorted flour
79. Mr. Sahl
80. "Casablanca" character
82. Forty winks
83. Judd and Willie
85. Sunset, for one
87. Koran faith
91. Established, as a foundation: 3 wds.
94. Indic vernacular
95. Bard's river
96. Goodman ——
97. Done
98. Feeds the kitty
99. Handwriting-on-the-wall word
100. Bobbsey twin
101. Actress Patricia
102. Dog-walker's need
103. Chem. suffixes
104. Explosive letters
105. Strays

DOWN

1. Friendship
2. One of "The Three Sisters"
3. Sylvia Plath work
4. 140 pounds, in Britain: 2 wds.
5. Greek beverage
6. Special people
7. Candies made of sugar paste
8. Famed coronation seat, with 85 Down: 2 wds.
9. Sulks
10. Foot part
11. Practice
12. Blackboards
13. British royal house
14. Poisonous fungi
15. Native of Aden, e.g.
16. Rds.
26. Desire
27. Adherent: suffix
28. Struck, old-style
32. Action
34. Achilles ——
36. "Happy Birthday ——": 2 wds.
38. Vend
39. Algonquian
40. Arabic letter
41. Sargasso et al.
43. Flower cluster
44. Indigent
47. Threw rocks at
49. Gloomy
51. —— of Cleves
53. Literary collection
54. Flower part
56. Father ——

260

57. Corrupt
58. Midday
59. Not any
60. Charles Lamb
61. IOU
66. Novelist Paton
67. Article feature
68. Huntress of mythology
69. Naughty, naughty!: 2 wds.

71. Prevailing
72. Finishing touch on a structure
74. Baptism receptacle
75. Just —— throw away: 2 wds.
77. Platform
79. Fashionable
81. ETA abbr.
84. "Both —— Now"

85. See 8 Down
86. State tree of Texas
88. "—— Come Back"
89. Lend ——: 2 wds.
90. Blackbirds
92. Level

93. Budget item
94. Lyricist David

PUZZLE 315

ACROSS

1. Shopper's paradise
5. Lamp necessity
9. "___ and the Fatman"
13. Yawn
17. Eye tunic
18. Bewildered
19. "It ___ Me Babe"
20. Norway's patron saint
21. Neighbor of Mo.
22. "The Odd Couple" playwright
24. Salamander
25. Eaten away
27. Triumphant cry
28. Prison bigwigs
30. Alias
31. Reduction
33. No-seats sign
34. Order
39. Roams
41. Yarn flaws
45. High-quality vineyard
46. Collars
48. Charged particles
50. Dwarf buffalo
51. Prefix with verse or son
52. Monastery head
54. Dolt
56. One of the dwarfs
57. Type of soprano
60. Playwright O'Casey
61. Hot dogs
63. Changes direction
65. Sci-fi servant
68. Costly
69. Payment
72. Follow
74. Postpone
77. ___ et ubique
78. Roman loan
79. Wheat grown for forage
81. Glacier covering
82. Cheese town
84. Make golden
87. English theologian
88. Teacher's org.
89. Psalms interjection
91. Sassy
93. Monotony
96. Blue
98. Part of speech
100. Motorist's gp.
101. Field event
105. Old French coin
106. Pleated trims
110. "Auntie ___"
111. Dumb-founded
115. Acclaim
116. In excess of
117. Extreme
118. Wild plum
119. Gumbo ingredient
120. Patton and MacArthur: abbr.
121. Night twinkler
122. Not new, in Edinburgh
123. Appear

DOWN

1. Soften
2. Affirm
3. Gauzy fabric
4. Four-wheeled carriage
5. Cowboy's handkerchief
6. Purpose
7. Kauai keepsake
8. Rose-red spinel
9. Fronton
10. Intend
11. Be aware of
12. Lab burners
13. Venice taxi
14. Helm position
15. Hock
16. Newts
23. Catch a fly
26. Scrape by
29. B & O and Penn.: abbr.
32. Ancient Tokyo
34. Slimy stuff
35. Sea eagle
36. Puzzled
37. Truck sections
38. Dwindled
40. TV eyesore
42. Emphasize
43. Clod
44. Pouches
47. Take wing
49. Spoke
53. Gov. bond
55. Nourish
58. Bombard
59. Molding

62. Highlander's refusal
64. Obstacle
66. Metrical foot
67. Small change
69. "___ a Woman" (Beatles tune)
70. Moon's pull
71. Trickle

73. Mother of Castor
75. Becker boomers
76. Votes for
80. Mentioned
83. Conquers
85. Coin spent in Sofia
86. Sideboard
90. Luck
92. Gait

94. Water, to Pierre
95. Mexican snacks
97. Couples
99. Sac
101. Los Angeles blight
102. Possess
103. Portent
104. Tease

107. Ocean fish
108. Ireland, in Gaelic
109. Shut loudly
112. Baseball stat
113. Eskimo knife
114. Mountain pass

PUZZLE 316

ACROSS

1. Mary's pet
5. Olive color
9. Broad valleys
14. Keep ___ to the ground
19. Nutmeg covering
20. Republic of Ireland
21. 1st German president (1919-25)
22. Ballroom dance
23. Scurried
25. Egg order
27. Use the cellular
28. Greek peak
29. Actress Debra ___
30. Comply
33. Baseball's Tommie ___
34. Draegermen
35. Female
36. Spoiler
39. Male deer
41. Wise herb?
43. Property
44. Three voices
45. Chalcedony
49. Indian rice
50. English queen
51. "___ Misbehavin'"
52. General Robert ___
53. Fragrant-flowered shrubs
58. Baseball's Trammell
59. Permit
60. Solo
61. Confined
62. Affect deeply
65. "Swan Lake" costumes
66. Elm and Main
68. Shipment
69. "Purple People ___"
70. Assignment
71. Composer Siegmeister
72. Breakfast dishes
78. Close
79. Chip in chips
80. Feast
81. Rhythm
82. Doctrines
83. Suffix with pun or gang
84. Look after
86. Toledo's lake
87. Kasparov's game
88. Vouches
91. When it's hot in Paris
92. Sagittarius, e.g.
95. Extra
96. Embossed
98. Flimsy
99. Ankle bones
100. Accompany
101. Evergreen
104. Fraud
109. Planet
110. Lease again
111. Cure
112. Lake bird
113. Win by ___
114. Old Hebrew measures
115. Hankers
116. Supplemented

DOWN

1. ___ Vegas
2. Rainbow
3. Peasant commune
4. Cutlass
5. Argue
6. Small brook
7. "Chances ___" (Mathis hit)
8. Garden plot
9. Bombe, e.g.
10. Misapplication
11. Sweet-sounding Horne
12. Aquatic bird
13. Duroc's digs
14. Supporters: suff.
15. Elbow
16. Moslem prince
17. Borders
18. Knock
24. Obey
26. Taps
28. S-shaped
30. Test
31. Disgrace
32. Actor George ___
33. Donkeys
34. Pine Tree State
37. 5-stringed instruments
38. Good ___
39. Blots
40. Threefold
42. Some copiers
45. Stinging jellyfish
46. "Kate & ___"
47. Perform again
48. English sand hills
50. Piercing tools
54. Dairy-case item
55. Fry
56. Modify
57. Rue
61. River in France
62. Ancient Celtic tribe
63. Hes
64. Legendary king of Troy

264

65. Spuds
66. Office workers
67. Floor piece
69. ____ Park, Colorado
70. Kill
72. Household appliances
73. Go in
74. "Golden Boy" playwright
75. Auto shoes
76. Cream
77. Spirited horse
84. Ancient helmets
85. Carrying case
87. Pizza topping
89. Sings
90. Jib
92. Pale
93. Horned animal
94. Con-stellation
95. Indiana cager
97. Hearth fire
99. Bulrush
100. Norma ____ Baker
101. Charleston's st.
102. Paid player

103. Radiation dosage: abbr.
104. Bashful
105. "____ Haw"
106. Perfect
107. A Stooge
108. Cease

PUZZLE 316

PUZZLE 317

ACROSS
1. Uncooked
4. Applaud
8. Arouse
12. In history
13. Ore vein
14. Opera feature
15. "A Few Good ___"
16. Finishes
17. Portable shelter
18. Pull behind
20. Tire features
22. Filmy
24. Bosc or Bartlett
25. Learning
26. Left, on a ship
27. Buddy
30. Imitated
31. "Just the Way You ___"
32. Duet plus one
33. Tie the knot
34. Bent the truth
35. Egg layers
36. 2000-pound units
37. Sticky substance
38. Fight against
41. Destiny
42. Steel component
43. Adam's garden
45. Believe it or ___!
48. Carpet feature
49. Theatrical part
50. Roofing substance
51. Looks
52. Market
53. Heavens

DOWN
1. Ewe's mate
2. Years of life
3. Was curious
4. Cloudless
5. ___ Island Sound
6. Do sums
7. Nagged
8. Common liquid
9. Neighbor-hood
10. Nice
11. Consumes
19. Film critic Rex ___
21. Pied Piper's follower
22. Cabbage salad
23. "Ryan's ___" (soap opera)
24. Skin openings
26. Monet and Manet, e.g.
27. Gifts
28. "___ Misbehavin'"
29. Be defeated
32. "___ Old Black Magic"
34. ___ Angeles
36. Prongs
37. Talk-show group
38. Tears
39. Buffalo's Great Lake
40. Shoe bottom
41. Tumbled
44. Female deer
46. Acorn bearer
47. Attempt

ACROSS

1. Hubbub
4. Undercover agent
7. Small wrinkly-faced dog
10. Cram
11. Twentieth letter
12. Half of a pair
13. "___ Baba and the Forty Thieves"
14. Gently strike a golf ball
15. Correct text
16. Go back
18. Experiments
19. Braid
22. Bride's partner
25. Basketball-goal part
26. Possessed
29. Deserve
30. Roll of money
31. Halo
32. Lamb's mother
33. Breakfast meat
34. Encouraged
35. Plane terminal
37. Servants
40. Six-legged animal
44. Shade trees
45. Leather-workers' tools
47. Television character Grant
48. Poisonous snake
49. False statement
50. Researcher's room
51. Votes against
52. In addition
53. Tavern beverage

DOWN

1. Slightly open
2. Hill's partner
3. Leave out
4. Wounded by a bee
5. Caress
6. Thus far
7. Pea containers
8. Segment
9. Fetches
14. Prissy
15. Snaky fish
17. On top of
18. Comedian Conway
20. Hobo
21. Help
22. Mild expletive
23. Uncooked
24. Metallic rock
26. Embrace
27. Exist
28. Pop
30. "___ and Peace"
31. Music and painting, e.g.
33. Belonging to him
34. Coffee servers
35. Magazine fillers
36. Lubricated
37. Cruel
38. Likewise
39. Mischief-makers
41. Singer Fitzgerald
42. Type of fossil fuel
43. Hose
45. Pie ___ mode
46. Victory

267

PUZZLE 319

ACROSS

1. Faucet
4. Qualified
8. Poker stake
12. Anger
13. Broadway beacon
14. Portal
15. Least heavy
17. Smell
18. Unsuccessful Ford
19. Rip
21. Up-to-date
23. Washed with clean water
27. Trot
30. Stop-sign color
32. Apprehensive
33. So be it!
35. I-topper
37. Cowgirl Evans
38. Chardonnay and Chablis
40. Auto fuel
42. "____ Miserables"
43. T-bone and sirloin
45. Small bite
47. Civil uprising
49. Judge's hammer
53. Not different
56. Lunch hour
58. Time periods
59. Al or Tipper
60. Earth's light source
61. Camper's shelter
62. Snow slider
63. Dangerous curve

DOWN

1. Flooring square
2. Like a desert
3. Wooden pins
4. Deer's horn
5. Honey-making insect
6. Misplaced
7. Go in
8. Decorated
9. Signal yes
10. Also
11. Misjudge
16. Rooster's mate
20. Be ill
22. Get hitched
24. Close securely
25. Author Stanley Gardner
26. Pigments
27. Spielberg shark movie
28. Leave out
29. Actor/dancer Kelly
31. Poodle, e.g.
34. Closest
36. Light brown
39. Hit the slopes
41. Wrote one's name on
44. Tunes
46. Butter portion
48. Screwdriver, e.g.
50. Clamp
51. Ostrichlike birds
52. Telescope part
53. Place
54. "You ____ There"
55. Chess piece
57. Metallic rock

ACROSS

1. Garden of Paradise
5. Constricting snake
8. Taxi
11. Entice
12. Bottle tops
13. Fib
14. Home-buyers' loans
16. Lyric poem
17. Knight's title
18. Blush
20. Near the bottom
23. Narrate
25. Hail, to Caesar
26. Gypsy Rose ____
27. Does sums
31. Newborn cow
33. Mouse's kin
35. Film spool
36. Singer Fitzgerald
37. Small drink
39. Boxer Muhammad ____
40. ____-of-fact
43. Illuminated
44. Thin and tasteless
47. Card spot
49. Hole in one
50. Hopeful thinkers
55. Wrath
56. Intend
57. Close tightly
58. Twice five
59. Venomous serpent
60. Askew

DOWN

1. Dutch ____ disease
2. Pair
3. Make a mistake
4. Butterfly catchers
5. Satchel
6. Sung drama
7. Valuable item
8. Lump of dirt
9. ____-de-camp
10. Has-____ (former star)
12. Life's work
15. Young woman
19. Darling
20. Shoestring
21. Racetrack shape
22. Satisfactory
24. Smallest amount
28. "Let's Make a ____"
29. Sandwich shop
30. Narrow opening
32. Renown
34. Cravat decoration
38. Formally proper
41. Odor
42. Varieties
44. Bide one's time
45. Real-estate unit
46. High schooler
48. Leaning Tower city
51. Spigot
52. Use needle and thread
53. Paving material
54. Cunning

PUZZLE 320

PUZZLE 321

ACROSS

1. Bandleader Lombardo
4. Hairless
8. Bikini top
11. Region
13. Butter substitute
14. Chest bone
15. Hindrance
16. Cat's cry
17. Hole in one
18. Recedes
20. Bordered
22. Groom's partner
25. Sneaky
26. Decay
27. Baseball event
30. Nights before
34. March date
36. Blemish
37. Rescue
38. Short note
39. Thought
41. Untruth
42. Gave food to
44. Meadow
46. Spaghetti, e.g.
49. Table doilies
51. Unrefined metal
52. Posterior
54. Noisy
58. ____ Pan Alley
59. Cut to size
60. Relieve
61. Unhappy
62. ____ Christian Andersen
63. Not many

DOWN

1. Car fuel
2. Large vase
3. Affirmative vote
4. Explosive device
5. Strong brews
6. Author Tolstoy
7. Fastening peg
8. Boast
9. Pilaf ingredient
10. Retired for the night
12. Matured
19. Plead
21. Coloring agents
22. Hat part
23. Went by bus
24. List entry
25. Dried up
28. Among
29. Furious
31. Singer Jerry ____
32. Malevolent
33. Plant starter
35. Plush
40. Toward the stern
43. Soil
45. ____ of Wight
46. Pans' partners
47. Opera solo
48. Dispatch
49. Primary
50. Weapons
53. Pitcher's stat
55. Blockhead
56. Take advantage of
57. Morning moisture

PUZZLE 322

ACROSS

1. Highway division
5. Tree fluid
8. Six-sided solid
12. Frosted
13. Even score
14. Parched
15. Poke
16. Fruit cooler
17. Hindrance
18. 12th-grader
20. Prim
22. Corn unit
23. _____ Diego
24. Crab's cousin
28. Temperamental
32. Actor Wallach
33. Little bit
35. Fish eggs
36. Looks after
39. Mechanical devices
42. Lout
44. Mongrel dog
45. Settle, as a dispute
48. Zoo employee
52. Teheran's nation
53. Boxer Muhammad _____
55. Alan _____ of "M*A*S*H"
56. Finger ornament
57. Dad's boy
58. Observed
59. Golf ball pegs
60. Harbor boat
61. Jerk

DOWN

1. Mouth parts
2. Land measure
3. Sign gas
4. Whirlpools
5. Played the lead
6. Help
7. Looks secretly
8. Gambling place
9. Large vases
10. Prejudice
11. Nervous
19. Stable morsel
21. Ewe's mate
24. Permit
25. Spanish cheer
26. Storage crib
27. Cloth shred
29. Mine yield
30. Speck
31. Affirmative word
34. Support
37. Activities
38. Unhappy
40. Expected
41. Oily
43. Banquet
45. Soil
46. New York canal
47. Walking stick
49. Appeal
50. Biblical garden
51. Military grade
54. Gehrig of baseball

PUZZLE 323

ACROSS
1. Barrels
5. Tree juices
9. Yes votes
13. Parisian river
14. Unaltered
15. Farmland measure
16. Unwarranted
17. Neighborhood
18. Huh?
19. Type of whiskey
20. Lady's title
22. Stuck-up one
23. Jamie ___ of "M*A*S*H"
25. Ceases
27. Subways' kin
29. ___ out (barely make)
30. Not many
33. Singer Ross
36. Sacred writings
39. Toward the center
40. Mine rock
41. Danger
42. Hidden passengers
44. Soothed
45. Swindle
46. Chart
47. Double curve
48. Cannoli filler
51. Rim
55. Certain woodwind
57. Gala
59. Free
60. ___ suey
61. Sandwich shop
62. Martini garnish
64. Staffer
65. Singer Guthrie
66. Crow's cousin
67. Lads
68. Howls
69. Pitcher

DOWN
1. Nairobi's site
2. Downy duck
3. Wildebeest
4. Look to be
5. Shovel
6. Ambiances
7. First performances
8. Dead ___ Scrolls
9. Gapes
10. Sound repetition
11. Saudi, e.g.
12. TV unit
13. Ride the waves
21. Classifieds
22. Grasslands
24. Refresh
26. Snow runner
28. Wyoming town
30. Mink and sable, e.g.
31. A Great Lake
32. Fuse
33. Record
34. Involved with
35. Soon
36. Daytime drama
37. Weep
38. Kid
43. Military female, formerly
47. Consume
48. Heavy cords
49. Score
50. Threesomes
52. Ambition
53. Contributor
54. First garden
55. Cleveland's state
56. Physique
58. Bygone time
60. Taxi
61. Little bit
63. Rule

272

PUZZLE 324

ACROSS

1. "____ on the Range"
5. Garden-watering tools
10. Father's Day month
14. Once ____ a time
15. Mature
16. India's continent
17. Animal fat
18. Idaho's capital
19. Loaned
20. Chicken ____ king
21. Soil
22. Dwellings
24. Rains ice
26. Swing loosely
27. Positive response
28. Tot's bike
32. Included
35. Trick
36. Lend an ____ (listen)
37. Necklace unit
38. Street talk
39. "____ and the King of Siam"
40. Shade tree
41. Heap
42. Nips
43. Cosmetic item
45. Scoundrel
46. Friendly
47. Art gallery
50. Comment
53. Musical with "Memory"
54. Short snooze
56. Above
57. Wed on the run
59. Israeli seaport
60. Ore source
61. Dinner breads
62. Request
63. +
64. Sugary
65. Experiment

DOWN

1. Hawaiian dance
2. Whitish gems
3. Virtuous
4. Cease
5. Nuns' garments
6. Scents
7. Clubs or hearts, e.g.
8. Chicago Loop trains
9. Pilfering
10. Junky car
11. Pre-owned
12. Supreme Court count
13. Snacks
21. Title of ownership
23. Rear
25. Stared at
26. Mr. Sinatra
28. Horse-race site
29. Penny
30. Highway division
31. Historic times
32. Cain's brother
33. Cold-cut shop
34. Moist
35. Locale
38. Decals
39. Clerk
41. Mix
42. Male voice part
44. Traps
45. Most adorable
47. Syrup source
48. Mother's brother
49. Foals' moms
50. Frolic
51. Wicked
52. Bill of fare
53. Songwriter Porter
55. Bog fuel
58. Near the ground
59. Appropriate

273

PUZZLE 325

ACROSS
1. Stuffed
5. Space
9. Crowd's sound
13. Cleveland's lake
14. Scallion's cousin
16. "___ Cinders" (cartoon)
17. Selves
18. Popular lady
19. Dart
20. Sight or taste, e.g.
22. Divide
24. Acorn-bearing tree
26. Humorist George ___
27. Mattered
31. Splashes
35. Mischief-makers
36. Pare
38. Shaved clean
39. Siesta
40. Platters
42. In favor of
43. Baby bird's comment
46. Beer or ale, e.g.
47. Cat call
48. Severely
50. Swiftly
52. Draw
53. "___ of La Mancha"
54. Like a fillet
59. Put off
63. On the sheltered side
64. Upset
67. Mature
68. Paper quantity
69. Extra
70. Hymn ending
71. Hits
72. Goulash, e.g.
73. Boys

DOWN
1. Lawyer's charges
2. Coax
3. Big tawny cat
4. School assignments
5. Steal from
6. "___ Day at a Time"
7. Lubricates
8. Burrowing mammal
9. Revitalize
10. Earthen pot
11. Dismounted
12. Pace
15. Tibet's neighbor
21. Have lunch
23. Commotions
25. Retained
27. Easy task
28. D-Day beach
29. Higher
30. Kentucky ___ (race)
31. More cunning
32. Wished
33. Swashbuckler Flynn
34. Like some winters
37. Corn unit
41. Did the backstroke
44. Admires
45. TV host Donahue
47. ___ spring (spa)
49. Rude stares
51. Cushion
54. Fishhook point
55. Margarine
56. Lowest tide
57. Little drinks
58. Mattress support
60. Peru's capital
61. Mimicked
62. Cravings
65. Before, to a poet
66. Morning droplets

PUZZLE 326

ACROSS
1. Marsh
6. Stalemates
10. Young grizzly
13. Himalayan nation
14. Upon
15. Southern cornbread
16. Supermarket lane
17. Horse's neck hair
18. Diva's solo
19. Ms. Garbo
20. Or ___! (threat)
21. Some rodents
22. Indian garment
24. Swiss cottage
26. Playful remarks
30. Campfire remains
32. Place
33. Canvas shelter
35. Droops
39. Ornamented
41. Brash newcomer
43. Red hair dye
44. Cowboy Autry
46. Pennsylvania port
47. Temptress
49. Insight
51. Cuddle
54. Snake's sound
56. Jai ___
57. At a distance
59. Furious
64. Tot's toy
65. Overly thin
66. Eat away
67. Fencing sword
68. "Of ___ and Men"
69. Legends
70. Thing, in law
71. Arctic transport
72. Go stealthily

DOWN
1. Hosiery problem
2. Small dam
3. Church recess
4. Soda fountain drink
5. Polite word
6. Not as wild
7. Venice native
8. Long time periods
9. Address
10. Reef material
11. Merge
12. Animal
15. Fleas, e.g.
23. Johnson of "Laugh-In"
25. Chops
26. Dull
27. Assistant
28. Las Vegas light
29. Subway-station item
31. Daze
34. "The Razor's ___"
36. Cooking fat
37. Group of three
38. Wineglass feature
40. Manicurist's concern
42. Church benches
45. Improve
48. Kingdoms
50. Small land masses
51. Consumer advocate Ralph ___
52. Wed secretly
53. Bargain events
55. Bothered
58. Flunk
60. Tehran's site
61. Mouselike animal
62. Notion
63. Student's seat

275

PUZZLE 327

ACROSS
1. Canvas cover
5. Casual talk
9. Swamps
13. Locale
14. Helpers
16. Director Kazan
17. Fibber
18. Trample
19. Semester
20. Bugs Bunny's treats
22. Pavement pit
24. Actor Brynner
25. Verbal
26. Thus far
29. Rod and ____
32. Power
36. Rowboat blades
38. Smacks
40. Jack rabbit
41. Salt Lake City's site
42. Title of respect
43. Nights before holidays
44. Make over
45. More unusual
47. Dole
48. Ahchoo!
50. Gush
52. ____ Palmas
53. Green bean
55. Admirer
57. Scuffed
60. Account examiner
64. Actor Baldwin
65. Actress Keaton
67. Walking stick
68. Weathercock
69. Alpine call
70. Young foxes
71. Goals
72. Bastes
73. Coin opening

DOWN
1. Bath powder
2. Operatic solo
3. Bring up
4. Dodge
5. Fortresses
6. Broadway smashes
7. Ruckus
8. Pace
9. Biblical birthplace
10. Butter substitute
11. Lass
12. Equivalent
15. Fern seeds
21. "____ Miss Brooks"
23. Sun-bronzed
26. Not mine
27. Gobbled up
28. Swap
30. "Born Free" star
31. Dens
33. Fray
34. Scacchi of "The Player"
35. Votes in favor
37. Footwear fasteners
39. Type of school
45. Cure
46. Gases up
49. Postal code
51. Crumple
54. Mexican farewell
56. Small cuts
57. Rescue
58. Family group
59. Tear
60. Once again
61. Mouse appendage
62. Aware of
63. Take five
66. Fruity drink

PUZZLE 328

ACROSS

1. Sizable
6. "Moonstruck" star
10. Iowa State's town
14. Sea
15. Exist
16. Sulk
17. Publish
18. Iridescent gem
19. "Carmen" solo, e.g.
20. Transmitting
22. Cut apart, as in biology
24. Before, in poetry
25. Horn sounds
26. Anyplace
30. Worries
33. Greases
34. Way out
36. Boise's site
38. Certain poem
39. Irritating
41. Relatives
42. Sticker
44. 5,280 feet
45. Roll-call response
46. Soda sipper
48. Domestics
50. Rubbish
52. Dog's doc
53. Most prying
56. Roosts
60. Hubbubs
61. Cassette
63. Divvy up
64. Look sullen
65. Ages
66. Spooky
67. Makes a mistake
68. Small hollow
69. Soak, as tea

DOWN

1. Prunes
2. Estate measure
3. Bridle part
4. Male geese
5. Whole
6. Obstruct
7. With it
8. Avoid
9. Alleviation
10. Gathered
11. Additional
12. Heroic tale
13. Chair
21. At no time
23. Small branch
25. ____ Columbia, Canada
26. Timber
27. Pelts
28. Vote into office
29. Test
31. Stolen
32. Blouse
35. Mosaic piece
37. Singles
39. Fierce look
40. Boldness
43. Monet and Degas, e.g.
45. Small ax
47. Squandered
49. Poems
51. Fixed gaze
53. Back of the neck
54. Aroma
55. Tart
56. Annoyance
57. Rabbit's relative
58. Ohio Indian
59. Ooze
62. Frying vessel

PUZZLE 329

ACROSS

1. Trickle
5. Sun-dried brick
10. Coal product
14. Steak order
15. Ward off
16. Lend a ____ (help)
17. Not entirely shut
18. Aide
19. Without moisture
20. Exiling
22. Foggy
23. Expected
24. Sunbathe
25. Hooded snake
27. Sprinkled
31. Toad features
33. Appear
35. Financial assistance
36. Had breakfast
37. Fashion
38. Employ
39. Christmas
41. Command to Fido
42. Striped cat
44. Type of sovereign
46. Public argument
48. Umpire's call
49. Owns
50. Used a broom on
53. Black and white, e.g.
59. Liquid rock
60. Arab chief
61. Pepper's partner
62. Again
63. Wedding walkway
64. Shower-wall piece
65. Take care of
66. Memos
67. Close with force

DOWN

1. Dreary
2. Indian prince
3. Iraq's neighbor
4. Green gem
5. Bowman
6. Pastrami seller
7. Forthright
8. Floating ice mass, for short
9. Broad-antlered beast
10. Shackled
11. Canoeist's needs
12. Make with yarn
13. Whirlpool
21. Underwater boats
22. Cushion
24. Domesticated
25. Inch along
26. Daisylike flower
27. Water holes
28. Cheek reddener
29. What ____ is new?
30. "The ____ Hunter"
31. Ebb
32. Tiny particle
34. Look at
37. Vaccination
40. Spotted cat
42. Afternoon socials
43. Demands
45. Groove
47. Throttles
50. Piggy-bank feature
51. Signal hello
52. Level
53. Buckeye State
54. Nuisance
55. Stack
56. Dog's wagger
57. Cinders of cartoons
58. Flower stalk
60. ____ Diego

278

ACROSS

1. Fragrant flowers
6. Jazz's Fitzgerald
10. Swiftly
11. Multicolored horse
12. Holland, with "The"
15. Modern: pref.
16. Moistened
17. Youngsters
21. Car fuel
22. On the ocean
26. Recruit
27. Dutch painter
33. Box
34. Holland export
35. Singletons
36. Debt note
37. Saucy
38. Evergreen tree
39. 2,000 pounds
40. ____ canto
41. Curvy letter
42. Pesky children
45. Frosted
48. Tantrum
49. Fruit stones
50. Composer Stravinsky
51. Taken ____ (surprised)
52. Auction offer
54. Father
57. Fleecy one
58. Commercials
61. Flight records
63. Strong brew
64. Escaped quickly
65. On
66. Colorado Indians
67. Dairy workers
70. Yield
71. Soothe
72. Ventilate
73. Trampled
74. Declare
77. Opposite of NNE
80. Sabots
83. Gymnast Korbut
84. Dirt
85. Curious
86. The things here

DOWN

1. Sprinted
2. Unlock
3. Glut
4. Reverberate
5. Visit
6. Epochal
7. "The ____ Ranger"
8. Actress Cheryl
9. Reply: abbr.
13. Lion's sound
14. Singer Stansfield
17. Those persons
18. Military assistant
19. Movable spans
20. Theologian's school: abbr.
21. "Pygmalion" playwright's monogram
22. Egyptian snake
23. Winter Olympics athlete
24. Corn spikes
25. Liberal ____
27. Seaport in Holland
28. Space chimp
29. Males
30. Tip
31. Female deer
32. Bulb plots
43. Dust cloth
44. In the past
46. Spy group: abbr.
47. And so forth: abbr.
51. Deeply impressed
52. Sad
53. Smidgen
55. Actress MacGraw
56. Delores ____ Rio
57. Inventor Whitney
59. Extinct bird
60. Drove too fast
62. Compass point: abbr.
64. Distant
65. Emote
68. Actress Jackson
69. Demeanor
74. Song for one
75. Clothes
76. An apple ____ . . .
77. Iranian ruler
78. Painful
79. Dampens
80. Took first place
81. Gel
82. "____ Done Him Wrong"

PUZZLE 330

• DUTCH TREAT •

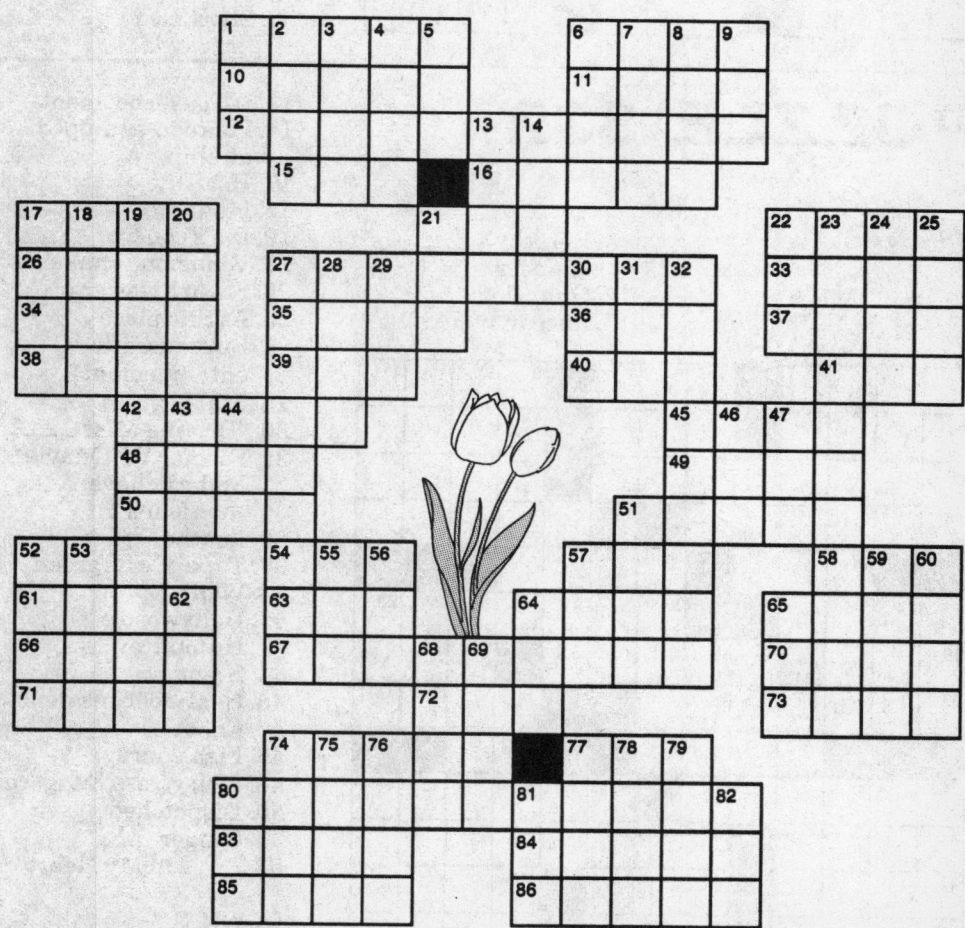

279

PUZZLE 331

ACROSS

1. Trumpet
5. Mysterious saucer
8. Indication
12. Concept
13. Tier
14. Run in neutral
15. Frolic
16. Unselfish
18. Geologic time unit
19. More prudent
20. Permit
21. Persia, today
23. Thorax bone
25. Doorway shelter
27. Tightly closed
31. ____-dish pie
32. Make weary
33. Most peculiar
36. Selected
38. And not
39. Talk wildly
40. Pig's home
43. Courted amorously
45. Chew and swallow
48. Pirate's hoard
50. "____ of Green Gables"
51. Greasy
52. Spigot
53. Folk singer Seeger
54. Shaft
55. Sneaky
56. Garden of Paradise

DOWN

1. Employ
2. Aroma
3. Stayed
4. Short sleep
5. Encouraging
6. Opponents
7. Proprietors
8. Knight's title
9. Golden calf, e.g.
10. Paste
11. Bird's home
17. Toledo's lake
19. Ashen
22. Develop, as fruit
24. Conductor's stick
25. "Much ____ About Nothing"
26. Marry
28. Heeded
29. Bard's before
30. Bear's lair
34. Plants seed
35. Rainbow and brook
36. ____-crawly
37. Once held
40. Cease
41. Musical group
42. Shout
44. Spoken
46. Feed the kitty
47. Adolescent
49. Nautical affirmative
50. Orangutan, e.g.

PUZZLE 332

ACROSS

1. Pile on
5. Apple cider girl
8. Dorothy's ____ slippers
12. Qualified
13. Race in neutral
14. Largest continent
15. Pontoon-equipped airship
17. Healthy
18. Magnate
19. Pin's cousin
21. Venomous snake
22. Future flowers
23. At this place
25. Bureaucratic entanglement
29. Stable grain
30. "Driving Miss ____"
32. Former VP Quayle
33. Make believe
35. Auctioned off
36. Loathe
37. Type of evergreen
38. Want
41. Hollywood's Humphrey ____
44. Scent
45. Next-door resident
47. Conceits
48. Fish snare
49. Songstress Fitzgerald
50. Dispatched
51. Ginger ____
52. "____ in My Heart"

DOWN

1. Final
2. Follow orders
3. Individually priced
4. Remove from office
5. Abadan's country
6. Relaxation room
7. Wide streets
8. Most crude
9. Secondhand
10. Comedian Cosby
11. New Haven university
16. Chop off
20. Whirlpool
22. Groom's lady
23. Short jump
24. Hearing organ
26. Very cute
27. Buddy
28. Goal
30. Cherished
31. Insect's feeler
34. Parched sensation
35. Breathed deeply
37. Thick mist
38. Carries out
39. Boundary
40. Before too long
41. Mouthful
42. Actor's part
43. Ambush
46. Snaky fish

PUZZLE 333

ACROSS
1. Woodsman's tool
4. Fashionable
8. Actress Markey
12. Shark feature
13. Uncouth
14. Singer Jerry ____
15. Spasm
16. Thicke of "Growing Pains"
17. Saga
18. Corn covering
20. Stripe
22. Cut drastically
24. Chimney deposit
25. Pitch
26. Predicted
30. Prone
31. Golfer Irwin et al.
32. Bill's partner
33. Beckoned
35. Soprano Lily ____
36. Aardvarks' morsels
37. Parson's home
38. Snow vehicle
41. Nimbus
42. Wolf's cry
43. Verve
45. Furious
48. U.S. author James ____
49. Warbled
50. Glacier material
51. Short talk
52. Uproar
53. Exam mark

DOWN
1. Toward the stern
2. Caesar's dozen
3. Charms
4. Collision
5. "The Incredible ____"
6. Mrs. Eddie Cantor
7. Suppressed
8. Turns inside out
9. Scruff
10. Hip bones
11. Pack of cards
19. Utilize
21. Foot digits
22. Doe's mate
23. Canter
24. Sandal bottoms
26. Most remote
27. Financial
28. Years and years
29. Snout
31. Like some juries
34. Followed
35. Sidekick
37. Tropical fruit
38. "Pygmalion" playwright
39. Company's symbol
40. Water jug
41. Penmanship
44. Tai language
46. Hole in one
47. Actress Sandra ____

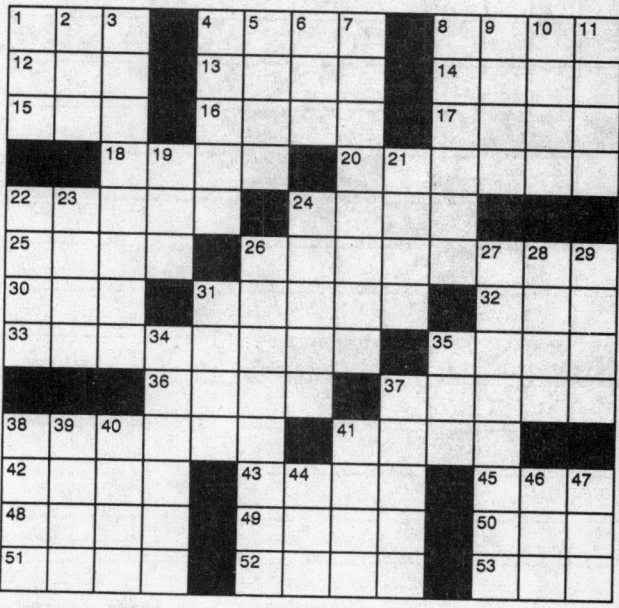

PUZZLE 334

ACROSS
1. Massage
4. African republic
8. Hunted animal
12. Gone by
13. Pueblo Indian
14. Relaxation
15. Reporter's question
16. Slaughter of baseball
17. October stone
18. Large bag
20. Embassy official
22. Forage plant
24. Wharf
25. Leave out
26. Elephant's tooth
27. Camp bed
30. Baking pans
31. Hasten
32. Cobbler's concern
33. Unit of work
34. Female sheep
35. Robert ____ Warren
36. Defeat
37. Great fear
38. Actress Hedy ____
41. Lock openers
42. Sour
43. Kite attachment
45. Author Fleming
48. Kiss-and-____
49. Educator Young
50. A Gabor
51. Guitarist Duane ____
52. Refuse
53. Confederate soldier

DOWN
1. Uncooked
2. Cry of disgust
3. Increasing
4. Prague native
5. Slab
6. Year: Sp.
7. Track-and-field plates
8. Showy flower
9. Knocks
10. Jacob's twin
11. Shout
19. ____ of the Apostles
21. Furniture wood
22. Ballot
23. Arab chieftain
24. Noiseless
26. Frustrated
27. Chintzier
28. Mrs. Chaplin
29. Minister to
32. Agile
34. Always, in verse
36. Poorly
37. Put off
38. Tardy
39. Got an A on
40. Bland
41. Pottery furnace
44. Tavern brew
46. "____ Maria"
47. Arrest

PUZZLE 335

ACROSS
1. Pack
5. Oddball
9. Cow's chew
12. Brainstorm
13. Kirgiz mountains
14. Barely make (a living)
15. Topples
17. Fresh
18. Locale
19. Seamstress Ross
21. Apron
24. Actress MacGraw
25. Roof part
26. Manitoba's capital
31. Whiskey
32. Caesar or Cobb
33. The Gay Nineties, for one
34. Once
36. Mine entrance
37. Shake
38. View
39. Socrates's forum
41. Soft cheese
43. Actress Wray
44. Near East region
49. Mimic
50. British school
51. "Stanley & ___"
52. Crimson
53. Cult
54. "L'il Abner" cartoonist

DOWN
1. Spasm
2. Fuss
3. Honey
4. King's home
5. Mane site
6. Adamson's lioness
7. "Norma ___"
8. Break up
9. Leggy insect
10. Polynesian instruments
11. Moist
16. Clumsy vessel
20. High priest
21. Feudal servant
22. BLT dressing
23. Elated
26. "___ and Peace"
27. Sickly
28. Vote against
29. Ireland
30. Attendance
32. Mexican garments
35. Damage
36. Vinegar's acid
38. Family mem.
39. Remotely
40. Ogle
41. Alliance
42. Let
45. Dined
46. Personal pension plan
47. Snap
48. Parapsychology concern

PUZZLE 336

ACROSS
1. Electrical unit
4. Informal talk
8. Soft drink
12. Style
13. Change
14. Storyteller
15. Ignited
16. Vicinity
17. Otherwise
18. Thick-skinned mammal
20. Health resort
22. Individual
23. Lasting forever
27. Swindle
29. Request
30. Earlier
31. Bustle
32. Heaths
33. Decade
34. Supporting limb
35. Poisonous serpents
36. Ascend
37. Newborn's outfit
39. Raspberry
40. Measure: abbr.
41. Grassy areas
43. House or robe
46. Unwritten
48. Diving bird
50. Medicinal plant
51. Specify
52. "Malcolm X" director
53. Whitetail
54. Mothers of wool
55. Pen

DOWN
1. Hooter
2. Tresses
3. Body of legends
4. Tall wading bird
5. Sandwich
6. Fruit beverage
7. Bread browners
8. Transparent
9. Linseed or olive
10. ___ Palmas
11. Exist
19. Writing liquid
21. Black-eyed vegetables
23. Marry on the run
24. Citizens
25. Periods in history
26. Solitary
27. Fete
28. Notion
29. Put off
32. Gym pads
36. Quarrel
38. Anesthetic
39. Large bundles
41. Ornate fabric
42. Tallow
43. Naughty
44. Malt liquor
45. Digit
47. Inexperienced
49. Low island

PUZZLE 337

• FOR THE TIME BEING •

ACROSS
1. Drink flavoring
5. Faucet
8. Biblical pronoun
11. First man
12. Puccini specialty
13. Actress Dawn Chong
14. For the time being
16. In the mode of
17. Fond du ____
18. Estate house
20. Less aggressive
23. Chirps
25. Long, long ____
26. Agitated
28. Emerald or ruby
29. Watchful
30. Misstep
32. Dishearten
34. Society page word
35. Observes
36. Mentioned
38. Inn
40. Make falsely larger
41. The Gay Nineties, e.g.
42. For the time being
48. Pitch
49. Actor Connery
50. Opera set in Egypt
51. Foxy
52. ____ Harbor, Long Island
53. Circle

DOWN
1. Feline
2. Poetic form
3. On the ____ (escaping)
4. Sufficient
5. Musical syllable
6. Broadcast
7. Compensation
8. For the time being
9. Angel's headgear
10. 12-month period
12. Curve
15. Rowboat's adjunct
19. Inclined
20. Childhood game
21. Ripened
22. For the time being
23. Squeeze
24. Pitcher handles
26. Retreat
27. Canadian Indian
29. Naive
31. Scarlet
33. Author of "The Gold Bug"
36. Turning part
37. Exemplary
38. New York team
39. Spoken
40. Enclosure
43. Legume
44. Crone
45. Spanish river
46. Hullabaloo
47. Race section

PUZZLE 338

• COOKWARE •

ACROSS
1. Neck part
5. Spinning toys
9. Church bench
12. Alack's partner
13. Mine entrance
14. A Gershwin
15. Crooked
16. Barrie character
18. Pickled flower bud
20. Dakota Indians
21. Glided over ice
23. Oriental coin
24. "The Road Not ____"
25. Selects
29. Native: suff.
30. Edgar Allan ____
31. Dined
32. Started again
35. "____ 66" (TV show)
37. Carp
38. Did the fox trot
39. Reporter Lane
41. Bottle dweller
42. Sleek cats
44. Iridescent gem
47. Circle segment
48. Actor Estrada
49. "____ That Tune"
50. West of Hollywood
51. Cozy rooms
52. Hindrance

DOWN
1. Collar
2. Pub order
3. Breakfast treats
4. Holdings
5. Put on cassette
6. River to the Baltic
7. Cherry stone
8. Sound system
9. Type of organ or dream
10. Baseball statistics: abbr.
11. Pallid
17. Nevada city
19. Writing implement
21. Hoosegow
22. "Kiss Me, ____"
23. "____ Devil"
25. Edible fish
26. Kitchen utensil
27. Diminutive suffix
28. Planter's need
30. Tent holder
33. Military group
34. Like some potatoes
35. Jogged
36. Pungent vegetables
38. Office furniture
39. Dr. Zhivago's love
40. Fairy tale beginning
41. Show amusement
42. Dawber or Shriver
43. Previous to, poetically
45. Doctors' group: abbr.
46. Journey part

PUZZLE 339

Two clues for each number and two puzzle diagrams—which answer goes where? That's your dilemma. Answer the clues and then decide in which crossword pattern the answer fits. The first two words have been entered for you.

ACROSS

1. Treaty
   Stalk
5. Astern
   "Born in the ___"
8. Wanderer
   Mr. Flynn
10. Tread
    Black bird
12. Spry
    Acid type
13. Wearies
    Begets
15. Cloaks
    Street show
16. Extinct bird
    Muses or Mets
17. Road turn
    Time periods: abbr.
18. American painter
    Artist Pablo ___
21. Gives up
    "___ & June"

22. Italian painter
    French painter
25. Terminal: abbr.
    Bat wood
28. Lebanese president
    Gemayel
    Actress Moran
29. Neck parts
    Slow, in music
31. Actress Blair
    Actress Burke
33. Actor Goodeve
    Tribe chief
34. Ripener
    Winter vehicle
35. Penetrate
    Challenges
36. Miscalculate
    Have being
37. This, in Spain
    Sole

DOWN

1. Trap
   Arctic explorer
2. Knight's wear
   Roman robes
3. Muslim rulers
   Beds
4. Man
   Sound
5. Behave
   Navy initials
6. Crusoe's pal
   Smarts
7. Nest
   Bulls, in Seville
9. Intensify
   Failures
11. Actor Sean ___
    Marries
14. ___ Canals
    Stage decor
19. Commercials
    Business abbreviation

20. Cower
    Staggered
21. Insinuator
    Coal
22. Father
    Singer Torme
23. Opera tune
    Iowa city
24. Pancho ___
    Color lightly
25. Shoe covers
    Netman Agassi
26. Belief
    Guide
27. Cowboy's mount
    Type of turf
30. Director
    Glimcher
    Bible country
32. Cool drink
    Timetable abbr.

PUZZLE 340

ACROSS
1. Small timepiece
6. Lamb's cry
9. Atlas entry
12. Maui greeting
13. Raised trains
14. Pitcher's stat
15. More primed
16. Authorize
18. Sloppy state
20. Calm
21. Soothsayer
24. Moth-repellant wood
25. Defeat
26. Pub missiles
28. Still
29. Mexican food items
30. The ___ of Reason
33. Military grades
34. Cozy
35. Smudge
38. Shrilly crying
40. Cake, e.g.
42. Sewn joint
43. Native of Moscow
45. Clutch
48. Hail, to Livy
49. Ransom ___ Olds
50. Up and about
51. Word of agreement
52. Adriatic ___
53. Suspicious

DOWN
1. Armed conflict
2. Actress MacGraw
3. Highest
4. Baby birds' comments
5. Severe
6. Spelling contest
7. Gifts to charity
8. Facets
9. Cried, as a cat
10. Coliseum
11. Kitchen utensil
17. Lode loads
19. Family car
21. Layer
22. Shad's output
23. Tasteless
27. Garden blooms
29. Lingers
30. Enliven
31. Firearm
32. Omelet ingredient
33. Ship deserters
34. Thinly scattered
35. Mist
36. Shade of violet
37. Road curves
39. Lawful
41. New Haven school
44. Actress Peeples
46. Galahad's title
47. Use a crowbar

PUZZLE 341

ACROSS
1. Cask part
6. Banquet
11. Culmination
12. Speaks
14. Montana's capital
15. Picturesque
16. Morays
17. Pulverize
19. Hot spring
20. Woman of Eden
21. Orderly
22. Toppled
23. People
25. Soothed
26. Washington bill
27. Boar's mate
28. Bridal contribution
31. Milers, e.g.
35. Real estate unit
36. Throngs
37. Ancient Egyptian king, for short
38. Born
39. Give lunch to
40. Divan
41. Call off
43. Elevate
45. Audience's call
46. Schools, in Paris
47. Gleamed
48. Horse

DOWN
1. Shirt part
2. Rudder handle
3. Singing brothers
4. Moving truck
5. Analyze
6. Finicky
7. Clearly outline
8. Dined
9. Sight and touch
10. Three-bagger
11. Fledgling's cry
13. Burn with hot water
18. TV spots
21. Actor Perkins
22. Doe's offspring
24. Painful
25. Years and years
27. Conquers
28. Fox trot, e.g.
29. Indian and Arctic
30. Twist sharply
31. Old-world deer
32. French star
33. ___ grouse
34. RBIs, e.g.
36. Brawl
39. Maidenhair
40. Blackthorn fruit
42. Pigeon's noise
44. Rate per hundred: abbr.

285

PUZZLE 342

Diagramless crosswords are solved by using the clues and their numbers to fill in the answer words and the arrangement of black squares. Insert the number of each clue with the first letter of its answer, across and down. Fill in a black square at the end of each word. Every black square must have a corresponding black square on the opposite side of the diagram to form a symmetrical pattern.

ACROSS
1. Daddy
5. Houston and Snead
9. Selves
10. Snares
12. Ragtime dance: 2 wds.
14. Collection
15. Pub quaff
16. Free
18. Before, in poems
19. Ending for young
20. Heads, in Le Havre
23. Untidy
24. Glowing gem
25. Afternoon drink
26. Melody
27. Ages and ages
28. Mine find
31. Without preparation: 2 wds.
34. Rock
35. Assistant
36. Resorts
37. Marries

DOWN
1. Cat and canary
2. Chills and fever
3. Harbor
4. Inquire
5. Fashion
6. Comic Johnson
7. Damage
8. Games
11. Pigpens
13. Listeners
17. Help with the dishes
18. Slithery fish
19. Ocean
20. One ___ customer: 2 wds.
21. Heroic stories
22. Magic cards
23. Waiter's offering
25. Big bags
27. Author Ferber
28. Migratory worker
29. Mr. Foxx
30. Stares at
32. Cut off
33. Cold and damp

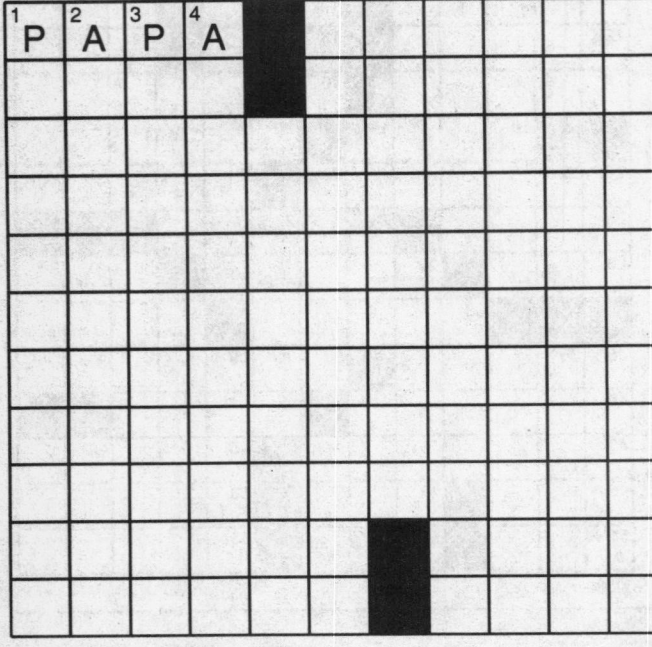

PUZZLE 343

ACROSS
1. Firmament
4. Alice's co-worker
7. Dead heat
8. Operated
9. Lease
10. Skier's place
12. Church seat
13. Mediterranean, for one
14. Chop
15. Grain for Dobbin
16. Bar order
17. Nureyev's art
20. Ditty
22. "We ___ the World"
23. Grade
26. Racecourses
28. Shrew
29. Fuss
30. Musician's engagement
31. Tin product
32. Sick
33. Clan emblem
36. Walk in water
38. Noteworthy age
39. Grease
40. Recede
41. Raw mineral

DOWN
1. Ragout
2. Relatives
3. However
4. To and ___
5. Baby's seat
6. First number
9. Feel contrite
10. Fasten securely
11. After a while
12. Prince Charles's game
13. Boot bottoms
14. ___ Vegas
17. Breakfast strips
18. Noah's boat
19. Snarl
21. Princess of Monaco
24. Appendage
25. Future chicken
27. First father
32. Inactive
33. Ball holder
34. Globe
35. Diner's check
36. Court
37. Tune

ACROSS

1. "The Tender ___"
5. Boring tool
8. Marathon, e.g.
9. Artist Man ___
10. Huron's neighbor
11. Looked over
13. Heckle
15. Reverberate
18. Water barrier
21. College gal
22. Type style
23. Has
24. Frosted
25. Urge on
28. Moistens
29. ___ and alack!
30. Bright star
33. Donate
34. Memorable periods
35. Work by Keats
36. Mailed
37. Proper
42. Enthusiasm
46. Celebration
47. Female sheep
48. Grasp
49. Morning moisture
50. Seven ___

DOWN

1. Acacia, for one
2. Uncommon
3. Caustic liquid
4. Fruit rind
5. Exist
6. Passage
7. Soap ingredient
12. Design scheme
13. Agrees silently
14. Proclamation
16. Milk source
17. Farm clucker
19. High cards
20. Crazy
22. Dessert treat
25. Slithered
26. Surfaced
27. Employ
28. Spend unwisely
29. Time past
30. Towhee's home
31. Mineral deposit
32. Delivery truck
38. Ova
39. Caution
40. Essayist's pen name
41. Snoozes
43. Went ahead
44. Amazement
45. Brand-___

PUZZLE 344

Starting box on page 525

GIVE AND TAKE

PUZZLE 345

Change the 4-letter words on the left to the 5-letter words on the right by giving and taking letters. Add one to the word on the left to form a 5-letter word. Then subtract one letter from that word to form a new 4-letter word. Next add a letter to form a new 5-letter word; subtract a letter to form a new 4-letter word. Finally, add a letter to form the word given on the right. The order of the letters may be rearranged in forming new words.

Example: VEST, STOVE, TOES, THOSE, SHOT, SHORT

1. CHIN ___ ___ ___ ___ STEIN

2. DIET ___ ___ ___ ___ SPIRE

3. ISLE ___ ___ ___ ___ FIEND

4. KEEL ___ ___ ___ ___ STOLE

5. LIEF ___ ___ ___ ___ HIKED

6. MEAL ___ ___ ___ ___ BREAK

7. NAPE ___ ___ ___ ___ LEAST

PUZZLE 346

ACROSS
1. Limb
4. That girl
7. Kind of moss
9. Cupolas
11. Divide evenly
12. Turn into
13. "The _____ Tourist"
16. All-purpose bag
18. Rex or Donna
19. Knievel, for one
21. "_____ Little Indians"
22. Head: Fr.
23. Terminate
24. Sprite
27. Skillful
29. Understands
31. Depots: abbr.
33. Refuse
36. Strike
37. Stone or Iron
40. Singing voice
41. Neighbor of Ga.
44. Six-shooters
47. Hold it!
48. Dill seed
49. Gospel preacher
52. Whole
54. Caper
55. Arrests
56. _____ de foie gras
57. Spanish lady: abbr.
58. "_____ and Peace"

DOWN
1. Plant louse
2. Scan
3. Colt's mom
4. Ad _____ committee
5. Speak grandly
6. Take out
8. Watch over
9. Erases
10. Begin: 2 wds.
11. Vistas
12. Uncovered
13. Singer Garfunkel
14. Curved letter
15. Bye-bye, in Birmingham: hyph.
17. Antiquity
20. Profundity
25. Rent
26. Wild
28. Mai _____ (cocktail)
30. Trays
32. Radio interference
34. Allen or Lawrence
35. Israeli dance
37. Southern constellation
38. Kelly and Hackman
39. Happenings
42. _____ Angeles
43. Liable
45. Aquatic mammal
46. Cookie
47. More crafty
50. Chew on
51. Kett of the comics
53. "_____ Little Teapot": 2 wds.

Starting box on page 525

PUZZLE 347   QUOTAGRAM

Fill in the answers to the clues below. Then transfer the letters to the correspondingly numbered squares in the diagram. The completed diagram will contain a quotation.

1. Meeting

$\overline{5}$ $\overline{43}$ $\overline{3}$ $\overline{26}$ $\overline{7}$ $\overline{28}$

2. Decatur's state

$\overline{39}$ $\overline{41}$ $\overline{35}$ $\overline{19}$ $\overline{44}$ $\overline{15}$ $\overline{46}$ $\overline{25}$

3. Mystifies

$\overline{13}$ $\overline{22}$ $\overline{2}$ $\overline{8}$ $\overline{31}$ $\overline{11}$ $\overline{49}$

4. Poult's parent

$\overline{10}$ $\overline{30}$ $\overline{47}$ $\overline{23}$ $\overline{4}$ $\overline{14}$

5. Muffled sound

$\overline{6}$ $\overline{16}$ $\overline{38}$ $\overline{36}$ $\overline{40}$ $\overline{24}$

6. TV's forerunner

$\overline{17}$ $\overline{33}$ $\overline{12}$ $\overline{1}$ $\overline{29}$

7. Restricted

$\overline{34}$ $\overline{42}$ $\overline{18}$ $\overline{9}$ $\overline{21}$ $\overline{27}$ $\overline{32}$

8. Peace of mind

$\overline{37}$ $\overline{45}$ $\overline{20}$ $\overline{48}$

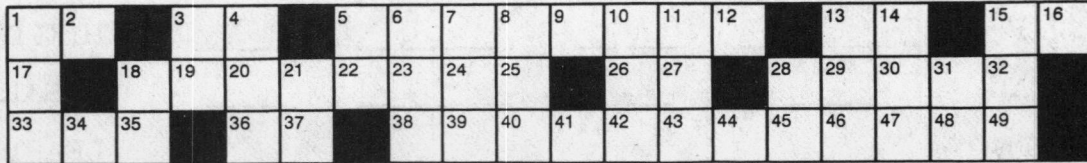

PUZZLE 348

ACROSS
1. Gorilla
4. Rooster's mate
7. Slack
8. Fuss
9. Verve
11. Assert
12. Look over
14. Prayer ending
15. Cravat
16. Play on words
17. Had lunch
20. Jumps
22. Abatement
25. Transparent
28. Real-estate contract
29. Choler
30. More unfavorable
34. Wear away
36. Drips
37. Banes
40. "____ the season ..."
41. Grassland
42. Bullfight shout
44. British nobleman
45. Dowels
47. Solo for Sills
48. Sketch
50. Knight's title
51. Plumb or Arden
52. "For ____ a jolly ..."
53. Kennedy or Weems

DOWN
1. Malt drink
2. Buddies
3. Correct
4. Shelter
5. Paradise
6. Neither's partner
10. Spike
11. Entertain
13. Society-page word
14. Fall fruit
17. Entire
18. Golf peg
19. Greek vowel
21. Farmland units
23. Utilize
24. ____ diem
26. Punching tool
27. Fish eggs
29. Utopian
31. Long-tailed rodent
32. Glide on snow
33. Double curve
35. Musical drama
38. Acme
39. Sleigh
41. Bear homes
43. White heron
44. A Great Lake
46. Rescue
47. Fire residue
49. Marry

Starting box on page 525

WORD MATH PUZZLE 349

In these long-division problems, letters are substituted for numbers. Determine the value of each letter. Then arrange the letters in order from 0 to 9, and they will spell a word or phrase.

1

0	1	2	3	4	5	6	7	8	9

```
              M U D
        ┌─────────────
E L L │ T Y P E D
         E L L
         P I D E
         M T N D
         P L M D
         P U E P
         D N P
```

2

0	1	2	3	4	5	6	7	8	9

```
                L E N
          ┌─────────────
L E S S │ V A L I S E
           E O S N
           O E L E S
           O L S S E
           L L V C E
           L P A S L
           O N E I
```

3

0	1	2	3	4	5	6	7	8	9

```
                R O E
          ┌─────────────
E G O │ S T E E R
         E G O
         R T H E
         R C G C
         H H U R
         C T R C
         I R E
```

PUZZLE 350

ACROSS

1. Actress Harper
5. La Scala melody
6. Spurn
7. Near miss: 2 wds.
11. Bogus
12. Sapling
13. Tropical fruit
14. Abadan's country
15. Scalpel
16. Pond sounds
18. Growing out
19. Burnished
20. Mount Ida's locale
21. Eddy/MacDonald songs
22. Plugs
23. Oath
24. Shock
26. Vatican dwellers
27. —— d'oeuvres
28. Frugal fellow
29. Toward shelter
30. Impersonated
31. London guard
34. Ne'er-do-well
35. Advance
36. Harrow's rival

DOWN

1. Washington port
2. Aphrodite's son
3. Father
4. Endorses
6. Drudge
7. Rankle
8. Collection
9. Faucet problem
10. Bifocal or zoom
11. Apartment
13. Campground pests
15. Toll
16. Kasparov's game
17. Ceremony
18. Epochal
19. More convinced
20. Armistice: hyph.
21. Hoodwinked
22. Binge
23. Lid
24. Moby Dick's foe
25. Totem ——
26. Document
28. Glossy fabric
32. Revise copy
33. In addition

Starting box on page 525

PUZZLE 351   CHANGAWORD

Can you change the top word into the bottom word in each column in the number of steps indicated in parentheses? Do not change the order of the letters, and change only 1 letter at a time. Proper names, slang, and obsolete words are not allowed.

1. LIVE (4 steps)　　2. LOST (4 steps)　　3. LIVE (4 steps)　　4. LOST (5 steps)

HOLE　　　　　　BORN　　　　　　LOAD　　　　　　TIME

ACROSS

1. Frosted
5. Bird of peace
6. Fitting
9. Priest's robe
12. S-shaped curve
13. In addition
14. Dessert option
15. Residences
20. Finale
21. Cereal grain
22. Far from each other
24. Nothing
25. Short in stature
26. See 13 Across
28. Fence door
29. Extinct bird
30. Painful
33. Pigpen
36. Ashen
37. Milky gem
38. Oolong
39. Magician's stick
40. Illuminated
41. Appear
42. Assist
43. Departed
44. Solar disk
45. Cunning
46. Employs
47. Grew older
48. Actor Arkin
51. Holstein or Jersey
52. Hat
53. Earth fuel
56. ____ de menthe
58. Picnic pest
59. Actress MacGraw
60. Put into words
65. Water barrier
66. Beams
67. Kiln
71. Be in debt
72. Single unit
73. Exhaust
74. Chair

DOWN

1. Wedding vow
2. Gear
3. Adam's mate
4. Land title
6. Everyone
7. Greek letter
8. 2,000 pounds
9. Mimic
10. Fuzz
11. Four-poster
13. Choir voice
16. Sorrow
17. Sound receiver
18. Festive
19. Locate visually
23. Amazement
24. Animal farm
26. Related
27. Lyric poem
28. Set
29. Fine and ____
30. Individual performances
31. Suppose
32. Scales of prices
33. Spirited horse
34. Adolescent
35. Sweet potato
36. Bucket
39. Used to be
41. Fret
43. Firearm
44. Time past
47. Perform
48. High card
49. Feeble, as an excuse
50. Pinnacle
53. Go by
54. Printers' measures
55. Dined
56. Talon
57. Hoarfrost
59. Fuss
61. Golf teacher
62. Jogged
63. Sight organ
64. Periods
68. Contend
69. Age
70. Seine

Starting box on page 525

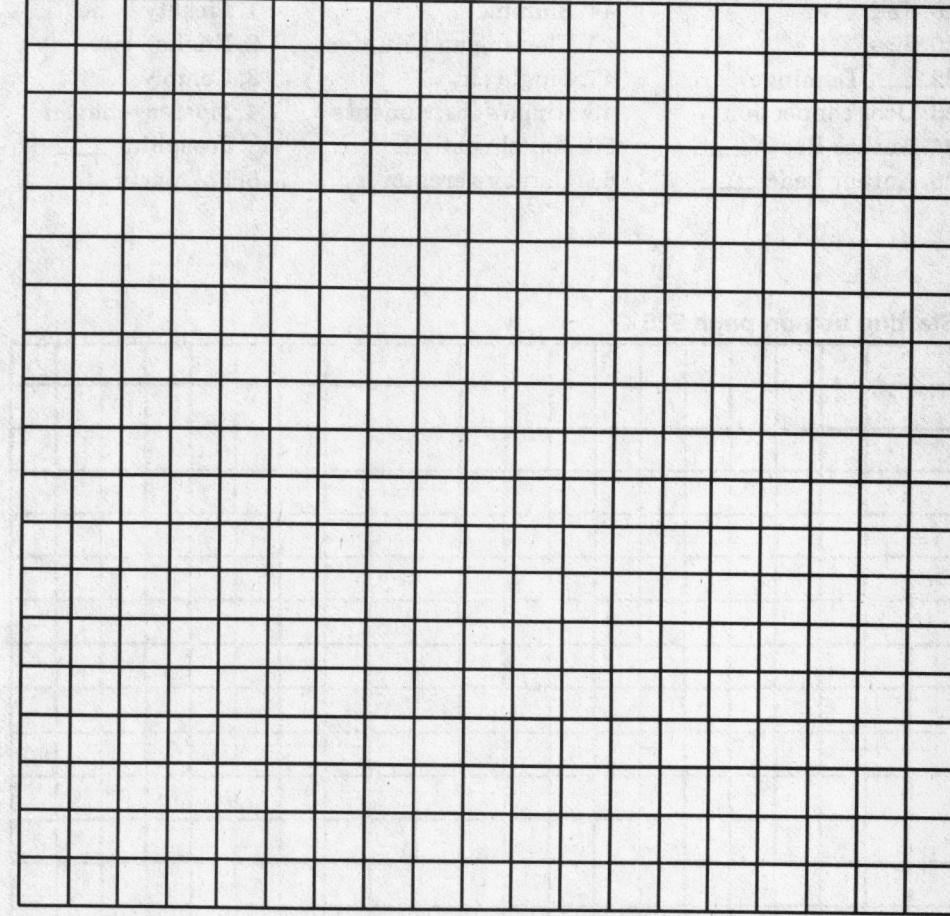

MISSING TRIOS

For each number below, fill in the same 3 missing letters (not necessarily in the same order) to complete a 7-letter, 6-letter, 5-letter, and 4-letter word. The Missing Trio is different for each number below.

1. P __ __ N T O __   __ __ __ __ P E R   C __ __ __ R __   __ __ T __
2. C __ N __ R A __   __ E __ T __ R   __ I T __ __ __   __ I __ __
3. C __ __ C __ I T   B __ Y __ __ D   T __ __ __ R __   N __ __ __ __
4. __ E S __ __ R E   B O __ __ H __   __ O __ H __   __ __ S __

291

PUZZLE 354

ACROSS

1. Conspiracy
5. Reckon
9. Judge's garment
10. Biblical witch's location
12. Capital
13. Lawn condensation
16. 17th-century steps
18. "Lucky" aviator
19. Fad
20. Jigs
22. ___ Domingo
23. Door connection
24. Author Booth ___
26. Author Pearl ___
27. ___ donna
28. Get cracking
29. Mocker
30. Promenade
31. Joad family's creator
35. Indigent
36. OPEC et al.
39. Canine's kin
40. Hester Prynne's creator
44. Slammer
45. Fleming and Hunter
47. Single out
48. Ringo's instruments
50. Knitting stitch
51. Gatsby's creator
56. Tire
58. Concur
59. Actress Stritch
62. Like Tucson's climate
63. Ached
64. Kind of measure
66. Osaka cash
67. Metal compound
68. Cheek
69. "The ___ Hunter"
70. Carries out
71. Miami's county

DOWN

1. Lickety-split
2. English city
3. Comply
4. Mystery-maven Josephine ___
5. Pol. party
6. Tennyson's lady
7. Ms. Ferber
8. Towering peak
11. Summarize
12. Catnip, e.g.
13. Damp and chilly
14. Breakfast item
15. Minute
17. ___ cotta
18. Delay
19. Mr. Little
21. Goes without
22. Trap
23. Shell
25. "___ a man . . ."
26. Magnitude
28. Bawdy
30. Marries
32. Opening, for short
33. Maiden-name indicator
34. Barbara ___ Geddes
36. Monastery garb
37. Cover-girl Carol ___
38. Yippee!
39. Daily delivery
40. Fawn ___
41. "The Bold and the Beautiful" character
42. Son of Loki
43. Accustom
44. Panel
46. Petite
47. Tofu
49. Bumped off
50. Agony
51. Bombed
52. Disregard
53. Playing card
54. Oxford letter
55. Took sustenance in style
56. Path
57. Bard's before
60. Roman fiddler
61. Roof's edge
63. Plaintiff's request
65. Legal thing
67. Figure up

Starting box on page 525

PUZZLE 355

ACROSS
1. "Alice" waitress
4. Like some data
5. Ms. Didrikson
9. Pub
10. Vestment
13. Cain's victim
14. Pungs
16. Sap
18. Cashews
19. ____ Cantrell
20. Work by 38 Across
27. French royalty
28. Expanse
29. Be obliged
30. Spanish year
31. Ages
33. Fort Knox units
37. Eastern prince
38. Famed American author
42. Strokes
43. Old hat
44. Western Indian
45. Merry adventure
46. Churchill's letter
47. ____ Anne de Beaupre: abbr.
48. Songs
51. Bishopric
54. Warms
57. Mediterranean port
58. 38 Across, e.g.
63. Fork part
64. Palestinian ascetic
65. "Rule Britannia" composer
66. Have a bite
67. ____-o'-shanter
69. Shower-stall unit
72. German article
73. Work by 38 Across
81. Turkish regiment
82. Susiana
83. Reverie
84. Musician Isaac
85. Meek one
86. Aurora
87. Possessive pronoun
88. Curling marks
89. Table leaving
90. WWII gp.

DOWN
1. Quaker
2. Old car
3. Admits
5. Kerchief
6. Touch against
7. Meg's sister
8. Or ____ (threat)
10. Swiss peak
11. Oahu neckwear
12. Phi ____ Kappa
14. Racing's Seattle ____
15. Singer Abbe
16. Creatures
17. Patriotic org.
20. Hold at bay
21. Gangster
22. Singer Sedaka
23. Affectation
24. Less plausible, as an excuse
25. Consolidate
26. Code name
32. Held a session
34. Wildebeest
35. Select
36. Boot part
37. Show up
39. Gorge
40. Mr. Guinness
41. Author Harper ____
45. Cook slowly
47. Timid
48. Church song
49. Mr. Heep
50. A votre ____
51. Method: abbr.
52. Shapely letter
53. French summer
55. Spanish aunt
56. Rivulet
58. Office missive, for short
59. Inters
60. Hold in check
61. Oklahoma city
62. Nevada city
67. Autocrat
68. Related
70. Brit. inc.
71. Cork's land
74. Provides food and drink
75. Warnings
76. Touched
77. Wings
78. Broadway's Auntie
79. Zodiac sign
80. ____ Cruces
84. Scare away

Starting box on page 525

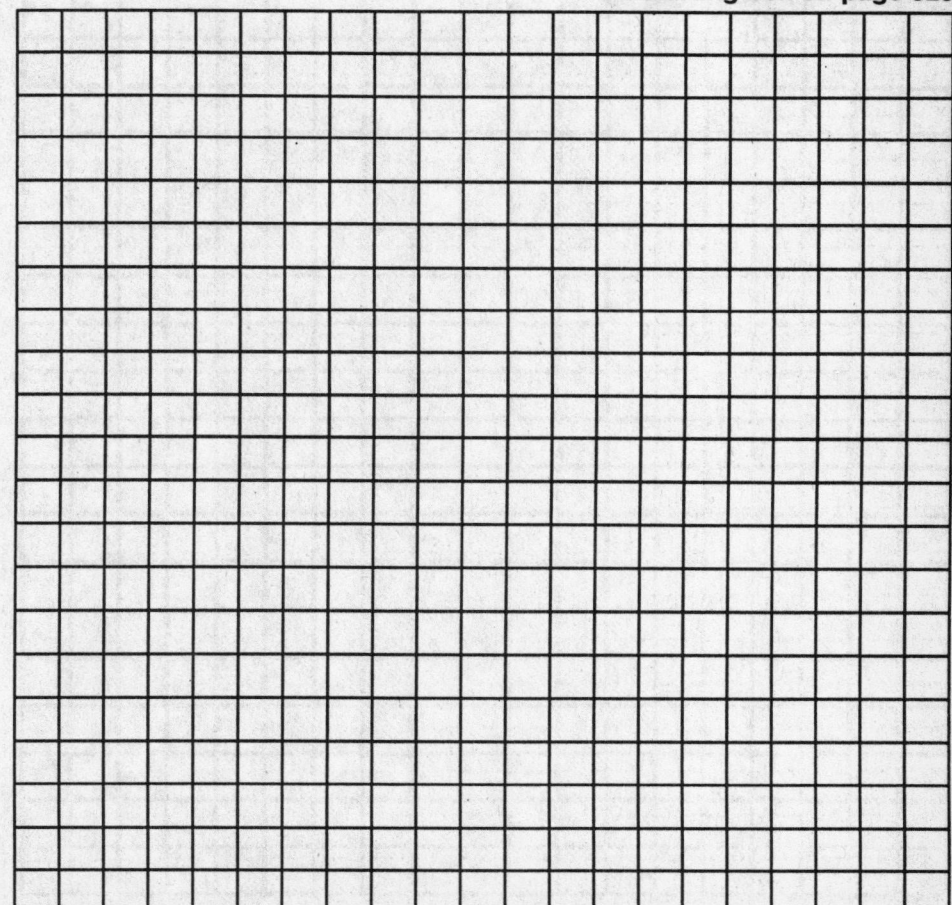

293

PUZZLE 356

• REVOLUTIONARY WAR •

ACROSS

1. Elec. unit
4. Tax agency: abbr.
7. ____ de mer
8. Pied Piper's follower
9. Comedian Olsen
10. "Rock of ____"
12. Eastern European
14. Type of apple, for short
16. Likely
19. Knock sharply
21. ____ vera
22. Ex of Frank and Mickey
23. Parts played
25. Held session
28. Youngsters
30. ____-Magnon
31. Dance step
34. Keats works
36. Bay window
38. Worsted
39. Revolutionary War battle sites
46. Territory
47. More painful
48. Witching, for one
49. Coterie
50. Turntable speed: abbr.
53. Murky
54. Snoop
55. Laminated rock
57. Excavation
58. Netman Lendl
59. That: Sp.
60. Cage
61. Flock member
63. Salver
67. Back of the neck
70. Exist
71. Knight's title
72. Aunt: Sp.
73. Decade
74. Pitcher handle

DOWN

1. Minor Prophet
2. Shopping center
3. Defendant's answer
4. Lyricist Gershwin
5. Tatter
6. Goblet feature
11. Revolutionary War battle site
13. Bravery
15. Make merry
17. Horseback game
18. Ball holder
20. Terrace
21. Curved line
24. Bridge
25. The sun
26. Hoosier humorist
27. Lone Star State
29. Japanese money
32. Playfully roguish
33. Busybody
35. Father horse
37. ____ Palmas
38. Revolutionary War battle site
40. Makes as profit
41. Drowse
42. Hang in folds
43. Cherry red
44. Capek play
45. Prohibitionist
50. Smash review
51. Factory
52. Males
56. Haunch
62. Toward the rising sun
64. Grade
65. Opera solo
66. Calendar cycle
68. Pizza ____
69. Sea eagle

Starting box on page 525

PUZZLE 357

ACROSS

1. Overly plump
4. Folder flap
7. Withered
8. Expert
9. Reimburse
12. Theater
14. Timetable
16. Amino _____
17. Hurry
18. Opera melody
19. Snoozing place
20. Fisherman's need
22. Clothing protectors
23. Inundate
26. Healthy
27. Start
28. Purchase
30. Cistern
31. Marsh
32. Cut wood
33. Kind of bar
35. Nerd
37. Quiver
39. Desertlike
41. Tempo
42. Clodhopper
45. Party pest
46. Cask
47. Trick
48. Fame
50. Boil
52. Four-legged pest
53. Grassland
54. Eye
55. Chess pieces
56. Lad

DOWN

1. Nourish
2. Slot-machine part
3. Camomile, for one
4. Implied
5. Throb
6. Busy insect
7. Malicious
9. Cleanse
10. Excuse
11. Leaven
12. Taxi
13. Rink stuff
14. Work period
15. Touch lightly
20. Shatter
21. Brew
24. Bright star
25. Chew on
28. Ray of sunshine
29. Open
31. Run for it
32. Ariel, for one
33. Platform for Hayes
34. Circle segment
35. Curved sword
36. Scent
38. Course
40. Study
41. Nut
43. Fire residue
44. Going rate
46. Leg joint
47. Depend
49. Tall tree
50. Weep
51. Conceit

Starting box on page 525

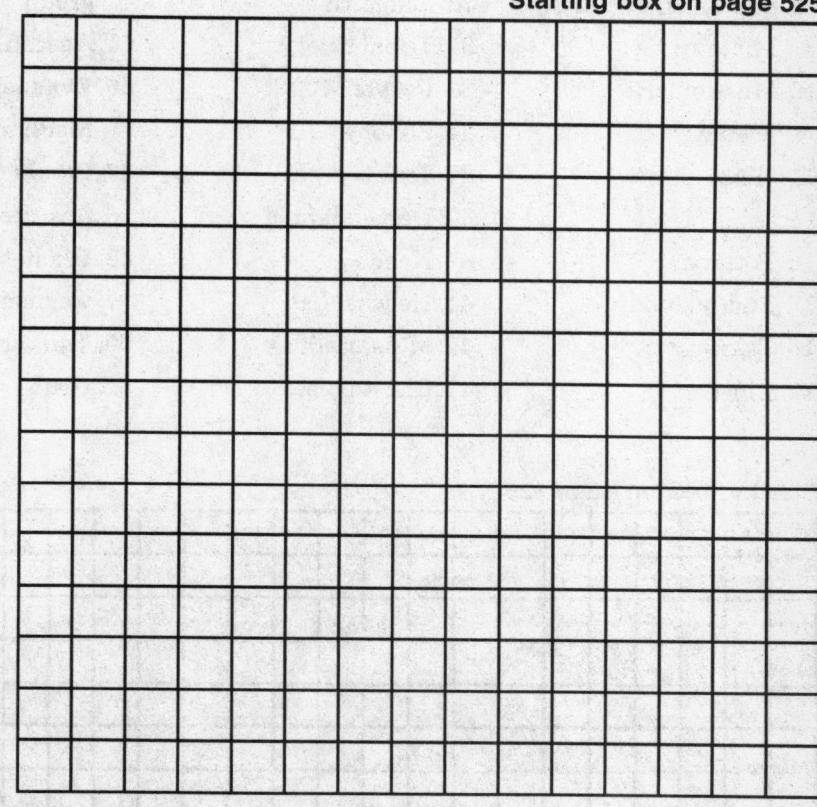

QUOTAGRAM   PUZZLE 358

Fill in the answers to the clues below. Then transfer the letters to the correspondingly numbered squares in the diagram. The completed diagram will contain a quotation.

1. Contributions
   15 30 49 21 38 33 45 34 43

2. Breakfast treat
   1 46 31 50 12 3 37 42

3. Flaky
   47 26 6 8 29

4. Morning brew
   44 16 25 32 13 20

5. Renowned
   17 41 22 36 9 18

6. Musket load
   10 2 5 35 28 7

7. Garland
   39 27 24 14 4 40

8. Decoy
   23 11 48 19

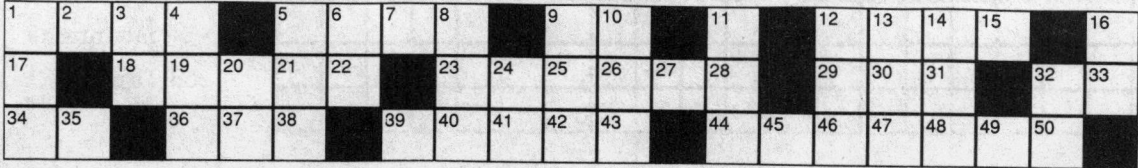

PUZZLE 359

ACROSS

1. Sail holder
5. Plant nutrient
6. Tuna
9. Southeast corner of Missouri
10. Muse of lyric poetry
11. "I Am ___"
15. "___ Mable"
16. Pottery
17. Fuddy-duddy
18. Take ten
22. Cinch
26. Mr. Kierkegaard
27. Skilled
28. Bitter: pref.
29. Clone
30. Songbird
31. Tribal chief
33. Part of MIT
34. Shabby
37. Tennis great
40. Descendant of Noah
41. He was: Lat.
42. Mets' stadium
43. Chest noise
44. As well
45. Sword
46. Silver quality: abbr.
47. Adolescent
48. Seed covering
49. Festive
50. Alexander's group
54. African antelope
56. Evangelist McPherson
57. Petula Clark favorite
59. Gladiatorial weapons
60. Tanker
61. Grub

DOWN

1. "Besame ___"
2. Medicinal plant
3. Wood fastener
4. Inside info
5. Dull finish
6. Sleeping
7. Old knowledge
8. Wild pig
12. New Zealand natives
13. Passionate
14. Broadway gas
18. Lousy treatment
19. River of Spain
20. Oodles
21. Wallet items
22. Get wet
23. Recess
24. Pain
25. Ready an oven
26. Strong cheese
31. Fence crossing
32. European blackbird
35. Amo, amas, ___
36. Facility
37. Of the stars
38. Singer E.
39. Walking race
45. Wise one
50. Mosquito, often
51. Egyptian deity
52. Eft
53. Lairs
55. "Andrea ___"
56. South American mountains
58. Droop

Starting box on page 525

296

PUZZLE 360

• MOVIE SONGS •

ACROSS

1. City of the Seven Hills
5. Exclamation of contempt
8. Food fish
11. "Who's the Boss?" character
15. Prayer ending
16. Nobelist Myrdal
17. Thin tie
18. Unvarying
19. Weight without cargo
20. "Have You Ever ____ Lonely"
21. Table spread
22. Gaunt
23. "You ____" ("Singin' in the Rain" song)
26. Sins
27. Anger
28. Dawn goddess
29. Vietnamese New Year
30. Intertwines
33. "____ Hideaway" ("Pajama Game" tune)
38. Fodder
41. Folk singer Phil ____
42. God of war
43. English opera composer
44. Actress Gabor
45. Mr. Onassis
46. Final passage
47. Attack on all sides
49. Overly proper
50. Belittle
52. Curling and polo
54. Thoroughfares
55. Wagons
57. Officeholders
58. Hindu religious title
60. Thai coins
62. Conical tents
65. Happenings
68. Baba and MacGraw
69. Wanderer
70. "____ kleine Nachtmusik"
72. Jazz style
73. ____ de guerre
74. Son of Jacob and Leah
75. Constituent
76. Small opening
77. Winter mo.
78. "The Sound of Music" song

81. Pulled
82. Bowler, e.g.
84. Grass bristle
85. Tree with needles
86. Stuntman Knievel
88. Classic from "Holiday Inn"
96. Take a chance
97. Whet
98. Very small degree
99. Architect Saarinen
100. Lulu
101. "Omnia vincit ____"
102. English school
103. South African currency
104. Convene
105. Perfect number
106. Private eye: abbr.
107. Ancient promenade

DOWN

1. Pro ____
2. Poet Khayyam
3. Lake
4. Foes
5. ____ cheese
6. With, in Arles
7. Yearns
8. Yearling
9. Olive genus
10. Portal
11. Free-for-all
12. "The Wizard of Oz" song
13. ____ miss
14. Beattie and Landers
16. Qualified
17. ____ nova
24. Time units: abbr.
25. Farther away
29. Mao ____-tung
30. Burden
31. Farm unit
32. "Mary Poppins" tune
33. Owned
34. Ages
35. Cartoonist Thomas ____
36. Gown
37. Ottawa's province: abbr.
39. Enthusiastic
40. Sweet potatoes
42. ____ Blanc
46. Roadsters
47. Goof
48. Scottish Gaelic
49. Fleshy fruit
51. Chow
53. Meerschaum, e.g.
54. Great review
56. Heated chamber
59. Left
60. Stripe
61. Medicinal plant
63. Immoral
64. North and Irish
66. Ripped
67. Raced
69. Sportscaster Barber
71. Tax agency: abbr.
74. Allow
75. Collared
76. Train attendants
79. Irrigate
80. Wool grower
81. "____ the season . . ."
83. Warn
85. Field of snow
86. Ancient country next to Palestine
87. Windmill blade
88. "____ You Need"
89. Residence
90. Aware of
91. Despise
92. Rampage
93. Substance
94. Florence's river
95. Fountain treat

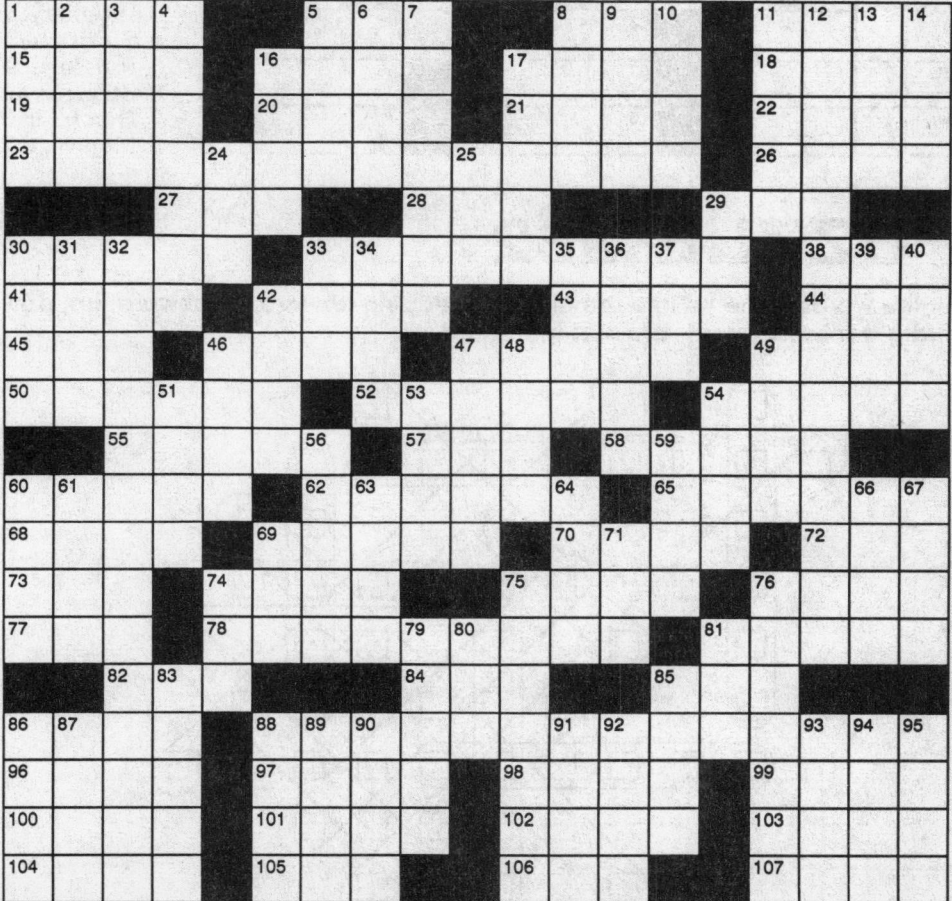

PUZZLE 361

ACROSS
1. Expansive
5. Ran away
9. Gentles
14. Genesis garden
15. Current fad
16. Drab-green color
17. Young plants
19. 39.37 inches
20. Gentle knock
21. Certain lodge member
22. Ocular orb
24. Compass pt.
25. Wicked
27. Ill-temper
28. Music and painting
29. Skeletal units
31. Involve
33. Amend copy
34. Small rug
35. Entrapped
39. Cargo weight
40. Mom and Dad
42. Actress Haddad
43. Debated
45. Light beam
46. Mind ____ matter
47. Mighty
49. Crooner Frankie ____
50. Foundation
53. Mimic
54. Wagers
55. Roe
56. Greek letter
57. Prepare a hide
58. Hasten
61. "A Fish Called ____"
63. Telling of a tale
66. Liquid measure
67. Sandusky's lake
68. One opposed
69. Bias
70. Water barriers
71. Mild oath

DOWN
1. Sunset direction
2. Mental impression
3. Intensifying
4. Story's last word
5. Ruffle
6. Straight and limp
7. Hen fruit
8. Mojave, e.g.
9. Thick volume
10. Cousin of beer
11. Bishop's hat
12. Happening
13. Dries up
18. Oahu garlands
23. Frothy
26. Dog's doc
27. Doctor in training
28. ____ carte
29. Alpha follower
30. Stench
31. Pitcher handle
32. ____ and outs
34. Plaid fabric
36. Very beautiful
37. Symmetrical
38. Take a chance
40. Household beast
41. Whine
44. Utilize
46. Horse's morsel
48. Expressed a view
49. Singer Horne
50. Oval stadiums
51. Serve
52. Mr. Claus
54. Strips
56. Component
57. Prune
59. Least bit
60. Arthurian lady
62. Place to relax
64. Coach Parseghian
65. Inventor's monogram

PUZZLE 362

Perfect Fit

Fit the words in the list into the diagram reading forward, backward, up, down, and diagonally, always in a straight line. The words cross as indicated.

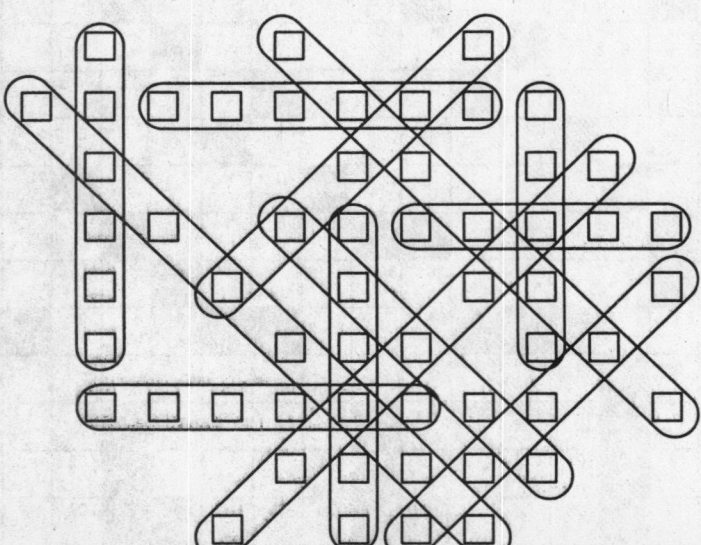

Breeze

Brief

Classy

Composer

Famous

Finesse

Forest

March

Plaza

Reflect

Skill

Spell

ACROSS

1. Baby's bed
5. Veranda
10. Ping ___
14. Actress Albright
15. Photographer Ansel ___
16. Chemical fertilizer
17. Of the ear
18. Mathematical comparison
19. Infrequent
20. Mountaintop
21. Id's companion
22. Antiseptic liquid
24. Helper
26. Canadian Indian
27. Wall surfacing material
30. Land measure
31. Mat
34. Terse
35. Insipid
36. Yale student
37. Overdue
38. ___ and desist
39. Anguish
40. Fury
41. Gold, frankincense, and ___
42. Winter jacket
43. Roofing substance
44. Article
45. Helen ___, teacher of the blind
46. Glasgow native
47. Tight closure
48. Current
51. Pig place
52. Metrical division
56. Ruth of baseball
57. Like some breakfast cereals
59. American author
60. Small nail
61. Glower
62. Docile
63. "Jane ___"
64. Tales
65. Amor

DOWN

1. Hoof sound
2. Repetition
3. Remus's mother
4. Lumbar discomfort
5. Texas city
6. Old saying
7. Defense organization
8. French chum
9. Synthetic rubber source
10. Blender setting
11. Algerian port
12. Pianist Peter ___
13. Celtic
23. Leader
25. Slick
26. Stock-market event
27. Rift
28. Pope's crown
29. Speak
30. Startle
31. Oyster find
32. Similar
33. Libyan money
35. Soft cap
38. Cell science
39. Alleviate
41. Mineral
42. Princess's annoyance
45. British economist
46. Brushed leather
47. Back of a ship
48. French priest
49. Actor Grant
50. Ski lift
51. Night sight
53. Ice-cream thickener
54. Notation
55. Social insects
58. ___ mode

PUZZLE 363

Progressions

PUZZLE 364

Can you follow the mathematical progression to find the fifth number in each series?

A.	14	23	19	28	___	33	29	38	34
B.	23	27	32	26	___	27	36	26	15
C.	8	24	72	12	___	108	18	54	162
D.	18	25	32	39	___	53	60	67	74
E.	9	4	16	11	___	39	156	151	604
F.	522	513	171	162	___	45	15	6	2
G.	32	36	9	5	___	24	6	2	8

PUZZLE 365

• MISSING •

ACROSS

1. Go by
5. Brood
9. Crustacean
13. Cut of meat
17. Director Martin ____
18. Mitchell mansion
19. Tennis's Mandlikova
20. Villain in Shakespeare
21. Rock's Brickell
22. Muddy
23. Winds up
24. Biblical you
25. Milton epic
28. Sixth planet
30. Race segment
31. Dist. above sea level
32. Ground
33. Shack
36. Gondola city
39. Round-tripper
43. School, in Paris
45. Preceding period
46. "More ____ You Know"
48. Dull person
49. As well
50. Actor Pesci
51. Football's Tarkenton
52. Gymnast Korbut
53. Intensity
55. Work hard
56. 10th president
57. Give it a go
58. Musical study
59. Falstaff's companion
60. Yankee slugger
63. Proclaim
64. Blake's "M*A*S*H" rank
68. Church response
69. Diving position
70. Show agreement
71. Aria
72. Theater award
73. Drummer Krupa
74. Cartoonist Keane
75. Sportscaster Hank ____
76. State police officer
78. Moniker
80. Collection of sayings
81. Zola novel
82. Fruit stone
83. Appendage
85. Block's partner
88. Station department
94. Twinge
95. Knight's neighbor
97. Mild oath
98. Sheriff Taylor's son
99. Salty drop
100. "____ of Green Gables"
101. Network
102. Acoustic unit
103. Very fast jets
104. Smirk
105. North Sea feeder
106. Cabell or Slaughter

DOWN

1. Make ready
2. Verdi heroine
3. Cooking direction
4. Pilfer
5. Band
6. New Mexico resort
7. Toledo's lake
8. Actor Beery
9. Storage box
10. Declaim wildly
11. Conjunction
12. Large woodwind
13. 1953 Crosby film
14. Hawaiian island
15. Inventor Sikorsky
16. Part of speech
26. Sam's singing partner
27. Corrida cry
29. Goal
32. Ladd role
33. Mound
34. Lew Alcindor's team
35. Fling
37. Rare gas
38. "____ Got the World on a String"
40. Tumble
41. Desire
42. Close at hand
44. Simon play
46. Type of winds
47. "I ____ Dreamed"
50. Rapture
51. Rampal's instrument
54. Tax org.
55. Wager
56. Chess champion Mikhail
58. Ireland, to a poet
59. Brick carrier
60. "____ Houston"
61. Love, to Ovid
62. Gambling city
63. "Carmen," e.g.
64. Nippy
65. Writer Ephron
66. Vigor
67. ____ Linda, California
70. Writer Anais ____
73. Across-the-board
74. Power source
75. Medieval peasant
77. Friend
78. Casual greetings
79. Firefighter's aid
82. Card game
84. Elk
85. Creates lace
86. Cards with single pips
87. Talk
88. Singular
89. "Rock of ____"
90. Basketball's Archibald
91. "____ the Roof"
92. Boy, in Madrid
93. Disc jockey Rick ____
96. "____ Foot in Heaven"

PUZZLE 366

ACROSS
1. Dog-paddle
5. Allegory
10. Grouch
14. Sentimentality
17. Easter flower
18. Tanker
19. Throw
20. Absorbed dose unit
21. Bothers
22. Final Greek letter
23. Hatch
25. Gobi, e.g.
27. "____ That a Time!"
29. Viewed
30. Chemists' workplaces
32. Parasite
34. Passenger car
37. Daring
41. Alter the length of
43. Gambling city
44. Resinous deposit
45. Pilgrim settler
47. Evans and Carnegie
49. Guitarlike instrument
50. Weary
52. Yellow fruit
54. Transitory
56. Forays
58. Disseminated
60. "High ____"
61. Compiling
63. Neck backs
65. Open plain
69. Powder
71. Pleasure craft
73. Mixture
74. Mister, in Rennes
78. Boxer Holmes
80. Respiratory organ
81. Harry's successor
82. Amber brew
84. Hawaiian feasts
86. Golfer's aid
87. Snatches
89. Large parrot
91. Cash carrier
93. Alpine region
95. Hues
97. Humorist Edward
____
98. Came to rest
100. Boise's location
102. Plucks
106. Clemens's sport
109. Singer Carr
111. Send
112. Moose
113. Toledo's lake

114. Miscalculated
115. Writer Gardner
116. Steeped drink
117. Actress Cheryl ____
118. Period of development
119. Large amount

DOWN
1. Slipped
2. Filament
3. Types
4. "All by ____"
5. Gridiron game
6. Ultimate goal
7. Gusted
8. Permissable
9. Correction aid
10. Small talk
11. Sprint
12. Circle parts
13. Doldrums
14. Magnificence
15. Cereal grass
16. Epic poem
24. Tavern fare
26. ____ avis
28. Shortcoming
31. Surfaces
33. Actress Hunt
35. Singer Paul ____
36. Playwright Coward
37. Extreme
38. Water nymph
39. Bitter
40. Villain
42. Notes
46. Absolutely not!
48. Espies
51. Annotates
53. Country in the Himalayas
55. "Paper Moon" actress
57. Slow mover
59. Sticker
62. Shine
64. Bush
66. Distant planet
67. Jury
68. Trimmed
70. Bandleader Xavier
____
72. Path
74. Brand-new
75. Approve
76. Cornhusker state
77. Drew back
79. Holiday season
83. South African coin
85. Cabbage salad
88. Flatfish
90. Zigzags
92. Devises
94. Slur
96. Blouse
99. Scarlett's residence
101. Gumbo vegetable
103. Undercover cop
104. ____ monster
105. Musher's conveyance
106. Wager
107. Porter or stout
108. Container's top
110. Barrel

301

PUZZLE 367

TWIN CROSSWORDS

Two clues for each number and two puzzle diagrams—which answer goes where? That's your dilemma. Answer the clues and then decide in which crossword pattern the answer fits. The first two words have been entered for you.

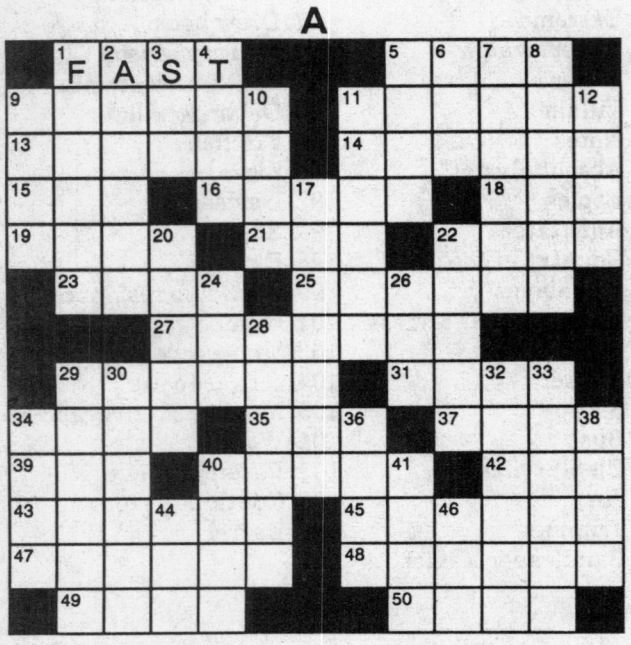

A

B

ACROSS
1. Rapid
   Like a snail
5. Store away
   Lids
9. Primer
   Mend
11. Gaps
   Refused consent to
13. Puzzle
   Crazy
14. Chant
   Spill a secret
15. Citrus beverage
   Commercials
16. Oversight
   Fortuneteller's card
18. Oklahoma city
   Clamor
19. Singer Garrett
   Actor Gregory ____
21. Lamprey
   Director Brooks
22. Healing plant
   Superior to
23. Actual
   Stagger
25. Male or female
   Warmhearted

27. Elegant
   Narrated
29. Waver
   Neck
31. Dimple
   Compass point
34. Serving dish
   Caution
35. Conducted
   Piggery
37. Kind of admiral
   Quarrels
39. Supply with weapons
   Aries symbol
40. Golden-touch king
   Moon period
42. Australian bird
   Sea inlet
43. Regard highly
   Compelled
45. Dodged
   Break
47. Looked closely
   Congressional body
48. Venerate
   Believes in
49. Caves
   Strong cart
50. Wagers
   Boys

DOWN
1. Car part
   "Return to ____"
2. Each
   Famous collie
3. Palace room, sometimes
   Stoop
4. Clock
   Departed
5. Box
   Portable shelter
6. A baseball great
   Make a doily
7. Group of eight
   Breed of dog
8. High school student
   Metalworker
9. Gather crops
   Iran's monetary unit
10. Uncommon
   Paper quantity
11. Pilfered
   Purple flower
12. Low hill
   Parch
17. Boat race
   Turned in
20. River boat
   Singer Carpenter

22. Common viper
   More bizarre
24. Author Tolstoy
   Permit
26. "____ Kelly" (Jagger film)
   Not old
28. Catlike
   Whipped
29. ____ and feathered
   Bartered
30. Weasel
   Carpenter's tool
32. Vital
   Most painful
33. Circus employees
   Contorts
34. Golf hazard
   Money rolls
36. Arrow
   North Sea feeder
38. Impolite
   Impudence
40. Baseball team
   Victim
41. Daredevil Knievel
   Balkan native
44. George Gershwin's brother
   Moving vehicle
46. Frank's ex
   Prompt

302

PUZZLE 368

• SPRINKLER SYSTEM •

ACROSS

1. Level
5. Pointed end
9. Bread
13. Eye part
17. Cilium
18. Neighbor of Kan.
19. Italian river
20. Tralee flower
21. Nice girlfriend
22. Straight
23. Posterior
24. Spy
25. Grin and ____
27. Movie theater sprinkler?
30. Mars
32. ____ Lanka
33. Politician Atwater
34. Bold
37. Ump
39. Actor McGavin
44. Hibernia
45. Shooting marbles
48. Border
50. Ingenuous
51. Name for a French poodle
52. Deceives
54. Quagmire
56. March date
57. High schoolers
59. Flag
61. Fashions
63. Aggregate
65. Jim's wife on "Murphy Brown"
67. Tribunal
68. Los Angeles athlete
72. Hysteria
74. Be silent, in music
78. Israeli dance
79. Depressed
81. Rubberneck
83. "Dies ____"
84. Shun
86. Neither's partner
88. Hymn response
89. Church section
90. Wrote
92. Have a burger
94. Endorsed
96. ____ Animas
98. Fetched
100. One of the Jacksons
101. Spring sprinklers?
107. Fastened tightly
111. Predict
112. Headquarters
113. Descended
115. Excavation timber
116. Divulge
117. Irish river
118. Work animal
119. Cry of dismay
120. German admiral
121. Diplomat Whitelaw ____
122. Chinese pooch
123. Pull

DOWN

1. Unwanted pounds
2. Evening gown fabric
3. Nepal's locale
4. Plain sprinkler?
5. Book chapters
6. Instrument for Don Ho, for short
7. Narrow board
8. Ways
9. Postal worker
10. Space
11. Mollusk
12. Like a bull
13. "My Friend ____"
14. Castle
15. Key
16. Psychic
26. One of David's warriors
28. Mess up
29. Signify
31. Remain valid
34. Skillful
35. Ohio county
36. High-pitched flute
38. White lie
40. Sprinkler stopper?
41. Depend
42. Continuously
43. Promontory
46. Expression
47. Hawk's action
49. May honoree
53. Rails
55. Yak
58. Dine
60. Ship for Columbus
62. Basketball's Holman
64. Honey
66. Thailand, once
68. Guy
69. Wimbledon score
70. Inflexible
71. Director Howard
73. Snuck
75. Steep rock
76. Roof part
77. ____ off (began)
80. Anguish
82. Army recruit
85. Vale
87. Allergy sufferer's bane
91. Dancer's cohort
93. Foot feature
95. Colorado Indian
97. Coast
99. Vagabond
101. Humanities
102. Furtive look
103. Chest sound
104. Inactive
105. All: pref.
106. Swing around
108. Tra ____
109. Flair
110. Office furnishing
114. Sort

PUZZLE 369

ACROSS
1. The in thing
4. Currency
8. Unit of matter
12. In earlier days
13. Woodwind
14. Doll's cry
15. Impulsive
17. By mouth
18. Greenish blue
19. Disregard
21. Fabled monsters
23. Type of party
24. Fall over one's feet
25. Ship
26. Current unit, for short
29. Metallic element
30. Fry lightly
31. Train segment
32. Lyrical poem
33. Unit of area
34. Water, in pharmacology
35. Cheers
36. Letter-closing word
37. Hold in regard
40. 103, to Caesar
41. Damsel
42. Artist Da Vinci
46. Formerly
47. Gape
48. Outcome
49. Witnesses
50. Sticks
51. "Major ____"

DOWN
1. "____ from the Madding Crowd"
2. Census stat
3. Ism
4. Soft drinks
5. Explorer Tasman
6. Distress signal
7. Waver
8. Surrounded by
9. Poi source
10. Legendary tentmaker
11. Masculine
16. Retain
20. Fence opening
21. German statesman Von Bismarck
22. Football field
23. Ferments
25. Unmarried man
26. Gained possession of
27. Hammer
28. Beseech
30. German river
34. Operatic solo
35. Carnival treats
36. Prongs
37. Famous cookie man
38. Hamlet, e.g.
39. "Of ____ and Men"
40. Frigid
43. Id's counterpart
44. Genetic material letters
45. Peculiar

PUZZLE 370

ACROSS
1. Food fish
4. Frosted
8. Franklin's mother
12. Wonderment
13. Not any
14. Iridescent gem
15. Move to another site
17. Limbs
18. Rub out
19. Cowboy jamboree
20. Epic
22. Corners
24. Let up
26. Fool
27. Small rug
30. Parking timers
32. Promotion technique
34. Observe
35. Tennis star Laver
37. Surgery beam
38. Blunder
40. Stalk
41. Voice above a baritone
44. Hindu social division
46. Table spread
47. With acrimony
50. Summit
51. Brainstorm
52. Optic organ
53. Matched groups
54. Glacier breakaway, for short
55. Cub Scout unit

DOWN
1. Wheeled vehicle
2. Be in debt
3. Representative
4. Early Peruvian
5. Shoreline
6. Goes in
7. Billy ____ Williams
8. Songs for one
9. Imitated
10. Fashion
11. In addition
16. Speak pompously
19. Drive back
20. Snead and Donaldson
21. Busy as ____
23. Corn unit
25. Baseball misstep
27. Learned
28. Suit to ____
29. Expression
31. Family member
33. Moisten with drippings, in cooking
36. Determine
38. Reading matter
39. Appraiser
41. Spinning toys
42. Gen. Robert ____
43. Tidy
45. Party line
47. Baby's apron
48. Caustic substance
49. Hankering

PUZZLE 371

ACROSS
1. Prepare wool
5. Nail
9. French friend
12. Healing plant
13. Enclosed area
14. Director Howard
15. Mexican river
17. Barbie's beau
18. Fit or fire starter
19. Killer whale
21. Corrode
23. Marine fliers
26. Hockey player
29. Pelion's base
30. I love, to Cicero
31. Reproductive body
34. Periodic table no.
35. Racecar driver Yarborough
37. Remove from power
39. Overact
41. In favor of
42. Tear
44. Certain legislative bodies
48. Feathered neckpiece
50. Chattanoogan river
53. Also
54. Spirit
55. Humdinger
56. Excessively
57. Anatomical network
58. Hawaii state bird

DOWN
1. Mystery writer John Dickson ____
2. "I cannot tell ____"
3. American statesman Elihu ____
4. B.A., e.g.
5. Bathing facility
6. Greek god of the flocks
7. Actor Ray
8. Plow pioneer
9. Little Rock river
10. A Stooge
11. Wayside stop
16. Wanders
20. ____-Magnon
22. Touch lightly
24. Town near Padua
25. "Casablanca" pianist
26. Mideast holy man
27. Grand Canyon river
28. Land east of Eden
30. Maven
32. Football off.
33. Type of poem
36. Summer on the Seine
38. Prayer
40. Stage direction
43. Prefix for far
45. Medieval serf
46. Baby-sitter, often
47. Dry
48. Cave dweller
49. Yoko ____
51. Composer Ayer
52. Opposite of SSW

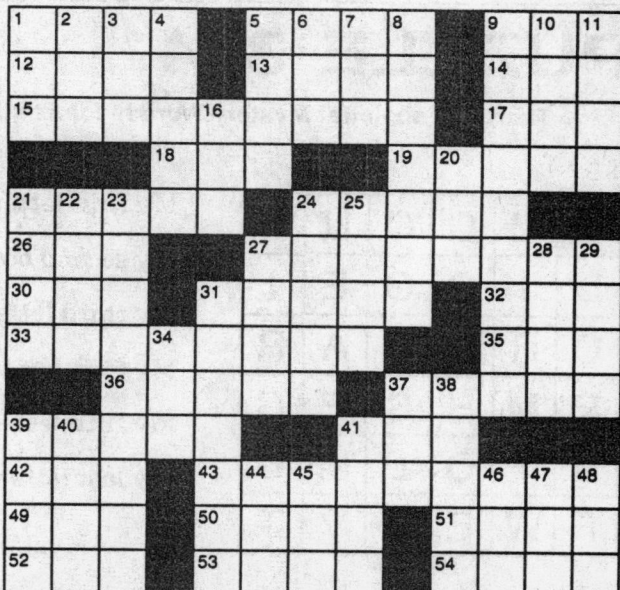

PUZZLE 372

ACROSS
1. Watering spot
5. Embroidery aid
9. TV's Rockford
12. Precinct
13. Irish river
14. Pindaric work
15. "American Gothic" painter
17. "Leave ____ to Heaven"
18. Flimflam
19. Thick
21. Tender
24. Muslim faith
26. ____ excellence
27. Budget accommodation
30. Refrain syllable
31. Cooks in liquid
32. Soak fibers
33. Hill workers
35. Traveler's haven
36. Caustic remarks
37. Devilfish
39. Else
41. Hebrew alphabet letter
42. Ballerina Slavenska
43. "Le Haras du Pin" painter
49. Entirety
50. At any time
51. Managed
52. Legal thing
53. Have the temerity
54. Witnesses

DOWN
1. Droll person
2. Misspeak
3. Grassland
4. Jouster's need
5. Carved
6. Conquistador's quest
7. Lennon's lady
8. Sells
9. "Maine Islands" painter
10. Caesar's fateful date
11. Scant
16. Craggy peak
20. Pitcher part
21. Elects
22. Bus cost
23. "Laughing Cavalier" painter
24. Roman ways
25. Overcasts
27. Cease
28. Chap
29. Lab burner
31. Featured
34. Lager's kin
37. Thickness unit
38. Peruvian range
39. Poet Khayyam
40. Mosaic piece
41. Unfailing
44. Actress Haddad
45. Above, to a bard
46. Stringed instrument
47. Greens toll
48. Football measures: abbr.

305

PUZZLE 373

Some of the clues in this crossword are In Twos. Fill in two different answers to the same clue in the squares indicated.

ACROSS

1. Adamson's lioness
5. Norman Vincent ____
10. Divests
14. Without dilution
15. Kingly
16. Adam's son
17. Foolish
18.]Eat
19.]Eat
20. Hurries
22. Legation
24. Satisfy
26.]Bring up
27.]Bring up
30. Certain speech sounds
34. Succulent plants
35. Exclamation of annoyance
38. Morse code sound
39. Tear
40. Cars
41. Use a strop
42. Eden resident
43. Highly seasoned
44. En ____
45. Constructs
47.]Hide
49.]Hide
51. Sewing case
52. Type of anoa
55. African fly
59. Appian Way, e.g.
60. Bacterial enzyme
63. Pinches
64.]Tops
65.]Tops
66. College official
67. Duel tool
68. ____ Park, Colorado
69. Commedia dell'____

DOWN

1. Finishes
2.]Vault
3.]Vault
4. Vouched
5. Magician's word
6. Always, to a bard
7. Past
8. Dock worker
9. Fundamentals
10. Electronic devices
11. Wading bird
12. Cozy rooms
13. Loom part
21. Platform
23. Lambs' laments
25. Tedium
27. Stallions' mates
28. Ecole attendee
29. Musical group
31. Cherish
32. Singer Ronstadt
33. Building material
36. And so forth: abbr.
37. Rolls-____
40. Sound of approval
41. Mexican ranch
43. Plaintiff
44. Wildebeests
46. Rarely found
48. Aquatic mammals
50. Doughnut-shaped figure
52. Roof piece
53. Slanted
54. Ancient Persian's kin
56.]Row
57.]Row
58. Feudal serf
61. Likely
62. Bishopric

PUZZLE 374

There is a six-letter Mystery Word hidden in the diagram. Can you find it in four minutes or less?

L	M	C	O	U	F
U	I	O	G	E	I
C	R	E	I	A	R
E	M	H	S	F	C
U	I	O	L	M	U
F	W	E	A	V	T

My first letter is in two corners of the diagram.

My second occurs twice in the same row.

My third letter begins and ends the same row.

My fourth letter is the only consonant in a row.

My fifth letters occurs exactly twice in the diagram.

My last letter is above my fifth.

Mystery Word: ___ ___ ___ ___ ___ ___

306

PUZZLE 375

ACROSS

1. Leaning Tower city
5. Hoist
9. Type style
14. Arabian gulf
15. Pennsylvania city
16. Imp
17. Yearn
18. Pepper's partner
19. Articles
20. Church officials
22. Misplaced
24. Witness
25. Prevaricates
27. Midday
29. Not many
32. Formerly
34. Wander
37. Egg-shaped
39. _____ Barbara
41. Roman emperor
43. Classify
44. Stadium sound
45. Famous essayist
46. Paradise
47. Trappings
49. Bawls
50. Author Jong
52. Woody plant
54. Bottom-line figure
55. Short letter
57. Pesters
59. Feline
62. Waistcoat
64. Gloomy
68. Solitary
70. Edible root
72. Roof edge
73. Gold digger
74. Verve
75. Region
76. Boils
77. Deposits
78. Tear apart

DOWN

1. Ashen
2. False god
3. Transmit
4. Cherub
5. Abates
6. Pensioner's acct.
7. Satisfy
8. Wyoming mountain range
9. Copy corrector
10. Allow
11. Singer Burl _____
12. Use a stopwatch on
13. You are something _____!
21. _____ de Janeiro
23. Fountain order
26. Frighten
28. Baseball teams
29. Golfer's cry
30. Dodge
31. Irrigate
33. Pass into law
35. Criminal
36. Pawnee or Cree
38. Russian leader
40. Rose's protection
42. Drying chamber
47. Social appointment
48. Motives
51. Lids
53. Self-esteem
56. _____ Park, Colorado
58. Malign
59. Gear parts
60. Came to earth
61. Sound
63. Saga
65. Naked
66. Tied
67. Interpret
69. Recent
71. Ship deserter

Halftime

PUZZLE 376

Pair off the groups of letters to form ten 6-letter names of tools.

ARE	HAM	SAN	SQU	_____	_____
ARS	KLE	SEL	TRO	_____	_____
CHI	MER	SHE	VEL	_____	_____
DER	NCH	SHO	WEL	_____	_____
ERS	PLI	SIC	WRE	_____	_____

PUZZLE 377

• HONOR ROLL •

ACROSS
1. Showoff
4. Spouse
8. Surmounting
12. Neighbor of Tenn.
13. "When I was ____ . . ."
14. Zola heroine
15. Set off casino bells
18. Fall bloomer
19. Cob or stag
20. Anjou or Bosc
23. Labor leader Chavez
26. Church recess
29. Fit together
31. Three, in Turin
32. Tart-theft victim
35. Ornamental vase
36. ____ Minor
37. No, to Yeltsin
38. "____ Came a Spider"
40. Neophyte
42. Course
44. Pianist Blake
48. Salutation to a monarch
52. Movie pooch
53. Screenwriter Anita ____
54. Ring decision: abbr.
55. "Younger ____ Springtime"
56. Slow canter
57. Ar's follower

DOWN
1. Garden boundary
2. MacGraw and namesakes
3. Marshal Dillon
4. Olympic ski family name
5. Porter
6. ____ Mahal
7. Dutch treat
8. Body joint
9. Wall hanging
10. Yoko ____
11. TV host Sajak
16. Powwow locale
17. Tuck away
21. Andy's pal
22. Equip anew
24. Commedia dell'____
25. Relax
26. Turquoise's kin
27. Knitting stitch
28. Spanish miss
30. Light carriage
33. Distress
34. Actress Aimee
39. Pitcher Ryan
41. Poet Lizette ____
43. Barbie, e.g.
45. "Love at First ____"
46. Squid fluids
47. Self-images
48. Pass the ____
49. Bat wood
50. Excessively
51. Car or bell follower

PUZZLE 378

ACROSS
1. ____ Alto
5. Tucker's companion
8. Strikebreaker
12. Congregation response
13. Single thing
14. Actor Franchot ____
15. Dissimilarity
17. Aware of
18. Laboratory test
19. Rachel or Tab
21. Machu Picchu site
24. ____ annum
25. Visage
28. Nullify
30. Mischievous child
33. Self-conceit
34. Form of protest
35. Golf mount
36. Came in first
37. Dye plant
38. Orion's heavenly wear
39. Greek letter
41. Lohengrin's love
43. Frame of mind
46. Pointed weapon
50. Say with certainty
51. Plan ingeniously
54. Appraise
55. "Golden Girl" McClanahan
56. Neck and neck
57. Mr. Kadiddlehopper
58. Shoshonean Indian
59. Let someone use

DOWN
1. Spotted, tailless rodent
2. Coach Stagg
3. Microscope part
4. Recorded
5. Large snake
6. Officeholders
7. Alcott heroine
8. Boulder
9. Penitent
10. Chip in chips
11. "To ____ not to . . ."
16. Certain grain
20. "Once ____ a midnight dreary . . ."
22. Devastate
23. Open
25. Not many
26. In the past
27. Tangible
29. Pickle seasoning
31. TV diner boss
32. Favorite
34. Ship's canvas
38. A ____ of laughs
40. Seraglio
42. Perched
43. Playwright Connelly
44. Elliptical
45. Light beige
47. Cleave
48. Pizzeria feature
49. Meander
52. Umpire's call
53. Maiden name indicator

• SKILLET SEARCH •

ACROSS

1. Prone
4. Cereal grain
7. Bench
9. Hodgepodge
10. Feature of Texas geography
12. Picnic pest
13. Mythical box opener
17. Psychic's gift: abbr.
20. Author Twain
21. Honest ___ Lincoln
23. Cushion
26. Squeezing snake
27. North ___ (Santa's home)
28. Fruit's soft part
30. Tavern beverage
31. Storage compartment
32. Respectful fear
33. Afternoon social
34. At this time
35. Temporary gift
37. Maternally related
39. Narrow inlet
40. Call out
41. April's preceder
43. Tooth ailment
45. Poorly lit
46. Snakelike fish
48. Pose a question
50. Nocturnal bird
52. Pie ___ mode
53. In a sheltered direction
55. Cleveland's lake
56. Mediterranean, e.g.
57. Affirmative word
58. Golf average
59. Enthusiastic
60. Unit of work
61. Put up wainscoting
64. Inventor Whitney
65. Tropical headwear
71. Above
72. Geometric ratio
73. Favorite animal
74. Coloring agent

DOWN

1. Cleopatra's viper
2. Pod vegetable
3. Sunbather's goal
4. Antique
5. Feel unwell
6. Shoe front
8. Express gratitude
9. Aware of
11. In addition
13. Light-colored
14. "Butterflies ___ Free"
15. Hit sharply
16. Border on
17. Recede
18. Stain
19. Scenic views
20. Cut grass
22. General Robert ___
23. Lingerie item
24. ___ vera
25. Morning condensation
27. Cure-all
29. Flapjack
36. Breathable mixture
38. Joan of ___
41. Highway measure
42. Assist
44. Wide-mouthed jug
45. Twenty-four hours
47. Long jump
48. Waterless
49. Comedian Caesar
51. Fall behind
54. Batter's stat
55. Night before
59. Assumed name
62. Draw closer
63. Dutch ___ disease
65. "___ Goes the Weasel"
66. "___ Maria"
67. Fisherman's mesh
68. Concealed
69. "___ Which Way You Can"
70. Casual shirt

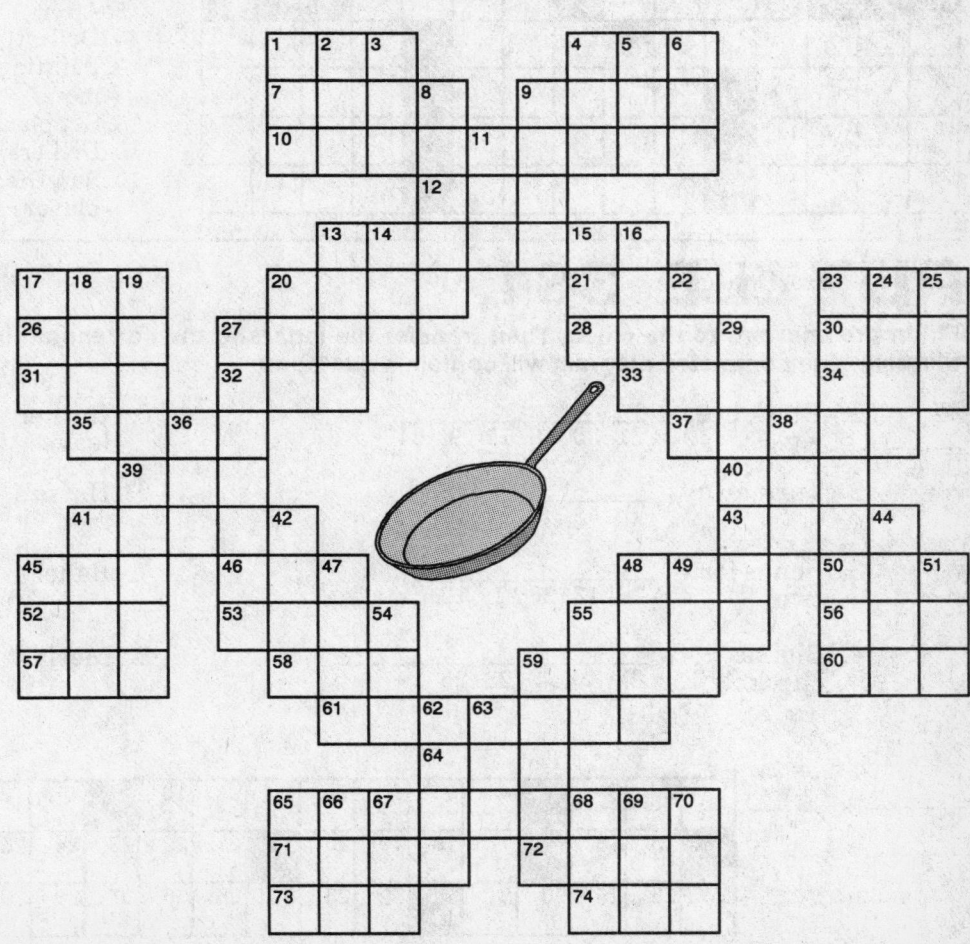

309

PUZZLE 380

ACROSS
1. Deep cut
5. Moderated
10. City map
14. Opposed
15. Call forth
16. Troubles
17. Hose hitch
18. Wife of Menelaus
19. Info
20. Way to go
21. Indignation
22. Holy ___
24. Complain loudly
26. Inferno
27. Dueling assistant
30. Calamitous event
34. Beseech
35. Dollar units
36. Numero ___
37. Fruit skin
38. Mongol leaders
39. Lackluster
40. Commercials
41. Touches
42. TV's Vincent ___
43. Most diminutive
45. Spies
46. Skiers' mountains
47. Flip through
48. Junky cars
51. Spasm
52. Fraternity, e.g.
56. Stead
57. Out of the way
59. Tortoise's foe
60. Scent
61. Ship bottoms
62. Rim
63. Actor Barry
64. Relaxes
65. Color changer

DOWN
1. Pant
2. Dancer Pavlova
3. RBI, e.g.
4. Moral way
5. After
6. Deflect
7. Painting on metal
8. Supplement
9. Drillers, often
10. San Diego players
11. Perjurer
12. Lowest female voice
13. Ivan, for one
23. Ages
25. Plus
26. Helsinki natives
27. Lean meat eater
28. Slur over
29. Burn perfume
30. Doled out
31. City on the Po
32. Make a law
33. Stately garments
35. Karpov's game
38. Souvenir
39. Soaked
41. Arrange in order
42. Arnold Palmer's org.
44. Temperament
45. Way in
47. Move obliquely
48. Impede the flow
49. Heckle
50. Indefinitely long time
51. Men's wear
53. "The ___ or the Tiger?"
54. Prod
55. Alcoholic drink
58. Ocean

PUZZLE 381   Quotagram

Fill in the answers to the clues. Then transfer the letters to the correspondingly numbered squares in the diagram. The completed diagram will contain a quotation.

1. Black eye, e.g.
$\overline{21}\ \overline{30}\ \overline{18}\ \overline{15}\ \overline{9}\ \overline{34}$

2. Turn away
$\overline{5}\ \overline{33}\ \overline{3}\ \overline{14}\ \overline{20}$

3. Songs for two
$\overline{36}\ \overline{13}\ \overline{26}\ \overline{1}\ \overline{16}$

4. Sign a check
$\overline{31}\ \overline{40}\ \overline{4}\ \overline{28}\ \overline{25}\ \overline{19}\ \overline{8}$

5. Gather leaves
$\overline{37}\ \overline{38}\ \overline{7}\ \overline{22}$

6. Horse's foot
$\overline{2}\ \overline{12}\ \overline{32}\ \overline{23}$

7. Panel
$\overline{17}\ \overline{29}\ \overline{6}\ \overline{27}$

8. Merit
$\overline{39}\ \overline{24}\ \overline{35}\ \overline{10}\ \overline{11}$

310

PUZZLE 382

ACROSS

1. Sousaphones
6. Duel reminder
10. Clothesline
14. Speechify
15. Weight allowance
16. A Great Lake
17. Contracts
19. Farmer's place?
20. Lair
21. Applies pitch
22. Free tickets
24. Leg front
25. Method
26. Fled
29. Spanish dance
33. Lily family plants
34. Wagers
35. Epoch
36. Speech impediment
37. Dish
38. Asian country
39. Night before a holiday
40. Thorny flower
41. Slice
42. ___ at arms
45. Hustlers after rustlers
46. Parched
47. Slant
48. Skinnier
51. Tantrums
52. Greek letter
55. Alert
56. Copies
59. To the sheltered side
60. Leisure
61. Sharp
62. "___ the Clock"
63. Solidifies
64. String instruments

DOWN

1. Frog's cousin
2. Goad
3. Cow shed
4. Devoured
5. Boils
6. Severe
7. Gives the axe to
8. Host Linkletter
9. Rejoinder
10. Parting place for Moses
11. Raw minerals
12. Heap
13. Morays
18. Young lady
23. Append
24. Dance instruction
25. Photograph finish
26. Bundles
27. Mediterranean fruit
28. Also-ran
29. ___ or famine
30. Approaches
31. Arbor
32. Fertile desert spots
34. Straw-colored
37. Grasslands
38. Highland girl
41. By the seashore
43. January's birthstone
44. Sooner than, to a poet
45. Flatbread
47. Morsels
48. Cotton-tipped applicator
49. Blanched
50. Neighborhood
51. Clenched hand
52. Journey
53. Chip in chips
54. Functions
57. Actress West
58. Frigid

LETTER SCORE

PUZZLE 383

In this game you seek the lowest score possible. Add letters to each side of the letter groups to form ten common words. You must add at least one letter to each side. To score, count 1 point for each letter you add and 7 points for each word you cannot form. We added a total of 28 letters.

1. _____ C M _____
2. _____ R G _____
3. _____ N J _____
4. _____ S K E _____
5. _____ F T _____
6. _____ C U U _____
7. _____ U X U _____
8. _____ U C C _____
9. _____ R C U _____
10. _____ N Y B _____

311

PUZZLE 384

ACROSS
1. Perform
4. Popular columnist
8. Influence
12. Shad's output
13. Sycamore, e.g.
14. Earring's locale
15. Fixed
17. She, in Salamanca
18. Scoundrel
19. Separate
20. Scents
22. Roof overhang
23. Got bigger
24. African country
27. Clod
28. Kegs
30. Frigid
31. Flaw
33. Joint
34. Profits
35. Filleted
37. Rice field
39. Bravo or Negro
40. Bad
41. Ketch
46. Prong
47. Designer Klein
48. "The Greatest"
49. Nervous
50. ____-in-the-wool
51. Ewe's mate

DOWN
1. Circle part
2. Dove's call
3. Sawbuck
4. Essence
5. Tacks
6. Actor Vereen
7. Thus far
8. Garment part
9. Michigan native
10. Adept
11. "____ of the Dragon"
16. Barge
19. Droops
20. Of the mouth
21. Protecting
22. Antlered animal
23. Sailor
24. Fire residue
25. Chilled
26. Vote in favor
28. Metropolis
29. Donkey
32. Hodgepodge
33. Handle
35. Sea water
36. Lubricated
37. Rose or Sampras
38. Keen
41. Gloomy
42. Some
43. Skiff's paddle
44. ____ carte
45. Comedian Conway

PUZZLE 385

ACROSS
1. Rotund
6. Medicinal quantities
11. Smeltery dross
12. Banished
14. Smooths out
15. Deep red
16. Inventor Whitney
17. ____ Range, Wyoming mountains
19. Flat-topped buoy
20. Finished
22. Youth
23. Duration
24. Iron setting
26. Disproves
28. Ramble
30. Weep
31. More sedate
35. Short intakes of breath
39. General Bradley
40. Inlet
42. Indian garb
43. Cyst
44. Spouses
46. Light brown
47. Pleases
49. Running easily
51. Signify
52. King's son
53. Used a VCR
54. Feel

DOWN
1. Spotted wildcat
2. Cowlike
3. Sooner than, in verse
4. Sediment
5. Art stand
6. Solves, as a cryptogram
7. Draft animals
8. Knight's title
9. Call forth
10. Bun seed
11. Snow coasters
13. Sandy tracts
18. Road surface
21. Anxious
23. Sousaphones
25. Scratch
27. Mist
29. Lowered in rank
31. Scattered seeds
32. Egg concoction
33. Tropical fruit
34. Squeal
36. Silks
37. Frolic
38. Burn slightly
41. Shrill barks
44. Hand out
45. Achy
48. Spinning toy
50. Bowling item

CODEWORD

PUZZLE 386

Codeword is a special crossword puzzle in which conventional clues are omitted. Instead, answer words in the diagram are represented by numbers. Each number represents a different letter of the alphabet, and all of the letters of the alphabet are used. When you are sure of a letter, put it in the code key chart for easy reference. Three letters have been given to start you off.

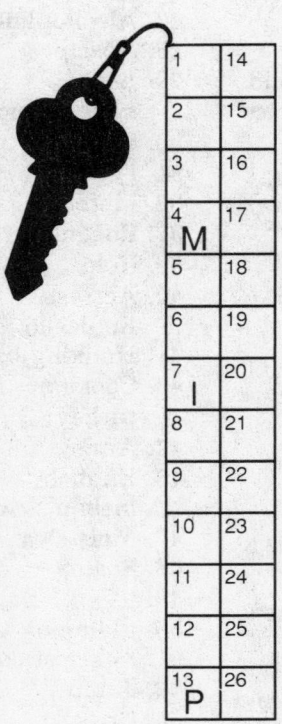

#	#
1	14
2	15
3	16
4 M	17
5	18
6	19
7 I	20
8	21
9	22
10	23
11	24
12	25
13 P	26

24	19	20	16	■	13	10	19	17	21	■	11	23	19	18
7 (I)	26	23	21	■	10	20	26	20	10	■	6	19	4	21
4 (M)	19	19	5	■	19	13	21	10	20	■	21	2	7	23
13 (P)	10	21	5	21	22	5	■	■	24	3	21	21	5	24
■	■	■	23	20	14	■	17	23	21	20	5	■	■	■
25	8	21	21	10	■	17	21	21	■	10	20	2	21	24
8	24	21	■	12	19	8	18	20	5	■	6	7	10	21
19	8	10	■	24	13	14	■	18	20	26	■	5	19	21
5	10	7	13	■	5	21	12	8	10	21	■	20	26	26
21	13	21	21	24	■	10	8	21	■	17	20	23	21	24
■	■	10	19	20	24	5	■	15	8	18	■	■	■	■
11	10	20	1	5	24	■	3	20	5	21	10	21	26	
23	19	10	21	■	6	20	9	21	21	■	12	20	2	14
21	13	7	11	■	21	23	19	13	21	■	5	10	21	21
1	21	23	5	■	24	13	19	5	24	■	24	21	12	26

HEADINGS

PUZZLE 387

Fill in the blanks with letters from the Headings to complete words pertaining to the Headings. You can use each letter in the Headings one time only, so cross out each letter as you use it. For example, the first answer is ROBIN. When you fill in the three blanks, cross out R, B, and I in BIRDS OF A FEATHER.

1. BIRDS OF A FEATHER

__ O __ __ N
__ __ L C __ N
__ I N C __
M __ R __ I N
__ __ A K __
O __ P R __ Y

2. TRAVEL IS BROADENING

__ __ S __
H __ T __ __ __
__ A __ S
__ O U __ __ S T
T __ A I __
P O __ T C __ R __
J U __ K __ T

3. HEARTY BREAKFAST MENU

P __ __ C __ __ __ E S
__ R __ I T
__ O __ __ T
__ U T __ __ __
__ A __
J __ L L __
C E __ __ __ A L

313

PUZZLE 388

ACROSS
1. ____ boy!
5. Church chorus
10. Health clubs
14. Fired a gun
15. Soup server
16. Use the telephone
17. Begin a journey
19. Largest continent
20. Vane dir.
21. State positively
22. Capital of Poland
24. Stalk
25. Halley's ____
26. Libertine
29. Breezed in
32. Group culture
33. "____ Two-Shoes"
34. Inventor Whitney
35. Once more
36. Noah's boat
37. Jaw projection
38. Cutting tool
39. Brief stop
41. Forest clearing
42. Alienate
44. Kicked
45. Songstress Lena
46. Debatable
47. Invent
49. By ____ and starts
50. Actor Bisoglio
53. Louts
54. Conform
57. Unruly child
58. In that place
59. Nick and Nora's dog
60. Matched groups
61. Chemical compound
62. Cry

DOWN
1. 1975 Wimbledon winner
2. Slim
3. Carry on the back
4. Old Siamese coin
5. Smart
6. Odalisque site
7. Aroma
8. Dockers' union: abbr.
9. Sequoia
10. Frightens
11. Take up a collection
12. Inter ____
13. Cabbage salad
18. Detests
23. Chinese island
24. Exhibition
25. Strangle
26. Rent
27. Alcohol lamps
28. Gossip
29. Less satisfactory
30. Slur over
31. Feasted
33. Meter
37. Coagulate
39. Role
40. Actress Funicello
41. Honking bird
43. Cooks a turkey
44. Annoy
46. English bishop's cap
47. Male swans
48. Scarce
49. ____ of clay
50. Clamping tool
51. Poker stake
52. Jump
55. Cries of surprise
56. Enactment

PUZZLE 389

Escalator

Place the answer to clue 1 in the first space, drop a letter, and arrange the remaining letters to answer clue 2. Drop another letter and arrange the remaining letters to answer clue 3. The first dropped letter goes into the box to the left of space 1 and the second dropped letter goes into the box to the right of space 3. Follow this pattern for each row in the diagram. When completed, the letters on the left and right, reading down, will spell related words or a phrase.

	1		2		3	
	4		5		6	
	7		8		9	
	10		11		12	
	13		14		15	
	16		17		18	

1. Mouse sound
2. Tsar's edict
3. Hawaiian guitars, for short
4. Arrow poison
5. Speedway car
6. Be concerned
7. Buccaneer
8. Small candle
9. Bog fuel
10. Finished (a puzzle)
11. Distributes charity
12. Snow coaster
13. Neighbor of Norway
14. Proceeds on a journey
15. Lairs
16. To coin a ____
17. Form
18. Pile

314

PUZZLE 390

ACROSS
1. Karate blow
5. Likely
8. Lascivious look
12. Tackle box item
13. Tiny, in Dundee
14. Monster
15. Word of woe
16. Argument closer
18. Graceful dance
20. Male deer
21. Plant seeds
23. Earn
27. Squeezing snake
30. Cosy home
33. Verdi opera
34. State of neatness
37. Tear down, sometimes
38. Snare
39. Have lunch
40. Desolate
42. Encountered
44. Blaze
47. V-shaped cut
51. Wealthy
55. Horseback game
56. New York canal
57. Fourposter, e.g.
58. Certain golf club
59. Sugar source
60. Finale
61. Give up

DOWN
1. Crab's pincer
2. Hawaiian dance
3. Spoken
4. Annoyances
5. Piercing tool
6. Pod contents
7. Examination
8. In _____ (slowly)
9. Self-image
10. Be mistaken
11. Scarlet
17. Highland hat
19. Area
22. Shed tears
24. Go by train
25. Concept
26. Small pie
27. Fishhook part
28. Milky gem
29. Cathedral part
31. Man's title
32. Sports unit
35. Printed sheet
36. Unseal
41. Frontiersman Carson
43. Discussion subject
45. Dressing gown
46. Genesis garden
48. Ripped
49. Lump of dirt
50. Sharpen
51. Spider's creation
52. Before, to a bard
53. _____ down (recline)
54. "The _____ Couple"

PUZZLE 391

ACROSS
1. Chum
4. Blueprint
8. Summon
12. Actor Wallach
13. "The _____ Ranger"
14. Europe's neighbor
15. Writing implement
16. Noshes
17. Film critic Rex _____
18. Pleased
20. Walks
22. Spirited horses
24. Bottle cap
25. Rotates
26. Sleeping place
27. Once held
30. Wallet stuffers
31. Gym mat
32. Actor's part
33. Join in matrimony
34. Gain
35. Not true
36. Each
37. Seaman
38. Reveries
41. Flooring unit
42. Receive a wage
43. Evangelist Roberts
45. Strike sharply
48. Farm measure
49. Cairo's river
50. Freudian word
51. Not as much
52. Went too fast
53. Period, e.g.

DOWN
1. Energy
2. Brewed beverage
3. Tarried
4. Begs
5. Burdens
6. Picnic invader
7. Cuddled
8. Felt concern
9. On the briny
10. Told an untruth
11. Fellows
19. Camera's eye
21. Disburden
22. Put away
23. Melody
26. Vampire _____
27. Shouted
28. Too
29. Stag or roe
31. Human beings
32. Fence bar
34. Jewel
35. Got an F
36. Window units
37. Not fresh
38. Business transaction
39. Speed contest
40. Is wrong
44. Mr. Van Winkle
46. Gone by
47. Saucepan

PUZZLE 392   Circular Crossword

Fill in the answers to the Around clues in a clockwise direction; for the Radial clues, from the outside to the inside.

AROUND (Clockwise)

1. Grass shacks
5. Be human
8. English baby carriage
12. Choose
15. Of sound
16. Thrash
18. Expunge
19. Polynesian tubers
21. Fitting no category
25. In that place
26. Loved ones
27. Insignificant
28. Fragrant seed
30. Radiate
31. Vast expanse

32. Drunkards
33. Expected
34. Metaphysical being
35. Classified items
36. Decompose
37. Eternally, in poems

RADIAL (Out to in)

1. Mortar mixer
2. Squadron
3. Contribute a tenth
4. Plot
5. Impish child
6. Sortie
7. Soar
8. Cellist Jacqueline du ____

9. Grate harshly
10. Fire remains
11. Wise counselor
12. Lout
13. Malay boat
14. Village
15. Scoff
16. Worries
17. Capital of Tibet
18. Actress Martinelli et al.
19. Lovers' rendezvous
20. Playground chute
22. Actress Moran
23. Actor MacMurray
24. Director Preminger
29. Take to court

ACROSS

1. Reindeer herder
5. Bowling score
10. Sod
14. Always
15. Argentine leader
16. Burma's locale
17. Roman fiddler
18. Omit
19. Repair
20. Alpert's horn
22. Blockade
24. Timeworn
25. Blue or flush
26. Vacant
29. ____ Vegas
30. Tutor
34. Field mouse
35. Female swine
36. Bay of ____
37. ____ Khan
38. Kareem's shot
40. Hurry
41. Centers
43. Ethan's brother
44. Wrenched
45. Doze
46. Humorist George ____
47. Swedish coin
48. Championship
50. Author Tolstoy
51. Parvenu
54. Certain canoes
58. Stead
59. Hank ____ of baseball
61. Entreaty
62. Writer Waugh
63. Wading bird
64. Remnants
65. Hawaiian goose
66. Colorado's ____ Park
67. Impetuous

DOWN

1. Period after Mardi Gras
2. Affirm
3. Lima's land
4. Advertise
5. Zoom
6. Skin
7. Mr. Onassis
8. Western shows
9. Foe
10. Tijuana treats
11. Patron
12. Bullfight venue
13. Portuguese folk song
21. Wield
23. Dyeing technique
25. Eastwood series
26. Swimmer Janet ____
27. Powerful person
28. Locate
29. Actress Myrna ____
31. Sneeze sound
32. Heap of stones
33. Spotted scavenger
35. Snow bunny's prop
36. Feather scarf
38. Brown pigment
39. Native mineral
42. Rabbit's fare
44. Police officer
46. Church platforms
47. Barrel
49. Vestige
50. Crescent-shaped figures
51. ____ Bator
52. Stack
53. Witnessed
54. Completed
55. Forearm bone
56. Koppel and Kennedy
57. Cummerbund
60. Mouse's cousin

Anagram Quotes

PUZZLE 394

Unscramble each set of letters below the dashes to complete the humorous quotations.

1. _____ _____ is the _____ of not _____ _____ _____.
   BNIGE DEMOTS   RTA   GABGNIGR GIHTR WYAA

2. _____ _____ has a way of _____ _____.
   ANPS DEGNJMTU   BMEGICNO ADNEFESUTN

3. _____ to _____ a _____ is like _____ to _____ a _____.
   GITNRY   ASQUHS   RMORU   TGYRNI   GINURN   LEBL

PUZZLE 395

ACROSS
1. River blockers
5. Sailboat
10. ___ facto
14. Disembarked
15. Henry Cabot ___
16. Ponder
17. Bantu language
18. Downy duck
19. Trudge
20. Editor
22. Jailbreak participant
24. Scruffs
26. "___ Miss Brooks"
27. Bishops' headdresses
30. Spark plug's job
35. Wear away
36. Author Ferber
37. Achy
38. Isle of ___
39. Submerge
41. Capp and Capone
43. Playing marble
44. Elevator name
46. Dapper
48. Cover with metal
50. Supported
52. Ferret's cousin
53. MGM lion
54. Indian, e.g.
56. Spreads out
60. Generosity
64. Nonclerical
65. Singer John
67. ___ Mountains
68. Diarist Frank
69. Hospital worker
70. Olympian Korbut
71. Espouses
72. Cornered
73. Pick a crop

DOWN
1. Stupefy
2. Grad
3. 5,280 feet
4. Amazed
5. Reposes
6. French river
7. Strange
8. Type of molding
9. Private
10. Divulges
11. Fruit part
12. ___ gin
13. Merrie ___ England
21. Challenged
23. Composer Cesar ___
25. Football's Luckman
27. Short notes
28. Furious
29. Bracer
31. Pesky insect
32. Tiny particles
33. Emulate Cicero
34. Handrail post
36. Rapier's kin
40. Slothful
42. Asparagus unit
45. Consoles
47. Tumult
49. Sluggishness
51. Novel
52. Freed from a habit
55. Actress Glenn ___
56. Type of salad
57. Window division
58. Lime's exterior
59. Aspersion
61. Perry's creator
62. "The Forsyte ___"
63. Smack
66. Three, in Turin

PUZZLE 396

Spelldown

The letters in each vertical column go into the squares directly below them, but not necessarily in the order they appear. Not all the letters in the top part will be used. When the squares have been filled in correctly, four popular TV moms will appear.

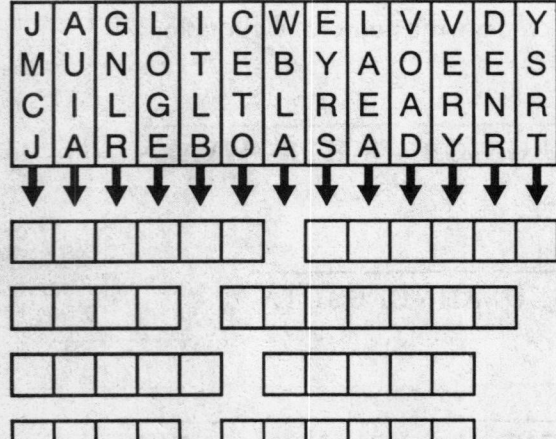

318

PUZZLE 397

ACROSS
1. Comedian Buttons
4. Cry loudly
8. Soup or jacket
11. Crude metal
12. Rose's beloved
13. Ride the waves
14. Moon, at times
16. India's continent
17. Carry
18. Anesthetic
19. Fortification
22. ___ whiz!
23. Love god
24. Inhabitants
29. Air pollution
30. Sprinted
31. King of beasts
32. Utopia
34. "___ la Douce"
35. Type of code
36. Sharply inclined
37. Black bird
40. Run away
42. "___ There"
43. Enjoyment
47. Male heirs
48. "___ She Sweet"
49. Caspian or Adriatic
50. Picnic pest
51. Resorts of sorts
52. Newt

DOWN
1. Mythical bird
2. Goof
3. Scottish river
4. Part of BLT
5. Egg on
6. Chablis, e.g.
7. Permit
8. Shove
9. New York canal
10. At a distance
13. Orbiting objects
15. Astronomers
18. Moray, e.g.
19. Coarse file
20. Madame Bovary
21. Entryway
22. Dancer Kelly
24. Faucet problem
25. Existed
26. Ireland
27. Caesar's home
28. Ginger cookie
33. "Gunga ___"
36. Benches
37. Marathoner Mota
38. Stratford's river
39. Air opening
40. Gymnast's feat
41. Singer Horne
43. ___ de deux
44. Employ
45. Ump's cousin
46. Dine

PUZZLE 398

ACROSS
1. Scorch
5. "___ No Evil"
8. Untidy condition
12. Go by horse
13. Golf standard
14. Word of opposition
15. Garden of Paradise
16. Organized
18. John Wayne film
20. Marsh bird
21. Writing fluid
22. Detective Charlie ___
23. Use money
26. Lad
27. Have lunch
30. Twinge
31. Butter square
32. Utah lily
33. "___ I Love Her"
34. Feline beast
35. Throw about
36. Evangelist Roberts
38. Chinese tea
39. Thong
41. Noble lady
45. Eavesdropped
47. Threesome
48. Not aweather
49. Nest egg plan
50. Rhythmic swing
51. Bunks, e.g.
52. Each
53. Congers

DOWN
1. Work gang
2. Pelt
3. Citrus drinks
4. Leasing
5. Fiery particle
6. Make money
7. Miscalculate
8. Heavenly food
9. Train driver
10. Staircase part
11. Flank
17. Wan
19. Last part
22. Portable sleeper
23. Bath, e.g.
24. Pot's partner
25. Signed, as a check
26. Slugger's stick
28. Mature
29. Pull along
31. Buddy
32. Surprise
34. ___ Cod
35. That woman
37. Fee schedules
38. Fragrant wood
39. Marble piece
40. Flooring material
41. French father
42. Great Lake
43. Window ledge
44. Drunkards
46. Pinch

PUZZLE 399

ACROSS
1. Scrape
5. Champions
9. Watcher
13. Belgrade denizen
17. ____-friendly
18. Achy
19. Nothing more than
20. "____ Stories"
21. Call
23. Baking dish
25. Army salutes
26. Apple and cherry
28. Rainbows
29. ____-Margret
30. Commanded
31. B-G connection
32. Legitimate
35. Leaf
36. Pot
40. Demonic
41. Civil servant
43. Yale student
44. TV's Selleck
45. Antitoxins
46. "Scenes from a ____"
47. Unobstructed
48. Winter wear
50. Artist Picasso
52. Slip
53. RBI, e.g.
54. Irritated
55. Quench
56. Furnish refreshments
58. Cutting beam
59. Captivate
62. Aliens' transports
63. Custom
64. Lexicographer Webster
65. Corrida shout
66. Cooling device
67. Kind of potatoes
70. Buffalo
71. Generosity
73. Long fish
74. Presentation
75. Actress Martha ____
76. Sugar stalk
77. Earl Grey, e.g.
78. Rice dish
81. Pierce
82. Angular rock
86. Exceptionally
88. Beginner
90. Ballet step
91. Spiral
92. German one
93. Part of QED
94. Back talk
95. Catch sight of
96. Specks
97. British tax

DOWN
1. Furrows
2. Lost
3. Hawk
4. Triumph
5. Pale
6. Doves' noises
7. Aquatic flyer
8. Discharge
9. Host
10. Some votes
11. Hesitation sounds
12. Leftover
13. Discord
14. Love god
15. Tenet
16. Drones
22. "On Golden ____"
24. Vertical
27. Brainstorm
30. Theda of silent films
31. Monte ____
32. Labs' doctors
33. Attest
34. Building material
35. Cat noise
36. Burn
37. Pizza topping
38. Malt beverages
39. Number of Muses
41. Borscht ingredient
42. Brown earth
45. Headliner
47. Declaration
49. Sweetsop
50. Nuisances
51. Chopping tool
52. Wood strip
54. Weathercocks
55. Hindrance
56. Sleeve feature
57. In the distance
58. Casual
59. Periods in time
60. Succulent plant
61. Loyal, in Scotland
63. Pallid person
64. Cleopatra's waterway
67. Mix-up
68. Rend
69. Backed out
70. Arizona Indians
72. Gets the lead out
74. Recognized
76. Demurely
77. Redwoods
78. Little dogs
79. "To Live and Die ____"
80. Baseball's Tiant
81. Snag
82. Disposition
83. Heart
84. Levin and Aldridge
85. Hill dwellers
87. ____ Alamos
89. Brazilian city, for short

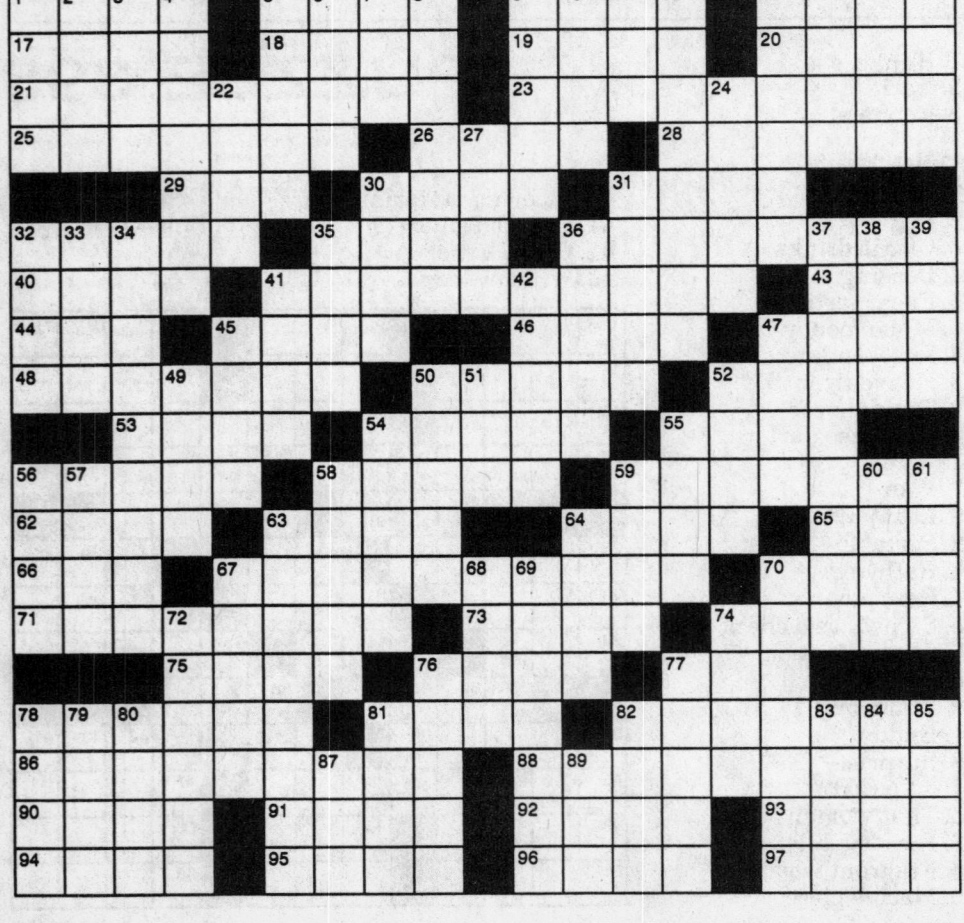

PUZZLE 400

ACROSS

1. Choral composition
8. NYC opera houses?
12. Gaza ____
17. Shunned
18. Wild way to run
19. Waste water
20. Artful ones?
21. Oar: prefix
22. Prayer
23. Wedding announcement word
24. Harbinger of spring
26. Ancient one et al.?
28. Hits from behind: hyph.
31. Residents: suffix
32. Grade
35. Lingerie item
36. Helen's abductor
38. Dry, in Reims
41. Foreign ____
42. Friendly word
44. Old-hat
45. Sloth
46. Soviets?
48. Turkish city
50. Greek letters
51. Certain Slav
52. Redactor
54. System of morals
56. South American birds
57. Tapered land?
61. Cartoon dog?
63. Praise highly
64. Notices
67. Stride
68. Excluding, in Ayr
69. Slipknot
72. Mr. Thomas
73. Baseball's Slaughter
74. Golf items
76. Fasting time
78. Ms. Lyon
79. Cub Scout pack
80. Plant with fragrant seeds
81. Started, poetically
82. Port of Rome
84. Cain's brother
85. Wall paneling
88. Sad birds?
92. Wireless set
93. Airline schedule abbr.
96. Alps et al.
97. Candid
99. Pilsner makers?
102. Charge formally
103. Talk wildly
104. Legume seed pods
105. Spew out
106. Ah, me!
107. Perpetual

DOWN

1. Rotter
2. British river
3. Stem joint
4. Jungle cats?
5. "Fables in Slang" author
6. Land: Latin
7. Gathered in a layer, chemically
8. Yacht basin
9. Fix, as a faulty text
10. The piper's son
11. Take off the top
12. Sequence
13. Gemini?
14. Tear down, in Leeds
15. Borodin prince
16. Corrals
19. Sudden attacks
25. Ohio city
27. Feeling queasy up among the clouds
29. Id ____
30. Bath, e.g.
32. Have concern
33. Was mendacious
34. Strong habit
37. Jellied stock
38. Most underhanded
39. Work for
40. Bruin bairns?
43. Solid
44. Gen. George and kin
45. Seizes improperly
47. Commences
49. Hummingbird's home
53. Yoko ____
55. Port of Hawaii
56. Laughing ____
58. With suspicion
59. Fairs, for short?
60. Hammer part
61. Like some cheese
62. Rational
65. Decorative case
66. Queen's field?
68. Movie fan
70. Chan portrayer
71. Rational
75. Unused
77. As well
80. Pathetic
81. Fairy-tale heavies?
83. Fretful one
84. Protection
86. Boxing site
87. French painter
88. Soft cheese
89. Director Fritz
90. Wavy, in heraldry
91. North American rail
94. Part of TVA: abbr.
95. Ionian gulf
98. Close friend
100. Aberdeen uncle
101. ____ soda

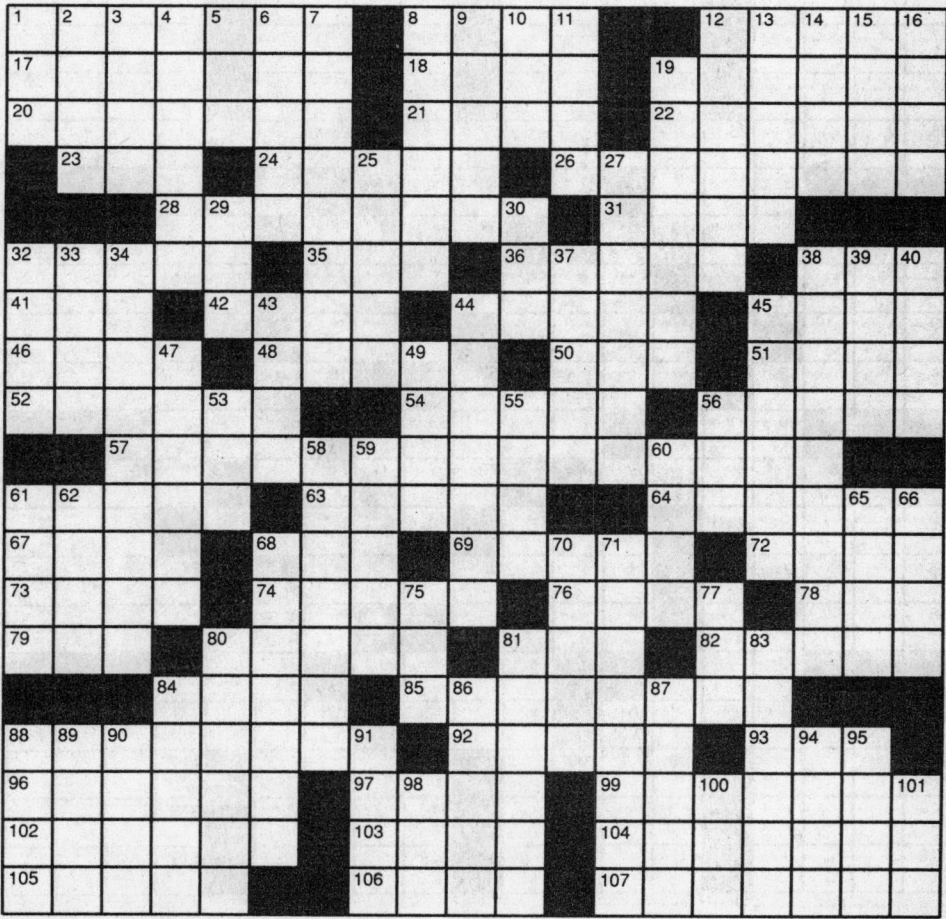

321

PUZZLE 401

• MUSIC TO MY EARS •

ACROSS

1. Social functions
5. Trade
9. Actor Newman
13. Prizefighter Max ____
17. Grate
18. Mosaic
19. Taj Mahal's city
20. Flight: pref.
21. Reverberate
22. Cognizant of
23. Cabin wood
24. Heat
25. Rodgers-Hammerstein musical
28. Gist
30. Expert
31. Grains
32. Academy for future generals: abbr.
33. Serious
37. Pro ____
40. Aggravates
44. More loyal
45. Rodgers-Hammerstein's "The ____ Music"
48. Toughen
49. Nothing
50. Play for time
52. Spanish queen
53. Ms. Osmond
54. Actor Baldwin
56. Stadium
58. Stifle
60. Whale
62. Actress Bernhardt
65. Doctrine
66. Stinging insects
70. "____ de lune"
72. Jib
76. Praying figure
77. German spa
80. Sea eagles
82. Musical syllable
83. More rational
84. Rodgers-Hammerstein's "South ____"
86. Thespian
88. Cut
89. Jog
90. Amaze
92. Faucet
94. Eight: pref.
97. Sawbuck
98. Concert
102. Rodgers-Hart's "____ Syracuse"
107. Oil cartel
108. Memo
110. Vend
111. Island off Scotland
112. Bill of fare
113. Always
114. Narrative
115. Sleuth Tracy
116. Paving stone
117. Permits
118. Amo, ____, amat
119. Gen. Robert ____

DOWN

1. Waste allowance
2. Apiece
3. Tennis notable
4. Washington city
5. Pebbles
6. Pinion
7. Shrine
8. Showy flower
9. Fortification
10. Past
11. Importune
12. Lariat
13. Rodgers-Hart musical
14. Long, long time
15. ____ the Red
16. Function
26. Cake decorators
27. Actor Bruce ____
29. Stints
33. Lab vessel
34. Seed coat
35. Reign
36. Autocrat
38. Heavy measure
39. At a distance
41. Entice
42. Goddess of discord
43. Espies
46. Spanish cheers
47. Arm bone
51. Diplomacy
55. New England state
57. Rainbow
59. Irish land
61. Fall back
63. Hebrew letter
64. Mata ____
66. Dan Blocker character
67. Spoken
68. Hindu queen
69. Labor Day mo.
71. Peruvian Indian
73. Aleutian island
74. Press
75. Cooking fat
78. Blemish
79. Two-wheeled vehicles
81. Surfeits
85. Hankering
87. Trust
91. Modes
93. Jury
95. Seed covering
96. Nautical term
98. Gypsy husbands
99. Fencing sword
100. Penny
101. Have affection for
103. Jug
104. Muddy
105. Formerly
106. Create
109. Asian holiday

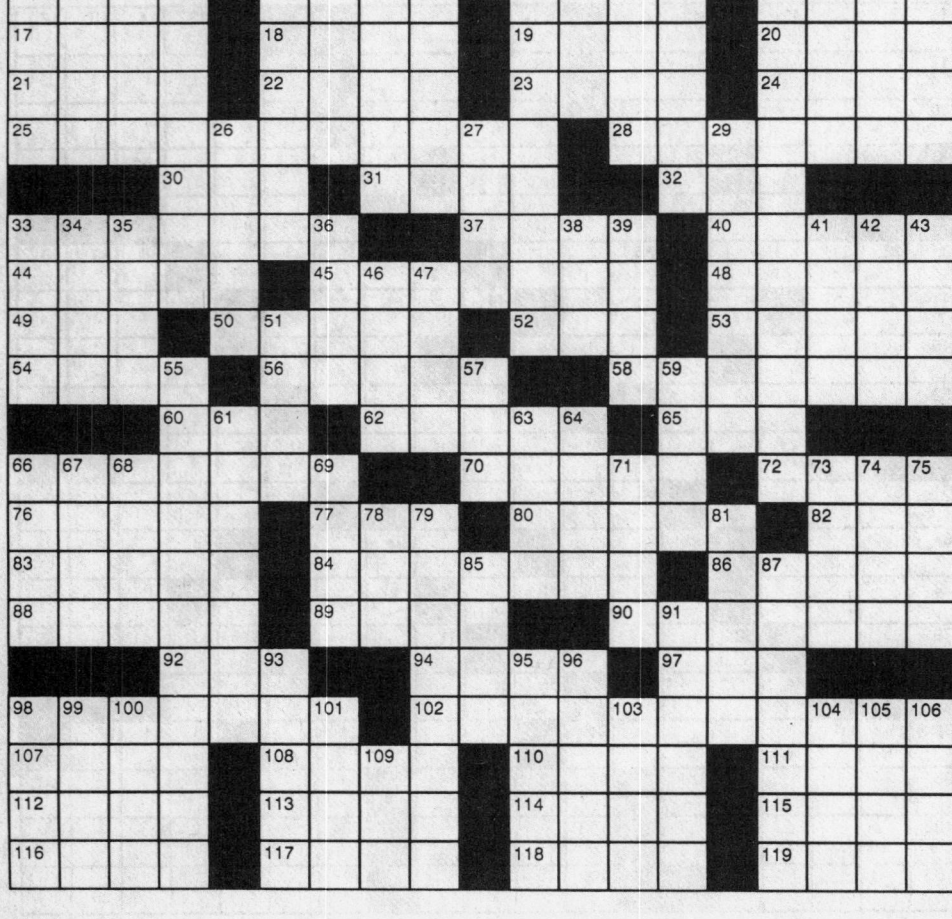

Double Trouble   PUZZLE 402

Not really double trouble, but double fun! Solve this puzzle as you would a regular crossword, EXCEPT place one, two, or three letters in each box. The number of letters in each answer is shown in parentheses after its clue.

ACROSS

1. Fair-haired ones (7)
4. Excuse (6)
7. Award (5)
10. Drunkard (5)
11. Peace advocates (5)
12. Ellipsoidal (4)
13. "Slammin' Sammy" ___ (5)
14. Go wrong (3)
15. Disgraceful (10)
16. Umpire's call (3)
18. Duck for down (5)
20. Prickly bush (5)
22. Navy officers (7)
24. Inclination (5)
27. Loots (8)
29. Pertaining to fishing (11)
31. Task (5)
32. Trio (9)
34. Acorn, e.g. (4)
35. Entertained (6)
36. President/chief justice (4)
38. Lab work (8)
41. Employ (3)
43. Chore (6)
46. Scottish poet (5)
47. Site (6)
48. Prison officials (7)
49. Rain water conduit (5)
50. Discover (6)
51. Capitol feature (4)

DOWN

1. Rorschach test items (5)
2. Goose egg (4)
3. Bandit (9)
4. Primer (6)
5. Ruler (9)
6. Switch positions (3)
7. Small lake (4)
8. Competitor (5)
9. Fervent (7)
15. Wound mark (4)
17. Tool (7)
19. Hates (8)
20. Wedding figures (6)
21. Once, once (4)
23. Narrow land connector (7)
24. Trick or ___ (5)
25. Scandinavian (5)
26. Phoned (6)
28. Tip (5)
30. Sky streaker (5)
33. Teach again (9)
35. Building curve (4)
37. Later (9)
38. Picture puzzle (5)
39. Parched (4)
40. Reply (6)
42. Choose (6)
44. Haphazard (6)
45. Thick (5)
47. Vein of metal (4)

Lettergrams   PUZZLE 403

Rearrange each line of letters to form a 6-letter word. Then rearrange the marked letters to reveal the name of a historical principle.

1. BALEGM   __ __ __ __ __ __

2. SNOREO   __ __ __ __ __ __

3. TRODCO   __ __ __ __ __ __

4. SCANRO   __ __ __ __ __ __

5. RGSONT   __ __ __ __ __ __

6. IPETOL   __ __ __ __ __ __

7. PETROX   __ __ __ __ __ __

8. NEDRIN   __ __ __ __ __ __

Historical principle: __ __ __ __ __ __ __ __ __ __ __ __

323

PUZZLE 404

ACROSS
1. Brilliant
6. With it
9. Spider's work
12. Stadium
13. Fuss
14. Corrida cheer
15. Famous
16. Word-for-word
18. Neither's pal
19. Court
20. Hollow
21. Sailor
23. Coffee holder
25. Unwell
28. Tree fluid
30. Boldness
34. Dove sound
35. Quickness
37. Lubricate
38. Additional
40. Hail, Caesar!
41. Moray
42. Consenting vote
44. Time span
46. Pawn
49. Sought office
51. Tier
54. Unlawful
56. Raid
58. Meadow
59. Employ
60. Reflection
61. Plaything
62. Born
63. Yarns

DOWN
1. Family vehicle
2. Press
3. Turn down
4. Sluggish
5. Pop
6. Corona
7. Colorful expression
8. Kettle
9. Had on
10. Spirit
11. Waist wear
17. Rim
19. Swaddle
22. Analyze
24. Below
25. Frozen water
26. Smoked salmon
27. Land parcel
29. Pod veggie
31. Fish eggs
32. Compete
33. Building wing
36. Level
39. Libertine
43. Rub out
45. Fragrance
46. Sword handle
47. Margarine
48. Modeler's medium
50. Toward shelter
52. Spoken
53. Salary
55. Pistol
56. Appropriate
57. Agreeable word

PUZZLE 405

ACROSS
1. Fashionable
5. Baste
8. Sphere
11. Steam bath
12. Eggs
13. Payable
14. Church instrument
15. Easygoing
17. Hammer part
18. Goof
19. Conceit
21. Switch position
24. Spat
27. Expectant
30. Brad
32. Ripen
33. Small donkey
35. Cunning
36. Pleased
38. Germ
39. Golf gadget
40. Supplement
41. Stir
43. Illuminate
47. Nuisance
51. Pasta
54. Cannes estate
55. Frozen cubes
56. Sawbuck
57. Start
58. Family pooch
59. Hill dweller
60. Unwanted plant

DOWN
1. Concern
2. Enormous
3. Foolish
4. Preserve
5. Fly alone
6. Tied
7. Decrease
8. Poem
9. Sprint
10. Wager
11. Soak
16. Metal
18. False
20. Chatter
22. Fleet
23. Dossier
24. Tatter
25. Leer
26. Insipid
28. Mine find
29. _____ Britain
31. Caustic
34. Unusual
37. Fast-food shop
42. Think
44. Jot
45. Valley
46. Clue
48. Other
49. Luge, e.g.
50. Make lace
51. Tear
52. Expert
53. Doggy doc
54. Promise

324

PUZZLE 406

ACROSS
1. Part of TAE
5. Mr. Coolidge, familiarly
8. Mr. Klemperer
12. Laugh
13. ____ of reason
14. Indigent
15. Marsupial
17. Dreadful person
18. Ref's kin
19. Argentine dictator
21. Senate workers
24. Like some apples
25. Alack!
26. Echoes mindlessly
29. Jose or Juan
30. Poets
31. Ginger beverage
33. Galapagos beasts
35. "The Man ____ Uncle"
36. Insect eggs
37. Road divisions
38. ____ Bend, Indiana
40. Precise time
41. Crow and sand
42. Pachyderm
47. Wings
48. Kurosawa epic
49. Gen. Robt. ____: 2 wds.
50. Manage
51. TV's "I ____"
52. Tease

DOWN
1. Biblical vessel
2. Mauna ____
3. Martin ____ Buren
4. Debates
5. Find fault
6. "Long, Long ____"
7. Spotted cats
8. Portuguese city
9. Like some orders: 2 wds.
10. Shredded
11. Pay dirt
16. Mornings: abbr.
20. Goes awry
21. ____ de deux
22. Kirghiz range
23. Work crew
24. "____ Bulba"
26. Pumas
27. Mountain lake
28. Wild plum
30. Lure
32. Type measures
34. New
35. June honoree
37. Cut off
38. Bargain chance
39. African port
40. Gainsay
41. Shea club
43. Fold over
44. ____ Baba
45. Mr. Sparks
46. Type of shirt

PUZZLE 407

ACROSS
1. Workers
5. Wash against
8. "The ____ Jar"
12. Inca's land
13. Broadcast
14. Famed canal
15. Magician's talent: 3 wds.
18. Click beetle
19. Cheers, e.g.
20. Sun
21. Ring out
22. Stimulus
24. Hanky-panky
28. Propel a boat
29. Electrified particle
30. Bombast: 2 wds.
31. Lets on
34. Uphill conveyance: hyph.
35. Bankrolls
36. Untilled land
37. Pillars
39. Fastened
42. Guile
44. Like some cars
45. Can. prov.
46. Proportion phrase: 2 wds.
47. Signs of assent
48. Gives the go-ahead
49. Gets the point

DOWN
1. Church section
2. Ms. Carter
3. "The ____ of the Sierra Madre"
4. Beau
5. Actor Bert
6. River isle
7. Nutrients required daily
8. On ____ of (representing)
9. Historic times
10. Dark suit's scourge
11. Showed the way
16. Solidify
17. Suds
21. Trudges
22. Bribe
23. Standard
24. "____ late that men betray" ("The Vicar of Wakefield"): 2 wds.
25. Beirut natives
26. Wing
27. Deface
32. Scottish woolens
33. Famed lawman
34. Love game
36. White item
37. Mexican coin
38. Glazed
39. Lowest-ranking GIs
40. This: Sp.
41. Brit. awards
42. Drab color
43. Sign

PUZZLE 408

• PLAY ON •

ACROSS

1. Flop
5. Drinkers
9. "____ the night . . ."
13. Silk-cotton tree
17. Medley
18. Thesaurus man
19. Street show
21. Marsh bird
22. Male voice
23. Musical play
24. Epic poem
25. Trieste wine measure
26. "Uncle Ned" and "Beautiful Dreamer"
30. "____ Night of Love"
31. Weird Sisters
32. Bring forth, as a lamb
33. Those against
35. Elector
36. Actor Woody
38. Annex
40. Fresher
42. Robinson, for one
43. Clarinet
46. Brings up
49. Pip
51. Louis XIV, e.g.
52. Father
53. Pago Pago's locale
54. "High Hopes" tree mover
55. Buckeyes
59. Ad ____
60. "Music Man" instrument
62. Purchases
63. "By the Beautiful ____"
64. Fast way to get there
65. Through
66. Krupa, for one
69. Newt
71. City trains
74. Some are classified
76. Seaport in Algeria
77. Actress Loni
82. College English class, for short
83. Matins division
85. "Flying Down to ____"
86. Treaty org.
87. Yugoslav
89. Can. province
90. Exploit
92. Exams
93. Continent
94. Skill
95. Curves
97. Chop suey sauce
98. Leontyne ____
100. "I'll Never ____ Again"
103. She rode on a bicycle built for two
106. Adherent
107. Strainer
108. Winter hazard
109. "Eroica" and "Pastoral"
117. Involved with
118. Peals
119. Vigilant
120. Lansbury musical
123. Fish-eater
124. Wrap
125. Squirrel's homes
126. Hoople's oath
127. Slave
128. War god
129. Poet Ogden
130. Lairs

DOWN

1. Hope
2. Palm leaf
3. Err
4. Rock group
5. Jr.-to-be
6. Curved molding
7. Sea swallow
8. Connecticut town
9. "Valse ____"
10. Cronkite
11. 3/21-4/19
12. Cause withering
13. 15 Down et al.
14. Deserve
15. Harry Lillis
16. First word of "Greensleeves"
18. Deceive
20. Famous lemons
27. Adjective suffix
28. Horse food
29. Frivolous gal of song
33. "Remember the ____"
34. City on the Meuse
35. Air duct
36. Some songs
37. Diamond and Young
38. Formerly, formerly
39. Shakespearean king
41. Decreased in strength
42. Cow sound
44. Troublemaker
45. Obligation
47. Gambol
48. Ancient native of Arabia
50. "Great Day" composer
51. Singer Stevens
56. Song of praise
57. "All You ____ Is Love"
58. Most secure
61. Calendar of masses
62. Actor Raymond ____
67. Disorderly retreat
68. Downpours
70. "Lemon ____"
71. Lanchester
72. "Little White ____"
73. Bare
75. Orchestrate
78. Famous
79. Fresh
80. Stevenson's "Prince ____"
81. Prying
84. Explosive inits.
85. Stratagem
88. Male voice
91. German composer
94. Board treaders
96. They come marching in
99. ____ Kabibble
100. Unwed
101. Unpleasant situations
102. College vine
104. Here, to Pierre
105. Appeared
107. Man who lives in a casa
109. Anger
110. Slaughter
111. Thames town
112. Life: Latin
113. Entreaty
114. Dame Myra
115. Straight: prefix
116. "Parsley, ____ . . ."
121. "The ____ I Love"
122. Ames et al.

ACROSS

1. Assam people
5. School groups: abbr.
9. Speed word
13. As much as a seated person can hold
19. Out of one's mind
21. Govt. org.: abbr.
22. Threatening words
23. Where A.A. met his sweetheart?
25. Hee-hawed
26. Constantine's birthplace
27. Two
28. Brings up
29. Bedouin's stopping place
30. Pollen holders
32. Wine
33. Urge
34. Perfect
35. Edward Everett's revoltin' development?
40. Some MDs: abbr.
43. County in Neb.
44. Bounder
45. Mouthward
46. Actor Gulager
47. Be patient
49. Be quick
52. Audibly active
53. Pt. or lb.: abbr.
56. Oscar and Joyce Carol's youthful capers?
58. Grip
59. Reduces to secular status
61. Dolt
62. Respiratory malady
63. Attains fame
64. "Oliver Twist" name
65. Flatfish
67. Dwarf count
68. Finch
69. Profundity
70. Guys
71. Thomas raises a false alarm?
73. Hwy.: abbr.
74. Pit-____
75. Touch tenderly
77. Residents: suffix
78. Fish paddle
79. Swiss river
80. Vast expanse
81. Titles of respect
86. Small boy
87. What Sir Richard saw in Pittsburgh?
92. Dvorak
93. A.B.A. member: abbr.
95. ____ out (erratic)
96. Steak ____
98. Words in 67 Across's refrain
100. Caper
101. Romanian city
102. Freed from taboo, in Hawaii
103. Pastry place
104. Thomas is an irritant?
107. Research paper
108. Golliwogg
109. Kind of writer
110. Messy
111. Elk
112. Heirs
113. Scent

DOWN

1. Shelley poem
2. Wyman's Johnny
3. Elderly person
4. Edge
5. Hairy
6. Chic
7. Actor Mischa
8. Draft letters
9. Actress Rita
10. ". . . against ____ troubles"
11. Magna ____
12. Overacting actors
13. Gray wolf
14. Decked out
15. "____ porridge hot"
16. Author from outer space?
17. Employs
18. Guided
20. In a mature way
24. Attempted
31. Gen. Arnold
32. Dish
36. Sour substances
37. False
38. Lode find
39. Beach acquisition
41. Least sylph-like
42. Cesspool
47. Become shrunken
48. Pub pints
49. Taxi drivers
50. Greek tourist mecca
51. Study groups: abbr.
52. Bitter drug
53. Fla. neighbor: abbr.
54. Kangaroos' pouches
55. Conrad is tuckered out?
56. Spouses
57. Husband of Isis
58. Mourning band
60. Certain feline
62. Musical signs
64. Dried up
65. Soccer great
66. Compass pt.: abbr.
68. Rock debris
69. Relating to a dowry
70. Foolish
72. Use skillfully
75. Tabby
76. Exist
79. Oregon seaport
80. Because
81. A Hemingway
82. Pismire
83. Over with
84. Rabat's land
85. Gym shoe
88. Certain printed matter measure
89. Whole
90. Portlander
91. ____ Island, NY
94. Things here
97. Dead embers
98. Nobel chemist Otto
99. Method: abbr.
100. Footless
101. Japanese box
103. Heat measure: abbr.
105. No ____, ands, or buts
106. Ship of old

PUZZLE 409

• WORDPLAY •

PUZZLE 410

• FRONTIER •

ACROSS

1. Biblical land
5. Hot dish
10. Martin et al.
15. "When I was ____"
19. Island east of Java
20. Glorify
21. Ike's opponent
22. Arizona Indian people
23. Wild guy
25. Chester Goode's boss
27. Guido's note
28. Clumsy boats
29. Gawk
31. Union between Cyprus and Greece
32. Fruits of the rose
33. Water closets
34. Sunnybrook, for one
35. Passions
38. Pacifies
39. Cover with streamers
43. Harvests
44. Wet, poetically
45. Ottoman Empire standard
46. Actress Merkel
47. Excommunication edicts
48. Inflamed
49. Fix firmly
51. Advanced degrees: abbr.
52. I hate: Latin
53. Dazes
54. Yellowish soil
55. Be appropriate for
56. Enlists anew
58. Malay laws
59. Ethiopian province
60. Navigation aid
61. Efts
62. Climbing plant
63. Nautical term
64. Rupee parts
65. Power failure
68. Reprove
69. Danger
70. Soup base
71. Chess pieces: abbr.
72. Cote sounds
73. Renewed a stamp pad
74. Darn it!
75. TV's Whelchel
76. Ode subject
77. Seines
78. Estranges from a habit
80. Harvesting machine
81. Breath: prefix
84. Summoning gestures
85. Leaps
86. Super star
87. Place for a bride
88. Curve
89. Yellowish-brown
92. Violin family
93. Spanish painter
94. Gorcey
97. Folksong subject
99. Legendary Grand Canyon digger
102. Potentates
103. Express thought
104. Cuttlefish
105. Irish-Gaelic
106. Match
107. Seasons
108. Atelier sight
109. Equal

DOWN

1. French cleric
2. Marsh hen
3. Actress Nazimova
4. Wire measure
5. Makes like a bird
6. Pawns
7. Fills a pen
8. Card game
9. Tedious
10. Israeli sheep
11. Biblical site et al.
12. "Der ____"
13. Turner
14. Pitcher's style of delivery
15. Self-possession
16. Diamond et al.
17. French possessive
18. Seals and Rowan
24. Head growths
26. Cross letters
30. Conrad TV show
32. Jumps
33. Wearies
34. Nourishes
35. Garden retreat
36. English author
37. American pioneer
38. Sea birds
39. Word to a sneezer
40. Cody
41. TV studio sign
42. Noted publisher
44. Archaic limit
45. Aids
48. Vapor
50. Castle ditches
51. Star of 10
53. Violin
55. Unit of cookies
57. Carols
58. High abode
59. Warms
61. British stool pigeons
62. Stains
63. Squirrel's treat
64. Slow, in music
65. Grain husks
66. Disturbed
67. Peter and Ivan
68. Food fish
69. Virgin Mary representation
70. Thicket
75. Praise
77. Arizona Indians
79. Overshadow
80. African tribe
82. Knock down a wasp's dwelling
83. Condition: suffix
84. Prejudices
85. Unwritten
87. Catkin
88. Misrepresent
89. Strikebreaker
90. Famous villain
91. Jacob's brother
92. Indigo
93. Dines
94. Stringed instrument
95. Comfort
96. Unique person
98. Govt. org.: abbr.
100. Bark cord
101. Cotton fiber knot

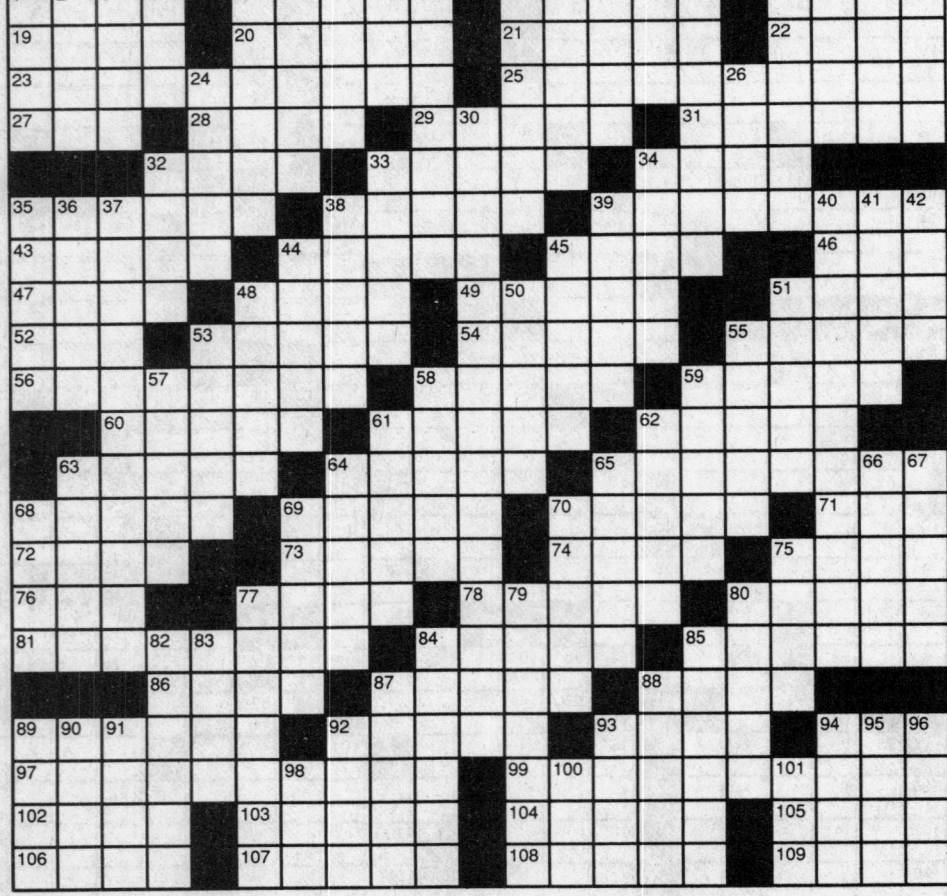

PUZZLE 411

• START THE WORDS •

ACROSS

1. Keen
6. Athletic group
10. Ages
14. Mexican money
19. Light boat
20. Earthen pot
21. Seldomly occurring
22. Ring
23. 5 MANS
27. Waver
28. Require
29. Lessen
30. Gershwin
31. Move
33. Near East chief
35. Drier
38. Droop
41. Tart
43. Elevator man
45. Feeds the fire
49. 4 TANS
54. Seed cover
55. Monica of tennis
56. N.Y. stadium
57. Wool cloth
58. Bundles
60. French summers
62. Latvian
64. Stockwell
65. Manors
68. Misfortunes
70. Competes
72. Parseghian
73. 3 RANS
77. Hanks
80. Attention-attracting call
81. Saarinen
82. Comes out
86. English river
88. Church part
90. Move rapidly
92. Characteristic
93. Ship's leader
95. Peruse
97. Thoughts
100. Korbut
101. 5 IANS
105. Second transaction
106. Clocks' Thomas
107. Central European
108. Upperclassmen: abbr.
109. Bottoms of oceans
112. 6 Across at 56 Across
114. Wise man
116. "____ Loves Me"
119. Heirs
121. Western town
123. Happy
127. 5 CANS
132. Clear the slate
133. Jewish month
134. Metal grating
135. Flower part
136. Female
137. Lease
138. Miss Kett
139. Mournful sound

DOWN

1. Gael
2. Despise
3. Poker term
4. Haley book
5. Spanish coins, once
6. ____ man
7. Spirit
8. French street
9. French maiden
10. Go wrong
11. Anger
12. Places
13. Feel
14. Friend
15. Before, long ago
16. Trucker's rig, for short
17. Wonder
18. Teasdale
24. Jong namesakes
25. Corrects papers
26. Brief
32. Frost
34. Tears
36. Greek letters
37. Lassoed
38. Room
39. Atmospheres
40. Ground grain
42. Carnegie
44. Comedian Mort ____
46. Former country in East Asia
47. Composer Sir Edward ____
48. Italian town
50. Of the jejunum-cecum section
51. Nerve networks
52. Actor Christopher ____
53. Countryman
59. Remain
61. Veered
63. Swarm
66. Thames school
67. Desert
69. Ruler
71. Let it stand
74. Van man
75. Great number
76. Flynn
77. Anteater
78. Sheeplike
79. Shaping forms
83. Aggravates
84. Alpine mountain
85. Male deer
87. Wanderer
89. Consumes
91. Sawbucks
94. Story
96. Consider
98. Comic Roscoe ____
99. Hide from view
102. Della ____
103. Isaac ____
104. Tall stone shaft
110. Conflicting
111. Sarcastic
113. Derisive sound
115. Black
116. Duck
117. Central character
118. Test
120. Look over
122. Leave out
124. Record
125. Latin inclusive abbr.
126. Pickling flavoring
128. "Rose ____ rose . . ."
129. Write
130. Painting
131. Ms. Lupino

329

PUZZLE 412

ACROSS

1. Inactive
5. Zuider ____
8. Out of danger
12. Chills, as champagne
16. Angler's item
17. Cupid
19. Cash drawer
20. Observe
21. Something other
22. Source of woe
23. Role model
24. Resume
25. Get rid of
27. One, in Munich
29. Wacky
31. Instruction
33. Gemstone
34. Serves perfectly
36. Pine nut
37. Guidance
41. Pleased
42. Tolled the bell
43. Fin follower
44. Challenge
45. Lamprey
46. Be overly fond of
47. Desires
48. "I cannot tell ____"
49. 1101, to Caesar
50. Gorged
51. Shows all
52. Mount
53. Stirrup or anvil
55. One who attempts
56. Now and ____
57. Bristles
59. Youngster
60. Memorable time
61. Beaver's forte
64. Vocalized
65. Sorties
66. Kind of hammer
67. Doctors' gp.
68. Oppositionist
69. Irish river
70. Svelte
71. Hope for strongly
72. Fuming
74. Join
75. Wild party
76. Let up
77. Emile Zola book
79. Where crops are raised
81. Manufactured
82. Gets rid of
86. Peru's capital
87. Branch
89. Salad
91. Earthly life
92. Entrance to a mine
93. Architect Saarinen
94. "Soap" family
95. Parisian magazine
96. Rx amount
97. Bambi, e.g.
98. ____ diem
99. 500 sheets of paper

DOWN

1. Angered
2. Eatery, for short
3. More or ____
4. Voted into office
5. Zoo attraction
6. Get rid of
7. A long time
8. Wasp bite
9. Staff assistant
10. Andy Capp's wife
11. Ovals
12. Quash
13. Quarter
14. Cigar or major follower
15. Black or Yellow
18. Looking at
26. ____ gratia artis
28. Chemical suffix
30. Afternoon snooze
32. Nothing
33. Evicts
34. Fish sauce
35. Gauge
37. Aka Lou Grant
38. List of court cases
39. Lake or canal
40. Plant
41. Diamond or ruby
42. Mechanical routine
43. Having handles
46. Rather and Dailey
47. Sobs
51. "Father of the ____"
52. George Bernard ____

54. Destroy
55. Inanimate object
56. London streetcar
57. Feathered neckpieces
58. "Rule, Britannia" composer
59. Chili con ____
60. Dispose of
62. Asian servant
63. Spring month
65. Published again
66. Mollusk
70. Driest
71. Discussion
73. Noah's boy
74. Mr. Koppel
75. Niblick holder
77. Everglades creature, for short
78. Not as old
79. Rover's friend
80. Author Kingsley ____
81. Morass
83. Saga
84. Ms. Cinders
85. Look
86. Young boy
88. Formerly named
90. Grandma's "chair"

PUZZLE 412

PUZZLE 413

ACROSS

1. Illuminating device
5. Wanes
9. Dad's partner
12. Wicked
13. Skinny
14. George Gershwin's brother
15. Scarlett's home
16. Stranded
18. "____ of Love" (1984 Australian film)
20. Elevate
21. Indy 500 contestant
23. Place
24. Wholly
25. Demolish
28. Actor Byrnes
31. Adam's home
33. Tropical constrictor
34. Wind instrument
36. Red ____ beet
37. Building wings
39. Singer Charles
40. Small rug
42. Skirt style
44. Colorado resort
47. Checked with a stopwatch
49. Glittered
51. Pretensions
54. Auricle
55. Spiel
56. Tizzy
57. Chowed down
58. "Born Free" lioness
59. Dairy products

DOWN

1. Give permission to
2. "Evening Shade" role
3. Extraordinary occurrences
4. Dish
5. Shade trees
6. Tempo
7. Prohibit
8. Sleep noise
9. Skirt length
10. Crude metals
11. Manufactured
17. Cowboy flick
19. Blunder
21. Actress Charlotte ____
22. Actor Alan ____
23. Emblem
26. Support
27. Impresario Hurok
29. Mocking
30. Actor Stockwell
32. Monicker designator
35. Pigment
38. Spade or Houston
41. Lower limb joint
43. Rent
44. Befuddled
45. Tiff
46. Carve
47. Decade units
48. Brainwave
50. "____ Abner"
52. Surrey
53. Rds.

ACROSS

1. Crony
4. Tabby
7. This woman
10. Draft animals
12. Above
14. Wages
15. Butter substitute
16. Cartoon dragon owner
17. Indignation
18. Guy in white
19. Irish lake
21. Lock need
24. Blue above us
25. Fib
28. Waterfowl
30. Supplemented
34. Emmet
35. Fishing gizmos
37. "____ Believer"
38. Take an oblique course
40. River duck
41. Press for payment
42. Fire leftover
44. Color
46. "Sunday in the ____ With George"
48. Rats!
52. Highland headgear
53. Cast or wrought
57. Happiness
58. ____ Grande
59. Cleo's river
60. Harrow's rival
61. Biblical craft
62. Mountain moisture
63. Entity

DOWN

1. Winnie the ____
2. Pivot
3. Stare rudely
4. Derby
5. Had a burger
6. Small child
7. Rotate
8. Bunny's kin
9. Potato bud
11. Cranny
13. Sneak a look
20. Dark bread
22. Building addition
23. Adolescent
24. Sam ____ of golf
25. ____ Vegas
26. Squid fluid
27. Summer, to Pierre
29. Raw metal
31. Small goat
32. Ratite bird
33. Comedian Aykroyd
36. Stealthy
39. Hostilities
43. Hide
45. Rim
46. Set of two
47. Haywire
49. Singing voice
50. Bright light
51. Hackman or Kelly
52. ____-la-la
54. Free
55. Cheer from a bullring
56. "Brave ____ World"

333

PUZZLE 415

ACROSS

1. Suspend
5. Health club
8. Jacob's twin
12. Medicinal herb
13. "I ____ a Teenage Werewolf"
14. Hole-making tools
15. Venomous snakes
17. Bargain event
18. Bind
19. Hardwood tree
20. Writing tool
21. Damage
22. "Number One with a ____"
25. Snooped
28. Martini ingredient
29. "Butterflies ____ Free"
30. Hue
31. Notebook
32. Hide
33. Colonizing insect
34. Grease
35. Bed linen
36. Ladybug, e.g.
38. Pig's home
39. Free
40. Feathered wrap
41. Unruly group
44. Appear
46. Wedding
48. Church's altar end
49. Atmosphere
50. Dreadful
51. Makes lace
52. Thickness
53. Lyric poems

DOWN

1. Stag
2. Jai ____
3. Memo
4. Obtain
5. Vow
6. "Jurassic ____"
7. Donkey
8. Painter's stand
9. Tchaikovsky ballet
10. "____ in the Family"
11. Employ
16. Burden
20. Play on words
21. Assembled
22. Auction offer
23. A Great Lake
24. Camper's shelter
25. Pierce
26. Cone-bearing tree
27. Bank's loan charge
28. Girl
31. Filled pastry
32. Bashful
34. Ancient
35. ____ of David
37. New York City newspaper
38. Repentant
40. Prisoner's release money
41. Female servant
42. Monster
43. Honey makers
44. Took a chair
45. Pollution-control dpt.
46. Chart
47. Bachelor's last words

ACROSS

1. Facts
5. Mist
10. Bird of prey
14. Showy spring flower
15. Fragment
16. Pang
17. Ooze
18. Lessens
19. Serving platter
20. Diner breakfast fare
21. Hard-working insect
22. Borscht ingredients
23. Curly hairstyle
25. Delighted
27. Mastery
30. Summer entree
32. Golf-course feature
35. Psychological
37. Poodle, e.g.
38. Owned
39. "Holiday ____"
40. Like Mr. Tanner in "Full House"
43. Hen's product
44. Soap-making substance
45. Blemish
46. Type of lottery
48. Play it by ____
49. Broaden
51. Software mogul Bill ____
52. Morsels
53. Eternally
55. Raise the shoulders
58. Round green vegetable
59. Sour substance
63. Frog's cousin
64. Droplets
66. Eroded
67. In the center of
68. Spry
69. Lamenting word
70. Depend
71. Shades, as of color
72. Jerk

DOWN

1. Plate
2. Zone
3. Cravats
4. Paving material
5. Javelin
6. Spinet and baby grand
7. Part of R and R
8. Expert
9. No's opposite
10. Loathed
11. Farmland measure
12. Huh?
13. Lock openers
22. Spoiled
24. Defect
25. Radiate
26. Light beer
27. Happy expression
28. Nairobi's nation
29. Circle or city beginner
31. Idolize
32. Burglary
33. National bird
34. Rims
36. Restriction
41. "My Two ____"
42. Violent anger
47. Distant
49. Toupee
50. Phonograph feature
52. Pal
54. Flower holders
55. Nighttime twinkler
56. Where the heart is
57. Train track
58. Nuisance
60. Fizzy-drink flavor
61. Islamic nation
62. Student's workplace
64. Baseball stick
65. Conceit

PUZZLE 416

335

PUZZLE 417

ACROSS

1. One from Belgrade
5. Worry
9. City north of Des Moines
13. Belgium river
17. Mishmash
18. Nurture
19. Travel about
20. Singer Jerry ____
21. Satisfactory
22. '60s do
23. Cartel acronym
24. Spicy stew
25. Mr. Mandela
27. John Candy film
30. Acorn trees
32. Actress Arthur
33. Piscivorous bird
34. Hoodwink
37. Cartoonist Kelly
39. Church part
43. Charged particles
44. Heisman-trophy winner Andre ____
45. Actress Phoebe ____ of "Gremlins"
47. Be under the weather
48. Nobel peace prize recipient, with 63 Across
49. Sort
50. Window ache?
51. Basin
52. Hermit
54. Family auto
55. Stubborn ones
56. Wrestling surface
57. Phase
58. Escort's offering
59. Heptad
62. Light or whale
63. See 48 Across
67. Affirm
68. God of war
69. Canadian hockey great
70. Arab chieftain
71. Backpack
72. Heavenly ram
74. Heed
75. Frog genus
76. Drool
78. Baseball's Speaker
79. Russian novelist Tertz
80. Stat for 78 Across
81. Sward
82. Arouse
84. Autumn period
90. Salem's locale
94. Urgency
95. Being: Fr.
96. Parade worry
98. Sailor's saint
99. Criminal band
100. Painter Bonheur
101. Singer Lovett
102. Fervor
103. Artist Roman ____-de Tirtoff
104. Practice pugilism
105. Twelve months
106. Sicilian town

DOWN

1. Part of ASAP
2. Actress Sommer
3. Iranian coin
4. Don Henley song, with "The"
5. Football's Gifford
6. Ump's kin
7. Wet behind the ____
8. Difficulty
9. Redolence
10. Brood
11. "The Greatest Story ____ Told"
12. Emit
13. Singer Elliman
14. Dieter's taboo
15. Spanish she
16. Bona fide
26. Cookie grain
28. New York athlete
29. "____ Tu"
31. 1984 Kentucky Derby winner
34. Spot
35. 3,600 seconds
36. Chip in a chip
38. Deluge refuge
39. British gun
40. Water holder
41. Queue
42. Lodge brothers
44. Skater Katarina ____
45. West Pointer
46. College course: abbr.
50. Texas river
51. Seals and Crofts song
53. Golfer Woosnam
54. Comedian Soupy ____
55. Robinson or Miniver
57. 1871 Chicago event

58. Ethereal
59. "Barefoot in the Park" director
60. Badder than bad
61. White House rejection
62. Twins
63. Prepare, as a turkey
64. Persian poet
65. Designer Ricci
66. Small amount
69. "Mikado" costume item
72. Israel's Eban
73. Carl and Rob
74. Nurse's aide
77. Golden Gate, e.g.
78. Roseanne's hubby
79. Part of RAF
81. Smudge
83. Copier fluid
84. "Picnic" playwright
85. Approaching
86. Noticeable effect
87. Discontinue
88. Bear: Lat.
89. Comedienne Martha ___
91. Narrow valley
92. Saudi Arabia's neighbor
93. Italian commune
97. Stevedores' org.

PUZZLE 417

PUZZLE 418

ACROSS

1. Work onstage
4. Label
7. Paper-mill need
11. Become dim
15. Words from Scrooge
17. Scotto song
18. District
19. Jannings of filmdom
20. Writer Harte
21. Trumpet-shaped flowers
24. Took for granted
26. Bump
27. Mountain ridge
28. Actress Merkel and others
29. Chanteuse Horne
30. Ending for kitchen or major
32. Coins
34. Roman track post
35. More sugary
38. Go by
39. Grazing lands
40. Rah, for one
41. Tatter
43. "Where the Spies ____"
44. Martin or Jones
45. Certain South Africans
46. Malacca
47. Leave high and dry
49. Flat fish
50. Photo finish
51. Soho socials
55. Sweat or night
58. Attain
59. Spirited mounts
62. " . . . valley of death ____ the six hundred"
63. River features
65. Twilight swoopers
66. Be under the weather
68. Sick
69. Moisten, as the turkey
70. Ancient home of Irish kings
71. Computer unit
72. Argues
74. Chains
75. Yielded
76. This: Sp.
77. "____ Train"
78. Boxer Max ____
79. Wall hanging
82. Twinkler
83. Divans' kin
86. TV's "In the ____"
90. Zhivago's love
91. Mine entrance
92. Cuckoopint plant
93. Old French coins
94. Send out
95. Physique
96. Quayle and Rather
97. Sandboxer
98. Get the picture

DOWN

1. Israel's ____ Eban
2. Gas eaters
3. "Red Sails in ____"
4. Walked on
5. Balloon filler
6. Sea birds
7. Ling-Ling, for one
8. Twist one's arm
9. Journey part
10. Crony
11. Polecat's kin
12. French girlfriend
13. Food plan
14. Other
16. Retards growth
17. Iowa college town
22. Hebrides island
23. Horse opera
25. Pas' mates
29. Mrs. Spratt's bane
30. Water pitcher
31. Stands for Palmer
32. Numbers man: abbr.
33. Pinnae
34. British economist
35. Gloss
36. Part of QED
37. Talk wildly
39. Fasting period
40. Punctuation mark
42. Turn to the right
44. Nutty
45. Dolts
46. Etui
48. Hard to find
49. Mamba, for one

50. Daisy and Fannie
52. Leases
53. Autocrats
54. Comics character Kett
55. ____ Lanka
56. Keep, as a poker hand
57. Not working
60. Reveries
61. Spot

63. Sheet of matted cotton
64. On the briny
65. Sob
67. Conducted
69. Singing voice
70. Traveler
71. Japanese ____
73. Actor Warren ____
74. Horse color
75. Witch's pet

77. Peony holders
78. Puts a fin on a filly
79. Pequod's captain
80. Decorator's advice
81. Foray
82. Give the cold shoulder to

83. Seal
84. Albany's canal
85. Fill to excess
87. Trend
88. Refrain syllable
89. Tacky substance

PUZZLE 418

PUZZLE 419

ACROSS

1. Rapids craft
5. Block
8. Indexed
14. Ill temper
18. Black
19. Bathroom covering
20. Colorful bird
21. Actress Sedgwick
22. Acrobatic feat
24. Riverboat adjunct
26. Frequently
27. Very large
28. Cables
29. Song of joy
30. Ultimate
31. Self
32. Type measures
33. Violin parts
34. Creek
36. Trim meat
37. Shoulder bags
41. Unwanted one
44. Shops
45. Sooner than, in verse
46. Monopolizes
47. Branding or wrought
48. Slime
49. Soprano Moffo
50. Smokey's concern
51. Once more
52. Bowl maker's apparatus
56. Concorde, for one
57. Caravansaries
58. Guitarlike instruments
59. Browning and Frost
60. Fish for garden pools
61. Gem's bed
62. Liniment
63. Balance
65. Temperate
66. German village
67. Spider's spinning
70. Attraction at 79 Across
72. Goofs up
73. "____ Got You Under My Skin"
74. Movie star
75. The lady's
76. Margarine
77. Chief Norse god
78. Rule
79. Carnivals
81. Miller's device
84. Snuggle
86. Cabs
87. Sounds of hesitation
88. Towering
89. Rubens's models
90. Jamaican music
92. College deg.
95. Diagonal pattern
97. Snakes
98. Stride
99. Deplore
100. Buffet item
102. Kingpins
104. Riches
105. Free from danger
106. Asian range
107. Rumor
108. Pismires
109. Marinates
110. Fuel
111. Activities

DOWN

1. Spy mission, for short
2. Toward the stern
3. Open
4. This is dynamite
5. San ____
6. A weather's antithesis
7. Singer Torme
8. Of local interest
9. Noah's mountain
10. Tarries
11. Physiques
12. Pipe joint
13. Lowest
14. Directive
15. Theory
16. Claim on property
17. Slippery one
19. Hoodlum
23. Grain crop
25. Earnings
28. Bride
32. Part of a hammer
33. Clearer
35. Possibilities
36. Arab boats
37. Labyrinths
38. Principle
39. Sea eagles
40. Fish eater
41. Dandies
42. Offspring of horses and donkeys
43. Songbirds
44. Lodging place
46. "____ Pinafore"
48. Playful animals
49. Polite cough
51. Garlic sauce
52. West Point freshmen
53. European blackbird
54. Short-winged hawk
55. Gobbles
60. Philosopher Marx
61. South African settlers
62. Shipworm

340

63. Family vehicle
64. Boasts
65. ____ Khan ("Jungle Book" tiger)
66. Editors' marks
67. Not rare
68. Bad
69. Kingsley or Vereen
70. Do one's nails
71. "Every ____ Way But Loose"
76. Singer Redding
77. Bard's above
79. Stymies
80. Fishermen
81. Emulates a duck
82. Tomahawks
83. Moor
85. Headmen
86. Mechanic's job
89. Sibling's child
90. Epics
91. Fruit or bird
93. Londoner's greeting
94. Classroom items
95. Not now
96. Swelling
97. Storage bldg.
98. Desert monster
100. Professional figurer: abbr.
101. Soggy
102. Sack
103. Timetable info.

PUZZLE 419

341

PUZZLE 420

ACROSS

1. Gifted
5. Judge's bench
9. Bone-dry
13. Cut
17. Dregs
18. A pop
19. Yucatan Indian
20. Activity
21. Stopping mechanism
23. Repairs
25. Gaits
26. Hurry
28. Lodestone
29. Picture border
30. Large piece
31. Undiluted
32. Biblical city
35. Ali ____
36. Tap dance
40. Malt drinks
41. Bunks
42. Hairdos
43. Acorn bearer
44. Japanese coin
45. Shells
46. Lahti folk
47. Speck
48. Flash attachment bracket
50. Boat hoist
51. Tracks
52. Pullet
53. Antique
54. Broom's cousin
55. Push aside
58. Lobster covering
59. Detective
63. Victuals
64. Etching fluids
65. Conceal
66. Ref
67. Sunbathe
68. Religious pictures
69. Buddies
70. High spirits
71. Arctic hare
73. Diva Gluck
74. Boom
75. Perched
76. Musical composition
77. "The Tell-Tale Heart" author
78. Catapult
81. Leaf cutters
82. Wiggly dessert
86. Infinite
88. Dobbin's footwear
90. Miner's way in
91. Clinton's canal
92. Revise
93. Gobbles
94. Sherpa sighting
95. Stock Exchange membership
96. Make over
97. Whack

DOWN

1. Priests' garments
2. Comedian Lahr
3. Tragic king
4. Yukon natives
5. Assail
6. Sighs of delight
7. Sgt. is one
8. Angels
9. Artist's cover-up
10. Roof part
11. Pastrami's bread
12. Winter warmers
13. Platforms
14. Part of speech
15. Inactive
16. Station
22. Dutch cheese
24. Male deer
27. TLC dispenser's org.
30. Hedda Hopper's accessories
31. Tip
32. Obi
33. Butter substitute
34. Bumper blemish
35. Presage
36. Kind of boom
37. Owl chatter
38. Pledge
39. Augments
41. Furry bandit
42. Courteous
45. Sigh of relief
46. Niagara or Victoria
47. Atlas contents
49. Not barefoot
50. Legal documents

51. Apple or quince
53. Cologne's river
54. Beauty packs
55. Salamanders
56. Lend
57. Cher's ex
58. Dart
59. ____ monster
60. Grass skirt
61. Sign
62. Rapier
64. Heel or tendon
65. Stage hogs
68. Key
69. More opulent
70. Gets out the squeaks
72. Elk
73. Quick
74. Nat King or Old King
76. Attack
77. Green sauce
78. Frolic
79. Tease
80. Exclude
81. Land west of the Pacific
82. Network
83. Soften
84. Whit
85. Bird's nursery
87. Previously, in verse
89. "____ on a Grecian Urn"

PUZZLE 421

ACROSS

1. Fitness resort
4. Neckwear items
8. Not as much
12. Malt drinks
16. Golfer's goals
17. Light beige
18. Yard
19. Papa's partner
20. Nights before
21. Close
22. Vietnam's continent
23. Wicked
24. Consequences
26. Many-seeded fruit
29. Colored eye part
30. Festive affair
31. Top
32. West Point student
34. Or ___! (threat)
35. Clip
37. Fixed charge
40. Small bills
41. Herbal drinks
42. Dilutes
43. Wash. neighbor
44. Lodging
45. Adventurous
46. Fork tine
47. Narrow opening
48. Notes
50. Goatee, e.g.
51. Leans
52. Egg-layer
53. Tub outlet
54. Not at home
55. Leather band
58. Gain knowledge
59. Gravely
63. Mideastern nation
64. Expenses
65. Stun
66. Sailor's yes
67. Convent resident
68. Wharves
69. Adjust, as a piano
70. "His ___ Friday"
71. Beer barrel
72. Writing liquids
73. Ditty
74. Talk-show group
75. Social insect
76. Cincinnati team
77. Grisham novel, with "The"
78. Spicy cake
83. Artificial
86. Fragrance
87. Astronaut Shepard
88. Tall-tale teller
90. Barely manages
91. "The Way We ___"
92. Brusque
93. New York canal
94. Current events
95. Moniker
96. Summer pullovers
97. Lairs
98. Attempt

DOWN

1. Rescue
2. Carter, e.g.
3. Guarantees
4. Campers' shelters
5. Frosts
6. Generation
7. Outshine
8. Camel's kin in the Andes
9. Comfort
10. Gulp
11. Entangling
12. Alter
13. Volcanic flow
14. Give off
15. Off-price offer
16. For each
25. Ignited
27. Mexican cheer
28. Directs at a target
30. Happy
32. Spiral
33. "___ of Green Gables"
34. Snaky fish
35. Rosebush's pricker
36. Citrus peel
37. Load
38. Correct copy
39. Gobbles up
41. Ripped
42. Wedding-dress feature
45. Horn's sound
46. Bosc and Bartlett
47. Locale
49. By comparison with
50. Naughty children
51. Toothpaste container
53. Pieces of office furniture
54. Seep

344

55. Basin
56. Genuine
57. Pealed
58. Door securer
59. Warbled
60. Indian medicine man
61. Harplike instrument
62. Bellow
64. Opposite of expand

65. Nags for payment
68. Wine and ____ (entertain)
69. Walked like a small child
70. Item of clothing
73. Mediterranean, e.g.
74. Brooch
75. Concur
76. Leases

77. Cabbies' charges
78. Graduate's garb
79. Notion
80. Standard
81. "____ Hawaii" (Elvis film)

82. Hard to come by
83. Primary
84. Moist
85. Double curve
89. Indignation

PUZZLE 422

ACROSS

1. Elderly
5. Leather-workers' tools
9. Statistics
13. Marketed
17. Equivalent
18. Part of a bridle
19. Leave out
20. Nautical greeting
21. Egyptian goddess
22. Chewing-gum flavor
24. Flank
25. Peach's relative
27. Lamented
28. Canyon's answers?
30. "Top ___" (Cruise film)
31. Hit-or-___
32. African antelope
33. Spectacle
36. Actor/dancer Kelly
37. Interfering
42. Volcanic flow
43. Haul
44. Melodies
45. Rust-prone metal
46. Army group
47. Elongated fish
48. Chowder ingredient
49. Leaning Tower site
50. Set free
52. Space
53. Positive quality
54. Sewing-box items
58. Latex or enamel
62. Actress Moreno
63. Clothes fasteners
68. Exist
69. Outlaws
70. Light brown
71. Actor Guinness
72. Some poems
73. Little lies
74. Take a chance
75. Entreaty
76. Cowboy movies
78. Actor Nolte
79. Distributed, as cards
80. "Little ___ Riding Hood"
81. Castle's ditch
82. Deface
83. Ready to pick
87. Queen's partner
88. One-story houses
92. Experts
93. Terrific
96. Enjoy
97. "Take Her, She's ___"
98. Territory
99. Johnson of "Laugh-In"
100. Brainstorm
101. Tacks on
102. Some evergreens
103. Forest-floor plant
104. Nuisance

DOWN

1. Japan's region
2. Struggle for breath
3. Arabian prince
4. Appoint
5. Firebug's crime
6. Sobbed
7. Deceive
8. Trapping
9. Rounded roofs
10. Surrounded by
11. Can metal
12. Waits on
13. Waist accessory
14. Cleveland's state
15. Metallic vein
16. Changes the color of
23. Sly trick
26. Stage signal
29. Cow's chew
31. Breakfast, e.g.
32. Microbe
33. Insult
34. Walking aid
35. Malicious
36. Unripe color
37. South Florida city
38. Facial features
39. Showy spring flower
40. Scents organ?
41. Tiny fly
43. Bandleader Arnaz
44. Honolulu hello
48. Expenses
51. Likely
52. Destroys
53. Cleopatra's viper
55. Fiddler and horseshoe
56. Arkansas mountain range

57. Baseball team
58. Cultivating tool
59. Clerk
60. Singer Burl ____
61. Robin's roost
64. Desk-drawer item
65. Actress Raines
66. Film spool
67. Shoo!
69. Tie up
70. Diplomacy
73. Thorough-fare
74. Blueprint
77. Go astray
78. Zilch
79. Rather or Aykroyd
81. Man with the golden touch
82. Bulls and bucks, e.g.
83. Papa's partner
84. Sour substance
85. Take care of
86. Purposes
87. Was aware
88. Grooves
89. Pelt
90. ____ out (barely makes)
91. Chair
94. Unrefined mineral
95. To and ____

PUZZLE 422

PUZZLE 423

ACROSS

1. Mop
5. Essay
10. Greenish blue
14. Former Berlin divider
15. Halos
16. Sidewalk edge
17. Not working
18. Marsh grasses
19. Pen
20. Old Faithful and others
22. Withdrew
24. Crafty
25. Ascended
26. Tricks
29. Nourished
30. Book of maps
34. Colonizing insects
35. Split ____ soup
36. Attack
37. Insect pest
38. "Of Human ____"
40. Director May Park
41. Plowed
43. Self-esteem
44. "Star ____" (TV show)
45. Guide
46. Exist
47. Outlaw James
48. Wampum
50. Noble title
51. Relieve an itch
54. Move from place to place
58. Raise ____ (make noise)
59. Lukewarm
61. Tehran's site
62. Toward
63. Wipe out
64. Locate
65. Nasty
66. Small depressions
67. Wild oxen

DOWN

1. Gulp
2. Walk through water
3. Actress Sheedy
4. Sanctifies
5. Delay
6. Colors
7. Before, to a poet
8. Capital of Spain
9. Curvy letters
10. Stresses
11. Campus square
12. Impulse
13. Snoozing
21. Overhead trains
23. Halt
25. Authors' audiences
26. Flat boats
27. Dark
28. Fashion
29. Marsh
31. Lions' homes
32. Staffers
33. Quench
35. Seed case
36. "Long, Long ____"
38. French cap
39. Ripen
42. Beirut's country
44. Frighten
46. Stick
47. Lively dance
49. Pretended
50. Aspects
51. Algae
52. Walking stick
53. Actress Moreno
54. Vapor
55. Diva's song
56. Armored vehicle
57. Stops
60. Cooking vessel

• SPREAD IT ON •

ACROSS

1. Garfield, e.g.
4. "Sanford and ____"
7. Atlas feature
10. Vigoda of "Fish"
11. Parisian's affirmative
12. Stuffing herb
13. Jelly's counterpart
16. Attempt
17. Require
18. Study
20. Quick swim
21. Tavern
24. Chat
27. Big ____, California
29. Hodgepodge
31. Exercise
32. Ostrich's kin
33. Paid athlete
34. Style
37. Metal container
38. Kindled
39. Van Winkle of literature
40. Peeper
41. Tier
43. Small amount
44. Mai ____ (cocktail)
46. Worship
48. First woman
49. Paddle
50. Relaxes
53. Color
54. Water barrier
56. Neckwear
57. Emulate Hammer
60. "____ and Away" (Cruise film)
62. Father
65. Jackie's second husband
66. "Absence of ____"
68. ____ Jima
69. News agency: abbr.
70. Diamond gal
71. Wager
72. Morning moisture
73. Writing implement
74. Wild ox
75. Append
76. Beer barrel
78. "The ____-Tale Heart"
80. Golly
82. Ice-cream topping
87. "____ the Fire"
88. ____ de Cologne
89. Afore
90. Afternoon social
91. Speck
92. Press for payment

DOWN

1. Tam
2. Help
3. Sign of sorrow
4. Old French coin
5. "Down and ____ in Beverly Hills"
6. Pointed end
7. Partner
8. Seasoned
9. ____ capita
12. Pace
14. Comedian Louis ____
15. Federation
19. Alaskan town
20. Eat
21. Flattered
22. Large continent
23. Break
24. Solidify
25. "____ Blue"
26. Dairy product
27. Most agile
28. Psychic Geller
30. Place
35. Epoch
36. Reel's companion
42. President Wilson
45. "____ Maria"
47. Beam
51. Conway of comedy
52. Ocean
54. Tyne of "Cagney and Lacey"
55. Diva's song
57. Lemon peel
58. Perform
59. Glimpse
60. Twitched
61. Reverence
63. Mimic
64. Noise
67. Soup scoop
75. Low voice
77. Self
78. Melody
79. James of jazz
81. Beige
82. Drill attachment
83. Crimson
84. ____ Paulo, Brazil
85. Trim
86. Female chicken

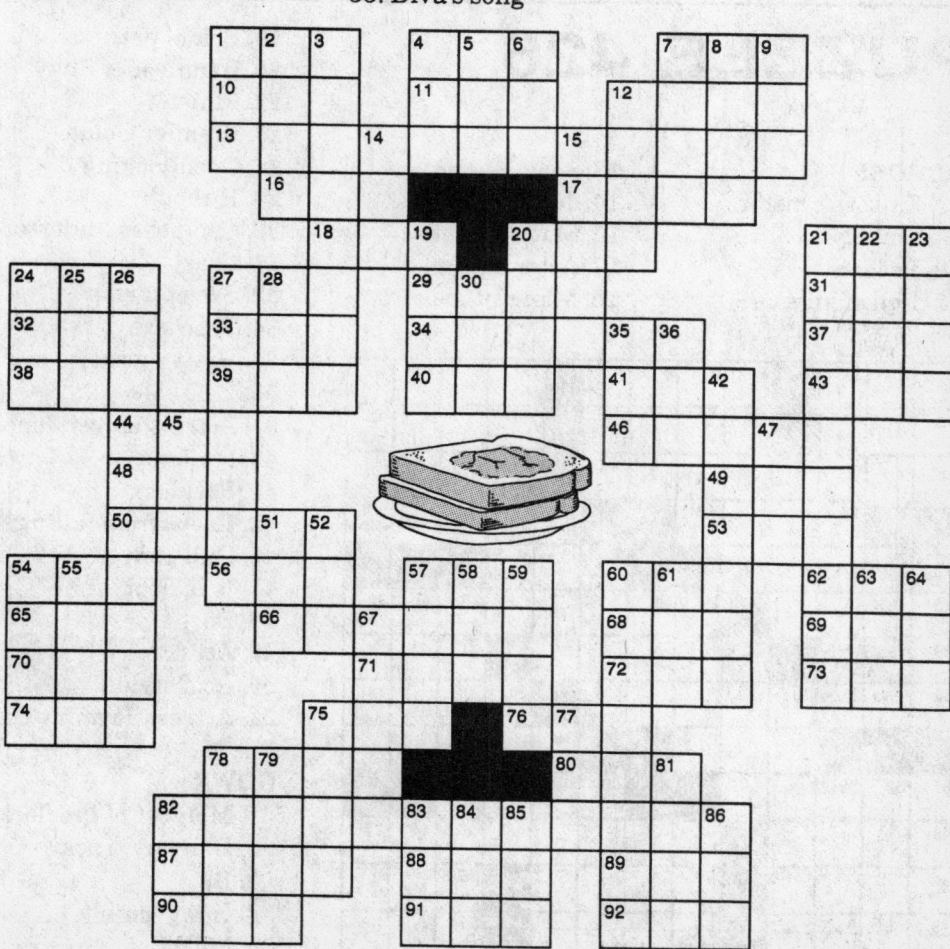

PUZZLE 425

ACROSS

1. Hones
6. Shy
11. Pay up
12. Worship
13. Isolated
14. Relating to birth
15. Kettle
16. Dwelling place
18. French summer
19. Afternoon get-together
21. ____ of the ball
23. Folklore dwarf
25. Ox
27. Beret
30. Doctors' org.
31. American Indian
33. Received
35. Crochet stitch
37. Student's rank
39. Slur over
40. Granted as true
41. Discourage
42. Silvery foodfish

DOWN

1. Shawl
2. Serf
3. Ham it up
4. Metallic element
5. Stair
6. Bicycle for two
7. Mountain in Crete
8. Overnight stop
9. Furious
10. Printer's direction
17. Terminate
20. Ripen
22. Permit
24. Gender
25. Facial expression
26. Implied
28. Desert plant
29. Cindy Crawford, e.g.
30. Imitated
32. Roe
34. Temporary shelter
36. Lyric poem
38. Outer edge

PUZZLE 426

ACROSS

1. Zsa Zsa's sister
4. Smear
8. Peasant
12. Roll of bills
13. Soar
14. Jacob's son
15. Made lovable
17. Actor Arkin
18. Mischief-makers
19. Bridal path
20. Bandleader Shaw
22. Finish
23. Premier Golda
24. Good-looking
29. Hubbub
30. Composer Anderson
31. Crazy
32. Sweet melon
34. Type size
35. Have a go at
36. ____ pole
37. Actress/singer Jones
40. Mailed
41. Reckless
42. Keeps from falling
46. Dull pain
47. Is in debt
48. Doze
49. Act
50. Roof style
51. Actress Jasmine ____

DOWN

1. Member of the flock
2. Delivery truck
3. Ell
4. Hang loosely
5. Melodies
6. Purpose
7. Cot
8. Tartans
9. Congers
10. Egg-shaped
11. Diamond team
16. Arab dignitary
19. Artist Warhol
20. Asian nurse
21. Update
22. Poet's sufficiency
24. Actress Lamarr
25. "You ____ There"
26. Leaving out
27. Apple-pie spice
28. Mild cheese
30. Stringed instrument
33. Inscribed
34. Frogs' haunt
36. Tantalize
37. Degree holder
38. 10K, for one
39. Netman Arthur ____
40. Appear
42. Land
43. Pair
44. Grenoble water
45. Mata Hari, e.g.

ACROSS

1. Masculine
5. Coat with metal
10. Frighten
12. Artist's stand
13. "The Mark of ____"
14. Backbone
15. The Queen's language: abbr.
16. Small child
18. What's up, ____?
19. Units of inheritance
21. Sassy
22. Worrier's complaint
24. Caution
27. Take as one's own
30. Hubbub
31. Three: prefix
32. Bend one's ____
34. Serious
36. Very small amount
38. Self-esteem
39. Anklets, e.g.
40. Rhyme and reason
41. Exam

DOWN

1. Labyrinth
2. ____ for the ride
3. Size
4. Be human
5. Annoying one
6. Track loop
7. Stage direction
8. Pavarotti, for one
9. Chosen few
11. Roadside inn
17. Film award
20. Convent member
21. Golf teacher
23. Prepares for publication
24. Yellowjackets, e.g.
25. Worship
26. Archer Hood
28. Tranquility
29. Approaches
31. Oak or elm
33. Remainder
35. Muskie and McMahon
37. Corrupt

PUZZLE 427

ACROSS

1. Touch down
5. Kind of year
9. Ocean
12. Aroma
13. Singer Guthrie
14. Law's is long
15. Miffed
16. Sham
18. Ripens
20. Pilgrim John
21. Saddle part
24. Thoroughfares: abbr.
25. Cease! asea
26. Capital of 33 Across
30. "____ o' My Heart"
31. Golly
32. Galley propeller
33. Grand Canyon State
36. Heavenly food
38. Debtor's letters
39. Denial of orthodoxy
40. Chan portrayer
43. Tardy
44. Novelist Lewis
46. Keen!
50. Tennis call
51. Sea eagle
52. Palo ____, Calif.
53. ____ to a customer
54. Goblet part
55. Seattle ____

DOWN

1. ____ Alamos
2. Commotion
3. Likewise not
4. Fantasies
5. Coat feature
6. Goes wrong
7. Pub drink
8. ____ salad
9. Hourglass contents
10. Gaelic
11. So be it!
17. Otherwise
19. Obtain
21. Mama's mate
22. More than
23. Christmas threesome
24. That girl
26. Shade of green
27. "____ but the Brave"
28. Fleming and Smith
29. Physician's photo: hyph.
31. African antelope
34. Metallic element
35. Lots and lots
36. Assembled
37. Sports buildings
39. Seraglio
40. Norway's capital
41. Property bond
42. Poker stake
43. Lothario's come-on
45. Mr. Carney
47. Building wing
48. Had a bite
49. Pull

PUZZLE 428

351

PUZZLE 429

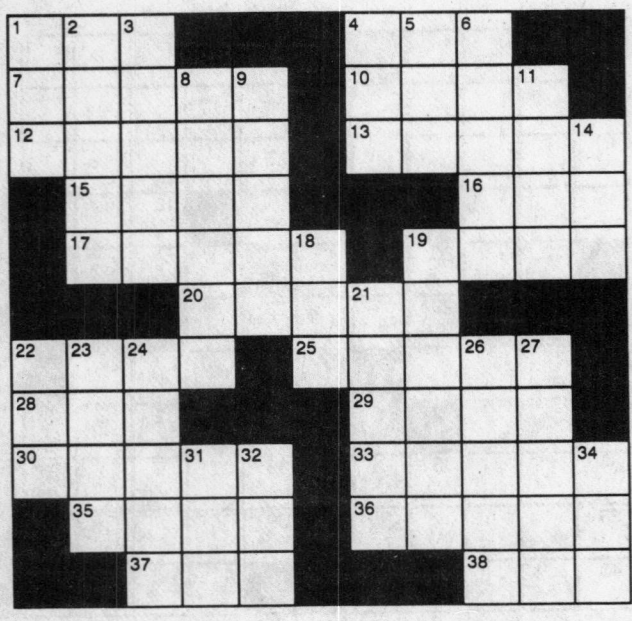

ACROSS
1. Groove
4. By
7. Torpid
10. Dry
12. Gold digger
13. Flutter
15. Carry
16. Ginger drink
17. Wipe out
19. Luge
20. Key
22. Prom dress
25. Primary
28. Roe
29. Be overly indulgent
30. Sire
33. Smooths
35. PBS series
36. Drive back
37. Seine
38. Piggery

DOWN
1. Brink
2. Wed
3. Singing voice
4. Foot
5. Epoch
6. Competitor
8. Save
9. Ringlet
11. Cancel
14. Crimson
18. Gnome
19. Tried
21. Duck down
22. Lump
23. Baker's need
24. Cart
26. Stairs
27. Doctrine
31. Night before
32. Make lace
34. Cunning

PUZZLE 430

ACROSS
1. Freeway
5. Barrel
9. Everyone
12. Egg on
13. Dash
14. Easy as ____
15. Electronic reminder
16. Palm fruit
17. Garden dweller
18. Paradise
20. Snake
22. Straightened
25. Lyric poem
26. Cheryl and Diane
27. Esteem
31. Cruising
32. That woman
33. Con man
34. Gored
36. Trojan ____
37. Order's partner
38. Tapering at both ends
39. Broaden
42. Papa's better half
43. Bustle
44. ____ tide
46. Smear
50. Suffering
51. Sea eagle
52. Path
53. Allow
54. Beams
55. Fencer's need

DOWN
1. Massage
2. Mine find
3. Grow old
4. Reliable
5. Yielded
6. Mr. Arkin
7. Perched
8. Works dough
9. Copied
10. "Saturday Night ____"
11. Ogle
19. ____ Moines
21. Horrendous
22. Sad cry
23. Endure
24. Brainstorm
25. Above, poetically
27. Scarlet
28. Ireland
29. Hurl
30. Spruce or willow
32. Chop
35. Flag
36. Restrain
38. Binds
39. Cry
40. Not working
41. Oaf
42. Scads
45. Time period
47. Circuit
48. Unit
49. Casual shirt

352

PUZZLE 431

ACROSS
1. Neap, e.g.
5. Lyric poem
8. Youngster
9. Carry on
11. Smooth talk
12. Opposed
13. ___ of Capri
14. Worry's supposed yield
15. Insulated bottle
18. Before, poetically
19. More novel
21. Droop
24. Put up with
28. Mature
30. Kind of skirt
31. Notion
32. Linen item
34. Rolltop, for one
35. Young hooter
36. Map abbr.
37. Garden intruder

DOWN
1. Book name
2. Young doctor
3. She-deer
4. Go wrong
5. Spoken
6. Do the tango, e.g.
7. Come in
8. Alda TV series
10. Weary
11. Fruit stone
14. Employed
16. Encounter
17. Possess
20. Wrinkle
21. Stated
22. Poisonous snake
23. Hotel visitor
25. Did autumn work
26. Go out
27. Clangor
29. Actress Veronica
32. This instant
33. Wonder

PUZZLE 432

ACROSS
1. Practice boxing
5. Actor Vigoda
8. Mr. Preminger
12. Prince Charles's sport
13. Write
14. "___ Here to Eternity"
15. Self: prefix
16. Tablet
17. Domesticated
18. Raceway horse
20. "The Magnificent ___"
21. Ocean
22. Singleton
23. Boohoo
26. Straight flier
29. Statute
32. Lyricist Gershwin
33. Grain unit
34. Actress Arden
35. Each
36. ___ Allan Poe
38. Comic Skelton
39. Car fuel
41. Vat
43. Looks over
45. Meeting records
49. Deposited
50. Summer sign
51. Sped
52. Ms. Boleyn
53. Motel's forebear
54. Story
55. GI's dining room
56. Ralph Kramden's vehicle
57. Paradise

DOWN
1. Tiff
2. Decant
3. Palo ___
4. Haley work
5. Seemed
6. Endure
7. Conclude
8. Frequently
9. One on the road
10. Weighty work
11. Portent
19. Pekoe, e.g.
20. Plant
23. Small drink
24. Mined find
25. Buying opportunities
27. Cloth scrap
28. Speeches
30. "___ Maria"
31. Join
36. Kind of curve
37. Operate
40. S.Amer. mountains
42. Montana city
43. Close noisily
44. Sugar source
45. Bill of fare
46. Frog's kin
47. ___ Stanley Gardner
48. Observed
50. Women's ___

353

PUZZLE 433

ACROSS
1. Desire
5. Highway
9. Beret's cousin
12. Repeat
13. Perry's creator
14. Countdown ender
15. Borscht ingredient
16. Washer part
18. Legislative group
20. Make amends
21. Slapstick
24. "Blame It on ____"
25. Endure
26. Steering
30. Birthstone
31. Style
32. Musical measure
33. Scrutinize
36. "Plaza ____"
38. Ostrichlike bird
39. Skylight
40. Nestling pigeon
43. Listen!
44. Fed
46. Not definite
50. Electron-deficient particle
51. Definite
52. Asta's mistress
53. Football scores: abbr.
54. Care
55. Fate

DOWN
1. Spider's creation
2. Glacier's material
3. Andress role
4. Cold frame's kin
5. Prepared
6. Wild party
7. Ring great
8. Spell out
9. Dorothy's dog
10. Shortly
11. Mother: Fr.
17. Molecular component
19. "____ to Billy Joe"
21. Pen
22. Follow
23. Marceau, e.g.
24. Rubicund
26. Linden or Holbrook
27. Same source: abbr.
28. Western alliance: abbr.
29. Increased
31. Winter malady
34. Wallop
35. Sneak attack
36. Knight's address
37. Cruel
39. Used the kiddy pool
40. Pique
41. Part of Q.E.D.
42. Footed vases
43. Roll call response
45. Bea and Betty's costar
47. Egg ____ yung
48. To's partner
49. Sweet potato

PUZZLE 434

ACROSS
1. One of Goldilocks's bears
5. Aspirations
9. Shoemaker's tool
12. Astronaut Shepard
13. Gossip bit
14. Born
15. Relax
16. Highway section
17. Butterfly catcher
18. Withdraw
20. Appointment
22. Feel concern
24. Domain
27. Box or side
30. Water game
32. Healing plant
33. "You ____ What You Eat"
34. Marsh bird
36. Topsy's friend
37. Stingy
39. Rung
40. Study
41. Relieved
43. Pennsylvania port
45. Sonnets' relatives
47. Insight
51. Veto
53. Play's players
55. Knowledge
56. Hoosier humorist
57. Bread spread
58. Lamb's pen name
59. Wand
60. Type of admiral
61. Chasm

DOWN
1. Young salmon
2. Toward shelter
3. Time gone by
4. Caper
5. Wing controls
6. Call ____ day
7. Fix
8. Defame
9. Tempered
10. Minuscule
11. Permit
19. Sentences
21. Afternoon custom
23. Type face
25. Treasure
26. Intend
27. Staff
28. Region
29. Deliberated
31. Agent
35. Saga
38. Embarrassed
42. Room ornamentation
44. Swiss mathematician
46. Bargain event
48. Burrowing rodent
49. The Emerald Isle
50. Undiluted
51. Tavern
52. Stir
54. Body of water

354

PUZZLE 435

ACROSS
1. Football term
5. Everyone
8. Uses oars
12. Got down
13. Female deer
14. Bad
15. Explode
17. Actor Barry
18. Male sheep
19. Peeled
20. Use a broom
23. Dictator
25. Amphibian
26. Rudolph, for one
30. Sin
31. Stove
32. "You ____ There"
33. Department of Defense building
35. Large continent
36. Consumer
37. Prohibitive, as cost
38. Acute
41. Make lace
42. Ripped
43. Groundskeeper
48. Toward shelter
49. "____ Life to Live"
50. Withered
51. Peruse
52. Good-____
53. Care for

DOWN
1. Cushion
2. Pub drink
3. Use a chair
4. Put in a warehouse
5. First man
6. Parcel of land
7. Actor Majors
8. Affection
9. Above
10. Claret or sherry
11. Snow vehicle
16. Snooze
19. Window glass
20. Stair
21. Had on
22. Merit
23. Singing voice
24. Omen
26. Fury
27. Comfort
28. Pennsylvania port
29. Harvest
31. File
34. Rotated
35. Swear to
37. Unhappy
38. Asterisk
39. Pit
40. Locale
41. Timber source
43. Mass or lump
44. Some
45. Born
46. Sea eagle
47. Crimson

PUZZLE 436

ACROSS
1. Matterhorn, e.g.
4. Competent
8. Flower of love
12. Anguish
13. Sketch
14. At any time
15. Assess
17. Anxiety
18. Plunge
19. Harbors
20. Remove from print
23. Long way off
24. Regions
25. Suffering
29. Cravat
30. Amend
31. Female deer
32. Like some exercise
35. Songs for two
37. Raced
38. Large wasp
39. One from the Himalayas
42. Farm laborer
43. Thickened lump
44. Ship's steerer
48. Carry
49. Small land mass
50. Bullfight shout
51. Oceans
52. Emotional state
53. Moist

DOWN
1. Wonder
2. ____ Angeles
3. Animal companion
4. Confesses
5. Courageous
6. Tardy
7. Female sheep
8. Change for the better
9. Above
10. Chair
11. Makes a mistake
16. Concept
19. Equality in value
20. Information collected
21. Sandusky's waterfront
22. Sly look
23. Sly dog
25. Twitch
26. Paradise
27. Memo
28. Exam
30. Fish part
33. Speaks
34. Outlaw
35. Destined
36. Vases
38. Telephone greeting
39. Performs
40. Fruit of the blackthorn
41. Very small quantity
42. Mexican money
44. That man
45. Cut grass
46. Malt drink
47. Profit

355

PUZZLE 437

ACROSS
1. Time frames
5. Young lady
9. Sate
13. Nessie's nest et al.
15. Lowest female voice
16. Main role
17. French revolutionary
18. "___ M for Murder"
19. Consumes
20. Protestors
23. Dry
24. Packed performance initials
25. Fold flock
28. Danger
33. Painted, for one
35. Type size
36. Gemstone
38. Harvests
41. Thing
42. Primitive dwellings
43. Observe
45. Golfer Sammy ___
47. Spotted
48. Self-esteem
51. Canyon sound
54. Lettering pros
60. Verbally summon
61. Thanks ___: 2 wds.
62. Kind of room or noodle
64. Messes up
65. "Nautilus" captain
66. Steeple
67. Orderly
68. Cable car
69. As it was

DOWN
1. Tree species
2. Street
3. Lots of space
4. Disgrace
5. Boys
6. Landed
7. Celebrities
8. ___ eclipse
9. Singer Laine
10. Shakespearean king
11. Dobbin's dinner
12. Footballer's distances: abbr.
14. Shops
21. More recent
22. Summit
26. "Able was I ___ ..."
27. Actor Laurel et al.
29. Saga
30. Traditional practice
31. Drink cooler
32. On the ___ (escaping)
33. Social event
34. "Born Free" heroine
36. Exclamations of surprise
37. Humorous wordplay
39. "Tell-Tale Heart" author
40. Sharply inclined
44. Moves slowly
46. D.C. neighbor: abbr.
49. Jumbo
50. Flirter
52. Assists
53. Satellite's path
54. Worry
55. Taj Mahal site
56. That
57. Italia's capital
58. Nuclear concern
59. Tender
60. Animal enclosure
63. Moist

PUZZLE 438

ACROSS
1. Noise
4. Quartet
8. Spouses
13. Correct
15. Alleviate
16. Motionless
17. Toward shelter
18. Phase
19. Actor's platform
20. New
22. Obligation
24. Cut the grass
25. Sell directly to the consumer
27. Negative words
29. Bee's abode
30. Discolor
34. Tit for ____
37. Express
39. Opera melody
40. Superior to
42. Weaken
44. Nautical direction
45. Delight
46. Cooking vessels
48. Society-page word
49. Calms
53. Spiral
55. Frolic
56. Trial
59. Flick
62. ____ moss
64. Purpose
66. Revere
68. Clock
70. Position
71. Of the sun
72. Adam's address
73. Head coverings
74. Shuts loudly
75. Dispatched
76. Forget-me-____

DOWN
1. Beloved
2. Lazy person
3. Eugenie, to Charles
4. Joyous
5. Cereal grain
6. Exploited
7. Regret
8. Man's title
9. Social insect
10. Sports group
11. Hence
12. Beef dish
14. Dentist's concern
21. Unsophisticated
23. ____ constrictor
26. Camera part
28. Break suddenly
31. Heavy metal
32. Father
33. Dislike
34. Designates
35. Competent
36. Three-____ sloth
38. Faucet
41. Wiener schnitzel meat
43. Somewhat, musically
44. Actor's whisper
47. Deluge
50. Slender candles
51. Before, poetically
52. Hockey players' needs
54. Collar attachment
57. Of a certain continent
58. Game of chance
59. Go by
60. Rocker Billy ____
61. Carbonated drink
63. High or low
65. Robin's home
67. Sheep
69. Males

PUZZLE 439

• SAILORS, AHOY! •

ACROSS

1. Night flier
4. Broadway musical
9. Pigpen
12. Turkish title
13. Lollobrigida et al.
14. Actor Marvin
15. Hold your position!
20. Actress Kendall
21. Also
22. Jolson and Hirt
25. Sailor's direction: abbr.
26. Old card game
29. The Matterhorn, e.g.
30. Teensy
33. Actress Ethel ___
35. Sharp remarks
37. Aft
39. Old stringed instrument
40. Canal transport
42. Ventilates
43. Sick
45. Operated
46. Aussie bird
47. Ostrich's output
48. Sort
50. Mrs. Cantor
52. Four-oared craft
54. Strike
57. "Norma ___"
58. Modern
59. Tennyson's "Crossing the ___"
60. Fuss
61. Commercials
62. Building wing
63. Singleton
64. Negative word
65. Tax month: abbr.
67. Historic time
70. Meadow
72. Twitch
74. Blond
76. Dinghy
78. So
81. Most competent
84. Bread ingredient
85. Select
87. ___ Moines
88. Foot digit
90. Stain
91. Pair
92. Uncooked
93. Finale
94. Onassis, for short
95. Wealth arrives!
104. Armed conflict
105. Close, old style
106. Plaything
107. Bandleader Brown
108. Trap
109. Take to court

DOWN

1. Evil
2. Past
3. Merchant vessel
4. Self
5. London's Old ___
6. Writing fluid
7. Make lace
8. Cigar residue
9. Single-masted craft
10. "___ and Sympathy"
11. Still
16. Sunburns
17. Deli bread
18. Greek letter
19. Gaucho's weapon
22. Boring tool
23. Medieval song
24. Down with the jib and spinnaker!
26. Greensward
27. Sphere
28. Woodwind
30. Get under way!
31. Make a mistake
32. Printers' measures
34. Wiggly fish
35. Feather scarf
36. Detective Spade
38. Label
40. Fishing craft
41. Harbor craft
44. Ocean craft
47. Heron
48. Lyricist Gershwin
49. Boy
51. Dolores ___ Rio
53. Author Fleming
55. Wedding words
56. Child
66. Before: pref.
68. Baseball's Campanella
69. Thunderstruck
70. Misplace
71. Chow down
73. Japanese statesman
74. Passing fancy
75. Actor Vigoda
77. Large inlet
79. "Born in the ___"
80. Stitch
82. Pilots
83. Masses
85. Heal
86. Lifts
89. Asner and Begley
91. Water barrier
95. Night hooter
96. Scottish negative
97. Owns
98. Tavern
99. Green veggie
100. Auto
101. Mine output
102. Debt initials
103. Comic Louis

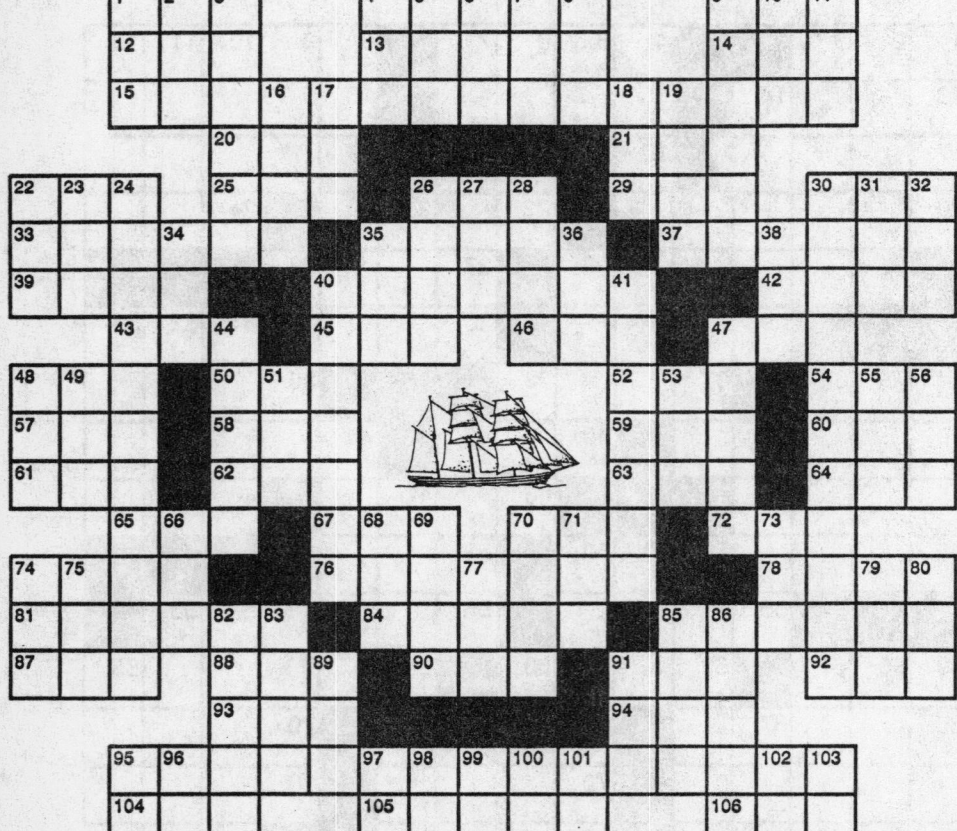

358

PUZZLE 440

• CANNERY ROW •

ACROSS

1. Overlook
5. Emulate a father-to-be
9. Frenzied
10. Spunk
11. Kitchen containers
13. Actress Peeples
14. Menorah fillers
18. "What's up, ____?"
21. Precise
22. Satisfy fully
24. Food fish
27. Singer Kabibble
28. Heap
29. Small pie
31. Orangutan, e.g.
32. Inventor Whitney
33. Building wing
34. ____ de Janeiro
35. A Bobbsey twin
36. Tame
38. Like a teddy bear
40. Businessman Onassis
41. Shy
42. Threat
45. French mathematician
48. Boulevard: abbr.
49. Biblical boat
51. Prohibit
52. Cry of discovery
53. Mal de ____
54. Nick's wife
56. Camera part
57. ____ de plume
58. Some
59. Sorrowful sound
61. Bench
62. Hurricane center
63. Chowder holder
65. Hive insect
66. Sea robber
72. India's continent
73. Oak or maple
74. Harvest
75. Vend

DOWN

1. Singer Davis
2. "____ Dreamer"
3. Male child
4. Lean
5. Daisy components
6. Strong beer
7. Freeway sight
8. Navy officer: abbr.
12. Comedian Caesar
14. Monastery room
15. Exist
16. Ingest
17. Night twinkler
18. Stopped, as a motor
19. Capital of Norway
20. Deception
21. Despicable
23. Skater Heiden
24. Christmas treat
25. Milky gem
26. Refute
28. Louisiana bird
30. Large-billed birds
37. Tax shelter: abbr.
39. Two, in Toledo
42. Papa's partner
43. Equal
44. Cupid
45. Gasp
46. Nautical shout
47. Like some excuses
50. Mr. Kristofferson
51. Lima or kidney
55. In the past
56. Pasture
60. Wheel ornament
61. Fragrances
64. Legume
66. Saloon
67. Function
68. Spy's letters
69. Before, poetically
70. Electric fish
71. Aunt or uncle: abbr.

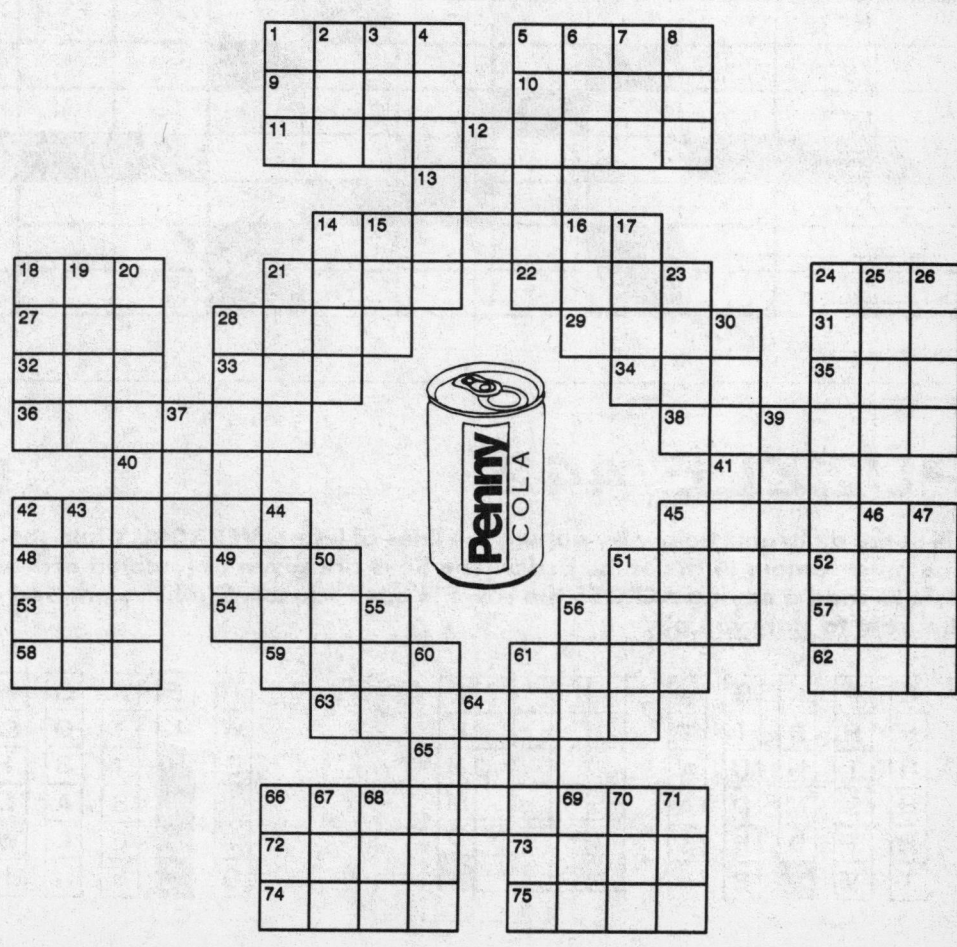

PUZZLE 441

DOUBLE TROUBLE

Not really double trouble, but double fun! Solve this puzzle as you would a regular crossword, EXCEPT place one, two, or three letters in each box. The number of letters in each answer is shown in parentheses after its clue.

ACROSS

1. Search (5)
4. Superstar quality (8)
7. Figure in Greek tragedy (5)
10. Thespian (5)
11. Guide (5)
12. Jot (4)
13. Nucleus (6)
15. Juvenility (10)
17. Religious image (4)
19. Singing voice (4)
20. Retreat (9)
24. Hamper (6)
28. Pair (3)
29. Unsteady (7)
31. Tease (5)
32. Polite one (9)
34. Misers (10)
36. Playwright Neil (5)
38. Interstice (3)
39. Responses (9)
42. Resolute (10)
46. Sting (4)
47. Angler's quarry (5)
50. Merchant (6)
51. Examined (6)
52. Evicted (6)
53. Pung (4)

DOWN

1. Phony (5)
2. Organic compound (5)
3. Ripped (4)
4. Pure (6)
5. Ascend (4)
6. Xylophones' kin (8)
7. Pith (4)
8. Bypass (6)
9. Friendship (5)
14. Draw out (6)
16. Puree (4)
18. Wild ass (6)
20. Betting ploy (5)
21. Litter's wee one (4)
22. Garden pest (4)
23. Epochs (4)
25. Get (6)
26. Baseball ploy (4)
27. Permits (4)
30. Mattress casing (7)
33. Estate house (7)
35. Speakeasy girl (7)
37. Frightful (9)
39. Deny (5)
40. Farm measures (5)
41. Dyed (6)
43. Factions (5)
44. Play for time (5)
45. Came in (7)
48. Umpire's call (3)
49. Actor Danson (3)

PUZZLE 442

BUILD-A-QUOTE

Fill in the diagrams below by putting the lines of letters VERTICALLY into their squares. The letters in each line must remain in the same order. The lines are given in jumbled order. When finished, you will be able to read a saying ACROSS the rows in each square. We have entered one line of letters in the first diagram to start you off.

1.

2.

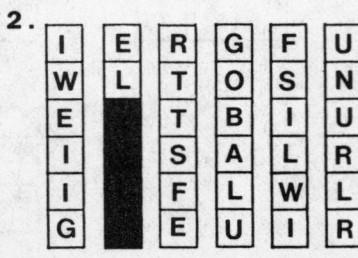

DOUBLE TROUBLE

Not really double trouble, but double fun! Solve this puzzle as you would a regular crossword, EXCEPT place one, two, or three letters in each box. The number of letters in each answer is shown in parentheses after its clue.

ACROSS

1. Those under age (6)
5. Take in (6)
9. Planet's kin (8)
11. Most sprightly (9)
12. That girl (3)
13. Audience members (9)
15. Actress Dawber (3)
16. Dross (4)
18. Agriculture goddess (5)
19. Snake (7)
20. Ritualistic (10)
22. Servants' wear (6)
23. Sinning (6)
24. Scouring rock (6)
25. Takes five (5)
26. Varying (10)
28. Silenced (5)
29. Fritter away (5)
30. Most insignificant (5)
32. Greek letter (3)
33. False show (8)
35. Quaker pronoun (4)
36. Relocate (8)
38. Kind of candle (5)
40. Meara's mate (7)
41. Brought up (6)

DOWN

1. Purees (6)
2. Weave (9)
3. Hockey-great Bobby (3)
4. Earth (4)
5. Louganis et al. (6)
6. Golly (3)
7. Like an eel (8)
8. Scriptures (9)
10. Perceptive (10)
11. Property attachments (5)
14. River duck (4)
17. Hailed (7)
19. Utilitarian (11)
21. Famed cat (6)
22. Key fruit (4)
24. Tangy (7)
25. Eating establishment (10)
26. Pure (6)
27. Mitt material (7)
28. Curs (5)
29. Tap yield (5)
31. Guided (7)
33. Lean toward (6)
34. Char (4)
37. Window part (4)
39. Pod veggie (3)

QUOTE FIND

Start at the circled letter and draw one continuous path moving from letter to adjacent letter, horizontally, vertically, and diagonally, to discover a humorous quotation. Each letter will be used once. The path does not cross itself.

Answer:

```
A G R A I O
I S R I T N
E N E A M D
C T A T O A
S (D) P M R F
I R O O T E
```

PUZZLE 445

ACROSS

1. Plant
4. Anti
7. Heroic poem
9. In the air
12. Impulsive
13. Confusion
15. Run away
16. Certain
17. Length times width
21. Heavy weight
22. Translate
25. Commotion
26. Info
27. Points
29. Flirt
33. 100 cents
36. Malevolence
37. Wee
38. Daft
39. Stain
40. Moist

DOWN

1. Vassal
2. Gem
3. Sage
4. Taxi
5. Corrida cheer
6. Silent acknowledgements
8. Swindle
10. Piccolo's kin
11. Seer's cards
14. Chess pieces
18. Crimson
19. Geologic period
20. Capable
22. Simpleton
23. Honorable
24. Fray
25. Too
28. Toboggan
30. Admit
31. Vermin
32. Scheme
34. Whichever
35. Grain

PUZZLE 446

ACROSS

1. Comedian Conway
4. Hemingway's nickname
8. Appendages
12. Distress
13. "Rock of ___"
14. Snout
15. Disorder
17. Large truck
18. Connection
19. Closed car
20. Arrange
23. Cliburn or Heflin
24. Toothed wheel
25. Throwing
29. New Haven tree
30. Cubicle
32. Brewed beverage
33. Kitchen cloth
35. Green veggies
36. Attention
37. Heat
39. Perspire
42. Threesome
43. Rend
44. Spanking place
48. Orient
49. Stake
50. In the past
51. Target
52. Observes
53. "I ___ Rhythm"

DOWN

1. Couple
2. Obligation letters
3. Encountered
4. French capital
5. Delegate
6. Apex
7. Query
8. Not here
9. Oboe's need
10. One of Goldilocks's bears
11. Pelt
16. Smear
19. Window part
20. Venerable
21. Sandwich shop
22. Bottlenecks
23. Container
25. Carpentry joint
26. Unit
27. Tidy
28. Incision
30. Naughty child
31. Scull's adjunct
34. Robust
35. Experts
37. Composed
38. Helpers
39. Phase
40. Erode
41. Loosen
42. Musical sound
44. Had being
45. Crone
46. Id's kin
47. Speck

ACROSS

1. Sail support
5. Coolidge's nickname
8. Lively party
12. Toward shelter
13. Exist
14. Pain
15. Sound a bell
16. Paid athlete
17. King of beasts
18. Classical language
20. Citrus coolers
21. Brick carrier
24. Pub
26. Commotion
27. Make a knot
28. Appeared in a play
32. Putrid
34. Fast
35. Primp
36. Dandy
37. Woman's secret
38. Helpful hint
40. Scarlet
41. Actor Baldwin
44. Slur over
46. Laundry
47. ___ de France
48. Nothing more than
52. Diminutive suffix
53. Give permission
54. News paragraph
55. Forest creature
56. Pigpen
57. Forbidden

DOWN

1. Road guide
2. Pub beverage
3. Ocean
4. Tattle
5. Ship's officer
6. Come
7. Sierra ___
8. Equilibrium
9. Etching fluid
10. Sandal
11. Biddies
19. Be present
21. Angel's instrument
22. Fragrance
23. Love unwisely
25. Knocked
29. Salty drop
30. Border
31. Colored the hair
33. Instructor
34. Fashionable group
36. Boneless cut of meat
39. Salome's costume
41. Overwhelmed
42. Tardy
43. Italian noble family
45. Radiate
49. Greek letter
50. Confederate soldier
51. Flightless bird

ACROSS

1. Hog fat
5. Bombard with laser beams
8. Arrived
12. Woodwind instrument
13. Actor Wallach
14. Opera solo
15. Alack
16. Spires
18. Relic
20. Make amends
21. Beam of light
22. Golf instructor
23. Humorous
26. Dawn
30. Metallic rock
31. Triumphed
32. Actor Gibson
33. Walks like a duck
36. Settle a loan
38. Help
39. Folding bed
40. Salt water
43. Bowmen
47. Tongue
49. False god
50. Prod
51. Massachusetts cape
52. Quote
53. Back end
54. Vanity
55. Soupy meat dish

DOWN

1. Rich soil
2. Competent
3. Wander
4. Sandy wasteland
5. Flavorful
6. Choir voice
7. Pizza
8. Prisoner taker
9. Singer Guthrie
10. Demeanor
11. Facility
17. Merit
19. Negative vote
22. Play on words
23. Cry of wonder
24. George Gershwin's brother
25. Actor Danson
26. Distress signal
27. Little devil
28. Mediterranean ___
29. English cathedral town
31. Marry
34. Peril
35. Stead
36. Fabulous bird
37. Morals
39. Belief
40. Smudge
41. Scarce
42. Actress Swenson
43. Open-mouthed
44. Blue-pencil
45. Fixed routine
46. Killed
48. High card

PUZZLE 449

ACROSS

1. Twosome
5. Muslims' religion
10. Manner
14. Hautboy
15. Like potato texture
16. Eager
17. Fondles
18. Flute player
19. Lack
20. Depots
22. Score and a half
24. Different
25. Dog's pest
26. Outlaw
29. Long-distance access
33. Stir
34. Weird
36. Stunned
37. Rounded roof
39. Cast parts
41. Places
42. Government funding
44. Stateroom bed
46. Forget-me-____
47. Signed the back of a check
49. Downy ducks
51. Peruse
52. Yield
53. Heated
56. Bothered
60. Mountain: prefix
61. Tee off
63. Therefore
64. Place
65. Cruise ship
66. Civil disturbance
67. Passing fashions
68. Gives off
69. Flip

DOWN

1. Bursts
2. Aid in wrongdoing
3. Modicum
4. Took a break
5. Deceiver
6. French river
7. Drinks like a dog
8. Ginger drink
9. Flowering evergreen
10. Insanely zealous
11. Above
12. Food plan
13. Small whirlpool
21. Tennis star Nastase
23. Leader
25. Less restricted
26. Emblem of authority
27. Decorate
28. Wilderness wanderer
29. Felt poorly
30. Fresh air
31. Room scheme
32. Works on manuscripts
35. Clothed with authority
38. Huge
40. Pittsburgh footballers
43. Forest plant
45. Conceal
48. Cowboy's seat
50. Barren spot
52. Desire jealously
53. Wild canine
54. Diva's solo
55. Hollow grass
56. Short skirt
57. Threesome
58. Swellheads
59. Specks
62. Circular edge

PUZZLE 450   Anagram Word Squares

A word square has the same words reading across and down. The first word across is also the first word down; the second word across is the second word down, etc. Can you form anagrams of the letter groups and place them in the diagrams to form word squares?

1. STEP
   SAGE
   PALE
   GEED

2. TIME
   METS
   MEET
   TEAM

3. MILE
   NEED
   SEAL
   DIVA

The answers for this crossword puzzle might be just around the bend! Solve the puzzle as you would a regular crossword. The clues for the words which bend in the diagram are listed under the heading BENDERS.

BENDERS

1. Spoken account
2. Sight-seeing trip
8. Stooge
9. Connected with: 2 wds.
17. Arthur, Morris, and Riley
18. Decides
28. Slaughters wholesale
29. ____ of the House
30. Pause in doubt
32. Solar-heat panel
43. Barrett with the inside info
49. Flyers or Braves

ACROSS

1. Of birth
6. Provide food
10. Part of FBI
13. Moves unsteadily
14. Legal thing
19. School gp.
21. Skill
22. Keats specialty
23. Survivor of Sodom
24. Pestered
25. "____ Boy" (Nat Cole hit)
26. Take food
33. ____ Aviv
34. Part of Congress
36. Involve
38. Deputy: abbr.

39. Shade tree
40. Three, in Roma
41. Lettuce type
42. Always-airborne force initials
44. Primped
50. Not graded
51. Chairs
52. Madagascar animal

DOWN

3. Fore's partner

4. Peggy or Pinky
5. Gel
6. Automobile
7. Jolson and Smith
11. Secret-message unscrambler
12. Takes umbrage at
15. Before
16. Declarations
19. Rulers by virtue of wealth
20. Craggy hill

27. Court-star Arthur
29. Helmsman
31. Radium or mercury
35. Self
37. Writer Levin
44. Place
45. M.D.s' assts.
46. Certain ring's locale
47. Moray
48. Ike's monogram

PUZZLE 452

ACROSS

1. Neon, e.g.
4. ____ Vegas
7. Brittle
12. Fruit drink
13. Fore and ____
14. Bart Simpson's dad
15. Prune
16. Harbor
17. Vacant
18. Biblical queen
20. Epoch
21. Snakelike fish
22. Emulated Monet
26. Actress Irving
27. Paves
28. Singer Charles
29. Wheel part
30. "____ or Dare"
31. "Butterflies ____ Free"
32. Wrath
33. Quiet
34. Consumer lures
35. Canned fish
37. Actress MacGraw
38. Bother
39. Emulates Sonja Henie
42. Daddies
45. Negative conjunction
46. Pension fund: abbr.
47. Happening
48. Flying saucer
49. Car engine's need
50. Return the favor
51. Beige
52. Tennis court divider

DOWN

1. Strong wind
2. Uproars
3. Ninth month
4. Tag
5. Distant
6. Piggery
7. Adore
8. Director Polanski
9. Brat
10. Place
11. Nose around
19. "____ Jude"
20. Globe
22. Take a break
23. Custom
24. Jug handles
25. Change color
26. Air
27. Elephant's snout
29. Not hers
30. Parched
34. Wing
36. Songstress Ross
37. Ohio city
39. Couch
40. Toledo's lake
41. Season
42. Each
43. Hail, to Caesar
44. Energy
45. Filbert, e.g.

ACROSS

1. Cover
4. Belly or garden
8. Aid and ___
12. Wrath
13. Encourage
14. Vanished
15. Fish propeller
16. Tramped
17. Motored
18. Personal property
20. Exploit
22. Stick
23. Deceives
27. Foreign
30. Quilter's gathering
31. Water tester
32. Soft drink
33. Dispose of
34. Skeleton part
35. Printing liquid
36. Breakfast cereal
37. Specified
38. Sahara, e.g.
40. Bear's burrow
41. Allow
42. Cash in
46. Enthusiastic
49. Excel
51. Exist
52. Recipe direction
53. Horrible
54. Preacher's subject
55. Antlered animal
56. Rational
57. Actor Cassidy ("The Addams Family")

DOWN

1. Existence
2. Garden bloomer
3. Parking-lot mishap
4. Shirt fastener
5. Did wrong
6. Conceit
7. Lost weight
8. Approve
9. Shout of disapproval
10. Cut short
11. Peg used by golfers
19. Length times width
21. "___ Loves You"
24. Powerful particle
25. Mood
26. Sow
27. Boric ___
28. Sole
29. Kinds
30. Chomped
33. Fazes
34. Dance orchestra
36. Lode yield
37. Sewing item
39. Senior citizen
40. Empty
43. "___ of Eden"
44. Part of HOMES
45. Patch
46. Include
47. Strive
48. Freezer cube
50. Ms. Peron

PUZZLE 454

ACROSS
1. Swabs
5. Actor Guinness
9. Negative
12. Region
13. Molten rock
14. Woolly one
15. Journal
17. By means of
18. Owns
19. Signs
21. Raise
24. Grow
26. Paddles
27. Philosophy
28. Imitate
29. More unusual
30. Lad
33. Intended
34. Get lighter
35. Plodded
38. Ties
39. Severe
40. Embrace
41. Hen product
42. Financial officer
48. Observe
49. Lounge
50. Gambling site
51. Road curve
52. Cheer
53. Swirl

DOWN
1. Operate
2. Prospector's find
3. Church bench
4. Soft belts
5. Sad cry
6. Circuit
7. "All About ___"
8. Yuletide singer
9. "___ on Sunday"
10. Being in debt
11. Make fun of
16. Tablet
20. Furious
21. Feather stole
22. Shoot the breeze
23. Sooner than, in poetry
24. Made a mistake
25. Lack
27. Arrived
29. Justly
30. Prohibit
31. Peculiar
32. Definitely!
33. Yellow pages, e.g.
34. Physique
35. The things here
36. Fads
37. Whims
38. Commuter vehicle
40. Corridor
43. Fish eggs
44. Building addition
45. Blushing
46. Finish
47. Actor Scheider

ACROSS

1. Fearless
5. High-school formal
9. Car type
14. Sills's solo
15. Enthusiastic review
16. Felony
17. Talk noisily
18. Vase-shaped jug
19. Ethnic groups
20. Scornful smirks
22. Victoria's principal outlet
24. Double curve
25. Window part
27. Rip
29. Bunny's jump
32. Assemble
34. Priest's vestment
37. Samoan port
39. Cocktail
41. Nine-____ battery
43. Jeans inventor Strauss
44. Dollar bill
45. New York canal
46. Cupid
47. Winged spirit
49. Darn!
50. Map book
52. Dutch cheese
54. Allow
55. Give off
57. Diamonds or spades
59. Rocky hill
62. Bucket
64. Fastened
68. Overweight
70. Jewelry metal
72. "A ____ of Two Cities"
73. Forty-niner
74. Dueling weapon
75. Similar
76. Rock
77. Backside
78. Tidy

DOWN

1. Pubs
2. Algerian port
3. Queue
4. Social appointments
5. Ironed
6. Uncooked
7. Baker's need
8. Deserve
9. Yell
10. Time period
11. Gaming cubes
12. Singing brothers
13. Loch ____ monster
21. Butt into
23. Plumbing problem
26. Wading bird
28. Rhine or Amazon
29. Healthy
30. Musical drama
31. Swivel
33. Trace
35. Reef material
36. Cream of the crop
38. Wedding walkway
40. Requires
42. Trial
47. Largest continent
48. Wash
51. Unit of current
53. Ms. Farrow
56. Striped cat
58. Mythological god
59. Jones and Selleck
60. Newspaper notice, for short
61. Nevada city
63. Prance
65. Large pond
66. Lamb's pen name
67. Ding
69. Japanese coin
71. Pasture

369

PUZZLE 456

BIBLE CROSSWORD

ACROSS

1. Thy ____ is brought down. (Isa. 14:11)
5. Shall say to his brother, ____. (Matt. 5:22)
9. And she took a ____. (2 Sam. 13:9)
12. Notion
13. And it became ____ in his hand. (Ex. 4:4)
14. ____ Grande
15. And ____ the book. (Dan. 12:4)
16. A fugitive and a ____ in the earth. (Gen. 4:14)
18. Let the proud be ____. (Ps. 119:78)
20. Topaz or opal
21. Who ____ tell him when it shall be? (Eccles. 8:7)
22. They knew that the island was called ____. (Acts 28:1)
25. Yet he restored the ____ unto his mother. (Judg. 17:4)
28. Owns
29. To him it is ____. (James 4:17)
30. They bring forth their young ____. (Job 39:3)
31. The ____ shall take him by the heel. (Job 18:9)
32. So that they ____ unto them. (Ex. 12:36)
33. And bring to pass his ____. (Isa. 28:21)
34. While Mordecai ____ in the king's gate. (Esth. 2:21)
35. They set the altar upon his ____. (Ezra 3:3)
36. ____ not him that wandereth. (Isa. 16:3)
38. Appointed with weapons of ____. (Judg. 18:11)

39. And all that handle the ____. (Ezek. 27:29)
40. Bind them upon thy ____. (Prov. 7:3)
44. Then Paul and ____ waxed bold. (Acts 13:46)
47. Shimei the son of ____. (1 Kings 4:18)
48. They set the ____ of God upon a new cart. (2 Sam. 6:3)
49. Tarry ____ to day also. (2 Sam. 11:12)
50. For his hand is ____ upon us. (1 Sam. 5:7)
51. Said unto him, ____, Lord. (Mark 7:28)
52. Then Asa was wroth with the ____. (2 Chron. 16:10)
53. They ____ unto it a lace of blue. (Ex. 39:31)

DOWN

1. Leaning Tower site
2. Lyric poems
3. Even unto the tower of ____ they sanctified it. (Neh. 3:1)
4. Because the ____ will be forsaken. (Isa. 32:14)
5. And black as a ____. (Song of Sol. 5:11)
6. And King ____ the Canaanite. (Num. 33:40)
7. Gear tooth
8. Maxims
9. To Abraham . . . were the ____ made. (Gal. 3:16)
10. And ____ with her suburbs. (Josh. 21:16)
11. Dwelt in the land of ____. (Gen. 4:16)
17. I will punish ____ in Babylon. (Jer. 51:44)

370

19. That utterance _____ be given unto me. (Eph. 6:19)
22. As if a _____ did flee from a lion. (Amos 5:19)
23. Fork prong
24. The _____ are a people not strong. (Prov. 30:25)
25. And Moses went up from the plains of _____. (Deut. 34:1)
26. Thou mayest not consume them at _____. (Deut. 7:22)
27. Two _____, to cover the two bowls. (1 Kings 7:41)
28. And the archers _____ him. (1 Chron. 10:3)
31. Respect . . . him that weareth the _____ clothing. (James 2:3)
32. Most spacious
34. Hagar the Egyptian, _____ hand maid. (Gen. 25:12)
35. Outlaw

PUZZLE 456

37. The herd _____ violently down a steep place. (Luke 8:33)
38. For he was _____ than all men. (1 Kings 4:31)
40. Look how thy brethren _____. (1 Sam. 17:18)
41. Jesus cried with a loud voice, saying _____. (Mark 15:34)
42. It is a _____ thing that the king requireth. (Dan. 2:11)
43. Their feet are swift to _____ blood. (Rom. 3:15)
44. Like a green _____ tree. (Ps. 37:35)
45. But these _____ written. (John 20:31)
46. For the _____ that is in the land of Assyria. (Isa. 7:18)

PUZZLE 457

ACROSS

1. Just manages
5. Moderate
9. Cinderella's dance
13. Zoo attraction
17. Toro
18. Put on a pedestal
20. Toast topping
21. Woody's son
22. Wall Street totes
24. Prince Charles's horses
26. Pittsburgh export
27. Step
29. Spiffiest
30. Mover's vehicle
32. Liner
33. Moisten
34. Broke a rule, in cards
38. Author Jong
40. Hoists
44. "Arabian Nights" name
45. Harmless slitherer
49. Author Levin
50. Newton fruits
52. Credible
53. Expanded
54. Greek cross
55. Western resort
57. Place for a watch
60. Gels
63. Facial spasm
64. U or good
66. Unbroken
68. Wharf pest
69. Three Dog Night song
70. Sail holder
72. Curbs
74. Scour
76. Spectator's cry
78. Lennon's wife
79. Busybody
81. Actress Capshaw
82. Inventor Whitney
83. Director Fritz ____
85. Barren
87. Race refreshment
90. Melmac native
91. Pandora's find
94. List of items
96. Get out of sight
97. Turned on
98. Layer of enamel
102. Conceit
103. Desert formations
106. Greek marketplace
107. Tantrums
109. To say the ____
112. Sculling equipment
114. Egyptian king, for short
115. Mobile home
118. Eskimo shelter
119. Melting snow
123. Doris Day film, with "The"
125. Inappropriate
129. Writer Hunter
130. Biblical weed
131. Jeer
132. Char
133. Foxy
134. J, F, or K: abbr.
135. Sluggers' stats: abbr.
136. Word-processing goof

DOWN

1. Diminishes
2. Author Vonnegut
3. Author Wiesel
4. Jacket part
5. Unidentified male
6. Lupino of films
7. Part of L.A.
8. Put on clothes
9. Lout
10. Winner's take
11. Hotel magnate Helmsley
12. Runs lightly
13. South Carolina river
14. Ontario's sister lake
15. Pub orders
16. Missing
19. Swimmer Williams
23. Writer Fannie ____
24. Pillow trimming
25. Solemnly sworn vow
28. Ventilates
31. Close at hand
33. Roasts
34. Huck's craft
35. Lamb's pen name
36. Factory work forces
37. Sketched
39. Gas guzzler
41. Furious
42. Work out
43. Bechamel, e.g.
46. Frigate hands
47. Poet T. S. ____
48. Pitchers
51. Broth
56. Actor Flynn
58. Do in
59. Uses a stopwatch
61. Strategy
62. Certain piggy's house

PUZZLE 457

65. Songstress Simone
67. Nick
71. Gin's go-with
73. Post office purchase
75. Orrin Hatch's state
76. Kingdom
77. Pitcher Reynolds
80. Location
84. Be a poor winner
86. Make a sweater
88. Verge
89. Old autos
92. Jet ____
93. Curly or Moe
95. Part of BTU
99. Type of exam
100. Radical
101. Confidence
104. City on the Hudson
105. Petticoat junction?
108. Finally!
110. Violin maker
111. Astronomer Carl ____
113. Submarine detector
115. Mimics
116. Launder
117. Trojan warrior
118. "____ Her on Monday"
120. Heed
121. Whack
122. Big sandwich
124. Uris character
126. Stand-in, for short
127. Prefix for cycle or corn
128. That thing's

373

PUZZLE 458

ACROSS

1. Certainly!
4. Closed
8. Laos's continent
12. Sail's support
16. Peel
17. Seize
18. Ringlet
19. Pain
20. One's old school
22. Valuables
24. Pekoe portion
25. Coral barrier
27. Kilt feature
28. Before, in verse
29. Small lake
30. Enemies
32. Expensive metal
35. Swiss _____ (beet variety)
37. Caution
38. Brief swim
41. "Much _____ About Nothing"
42. Christmas
43. Cut, as a cake
45. "It Had to Be _____"
46. Haze
47. Certain noblemen
49. Nights before holidays
50. Stitched
51. Romps
53. Modeled
55. Soft drinks
56. Cry of disgust
57. Mirror
58. Ruby, e.g.
59. Nab
62. Egypt's capital
63. _____ spring (spa)
67. Submit to
68. Marshal Dillon
69. Middays
71. _____-Wan Kenobi
72. Tavern beverage
73. Broadest
75. Craving
76. Filmmaker Spike _____
77. Half a score
78. Point-scoring serves
79. Consent
81. African grassland
82. Eating plan
83. Frosts
84. "Comin' Thro' the _____"
86. Petite
89. Rust-prone metal
90. Peaceful
94. Cattle and sheep, e.g.
97. Twin
100. Zone
101. Sunburn soother
102. Atmosphere
103. Clip
104. Hair wave
105. Fix
106. Jump
107. Actor Brynner

DOWN

1. Ivy League school
2. Columnist Bombeck
3. Ocean floor
4. Horse-drawn vehicle
5. Head topper
6. Hawaiian guitar, for short
7. Extreme fear
8. Played a part
9. Ride the waves
10. Outrage
11. Pie _____ mode
12. Heavy hammers
13. Land measure
14. Mets' stadium
15. Exam
16. TV host Sajak
21. Deface
23. Pay out
26. Concludes
29. Gloom
30. Confronted
31. Unrefined metals
32. Fisherman's hook
33. Smell
34. Trademark
36. Belonging to that girl
37. "Husbands and _____"
38. Changed the color of
39. Hawkeye State
40. Word plays
42. Whinny
44. School assignment
48. Divides
50. Not all
52. "Peanuts" character
54. Canoe paddle

55. Common or sixth
57. Fence doors
58. Spicy cookie
59. Outer garment
60. Capable
61. High schooler
62. West Point student
63. Additional
64. Audition goal
65. Cain's brother
66. Bent the truth

68. "Of ___ and Men"
70. Belonging to us
73. Stands in line
74. Mexican dish
80. Friendly
81. Truth
82. "I ___ of Jeannie"
83. Annoyed

85. Still
86. Smack
87. Put on the payroll
88. Mind ___ matter
89. Sacred image
91. Off-white

92. Hammer's target
93. Shade tree
95. Scot's cap
96. Bullfight cheer
98. Expected
99. Gay Nineties, e.g.

PUZZLE 459

ACROSS
1. Object
5. Part of CD
9. Cut the grass
12. Burrowing rodent
13. Locale
14. Politician Beame
15. Arctic animal
17. Bumped into
18. Pump purchase
19. Approves
21. "Little ___"
24. Patriot Nathan ___
26. Smell
27. Hot pepper
30. Seine
31. Added liquor to
32. Nincompoop
34. Decreases in size
36. Melt together
37. Frosts
38. Took ore
39. Swap
42. Barnyard female
43. Possessed
44. Elected
50. Id's kin
51. Disparaging remark
52. Volcanic output
53. Word of assent
54. Brink
55. Raced

DOWN
1. Little demon
2. Also
3. House wing
4. Scanty
5. Bits
6. Infuriate
7. Sargasso or Adriatic
8. Sang
9. "I Remember ___"
10. Heed
11. Moistens
16. Bled, as a color
20. Barbie's friend
21. Was victorious
22. Pindar products
23. Wool-eater
24. Chops
25. Votes for
27. Walking stick
28. Part of speech
29. Relieve
31. Permit
33. Nourished
35. Eliminate
36. Certain exams
38. "A Few Good ___"
39. Those people
40. Frenzy
41. Fusses
42. Charter
45. Timeworn
46. Coffee cup
47. Knock
48. Night before
49. Pa

PUZZLE 460

ACROSS
1. Have
4. Not hot
8. Talks
12. Court
13. Head covering
14. Stead
15. ____ Angeles
16. Neighborhood
17. Prayer ending
18. TV's "____ John"
20. Battle
22. Mix
25. "____ Pan"
29. Allergic reaction
32. Go out with
34. Less than two
35. Honest ____ Lincoln
36. Bizarre
37. Assist
38. Not well
39. Comfort
40. Advantages
41. Secluded valleys
43. Rubbernecked
45. Had breakfast
47. Sparrow's home
50. Reimbursed
53. Empty
56. Worry
58. Movie hero
59. Irish land
60. Born
61. Hue
62. Snow toy
63. Generation

DOWN
1. Night bird
2. Timber
3. Sniffer
4. Graph
5. Boat paddle
6. Tell a whopper
7. Sketch
8. Harsh light
9. Point
10. Spelling contest
11. "The ____ Also Rises"
19. Cinders
21. Mimicked
23. Thought
24. Pay increase
26. Amphibian
27. Oklahoma town
28. Crimson and scarlet
29. Surprise attack
30. Ready, willing, and ____
31. Merchandise
33. Canasta card
36. Sunset direction
40. "____ to Billie Joe"
42. Scoop
44. Concluded
46. Plumb and Arden
48. Of sound mind
49. Cake layer
50. Olive center
51. Bustle
52. Atom
54. Corn or safflower
55. Anger
57. Meadow

PUZZLE 461

ACROSS
1. Fido's treat
5. Etching fluid
9. Disencumber
12. Waterless
13. Solo
14. Byron's before
15. Sets of beliefs
17. French negative
18. The Boston ____ Party
19. Very dark wood
21. Bus stations
24. Blunder
25. ____ and above
26. School's list of courses
30. Allow
31. Paving material
32. Self-esteem
33. State crime
36. Protagonist
37. Pool stick
38. Worshipped
40. Savor
43. Long-nosed fish
44. Be sorry
45. Wary of attack
51. ____ you kidding?
52. Uniform
53. ____ go bragh!
54. Golf score
55. Shipped
56. Kernel

DOWN
1. Salad ____
2. Galena, e.g.
3. Zero
4. Revisor
5. Pseudonym
6. Pigeon's call
7. Country hotel
8. Sahara, e.g.
9. Gambling city
10. Pressing tool
11. Gainsay
16. Understand
20. Lingerie item
21. Dunce
22. At any time
23. Baseball's Rose
24. Hearing organ
26. Is able to
27. Lascivious look
28. Fairy-tale monster
29. ____, better, best
31. Foot digit
34. Play a part
35. Napped leathers
36. Equine beasts
38. Broker
39. Comedian Aykroyd
40. Snare
41. Emanation
42. Oracle
46. Night before
47. Bog
48. Rage
49. Contend
50. Stop

PUZZLE 462

ACROSS
1. Dunks
5. "My Three ____"
9. Ruckus
10. Apartments
12. Cottonwood
13. Take back
15. Native metal
16. Sod
18. God of love
19. Beach feature
21. Assemble
23. Geologic division
24. Church official
26. Bedroom furniture
28. Cup handle
30. Movie backdrop
31. Began
35. Men
39. Circle part
40. Collar type
42. Pound
43. Tanks
45. Component
47. Sinatra's ex
48. Newspaper person
50. Weld together
52. Dodge
53. Strives
54. Watched
55. Prophet

DOWN
1. Trust
2. Unwell
3. Bog fuel
4. Antitoxin
5. Wave riders
6. Song from "A Chorus Line"
7. Pleasant
8. Unblinking looks
9. Ethical
11. Saw wood
12. Sit for a portrait
14. Autocrat
17. Rouge color
20. Whitetail
22. Abound
25. Classify
27. Pierce
29. Called it a day
31. Hoard
32. Swap
33. On the go
34. Speck
36. Commander
37. Roof overhangs
38. Celebrity
41. Birds' abodes
44. Stick around
46. Additional
49. Lyric poem
51. Untruth

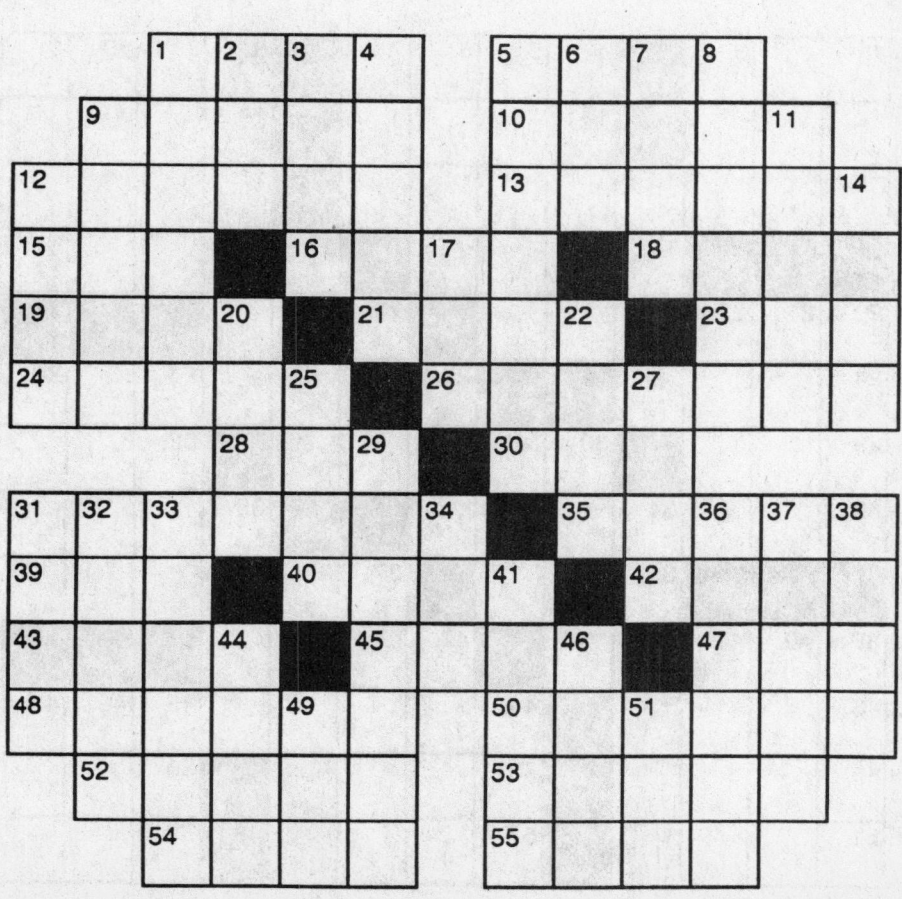

PUZZLE 463

ACROSS

1. Tam
4. Futons, e.g.
8. Quote
12. Pastoral poem
13. Medicinal lily
14. Think-tank product
15. Television offering
17. Snug retreat
18. Carry
19. Sleeveless garments
20. Scarcity
23. Objective
24. Fibber
25. Shopping malls
29. Faux pas
30. Rubbish
32. Saloon order
33. Nonsense
35. Gratis
36. Clumsy vessel
37. Automobile pedals
39. Enhance
42. Listen
43. Curve
44. Accepted
48. Shoestring
49. Lampreys
50. "We ____ the World"
51. Blissful abode
52. Gaiety
53. Countdown start

DOWN

1. Pro's opposite
2. Lemon drink
3. Church seat
4. Breakfast meat
5. Make jubilant
6. Medicinal portion
7. Stage scenery
8. "____ Paradiso"
9. March date
10. Exam
11. Chows down
16. Agitate
19. "Miami ____"
20. Split
21. Windy
22. Equine female
23. Matisse's forte
25. Bat wood
26. "____ Eyes"
27. Robt. ____
28. Witnesses
30. Caution
31. Question
34. Prison employee
35. Bill of ____
37. Songstress Regina ____
38. Bring up
39. Adept
40. John Huston film with "The"
41. Formerly
42. Bounder
44. Implore
45. Large tub
46. Sooner, to Keats
47. Cozy room

PUZZLE 464

ACROSS

1. Floor-cleaning tool
4. Lively party
8. Enthusiastic
12. A Gabor
13. Norwegian capital
14. Heap
15. Prolong
17. Ashen
18. Trick or ____
19. Raggedy Ann, e.g.
21. Layer
23. Purpose
27. ____ the wrong way
30. Devour
32. Tour leader
33. Messes up
35. Dad
37. Sleuth Nancy ____
38. Once more
40. Thus far
42. Snaky letter
43. Of the teeth
45. Golfer's peg
47. Component
49. Crimes
53. China's continent
56. Lipstick or blush
58. Mailed
59. ____-slapper (joke)
60. Historic period
61. For Pete's ____
62. Kernel
63. Damage

DOWN

1. Thaw
2. Finished
3. Window section
4. Wine container
5. Fire residue
6. Toboggan
7. High respect
8. Clap
9. By means of
10. Under the weather
11. Ruby or Sandra
16. Empty interval
20. Lower limb
22. Bark sharply
24. Father
25. Lyric poems
26. Information
27. Enjoy a novel
28. Yearning
29. Type of muffin
31. Plaything
34. Place
36. Favorite
39. A Bobbsey twin
41. Abounded
44. Moistens, as a stamp
46. Adam's wife
48. Pitch
50. Topic of gossip
51. Italian money, once
52. Wound mark
53. Donkey
54. Caribbean, e.g.
55. Pen filler
57. Observe

PUZZLE 465

ACROSS

1. "____ to Joy"
4. Football's Sayers
8. Stubborn animal
12. Annoy
13. Single bills
14. October birthstone
15. ____ Baba
16. "Rock of ____"
17. Hounds
18. Smaller
20. Sight or smell
21. Black gold
22. Part of MPH
23. Actress Midler
26. Blitzen's companion
30. Savings plan
31. Baled commodity
32. Chicken ____ king
33. Splashed a bit
36. Woefully
38. Lend an ____ (listen)
39. Retired soldier
40. Rose and Cotton
43. Difficult problem
47. Malevolence
48. Rate of stepping
49. Intention
50. Roman emperor
51. Actor Guinness
52. Frozen water
53. Sketched
54. Bird's home
55. Informal room

DOWN

1. Egg-shaped
2. Sandwich shop
3. Way out
4. Soccer's net-keeper
5. Celestial harpist
6. Lascivious grin
7. Double curve
8. Up-to-date
9. On top of
10. Falls behind
11. You are something ____!
19. Small child
20. Sargasso ____
22. Use a crowbar
23. Offer a price
24. Cenozoic, e.g.
25. Small flap
26. Writing tablet
27. Scoundrel
28. Building shape
29. Boxer Sugar ____ Robinson
31. "Take ____, She's Mine"
34. Yell
35. ____ Vegas
36. Choose
37. Dined
39. Bad habits
40. Curve
41. Above
42. Telegram
43. Cowgirl Evans
44. Female servant
45. "Three Blind ____"
46. Prayer ending
48. Skillet

ACROSS

1. Total
4. Bring civil action against
7. Mineral spring
10. Regret
11. Wagon
12. Pass over
13. Perfect score
14. Designer Klein
15. Father's sister
16. Fuel container
18. Firearm
20. Grin
22. Playwright Coward
23. Smart
24. Preserves food
25. Newspaper spot
27. Colony insect
28. Rake over the ____
30. Countdown ending
31. I
32. British nobleman
33. Kismet
34. Finch
35. Provide
36. Airport sight
37. Heat
38. Wash and ____

39. Gorillas
41. Make a mistake
44. Egg layers
45. Underscore
46. Sailor's yes
47. Elderly
48. Establish
49. Conducted

DOWN

1. Actor Carney
2. Payable
3. Tooth man
4. Descended
5. Vase
6. Everlasting
7. ____ and crossbones
8. Yearn
9. Befitting
11. Sugar source
12. Money vaults
17. Tavern order
19. Charged particles
20. Did the backstroke
21. Not yours
24. Heel
25. Pay your share
26. Gentle animal
28. Breakfast flake
29. Adventures
30. Cookie grain
32. Fibbers
33. Not near
34. Tasteless
35. Federal ____
36. Strip
37. Exited
38. Reporter's question
40. Slapstick prop
42. Sandwich bread
43. Santa's suit color

PUZZLE 466

383

PUZZLE 467

ACROSS
1. Layer
5. Pea's home
8. Snatch
12. Persuade
13. Recline
14. Pudding or paper
15. Pour
16. Everybody
17. Lemon drinks
18. Income
20. First born
22. Rolls with holes
25. Sock part
26. Blazing
27. Bench
28. Bumped into
31. Retrievers
32. Contemptible fellow
33. Fly high
34. Sooner than, to Shelley
35. Unhealthy
36. Market
37. Dynasty
38. Raspy
39. Flat-bottomed boats
42. Subside
43. Taleteller
44. Heavy-hearted
46. Lantern
50. Boundary
51. Souffle ingredient
52. Fencer's weapon
53. Sundown direction
54. Jane or John
55. Posted

DOWN
1. ____-and-dried (routine)
2. Gold source
3. Stone or Iron
4. Mellows
5. Broadway events
6. Canola or corn
7. Erased
8. School mark
9. Sally ____
10. King toppers
11. None better
19. Pub drink
21. Humble
22. Large bundle
23. Remote
24. Taunt
27. Friend
28. Othello, e.g.
29. Corn servings
30. "A ____ Grows in Brooklyn"
32. Grouped
33. Mews
35. Rage
36. Weep
37. White heron
38. Avoid
39. Tooted
40. ____-de-camp
41. Cloth scraps
45. In days past
47. Copy
48. Crew
49. Domestic animal

384

PUZZLE 468

ACROSS

1. Slugger DiMaggio
4. Netting
8. Quiet down
12. Everything
13. Brainstorm
14. Largest continent
15. Memory jogger
17. Air opening
18. Actor Scheider
19. Span
21. Film award
24. Part of speech
25. Navy or pinto
26. Lasagna seasoning
30. Rower's need
31. Amount before taxes
33. Writing tool
34. Removes the contents of
36. Ground grain
37. Single time
38. Savory
39. Go against
42. Comedian Conway
43. Coin opening
44. Mimicked
49. Be defeated
50. Opinion sample
51. Actor Wallach
52. Was in arrears
53. Lug
54. Viper

DOWN

1. Wide-mouthed bottle
2. Bullring cheer
3. Dutch ____ disease
4. Of small importance
5. Vortex
6. View
7. Ports
8. Possessing
9. Manipulated
10. Croon
11. Loathe
16. Teheran's site
20. Regrets
21. Reed instrument
22. Sewing joint
23. Complain
24. Hangman's loop
27. Orangutans, e.g.
28. Tidy
29. Nothing but
31. Game traps
32. Buyer's chit
35. Whistled
36. "I Remember ____"
38. Book's name
39. Norway's capital
40. Turn the soil
41. Sit for a painting
42. Lean
45. Cow's noise
46. Pekoe, e.g.
47. Overhead trains
48. Immerse briefly

PUZZLE 469

ACROSS
1. Timeworn
4. Totals
8. Part of A.M.
12. Lament
13. Demolish
14. Opinion
15. Bikini part
16. Notation
17. "En garde" weapon
18. Wait on
20. Storage box
22. Matinee figure
25. Dolt
29. Bistro
32. Gangster Capone
33. Find out
34. Chop
35. Platform
37. "The ___ Squad"
38. Freezing rain
40. "All of ___"
41. Certain Hill workers, for short
42. Shrub wall
43. Downwind
45. Obligated to
47. Venomous snake
51. Skirt length
54. Race type
57. First woman
58. King beaters
59. Rubberneck
60. Lamprey
61. Brilliantly colored salamander
62. Wide-mouthed jar
63. Dishwasher cycle

DOWN
1. Spheres
2. Decoy
3. Letter opener
4. Furnished with weapons
5. Outstanding
6. Faintly lit
7. Stuck-up person
8. Madison or Fifth
9. Bite
10. Palmer's peg
11. Female sheep
19. Compete
21. Inactive
23. Type of bran
24. Andes animal
26. Moniker
27. Harvest
28. Comes to a close
29. Loose change
30. Spindle
31. Nourish
35. Simmer
36. Jellylike substance
39. Self-centered person
41. "The ___ Badge of Courage"
44. Impatiently longing
46. Boundary
48. Achievement
49. Perpetually
50. Depend
51. "Cadillac ___"
52. Skating surface
53. Of late
55. Crude
56. Gorilla

ACROSS

1. Deeds
5. Jungle dweller
8. Region
12. Ark skipper
13. Lass
14. Fibber
15. Sightsee
16. Cereal grain
17. Farm measure
18. Play platform
20. Flower containers
22. Once named
23. Lodge member
24. Used the horn
27. Close
31. Female sheep
32. Sight organ
33. What flower girls toss
37. Grooms' ladies
40. Batter
41. Intend
42. Shipment
44. Potato type
47. Manner
48. Hooter
50. Donated
52. Track numbers
53. Summer shirt
54. Level
55. Finest
56. "____ Jude"
57. Transmit

DOWN

1. Aardvark's tidbit
2. Makes like a dove
3. Tense
4. Got smaller
5. Consented
6. Salary
7. Football number
8. Nome's state
9. Wedding confetti
10. Corn units
11. "We ____ the World"
19. Golly!
21. Pub brew
24. With it
25. Be liable
26. Tennis barrier
28. Herring or maple
29. Farewell
30. Yup!
34. Lock up
35. Fall behind
36. Not rough
37. Singer Pearl ____
38. Remove
39. Pictures
42. Secret message
43. Increases
45. Latch onto
46. Kitchen appliance
47. Crowd
49. Tiny
51. Conclusion

PUZZLE 471

ACROSS

1. Delay
5. Berets
9. Commotion
12. Crooked
13. Actress Barbara ____
14. Was in front
15. Harvest
16. Mixed
18. Bungle
20. Soldiers
21. Razor features
24. Pigpen
25. Rowboat tool
26. Pat
28. Bags
32. Iowa city
34. Chatter
36. Bowler's path
37. Portugal's neighbor
39. Butterfly catcher
41. Permit
42. Burrow
44. Birds of prey
46. ____ of the action
49. In favor of
50. Rubbish!
52. Rome's fiddler
56. 2,000 pounds
57. Tall-tale-teller
58. Got bigger
59. Urban trains
60. Evergreens
61. Rescue

DOWN

1. Armed conflict
2. Overwhelm
3. Pension plan: abbr.
4. Did secretarial work
5. Rumor
6. Sales pitches
7. Exams
8. Horses' sounds
9. Palo ____
10. Mysterious
11. ____ and ends
17. Fit for a king
19. Scarlet
21. Constrictors
22. Reading light
23. Territory
27. Censor
29. Shout
30. Leg part
31. Places
33. Margins
35. Zoo employees
38. Pleasantly
40. Sailor
43. Aladdin's slave
45. Bells
46. Poker stake
47. Lifeguard's beat
48. Taverns
51. Noticed
53. Dynasty
54. Gun a motor
55. Be in debt

PUZZLE 472

ACROSS

1. Poor actor
4. Her, subjectively
7. Very bad
12. Bullring cheer
13. Buddy
14. Pay hike
15. Tot's outfit
17. Bordered
18. Drove away
19. Conclusion
20. Alleviated
21. Native of Rome
25. Instruct
27. Great Lake
28. Mineral spring
31. Dehydrated
33. TV host Linkletter
34. Conger and moray
36. Frenchman's cap
38. Farm vehicle
40. Smelling ____ (swooner's restorative)
44. Boat blade
45. Squab
46. Tramps
49. Abandon
50. Burst forth
51. Before, poetically
52. Sandwich bread
53. Disordered
54. Unite in marriage
55. Likewise not

DOWN

1. Equine animal
2. Hello, in Hawaii
3. Notes
4. Moved swiftly
5. Difficult
6. Chicago Loop trains
7. Stadium
8. Duck's walk
9. Not worth a ____
10. Take advantage of
11. Guided
16. Keats or Shelley
19. Anesthetic inhalant
21. Frostier
22. Lyricist Gershwin
23. Melody
24. Fish snare
26. Leafy bower
28. Matched group
29. Each
30. Pie ____ mode
32. Wanted
35. Ice cream measures
37. Labels
39. Delectable
41. Acquire knowledge
42. Japan's capital
43. Smile of contempt
45. Read steadily
46. Skirt border
47. Prospector's find
48. Public transport
49. Not many

1	2	3	■	4	5	6	■	7	8	9	10	11
12			■	13			■	14				
15			16				■	17				
18					■	19			■	■	■	■
20				■	21			■	22	23	24	
■	■	25		26			27					
28	29	30	■	31		32	■	33				
34		35	■	36			37	■	■	■	■	■
38			39		■	40		41	42	43		
■	■	44		■	45							
46	47	48		■	49							
50				■	51		■	52				
53				■	54		■	55				

389

PUZZLE 473

ACROSS

1. North or Red
4. Change position
8. Unwritten
12. Limb
13. Corrupt
14. Michelle Phillips, e.g.
15. Reverie
17. High cards
18. Footed vase
19. Bureau
20. Muscular
23. Actress ___ Jessica Parker
25. Crooked
26. Deteriorate
27. Dated
30. MGM lion
31. Permit
32. Caviar source
33. Windy curve
34. Performs
35. Snakes
36. Pitfalls
38. "The ___ Tycoon"
39. Scrapbook
41. Cavity
42. Surprise attack
43. Freeloader
48. Poker stake
49. Cast or wrought
50. Blokes
51. Norm's drink, on "Cheers"
52. Robin's home
53. Bachelor's home

DOWN

1. Blue
2. Epoch
3. Actress Irving
4. Festive
5. Baker's need
6. By means of
7. "Nightmare on ___ Street"
8. Nebraska city
9. Thorough-bred
10. Iowa college town
11. Remain
16. Obligation
19. Personnel
20. Robust
21. Mas that baa
22. Winter's nip
23. Clearances
24. Commotions
26. Complete failure
28. Run easily
29. Writing table
31. Doc Bricker of "The Love Boat"
35. Painting and sculpture
37. Less polite
38. Enormous
39. Certain Middle Easterner
40. "Superman" reporter Lois ___
41. Paid athletes
43. Brooch
44. Have being
45. Brat
46. Earl Grey, e.g.
47. Goal

ACROSS

1. Ten-gallon ____
4. Talk wildly
8. Imitates
12. Rage
13. Margarine
14. Grotto
15. Male horse
17. Unzip
18. Gusto
19. Trademark
20. Touch tenderly
23. Malleable metal
24. In excess
25. Pauper
29. Triumphed
30. Fencing swords
32. Falsify
33. Tumid
35. Confront
36. Cleopatra's viper
37. Relax
39. Clan
42. Duet
43. Tortoise's competitor
44. Large kettle
48. Fiendish
49. Israeli seaport
50. Overwhelm
51. Clutter
52. Rosary component
53. Drenched

DOWN

1. Casual greetings
2. Museum display
3. Hot beverage
4. Buns
5. Pseudonym
6. Broadway light
7. Large weight
8. Squirrels' staples
9. Hemingway's nickname
10. Steven's beginning
11. Convey
16. Suggestive look
19. Slant
20. Milk producers
21. Affirm
22. Gambling town
23. Golfing peg
25. Pigsty
26. Woeful expression
27. Riviera resort
28. Juvenile
30. Or ____!
31. Vitality
34. Tags
35. A president
37. Author Ingalls Wilder
38. Lubricated
39. Him and her
40. Great review
41. Eye part
42. Speed
44. Taxi
45. Natural
46. Part of IOU
47. Seine

PUZZLE 474

PUZZLE 475

ACROSS
1. Credit ____
5. Dagwood's dog
10. Labels
14. Away from the wind
15. Sam or Remus
16. Irritate
17. Thick piece
18. "____ Magnolias"
19. Prayer word
20. Oppressive rulers
22. Passed by, as time
24. Spinning toy
25. Skier's stick
26. Military leaders
31. Magician
35. Notice
36. Finger ender
38. Tent of skins
39. Valuable dirt
40. Divide
42. Pilot's pilot
43. Surfaces
46. ____ gin fizz
47. Pond film
48. Analyzed
50. Tennis shoes
52. Dumbo's wings
54. Even score
55. "The ____ Letter"
58. Bureaucratic routine
62. Ripped
63. Ann ____, Michigan
65. Cat's weapon
66. Brain wave
67. Perhaps
68. Famed diamond
69. True
70. Swiftness
71. "____ of the Dragon"

DOWN
1. Throw
2. Actress Sheedy
3. "____ Window"
4. Argued
5. Brooms' companions
6. Farm insects
7. Drink chiller
8. Nap
9. Canary color
10. Circus swing
11. Strives
12. Merriment
13. "____ in the Clowns"
21. Oslo's land: abbr.
23. Touched down
26. Casper, e.g.
27. Weird
28. Requires
29. Running circuits
30. Opera singer Beverly ____
32. Quickly
33. Happen again
34. Considers
37. Maned animal
41. Seesawed
44. Endless
45. Make waterproof
47. Incomplete
49. Fantasies
51. Help
53. Purse band
55. Blend
56. Secret language
57. Zone
58. Judge's attire
59. Soothing succulent
60. Mate for mama
61. Water jug
64. Brief farewell

PUZZLE 476

ACROSS
1. Large bag
5. "Betsy's Wedding" director
9. Fellow
12. Pride member
13. Mend
14. Mining product
15. At rest
16. Views
18. Rhythm
20. Equal
21. Soup scoop
23. Taps
27. ____ and running
30. No longer is
31. French cap
32. Simmered
34. Dinner jacket
35. Exterior
36. Oriental sauce
37. Cleopatra's snake
38. Other
39. Craftier
41. Lasso
43. Oared
47. Ascertained the dimensions of
51. Bog
52. Antique
53. Rant
54. Actor Thicke
55. Corrida shout
56. Fume
57. Bird's home

DOWN
1. Slender
2. Assistant
3. Male foal
4. Bow down
5. Flurry
6. Suit parts
7. ____ a hard bargain
8. Archer of "Fatal Attraction"
9. Gunk
10. Vase
11. Permission granter
17. List in a book
19. Cruder
22. Papa
24. Section
25. Fourposters
26. Halt
27. Clarinet's relative
28. Grossly offensive
29. Temper tantrums
31. Customer
33. Ogles
34. Plaything
36. Shirt section
39. Herring
40. Caesar, e.g.
42. Belonging to us
44. Sly trick
45. Epochs
46. Dimple
47. Elsie's call
48. Building wing
49. Citrus cooler
50. Mountain moisture

393

PUZZLE 477

ACROSS
1. Gears
5. Actor West
9. Bunk or canopy
12. Frank
13. Full-strength
14. Poet's before
15. Tresses
16. Semester
17. Fabrication
18. Ooze out
20. Edible crustacean
22. Animal park
24. Petite
25. Oil's partner
29. Prepared
33. Commotion
34. Rival
36. Misfortune
37. Sample
40. Cuddles
43. Coffee server
45. Zodiac sign
46. Got too big
50. Pincers
54. Mata Hari, e.g.
55. Astounds
57. Anecdote
58. Prune
59. Famous fiddler
60. Balanced
61. ____ of a kind
62. Sketched
63. Changed colors

DOWN
1. Rooster's feature
2. October's stone
3. Critic Shalit
4. Ahchoo!
5. Liable
6. Fight for two
7. Direction marker
8. Part of a club
9. Haber-dashery item
10. Famous canal
11. Whitetail
19. Pooch
21. Look
23. Blockhead
25. Tank
26. Rhoda's mom
27. Negative votes
28. Rolling Stones guitarist Wood
30. Leather worker's tool
31. Bambi's mom
32. Of course
35. Snaky fish
38. Harbor boat
39. Chore
41. Put down
42. Blew a horn
44. More modern
46. Capital of Norway
47. Once ____ a time
48. Category
49. No longer are
51. Nautical defense arm
52. Exultation
53. Transmit
56. Plant

394

ACROSS
1. Statute
4. Actor Lugosi
8. Cease
12. Yoko ____
13. Matures
14. Ice-cream holder
15. Fortitude
17. Forthright
18. Family car
19. Vend
21. TV unit
23. Calm
27. Provided food
31. Colorado resort
32. Recline
33. Golfer Trevino
35. Downcast
36. Thoughts
39. Blackboard cleaners
42. Bother
44. Grabbed a bite
45. Inheritor
47. ____ d'hote
51. Sit for an artist
54. Choice
56. Elvis ____ Presley
57. Chemical compound
58. Black cuckoo
59. Marries
60. Fizzy water
61. Funnyman Caesar

DOWN
1. Defeat
2. Poker stake
3. Sentence part
4. Pennant
5. Hen product
6. Permits
7. Cinders
8. Reprimands
9. Do better than
10. Washington bill
11. Enclosure
16. Soothe
20. Meadow
22. ____ Aviv
24. Church recess
25. Rend
26. Concludes
27. Paper fastener
28. Assistant
29. Crossed letters
30. Billy ____ Williams
34. Precambrian, e.g.
37. Greek capital
38. Understand
40. ____ the Hun
41. Briny expanses
43. Gets a lift
46. Nevada city
48. Prejudice
49. Actress Anderson
50. Oklahoma city
51. Dog's foot
52. Neighbor of Wash.
53. Turf
55. New England cape

PUZZLE 479

• INTERNATIONAL CUISINE •

ACROSS

1. Gentle ____ lamb
4. ____-de-camp
8. Biblical king
13. Normal quality: abbr.
14. Tiny pests
16. Twist of fate
17. Asparagus topping
21. ____ de Janeiro
22. Canine
23. Senator Kennedy
24. Ground beef patty
30. Tender
33. Singer Clapton
35. Conger fisherman
37. Choir voices
41. Tedious person
42. Breakfast rounds
46. Honey maker
47. ____ Paulo
48. Publicize
49. Command to a horse
50. Wall component
51. Tightly packed
54. Golfer's peg
55. Face flanker
56. Romulus and ____
59. Extremely
61. Japanese sash
63. Prod
66. In the past
67. Not many
70. Type of salad topping
76. Mock butter
77. Puccini opera
78. Choose by vote
79. Unusual
80. Pitcher Hershiser
83. Particular ragout
87. Actress MacGraw
90. Agent: abbr.
92. Pie ____ mode
93. Meat and noodle dish
101. Change
102. Implements of work
103. Native: suff.
104. Smudges
105. Came by horse
106. Novel

DOWN

1. Cigar residue
2. Gale
3. Impromptu
4. ____ Khan
5. Small hotel
6. Mom's spouse
7. Airport abbr.
8. That guy's
9. Mesozoic, e.g.
10. Total defeat
11. ____ in a lifetime
12. Tinted
15. Comedian Caesar
18. TV's "____ Grant"
19. Distress letters
20. Self
24. Employ
25. Top pilot
26. Sign up: abbr.
27. Set
28. Yale grad
29. Take five
31. British flyers: abbr.
32. Santa's helper
33. Subside
34. Fish eggs
36. Greek R
38. Striped cat
39. Single
40. Opposite of NNW
42. ____ de cologne
43. Gesture of assent
44. Stick-in-the-____
45. Colorado Indian
47. Plant stalk
50. Observe
52. Sleuth Wolfe
53. Utter
54. Attempts
57. Cry of disgust
58. Lay lawn
59. Small bus
60. Quiche ingredient
61. Frequently, to Keats
62. Sis's sibling

396

64. "We ____ the World"
65. Sandwich shop
67. Defect
68. Always, to a poet
69. Sorrow
71. Cpl. or sgt.
72. Pullman, e.g.
73. Preacher's talk: abbr.

74. Chemistry, e.g.: abbr.
75. "____ Now or Never"
76. Raw metal
81. Be mistaken
82. Hawaiian wreath
84. Actor Holbrook
85. Killed
86. Sample

87. Moby Dick's foe
88. Calm
89. Involved with
91. Singer Boone
94. Obtain
95. "____ longa . . ."

96. Likewise not
97. Sticky stuff
98. "This ____ House"
99. Function
100. Chop

PUZZLE 480

ACROSS

1. Grand ____
5. Graceful bird
9. Asterisk
13. Experiment
17. Word from the crib
18. King of the road?
19. Ripped
20. Mane
21. Sign of the future
22. Misses
24. Norwegian seaport
25. Sincere
27. Moo juice
28. To a degree
30. High card
31. Strong wind
32. Patched
33. Not flat
36. Soda flavor
37. Forefather
41. Poems
42. Possessed
43. West Point students
45. Baseball stat
46. Spanish cheer
47. Cowboy's rope
49. Slant
50. Stew ingredient
51. Rich
53. Creek
55. Bride's walk
56. Celestial sighting: abbr.
57. Trudges
58. Beat the competition
59. Building material
62. ____ Island
63. More distant
67. For Pete's ____!
68. Furry bandit
69. Like a fish
71. Picnic refresher
72. Self-made pension: abbr.
73. Transform
75. Olive product
76. Yearning
77. In no certain place
79. Parmigiana ingredient
81. Hard metal
82. Targets
83. Auction
84. In good shape
85. Beachwear
88. Adjust
89. Engineer's assistant
93. Fix copy
94. Farmer's crop
97. Dressing gown
98. Haul
99. Prince in disguise?
100. Wood source
101. Singer Fitzgerald
102. Winter toy
103. Several
104. Parakeet's meal
105. Doe's mom

DOWN

1. Pollution
2. Flimsy, as an excuse
3. Prayer response
4. How-to books
5. Shed light
6. Made cloth
7. Actor Vigoda
8. Everyday
9. Mink wrap
10. Grabbed
11. Noah's craft
12. Appreciates
13. Rosebush prickles
14. Toward the rising sun
15. Threshold
16. Helen of ____
23. Reddish purple
26. Frozen
29. Impresses
31. "The ____ Must Be Crazy"
32. Creep about
33. Horse foot
34. Lazy
35. Smirk
36. Crate
37. Mexican farewell
38. Golfers' items
39. Not written
40. Proportion
42. Ring of light
44. Homes
47. ____ of Riley
48. Tablecloth shape
50. Julep flavor
52. Inner ____
54. Curtain holder

398

55. Spacious
57. Call
58. Humpty Dumpty's seat
59. Largest continent
60. Mend
61. All right
62. Laughs loudly
63. Flunk

64. Hound's prey
65. Trim
66. Movie spool
68. Lab workers
70. Burned wood
73. Face part
74. Happening
76. Stated
78. Hung around

PUZZLE 480

80. Chooses by vote
81. Knight's title
83. Soft leather
84. Penalized
85. Gambles
86. Matinee hero
87. Wind toy

88. Pair of horses
89. Liberate
90. Lawn tunneler
91. Competent
92. Close
95. Court
96. Pay dirt

PUZZLE 481

ACROSS

1. Fireplace residue
4. Holder
8. Lima's nation
12. Tell a whopper
13. Clarinet's relative
14. Purple flower
15. Annex
16. Croon
17. Shoestring
18. Russian pal
20. Presented
21. "Just the Way You ____"
22. Obtain
23. Amusingly clever
26. Turn bottom up
30. Hubbub
31. Sauté
32. Neither here ____ there
33. Brief bloomer
36. Landed property
38. Singer Grant
39. Heel
40. Peep
43. Speak softly
47. Car part
48. Manhandle
49. Inventor Whitney
50. Chip in chips
51. Anagram for race
52. Cleopatra's snake
53. Salty drop
54. Swimming hole
55. Kind of shirt

DOWN

1. Actor Baldwin
2. Fodder tower
3. Tiller
4. Bead string
5. Stay
6. Ice-cream container
7. Cask
8. Airplane operators
9. Geologic divisions
10. Paella ingredient
11. Like some cars
19. Stool pigeon
20. Vigor
22. Happy
23. Mass
24. Journalist Wells
25. Fiddle
26. Wail
27. Lodge
28. Menagerie
29. Miscalculate
31. Pop-up, as a ball
34. Pantry
35. Young hellion
36. Sent
37. Paid announcements
39. Make butter
40. Converse informally
41. Sharpen
42. Bit
43. Texas town
44. Bog fuel
45. What ____ is new?
46. Ready to pick
48. Atlas feature

ACROSS

1. Demonstrate
5. Ungentlemanly fellow
8. Ceremony
12. Molten rock
13. Kind of poem
14. Biblical garden
15. ____ and above
16. Steal
17. Sell
18. Sinew
20. Tire grooves
22. Sprite
23. Knight's title
24. Modified
28. Sandy shore
32. And not
33. Accomplished
35. Sheep's sound
36. Browned bread
39. Bothers
42. Used to be
44. Not against
45. Spud
48. Puts into effect
52. Eve's mate
53. Amusement
55. Castle ditch
56. Business abbr.
57. Donkey
58. Tempo
59. Cafeteria item
60. Discern
61. Put away

DOWN

1. Coin opening
2. ____ a nice day!
3. Baking chamber
4. Prison overseer
5. Grain fattened, as beef
6. Commotion
7. Unpaid bills
8. Patriot Paul ____
9. Notion
10. Lean
11. Finishes
19. Elderly
21. Torso bone
24. Hill insect
25. Cow's call
26. Baseball stat
27. Immerse briefly
29. Lincoln's nickname
30. Sedan, e.g.
31. Possesses
34. Protection
37. Marshy
38. Make lace
40. Male heir
41. Hobos
43. Couches
45. Agreement
46. Aroma
47. Scarlett's plantation
49. Winter garment
50. Tortilla item
51. Goulash
54. Employ

401

PUZZLE 483

ACROSS
1. Give food to
5. Dirty Harry, for one
8. Loathe
12. Otherwise
13. Flabbergast
14. Amiss
15. Record
16. Cozy room
17. Azure
18. Choler
20. Comes up
22. Kind of card
25. Fate
26. Wild West show
27. Piggery
28. Groove
31. Copied
32. Dried grass
33. Make well
34. Males
35. "____ Goes the Weasel"
36. Kitchen appliance
37. Painting or photography
38. Pintos and palominos
39. Vote
42. Term of agreement
43. Spoken
44. Sooner than, poetically
46. Presidential "no"
50. "The Way We ____"
51. Earth's star
52. Matured
53. "____ and the Tramp"
54. Orange pekoe
55. Zilch

DOWN
1. Law-enforcement off.
2. Yale grad
3. Snake shape
4. Made up one's mind
5. West Point student
6. Feel obligated to
7. Fine
8. Nun's garment
9. Leather workers' tools
10. Accurate
11. Windows to the soul
19. ____ Grande
21. Singer Orbison
22. Stuff
23. Cowboy's gear
24. Biblical garden
27. Drain
28. Operates
29. Impulse
30. Pullovers
32. Spiciest
33. Gypsy wagon
35. Expert
36. Fish delicacy
37. "Gasoline ____"
38. Laughing animal
39. Play at the lanes
40. ____ code
41. Fat
45. Mourn
47. Conceit
48. Decimal unit
49. Lyric poem

PUZZLE 484

ACROSS

1. Female knights
6. Thin rock
11. Total ____
12. Eagle's weapons
14. Save for future use
15. Small waves
17. Jane Goodall's concern
18. Barely balances
20. Union gp.
21. Business benefit, for short
23. Ranch roamer
24. For keeps
25. Put away
27. Orange potato
28. Choose
29. Russian leader
31. Hanging ornaments
33. "For want of a ____ . . ."
35. Scruffy dog's name
36. Claimant
40. Addle follower
43. Ocean or Martin
44. Clear the ____
46. Frosted
48. Forum date
49. Subsequently
51. Mackerel
52. Uproar
53. Of Moslems
55. Toss onto the scrap heap
56. Express approval
58. Guacamole fruit
60. Bottled spirits
61. Mrs. Black, nee ____
62. Lays back
63. Golfer Sam ____

DOWN

1. Be worthy of
2. Part of a royal flush
3. Trading center
4. Santa's helpers
5. Like winter rain
6. Newspaper headline
7. Shaggy
8. Swiss sights
9. Cut off
10. Animate
11. 21st amendment
13. Specify
14. Gavel noises
16. Out of ____
19. Tourist ____
22. Places for pooches
24. Resilient
26. Pepys's log
28. Mystery writer's award
30. Young insect
32. Afternoon rest
34. Like a winter tree
36. Tolerate
37. House exterior
38. Willowy
39. Actress Moreno
41. Green stone
42. Tease
45. Frames again
47. Large extinct bird
49. Thing of value
50. Torn apart
53. Rainbow
54. Hit town
57. ____ for the road
59. Professional figurer: abbr.

403

PUZZLE 485

ACROSS

1. Illicit profit
6. Evaluates
11. Lanchester and Maxwell
16. Bind again
17. To the side
18. Gratify completely
20. Turkish city
21. Worry needlessly
23. Worth wanting
25. Wharf
26. Shaver
27. Feeds one's face
28. Nothing
29. Affirmative vote
30. Dick Tracy's wife
31. Wild plum: var.
32. "___ Buddies"
34. Folksinger Pete ___
36. Hair covering
38. Goddess of fertility
40. "Lawrence of ___"
44. Laundry appliance
46. Leather color
47. Glossy paints
48. Fogs
50. Sanction
52. Makes edging
53. Coterie
54. "B.C." insects
55. Professions
57. Military helper
58. Amin
59. Went rapidly
61. Buffalo's lake
62. ___ but wiser
63. President between Zachary and Franklin
65. Columnist Landers
66. Burn slightly
68. Like teardrops
69. Seine tributary
70. Pork and beef
72. Organic compounds
74. Duel provocations
77. That guy
79. Fur pieces
82. Eggs
83. Spanish cheer
84. Take out, in printing
85. River to the Rhine
86. Have a tantrum
88. Shea events
90. Means for advancement
94. Accumulate
95. Ladies of Spain
96. English forest
97. Donny's sister
98. Make a speech
99. Donna and Oliver
100. Singer Paul and family

DOWN

1. Test marks
2. Distributes the cards again
3. Not moving
4. French film ending
5. Go like the wind
6. Synagogue VIPs
7. God of light
8. Noxious weed
9. Drop a fly
10. Intersection sign
11. Ike's command: abbr.
12. School letters, in Brooklyn
13. Black-furred animal
14. Earth holder
15. Sunflower products
18. Metric unit
19. Overbearing
22. Rubs lightly
24. Battery terminal
30. Mine car
32. "The ___ from Brazil"
33. Bishop's headdress
34. Religious offense
35. Important periods
37. Food scraps
39. Glossy fabrics
41. Irrelevant
42. ___ France
43. Garden blossom
45. Ran the marathon
47. Alleviates
48. Mutilates
49. Home of some elephants

404

51. Disagreeable
52. Numerical prefix
56. Sea eagles
57. Kelp or diatom
59. Without, to Pierre
60. Capital of Transvaal
62. Five to the fin

64. Taradiddles
65. Three-toed sloths
67. Force
69. Manlike ape
71. Central European region
73. Dale or Maurice
75. Gave to, temporarily

76. Steve, Woody, and Mel
78. Predicaments
79. Deep-voiced singer
80. Horse opera
81. Sports palace
84. Cony
87. Autocratic ruler

88. Presage
89. Vasco da ___
91. ___ of gold
92. Before historic or pare
93. Naples number

PUZZLE 486

ACROSS

1. ____ the way
5. Winesap, e.g.
10. Immense
14. Wild goat
15. Punctuation mark
16. Notion
17. Doubtful
19. Abel's father
20. Clothing
21. Papal name
23. Wrath
24. Wedding exchange
26. Burst forth
28. Deprived (of)
32. Heroine of children's books
35. Prefix with corn or cycle
36. Harkens
38. Small hill
39. Great quantity
41. Sag
43. Actress Markey
44. Russian guild
46. Young herring
48. Becker boomer
49. Saws wood
51. Toddler transport
53. Breathing spells
55. "____ Smile" (Hall and Oates tune)
56. Cuckoo
58. African antelope
60. Leather legging
64. Niche
66. Pick-me-ups
68. Small case
69. French painter
70. Discord goddess
71. Toward the setting sun
72. Comedy sketches
73. Snick and ____

DOWN

1. City on the Arno
2. Border upon
3. Article of clothing
4. Lapse, as a subscription
5. Emphasized
6. Luau food
7. Fall heavily
8. Donald Duck's nephew
9. Guarantee
10. Through
11. Extra
12. Burn
13. Domesticate
18. Kind of coffee
22. Pout
25. Toothed wheels
27. Corn cake
28. French author
29. Bury
30. Triumphant
31. Decreases
33. Sliver
34. Church official
37. Classifies
40. Not there
42. Fort's walls
45. For fear that
47. Molding
50. Hurricanes
52. Factory machines
54. Disclose
56. Once again
57. Keep in mind
59. Former Spanish province
61. Sea bird
62. ____ Canal
63. Being: Lat.
65. Scout Carson
67. Soak hemp

PUZZLE 487

ACROSS
1. Chunk
5. Pronoun
8. Conspiracy
13. Appraiser
16. Roman magistrate
17. "Roll out ___ ..."
18. French painter
19. Buddhist sect
20. Mauna ___
21. Comes forth
23. Stinging insect
24. Chemical suffix
25. Olive's beau
28. Egyptian city
33. Boston and English
34. Cask stoppers
35. Three, to Loren
36. Missing ___
37. Mockery
38. Hula ___
39. Single
40. Suit material
41. Japanese emperor Jimmu ___
42. Court proceedings
44. Most tender
45. Expressions of doubt
46. Remnant
47. Diving birds
51. Faucet
52. Dine
55. Nautical term
56. Tie in
59. Swiss capital
60. Too zealous
61. Grooves
62. Playing marble
63. Expense

DOWN
1. French city
2. Tennis great
3. British gun
4. Relative
5. Leather band
6. Garden tool
7. Director Kenton
8. Binds
9. Thinks highly of
10. Singer Crosby
11. Not windward
12. Sits still for
14. Asiatics
15. Got up
22. Meld
23. Calendar division
25. Aviator
26. Sheeplike
27. Languishes
28. Clean out
29. Way back when
30. Pay the penalty
31. Presses
32. Stop
34. Night spots
37. Banquet
38. Tarragon, e.g.
40. Plots
41. Hairpiece
43. Occupant
44. Bart or Ringo
46. Toss around
47. Yakety-yaks
48. Biblical brother
49. Claudius's successor
50. Inverness man
52. Palm tree
53. Indian tribe
54. Brazen
57. An avis lays them
58. Resin

PUZZLE 488

ACROSS
1. Underwater craft
4. That woman
7. Constricting snakes
11. Miner's find
12. Distinctive air
14. Competent
15. Athletic shoes
17. Tree's anchor
18. Males
19. Bouts of indulgence
21. Calls of disapproval
23. Positive
24. Breezy
25. Registered
29. Chatter
30. Leg joints
31. Hubbub
32. Basic aspects
34. Little stick
35. Hindmost
36. Kind of sculpture
37. Drinking tubes
40. Earth's star
41. Apple and mince
42. Dig in
47. In a sheltered direction
48. Beloved
49. "Chances ____"
50. Cincinnati team
51. Conceit
52. Exercise place

DOWN
1. Distress signal
2. Ornamental vase
3. Honey maker
4. Land ____ alive!
5. Tints of color
6. Be wrong
7. Keg
8. Wind instrument
9. Medicinal plant
10. Matched groups
13. Guarantees
16. Sailor's greeting
20. Experts
21. Prejudice
22. Globes
23. Derisive smile
24. Ripen
25. Wrapped
26. Statutes
27. Revise
28. Great Dane, e.g.
30. Was aware of
33. Wipes out
34. Adjust for sound
36. Small donkey
37. Ship's mast
38. Floor covering
39. Actress Donna ____
40. Doe's mate
43. Society page word
44. Broken-down horse
45. Weep
46. Skirt edge

ACROSS

1. Tennis shot
4. Chamber
8. Father
12. Indignation
13. Surface space
14. Eve's garden
15. College party
16. Kid's mom
18. Literary composition
20. Dachshund
21. Seed containers
24. More recent
28. Comment at the bottom of a page
32. Challenge
33. TV spots
34. Work hard
36. ____ and reel
37. Exclusive
39. Fairness
41. Fish
43. Therefore
44. Assistant
46. Book of maps
50. Swapping
55. Malt liquor
56. Comic Johnson
57. Opposite of aweather
58. Fish beginning
59. Accomplishment
60. Ran, as colors
61. Lion's retreat

DOWN

1. Admire
2. Metals
3. Implores
4. Deep valleys
5. Period of time
6. Football's Dawson
7. Country
8. Identified
9. Commotion
10. Split ____
11. Snack for an aardvark
17. Distant
19. Leaning toward
22. Dispense
23. Staff
25. Merchandise
26. Cupid
27. Ruby and rose
28. Speedy
29. Fragrance
30. Norway's capital
31. At all
35. Occupied
38. Filled with joy
40. Forget-me-____
42. Tell a whopper
45. Lackluster
47. Cooking fat
48. Medicinal plant
49. Looked at
50. Defective
51. "You ____ Mine"
52. Highway: abbr.
53. Feeling rotten
54. Once named

PUZZLE 489

PUZZLE 490

ACROSS

1. Military group
5. Nipped
8. Simmer
12. Aching
13. Far down
14. Conceal
15. Pitcher
16. Single
17. Surrounded by
18. Dashed
20. Long-plumed herons
22. Order
25. Strike suddenly
26. Once more
27. Lower limb
28. Writing tablet
31. Shredded
32. Jolt
33. Center
34. Beast of burden
35. Early drops
36. Primp
37. Mandible
38. Allotments
39. Covered passageway
42. ____ and downs
43. Virtuous
44. Actor Van Cleef
46. Long tale
50. Otherwise
51. Hearty bread
52. Mas that baa
53. Positions
54. Longing
55. Leak slowly

DOWN

1. Take advantage of
2. Every ____ and then
3. Intense anger
4. Tract of land
5. Fair-haired
6. Charged particle
7. Small pincer
8. Piercing
9. Clock, as a race
10. Revise and rewrite
11. Marries
19. Columnist Landers
21. Prevent from speaking
22. Information
23. Self-images
24. Blemishes
27. Established rule
28. Bard
29. Vicinity
30. Lairs
32. Adornments
33. Thwarts
35. Mom's hubby
36. Young dog
37. Green minerals
38. Fertile female ant
39. Bronze and Ice
40. Part to play
41. Expense
45. Organ of sight
47. Reverent fear
48. ____ whiz!
49. Cleopatra's snake

ACROSS

1. Hullabaloo
5. Mode
8. Defeated
12. President James ____ Carter
13. ____ of a kind
14. Had on
15. Place
16. Scraggly-faced
18. Crush underfoot
20. Supplement
21. Spoiled
22. Hot dog
25. Eroded
28. Conjunction
29. Stir
30. Trudge
31. " . . . three ____ in a tub"
32. Prune
33. Apple cider girl
34. Shad's offspring
35. Ms. Davis
36. Nut
38. Light bed
39. ____ the line
40. Bliss
44. Quick-tempered person
47. Brim
48. Rind
49. By means of
50. Singer Fitzgerald
51. Askew
52. Strong desire
53. Clairvoyant

DOWN

1. Hat material
2. Cave
3. Precinct
4. Probed
5. Was willing to
6. Actress Bancroft
7. Of course!
8. Up and about
9. Pact
10. Before, to poets
11. Study
17. Descendant
19. Criticize harshly
22. Triumphed
23. Proofread
24. Lasso
25. Chronicle
26. "The Four Seasons" actor
27. Warmer
28. Wedding announcement word
31. Trim the lawn
32. Couches
34. "Donovan's ____"
35. Tropical snake
37. Feverishly
38. Wash up
40. Great Lake south of Huron
41. At rest
42. Coquettish look
43. Close by
44. Hot tub
45. Church seat
46. Poison ____

PUZZLE 492

ACROSS

1. Mandible
4. Piercing tool
7. Supplemented
11. Lyric poem
12. Placed
14. Electricity carrier
15. High-schooler
17. Vivacity
18. "Chances ____"
19. To the other side
21. Prospector's territory
24. "Rock of ____"
25. Put to sleep
26. Wearing footgear
27. Uncooked
30. Cereal grain
31. Play's setting
32. Woodchopper's implement
33. Pair
34. Pod vegetables
35. Lubricants
36. Fairy's scepter
37. Manservant
38. Hardening adhesive
41. Strike
42. Presidential office shape
43. Jungle trumpeter
48. Gentle
49. Urgent
50. Baltic or Adriatic
51. Bullfight cheers
52. Part of RPM
53. Ink writer

DOWN

1. Scribble hastily
2. Citrus beverage
3. ____ Willie Winkie
4. Frighten
5. Salary
6. Fib
7. Pitchers
8. Metric weight unit
9. Historic time periods
10. Lairs
13. Mythical fire-breathers
16. Carpenter's spike
20. Yield
21. Lump of earth
22. Hawaiian feast
23. Choir voice
24. In front
26. Aromatic
27. Banister
28. Wheel shaft
29. Sunset direction
31. Bridge
35. Pledge
36. Fuses together
37. Venomous serpent
38. Singer Perry ____
39. Malevolent
40. Stallion or buck, e.g.
41. This place
44. Fleshy mouth part
45. Cleopatra's snake
46. Born
47. Turn into leather

ACROSS

1. Touched
5. Zoo enclosure
9. Soft hat
12. Vicinity
13. Engage
14. Actress MacGraw
15. Social standing
16. Charming
18. Regard highly
20. ____ rummy (card game)
21. Arrests
23. Trimmed
27. Machine part
30. Genuine
32. Days of old
33. Lyric poem
34. Uses a lever
36. Be victorious
37. Burden
39. Strip of wood
40. Mesh
41. Cupid's weapon
43. Bridge
45. ____ Cruces
47. Nation of De Gaulle
51. Makeup item
55. Lunch or dinner
56. Golly!
57. Singly
58. Miscalculates
59. Hooting bird
60. Thin stick
61. Prescribed amount

DOWN

1. Price of passage
2. Historic periods
3. Time before Easter
4. Removed
5. Judge's office
6. Help
7. Sailor's beverage
8. Spooky
9. Taxi
10. "____ in the Family"
11. Cherry or mince
17. Artist Warhol
19. Marshal Wyatt ____
22. Spinnakers, e.g.
24. Formal dress
25. Huron's neighbor
26. Dimple
27. Soft drink flavor
28. Smell
29. Equipment
31. Kids' jumping game
35. Celebrity
38. Raggedy Ann, e.g.
42. Torso's narrowest part
44. Called
46. Winter white stuff
48. Roman fiddler
49. Autos
50. What ____ is new?
51. Conceit
52. Longbow tree
53. Snaky fish
54. Inventor Whitney

PUZZLE 493

PUZZLE 494

ACROSS
1. Faucet
4. Agt.
7. Make merry
9. Bravery award
11. Kitchen gadget
13. Gully
14. Big ___ (London landmark)
15. Character Pyle, played by Jim Nabors
17. Neckwear
18. Self
20. "The Old Man and the ___"
21. "What's up, ___?"
22. Make ___ meet
24. Gateway
26. ___ what?
27. Near
28. Baseball's Rose
30. Soupy meat dish
32. Headgear
33. ___ mode
35. Pat gently
37. Male child
38. Collision
40. Comedian Skelton
42. General George S. ___
44. Ice cream concoction
46. Direction sign
47. Actor Wallace
48. Artificial coloring
49. Printers' letters

DOWN
1. Wigwam
2. Retaliate for
3. Ballpoint ___
4. Accelerate
5. Newspaper employee
6. Sudden fear
7. Mr. Petrie of "The Dick Van Dyke Show"
8. Break a ___!
9. Damage
10. Gypsy Rose ___
12. Flagmaker Betsy ___
13. Enjoy a book
16. "Love ___ Tender"
19. Beginning
21. Bestowed excessive love
23. Speck
25. Cereal grain
28. Food closet
29. Make money
30. Back talk
31. Prison official
32. Store up
34. "___ Law"
36. Chicago team
37. Health club
38. Elsie, e.g.
39. Core
41. Actress from 34 Down
43. Foot digit
45. Born

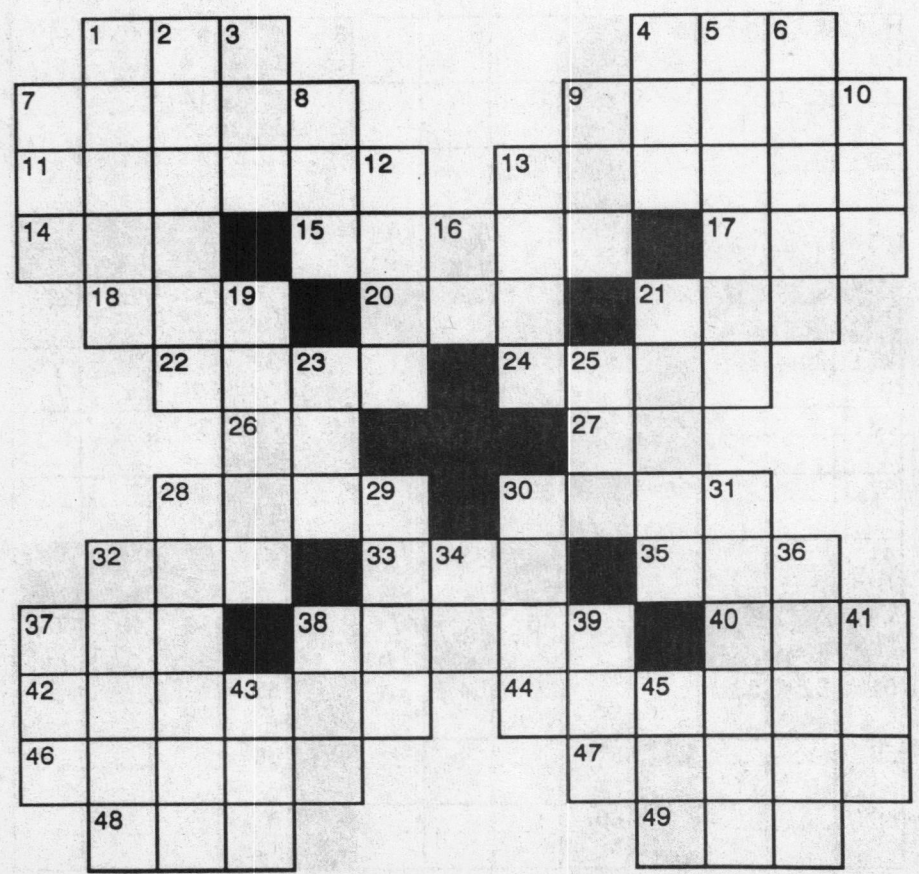

414

ACROSS

1. Shade tree
4. Fast plane
7. Transmitted
11. Paper measure
13. Mine yield
14. Defined space
15. Nevada resort
16. Egg layer
17. Linen fiber
18. Room for relaxation
20. Social equal
21. Notion
23. Reverent fear
25. Pastoral poem
26. Dutch bulb
28. Apple seed
31. Tavern drink
32. Turf
33. Baseball stat
34. Comedian Skelton
35. Subscribe again
37. Pull behind
38. Lemon refresher
39. Place for a roast
41. Failed play
44. Afternoon beverage
45. Encase
46. Chimpanzee, e.g.
48. Some resorts
52. Where the heart is
53. Untruth
54. Follow
55. Portent
56. Traveler's lodging
57. Attempt

DOWN

1. Be human
2. Confederate general
3. "The Invisible ____"
4. Everyman Doe
5. Sooner than, in poems
6. Decade number
7. Out of danger
8. Perry's creator Gardner
9. Close-by
10. Tariff
12. Style
19. Take nourishment
20. Vigor
21. Inactive
22. Feat
23. Solo
24. Broad
25. Rower's implement
27. Secondhand
28. Rose of baseball fame
29. Wrought ____
30. Fido's foot
35. Knock sharply
36. Sorrow
40. Extensive
41. ____ the heart (sincerely)
42. Limping
43. Accessible
44. Adolescent
45. Which person
46. Boxer Muhammad ____
47. Needle's cousin
49. Singer Boone
50. Ventilate
51. Cunning

PUZZLE 495

PUZZLE 496

ACROSS

1. Blemish
5. To and ____
8. Criticizes
12. Huron, e.g.
13. Edge
14. Verbal
15. Land measure
16. Song of praise
17. "Better Luck Next ____"
18. Defeated
20. Packed
22. Derby, for one
23. Ingest
24. Tier
27. Footstool
31. Period in history
32. Oxygen or helium
33. Fuss
34. Beverage maker
37. Totaled
39. One billion years
40. Hot tub
41. Mechanic's place
44. State of mind
48. Porter and stout
49. Red deer
51. Small opening
52. Snout
53. Astonishment
54. Verve
55. Obtains
56. Conducted
57. Bird's home

DOWN

1. Thick slice
2. Walk impatiently
3. Gumbo ingredient
4. Cut a tooth
5. Facade
6. Disencumber
7. Egg dishes
8. Tuber
9. Very dry
10. Moniker
11. Winter vehicle
19. Lend an ____
21. Cereal grass
24. Testing place
25. In the past
26. Thus far
27. Sculler's need
28. Angry
29. Summer drink
30. Motion of agreement
32. Universal
35. Pokes fun at
36. Record
37. Mimic
38. Moisten
40. Horse
41. Group of bandits
42. ____ vera
43. Take five
45. Column
46. Cenozoic and Paleozoic
47. Let
50. Be indebted to

ACROSS

1. Snoop
4. ____ work and no play . . .
7. Feline sound
10. Casual shirts
12. TV's "____ John"
14. "____ Maria"
15. Spoken
16. Father, to the crib set
17. Illuminated
18. Undiluted
19. Prison chamber
21. Dawn to dusk
24. Spider's trap
25. Hi-fi component
28. Sandwich shop
30. Make ale
34. Distant
35. Ship's canvases
37. Time period
38. Leisurely gait
40. Fashion anew
41. ____ cleaning
42. Container
44. ____ of the line
46. Ruth the legend
48. Gambler's concern
52. Neither's companion
53. Small letter
57. Enthusiasm
58. Dine
59. Tuneful threesome
60. Singer Fitzgerald
61. Give it a whirl
62. Franklin, to friends
63. Keep a stiff upper ____

DOWN

1. Cease
2. Lima's land
3. Twelve months
4. Tack on
5. Meadow
6. Fellow
7. Shopping area
8. Wickedness
9. Sopping
11. Luge
13. Relay, for one
20. Wane
22. Madison Avenue products
23. Crave
24. Playwright Oscar ____
25. Rearward
26. Spoil
27. Sport instructor
29. Misrepresent
31. Angry color
32. Be inaccurate
33. Pave the ____ for
36. Alan, to Robert Alda
39. Bathing need
43. Monthly due
45. Slumber
46. Wild pig
47. Pretentious
49. Vale
50. Surrealist painter
51. Strike
52. Mesh
54. Globe
55. Cravat
56. Long time

PUZZLE 497

PUZZLE 498

ACROSS
1. Flower holder
5. Kind of bed
9. Dove's sound
12. Concert solo
13. Unwrap
14. Wise bird
15. Camera eye
16. Agreed
18. Enthusiastic
20. Golf gadget
21. Recline
24. Tilts
28. What snowflakes are
32. Frog or year
33. "Flying Down to ____"
34. Examines by radar
36. Pub offering
37. " . . . three men in ____"
39. Imitated
41. Artist's cap
43. Matured
44. Minstrel's song
46. ____-case scenario
50. A fly in the ____
55. Raise
56. Fruit cooler
57. Cultivate
58. Boundary
59. Chubby
60. Choir member
61. Medicine unit

DOWN
1. Earthly life
2. Territory
3. Vocalize
4. Art stands
5. Feather scarf
6. ____ and downs
7. Sparrow's home
8. Genuflect
9. Folding bed
10. Feel obligated
11. Ancient
17. Singer Young
19. Spoils
22. Chantilly
23. Pack animal
25. Subway scarcity
26. Narrative
27. Drove too fast
28. Lobster's kin
29. Ritual
30. Thine
31. Cozy
35. Seattle ____
38. Waistband
40. Worshiped
42. City in western Florida
45. Holler
47. Make over
48. Stoops
49. Coatrack
50. Simpleton
51. Asian peak
52. Lacrosse goal
53. Wayne's word
54. Deuce

ACROSS

1. Through
4. Bakes
9. Keats poem
12. Painting, for instance
13. Hangout
14. Neither's partner
15. Fate
16. Blunder
17. British beverage
18. Join together
20. Band instrument
22. Evaded
25. Fable message
28. Foot lever
30. Roomy
31. ___ and tonic
34. Imp
36. Out of the ordinary
37. Cracker-jacks
39. More congenial
41. Summits
43. Patterns
47. Wedding band
49. "Jack ___ could eat no fat"
50. Itty-bitty
52. Texas shrine
55. Blvd.
56. Overhead trains
57. Havana native
58. Golf gadget
59. Whit
60. Retains
61. Pipe joint

DOWN

1. Worth
2. Shackles
3. Garret
4. Chirped
5. Paddle
6. "___ Town"
7. Granny, for one
8. Play a guitar
9. Canadian province
10. Bambi's mom
11. Period
19. Knock
21. Hair decoration
23. Actress Barbara ___
24. Comedian Letterman
26. Append
27. Went in front
29. Parasites
31. Opening
32. Frost
33. ___ and dearest
35. Exercises
38. Winter transport
40. "___ Van Winkle"
42. Nibble
44. Bother
45. Orange type
46. Stainless ___
48. Paste
50. "Charlotte's ___"
51. Hebrew priest
53. Politician Ribicoff
54. Motorist's guide

419

PUZZLE 500

ACROSS
1. Bivouac
5. Additional
9. Cook in oil
12. Smell
13. Imitates
14. Pastureland
15. Dog's treat
16. Baby's powder
17. Unit of corn
18. Take advantage of
20. Large spotted cat
22. Maiden
25. Epoch
26. Mineral-bearing rock
27. Once around a track
29. Swap
33. Shade of color
35. Roll of cash
37. Stumble
38. Glossy fabric
40. Armed conflict
42. Command to a horse
43. Dawn dampness
45. Water down
47. Sticks
51. Beaver's construction
52. Golfer Trevino
53. Singer Jerry ____
55. Stingy
58. Rowboat propeller
59. Wicked
60. Poker starter
61. Last word
62. Matched groups
63. Ragout

DOWN
1. Corn on the ____
2. Commotion
3. Memorial structure
4. Push
5. Wrestling surface
6. October's stone
7. Confederate general's signature: abbr.
8. Accompany
9. Circus insect
10. Back side
11. Three feet
19. Moray, e.g.
21. Hair division
22. Morse code symbols
23. Opera solo
24. Attorney's subject
28. Animal foot
30. Dispute
31. Way to lose weight
32. Fencer's weapon
34. Moon's pull
36. Mom's spouse
39. You get on my ____!
41. Divest
44. Operate a loom
46. Tibetan monks
47. Succulent plant
48. College official
49. Group of cattle
50. Incision
54. Overhead trains
56. Dined
57. Turn over a ____ leaf

420

ACROSS

1. Decay
4. Price paid
8. Filled tortilla
12. Commotion
13. Head growth
14. Winter flakes
15. Euclid's field
17. ____ and now
18. Cigarette residue
19. Candle cores
20. Carries on
22. Rendered fat
23. Lawyer's assignment
24. Bugs Bunny's celluloid world
27. Singer Garfunkel
28. Long family quarrels
30. Fasten with a knot
31. The ____ State (Utah)
33. Touched
34. Ceremonial garment
35. Unsatis- factory
37. Pours down
39. Matador's cheer
40. You are something ____!
41. Interfering
46. Questions
47. Impulse
48. Pair
49. "____ Horizon"
50. Stag or roe
51. Red or carpenter

DOWN

1. Cloth shred
2. Type of poem
3. As well
4. Bureau
5. Promises
6. Knight's title
7. Attempt
8. Pullover
9. Amusing tales
10. Bottle stopper
11. Is in debt
16. Lion's head fur
19. Large conflicts
20. Hard to find
21. Printer's stars
22. Young fellow
23. Hired car
24. Billiards stick
25. Greasy
26. Tennis court divider
28. White lies
29. First woman
32. Truthful
33. Gasoline, e.g.
35. Hunter's cabin
36. More aged
37. Genuine
38. In addition
41. Wet dirt
42. Bard's before
43. Peak on Crete
44. Religious sister
45. Acquired

PUZZLE 501

PUZZLE 502

ACROSS

1. Wipe
4. Forfeit
8. Acts
12. Cooling beverage
13. Sowing wild ____
14. Hamburger order
15. Steps
17. Gumbo ingredient
18. Requested
19. Texas city
21. Broad-antlered deer
23. Jabbered
27. Spaceship
30. Affirmative vote
32. Loom
33. Siestas
35. Bark
37. Nancy ____ (girl detective)
38. Standard of perfection
40. Trashy newspaper
42. Sample
43. Becker's game
45. Bear cave
47. Distribute cards
49. Titles
53. To ____ it may concern
56. Steelers' sport
58. Ames's state
59. Sinister
60. Need
61. Adolescent minor
62. Trust
63. Was in front

DOWN

1. ____ mia!
2. Lyric poems
3. Pikes ____
4. Noisily
5. Scull
6. Fret
7. School paper
8. Wilted
9. Kind of paneling
10. Make a gaffe
11. Body of water
16. Understand
20. Raucous cry
22. Crucial
24. Role
25. "If ____ I Would Leave You"
26. Moist
27. Component
28. Wash out
29. Store sign
31. Light breeze
34. Visitor who brings sleep
36. Writing tablet
39. Speak falsely
41. Daintily
44. More secure
46. Grab
48. "All You Need Is ____"
50. Manhandle
51. Alternative
52. Winter vehicle
53. Humor
54. Garden tool
55. Have creditors
57. Fossil fuel

ACROSS

1. Stroke
4. Swerve
7. Taken
10. Ultimate
12. Pennsyl-
    vania port
14. "The
    Greatest"
15. Ogle
16. Soothe
17. Staff
18. Arizona city
19. Huge pond
21. Certainly!
24. Cleopatra's
    viper
25. Belfry
    dweller
28. Vamoose!
30. Subdued
34. Cool drink
35. Apologetic
37. Non-
    professional
38. Went on
    horseback
40. Dog in
    "Our
    Gang"
41. Caustic
42. Bandleader
    Brown
44. Morsel for
    an aardvark
46. Resign
48. "God's
    Little ____"
52. Jog
53. Finished
57. Victuals
58. Roman
    three
59. Diamond
    number
60. Loyal
61. Select
62. Cooking
    direction
63. Room for
    relaxation

DOWN

1. What a
   psychic
   might read
2. Fencing
   sword
3. Plumbing
   joints
4. Last letter
5. Lyricist
   Gershwin
6. Dogfaces
7. Listen
8. Century
   plant
9. Acted
11. Doctor's
    picture
13. Morays
20. Suitable
22. Road curve
23. Stores
24. Main artery
25. Exclude
26. Bedlam
27. Senator
    Kennedy
29. Unrefined
    metal
31. Entirely
32. Mother ____
    I? (child's
    game)
33. Storm
    center
36. Hankering
39. Inventor
    Whitney
43. Collar type
45. 27th
    president
46. Witticism
47. Squadron
49. Heavy
    string
50. Rake
51. First garden
52. ____ de
    Janeiro
54. By
55. Cease
56. Jazz pianist
    Garland

PUZZLE 503

PUZZLE 504

ACROSS
1. Drink slowly
4. Hershfield's agent
8. Handkerchief material
12. Rhoda's mom (Nancy Walker role)
13. Shortly
14. Ellipse
15. South's opposite: abbr.
16. Spring cleaning
18. Slenderize
20. Front-page stories
21. Smells
23. Luminary
25. Skating arena
26. Heroic tale
27. Adverse review
30. Exist
31. Begin
32. Before, to a poet
33. Escorted
34. Sharpen
35. Adrift
36. Military grade
37. Crucial
38. Cut remnant
40. Window ledge
41. Advocates
44. Tail
47. "____ and Circumstance"
48. Laugh a minute
49. Respectful title
50. "Planet of the ____" (Heston film)
51. Exile island
52. 007, e.g.

DOWN
1. Moral transgression
2. Marriage vow
3. Excused
4. Cinders
5. Cowboy's wear
6. Debt letters
7. Metaphysical being
8. Demote
9. State positively
10. Train units
11. Large deer
17. Legislate
19. Rile
21. Kind of exam
22. Tragic
23. Paddle
24. Exhaust
26. Short jacket
27. Fidgety
28. ____ code
29. Chime
31. Acute
35. Trouble
36. Turnpike exits
37. Landscape
38. "The Little ____ of Horrors"
39. Arrived
40. Social climber
41. Auditor: abbr.
42. Indignation
43. Black gold
45. Imbibe
46. Parched

PUZZLE 505

ACROSS

1. Where the heart is
5. Welcome ____
8. ____ rummy
11. Summit
12. Building ____
13. Exist
14. Small pie
15. Italy's capital
16. Put down
17. Arm covering
19. Penetrating
21. More up-to-date
23. Otherwise
26. Leans
29. In front
31. Summer drink
32. Lock of hair
34. Find fault constantly
35. Basic
37. Makes like a chick
39. Use a keyboard
40. Beer mug
42. He played Columbo
44. Astir
48. And not
50. Goals
52. Disturb
53. Fuss
54. Chair
55. Nuclear particle
56. Plead
57. ____ on for size
58. Cohorts

DOWN

1. Caps
2. October stone
3. Only
4. Magnitude
5. Pasture sound
6. Looks up to
7. Adolescent
8. Motorcycle fuel
9. Anger
10. New Jersey cager
12. Work gang
18. Waistcoats
20. Newsman Koppel
22. Choose
24. Easy task
25. Omelet ingredients
26. Diplomacy
27. In a lazy manner
28. Kid's jumping game
30. Molded salad
33. More hazardous
36. Bounding main
38. Catch in a snare
41. Compass direction
43. At the tail end
45. Jot
46. Stringed instrument
47. Shade providers
48. Arrest
49. Kind of poem
51. Spring month

PUZZLE 506

ACROSS
1. Waiter's bonus
4. Arab garb
7. Baby food
10. Mine access
12. "____ Dawn" (Reddy song)
15. Bristle
16. Actress Anderson
17. More aged
18. Poker holding
19. Tribe
20. Mountains in South Dakota
22. Adversaries
24. Ridge
25. Bar seats
28. Singer Midler
31. Eaglet's home
32. Adjutant
33. ____ Moines
36. Popular western vacation spot
40. Opposite of NNW
41. Throat clearer
42. Longest European river
43. Storms
45. Best
46. Atoll material
49. Shaker's filling
50. Miami stadium
54. German king
58. "The Big Heat" director
59. Gentleman's gentleman
60. Spoken
61. Suit to ____
62. Stage whisper
63. River at Cairo
64. "Oh, say can you ____ ..."
65. Poet's above
66. Nail

DOWN
1. Powder ingredient
2. Graven image
3. ____ colada cocktail
4. Certain brick houses
5. Ringers
6. "The Four Seasons" actor
7. Norman Vincent ____
8. Slanting
9. Describe grammatically
11. Food wrap
13. Gumshoe
14. "Raiders of the Lost ____"
15. Turret
21. Derby
23. Bread spread
25. Utters
26. Duffers' gadgets
27. Border, in heraldry
28. Gnaws
29. Esau
30. Sawbuck
32. 1975 Wimbledon winner
33. Robertson or Evans
34. Work units
35. Old card game
37. Oscillate
38. Malevolent
39. Boat for a temporary bridge
43. Scope
44. Math subj.
45. Waver
46. Soft drinks
47. Harangue
48. Rajah's mate
49. Stockholm native
51. Topsy's playmate
52. ____-relief (sculpture)
53. Hodgepodge
55. Excursion
56. Yarn
57. Mr. Cassini

PUZZLE 507

• TIMELY MOVIES •

ACROSS

1. Op. cit. relative: abbr.
5. Type of beetle
9. Portable breathing device for divers
14. Contradict
15. Where the heart is
16. Singer John
17. Star in Taurus
19. Pursuit
20. Earp brothers movie
22. Be beholden for
23. Geddy _____ of Rush
24. Entertain lavishly
28. Part of MPH
29. Pertaining to a grandparent
31. Gibson of film
32. Despise
35. Store sign
36. "_____ Las Vegas"
37. Cimino crime drama
40. Carry on
41. Redding of R&B
42. Charlie Chan portrayer
43. "Evil Woman" group: abbr.
44. Sexual desire
45. Tennis point
46. Intersecting line
48. Question
49. See ya!
52. George A. Romero thriller
56. Hannibal Smith's squad
59. Breaks up soil
60. Simpson matriarch
61. Seaweed product
62. Sound follower
63. Cherub
64. Bard's instrument
65. Insignia

DOWN

1. Sun Valley's state
2. Under
3. Put on
4. Textile worker
5. Host of '90s "The Match Game"
6. Rich treat
7. Nursemaid
8. Rayburn of '60s "The Match Game"
9. Follow-up movie
10. Held tightly
11. Shoshonean
12. Athlete Jackson et al.
13. Harvester or red
18. Waist-length jacket
21. Kind of piano
25. Juanita's friend
26. Song by 16 Across
27. African antelope
28. Study intensely
29. Plant louse genus
30. Peace symbols
32. "Young Doctor Kildare" actor
33. "_____ Street Blues" by Handy
34. Great destruction
35. Director Preminger
36. Singer Jerry _____
38. Two score
39. Missile
44. Tooth coating
45. On land
47. Proverb
48. Flower extract
49. Misrepresent
50. Seaport in Crimea
51. A Ford
53. Unwritten
54. Ultraconservative
55. Claims
56. "I _____ Rock"
57. Beach color
58. Unit of energy

Multipliers

PUZZLE 508

In these multiplication problems letters are substituted for numbers. Determine the value of each letter. Then arrange the letters in order from 0 to 9, and they will spell a word or phrase.

1.

```
  MOAT
x  PEN
  ETTT
 MPPCT
 PNOI
RITRIT
```

0 ___
1 ___
2 ___
3 ___
4 ___
5 ___
6 ___
7 ___
8 ___
9 ___

2.

```
   LOUD
x   POD
  OEHEN
  NPDPH
   ESNE
 NUPDEIN
```

0 ___
1 ___
2 ___
3 ___
4 ___
5 ___
6 ___
7 ___
8 ___
9 ___

3.

```
   RAIL
x   OUR
  VULLC
  LHACC
  AASOL
LCLCCLC
```

0 ___
1 ___
2 ___
3 ___
4 ___
5 ___
6 ___
7 ___
8 ___
9 ___

Solve this puzzle as you would a regular crossword. Then read the circled letters from left to right, and they will reveal a quotation.

ACROSS

1. Robber ____
6. Person
11. Alleviates
16. Informed
17. Firebug's crime
18. Writer Boothe Luce
19. Poise
21. Take five
22. Choler
23. British elevators
24. Chit
26. Language suffix
27. Actress Best
29. TV sitcom character on "Alice"
30. Venomous snake
31. Functions
32. Kismet

34. Vaporize and condense
36. Pens
39. Sesame plant
40. "The Night of the ____"
43. ____ space
44. Beatty film
46. French preposition
47. Lulu
48. Evergreen
49. Billions of years
50. Business-letter opener
51. Faint
52. Pupa cases
54. "____ Canyon"
55. Hannibal's defeater
57. Kook
58. Research papers
59. More tangy
61. Per ____
62. Ulster

64. Bad ____ (famous spa)
65. Prickly sticker
66. Ilk
70. Quonset ____
71. Italian monk's title
72. Shades
74. Misery
75. Spry
77. Pit audience
80. Did a farrier's job
81. Tidal bore
82. Alaska native
83. Alcohol lamps
84. Position
85. Leaf openings

DOWN

1. Count of jazz
2. Tony or Oscar
3. Bird of poem

4. Spanish gold
5. Singer Sedaka
6. Confuse
7. Muse of poetry
8. Wife of Osiris
9. And not
10. Foliated rock
11. Pastel color
12. Pub potion
13. Store clerks, sometimes
14. Obliterate
15. "The Battle of the ____"
20. Breaches
25. Choice
28. "____ the Ball"
30. Illness
31. Eskimo knife
33. Prefix for gas
34. Circle meas.
35. "Here ____ Again"
36. "Into the ____"
37. Mystical
38. Inventory listing
39. Regal seats
41. Gumption
42. Fools
44. Attack term
45. Opposite of neg.
48. Header's counterpart
50. Emanates
52. Isomer prefix
53. "____ Man in Havana"
54. Haggard heroine
56. Favorite
58. Done in
60. Reflections
61. Pressed for payment
62. Pursue
63. Should
65. Brook
67. Proprietor
68. Rake
69. Tries out
71. Certain agts.
72. Tunic, to Tacitus
73. Rebuff
76. Actress Thompson
78. Spill the beans
79. UN agency

ACROSS

1. Stole
5. Popular seafood
9. Tied up
13. Relieve
14. 747, e.g.
15. Grandma Moses
16. Alternative to snowshoes
17. Cousins' mothers
18. Stash
19. Wood used for salad bowls
20. Plant life
22. Caesar's date
24. Squeals
25. Consented
28. Field mice
31. Loamy deposit
32. Present
33. Dejected
36. East Coast bird
40. Wily
41. Diminishes
42. Alliance
43. Goes it alone
45. Sir and Ma'am
46. Enclose
49. Trait carrier
50. Knights of the ____
54. Gossips
58. Serling and Stewart
59. Neighbor of 60 Across
60. Toledo's lake
61. Hem
62. Saudis, e.g.
63. Let
64. ____-in-the-wool
65. Tennis great Virginia ____
66. Bends downward

DOWN

1. "Go ____, young man"
2. Knave
3. China's site
4. Most bothersome
5. Whodunit leads
6. Phoned
7. Start a poker hand
8. Most superb
9. Sews loosely
10. Up to
11. Investigate
12. Exhibits ennui
14. Surfaced a road
21. Vote for
23. Lucy's partner
25. Priests' wear
26. Soccer score
27. Swear by
28. Action words
29. Minerals
30. Baseballer Durocher
32. Vagabond
33. Dirt
34. ____ vera
35. Studies
37. Actress Harris
38. Destroy
39. Numbers
43. Felt
44. Out of the ordinary
45. Young people
46. Slipped up
47. Gloomy
48. Move slightly
49. Sphere
51. Defrost
52. Nimbus
53. Actor Dillman
55. Field of study
56. Crooner Crosby
57. Stage decorations

Alpha Quotes

Reveal the quotes by eliminating the letters of the alphabet that are not part of the quotes. The unused letters go in alphabetical order from A to Z.

1. A T H B E B C E D S T E T F H G I N H G I W E J C K A N L

G M I V E N O A P E P R Q S R O N S I S T O N U E M O V R

W E C H X A Y N Z C E.

2. C A I V B I C L I D Z A T E I O F N G I H S J I U S J T K A

L S M L O N W P O R P O C Q E S S R O S F L E T A R U N I

N V W G T O X B E K Y I Z N D.

PUZZLE 512

ACROSS
1. Suitable
4. Aid a felon
8. Current trends
12. Caviar
13. Bus fee
14. Russia's ____ Mountains
15. Medieval performer
17. Stir up
18. Robert E. ____
19. Worn away
21. Solemn
24. Assert with confidence
25. Declare openly
26. Twirl
27. Orthodontist's group: abbr.
30. Marshy ground
31. Before all others
32. Female ruff
33. Final purpose
34. ____ vera
35. Saloon beverage
36. Demeanor
37. Sordid
38. Aft
41. Had breakfast
42. Tree's anchor
43. Establish a settlement
48. At a distance
49. Wicked
50. Dog's doc
51. Commanded
52. Social engagement
53. Affirmative vote

DOWN
1. Provide with weapons
2. Hawaiian dish
3. Decade number
4. Following
5. Without covering
6. Before, in poems
7. Broadcast visually
8. Frenzy
9. Hot and dry
10. Cowgirl Evans
11. Snow coaster
16. Large amount
20. Lease
21. Out of danger
22. Baking chamber
23. James ____ (007)
24. Cook's garb
26. Rendered soundless
27. Region
28. Reckon
29. Eagle's nest
31. Impartial
35. Existed
36. English measure
37. Robbed
38. Saudi, e.g.
39. Couch
40. Frog's cousin
41. Dismounted
44. Eggs, to Ovid
45. Climbing vine
46. Last letter
47. Airport abbr.

PUZZLE 513

ACROSS
1. Small jumps
5. Auto
8. Messy person
12. Leave out
13. Tell a falsehood
14. Breach
15. Actor Hackman
16. Commercials
17. Arrow poison
18. Moves stealthily
20. Latin-American dances
22. Supple
24. Deep gorge
27. Jails
31. Rowboat adjunct
32. Miner's find
33. Decimal point
34. Pacify
37. Reddish
39. "____ the Wind"
41. "Jane Eyre" author
44. Idolize
48. Attract
49. Table support
51. Individuals
52. Man of Eden
53. Golfer Trevino
54. Begone!
55. Lugosi of films
56. Ancient
57. Story

DOWN
1. Swine
2. Sign of the future
3. Soft wood
4. Robs
5. School section
6. Assist
7. Renovate
8. Polishes
9. Of great length
10. Margarine
11. Honey-makers
19. Actress Basinger
21. French friend
23. Period of indulgence
24. Beat walker
25. Actor Holbrook
26. Mr. Parseghian
28. Not even
29. Doze
30. Home for a pig
32. Shakespeare's moor
35. Movie theater
36. Carpenter insect
37. Disencumber
38. Greatest degree
40. Stormed
41. Tattle
42. Impolite
43. Of the mouth
45. Andean native
46. Authentic
47. Famous Italian family
50. Conger, e.g.

430

PUZZLE 514

ACROSS

1. Christens
6. Hit and rebound
11. Govt. power agency
14. Ask earnestly
17. Overact
18. Animated
19. Expand
21. Shower
22. Custom-fitted
24. Gland
26. San ____, Italy
27. Anglo-Saxon laborers
28. Touch
29. Teased
31. Foal's father
33. Feminine suffix
34. "____ Miss Brooks"
35. Mussolini
37. Absolute rulers
39. Investigations
41. Of the sea: abbr.
43. Obliteration
47. Strength
49. Portico
51. Drive onward
52. Chooses for a jury
55. Highly spiced stew
57. Moslem weight units
58. Soap ingredient
59. Stingy one
62. Harem room
63. Cover
66. Large, silvery fish
67. Brings to life
70. Signs up
72. Mineral springs
74. Browbeat
75. Came together for united action
77. Slaughter
79. Winding, narrow ridges
82. Fodder plants
84. Air currents
86. Extinct flightless bird
87. Sound of contentment
90. Hurried
92. Samoan seaport
93. Main point
94. Sundry assortments
96. Sweeps
98. Hanging
100. Became resolved to
103. Habituate
105. Issue
106. Vandyke, for one
107. Original position
108. Prosecutors: abbr.
109. Pea container
110. Bulb plants
111. Swarms

DOWN

1. Animal snout
2. Nonprofessional
3. Nacre
4. Kind of gasoline
5. Prophet
6. Dray
7. Magic-lamp owner
8. Unburden
9. "____ the river and . . ."
10. Distributes
11. Regret
12. Direction: abbr.
13. Wings
14. Impact
15. Heron
16. Silly ones
20. Tax estimator
23. Leave out
25. Electra's brother
28. Dandy
30. Greek letters
32. Wyatt
35. Swiss capital
36. Beyond control
38. ____ avis
40. Constrictor
42. Road-use charge
44. The latest
45. 19th-century English novelist
46. Fitzgerald and Logan
48. Nevada city
50. Inter ____
52. Mormon church official
53. Actress Loy
54. Small drinks
56. Indian coin
60. Back of the neck
61. Lhasa native
64. Wretched coward
65. Lamb
68. Church service
69. Inquire
71. Indian weight units
73. Rail bird
76. Unseated
78. Japanese city
80. Pulpit
81. Took a chair
83. Sewing line
85. Devils
87. Masqueraded
88. Moslem scholars
89. Hayworth and Gam
91. ____ and drabs
93. Spirit
95. Ginger cookie
97. Snick and ____
99. Section: abbr.
101. WWII area
102. Hammarskjold
104. Snaky letter

PUZZLE 515

• MOVIE GREATS •

ACROSS
1. Indian prince
5. Bored
10. Boone or O'Brien
13. Type style: abbr.
14. Fix the clock
15. Oklahoma city
17. Movie great
20. Gibbon
21. George C. Scott film
22. Muscular Charles
23. Robert De ____
24. Finish line
26. Granny and others
28. Registrants
32. Duplicate
33. Star of 17 Across
35. Gun owners' org.
36. Detroit product
37. Polynesian kingdom
38. Look over quickly
39. Actor Erwin
40. Pup
41. Creator of the Grinch
42. "The African Queen" star
44. Gape
45. Martial ____
46. ____ does it!
47. Food regimens
50. College instructor, for short
51. Fuel
54. Movie great
58. Ash or elm
59. ____-garde
60. Victor Borge, e.g.
61. Road curve
62. Takes a siesta
63. Shut violently

DOWN
1. Latvian capital
2. Sleep like ____
3. Oscar winner Wyman
4. Frothy beverage
5. Brambles
6. Release
7. Tennis great
8. Matched luggage
9. Ordinal suffix
10. Silver-gray metal
11. Indigo plant
12. Turner or Louise
16. Med. title
18. Correspond
19. "The Good ____"
23. "____ Nanette"
24. Use a scale
25. Swenson on "Benson"
26. Jane Fonda film
27. ____ to snuff
29. Bring upon oneself
30. Clear the tape
31. ____ souci
32. Bucks
33. Diving birds
34. Business letter abbr.
37. Wrongful act, in law
38. Catbird for one
40. Prize money
41. Chief of ____
43. Washes
44. Summer wear
46. Helen of radio fame
47. Period
48. Concerning
49. Hot times abroad
50. School orgs.
51. Aim
52. ____ Magnani
53. Flower part
55. ____ correspondent
56. Ciceronian greeting
57. Sts.

PUZZLE 516   Suspended Sentence

The words in each vertical column go into the spaces directly below them, but not necessarily in the order they appear. When you have placed all the words in their correct spaces, you will be able to read a quotation across the diagram from left to right.

A GOES MIDNIGHT A	INTO WITHOUT BLACK META-PHYSICIAN	IS A A CAT	LIGHT THAT A DARK	CELLAR PERSON ISN'T LOOKING	FOR AT THERE WHO

432

ACROSS

1. Bolo a wolf
5. Reaps extra
10. Cut 151 pence
14. Made cheese
15. Reduce recorder?
16. In dire need of transportation
17. Not a single sister, I hear
18. Stare at flower
19. Scatter?
20. Lattice is stiller
22. Finds lost ace
24. Downer?
26. Irate without, i.e., scoundrel
27. Sad, it lets in miners
30. So, why tofu source?
32. I'd pet, but it's warm
36. Reynolds and Lancaster hide second breaks
38. Knock spigot
40. Read the challenge
41. Not a don't
42. Tris, the orator
45. Capture ink
46. Care for 10, and 500
48. Tar pictures
49. Mailed over?
51. Curves before tees
53. Neither mate
55. Peels pears
56. Backpack without Kay
58. Stormed up a grade
60. Expected at a wide place
64. Scot led least friendly
68. Twine company road
69. Rise above tugboat
71. 51 New Englanders queue
72. In the middle of Elm Street
73. Rode a love
74. Goddess of strife, sire
75. Watery asset, without tea
76. Soles on good earth
77. Places tennis divisions

DOWN

1. Loaned the French New Testament
2. Door scent
3. What ails a bean
4. So let me make eggs
5. Tad is solemn
6. Goes by EPA's steamship
7. Pat is liable
8. Leer at fishing gear
9. Headless terror is wrong
10. Made Ted race
11. Tune till
12. Lied still
13. Apes pod vegetables
21. Itemizes slits
23. Feline bulldozer
25. Tarot, or spinner?
27. Lessen a beat
28. Greenhorns: duds with energy
29. Presses on, sir
31. Gab with hairy ox
33. Reap phosphorus sheet
34. Conceal fire near Castle
35. Depresses teeth?
37. Pa's bath
39. For each rep
43. Ocean bird heard to work for money
44. Fend off Perle
47. Chooses 12th mo. or 15th day
50. Add less burdens
52. Took a chair on top of Saturn
54. Rears 100 snakes
57. Flowery piece of plate
59. Runs through ogres
60. Play parts, as around Connecticut
61. Was dressed in row E
62. Neighborhood of arena without nitrogen
63. Extinct bird performs twice
65. Ere I saw Ireland
66. Isn't in a tizzy
67. Harper is carless actress
70. Owe distress

PUZZLE 518

ACROSS
1. Karate hit
5. Storms
10. Russian, e.g.
14. Bagel
15. French school
16. Bark cloth
17. Tony's cousin
18. Gepetto, e.g.
20. Actress Joanne
22. Milk-producing farm
23. Sea eagle
24. Supplies with fuel
26. Glued
30. Lyon's river
31. "____ Karenina"
32. Generous fellow
33. Three, in Roma
36. Satyrs: 2 wds.
40. ____ and order
41. Sicily's land
42. Word of regret
43. Tall tale
44. Baseball's Mickey
46. Author Du Maurier
48. Hawaiian food
49. Shinto gateway
50. Sorrel tree
55. Ground hogs
58. ____ mater
59. Handle on an urn
60. Century plants
61. Luge
62. Soothsayer
63. English measure
64. ____ Krishna

DOWN
1. Brag
2. Nomad
3. Medley
4. Begged
5. Bounty
6. Chipmunk's snack
7. Acceptable
8. Days of yore
9. Dry, as wine
10. Hull planking
11. C'est ____: 2 wds.
12. Copycats
13. Fluctuate
19. Hebrew God
21. Tiny
24. Annie's pet
25. Student's carryall
26. Pivoted object
27. Sulawesi ox
28. Winter precipitation
29. Little one
30. With gloom
32. Trap
33. Lean to one side
34. Genuine
35. Being, to Cato
37. Made of stone
38. Solar god
39. Use a sunlamp
43. Arachnid
44. Rich dessert
45. Atmosphere
46. Lorna of Exmoor
47. Stood up
48. Gambling game
49. "____ the night before . . ."
50. Edinburgh man
51. Scrub
52. Mexican pot
53. Hebrew measure
54. Miami's county
56. Son of Noah
57. Diminutive ending

PUZZLE 519   SLIDE-O-GRAM

Place the seven words below into the diagram, one word for each across line, so that one of the rows reading down will spell out a 7-letter word that is related to the others.

Beetle
Butterfly
Cricket
Grasshopper
Mosquito
Moth
Spider

CODEWORD

PUZZLE 520

Codeword is a special crossword puzzle in which conventional clues are omitted. Instead, answer words in the diagram are represented by numbers. Each number represents a different letter of the alphabet, and all of the letters of the alphabet are used. When you are sure of a letter, put it in the code key chart for easy reference. A group of letters has been inserted to start you off.

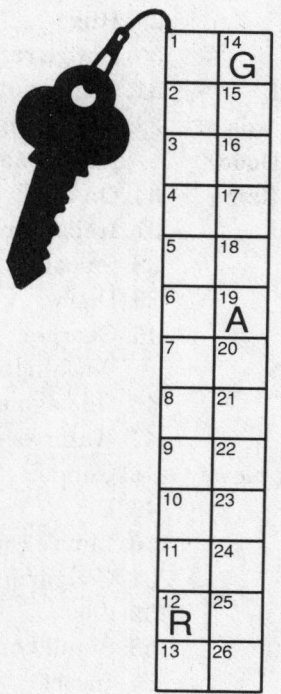

CODEWORD

PUZZLE 521

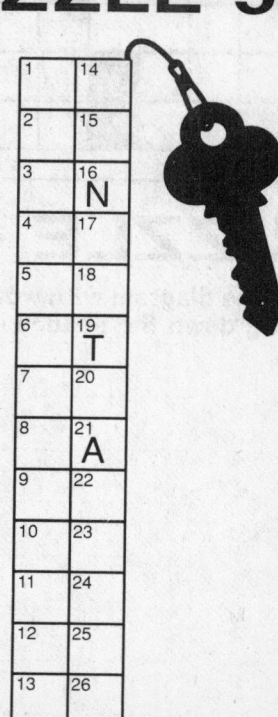

435

PUZZLE 522

ACROSS

1. Sluggish
5. Valuable
10. Leftover fare
14. Volcano output
15. Task
16. Resound
17. Gershwin composition, with "An": 3 wds.
20. Writing utensil
21. Brink
22. Expert
23. Lean
24. Use a lever
25. Modern
28. Greedy
30. Opening
33. Actor Alda
34. "Remember the ___"
35. Reverential fear
36. Song of 1920, with "The": 2 wds.
40. Dined
41. Prevent
42. Emanation
43. That woman's
44. Irish fuel
45. OPEC, e.g.
47. Jailbird
48. French glove
49. Dismay, in Britain
52. Apparent
54. Revolver
57. Sherwood drama: 3 wds.
60. "___ La Douce"
61. Warning flame
62. Conceited
63. Twofold
64. Mary ___ Moore
65. Miss Kett

DOWN

1. Insulting blow
2. Disabled
3. Kiln
4. Conflict
5. Emphasis
6. "Jaws" star
7. Melody
8. Great Lake
9. "___ Little Indians"
10. Intoxicating
11. Land measure
12. Vessel
13. Party giver
18. Russian tsar
19. Forgive
23. Miss Horne
24. Kind of cotton
25. Indian ruler
26. Cheer up
27. Prank
28. Warn
29. Huge
30. Entire range
31. Cognizant
32. Regarding punishment
34. On the briny
37. Italian province
38. Smooth
39. Dash
45. George Washington ___
46. One against
47. Waterway
48. Genus
49. Dry
50. Lima's country
51. Cougar
52. Just
53. Small bottle
54. Insect
55. Standard quantity
56. Zola novel
58. Frequently, to a poet
59. Adam's mate

PUZZLE 523

HOCUS POCUS

Fill in the diagram with words formed by unscrambling the letters so that an 8-letter word will be revealed reading down the shaded column. This is a bit tricky as the scrambled letters may form more than one word.

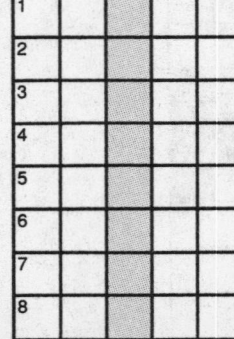

1. A E L P T
2. A E M N S
3. A I N S T
4. A E G L R
5. A E P R S
6. A C E R T
7. E I M S T
8. E I N R S

PUZZLE 524

ACROSS
1. Put away aboard
5. "____ Spee"
9. Nile dam site
14. West African country
15. Rivulet
16. Call
17. Ireland, fondly
18. Play part: 2 wds.
19. Laborers
20. Troy's undoing: 2 wds.
23. Speck
24. ____ hat
25. ____ as she goes
27. Flanked by
31. Tests
34. Masjid or Pasha
35. Halt
38. Beauty shop
39. Skating area
41. Lance
43. Wild plumlike fruit
44. Wooden peg
46. Full
48. Language suffix
49. Markets
51. Top
53. Speaks
56. Hail, to Caesar
57. Graduate degree letters
59. "Gypsy" star: 2 wds.
64. Send payment
66. "The Children's ____"
67. Patron saint of sailors
68. One of the Muses
69. Fairy-tale opener
70. Plod
71. Corn breads
72. Sow
73. Pueblo Indian

DOWN
1. Merganser
2. Poi source
3. Medley
4. Oriel, e.g.
5. Eminent Iberians
6. Affluent
7. Choir members
8. Coquette
9. Seems
10. "____ Done Him Wrong"
11. "Sleeper" star: 2 wds.
12. In the year: Latin
13. Sparrow's abode
21. Kind of energy: abbr.
22. Collection
26. Buenos ____
27. Poets
28. George or T.S.
29. "Wizard of Oz" character: 2 wds.
30. Drowses
32. Free
33. Derisive look
36. Black or Red
37. Chows
40. Actress Deborah
42. Fixed
45. Sheds: hyph.
47. Nose or swan
50. Penn, e.g.
52. Most recent
54. Group character
55. Rhone feeder
57. Certain sch.
58. Public idol
60. Publisher Henry
61. Southwest stewpot
62. Melville book
63. Corgis, e.g.
65. Inhabitant: suffix

KEYWORD

PUZZLE 525

To find the KEYWORD fill in the blanks in words 1 through 10 with the correct missing letters. Transfer those letters to the correspondingly numbered squares in the diagram. Approach with care—this puzzle is not as simple as it first appears.

1. S T _ R T
2. V A L _ E
3. F O R _ Y
4. B _ A S T
5. B L O O _
6. S P _ R T
7. _ A T C H
8. S H _ R K
9. _ O D G E
10. L E A S _

1	2	3	4	5	6	7	8	9	10

437

PUZZLE 526

ACROSS

1. Hoist
6. Munches
11. ___ bleu
12. Cheer
14. Atlanta, Ga.
17. Historical periods
18. Abound
19. Belfry
20. Sothern
21. Containing iron
23. Winter stuff
24. Canning gel
26. Strikebreaker
28. Pentagon VIP
29. Discoloration
30. Intrepid
32. Hiker's path
34. Vicuna's kin
35. Glossy coats
37. Metric measures
40. Lunched
41. Son of Eve
42. Composer Johnny
43. Decorator's advice
45. Hid away
47. Japanese sash
48. Merits
50. Ancient Ireland
51. Double
52. Eskimos
55. Garment part
56. System of self-defense
57. Arabian horse
58. Aspersions

DOWN

1. St. Peter's and Lateran
2. God of war
3. Bachelor's last words
4. Melt
5. Go in
6. Laboratory substances
7. Center
8. Goofs
9. Stoles
10. Nest eggs
11. Band instrument
13. Champions
14. Piles
15. Daughter of Cecrops
16. Seamed and tucked
21. Last exams
22. Actor Reiner
25. Spare, for one
27. Reproached
30. Complimented
31. Asian ruler
33. Cays, to the French
35. Takes without right
36. Daily task
38. Discount
39. Seed coverings
40. Neighborhood
42. Servile
44. Attack
46. Gambles
49. Snow glider
51. Honey
53. Hail, to Caesar
54. Actress Joanne

PUZZLE 527

SHARE-A-LETTER

Fill in each diagram with the words that correspond to each subject. Letters to be filled into the larger areas will be shared by more than one word. Words read across only.

1. ANIMALS

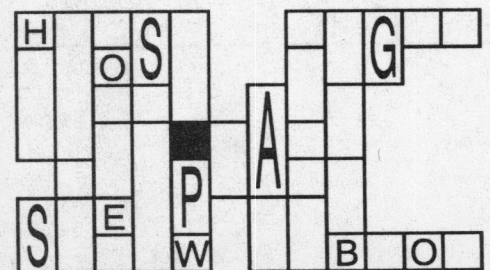

2. COLORS

438

ACROSS

1. Actress Kelly
6. Head covers
10. Spool
14. Drives fast
15. Leave out
16. Medicinal plant
17. Special occasion
18. Irritate
19. Baseball team
20. Oater
22. Trickle slowly
24. Before, poetically
25. Floor cleaners
26. Craft
29. Pine tree
31. Defect
33. Turret
35. Beavers' creation
36. Wharf
37. Mexican blanket
38. Makes known
40. Caresses
41. Stringed instruments
42. Made thread
43. Printers' measures
44. Thesis
45. Jump
46. High explosive
47. "____ Loves Me"
48. Great Lake
50. Unlocked, to a bard
52. Impudent child
53. Uneven
57. Confront
60. Roma's language: abbr.
62. Musical drama
63. Level
64. Stitches
65. Conflicting
66. Requirement
67. Sea eagle
68. Rock

DOWN

1. Became larger
2. Rant
3. High cards
4. Middle
5. Organic compound
6. Cereal grain
7. French friend
8. Head rest
9. Precipitous
10. Social class
11. Inventor Whitney
12. Vast age
13. Southern general
21. Makes ready for use again
23. Backward
25. Disfigure
26. Rouse
27. Regret
28. Lock of hair
29. Starve
30. Inflict
32. Guitarist Paul
34. Spanish gold
35. Jackknifes
36. Entreaty
37. Daze
39. Georgia's neighbor: abbr.
40. Resort
42. Visualize
45. Untidiness
46. Kettle
49. Elevate
51. Supports
52. Curve
53. Otherwise
54. Distant: pref.
55. Persia, today
56. Look after
57. Marsh
58. St.
59. Passing grade
61. Grain beard

WHAT AM I?

My first is in father, but never in mother.

My second's in aunt, but never in brother.

My third is in grandma and also in mate.

My fourth is in sister, but never in Kate.

My fifth is in uncle and also in clan.

My sixth is in baby, but never in man.

I've room for many, from sibling to spouse.

If you want to find me, look in most any house.

PUZZLE 530

ACROSS
1. Worn out
5. Trite
10. Cranky one
14. Ornamental fabric
15. Heals
16. Govern
17. Actor Arkin
18. Dwell
19. Eastern continent
20. Abutted
22. Additional
23. By way of
24. Budge
26. Folds
30. Drink
34. Hawk's nest
35. Do gardening work
36. Actor Steiger
37. Hits solidly
38. Heed the alarm
39. Amphibian
40. Actress Bartok
41. Seedy joints
42. Type of writing
43. Presented payment
45. More sluggish
46. Chilled
47. River: Sp.
48. Fiery particle
51. Wound dressings
56. Rub lightly
57. Arm support
59. Big bundle
60. Fish sauce
61. Color
62. Actress Lanchester
63. Assay
64. Put 2 and 2 together
65. Consider

DOWN
1. Chunk
2. Angelic headwear
3. Actor Sharif
4. Baby-sit
5. Frightens
6. Potato, e.g.
7. Like the Gobi
8. Guided
9. Compass dir.
10. Moon feature
11. Big hurry
12. "I cannot tell ___": 2 wds.
13. Bruin
21. Dueling swor[d]
22. More than
24. Allots
25. Baker's need[s]
26. Provide food
27. Depart
28. Church instrument
29. Bro's sib
30. Made cookies
31. Bow missile
32. Silly bird
33. Lawn tool
35. Fluttered
38. Telegram
39. To and ___
41. Pack of cards
42. Trudge
44. Guide
45. Charred
47. Buffalo's ho[rn]
48. Hit hard
49. Heap
50. Mimics
51. Tie
52. In the sack
53. Storm
54. If not
55. Connecting stitches
57. Depot: abbr.
58. Box top

PUZZLE 531

WORD SPIRA[L]

Fill in the spiral diagram in a clockwise direction with the 4-letter answer words. The last letter of [each] word will be the first letter of the next word. When the diagram is completed, a 7-letter word will read d[own] the shaded center column.

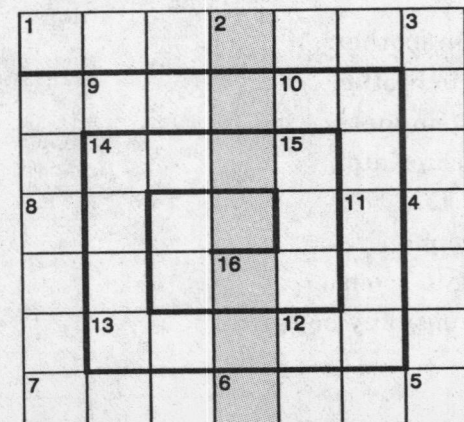

1. Musical sign
2. Heating need
3. Extensive
4. U.S. territory
5. Actress Marjorie
6. Waiting-room call
7. Stumble
8. Trail
9. Make a rug
10. Chicken ___
11. Action word
12. Small nail
13. Platform
14. Adventure story
15. Choir member
16. Swear word

440

PUZZLE 532

ACROSS
1. Damage
4. Insult
8. Land measure
12. Pub drink
13. Ancient weapon
14. Put down
15. Poetic contraction
16. Bakery worker
17. Against
18. Ceramic square
20. Resource
21. Rich cake
23. Scratch
25. Sad expression
26. Says again
30. Garland
31. Paces
32. Topsy's playmate
33. Changes
35. Type of school
36. Raw minerals
37. Singes
38. Revenge
41. Castro's land
42. Own
43. Needy
45. Swindle
48. State
49. Goals
50. Age
51. Military meal
52. Bed support
53. Got off one's feet

DOWN
1. Small rug
2. Muhammed ____
3. Hold back
4. Grin
5. Decorative edging
6. Playing card
7. Each
8. 49th state
9. Containers
10. Ceremony
11. Prepare copy
19. "____ a Miracle"
20. Skills
21. Soft mineral
22. Margarine
23. Defrosts
24. Queries
26. Hard to find
27. Patios
28. Level
29. Weakens
31. Existed
34. Electors
35. Tavern
37. Explode
38. Fake
39. Overlay
40. Currier and ____
41. Stupor
43. Dance step
44. Lubricate
46. Mouths
47. ____ King Cole

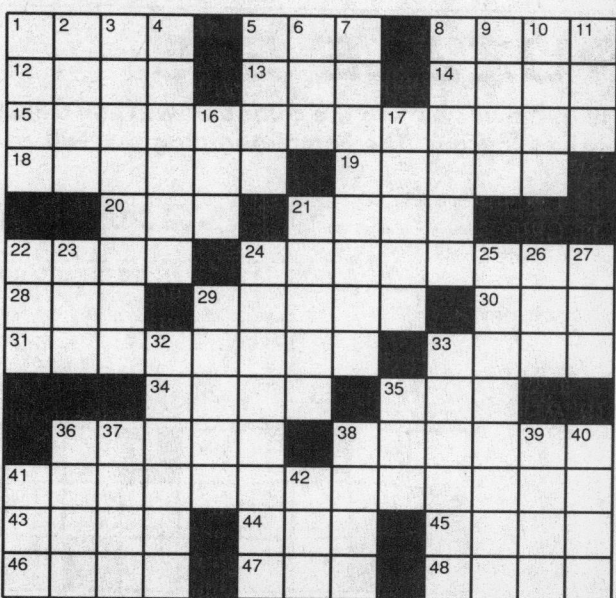

PUZZLE 533

ACROSS
1. Red vegetable
5. Beret
8. Surfeit
12. Wild buffalo of India
13. Actress Lupino
14. Conceal
15. Start of quotation: 2 wds.
18. Merchant
19. Goddess of agriculture
20. Teachers' org.: abbr.
21. New York stadium
22. Breakfast option
24. Sleuth Mickey
28. Mineo
29. Forelegs
30. 149, to Caesar
31. Voting into office
33. Western college: abbr.
34. Bee's home
35. Yoko
36. "____ Romance": 2 wds.
38. Texas city
41. End of quotation: 3 wds.
43. Spoken
44. Sea eagle
45. Mine entrance
46. Swamps
47. Billy ____ Williams
48. Hideaways

DOWN
1. Hairless
2. Great Lake
3. Enmesh
4. Names
5. Row
6. Paid notices
7. Corresponding
8. Sung by a choir
9. Admire
10. Poems
11. Affirmative reply
16. Meadow
17. Spools
21. Backbone
22. Compass pt.: abbr.
23. Lass
24. Quaked
25. Praise
26. Nothing
27. Guido's note: 2 wds.
29. Ex-Police member
32. Ices
33. Lighten
35. Cereal grain
36. Of flying
37. Banner
38. Copenhagen native
39. Similar
40. Fast jets: abbr.
41. Watch piece
42. Before, to poets

PUZZLE 534

ACROSS
1. Mile's equal
5. Prophet
9. Mountain tops
14. Redact
15. Greek mountain
16. French mountains
17. Italian mountains
19. Thin candle
20. Romantic runaways
21. Gates
23. Golly!
24. Henri's heaven
25. Century parts
29. Singing group
32. Harvests
33. Insertion mark
35. Concrete ingredient: abbr.
36. Hockey great and '49 Nobelist
37. Gaffe
38. Ersatz
39. Imbibe sparingly
40. Aligns
41. Minion of Oberon
42. More disreputable
44. Headwear for Sikhs
46. Kenya's longest river
47. Life story, for short
48. Rifts
51. Mohican drums: hyph.
55. Cream of the crop
56. Of K2's range
58. Actress White
59. "L'____, c'est moi"
60. Actor Richard
61. Whole notes
62. Lairs
63. Beatrice d'____

DOWN
1. Ancient Persian
2. Baal
3. Rural structure
4. Makeshifts
5. Evening party
6. Superlative suffixes
7. Wind dir.
8. Kind of file
9. New England athlete
10. Click beetle
11. American mountain region
12. Sloop part
13. Latvia and Kirghiz, formerly
18. Rewards, of yore
22. Earth pigment
25. Smelting waste
26. Otherworldly
27. Central European mountain range
28. Scrub
29. Mountain extreme
30. Discover
31. TV awards
34. Deauville donkey
37. Sunfish
38. Undercover undermining
40. Decorates gaudily
41. Composer Rudolf
43. ____ d'hotel
45. Subs: hyph.
48. Equinox mo.
49. Role for Liz
50. Molt
51. Govt. agent: hyph.
52. Court crier's cry
53. Trading center
54. Partner of snick
57. Native: suffix

PUZZLE 535   QUOTAGRAM

Fill in the answers to the clues below. Then transfer the letters to the correspondingly numbered squares in the diagram. The completed diagram will contain a quotation.

1. Exaggerated

  $\overline{37}\ \overline{42}\ \overline{4}\ \overline{21}\ \overline{8}\ \overline{31}\ \overline{14}\ \overline{1}\ \overline{43}\ \overline{11}$

2. Dared

  $\overline{22}\ \overline{33}\ \overline{18}\ \overline{40}\ \overline{26}\ \overline{17}\ \overline{35}\ \overline{15}\ \overline{39}\ \overline{44}$

3. Superior

  $\overline{38}\ \overline{10}\ \overline{19}\ \overline{32}\ \overline{20}\ \overline{6}$

4. Advance

  $\overline{25}\ \overline{16}\ \overline{2}\ \overline{28}\ \overline{41}\ \overline{5}\ \overline{29}$

5. Fine rain

  $\overline{24}\ \overline{27}\ \overline{13}\ \overline{36}$

6. Military body

  $\overline{7}\ \overline{30}\ \overline{12}\ \overline{9}$

7. Feathered wrap

  $\overline{3}\ \overline{23}\ \overline{34}$

442

PUZZLE 536

ACROSS
1. Two-masted ship
5. Cut
10. Necktie
12. Entrance
14. Ebb
15. Spin
16. French friend
17. Lash
19. Oolong
20. Inclination
22. Dobbin's dinner
23. Istanbul resident
24. More tidy
26. Peppery plant
27. Small, open carriage
29. Lodge
32. Hardships
35. Smell ____
36. Spree
37. Farmer's place, in rhyme
39. Operated
40. Run-of-the-mill
42. Contend
43. Expunged
45. Be aware of
47. Israelite tribesman
48. Treats with malice
49. Farewell words
50. Beginning

DOWN
1. German seaport
2. Wisconsin city
3. "____ Got a Secret"
4. Wanders
5. Hose setting
6. Chicago section
7. Knack
8. "The Thinker," for one
9. Detesters
10. Kind of apple
11. Restraint
13. Piping failures
18. New Jersey river
21. Silent
23. Tire feature
25. Make leather
26. Caesar's 151
28. Hurdy-gurdies
29. Felt concern
30. Biblical mount
31. Fruit
33. See 47 Across
34. Carved
36. Gemstones
38. Dregs
40. Alpha's tagalong
41. Cuts off
44. Pose
46. Fasten

PUZZLE 537

ACROSS
1. Rum cake
5. Matterhorn, for one
8. Arab cloaks
12. Too bad!
13. College cheer
14. Filled tortilla
15. Be clamorous
18. Explosive: abbr.
19. Char-____ (London tourist bus)
20. Large parrot
21. Lao-____
22. Part of BPOE
24. In conflict
27. Became unavailable
30. Ancient France
31. Belonging to us
32. Fugitive
35. Leave a bigger gratuity than
37. God or tasse starter
38. Wts.
39. Angelico
41. Musical piece
43. ____ de la Cite
46. Scottish isles
49. Freshly
50. Workers' group: abbr.
51. Brewed drinks
52. Ancient Persian's kin
53. Napoleon's marshal
54. Rice wine

DOWN
1. Bret Maverick's brother
2. Funny King
3. Fish's temptation
4. Donkey
5. Algerians, in Paris
6. Turner
7. Dialer
8. Lawyer: abbr.
9. Has second thoughts
10. Farm unit
11. Asiatic bean
16. Vane direction
17. Home of the Bruins
21. Delicate fabric
23. Nautical units of speed
24. In the past
25. Sigma's follower
26. Passe
28. Psychic Geller
29. Cookbook abbr.
33. U.S. citizen: abbr.
34. Ziner's "____ This Wilderness"
35. British alumnus
36. Over, in Berlin
39. Froth
40. Mystic poem
42. Ubangi tributary
43. Inspiration
44. Faucet drip
45. Existence: Latin
47. Sheep
48. "____ a Wonderful Life"

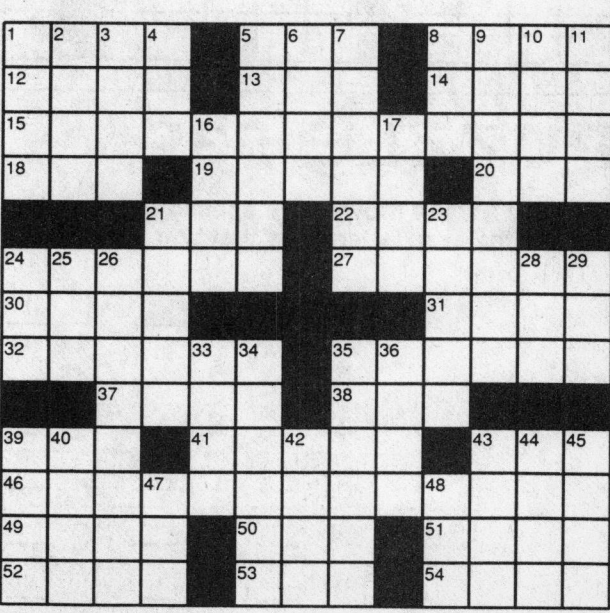

PUZZLE 538

ACROSS

1. Take off the top
5. Fall flower
10. Chatters
14. Verdi opera
15. Soupcon of snow
16. Prayer ending
17. Sense
18. Citrus fruits
19. Agitate
20. Appraise
22. Walk like a baby
24. Provides guns
25. Walesa, for one
26. Fee
29. Love song
33. Multitude
34. Locations
35. Clump
36. Rosary prayers
37. Tender spots
38. Ache
39. Bog
40. Tanker
41. Comedy
42. Philadelphia printer
44. Smoothed down
45. Angered
46. Army division
47. French dance
50. Featuring
54. Great Lake
55. Seat
57. False god
58. Short swims
59. National bird
60. Ms. Lanchester
61. Sunrise direction
62. Mighty horse
63. Germ

DOWN

1. Secure
2. Ukrainian city
3. Thought
4. Ducks
5. Burning
6. Small openings
7. Gentle
8. Piece out
9. Makes new again
10. Eden, e.g.
11. With a group
12. Phone inventor
13. Dagger
21. Strong desire
23. Mexican cheers
25. First pope
26. Threshing residue
27. Hang around
28. Stadium
29. Warning signal
30. Prize
31. Ballet, e.g.
32. Rimmed
34. Firm
37. Periods of quiet
38. Larders
40. Soup vegetable
41. Country event
43. Most pleasing
44. Trapped
46. Useful
47. Admit defeat
48. Opera highlight
49. Bites
50. Wise
51. Not working
52. Snout
53. Happy
56. Chapeau

PUZZLE 539   You Know the Odds

Six Fred Astaire movies are spelled out, but they are missing every other letter. It shouldn't be too difficult to fill in the even letters now that You Know the Odds!

1. T _ P _ A _
2. S _ A _ L _ E _ A _ C _
3. Z _ E _ F _ L _ F _ L _ I _ S
4. R _ Y _ L _ E _ D _ N _
5. F _ N _ Y _ A _ E
6. B _ U _ S _ I _ S

444

ACROSS

1. '60s musical
5. Electrical units
9. Friend for Francois
12. Make eyes at
13. Trading center
14. Rent
15. Former Israeli leader
17. "A Chorus Line" song
18. Shakespearean villain
19. The Prado, e.g.
21. Twyla Tharp's milieu
23. Crosiers
24. Violent melee
25. Comes to light
29. "Exodus" hero
30. Design transfer
31. Through
32. Spiritually symbolic
34. Eye part
35. Store sign
36. Funeral heaps
37. Strand at sea
40. Drug agent
41. Woodsman's tool
42. Offensive
46. Offer
47. Run into
48. Singer Johnny ____
49. Had dinner
50. Zone
51. Remain

DOWN

1. Swine
2. In the past
3. The Prairie State
4. Edit
5. Bullets
6. Fannie or Ginnie
7. Ancient
8. Flaky pastry
9. Agave's kin
10. Cafe card
11. Article
16. Grow older
20. Pitcher Maglie
21. Liquid measure
22. Ethereal
23. Pie nut
25. Month for gifts
26. Topper
27. Coniferous tree
28. Fresh talk
30. School certificate
33. ____ T (exactly)
34. Words to a show
36. ____ vobiscum
37. ____ au rhum
38. Way out
39. Surrender
40. ____ bene
43. Born
44. Neighbor of Mex.
45. Bashful

ACROSS

1. State positively
5. Actor Baldwin
9. Inquire
12. Carte du jour
13. Twofold
14. Meadow
15. Certain votes
16. Man-made object
18. Enormous
20. Social class
21. Pizza topping
24. Short a few
25. Mississippi landing place
26. Traffic cop's catch
30. Spoon-bender Geller
31. ____ Fawkes' Day
32. Lizzie Borden's tool
33. Hotel employee
36. Extreme danger
38. Feedbag tidbit
39. Fastidious
40. Squirrel away
43. Terse
44. Tread
46. Downs or Hefner
50. Blyth or Jillian
51. Metal vein
52. Biblical brother
53. Actress ____ Dawn Chong
54. Gave the once-over
55. Engrossed

DOWN

1. Golfer Alcott
2. Victory sign
3. Spanish queen
4. Frat candidate
5. Saw
6. Tackle-box item
7. Nosh
8. Trite phrase
9. Ah, me!
10. Cult
11. "Kiss Me ____"
17. Dunaway or Emerson
19. Put into service
21. Cudgel
22. Present!
23. Depraved
24. CIA employee
26. Dine late
27. Drat it all!
28. Highway sign
29. Depend
31. Obtained
34. "____ in Space"
35. Squabble
36. Equality
37. Choice word
39. Conned
40. At a distance
41. "____ Lisa"
42. Perfect
43. Relinquish
45. Yo-yo, e.g.
47. "Born in the ____"
48. Opening
49. Cabin

PUZZLE 542

• BRAINTEASERS •

ACROSS
1. Actor Mineo
4. Uninteresting
8. Cotton bundles
13. Unsymmetrical
15. Actress Gam
16. Overact
17. Emilia's mate
18. Fragrance
19. "Call Me ____"
20. Cruciverbalist's pastime
23. Heredity factors
24. "____ fan tutte"
25. ____ and feathered
27. Shushes
31. "Fur ____"
32. Miami's county
33. Festive
34. Pinch
35. Pleasant-looking people
38. Embargo
39. U.S. publisher
41. Declare positively
42. Harangue
44. Puts in other words
46. Cargo ship
47. Unique person
48. Songstress Page
49. Code experts
55. Jeweler's eyeglass
56. Architect Saarinen
57. Of the ear
58. More adept
59. Political cartoonist
60. Actress Naldi
61. Wing: prefix
62. Shoe form
63. Deceive

DOWN
1. Levantine ketch
2. Wing-shaped
3. Anagrams
4. Having a steep edge
5. Beach resorts
6. Performer: suffix
7. Fermented apple juice
8. Confound
9. Wonderful
10. Polish city
11. Kin of etc.
12. Decorated with a small pattern
14. Tough questions
21. Dirks, of old
22. Raft helmsman
25. Opera hero
26. Wonderland girl
27. Bargain events
28. Occult
29. Cheer up
30. More logical
32. Branching off
36. San ____, California
37. Truth, of old
40. Cork
43. Allot scarce items
45. In front: prefix
46. Writer Truman
48. Analyze grammatically
49. Applaud
50. Lee's first name: abbr.
51. Christmas
52. Raise
53. Singer Gobbi
54. Read quickly

PUZZLE 543   SATELLITES

Form 9 words by placing one syllable in each circle below. The center circle will contain the first syllable for each of the 9 words. All the syllables will be used once. Words read outward from the center.

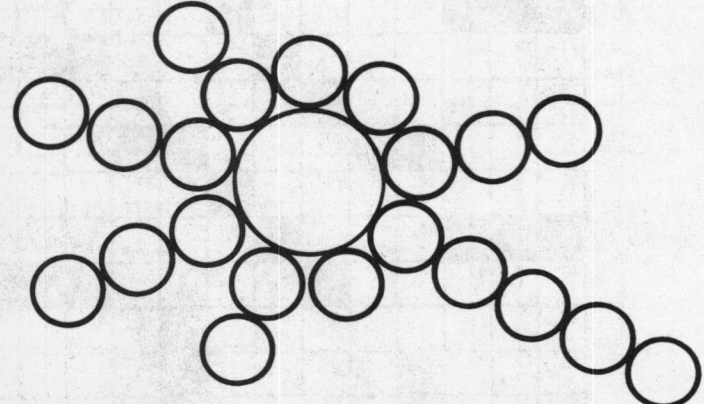

A	A	A	AL	AN
BOD	CAL	CON	DA	GE
GEL	GRAM	I	LOPE	
LY	LYT	SIC	SWER	
TE	TIQUE	Y	Y	

446

Here is a puzzle with more than the expected crossword challenge—and rewards. Each clue involves a pun or some form of nuttiness. Look out for traps! With a little practice, you will soon catch on to these tricky clues and enjoy the extra challenge.

ACROSS

1. Singular victory
4. What Mimi will do in the end
7. Money to ola
10. Back in the saloon
13. Sounds like one flying insect, Lincoln
14. A color of another color
15. Aw, I am in wondrous respect
16. Come up and get this
17. 1066, 1492, 1776: abbr.
18. Not pres.
19. Sailor returns for rodent
20. Miss Hogg likes to eat a lot
21. Item dat does de waggin'
23. Contest, in green—back
24. Unspecified alternative
25. It's common knowledge that Truman was one for years
28. What you earn when you shake a tail and grow old
31. Poem written to your creditors
32. Main arterychoke
36. A drink for the sick man
37. Like June 1 or June 30—or any of the days between
39. Club members who eat now and pay later
40. Author of K, TI, DJAMH and ACGOV
41. Summer hours, for Koch: abbr.
42. The bottom (of a sack in a blind alley)
43. What Paris is if it's pronounced Paree and spelled Paris
44. Reason for owning an auto?
46. If we wrote Joyce's last name this way, we'd start the letter "Gentlemen"
47. Commerciall messagee, for short?
48. Scandinavian who was wed inside
49. Southern constellation that looks the same backwards
50. Leave before the going-away party
51. Queen of New Jersey
55. Suckers keep coming back to them to be cured
58. Negative, to a pecan?
59. More and more like a pin (get the point?)
63. Cheer for a Norse toreador
64. Just up the road a piece, a piece, a piece . . .
65. Sit with the head at the end
66. taob ruoy wor, wor, wor ot desU
67. The time dinner was at?
68. Tea and this . . . seems sound
69. Profit or loss, it's all you've got left
70. It follows the leader
71. Short resident of Seoul
72. It's a matter of law
73. What gin makes a martini (a prohibitionist might object)
74. It keeps teachers after school

DOWN

1. Became pale like a fairy-stick
2. Ill wind no one blows good
3. Home for the birds
4. Address of that pompous gentleman sitting up front
5. For the pay-off in Moscow
6. Rutherford B. Hayes always ended with this
7. Macy's made a spectacle of itself on Thanksgiving
8. I was cognizant of the fact that the merchant had only one left
9. Thus far, according to the Frenchman in the American Revolution who lost his chuckle
10. They road me out of town on one
11. What one does to please
12. Carry around on a Scottish hillside
22. It's curtains for Dr. Kong
23. ____ A. Wake, a chunky but alert man
24. Came up on memo about type of jacket
26. Con man for a Queen
27. Cigarettes can start you to coffin
28. Makes leftover coffee
29. Welcome dogs, children, smoking, etc.
30. Daring deed my beau did
33. Made beer backwards in a kingly fashion
34. I'll swap Mark for your secret
35. Where all joking is
37. Pry up to take great delight in
38. As a cooling beverage this drink can be a real lemon
39. In music, living proof that two heads are worse than one
42. Crustacean that likes apples and grass
45. When Caesar fishes for a compliment
46. Someone else's child
49. Blues, Monday morning or any other time
50. Insures a home on your range
52. Like this puzzle?
53. Take advantage of an open-door policy
54. On edge from too many exams
55. Basic principle of a graduated income tax, according to the rich
56. She used to be a tenor
57. An equal, don't you see
60. Fall flat, on vacation
61. Where it's easiest to orient yourself
62. When in Rome, spell as the Romans do
64. Bid prohibited in advance
65. Neither flesh, fowl, nor good red herring, politically: abbr.

PUZZLE 545

ACROSS
1. Ms. Zadora
4. Crow's call
7. Sore
10. Margarine
12. Do cobbler's work
13. Unusual
14. Address abbr.
15. Certain lure
17. Sea: Fr.
18. Singleton
19. Large dog: 2 wds.
24. Cereal grain
25. Always, to a poet
27. They're not hip
31. Dogpatch's Daisy ____
32. Relative
33. Shape anew
35. Having breadth
36. Barrel slats
37. Whale group
38. By way of

DOWN
1. Complaints
2. Newspaper addendum
3. Fuss
4. Eye part
5. Actor Ladd
6. Existed
7. London trolley
8. Subways' kin
9. Newspersons
11. "____ the land . . ."
16. Hostelry
20. Went sailing
21. Grain unit
22. Take away
23. Blackjack figure
26. Cincinnati nine
27. Spotted
28. Witty remark
29. Take out, as a knot
30. Establish
34. Chart

PUZZLE 546

ACROSS
1. Swiss peak
4. Eskimo craft
9. Saratoga, e.g.
12. ____ annum
13. Martini garnish
14. Youngster
15. Self
16. More mature
17. Before, poetically
18. That girl
20. Go with stealth
22. Seems
26. Shade trees
27. Abound
28. Coral island group
30. Lend an ____
31. Regions
32. Vintage auto
35. Dozed
36. Meadow youth
37. Certain horse
39. Lawman
41. Heavenly blazer
43. With: prefix
44. Actor Reiner
45. Automaton
48. Baseball club
51. Mined find
52. Swap
53. Be in debt
54. Printers' measures
55. Wrath
56. Marry

DOWN
1. Gorilla, e.g.
2. Journey segment
3. Get ahead
4. Asian peninsula
5. Actress MacGraw
6. Kennel sound
7. Thoroughfares: abbr.
8. Corn units
9. Kind of bath
10. City oases
11. Summer drink
19. Haw's partner
21. Pipe bend
22. Had a bite
23. Shade of green
24. Unusual
25. Directions units
29. Drat, e.g.
31. Calgary's province
32. "Finian's ____"
33. Sprite
34. On one's way
35. Golfer Snead
36. Holler
37. Oak-to-be
38. Judicial wear
40. Fragrant compound
42. Actor Rip
44. Fish eggs
46. Hunt successfully
47. Keats poem
49. Wonder
50. Mr. Danson

PUZZLE 547

ACROSS
1. Dole out
5. Hole in the wall
8. Damage
11. Related
12. Opera star
13. Raw mineral
14. Care for
15. Finished
16. Be unwell
17. Goad
19. Nougat, e.g.
21. Music-loving snake
24. Cask
25. Strange
26. Cherished one
30. Moral offense
31. Carefree
32. Be in debt
33. Two-year-old
36. Frequently
38. Sup
39. On the qui vive
40. Pass out
43. Information
45. Pot top
46. Spirit
48. Catches
52. Commotion
53. Salamander
54. Pesky insect
55. Solidify
56. Decade
57. Whirlpool

DOWN
1. Pad
2. Supply a lack
3. Can
4. Last
5. Donate
6. Blvd.
7. Package
8. Sound of pain
9. Desertlike
10. Depend
12. Follow closely
18. Sprinted
20. Past
21. Throw
22. Hodgepodge
23. Real fix
24. Locker
26. Saloon
27. Ballot
28. Jug
29. Hollow
31. Acquire
34. Study
35. Hidden
36. Cereal grain
37. Projecting rim
40. Banner
41. Helper
42. Fan's favorite
43. Sunrise
44. Picnic pest
47. Confederate general
49. As well as
50. Naughty
51. Pig's home

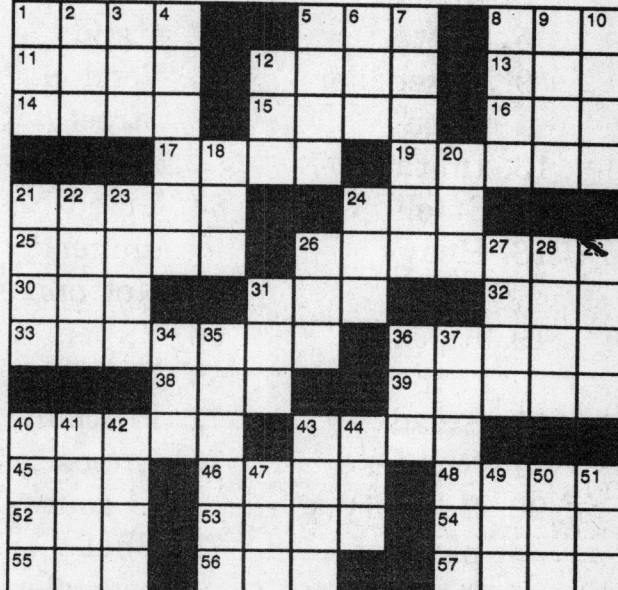

PUZZLE 548

ACROSS
1. Dutch cheese
5. Ampersand
8. Elephant boy of film
12. Western monster
13. ___ Grande
14. Cupid
15. Narrow valley
16. Building extension
17. Wretched
18. Hear
20. Dress fold
22. School VIP
24. Horse
27. Slap
28. Loiter
31. Unadulterated
32. Transgression
33. Nibble
34. Ripen
35. ___ Aviv
36. Miserable dwelling
37. Bird
39. Reel
41. Different
44. Concrete piece
45. Lyricist Gershwin
47. John-Boy's sister
49. Sharpen
50. Umpire's call
51. Singing voice
52. Widemouthed jug
53. Utmost degree
54. Feat

DOWN
1. ___ cream
2. Pickle type
3. On the sheltered side
4. Sea cow
5. Contest site
6. Nothing
7. "Boy on a ___"
8. Cut
9. "Aida" highlight
10. Lightning stroke
11. Manipulate
19. Barber or Buttons
21. Lease
23. Cool
24. Resort
25. Harbor craft
26. Before, to a poet
28. Actress Ullmann
29. Had brunch
30. Set
32. Pacific Ocean mammal
33. Type of whale
35. Duo
36. Torrid
37. Serious
38. Reluctant
39. Like a snail
40. Sheet of glass
42. Author Gardner
43. Baptism, for one
44. Haggard novel
46. Well-worn groove
48. Show assent

PUZZLE 549

ACROSS

1. Become weary
5. Butte
9. Baseballer Rose
13. Imitated
17. Smell
18. Heavy metal
19. Russian tsar
20. Stead
21. Not far
22. Beautify a piece of land
24. Soften
25. Car home
27. Observed
28. Ambassador's place
30. Orderly
32. Use a catamaran
34. Japanese currency
35. Dresses a wound
39. Burn mark
41. Stories
45. Great anger
46. Domain
48. Trade
50. Kind of soda
51. Baby foxes
53. Post
55. Father
57. Sprinted
58. Artist's stand
60. Tendon
62. Street with no exit
64. Go to dinner
66. Not once
68. Expert
69. Tremble
73. Postpone
75. Opposite of south
79. Boat propeller
80. Highbrow
82. Brink
83. Actress Winningham
84. Newton ingredients
86. Comet feature
88. Burns
91. Look upon
92. Pick up the check
94. Fingertip feature
96. Doused
98. Uno, ____, tres, . . .
100. Mix
102. Shadowbox
103. Custodians
107. Journey
109. "Carmen" and "Aida", e.g.
113. Medicinal lily
114. Wifeys or mamas
117. Motivator Carnegie
118. Tie fabrics
119. Rake
120. Fencing weapon
121. Neighbor of Turkey
122. Encounter
123. Water jug
124. Hollow grass
125. Watch over

DOWN

1. Chinese association
2. Notion
3. Simba's sound
4. Chore
5. Distance traveled
6. Generation
7. Male offspring
8. South American mountains
9. Outdoor meals
10. Topsy's playmate
11. Masking or adhesive
12. Foe
13. Yearbook
14. Pastries
15. Slippery fish
16. Obligation
23. Red, Yellow, and Black
26. Toothed wheel
29. Gamble
31. Sports groups
33. Edicts
35. Two-wheeler
36. Formal solo
37. Fishing boat items
38. Destroyed
40. Foray
42. Legends
43. Dash
44. Beach-castle material
47. Dug out ore
49. Type of school
52. Kernel
54. River embankment
56. Make money
59. Boys
61. Fuses together
63. Condemn

65. Canvas shelter
67. Stormed
69. Plush
70. Scalp growth
71. Strong desire
72. Horse color
74. Century units
76. Foolhardy
77. Maple, e.g.
78. Obey
81. Prejudice
85. Unhappiest
87. Smaller
89. Refreshed by rest
90. Break suddenly
93. Foot end
95. Italian coin, once
97. Recognition
99. Sleep noise
101. Horseman
103. Heat-up
104. Away from the wind
105. Strong cord
106. Moving with little speed
108. Water main
110. Unique
111. Astronaut Shepard
112. Ship
115. Merited
116. Wide shoe size

PUZZLE 550

ACROSS

1. Settled a debt
5. Cunning
8. Metal sources
12. Piece of farmland
13. ____ is me!
14. Aviation prefix
15. If the ____ fits . . .
16. Watched
18. "Love Me ____"
20. Tiny
21. To the bitter ____
22. Actor Hardwicke
25. Lawn-mower part
28. Golfer's goal
29. Depot: abbr.
30. Actor Torn
31. Risk
32. Roman loan
33. Elec. unit
34. Label
35. Confuse
37. Seesaw
39. Jungle swinger?
40. Airport abbr.
41. Noble mounts
45. Cellar
49. Scheme
50. Territory
51. Actress Grant
52. Republic of Ireland
53. Screen ____
54. Pro
55. Turnpike incline

DOWN

1. Bygone
2. Need a rubdown
3. Press
4. Gave title to
5. Zorro's tool
6. Tennis shot
7. Affirmative
8. Paddled
9. Flip-flopped
10. Before, to a bard
11. Turf
17. Water jug
19. Chemical suffix
22. Felix, e.g.
23. Type type: abbr.
24. Mind
25. Unruly child
26. Key ____ pie
27. Satisfies
28. Al Bundy's wife
31. Saloon
34. Condition
35. Likely
36. More profound
38. Trick or ____
39. Fall flower
42. Director Kazan
43. Frosh's residence
44. ____ on the gas
45. Baseball club
46. "You ____ My Sunshine"
47. Sprite
48. New: pref.

PUZZLE 551

ACROSS

1. Flit about socially
4. ____ de deux
7. Space
10. Sheep mothers
12. Friend: Fr.
13. Tag ____
14. Net
15. "____ Van Winkle"
16. Dock
17. Bone-dry
19. Musical sound
20. Farm units
22. In favor of
23. Applauds
24. Green-eyed
28. Stable morsel
29. Spotless
31. Santa ____
32. Small, flaky bread
34. Twig
36. Guided
37. Second's preceder
38. Goad
40. Tardy
41. Sight
42. Heel
43. Aquatic animal
47. Spirit
48. Highest card
49. Rescue
50. Actor Danson
51. Danger color
52. Large rodent

DOWN

1. Precious stone
2. Reverence
3. ____ Moines
4. Capital of France
5. Surrounded by
6. Small drink
7. Acquire
8. Away from the wind
9. For each
11. Keen
13. Bobbin
18. Carried to safety
19. Act of passing through
20. Jai ____
21. Felines
22. Pod vegetable
23. Corn holder
24. Fast plane
25. Paddles
26. Component part
27. Droop
30. Box top
33. Circus comic
35. Iron
37. Bleached
38. Heap
39. ____ between the lines
40. "Arsenic and Old ____"
41. Puppy doc
42. Jalopy
44. Lend an ____
45. A Gardner
46. Allow

453

PUZZLE 552

• NEWS THAT FITS •

ACROSS

1. Cheer-leader's cry
4. Golf score
7. Damage
10. Before, in verse
11. "Where the Boys ___"
12. Cowgirl Evans
13. "Help wanted," e.g.
16. Lyric poem
17. Donna or Rex
18. Busy as a ___
21. "___ Miserables"
23. Fashion of the moment
24. Elderly
25. 102, to the Romans
27. Abel's brother
29. To's partner
32. Actress MacGraw
33. Columnist Landers
34. Counselor
38. Knock smartly
39. Tit for ___
40. Road map abbr.
41. "Norma ___"
42. Three, in Italy
43. Stop ___ dime
44. Director Preminger
46. Colorado ski resort
48. ___ Speed-wagon (rock band)
49. Baseballer Mel ___
50. Objects of worship
53. Let fall
54. Crazy ___ loon
56. Short sleep
57. Citrus beverage
60. Encountered
61. Pub brew
64. "My ___ Sal"
65. Gossip's delight
67. Opposite of WNW
68. Ramble in search of fun
69. Sullivan and Asner
70. Rower's propellers
71. Title of respect
72. Epoch
73. Rita Hayworth's husband Khan
74. Donkey
76. Director Peckinpah
77. ___ and pepper
79. "Hee ___"
81. Wedding announce-ment sites
86. Leave out
87. Have lunch
88. Actress Gabor
89. Marry
90. Doctor's group: abbr.
91. Ready, ___, go!

DOWN

1. ___ room (family's fun place)
2. Woody Guthrie's son
3. Newspaper's eye-catcher
4. ___ de deux (dance for two)
5. Jackie O's second
6. Football official
7. Fabricated
8. "When I was ___"
9. Comedian Skelton
12. Legal document
14. Observe
15. Native of Teheran
18. Small ship
19. Jazz's Fitzgerald
20. Periodical's opinions
22. Mark of a wound
23. "___ Easy Pieces"
25. Humorous drawings
26. Insertion word
28. Nabokov heroine
29. Big-news locales
30. Sprinted
31. WWII or-ganization: abbr.
35. Depot: abbr.
36. Hesitation sounds

PUZZLE 552

37. Clark Kent, e.g.
45. Actor Knight
47. Ike's field of command: abbr.
51. Varnish ingredient
52. Health resort
53. Actor Arnaz
54. Years of life
55. Melancholy
57. An apple ____ . . .
58. Women's patriotic group: abbr.
59. "Born Free" lioness
60. Telegrams, e.g.
62. "Doctor Zhivago" heroine
63. Dutch cheese
66. Actor Nick ____
73. Landed
75. ____ Na Na
77. Any
78. Sulfuric or prussic
80. "____ Only Just Begun"
81. Plant
82. Earl Grey, e.g.
83. Sweet potato
84. School group: abbr.
85. Used a chair

455

PUZZLE 553

ACROSS
1. Miff
5. Source of energy
9. Spider's creation
12. A long way off
13. Pop
14. Musical sense
15. Extinct bird
16. Maintain
18. Reel
20. Professor's choice in blazer?
21. Frigid
24. Honey producer
25. Incite
26. Garnish
30. Unruly crowd
31. Actor Aykroyd
32. Peak on Crete
33. Shea ____
36. Paramour
38. Also
39. Rely
40. Awry
43. Fence opening
44. Single man
46. Captures
50. Before
51. Penny
52. Work on copy
53. Conducted
54. Ball holders
55. Contradict

DOWN
1. Owned
2. Alien spacecraft?
3. Trendy movement
4. Ices a cake
5. Tomato jelly
6. Actor Rip
7. Poem
8. Conquer
9. "____ off to see the wizard . . ."
10. Roof overhang
11. Raised dogs
17. Mas that baa
19. Pizza ____
21. Crest
22. Base
23. Caribbean country
24. Outlaw
26. Actress Dawber
27. "Saturday Night ____"
28. Utopia
29. Football distance
31. Defective bomb
34. Smidgen
35. Bug
36. Tennis call
37. Unlocked
39. Pub game
40. Cain's brother
41. "The Old Gray ____"
42. Like some tea
43. Left
45. Confederate general
47. Lime beverage
48. Storage box
49. Porky's pad

CRISS-CROSSWORD

The answer words for Criss-Crossword are entered diagonally, reading downward, from upper left to lower right or from upper right to lower left. We have entered the words BALD and GAL as examples.

TO THE RIGHT

1. Hairless
2. Styling goo
3. Mustang, e.g.
4. Popcorn seasoning
5. Largest planet
6. Lone Star State
7. Tree fluid
9. Hawaiian garland
11. At no time
12. Caution-light color
14. Knock loudly
16. Begin again
17. Winged mammal
19. Dimples
20. Used to be
22. Bank clerks
24. Crazy
26. Royal rule
28. Scarlet
31. Fence door
32. Cain's father
33. ____ on your life!
35. Catch

TO THE LEFT

2. "My ____ Sal"
3. Actress Hayes
4. Warrior
5. Wide-mouthed bottle
6. Oklahoma city
7. Ninth month
8. Cab
10. Singer Boone
13. Seamstress
15. Large tub
16. Drive back
18. Prohibit
19. Soap
21. ____ after (pursued)
23. Unfamiliar
25. Horror actor Chaney Jr.
27. Tired
29. Car type
30. Weaver's machine
34. ____ a boy!
36. Small quantity

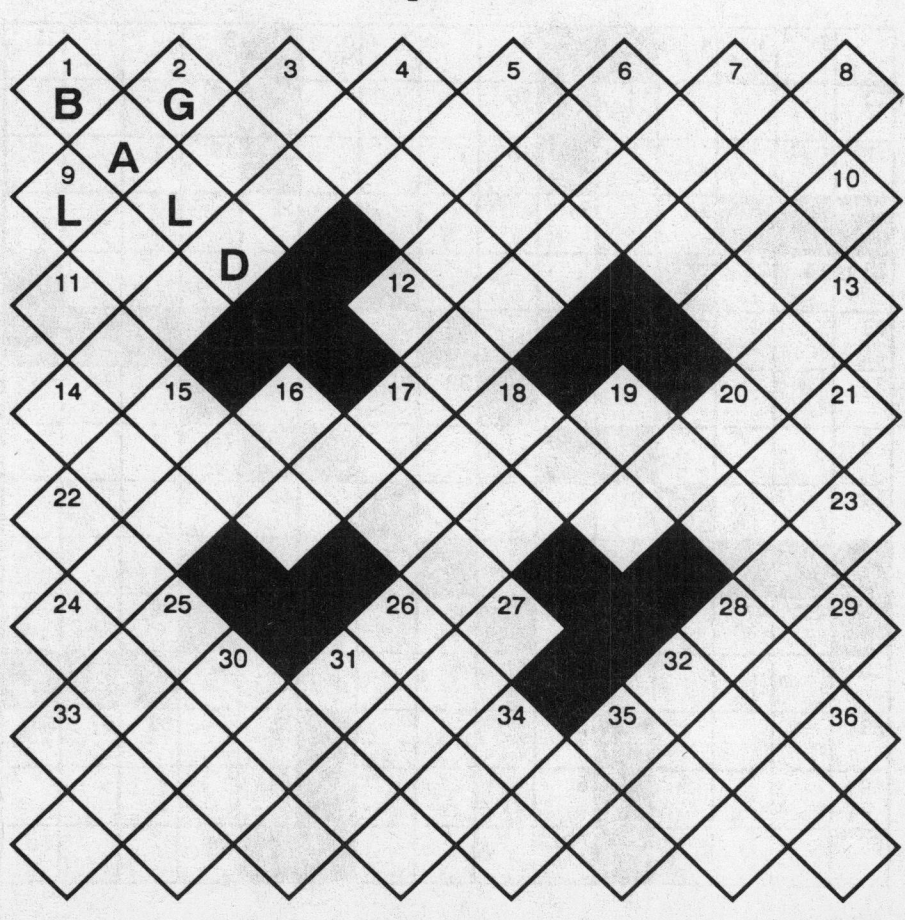

457

PUZZLE 555

ACROSS
1. Vagrant
5. ____ Cod
9. Papas
13. Use
15. Nameless: abbr.
16. Elliptical
17. Heavenly food
18. Window part
19. Mrs. Chaplin
20. "Dallas" spinoff
23. Tabby, e.g.
26. Broad valley
27. All set
28. Sports player
30. Matured
31. Plaits
32. Engendered
33. Conservative's foe: abbr.
36. Tie up
37. Portable bed
38. Mosaic piece
39. Tibetan ox
40. Hammer part
42. Gum arabic tree
44. Pork cut
45. Mideast sea
46. Sacred song
48. Still sleeping
49. Football scores: abbr.
50. California city
53. Jerky joint
54. Author Wiesel
55. Build
59. First garden
60. Singer Diana ____
61. Tennis shot
62. Section
63. Witnesses
64. Spoke

DOWN
1. Bad actor
2. Eggs
3. Forbid
4. Piggy's noise
5. Chess move
6. Licorice-tasting seed
7. Gallup product
8. Make bigger
9. Trinket
10. Go around
11. Actor Glover
12. Smelting waste
14. Alit
21. Stable morsels
22. Lack
23. Taxi driver
24. Skylit courtyards
25. Express gratitude to
29. Jar top
30. Columnist Buchwald
32. Boat front
33. Lawful
34. Homeric work
35. Pinto and navy
37. Is able to
38. Small flap
40. Soft drink flavor
41. ____ up (loosens up)
42. Zone
43. Core groups
44. Present but dormant
45. Convent head
46. Ling-Ling, e.g.
47. Derisive smile
48. Get up
50. Round farm basket
51. ____ vera
52. War god
56. Historic time
57. 106, to Livy
58. Newsman Koppel

PUZZLE 556

ACROSS
1. Twinge
5. Sear
9. Shut noisily
13. Toward the sheltered side
14. Infrequent
15. Vista
16. Donate
17. Emanation
18. Throw away
19. Makes do
20. Tire mishap
21. Map overlay
22. Build
24. Gape
26. Sailor's yes
28. Appalled
33. Baffle
37. Dressed
40. African lily
41. Comfort
42. Orange orchard
43. Key ___ pie
44. Waste allowance
45. Car
46. Writes down
47. Brook
49. Court
51. Wheat ___
54. Top-notch
58. Selected
62. Seep
64. Rant
66. Blackbird
67. Roast cooker
68. Again
69. Watchful
70. Location
71. Fork prong
72. Only
73. Eye drop
74. Has food

DOWN
1. Book leaf
2. Similar
3. At no time
4. Silly birds
5. Sly
6. Pull
7. Attire
8. Lariat
9. Look through
10. Fewer
11. Feed the kitty
12. Measure up to
15. Playground item
23. Baseball ___
25. Walk through water
27. Tan
29. Circle of light
30. Got down
31. Several
32. Summer shirts
33. Matched groups
34. Sour
35. ___-friendly
36. Distribute
38. Land parcel
39. Declare
42. Sport
46. Neither's partner
48. Actor's go-between
50. Kitchen gadget
52. Perch
53. Picture show
55. Very angry
56. Craze
57. Incident
58. Stuff
59. Robust
60. "___ the Rainbow"
61. Like a desert
63. Greek Z
65. Meadow mamas

PUZZLE 557

ACROSS
1. Distant
4. Identical
8. As well
12. Become older
13. Entreaty
14. Planted
15. Dickens or Hardy
17. Go with the wind
18. Wealthy
19. Comedian Durante
20. Formal argument
23. ____ Vegas
24. Sherbets
25. Slow reptiles
29. That woman
30. Boasts
32. "____ Maria"
33. Hold within
35. Kitchen cooker
36. Provide with weaponry
37. In the direction of
39. Milky gems
42. Green citrus fruit
43. Hay package
44. Lingerie garment
48. Unlock
49. Single entity
50. Actress/singer Doris ____
51. Orient
52. Garden plots
53. Pigment

DOWN
1. Admirer
2. "Long, long ____ . . ."
3. Race in neutral
4. Divide
5. "____ in Wonderland"
6. Screen
7. Consume
8. Help
9. Fertile soil
10. Do the backstroke, e.g.
11. Sole
16. Historic periods
19. Causes to shake
20. Phonograph record
21. Sound re-verberation
22. Has-____ (former star)
23. Pull laboriously
25. Light brown
26. Molten rock
27. At any time
28. Transmit
30. Taverns
31. Outer edge
34. Natural ability
35. Is in debt
37. Fainthearted
38. Leaves out
39. Reed instrument
40. Mama's hubby
41. Cousins of beer
42. Highway division
44. Baby bear
45. Out of the ordinary
46. "Now I ____ me down . . ."
47. Needle hole

ACROSS

1. ____ Wednesday
4. Fedora
7. Best friend
10. Bellow
12. Kimono sash
13. A few
14. Yarn
15. Fisherman's trap
16. Bread spread
17. Juliet's lover
19. Singer Neville
21. Adjust
23. Craze
26. Dessert choice
27. Knock sharply
30. Once ____ a time . . .
31. Circle part
32. Hideout
33. Mountain ____
34. Self-esteem
35. Actor John ____ ("Planes, Trains, & Automobiles")
36. " . . . over the ____ "
38. Athletic game
40. Noble
43. Thick slice
44. Of all: Scottish
46. English school
48. Cavity
49. Summer color
50. Type of wine
51. Lamb's mom
52. Football player
53. Kitten sound

DOWN

1. Actor Carney
2. Take to the air
3. Angel's headdress
4. Integrity
5. Honest ____
6. Ill-fated ship
7. Prince Charles's game
8. Prayer ending
9. Writer Tolstoy
11. Continue
13. A sight for ____ eyes
18. Period of note
20. Years of life
22. Chef's garment
23. Sludge
24. Mimic
25. At once
27. Dashed
28. Abet
29. Jimmy
31. Arouse
32. Barrister
34. Auricle
35. Talk fondly
36. Judge's garb
37. Trademark
38. Poky
39. "____ Rider" (Eastwood film)
41. Tiny particle
42. Misplace
43. Haggard heroine
45. Martin ____ Buren
47. Recent

PUZZLE 559

ACROSS

1. Stretch over
5. Exhibits
10. Black suit
12. Red suit
14. Become caked
15. All
16. Crude mineral
17. Sees
19. Hosiery color
20. Cages
22. "Willard" subject
23. Sunday seats
24. Less fresh
26. Not as good
27. Youngster
28. Pen ____
29. Scatter
32. Fondle
35. Chops weeds
36. Guy's date
37. From ____ to stern
39. ____ of this world
40. Window squares
42. Have unpaid bills
43. Of an Indian group
45. Gazes fixedly
47. Calm
48. Small candles
49. Dimples
50. Sleeping places

DOWN

1. 300 spoilers
2. Part of PTA
3. Do sums
4. Require
5. Piece of paper
6. Coop residents
7. Cereal grain
8. Author
9. Soda sippers
10. Close up ____
11. Trapped
13. Horse ____
18. Paving liquid
21. Reductions
23. Fishing rods
25. Long arm of the ____
26. Armed conflict
28. Faintest in color
29. Inoculations
30. Took a guided trip
31. Go on a pension
32. Catch as catch ____
33. Warehoused
34. City drains
36. Storm winds
38. Disorder
40. Breathe heavily
41. ____ in the back
44. Actor Vereen
46. Chimpanzee

PUZZLE 560

ACROSS

1. V
5. Fawn's mother
8. Fail
12. Think tank product
13. Country hotel
14. Fencing tool
15. Milwaukee product
16. Harshest
18. Cleave
20. Bread bakers
21. Writer Levin
22. Nevertheless
23. Filters
27. Elbow poke
30. Stream
31. London brew
33. "A ____ of Two Cities"
34. King Kong, e.g.
35. Held in regard
37. ____ soup (thick fog)
40. Vixen
41. Bucolic
43. Sinned
46. Traitor
48. Australian birds
50. Poetic works
51. Astonishment
52. "West ____ Story"
53. Mix, as a salad
54. Comedian Skelton
55. Goulash

DOWN

1. Cock and bull story
2. March 15
3. Al Gore, e.g.
4. Hitherto
5. Aloof
6. "A Chorus Line" song
7. Agent
8. Visorless cap
9. Ready for business
10. Jam
11. Gamble
17. Dusk
19. Dander
23. Spring
24. Policeman
25. Bemoan
26. Neptune's kingdom
27. Jolt
28. Stout
29. ____-and-breakfast
32. Clung
33. Fierce female feline
36. Tarnish
37. News medium
38. Hearing organ
39. Sacrifice table
41. Make over
42. Applies
44. Radiate
45. Type of ranch
46. Speck
47. Meadow mama
49. Take stitches

PUZZLE 561

BATTLESHIPS

The diagram below represents the sea which contains a crossword puzzle—the answer words are Battleships. The letter-number combination to the left of each clue indicates the location in the diagram where a Battleship has been "hit" (for example, A8 is in the first row, eighth column). A "hit" is any one of the letters in the answer word. Using this clue you must determine the exact location of each answer and whether it is an across or a down word. Fill in black squares to separate words as in a regular crossword. We have filled in the first two answers for you.

A3 Subsequently	D13 Source of wisdom	H4 Actor Thicke
A3 Talon	D14 Convent room	H7 Brown ermine
A7 Single step	E1 Packing box	H9 Lofty goals
A9 Frozen water	E4 Wandering	H13 Chamber music group
A14 Fourth of a bushel	E11 Flowering shrub	H13 Son of Loki
B2 Prevalent	E12 Royal residence	I1 Coin opening
B2 Passenger ship	F6 Told tales	I2 Choose
B8 Seraph	F6 Pixie	I8 Relieve
B10 Puerto Rico city	F11 Engrossed	I13 Used a broom
B12 Vicinity	F14 Relies	I14 Faucet leak
B15 "Kiss Me ___"	F15 Highlander	J3 Fixed routine
C1 Contribute a share	G4 Waste metal	J7 Wavers precariously
C4 Minuscule	G5 Small cut	J12 Taunt
C7 Amphibian	G8 Occurrence	J12 H.H. Munro
C9 Stormed	G8 Tenn. athlete	K5 Sends out
C13 Writer Ambler	G10 Fragrant	K5 Truck trailer
C15 Merry tune	G15 Circle segment	K7 Abhor
D2 Golfer's peg	H1 Diving bird	K12 Vitamin C source
D5 Faction	H2 Contend	K14 Extreme
		L3 Hour and minute
		L4 Acquire
		L10 Diplomacy
		L11 Revue scene
		L14 Totality
		M2 Malay dagger
		M6 Rain lightly
		M6 Rascal
		M10 Give consent
		M12 Tavern
		M13 Division word
		M15 Sailboat
		N1 Frozen dew
		N1 Gumbo
		N7 Convent dweller
		N8 Begin
		N8 Tempted
		N9 Maintain
		N15 Roman emperor
		O2 Matured
		O2 Ship's jail
		O4 Ragged
		O9 ___ nous
		O12 Tide of least height
		O13 Hindu queen

	1	2	3	4	5	6	7	8	9	10	11	12	13	14	15
A	C	L	A	W	■										
B			F												
C			T												
D			E												
E			R												
F			■												
G															
H															
I															
J															
K															
L															
M															
N															
O															

464

PUZZLE 562

ACROSS
1. Singer Redding
5. Health resort
8. Component
12. Visage
13. Auricle
14. Knot
15. Regular
17. Soft drink
18. Vase
19. Mangle
21. Circle parts
24. Remote
25. Draft animals
26. Road surface
30. Comedian Olsen
31. Earthenware jar
32. Yoko ____
33. Dealer
35. Mexican food
36. Draw the ____
37. More adorable
38. Nantucket, e.g.
41. Producer Peters
42. B-52's song
43. Flood
48. Choir singer
49. Sargasso ____
50. Frenzy
51. ____-do-well
52. Female fowl
53. Length times width

DOWN
1. Amiss
2. Roofing liquid
3. Frost
4. Spangle
5. Witnessed
6. Piping god
7. Remnant
8. Open, as champagne
9. "High ____"
10. Dormant
11. Salty drop
16. Psychic Geller
20. Billiards need
21. Alcove
22. Pivot
23. Stag
24. Solitary
26. Shake
27. Exactly
28. Fairy-tale starter
29. Inferior
31. Asian dynasty
34. Noise
35. Treeless plain
37. Against
38. Persia, today
39. Dover or lemon
40. Overdue
41. San ____
44. Betty Ford, ____ Bloomer
45. Cushion or pocket
46. Foot part
47. Greek letter

PUZZLE 563

ACROSS
1. Frolic
5. Power source
9. Lily or knee
12. Ore vein
13. Diva Ponselle
14. Hasten
15. Arizona city
16. Midge
17. Tavern
18. Paris suburb
20. Jury's verdict
22. Holland or Lincoln
24. Be human
25. Financier Onassis
26. Coagulate
28. Art stand
32. Gamble
34. Vast amount
36. Pianist Peter ____
37. Campfire residue
39. Flop
41. Excavate
42. Station letters
44. Tile game piece
46. TV PI
49. Article
50. Hockey great
51. Plant part
53. Campus figure
56. "Arabian Nights" name
57. Bond's adversary
58. Swenson of "Benson"
59. Kindergarten attendee
60. "____ of the Dragon"
61. Upon

DOWN
1. Strand of yarn
2. Baseball's Gehrig
3. Rebuke
4. Desire
5. Some patterned socks
6. Heavy weight
7. Orange variety
8. Age
9. Iceman Esposito
10. "____ Misbehavin' "
11. Disavow
19. Gam
21. Tehran's land
22. Scarlett's home
23. Author Leon ____
27. ____ Zeppelin
29. Sludge
30. Actress Moran
31. Emblem
33. Eager
35. Accountant
38. Strong
40. Period
43. Love, in Roma
45. Magazine and radio
46. Castle feature
47. Singer Guthrie
48. Moxie
52. Stop ____ dime
54. Gone by
55. Snooze

PUZZLE 564

ACROSS
1. Woodland abode
6. Annoy
9. Martini garnish
10. New York canal
11. Dishes
12. Time-consuming
13. Subways' kin
14. Marionette controllers
16. Game fish
18. Turf
19. I'm all ____!
21. Superlative
24. Knock
26. Like a lawn at dawn
28. Marches in review
32. Golf implement
33. Bakery mainstay
34. Emulates Hans Brinker
36. Show the way
37. Weary
38. "To ____ is human . . ."
39. Pigpens

DOWN
1. Lassie, e.g.
2. 49th state
3. Jot
4. Actor Burl
5. They're for the birds
6. Steel metal
7. Wedding item
8. Beer barrels
10. Omitted phonetically
11. Vim
15. Mr. Reiner
17. Task
20. Melancholy
22. Couch
23. Certain woolens
25. Bothers
27. ____ sirree!
28. Vaulter's need
29. Declare
30. Admiral or echelon
31. Comic routine
35. Mr. Onassis

PUZZLE 565

ACROSS
1. ____ the line (behave)
4. Went by SST
8. Highway approach
12. Samovar
13. Enthusiastic review
14. Cleveland's lake
15. Has faith
17. River deposit
18. Neck of the woods
19. Court events
21. Canine sounds
23. Chief
24. Sets up
25. Attire
29. Summer drink
30. Rural buildings
31. Bard's before
32. Body talk
34. Lowdown sort
35. Goals
36. Archetype
37. Invent
40. It's a ____!
41. Certain paintings
42. Tidy quality
46. Empty
47. Otherwise
48. Small drink
49. Heavy metal
50. Tears
51. Porker's home

DOWN
1. Vat
2. Mined find
3. Blows up
4. Liberates
5. Molten rock
6. Night prior
7. Horse operas
8. Live
9. Opera highlight
10. Flour source
11. Favorites
16. Angers
20. Ewes' mates
21. Boast
22. Military sidekick
23. Jack rabbits
25. Rose tender
26. Unnecessary
27. Maple, e.g.
28. Convince
30. Baseball maneuver
33. Kidded
34. ____ of plenty
36. Little bits
37. Wind
38. Go on horseback
39. Singer Fitzgerald
40. Pant
43. Actor Wallach
44. Pose
45. Secret agent

PUZZLE 566

ACROSS
1. Edge of an opening
4. Derby
7. Levy
11. Actress Gardner
12. Steep
13. Margarine
14. Marsupial
16. Moistens
17. Whole
18. Function
20. Headed
21. Yard feature
25. Ringlet
28. Timid
29. "Much ____ About Nothing"
30. Yoko ____
31. Stays inactive
33. Seine
34. Actor Hutton
35. Make a mistake
36. Window part
37. Director Spielberg
39. School organization: abbr.
41. Words at a wedding
42. Heart arteries
46. Pillar
49. Chewy candy
51. Region
52. Regimen
53. Period of history
54. Bargain
55. Comedian Caesar
56. Collection of like things

DOWN
1. ____ Ontario
2. Tennis star Lendl
3. Breathe heavily
4. Employed
5. In the past
6. Idea
7. Steeple
8. Bullfighter's cry
9. Allow
10. ____ Alamos
12. Rabbit
15. Aquatic respiratory organ
19. States
22. Actor Andrews
23. Biblical paradise
24. Written message
25. Beds
26. Military group
27. Italian city
28. Title of respect
31. Unwanted plant
32. Traitor Benedict et al.
36. Young salmon
38. Healthy
39. Walked back and forth
40. Horn sound
43. Knots
44. Land measure
45. Chair
46. Cushion
47. Valuable mineral
48. Caspian, e.g.
50. Three, in Roman numerals

PUZZLE 567

ACROSS
1. Love: Latin
5. Dejected
8. Pitcher
12. Representative
14. Clock part
15. Raised
16. Discharge
17. Dutch commune
18. Helpful
20. Heavenly bodies
23. Shoo!
24. Serf
25. Withdraw
28. Make lace
29. Ranted
30. Gave permission to
32. Proved wrong
34. Tender
35. Norse god
36. Play section
37. Record player
40. Ginger-flavored drink
41. Cavity
42. Appoint
47. Epochs
48. Taking as one's own
49. Slight impression
50. Bandleader Brown
51. Winter vehicle

DOWN
1. Fruit drink
2. Mr. Brooks
3. Spanish cheer
4. 1775 rider
5. Fill
6. Dined
7. Subtracted
8. Sapped of vigor
9. Foundling
10. Light tan
11. Spool
13. Wanders
19. Reddish-brown chalcedony
20. Place
21. Former Russian ruler
22. Poker stake
23. VII
25. Sane
26. Medicinal plant
27. Sea bird
29. Impolite
31. Golf need
33. Woods
34. Aromas
36. Slide
37. Lean-to
38. Ripped
39. Ardor
40. Old Testament book
43. Lyric poem
44. Be unwell
45. Foot part
46. Finish

PUZZLE 568

• WOODEN'T YOU LIKE TO KNOW •

ACROSS
1. Lively dances
5. Cook's measures: abbr.
9. "The ____ on Main Street"
13. Speak publicly
15. Suit to ____
16. ____ Alto (Azores volcano)
17. Sub's defense
18. "Me and My ____"
19. A weather's opposite
20. Motor
22. Brief musical finales
24. Goody-goody
25. Clove hitch, for one
26. Ship's upward curve
27. Entire
29. Compass point
31. Parent, lovingly
33. Perjuror
35. Unfavorable destiny
37. ____ Peace Prize
41. Bills and coins
43. Yes, captain!
44. Keep in the warehouse
45. Foot-leg connector
46. Ritzy
48. Easter meats
49. Course deviation
51. Consumer
53. "Norma ____"
54. French friend
57. Surf sound
59. Starring role
61. Monotonous cadence
63. Unites
66. Have memorized
67. Churl
69. Actress Keaton
70. Word written on the wall
71. Ms. Ferber
72. South Seas island
73. "East of ____"
74. Oriole home
75. Stitched

DOWN
1. Singer Feliciano
2. Steel ingredient
3. Dockside incline
4. Step
5. Label
6. Refuse to back down
7. Big name in Argentina
8. Infrequently
9. Minor quarrel
10. Tool handles
11. Earth's surface, largely
12. Art of verse, once
14. Bert's partner
21. Mild expletive
23. Short jackets
27. ____ mater
28. Pride leader
30. Cleansing bar
32. Closet dweller
34. Depend
36. Untidy condition
38. Chess, for one
39. Ms. Bombeck
40. ____ majeste
42. Long time
47. Steering wheel
50. Of a natural fabric
52. Donna and Willis
54. ____ no questions . . .
55. Dug for minerals
56. Hole ____
58. Electrical terminal
60. Operatic songs
62. Ms. Verdon
64. Ample, to Shakespeare
65. Madonna's ex-husband
68. Make lace

PUZZLE 569

KEEP ON MOVING

Your goal is to move from the outlined square to the asterisk. The outlined square has the number 2; therefore, you must move 2 squares north, south, east, west, or diagonally to another square. In the new square is a number; move that number of spaces north, south, east, west, or diagonally. Continue moving in this way to reach the asterisk.

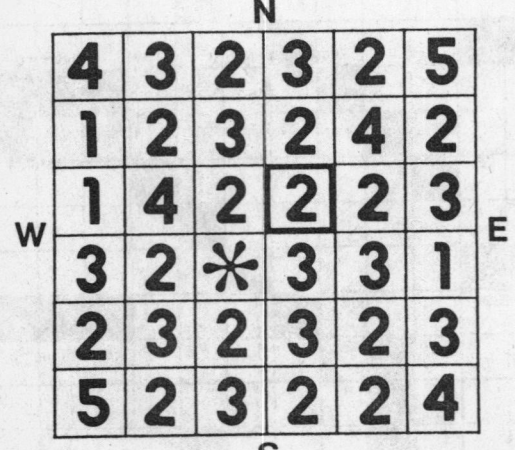

PUZZLE 570

ACROSS

1. Regarding: 2 wds.
5. Poisonous snakes
9. Field day
13. ____ En-lai
14. Camera term: hyph.
15. French friend
16. Snitch
18. Bakery product
19. "____ Loves Me"
20. God of love
21. Main course
23. City in Germany
24. Pop star
25. "Friends, ____, countrymen . . ."
28. Splinters
31. Make happy
32. Chutzpah
33. Sound loudly
35. Sensed
36. Cunning
37. Redneck
38. Door part
39. Finished
40. Lawyer's work
41. Pine leaves
43. Thorny shrubs
44. Bun
45. Have in mind
46. Down in the dumps
49. Pepper's mate
50. School group: abbr.
53. Toe the line
54. Bovine transports: 2 wds.
57. Singer Turner
58. Run-of-the-mill
59. Suit to ____: 2 wds.
60. Obedience-training command
61. Father
62. Phi ____ Kappa

DOWN

1. New Testament book
2. Former Iranian bigwig
3. Carry
4. Not at home
5. Bond car ____ Martin
6. Depots: abbr.
7. Eur. country: abbr.
8. Quickly
9. Silly person
10. Bradley or Sharif
11. Mud
12. Baseball's Rose
14. Feathery plants
17. Sierra ____
22. Turkey month: abbr.
23. Melee: 2 wds.
24. More sick
25. Umps' counterparts
26. Liquid part of fat
27. French director Louis
28. Socrates and Solomon
29. Ignite a spark
30. Abstinent
32. Judge's hammer
34. Make untidy
36. Hoards
40. Basket
42. Uno, ____, tres
43. Southern beauty
45. Dull surface
46. Flame pursuer
47. Theater award
48. Philosopher Descartes
49. Recipe verb
50. ____ de foie gras
51. Waste allowance
52. Floundering
55. "Exodus" hero
56. Vehicle for hire

CRACKERJACKS

PUZZLE 571

Find the answer to the riddle by filling in the center boxes with the letters needed to complete the words across and down. When you have filled in the Crackerjacks, the letters reading across the center boxes from left to right will spell out the riddle answer.

RIDDLE: How does one wait for the doctor?

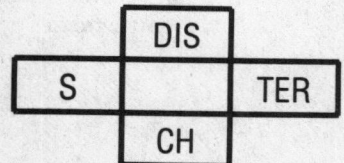

ANSWER: _____

469

PUZZLE 572

Stoplines

A heavy black line is used to indicate the end of a word rather than the usual black square. This is a type of diagram popular with our friends across the seas. Since there are no black squares, letters fill the entire diagram.

ACROSS

1. "____ the Ball"
6. Garbage
11. Stops the flow of
16. Suit maker
17. Deep hurt
18. Former Egyptian President
19. Made angry
20. Actress Mary
21. Gaze at fixedly
22. Put up
24. Beatles' Sgt.
27. Singer-actress Adams
29. Give off
32. Changes, as a hemline
37. Change, as a law
39. "Vic and ____"
40. "9 to 5" actress
41. Longs for
43. Before mark or wind
44. Symbols of folly
45. Prefix with mural
46. Aide: abbr.
48. Noted critic
51. French comic-actor Jacques
54. Street show
57. Allude (to)
60. "As You Like It" forest
62. Banal
63. Certain computer
64. Oven
65. Place for a carnation
66. One who idles
67. Film dog
69. Vigoda and Beame
71. Author Bram ("Dracula")
76. Actor John
79. Ms. Keaton
82. Kind of oil
84. Ancient age
85. Singer Bobby
86. Clearance event
87. Outlays
88. Ginger cookies
89. Horse sound
90. Thieves' talk

DOWN

1. "____ Grows in Brooklyn"
2. "State ____"
3. Ceramic piece
4. Chosen by vote
5. Lightning ____
6. Pitfall
7. Tear down: var.
8. Play division
9. Mall unit
10. TV's "____ Come the Brides"
11. Draft inits.
12. London gallery
13. Writer-educator Le Shan
14. U.S. spacecraft name
15. Silver, e.g.
23. Use a cassette recorder
25. "Columbo" star
26. Fast
28. Impression
30. Remus's father
31. Cantor and Lupino
33. Fall behind
34. Three to Luigi
35. Before hip or quartz
36. Snicker ____
38. Jelly variety
39. Begin
42. ____ Bernard
47. Head to Henri
48. Staggers
49. Of an historic time
50. Foreign: prefix
52. Mrs. Jeeter Lester and others
53. Examine
55. Citizen of Dhahran
56. Mature
58. Building extension
59. Caviar
60. Taj Mahal site
61. Poultry item
65. Alan and Cheryl
68. "____ of robins in her hair . . ."
70. Small cut
72. Throw lightly
73. Pearl Buck heroine
74. Always
75. Remainder
77. Secret society
78. Asian prefix
80. Parshegian
81. Naval rank: abbr.
83. Labor union inits.
84. Health farm

470

ACROSS

1. Leg part
5. Applies gently
9. "Do ____ others . . ."
13. Perjurer
14. Gladden
16. Crucifix
17. Small whirlpool
18. Gershwin musical
20. Enchanted
21. Walk restlessly
22. "____: The Great Robbery"
23. Candid
25. Jazzman Getz
26. Quaker
28. Roofing piece
31. Fruit skins
32. Town: Ger.
33. Elec. unit
35. Shakespeare villain
36. Foam
37. Songstress Adams
38. Singleton
39. Make amends
40. Fashion
41. Small earthquakes
43. Tarry
44. Rice wine
45. Chinese peninsula
46. Unsullied
49. Sewing machine inventor
50. Society girl
53. Lerner and Loewe musical
55. Quintet
56. "Now ____ me down . . ."
57. Musical bridge
58. Currier & ____
59. Mutations: abbr.
60. Beatles' "Back in the ____"
61. Talk wildly

DOWN

1. Musical symbol
2. Confidential assistant
3. Small sponge-cake
4. Small or fish
5. Florida city
6. Old cry of sorrow
7. Commanded
8. Pig's home
9. Entreating
10. Midday
11. Accepted
12. Betting quotations
15. Lenny Welch song
19. They were: Latin
21. Reviews unfavorably
24. Decorate again
25. Embarrass
26. Cold: Sp.
27. Laughing
28. Shocks
29. Coventry protester
30. Writer Zola
32. Fern seed
34. Equal
36. Furnace tenders
37. Sicilian volcano
39. Violinmaker
40. Indian stableman
42. Literary compositions
43. Attorney
45. ____ operandi
46. Roman 904
47. Tree frog
48. From a distance
49. Crones
51. Flat
52. Outdo
54. Romanian coin
55. Douglas, for one

• CHERCHEZ LA FEMME •

CRYPTO-LIMERICK

To read this humorous verse, you must first decode it as you would a regular cryptogram (other letters are substituted for the correct ones).

QEHNH GFAH VMP M ZGSFO DMF FMDHC OMBH,

VEG AEHNRPEHC QEH QEGSOEQ GT M PMRB.

EH YGMNCHC M ZMAEQ,

YSQ NHDMRFHC GF ERP AGQ,

HWAHJQ VEHF EH ESFO G'HN QEH NMRB.

PUZZLE 575

ACROSS

1. Vegetable dish
6. Weasel
11. Russian fighter jet
14. By oneself
15. Scanty
16. Anon
17. Courtois's discovery
18. The Sioux State: 2 wds.
20. English river
21. Trembles
23. Crescent-shaped
24. Music makers, for short
25. Facial feature
27. Ms. MacGraw
30. So be it!
31. Laughed
35. Egyptian deity
37. Bog bird
38. Hail!
39. Peeped
40. Judging place
41. Remain
42. "A Shropshire ____"
43. Explode
44. Charge
45. Biblical land
47. Gem weight
48. Floated
51. Miller or Sheridan
52. Swiss city
53. Costa Rican province
54. Blushed
56. Horseshoe projection
57. Beaten-egg beverage
58. Pismires
59. Wrap
60. Frighten
63. Rebounds
65. Immerse
68. English royal family member
71. Castle
73. Belonging to us
74. Calm
75. White poplar
76. Popular shirt
77. Ship sections
78. Runner

DOWN

1. Port ____
2. Century plant
3. Metal deposit
4. Blackbird
5. Animal abodes
6. Uttered
7. Weeds
8. Table scraps
9. Hardwood
10. Lewis or Mack
11. Gaze dreamily
12. Tiny bit
13. Growl
15. Twists
16. Polecat
19. Carroll heroine
22. Weather forecast
25. Map
26. Chase
27. Crawly creature
28. Southern general
29. Actress Jill
30. Imitated
31. Pie part
32. Church in Rome
33. Miss Gabor
34. "L.A. Law" star
36. Desert dweller
37. Pacific sea
40. Preserved
41. County ____
43. Foundations
44. Branch
45. Spoil
46. Greenback
47. Isn't able to
48. Oregon's capital
49. Conceit
50. Follow
52. American poet
53. Author Truman
55. Mends
56. Proofreading marks
59. Waterway
60. Locate visually
61. Solving guide
62. Swiss river
63. Yield
64. Counterfeit
65. Fight
66. Capri or Man
67. Equal
69. Inquire
70. Horse command
72. Japanese sash

ACROSS

1. Pesky insect
5. Birds' abodes
10. Swap
15. Book of maps
17. Notions
18. Circled high
19. "____, for me and my gal": 4 wds.
22. Actress Grant
23. ____ de France
24. Had dinner
25. Husband, to wife
28. Weightlifter's equipment
34. Boxing wonder
35. Derisive wit
36. Forbid
39. Sunbather's desire
40. Most primitive
42. Actress Gabor
43. Inquired
46. Cigar residue
49. Reclined
50. Ireland
52. Silent
54. Track events
56. Anwar
57. Sheep cry
58. Model again
59. Fruit drink
61. Health resort
62. Dampen once more
65. Become firm
66. To a large extent
73. Botch things up
74. House wing
75. More spooky
76. ____ de Janeiro
77. Combative
80. Not new, as a car
81. Actress Arden
84. Exist
85. Republican party initials
87. Wartime hit about a sailor: 2 wds.
97. Depends
98. Stranger
99. Kindled the fire again
100. Semiprecious stones
101. Cowboy's home
102. Neat

DOWN

1. Gangster's gun
2. To the ____ degree
3. Pub brew
4. Dining-room need
5. Nothing
6. Sullivan and Koch
7. Ocean
8. Paving material
9. Wind direction: abbr.
10. Sounds
11. Old cloth
12. Operatic solo
13. Fender-bender
14. Rim
16. Observe
18. Window ledge
20. Guided
21. Rouses
25. ____ Hari
26. Woe!
27. "Peter Pan" fairy
29. L.A. university: abbr.
30. Damage
31. Measure of cooling capacity: abbr.
32. Auction offer
33. Before, to a poet
36. Homes for carillons: 2 wds.
37. Actress Gardner
38. "No" vote
41. Russian news agency
44. Of an historic period
45. Cuts vegetables
47. Nova
48. One who conceals himself
51. Certain tide
53. Put on, as cargo
55. For men only
59. Grow old
60. Dolores ____ Rio
63. PA port
64. Walked on
67. Lease again
68. Conger
69. Onassis
70. Twitch
71. Zodiac sign
72. Many moons: abbr.
77. Little ones
78. Love god
79. Self
80. In a dither
81. Madrid's river
82. Al Gore, e.g.
83. Fitzgerald
86. "____ Town"
88. "____ Abner"
89. Make lace
90. Bullring cheer
91. Cookbook direction
92. "____ and Sympathy"
93. Hospital workers: abbr.
94. Inventor Whitney
95. Free from
96. Pigpen

PUZZLE 576

• YOU RANG? •

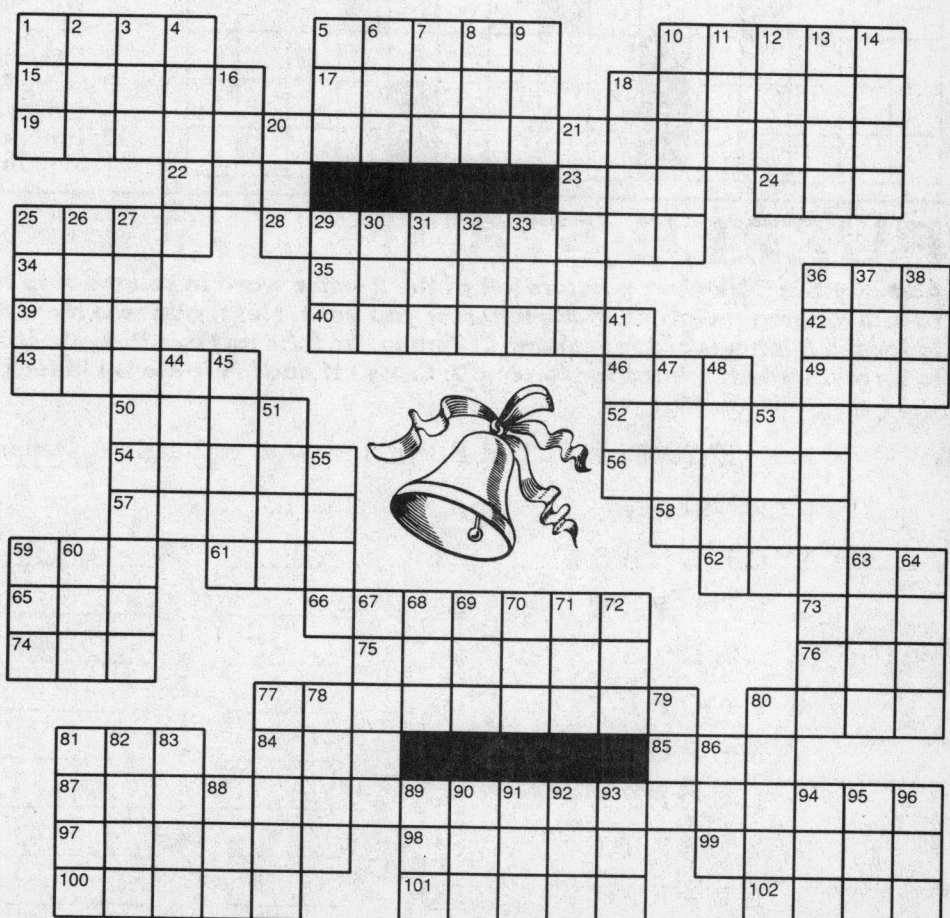

473

PUZZLE 577

ACROSS

1. Quartet member
5. TV's "____ Girl"
9. Geisha's land
14. Clever remark
15. Speed
16. Banishment
17. Hazy
19. Extend a subscription
20. Vital statistic
21. Kid
22. Sort
24. Obtain
25. Guy's date
26. Take to court
27. Linger
30. "I Am ____"
32. Pep
35. English horn
36. Melancholy
37. Singer Fats
39. Need
41. Part of FBI
42. Thoroughfare
43. Prohibit
44. Salad fish
45. Last English letter
46. Interweave
48. Cutting beam
49. Aim
50. Good buddy
51. Ems, for one
54. Tiny bit
55. Turkish topper
56. ____-been
59. Expansive
61. Garden bloom
64. Assumed name
65. Correct copy
66. One opposed
67. "Beauty and the ____"
68. N.Y. nine
69. Try out

DOWN

1. Greenish blue
2. Respiratory organ
3. Neap or spring
4. Unshut, poetically
5. Ordeal
6. Suspend
7. Wimbledon whistler
8. Irksomeness
9. Steve Martin film, with "The"
10. Hatchet
11. Metallic sound
12. Opposite aweather
13. Salamander
18. Ravel
23. Heavy
25. "How ____ Was My Valley"
26. Turf
27. Gem
28. Over
29. Wandered
30. Method
31. Signal approval
32. Illness source
33. Senseless
34. Grinding tooth
36. Sound system
38. Iron, e.g.
40. " . . . ay, there's the ____"
41. Craze
43. Make an offer
47. National song
48. Indolent
50. Stones
51. Thick piece
52. Ashen
53. Opera solo
54. Be witty
55. Dart about
56. Whet
57. New Testament book
58. Comic bit
60. Chat
62. "____ to a Nightingale"
63. Chapeau

[Crossword grid with numbered cells 1–69]

PUZZLE 578   PICK-ME-UPS

Add any two Pick-Me-Up letters left of the 2-letter word in column A to form a 4-letter word in column B, rearranging the order of the letters if you wish. Next, add two more Pick-Me-Up letters to column B to form a 6-letter word for column C. Finally, add the last two Pick-Me-Up letters to your column C word to form an 8-letter word for column D. Cross off each Pick-Me-Up letter as you use it.

EXAMPLE:	D E E P R T	Ad	Read	Depart	Departed
PICK-ME-UPS	A.	B.		C.	D.
1. C E H K L S	As	___		___	___
2. C D I M N O	Be	___		___	___
3. A E R S S T	Do	___		___	___
4. E N O P R T	Is	___		___	___
5. M E I O N T	Do	___		___	___
6. I G O N S Z	No	___		___	___
7. E N R S T U	Of	___		___	___
8. E L M R S T	Pa	___		___	___

PUZZLE 579

• INTERNATIONAL •

ACROSS

1. Czech
5. Wither
9. Celebrations
14. ____ prius
15. Learned Muslim
16. Few: prefix
17. Turkish official
18. Amatory precipice: 2 wds.
20. Sun-dried currant
21. Shed: hyph.
22. Book-catalog initials
23. Fuel
25. Tunney opponent
27. Stately
32. Bishopric
33. Biblical judge
34. Islamic god
36. Fury
40. Modern dwelling: 2 wds.
43. Canines
44. Ms. Osmond
45. Saloon
46. French pronoun
48. Those who don't give up
50. Asian state
54. Your, in Paris
55. Canadian province: abbr.
56. Truer
59. Halting
63. Connect surgically
65. Andy's pal
66. Author Jones
67. Dwellings: abbr.
68. Zeros
69. Loft
70. Trevino et al.
71. Printer's word

DOWN

1. Cookie
2. Peruvian city
3. Sale sign: 2 wds.
4. Shrew
5. Gets sick: 2 wds.
6. Burn plant
7. Singing star
8. Correct
9. Get ahead: 2 wds.
10. Total
11. Property charges
12. Marble
13. Mushy
19. Travel lanes: abbr.
24. Hateful
26. But, in Spain
27. Edna ____
28. French mountain
29. Upset
30. Turkish flag
31. To wash, in Madrid
35. Present
37. Dawn, in Cherbourg
38. Old ruler
39. Towel word
41. Yen
42. Smooth cartridge paper
47. Grain holder
49. "Treasure ____"
50. Australian marsupial
51. Kittiwake
52. Begin
53. Fissurelike
57. Slangy denial
58. Italian family
60. French friend
61. Gangster's girl
62. Existence
64. Oneself, in France

SPLIT PERSONALITIES   PUZZLE 580

The names of eight entertainers have been split into two-letter segments. The letters in each segment are in order, but the segments have been scrambled. For each number below, can you put the pieces together to identify the entertainers?

1. IE EL CH LI RI ON
2. KS RA FR AT AN IN
3. LL MS DY IA WI AN
4. AN RR OW BA YM IL
5. KA DA NE SE IL
6. RE EL SL VI EY SP
7. CA BE MP EN LL GL
8. AE KS AC ON MI LJ CH

475

PUZZLE 581

ACROSS
1. Dined
4. "My ___ Sal"
7. Boxer's move
10. Thyme or rosemary
12. Kind of card
14. Vendition
15. Ms. Boleyn
16. NBA structure
17. ___ of Knowledge
18. Postpones
20. Bare
22. Eggs
23. Court proceeding
24. Challenge
26. Vocal hesitations
27. Yield
30. Assistant
31. Ms. Gardner
32. Open ___!
34. Author Tolstoy
35. Young bluefish
37. Pull
38. Avenue
40. "Raven" poet
41. Baseball's Rose
42. Dried up
43. Mr. Skelton
44. Model's stance
45. Kind of snake
47. Pro
48. Made the grade
50. Sends a letter
53. Do KP work
54. Spooky
56. Wicked
58. Dark brews
59. Paris's river
60. Nerve network
61. Grassy tract
62. Bovine comment
63. Society-page word

DOWN
1. Eureka!
2. Incline
3. Sea eagle
4. Needlefish
5. TV's "You ___ There"
6. Reclusive types
7. Preserves preservers
8. Away from aweather
9. Quilting party
11. Ere
12. Scarlett's home
13. Judd Hirsch show
14. Fur pieces
19. Night prior
21. Raceway horse
23. Woodsman
24. Food regimens
25. Love excessively
26. Actress Gabor
28. Goes out with
29. Overact
30. Kaline and Hirt
31. Picnic crasher
32. Get the point
33. Lamb's mom
35. Flowers-to-be
36. Pea envelope
39. Cleans the slate
41. Redcap
43. Save
44. Hawaiian dish
46. Sandra and Frances
47. Liberate
48. Ashen
49. Neck of the woods
50. Sot
51. Tied
52. Locale
53. Chum
55. ___ Grande
57. Actress Remick

PUZZLE 582 — ANAGRAMS PLUS

Find ten things that are grown by adding the given letter to each word and rearranging all the letters. For example, G + SPARE = GRAPES.

1. L + COVER _____
2. C + LEERY _____
3. E + ORGAN _____
4. R + ACTOR _____
5. D + CHOIR _____

6. H + RAIDS _____
7. U + PRINT _____
8. B + RELAY _____
9. L + TENET _____
10. C + PAINT _____

PUZZLE 583

ACROSS

1. Rim
4. Very proper
8. Ceremony
12. Mine product
13. Tiny amount
14. Biblical prophet
15. Thing, in law
16. U.S. citizens
18. German city
20. Female religious figure: abbr.
21. Mangles
24. Love to excess
28. Arrived
30. And others: abbr.
32. Mr. Chaney
33. Famous boxer
34. Singer Como
35. Old Tokyo
36. "____ Girls"
37. Dutch cheese
38. Church service
39. Parking ____
41. Egyptian-temple entryway marker
43. Toss
45. Peruvian mountain range
48. Soaked in sauce
53. Building addition
54. Dill seed
55. Close tight
56. Inlet
57. Ocean movement
58. Gratify
59. Opinion

DOWN

1. Homespun knowledge
2. Angers
3. One who looks on the dark side
4. Large musical instrument
5. Gypsy man
6. Resident: suff.
7. Planet
8. Sped
9. "____ Yankee Doodle Dandy"
10. Great weight
11. Road curve
17. European country
19. Before, poetically
22. Requirement
23. Leather thong
25. Mediterranean shrubs
26. Engine parts
27. Seth's son
28. Serene
29. To the sheltered side
31. Military branch
34. Argentine name
38. Day of the week: abbr.
40. Cream of society
42. Soup server
44. Kind of fish
46. Lamb
47. Kill
48. Small rug
49. Cuckoo
50. Color of embarrassment
51. Brewed beverage
52. Dine

PUZZLE 584

ACROSS

1. Time spans
5. Court divider
8. Emcee
12. Endure
13. "We ____ the World"
14. Sheltered
15. Film presentations
18. Another time
19. Actor Jeremy ____
20. Ump's kin
22. Pouch
23. &
26. Verve
28. Beehive State
32. Film presentation
35. Smell
36. List shortener
37. Receptacle
38. Emmet
40. "____ Kapital"
42. Harriet Beecher ____
45. Less cooked
49. Film presentation
53. Jackson or Archer
54. Ages and ages
55. Brad or spad
56. Suds
57. Put two and two together
58. Low card

DOWN

1. Actress Lanchester
2. Phoned
3. On the briny
4. Part of a flight
5. Siesta
6. Bungle
7. Duffer's gadget
8. Ducktail
9. Butter substitute
10. Stitched
11. Polanski film
16. Prepare to pray
17. By way of
21. Armada
22. Golfer Sam ____
23. "Much ____ About Nothing"
24. Doze
25. Pair
27. Toward the stern
29. Clumsy boat
30. Actress Meyers
31. Layer
33. Fighter
34. Morning noisemaker
39. Beatty
41. Eva Marie ____
42. Mop
43. Color
44. Writer Sarah ____ Jewett
46. Garb
47. American Indian
48. Depend
50. Legume
51. Steiger
52. Finale

PUZZLE 585

ACROSS
1. Record
5. Flower containers
9. Fountain order
13. Vocal
14. River craft
15. State
16. Mix a salad
17. Unlocks
18. Ash Wednesday's time
19. Behind, on a ship
21. Spices up
23. Actor Marvin
24. ____ a boy!
26. "Of Mice and ____"
27. Vim and vigor
28. Morning moisture
29. Historic period
32. Apiece
36. "____ That Tune"
38. Hemingway product
40. Pain
41. Hobo
43. Adjudge
44. Kick off
46. Dueling sword
47. Make ____ meet
48. Psychic power: abbr.
49. Possessive pronoun
51. Have being
53. Lend a hand
54. Bird's beak
55. Fuel
58. Trial figure
62. Get
64. "Me and My ____"
65. Trophy
67. Wile
68. "Un Bel Di," e.g.
69. Country roads
70. Eye amorously
71. Minus
72. Went eighty
73. Woods animal

DOWN
1. Complete
2. Originated
3. Classroom adhesive
4. Otherwise
5. Baby food
6. Singles
7. Musical sound
8. Open ____!
9. Elegant room
10. Kiln
11. Family rooms
12. Actor Carney
14. Satisfied
20. ____ Van Winkle
22. Stitched
25. Extras
28. Abase
29. Flush
30. Critic Rex
31. Charity
32. Soothe
33. Behaves
34. Gent
35. That woman
37. Chart
39. Pindaric
42. Spells
45. Slender
50. High hopes
52. Kind of tide
53. Strongman Charles
55. Measure
56. Bridal path
57. Scoff
58. Telegram
59. Writer Murdoch
60. Exchange
61. Not crazy
63. Walked on
64. Guy's mate
66. Eric the ____

PUZZLE 586   ESCALATOR

Place the answer to clue 1 in the first space, drop a letter, and arrange the remaining letters to answer clue 2. Drop another letter and arrange the remaining letters to answer clue 3. The first dropped letter goes into the box to the left of space 1 and the second dropped letter goes into the box to the right of space 3. Follow this pattern for each row in the diagram. When completed, the letters on the left and right, reading down, will spell related words or a phrase.

1. Color band
2. Ceremonies
3. Weary
4. Court actions
5. Coin-toss outcome
6. Lath
7. Lubricate
8. Storms
9. I'm all ____
10. Goose or Hubbard
11. Greek poet
12. Additional
13. Nursery toy
14. Anon
15. Genuine
16. Aches (for)
17. Trap
18. Close

478

PUZZLE 587

ACROSS
1. Swat
5. Cyst
8. Jog
12. Sleeveless garment
13. Under the weather
14. Sat on a horse
15. On high
16. Pub order
17. English boy's school
18. Chaos
20. Einstein
22. Indian
23. Sesame seed
24. Least nervous
28. Station
32. Stir
33. Erode
35. Before, poetically
36. Hen
39. Show disgust
42. Toss
44. Collection
45. Football kick
48. Brings together
52. Emptiness
53. Pep
55. Run
56. Feminine ending
57. Age
58. Otherwise
59. Swamp grass
60. ____ Vegas
61. Require

DOWN
1. Wound covering
2. Behindhand
3. Footless
4. Dress extra
5. Breed of cat
6. Everyone
7. Athletic-shoe spike
8. Threefold, musically
9. Mechanical course of procedure
10. Aroma
11. Outdoor shelter
19. Supped
21. Cover
24. Silent ____
25. Oklahoma city
26. Actress Myrna
27. Children's game
29. Legume
30. Grampus
31. Golfer's need
34. Severe bodily shocks
37. Omitted
38. Pole
40. Hostelry
41. Unmarried female
43. Tool to draw angles
45. Ended
46. Jot down
47. Locale
49. Story
50. Latin being
51. Lean-to
54. Mr. Gershwin

PUZZLE 588

ACROSS
1. Opera song
5. Cup edge
8. Go by
12. Camera's eye
13. Guido's high note: 2 wds.
14. Notion
15. Behind one's back: 3 wds.
17. Study
18. Anesthetic
19. Harem room
21. Anglo-Saxon slave
23. Turn on an axis
27. Moisture
29. Sprite
31. Cantaloupe
32. ESP devotee Geller
33. Young boy
35. Fortune
36. Produces coal
39. Hosiery shade
41. Consumed
42. Wild confusion
44. Castle ditch
46. Tart
47. Hawaiian farewell
50. Upholstered couch
53. Profit from: 3 wds.
56. God of war
57. U.S. cloak-and-dagger agency: abbr.
58. Land measure
59. Bustle: hyph.
60. Bowlike curve
61. Dispatched

DOWN
1. Century plant
2. Torn
3. Impending: 3 wds.
4. Cigarette residue
5. Legal thing
6. Under the weather
7. City boss
8. Blackbeard, e.g.
9. Fruit drink
10. Ocean
11. Melancholy
16. Sea eagle
20. Portuguese title
22. Cloth measure
24. Suddenly: 3 wds.
25. Horn sound
26. Grafted, in heraldry
27. Slow on the uptake
28. New York canal
30. Pudgy
34. Water barrier
37. Texas city: 2 wds.
38. Capuchin monkey
40. Ark's builder
43. Muslim holy city
45. Assumed name
48. Antler
49. Dill
50. Remained inactive
51. Spanish gold
52. Nourished
54. Melody
55. Pocket

PUZZLE 589

ACROSS
1. Garden tool
5. Dull
9. Novice
13. Zone
14. Scrape
15. Donna or Rex
16. Slapstick props
17. Main artery
18. Opposite of aweather
19. Narrows
21. Purify
23. Building sites
25. Genuine
26. Taxi
29. Host Linkletter
30. Sixth sense: abbr.
31. Toddler
34. Of farmers
37. Range
39. Wharf
40. Like gingersnaps
43. Not settled
44. Pick by ballot
46. Sweat
48. Vermilion
49. Commercials
52. Haul
53. Grimalkin
54. Became larger
55. Diagnostic aid
57. Symmetrical solid
60. Plays the ham
64. Profound
65. Musical study
67. Small container
68. Bad day for Caesar
69. Fragment
70. As well
71. Challenge
72. "Harold ___"
73. Fume

DOWN
1. Preoccupied
2. Sills solo
3. Castle fortification
4. Painting holder
5. To and ___
6. Pig fat
7. Garb
8. Beleaguers
9. Path
10. Howl
11. Line dance
12. Keats poem
14. Of the stomach
20. Lion's call
22. Evening bugle call
24. Twinkler
26. Escapade
27. Deft
28. Produce
31. Theme
32. "La Boheme," e.g.
33. Dogma
35. Curve
36. Sever by pinching
38. Beat walker
41. Congeals
42. Push on
45. Tobacco smoke solids
47. Stayed afloat
50. Hate
51. Wrap
54. Type of moth
56. Variable stars
57. Relinquish
58. Coral ridge
59. Bait
61. Cant
62. Slacken
63. Sluggish
64. Performed
66. Retreat

PUZZLE 590   Honeycomb

The small arrows indicate the beginning of each 6-letter answer, which will circle its number in either a clockwise or counterclockwise direction.

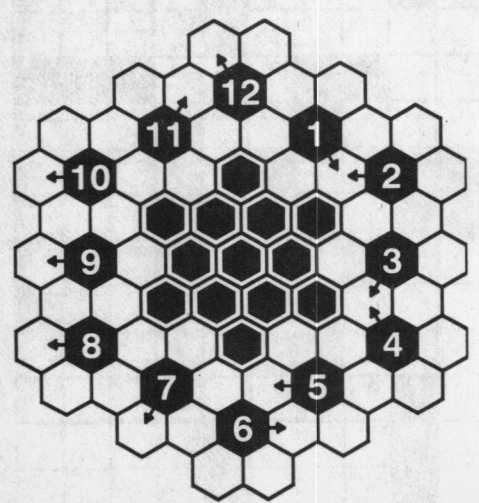

1. Nabokov heroine
2. Timmy's canine pal
3. Romeo's love
4. Dame Anderson
5. Mrs. Washington
6. Aviator Earhart
7. Environmentalist Carson
8. George Burns's sidekick
9. "Portrait of ___"
10. Comedian May
11. Sister of Moses
12. A Dionne

480

BRICK BY BRICK

PUZZLE 591

Rearrange this stack of bricks to form a crossword puzzle. The clues will help you fit the bricks into their correct places. Row 1 has been filled in for you. Use the bricks to fill in the remaining spaces.

ACROSS

1. Scorch
   Punctuation
   Snatch
2. Ear part
   Regions
   Portrayal
3. Actor Baldwin
   Files
   Milky stone
4. BLT home
   Athens vowel
   Critical
5. Ashen
   Exist
6. Placid
   Introduces
7. Soho repast
   Royal Russians
   Follow
8. Scotto song
   Sailing craft
   Ireland
9. Cotton thread
   Enclosed
   Victory sign
10. Memento
    Most kind
11. Quiche
    Seasoned
12. Calms
    Acquired
    Israel port
13. Garden soil
    GI's holiday
    Glide
14. Opposed
    Actress Barkin
    Amor
15. Pip
    Brainy
    Glut

DOWN

1. Clothed
   Stem
   Alack
2. Perforation
   Spooky
   Solitary
3. Seth's sib
   Poker action
   Delayed
4. Chef's guide
   Swiss peak
   Amongst
5. Pismire
   Spot
6. Negligent
   Walkways
7. Sermonize
   Matching
   Slippery tree
8. Plateau
   Liable
   Festive
9. Chart
   Forest felony
   Canine name
10. Guarantee
    Sorry
11. Time-out
    Tear
12. Tar's quaff
    Before
    Halts
13. Lasso
    Artless
    Irene of "Fame"
14. Arkin
    Wearies
    Fracas
15. Sash
    Icy downpour
    Different

BRICKS

ESE / _TR	N_E / T_S	DEL / _	ANT / SEE	LOB / ALE
ENT / _	IRE / VEE	LLE / MAR	KE_ / E_R	_PR / ARS
ROS / ATE	E_A / C_R	GO_ / EAV	A_S / LE_	OLE / PAL
TA_ / E_A	NIC / IPE	KEE / _	URG / RE_	T_A / E_S
ALL / LOA	EST / _	LOO / INN	S_S / S_O	SER / TEA
REA / ASP	I_E / PAL	I_E / D_S	AYS / M_L	P_E / ER_
ARI / LIS	PSA / _PI	ENE / _TS	CRE / AIL	NTS / AIL

DIAGRAM

	1	2	3	4	5	6	7	8	9	10	11	12	13	14	15
1	C	H	A	R		C	O	M	M	A		G	R	A	B
2															
3															
4															
5															
6															
7															
8															
9															
10															
11															
12															
13															
14															
15															

481

PUZZLE 592

• CHEMISTRY BASICS •

ACROSS

1. "____ the season . . ."
4. Sargasso ____
7. Fire a gun
9. Indonesian island chain
11. Easels, e.g.
12. Most ancient
14. Frying utensil
15. Golfer Woosnam
17. Santa's helper
18. Depot: abbr.
19. "____-Hur"
20. Certain
21. Part of speech
23. Venomous viper
25. Daughter's brother
26. Electricity measure
27. Victory sign
29. Road map abbr.
31. Foot part
33. Antiseptic element
35. Make a mistake
36. Balloon gas
38. Shorthand specialist
39. Light bulb gas
41. Suggestive grins
42. Mrs., in Spain
43. Naughty
45. Have creditors
48. Physicians: abbr.
49. Building addition
50. Fifth month
51. Dehydrate
54. "Agnus ____"
55. Exist
56. TV spots
59. ____ of the crop
61. Nonmetallic element
65. Michelangelo statue
67. Wire and pipe metal
69. Sought election
70. Diamond substance
71. ____ de France
72. Be victorious
74. French friend
75. Squealer
76. Sculpture, e.g.
77. Attorney's concern
79. Money mill
81. Evangelist Roberts
83. Mao ____-tung
84. Scientist's room
86. Third letter
87. Head gesture
88. Before, in poems
89. Reeks
91. Cold season
93. Maple and fir
94. Cheerful
95. Marina ____ Rey
96. ____ culpa

DOWN

1. Holier-____-thou
2. Charged particle
3. ____ chloride (salt)
4. Flammable yellow element
5. Terminate
6. Citrus coolers
7. Comedian Laurel
8. Russian ruler
9. Fly alone
10. Famous movie dog
11. Money user
13. More savory
16. At no time
17. January, in Madrid
19. "Puss in ____"
20. That woman
22. ____ degree (ultimate degree)
24. Serves wine
25. Bro's sibling
26. Yoko ____
28. Unit of work
30. Moray or conger
32. Typesetter's measures
34. One ____ million
37. Went in front
39. Improvise
40. "____ is an island"
43. Canopy or fourposter
44. Beer's cousin
46. Armed conflict
47. Organ of sight

482

PUZZLE 592

51. Oddly amusing
52. Officially revokes
53. Jabber
56. Melody
57. One who devalues
58. Boutique, e.g.
59. 201, to Caesar
60. Cat's cry

62. Give a speech
63. Male sheep
64. Scallion's kin
65. TV host Sajak
66. Hill insect
68. Outer edge
70. Coolidge's nickname
73. Coin metal

75. Curies' discovery
78. Electrical power unit
80. Loch ____ monster
82. Tiers
83. Three, in cards

85. Feathery flier
88. Sicilian volcano
90. Formerly named
92. Opposite of SSW

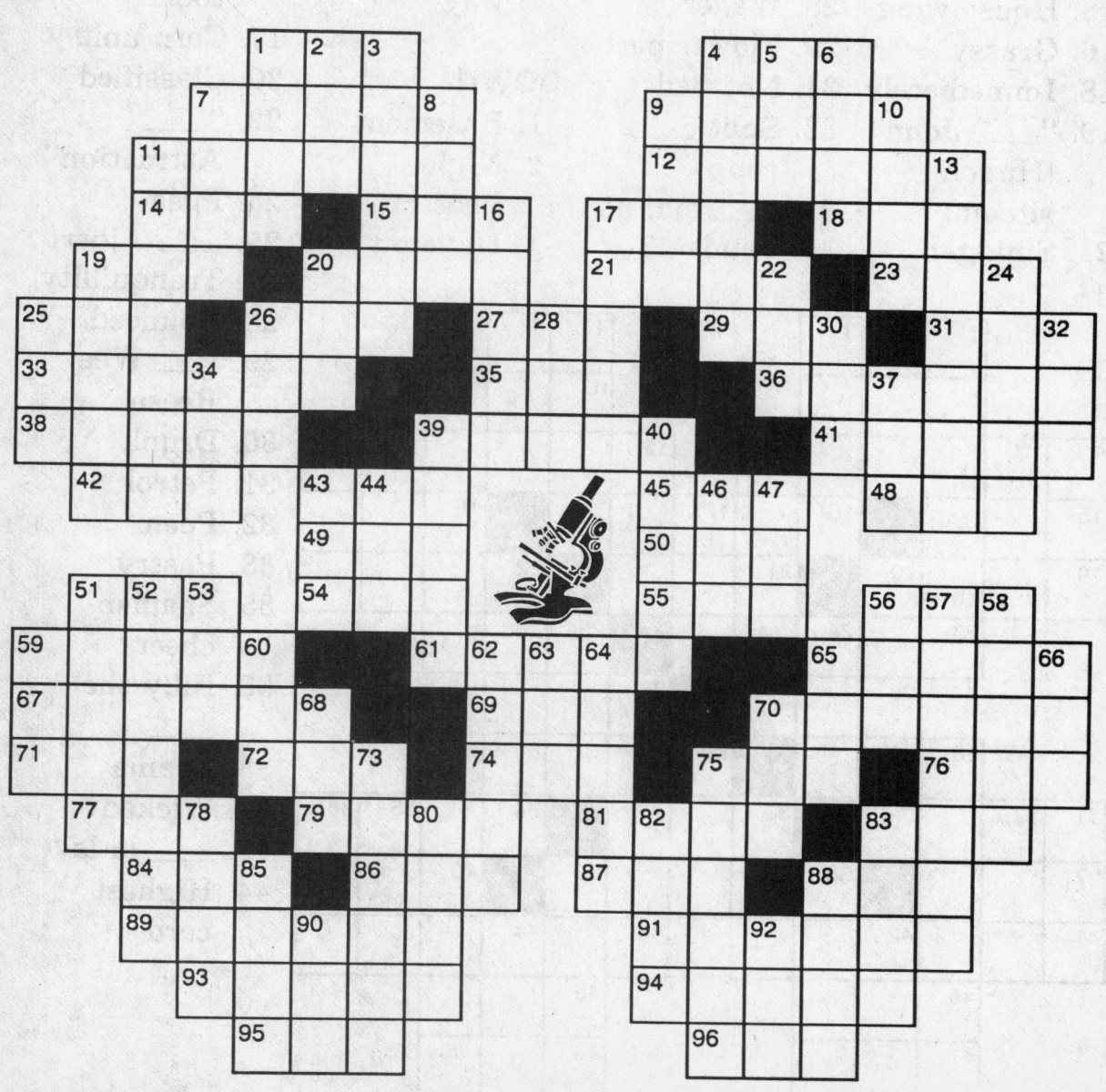

483

PUZZLE 593

ACROSS

1. Heifer
4. Animal foot
7. Female sheep
8. Mine output
9. Love song
12. New York Indian
15. House wing
16. Grassy
18. Immediately
19. "___ John" (Hirsch sitcom)
21. Smidgen
22. "I ___ Pretty" from "West Side Story"
23. Sports car
25. Distant
26. Paving liquid
27. Mrs. Nixon
28. Wager
29. Flower part
31. Not bad
33. Split ___ soup
34. ___ ma, no hands!
37. Bustle
38. Section
40. Clay, presently
41. Decide
43. Shunned
45. Time period
46. Hockey surface
47. Night and ___
48. Showed the way

DOWN

1. Basement
2. Night hooter
3. Have on
4. Child's steed
5. Exist
6. Hot dog
9. ___ of roses
10. Beer's cousin
11. Discourage
12. Bizarre
13. Female deer
14. Piercing tool
17. Corn unit
20. Classified
22. "___ Attraction"
24. Puss
25. ___ Albert
27. Tranquillity
28. Bounced
29. ___ Wee Reese
30. Drunk
31. Petrol
32. Poem
33. Pastry
35. Spanish cheer
36. Billy the ___
38. Drama
39. Wicked
42. ___ la la
44. Highest card

484

PUZZLE 594

ACROSS

1. Strokes lightly
5. Dried grass
8. Willing's partner
12. Range
13. Third person singular pronoun
14. Divulge
15. Handbills
17. Labyrinth
18. Man Friday
19. Canons
20. Twenty
23. "Peter ____"
24. Judd Hirsch series
25. Waned
30. Metallic dirt
31. Downpours
32. Actress Plumb
33. Pittsburgh skaters
35. Dominant
36. Notices
37. Wistfully
38. Dark fur
41. Casanova
43. Evangelist Roberts
44. Encourages
48. Huron, e.g.
49. "Gunga ____" (Grant film)
50. Colt's mom
51. Command to a child
52. Choose
53. Foil's kin

DOWN

1. Cohort
2. "You ____ My Sunshine"
3. Afternoon beverage
4. African hunting expedition
5. Weeded
6. Before: pref.
7. Certainly!
8. Nut type
9. Rosary part
10. Lounge
11. Just manages to earn
16. Fib
19. Tins
20. Traffic sign
21. Be concerned
22. Yoked animals
23. On ____ and needles
25. Soapbox
26. Triumph
27. Starring role
28. Sinister
29. Refuse
31. Ill-mannered
34. Ship's kitchen
35. French lady
37. Amount
38. Fly alone
39. Regal steed
40. Make cookies
41. Trim
42. Shade of color
44. "Much ____ About Nothing"
45. Draw on
46. Before, to poets
47. Admit as a visitor

485

PUZZLE 595

ACROSS
1. Wonder
4. Cross one
8. Hit sharply
12. Chum
13. Misplace
14. Ring of light
15. Ogle
16. Comfort
17. Again
18. Scheme
20. Become solid
22. Pale
24. ___ of day
25. Gab
26. Lay macadam
27. Narrow opening
30. Heavy weight
31. Strange
32. Prospector's find
33. Matched group
34. Camera part
35. State
36. Deed
37. Pick up the tab
38. Go around
41. Active person
42. Pack up
43. Single thing
45. Snooze
48. A Great Lake
49. ___ and shine!
50. "___ to Billy Joe"
51. Fuse together
52. Large deer
53. Tier

DOWN
1. Big monkey
2. Path
3. Dumbo, for one
4. Not dirty
5. Bay horse
6. Donkey
7. Busy places
8. Be generous
9. Fairy's baton
10. Toward the sheltered side
11. City
19. ___ the good times roll
21. Hymn ending
22. Performs
23. Sandal
24. Poison
26. Enjoyment
27. Head of state
28. Neighborhood
29. Saucy
31. Ginger drinks
35. Exist
36. Lost color
37. Carries
38. Huffed and puffed
39. Long ago
40. Bucket
41. Computer storage platter
44. Nothing
46. Fuss
47. Church bench

PUZZLE 596

ACROSS
1. Deposit
4. On top of
8. Drill
12. "____ on a Grecian Urn"
13. Claudius's successor
14. Brainstorm
15. Large snake
16. Adolescent
17. "My Three ____"
18. Banister
20. Dashing
22. Extent
24. Bridle strap
25. Toledo's lake
26. Penalty
27. Escorted
30. Mail
31. Snake shape
32. Not taped
33. Chasing game
34. Swipe
35. Candid
36. Inquisitive
37. Like a tree-trunk growth
38. First aid for a broken bone
41. Kick
42. Bark
43. Blue bloom
45. Little demon
48. Cousin's mother
49. Egypt's river
50. Automobile
51. Hunted animal
52. There's ____ in them thar hills!
53. Lock opener

DOWN
1. Arched toss
2. Flurry
3. Hankering
4. Loosen
5. Fruit skin
6. Unrefined mineral
7. Gobbledy-gook
8. Shaggy bovine
9. Scent
10. Apartment fee
11. Uncompli-cated
19. Ripened
21. Pizza
22. Relax
23. Territory
24. "____ Business" (Cruise film)
26. Dining
27. Cosmetic item
28. Arden and namesakes
29. Refuse
32. Diving bird
34. 2,000 pounds
36. Excellent
37. Pondered
38. Exchange
39. Rain hard
40. Sole
41. Tablet
44. ____ de Janeiro
46. Actress West
47. Snoop

487

PUZZLE 597

• BACK IN THE SADDLE •

ACROSS
1. Feud
4. Father
7. Young dog
10. To's mate
13. Chicken ___ king
14. Ethan Allen's brother
15. GI's address
16. ___ Palmas
17. Gary Cooper film, with "The"
21. Buttermilk's rider
25. Huron's neighbor
26. This, in Barcelona
27. Gave temporarily
30. Type of cross
35. Living room
39. Shade trees
40. Avoid
41. Days gone by
42. Peak on Crete
43. Silver's rider
48. Squealer
49. Titled
52. Foreigner
54. Wiped
55. Actor Clark ___
56. Columnist Landers
57. Tom Hanks film
58. Ties
61. Base
63. Sierra ___
64. French income
65. M.D.'s group
67. "___ or Alive" (TV series)
73. Sullivan and Ames
76. Champlain or Tahoe
78. Zodiac ram
79. Premed course: abbr.
80. Producer Spielberg
83. Ruffs
84. Barkin and Burstyn
86. English school
88. Stomped
89. Trigger's rider
94. "Stagecoach" star
99. Fruit beverage
100. Small taste
101. ___ Jima
102. Affirmative vote
103. Take nourishment
104. Kind of bean or sauce
105. Sea, in Sevres
106. Actor Brooks

DOWN
1. Inexperienced
2. Bullfight cheer
3. Had being
4. Sup
5. "You ___ My Sunshine"
6. Patriotic group: abbr.
7. Apartment
8. ___ tree (stumped)
9. Fishing rod
10. Sunshine State: abbr.
11. Scurried
12. WWII intelligence group: abbr.
18. Hamilton bills
19. Before, to a poet
20. Disencumber
22. Sixth sense: abbr.
23. Delphi letter
24. Deviate
27. Hawaiian necklace
28. Antique
29. Miss Kitty of "Gunsmoke"
30. Write
31. "___ Maria"
32. Golf standard
33. Nabokov novel
34. Writer Deighton
36. "Bonanza" star
37. "___ pro nobis"
38. Soak flax
43. Pinky ___
44. Weird
45. Wisecrack
46. Musical note
47. Hair adornment
50. Attorney Becker on "L.A. Law"
51. Small fish
53. Author George ___
59. Genetic factor: abbr.
60. Member of Congress: abbr.

488

61. Brother's title
62. Guided
65. Jolson and Capone
66. Rug
68. Beret's kin
69. Historic time
70. Noise
71. Poor grade
72. Lion or baron suffix
74. Newsman Rather
75. Avenues: abbr.
77. Continuously
79. Actor Alan ____
81. DDE's command
82. Eggy drink
84. Sea bird
85. Base
87. Loch ____ monster

PUZZLE 597

88. Norse god of thunder
89. Actress ____ Dawn Chong
90. Harem room
91. Up until now
92. ____ de Janeiro
93. Secret agent
94. "Jules and ____"
95. Have an obligation to
96. Southern potato
97. Comedian Louis ____
98. Lamprey

489

PUZZLE 598

ACROSS

1. Employer
5. Ocean vessel
9. Make happy
14. Prepare for publication
15. Couldn't ____ less
16. Instruct
17. Ripped
18. Location
19. Hag
20. Prize
22. Plot
24. Spelling contest
25. Was ahead
26. Olympic trophy
30. Swift
33. Weasel sound
36. Martini garnishes
38. Be untruthful
39. ____ the slate clean
40. Single
41. Frequently
43. Descended
44. Copier
45. Regret
46. King's seat
48. ____ in the face
49. Cheerful
51. Come in
52. "The Night ____ a Thousand Eyes"
53. Make a blunder
55. Explosions
58. Hook and ____
62. Banquet
63. Lounge around
65. Enjoy a book
67. Cream of the crop
68. Adored one
69. Military division
70. Senior
71. Moist
72. Use a keyboard

DOWN

1. Gamble
2. Smell
3. Father
4. Fret
5. Frighten
6. More difficult
7. Anger
8. Like two ____ in a pod
9. Engraved
10. Enticed
11. Nuclear particle
12. Musical pitch
13. Before, in poetry
21. Competent
23. Customer
26. Tooth
27. Wed on the run
28. Ate
29. State
31. Change
32. Pumpkin dessert
33. Aviator
34. Say
35. Singer Cetera of "Chicago"
37. Most tender
39. Alert
42. Mink, for one
47. Cattle group
49. Expert
50. Lemon color
52. Speed
54. Pep gathering
55. Saved by the ____
56. Put down
57. Slipped
59. Mild oath
60. Strange
61. Incline
62. Cover charge
64. "____ to Billy Joe"
66. Add color to

490

ACROSS
1. Grant
5. Performed
10. Equal to the task
14. In the midst of
15. Credulous
16. Table game
17. Best man's concern
18. Inexperienced
19. Playground
20. Belfries
22. Joshes
24. Went first
25. "___ M for Murder"
26. Fragrances
30. Snuggled
33. "Little ___"
34. Frequently
35. River bottom
37. Alter
38. Saute
39. "And Then There Were ___"
40. Clique
41. Feline animal
42. Taut
43. Two-toed flightless bird
46. Attorney
47. Uncle's wife
48. Hiatus
49. Vitamin C source
52. Love ballad
57. Anguish
58. Prospected
60. Environs
61. Stream
62. "___ by any other name . . ."
63. Partiality
64. Toboggan
65. City drain
66. Rational

DOWN
1. Sedans and coupes
2. Give off
3. Take a meal
4. Periphery
5. Obtuse and acute
6. Worried
7. Ascots
8. Dusk
9. Molar man
10. Dismay
11. Feathery stoles
12. Folk mythology
13. Lodge members
21. Blueprint
23. Nosh
25. Challenge
26. Overwhelms
27. Cowboy contest
28. Fails to mention
29. Was introduced to
30. Actor Jay ___ (Dennis the Menace)
31. "___ and Ivory" (Wonder song)
32. Thick
36. Stag or roe
38. Truth
39. Novel
41. Movie houses
42. Record
44. Sunbathed
45. Carpet
46. Pantry
48. Honking birds
49. Picks
50. Complain bitterly
51. Helper
52. Singer Phoebe ___
53. Arrests
54. Scotto song
55. College official
56. Alleviate
59. Choler

491

PUZZLE 600

ACROSS

1. Random try
5. Toward the stern
8. Breaches
12. Summon
13. Lobster eggs
14. Solo for Sills
15. "____ Graffiti"
17. Restrain
18. Change
19. Parking site
21. Poet's before
22. "____ Little Indians"
24. Crowd noise
26. Playmate
29. Wet dirt
31. Jot down
34. Fast horse
36. Every ____ and then
38. Quick-witted
39. Nary a once
41. Forty winks
43. Downcast
44. Well-known garden
46. ____ whiz!
48. Tin container
50. Solemn promise
52. Sports palace
56. Ungracious
58. Improved
60. Locale
61. Grant's foe
62. Point out
63. Shopping center
64. Piece out
65. Kinski film

DOWN

1. Ship's mast
2. Unexciting
3. "Rock of ____"
4. French hat
5. Rainbow
6. Colt
7. Pavarotti, e.g.
8. Car fuel
9. Blood carriers
10. Wharf
11. Identical
16. Bit of gossip
20. Pull behind
23. Type of buoy
25. "Raiders of the Lost ____"
26. Skillet
27. Have being
28. Lilac
30. Singer Henley
32. Reception
33. Finale
35. Fourposter, e.g.
37. Move back and forth
40. Race
42. Bog fuel
45. Princely
47. Assemble
48. Study for finals
49. Distinctive air
51. Seven days
53. Pennsylvania port
54. Profits
55. Thirst quenchers
57. Have a snack
59. To a ____

492

PUZZLE 601

ACROSS

1. Eroded
4. Food fish
7. Garden tool
12. Floor-shiner
13. Mickey's ex
14. TV host Funt
15. Was
17. Carried
18. Nanny
19. Quote
20. Tennis star Ashe
22. Johnny ____
25. Hurls
28. Raw metal
29. Dander
30. To the sheltered side
31. Copycat
32. Tizzy
33. Map abbr.
34. Falsehood
35. Storms
36. Author Tolstoy
37. Reply
39. Sleep
41. Provokes
45. Steer
47. Playing marble
48. Fall bloomer
49. Wooden nail
50. Actress Bartok
51. Pinto and lima
52. Metric land unit
53. Sniggler's quarry

DOWN

1. Impresses deeply
2. Cab
3. Way out
4. Furnishes the food
5. Obvious
6. June honoree
7. Wit
8. Scheme
9. Changing
10. Ruby or Sandra
11. Wrap up
16. Ohio or Utah
19. Heal
21. Wishes
23. Famous canal
24. Wagers
25. Phone
26. Soothing plant
27. Spanish miss
31. "____ She Sweet"
32. Beetle Bailey character
34. Beams of light
35. Go back on one's word
38. Thirst quencher
40. Serene spot
42. General Robert ____
43. Split
44. Playful sea creature
45. Chat
46. Apply
47. Workout site

PUZZLE 602

ACROSS

1. First woman
4. Health resort
7. ____ voyage
10. Food for an aardvark
13. Fall behind
14. Long ____ Sally
16. Destiny
17. Weeding tool
18. Place for petunias
21. Till
23. Grower
24. Baltimore bird
25. Workout locales
26. Expressions of surprise
28. Opposite of NNW
29. Neither's partner
31. Santa ____ Race Track
33. Sunbeam
36. Ginger drink
37. Carrot or cucumber
41. Native metal
42. Hive dweller
43. Orange drink
44. Goddess of the dawn
45. Collection of dishes
46. Leek's kin
49. Shovel
52. Foot digit
53. Dust cloth
54. Feels sore
57. "This Is ____ Tap"
60. Flightless bird
62. Walking on ____
64. Mauna ____
65. Fishing pole
67. Male sheep
68. Lawn weed
72. Expire
73. Director Reiner
74. Oaks and elms
75. Curvy letter
76. "____ a Living"
79. Chicken ____ king
80. Cereal grain
83. Transplants
86. Sell to consumers
89. Edible spear
92. Plant beginnings
96. Caribbean, for one
97. Sediment
98. Storm
99. Cookie grain
100. Household animal
101. Opposite of WSW
102. Scarlet
103. Not wet

DOWN

1. Santa's helper
2. Actor Kilmer
3. Self
4. Water vapor
5. Capital of France
6. Linen vestments
7. Indonesian island
8. German kings
9. Singers Young and Sedaka
10. Cry of triumph
11. Forget-me-____
12. Kind of summer shirt
15. Confederate general
16. Animal hair
19. Twisted
20. Humming sound
21. ____ Rica
22. Victory sign
25. Talent for growing plants
27. ____ the road
29. Capture
30. Bread spread
31. Become older
32. Lincoln's nickname
33. "I Never Promised You a ____"
34. "Butterflies ____ Free"
35. Still
37. Moving truck
38. McMahon and Asner
39. ____ Alamos
40. Sixth sense: abbr.
47. Memo of a debt
48. "____ the land of the free"
50. Hero of "Exodus"
51. Newsman Rather
55. Tic-____-toe
56. Knight's title

494

PUZZLE 602

57. Call for help, on the ocean
58. Dads
59. Actress Nettleton
60. Go wrong
61. ____ Tse-tung
63. Large rodent
64. ____ Vegas
66. ____ Moines
69. Knuckles or ring
70. Congeal
71. Brings up
76. Writer Levin
77. Concise
78. Neighbor of Portugal
80. Policeman's emblem
81. Irked
82. Actress MacGraw
84. Flirt with the eyes
85. Egyptian king, for short
87. Always, in poems
88. Salty drop
89. Cleopatra's snake
90. Look at
91. Square of butter
93. Auction signal
94. Needlefish
95. Hog's haven

PUZZLE 603

ACROSS

1. Actor Pendleton
4. Babble
8. Actress Raines
12. Clockmaker Terry
13. Body of knowledge
14. Advertising light
15. Took nourishment
16. Caretaker
18. Emulated Cindy Crawford
20. Lower digit
21. Marsh plant
24. Seasons
28. Fare
31. Linen, e.g.
33. Long, long ____
34. Nibbles
35. Hollywood's Farrow
36. Makes proportional
38. Kind of tree
39. Gluts
40. Marquee name
42. Veggie
44. Noise
48. Take back
53. Black or Yellow
54. Atop
55. Singer Seeger
56. Be mistaken
57. Left
58. Blind part
59. "Native ____"

DOWN

1. Kind of tide
2. Tall, in Tijuana
3. TV's "Family ____"
4. Ice-skate feature
5. Homesite
6. Sculpture, e.g.
7. Root vegetable
8. Make esteemed
9. Meadow
10. Silent screen's Chaney
11. Picnic invader
17. Pries
19. Bard's before
22. Discharge
23. Appointments
25. Kind of bean
26. Follow
27. Bridge triumph
28. Yaks
29. Taj Mahal site
30. Horn's contribution
32. Examination
34. Army posts
37. Manuscript
38. Master
41. Resource
43. Cobras
45. Exploits
46. Famous fiddler
47. Mild oath
48. Tier
49. Genesis name
50. Enclosure
51. Slippery one
52. Depot: abbr.

ACROSS

1. Is in debt
5. Pretends
9. Dined
12. Curved doorway
13. Billiards' kin
14. Irritate
15. Bettor's card game
16. Appeal
17. Regret
18. Rejected
20. Records on cassette
22. Small child
23. Building shape
24. Naught
27. One of ten in a dollar
30. "The ___ of the Mohicans"
33. Exist
34. Small rock
36. Named formerly
37. Rosary segment
39. Whirling current
40. Female sheep
41. Dense mist
43. Snakelike fish
45. Whiter
47. Gambling halls
51. Citrus drink
52. At a distance
54. Horse's neck hair
55. Deep cooking vessel
56. Snout
57. Grab with one's teeth
58. Burro
59. Feat
60. Spill liquid

DOWN

1. Louts
2. Wind in cloth
3. Neutral color
4. Brief in time
5. Desire for a meal
6. Frigid
7. Foot digit
8. Blue roofing material
9. Flying machine
10. Not false
11. Supplements
19. Dozes off
21. "___ My Children"
24. Capture
25. Wrath
26. Handbills
28. "The ___ Squad"
29. Made oneself beloved
31. Do embroidery
32. Golfer's peg
35. Orbs of sight
38. Female deer
42. The ___ Canyon
44. Branches
45. Mama's spouse
46. Commotions
47. Lawyer's assignment
48. Carpenter's spike
49. Aware of
50. Ooze
53. Adversary

PUZZLE 605

ACROSS

1. Kermit, for one
5. Ship's record
8. 100-yard dash
12. Untaped
13. "___ Town"
14. Track shape
15. Thing
16. Nosy ones
18. For each
19. Gets back
20. Even score
22. "Did You ___ Have to Make Up Your Mind?"
23. Bundle
25. Sun. talk
26. Bottle top
29. "___ People Eater"
31. Moe, Larry, or Curly
33. Wide street: abbr.
34. King Kong, for one
36. ___ box (TV)
37. Tart
38. ___ at Work ('80s rock band)
39. Cautious position
42. Yogi, once
45. Poison remedy
46. "Spenser: For ___"
47. Boxer Max ___
48. Bambi's mom
49. Brink
50. Dueling tool
51. Blunder
52. ___ halfway

DOWN

1. Comic Wilson
2. Ceremony
3. "William Tell ___"
4. Jewel
5. Misplace
6. Units of weight
7. Ruts
8. Cowboy, at times
9. State
10. "Shake It Up" rock group
11. Overhead trains
17. Additional period of play
19. Substituted
21. Little devil
23. Auditor: abbr.
24. Jack Lemmon film
26. Occur at the same time
27. Past
28. ___ Shop Boys (British duo)
30. Incident
32. Poem
35. Newspaperman
37. Burning
39. Easy job
40. Suit to ___
41. Bambi, for one
43. Force
44. Borscht ingredient
45. Honest man
46. Dress bottom

498

ACROSS

1. Grade
5. Go by
9. Yoked animals
10. Toward shelter
11. Lately done
13. Sewing spike
16. Noah's boat
17. Inventor Whitney
19. Help
20. Even score
21. Huge mythical bird
22. Label
23. Argument
26. In what place
28. "The Cat ___ the Hat"
29. Santa's chuckle
30. Form
33. Leavening agent
37. Spinning toy
38. Explosive initials
41. Cow's comment
42. Swiss mountain
43. Steal
44. "___ the King's Men"
45. "___ Bailey" (comic strip)
48. Made accessible
51. Diva's solo
52. Dull, unattractive person
53. Engrossed
54. Sicilian volcano

DOWN

1. Spaceship
2. Wood-cutter's tool
3. Hamilton bill
4. Go in
5. Overwhelming fear
6. Ginger ___
7. Witness
8. Calm
11. Rodents
12. Great Lake
14. Untruthful person
15. Advantage
18. ___ and behold
24. Point
25. First digit
26. For what reason
27. Garden implement
30. Pierce
31. Ace in the ___
32. Seem
34. Actress Plummer
35. Shoe bottom
36. Recounted
38. Trick or ___
39. Dr. ___ (Bond's enemy)
40. Kind of steak
46. ___ la la
47. Fleshy mouth part
49. Cherished animal
50. Sea eagle

PUZZLE 606

PUZZLE 607

ACROSS
1. Enjoyable
4. Suits
8. Experts
12. Self
13. Graven image, e.g.
14. Move on wheels
15. Shade tree
16. British noblewoman
17. Actor Griffith
18. Fibbing
20. Yale grad
22. Want
24. Play ____ (feign death)
28. Disperse
31. Honking birds
32. Small child
33. Shake
35. Each
36. Choose
39. Formed by humans
42. Laundered
44. Fly
45. ____ of a kind
46. October birthstones
49. Swabs
52. Periods in history
55. Faucet
56. Buffalo's lake
57. Broad valley
58. First woman
59. High-schooler
60. Hot tubs
61. Mom's spouse

DOWN
1. Touch
2. Unsightly
3. Puts up for office
4. Squirm
5. Actress Lupino
6. Baseball's Seaver
7. Slumber
8. Extol
9. Actor/director Howard
10. Elderly
11. Wily
19. Butterfly catcher
21. Journal
23. Morning moisture
25. Drawn apart
26. Secondhand
27. Only
28. Simmer
29. Soft drink flavor
30. Male sheep
34. Auto fuel
37. Picked
38. Twice five
40. Lariat loops
41. Atlas entry
43. Acts
47. Volcano's output
48. Went fast
49. Encountered
50. Mine yield
51. Fruited pastry
53. Knock sharply
54. Chicken ____ king

ACROSS
1. Unhappy
4. Lend an ____
7. Kind of resort
10. Rich lodes
12. Swill
14. Gymnast's goal
15. Orderly
16. Ditto
17. Sugar ____ Leonard
18. Tempests
20. Merchant
22. Court
24. Beverage
25. Devoured
30. Send out
33. Tumult
34. Less common
36. Time period
37. Twit
39. Prepared to fire again
41. "The ____ Also Rises"
43. Young fellow
44. Completely revised
47. Drive
51. Family member
52. Solemn promise
54. Ready to pick
55. Snacked
56. High flyer
57. Shangri-la
58. Family room
59. Not strict
60. Finale

DOWN
1. Aria
2. Space
3. Bargain
4. Dangerous curve
5. Pity!
6. Type of apple
7. Flowed
8. Bosc
9. Some
11. Frets
13. Stone
19. Bitter
21. TV's Kathie ____ Gifford
23. Poet Khayyam
25. Ont.'s locale
26. Verse form
27. Scandinavians
28. Sooner than, in poetry
29. Valley
31. Choler
32. Youth
35. Wander
38. Faulty product
40. Idolize
42. Comfortable corner
44. By ____ (mechanically)
45. Carpenter's need
46. Singer James
48. Ocean motion
49. Candid
50. Tear
51. Insane
53. Jinx

PUZZLE 609

ACROSS
1. Disconcert
5. Smack
9. Fisherman's hook
13. Moist
17. Golf club
18. Ballet skirt
19. Lamb's pen name
20. Fencing weapon
21. Durocher and Tolstoy
22. Gets older
23. Makes into leather
24. "The Way We ___"
25. Ingredients
27. Head of the family
30. Companions of ids
31. Swallow hard
32. Actress Lupino
33. Renders accessible
35. Record on cassette
36. Stack of stove fuel
41. Small bites
42. Burrows
43. Deserves
44. Guided
45. Average grade
46. Drains, as of energy
47. Female servants
48. Supplemented
49. Chore trips
51. Painting surface
52. Domineering
53. Bleat
54. West Pointer
55. Bowler's target
56. Holy water basin
59. Cougars
60. Tightly embraced
64. Promote
65. Roadside lodging
66. Papal name
67. Genetic substance
68. ___ a girl!
69. Regions
70. Keg's cork
71. Laborer
72. Lawyer's fee
74. Trick
75. Out-of-date
76. Yell of disapproval
77. Angelic instrument
78. Yawn
79. Redeeming feature
84. Pyrenees republic
87. Roman poet
88. Tree anchor
89. Filled tortilla
91. "___ There"
92. Flatfish
93. Qualified
94. Decorate, as a tree
95. Sewing joint
96. Was in the red
97. Bland
98. Assistant
99. Catch sight of

DOWN
1. Camera ammo
2. Length times width
3. Menagerie worker
4. Navy officers
5. All-male parties
6. Pulls laboriously
7. Dined
8. Workout exercises
9. Costume
10. Cry of dismay
11. Monetary penalty
12. Clothing styles
13. Fowl's wattle
14. Mimicked
15. Only
16. Social equal
26. Integers: abbr.
28. Bullring cheers
29. Gambler's concerns
31. Jokes
33. "___ upon a time ..."
34. Wharf
35. Hints
36. Belt site
37. Church calendar
38. Kinds
39. Robert E. and family
40. Swirling current
42. Baby's father?
43. Alleviates
46. Break sharply
47. Decoration for bravery
48. Long periods of time
50. Border on
51. Amusing pastimes
52. Prejudice
54. More adorable
55. Drain stopper
56. Mix
57. Carry

58. Evict
59. Cornbread
60. Motion picture
61. Keeps in existence
62. Baseball's Slaughter
63. Copenhagen native
65. Fancy initials
66. Fruit's soft part

69. Jerusalem hill
70. Ecclesiastical hat
71. Native American baby
73. Stayed
74. Female military initials
75. Writing tablet
77. Loathed

78. Subterranean sprite
79. Mediocre
80. Declare openly
81. Highly offensive
82. Mongolian desert
83. Bread item

84. Burning liquid
85. Cut grain
86. Military force
90. Onassis, to pals

PUZZLE 610

ACROSS
1. Scan
5. Seafood
9. Entitle
12. Muscle strain
13. Cleveland's lake
14. Pay dirt
15. Karate ____
16. Meticulous
18. Toys for "walking the dog"
20. Fountain treat
21. Make a lap
23. House of snow
27. Money earned on money
32. Harmonize
33. Milk provider
34. Use
36. Conger
37. Heroic poem
39. Oriental cafe
41. Jeans fabric
43. Score to beat
44. Vocal sound
47. Bellybutton
51. Gaily
55. Pianist Peter ____
56. "____ Town"
57. Zenith
58. Encircle
59. Princess's annoyance
60. ____ we forget
61. Alternatively

DOWN
1. Zesty
2. Sound reverberation
3. Nautical shout
4. Oust
5. Provided sustenance to
6. Eye part
7. Missile housing
8. Johanna Spyri's heroine
9. Bambi's mom
10. Footed vase
11. Wager
17. Jokes
19. Horse father
22. Required reading
24. Stead
25. Billfold bills
26. Make eyes at
27. Frosted
28. Yep's antonym
29. Look-alike
30. Grasp
31. Capture
35. By comparison with
38. Quote
40. Juice fruit
42. Virtuous
45. French resort
46. Shade sources
48. Conceal
49. Misplays
50. Rich source
51. Policeman
52. Tint
53. Period in history
54. Notwithstanding

504

PUZZLE 611

ACROSS

1. ___ of roses
4. Sawbucks
8. Make over
12. Mine output
13. Slanted
14. Eager
15. Strawberry's sport
17. Sell
18. Pacino and Molinaro
19. Copycat
21. Pool shot
24. Wasp
27. Feed the kitty
28. Fixed routine
29. "Norma ___"
30. Galahad's title
31. Yields
32. Eden dweller
33. Bullfight cry
34. Fibster
35. Passing grades
36. Sets in order
38. Uptight
39. Humor
40. Suffer
41. Lose weight
43. Wages
48. Farm measure
49. Great Lake
50. Alley ___
51. GI's lunch
52. Cubs rival
53. Plaything

DOWN

1. Comedian Hope
2. Generation
3. ___ Moines
4. Dining-room furniture
5. Greek letters
6. Zilch
7. Scatter
8. Poe's bird
9. Fir
10. Noise
11. Bizarre
16. Soothe
20. Bakery offerings
21. Bricklayer
22. Old womanish
23. Flags
24. Soft drinks
25. Roof overhangs
26. Songstress Della ___
28. Sleigh puller
31. Egyptian queen, for short
35. Food shop
37. Carries
38. Fork prongs
40. Very dry
41. Barrier
42. Frozen water
44. Exist
45. Negative word
46. Sticky substance
47. 007, e.g.

PUZZLE 612

ACROSS

1. ____ soldier
4. Locale
8. Bat an eye
12. Grief
13. Campus official
14. Mideast nation
15. Cleverly defeat
17. Judge's garb
18. Pot covers
19. Cleanse
20. Blockhead
23. Grown boy
24. Change for a nickel
25. Pharmacist
30. BPOE member
31. Fiend
32. Bering or Red
33. Price reduction
35. Pennant
36. Shade tree
37. Spins
38. Grownup
41. Rocky place
43. Attract
44. School for chefs
48. Expensive
49. By mouth
50. Caustic liquid
51. Partner
52. Valuable stones
53. Rent

DOWN

1. Brace
2. Debt letters
3. Trap
4. Acknowledge
5. Peruse
6. Roman loans
7. Picnic pest
8. Electrician's concern
9. Press
10. Captures
11. Place for a patch
16. Groove
19. Tantrum
20. Chilled
21. Lunch spot
22. Signs
23. Mongrel
25. Percussion instrument
26. Flee
27. ____ of Capri
28. Block completely
29. Labels
31. Fastener
34. Dieter's "stick"
35. Leafy plant
37. Ride the ____
38. "The Four Seasons" actor
39. Burr-Hamilton combat
40. Russian mountain range
41. Certain
42. Bivalve
44. Toothed wheel
45. Entire
46. Corned beef on ____
47. However

ACROSS

1. Actor Bogarde
5. Layer
8. Nervous
12. Persia, today
13. Old World deer
14. Function
15. Lavish
17. Adam's home
18. Command to a mule
19. Minor clergy
21. Ribbed cloths
24. Take a chair
25. Bauxite, for one
26. Sweet potato
28. Award
32. Cozy dwelling
34. Index
36. Snacker's haunt
37. Join
39. Bark
41. Delivery truck
42. Vote in favor
44. Shoo!
46. Beams
50. Columnist Buchwald
51. Neighborhood
52. At a higher level
56. Not short
57. Baby seal
58. Poe or Browning
59. Boundaries
60. Sample
61. Covet

DOWN

1. Excavate
2. Fury
3. Tallest
4. Bow down
5. In favor of
6. Flashy
7. Affirmatives
8. Built
9. Extinct bird
10. Valley
11. Inclinations
16. Depend
20. Point a gun
21. Hue
22. Songbird
23. Perched
27. Actress Britt
29. Ardor
30. Arkin or Ladd
31. Rope
33. Pekoe portions
35. Apron
38. Hearty bread
40. Form of fuel
43. Burst forth
45. Fruit of the vine
46. Account
47. Household appliance
48. Heal
49. Urge
53. Undercover man
54. Race, as an engine
55. Pigpen

PUZZLE 613

PUZZLE 614

MOVIES AND TELEVISION

ACROSS

1. Singer Davis
4. "Alice" waitress
7. "___ the Wild Wind"
11. Cosby kid Bonet
12. "The Tender ___"
13. Maison room
14. Sale term
15. "The ___ Is Silence"
16. Actor Williams
17. "Those ___ from Seattle"
19. Lorne of "Bonanza"
20. "We ___ Not Alone" (Muni film)
21. Through
22. "The Great ___"
23. Molinaro and Pacino
24. Powell of "Born to Dance"
29. Rich Little, e.g.
33. Greek vowels
35. "___ Winds" (Fredric March film)
36. "The ___ Show"
37. Carries on
39. Peck film, with "The"
40. Clarinetist Shaw
42. "Each Dawn ___"
43. See 54 Down
44. Actor Lionel ___
46. Before, to a bard
48. "Meet John ___"
49. Numbers man: abbr.
50. "For Me and My ___"
53. "___ Heaven"
57. Bendix-Hayward film, with "The"
59. Sister of 4 Down
60. Actor Singer of "The Beastmaster"
61. "Jane ___"
62. Actor Malden et al.
63. Melville work
64. Actress MacGraw et al.
65. Actress Samms of "The Colbys"
66. Fielding of "Night Court"
67. Magnetism unit

DOWN

1. Scrooge
2. Stage device
3. Singer Johnny ___
4. Star of "Daddy Long Legs"
5. "Brigadoon" girl
6. Choose
7. "The ___ Breed"
8. General Robt. ___
9. Thicke of "Growing Pains"
10. TV's "___ and Gladys"
11. Zhivago's love
12. "The Long, Long ___" (Ball-Arnaz film)
13. "Sesame ___"
18. Gabor of "Green Acres"
19. Actor Gerard
22. "Gigi" star
25. "Pretty Maids All in ___"
26. TV's "___ That Tune"

27. Pindaric works
28. Torn
29. Woeful word
30. Actor's quest
31. Singer James
32. Harness strap
34. Help
38. Pacino film
41. Cantor and Fisher
45. Long, long time
47. Otic organ
50. Actress Hunnicutt
51. "The ____ Fools"
52. Majors and Remick
53. "Let's ____ a Deal"
54. TV's Batman, with 43 Across
55. Skin: pref.
56. Actress Raines
57. Syrian city
58. "Same Time, Next ____"
60. TV's "The ____ Squad"

PUZZLE 614

509

PUZZLE 615

ACROSS
1. Per
5. Drake or stag
9. Dismounted
13. Scarce
14. Wise lawgiver
15. "Adam ____"
16. Essential mineral
17. Glide
18. Wallet items
19. Stitch
20. Pungent root
22. Gawk
24. Concerning
25. Dog
27. Church announcement
29. Correct
30. Jitterbug
31. Subway depot: abbr.
34. Dennis the Menace, e.g.
35. Italian poet Alighieri
36. Wound cover
37. Carpenter or soldier
38. Composer Prokofiev
39. Ignite
40. Lawsuits
41. Lathered
42. Toil
44. Harbor sight
45. Wood-fiber sheeting
48. "I ____ Rhythm"
51. Chalet feature
52. Chapter's partner
53. Only
54. Young or old ending
55. Make joyful
56. Transaction
57. Tattered
58. Hamlet, e.g.
59. Jazzman Kenton

DOWN
1. Goddess of discord
2. River through Bern
3. Ship's lookout site
4. Pullet
5. Bond portrayer
6. So sorry!
7. Place or show
8. Captivate
9. Residences
10. Communist hero
11. That is: Lat.
12. Gibbon's former co-host
14. Orchestrate
20. Round of applause
21. English princess
23. Colorize
25. Torero's cape
26. Final word
27. Hits
28. Sweeten the pot
30. Venture
31. Butt of blame
32. Mild
33. Retired
35. Was worthy of
36. Metal dross
38. Emulate a pack rat
39. Cross a stream
40. Underground chamber
41. Bombay wear
42. " . . . from ____ shining . . ."
43. Rod of the courts
44. Sew temporarily
45. Top grade
46. Lugosi of films
47. Mediterranean port
49. Clay jar
50. "Bandstand" viewer
53. Draft letters

ACROSS

1. Soda fountain drink
5. Tabby
8. Necklace piece
12. Lotion ingredient
13. Tint
14. Unsightly
15. Chief
16. Story
18. Picnic bug
19. Likewise
20. Instant lawn
21. Flightless birds
23. With it
25. Secretary of ancient times
27. Votes in
31. Sonnet
32. Chess piece
33. Summing up
36. Convicted
38. Limo
39. ____ of Capri
40. "Peggy ____ Got Married"
43. Estimate
45. Blue
48. Against
50. Or ____!
51. Dirt
52. None
53. Umbrella weather
54. Previously
55. Hog's home
56. Not at home

DOWN

1. Papa's mate
2. Actor Arkin
3. Hung around
4. Decade number
5. Lounge chair
6. Em, to Dorothy
7. Grow incisors
8. Flower-to-be
9. Selves
10. Choir voice
11. Colored
17. Mattress spring
19. Add to a soundtrack
22. Copy
24. Danger
25. Health resort
26. Cape ____
28. Tangy salad
29. Wee one
30. The blue
34. Harps
35. Rye and corn, e.g.
36. Silly
37. Function
40. Just fair
41. On top of
42. Saga
44. Component
46. Orient
47. Refuse
49. Spanish cheer
50. Generation

PUZZLE 617

ACROSS
1. Very long time
4. Persian king
8. Flunk
12. Pie ___ mode
13. Nutmeg spice
14. Neutral color
15. Shopkeeper
17. Revolve with a hum
18. Lazy
19. Canada flocks
20. Wear away
22. "___ Miniver"
23. Coops
24. Picking up the tab
29. Apple cider girl
30. Sooty
31. Comedian Costello
32. Grand Canyon's river
34. And
35. Laddie
36. Dishearten
37. Fastener
40. Knights' titles
41. Hello, matey!
42. Midday
46. Broad
47. Efficient
48. Belonging to us
49. Sprinted
50. "The ___ Piper"
51. Born, in Paris

DOWN
1. Hearing organ
2. Bullring cheer
3. "___ Velvet"
4. Grin
5. ___ and hearty
6. Highest card
7. She, objectively
8. Least
9. Pain
10. Rainbow goddess
11. Entice
16. Tacks on
19. Dingy
20. Hero's tale
21. Make over
22. Written reminder
24. Waiter's item
25. Free
26. Magic trick
27. Common or proper word
28. Blow
30. Flourish
33. Minded
34. Divide
36. Ate
37. Cuts wood
38. Computer component
39. Went by rail
40. Exclusive
42. Forty winks
43. Japanese sash
44. Expected
45. Before, in poems

512

ACROSS

1. Far and ____
5. Polite cough
9. ____ carte
12. Notion
13. Alone
14. Spoil
15. Bar bills
16. Family possession
18. ____ the line (obeyed)
20. Unkempt
21. Mouselike mammals
24. Actor Max ____ Sydow
25. Acquire knowledge
26. Thieves
30. Vase
31. Speck
32. Prospector's find
33. Crown and scepter
36. Engine
38. Old horse
39. Leave
40. Serious
43. Assistant
44. Stringiest
46. Frontal ____ (brain part)
50. Tune
51. Region
52. Heed
53. Where cranberries grow
54. Greenish blue
55. Moon's pull

DOWN

1. Keen humor
2. Actress Lupino
3. Society gal
4. Spring holiday
5. Fireplace leftovers
6. Cultivated
7. Inventor Whitney
8. Utah settler
9. Andy's partner
10. Thailand's neighbor
11. Military group
17. Give temporarily
19. Hold title to
21. Aspersion
22. Roll call response
23. Tolled
24. Large tank
26. Feathery wrap
27. Tiny particle
28. Horse's gait
29. Bone-dry
31. Excavate
34. Again
35. Noosed rope
36. Angry
37. Spotted wildcat
39. Essential
40. Strike-breaker
41. Buckeye State
42. Piece of a glacier, for short
43. On the briny
45. Before, in poetry
47. Japanese sash
48. Garden plot
49. Organ of sight

PUZZLE 618

PUZZLE 619

ACROSS
1. Worn-out
5. Aid
9. Packed away
11. Chain
13. Nook
14. Hypnotic state
15. Director Howard
16. With long hair
18. Singer "King" Cole
19. Ripened
21. Honey maker
22. Hamilton bills
23. Flower part
25. Rains down icy pellets
27. Break takers
29. Comic Howie ___
31. Begin
35. Red planet
36. Type of neckline
38. Large amount
39. Curved path
40. Shelf
42. Golfer Trevino
43. Merchant
45. Mourn
47. Demure
48. Charred
49. Newcomers to society
50. Supplements

DOWN
1. Larry or Curly, for example
2. "The Green ___"
3. Possess
4. Abound
5. Group of cattle
6. Historical period
7. Small finch
8. Hickory nuts
9. Discard
10. Colorless
11. "Remington ___"
12. Hardens
17. Cuddled up
20. Mends
22. Examinations
24. Conducted
26. Hesitation sounds
28. Harsh
29. Blemished
30. Penny ___
32. Claim without proof
33. Female ruffs
34. Wool fabric
35. Small rugs
37. Hen products
40. Allows
41. New York canal
44. Smidgen
46. Writing fluid

514

PUZZLE 1

```
ROE  IMP   OLE    EWE
IRE  DREW  NOSEGAY
CALLASPADEASPADE
ELSE    PRO    EINE
      OGLE  RAIN
WAG  LAR  ADO   GAP
ALA  ESS  ENROLL
TERRA       ELBOW
ATE  DAN  MAD   WAS
FIR  EKE  APE   UNA
TED  NED  KEN   NEW
ROWER      ERRED
WORSEN   PAH   ORE
NOS  LEG  AGA   DAR
     SLOE  ROYS
STAT  ADS     ASEA
TURNOVERANEWLEAF
UPATREE  DIVE  EVA
TSP  MEG  PET   PER
```

PUZZLE 5

```
LIP   BOTH   AFAR
ALE   LURE   CAME
PLATINUM    TREE
     ONCE  FIEND
INVADE   BIN
DEAD    BAGGAGE
LOT  BEERS   TEA
ENSLAVE    MOMS
     AGE  ELAPSE
CRIBS    BAIL
HIRE   MAGNETIC
IDOL  ABLE   WOO
PENS  TEEN   OUT
```

PUZZLE 9

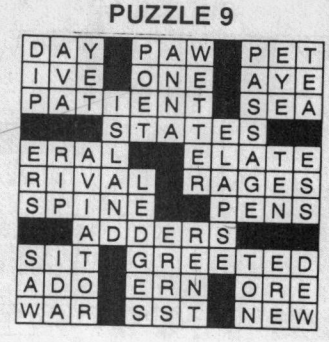

```
DAY  PAW    PET
IVE  ONE    AYE
PATIENT    SEA
      STATES
ERAL    ELATE
RIVAL   RAGES
SPINE    PENS
     ADDERS
SIT   GREETED
ADO   ERN   ORE
WAR   SST   NEW
```

PUZZLE 2

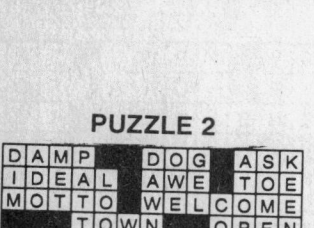

```
DAMP    DOG   ASK
IDEAL   AWE   TOE
MOTTO  WELCOME
    TOWN    OPEN
CINEMA   BOY
ODOR  LEAN   HAT
MOO  ALONE   EGO
ELK  RENT   LION
    ACT   EMERGE
JAIL     BRAG
OBSERVE   RECAP
ILL  OIL   KNAVE
NEE  BAT   DREW
```

PUZZLE 6

```
              HIT
         STY  ATO
         TRA  REP
        DOER  TRE
      ROWAN  FAKE
      DIVED  OTARY
ARTE     IRE   RED
HEARD    AND   OAR
ADS  OOPS    MARRY
       PHOENIX
SALEM  CULL   CPA
EVE   CTS   ETHIC
TIE   PHS    HATE
SCARE      PRESS
HUEY       BOISE
SSE        LINE
TAN        ESS
IGN        WEE
NEE
```

PUZZLE 10

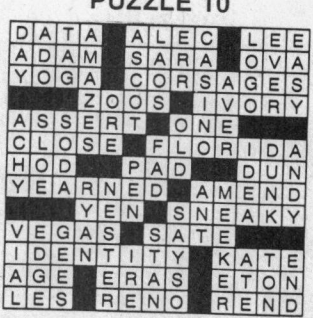

```
DATA    ALEC   LEE
ADAM    SARA   OVA
YOGA   CORSAGES
      ZOOS  IVORY
ASSERT   ONE
CLOSE  FLORIDA
HOD   PAD    DUN
YEARNED    AMEND
      YEN  SNEAKY
VEGAS    SATE
IDENTITY   KATE
AGE  ERAS   ETON
LES  RENO   REND
```

PUZZLE 3

```
HOSE   FEN   DAMS
ABLE   AXE   ORAL
ROULETTE    ZERO
PER  PAR    YEAST
     RELATE
VALUE   OUT   SIP
EDIT   ORB   COLA
TOT   KID   JOLLY
      ELICIT
PICKY   NAB   HUG
EDEN   BASEBALL
GENE   ART   ERNE
SATE   DYE   DEAN
```

PUZZLE 7

```
SARA   LOB   TEST
EDEN   OPERATOR
TICK   PARABOLA
ATOLL   LEG   NAY
     VEAL  TED
GEE   GIN   SEDAN
ERRS   PAH   WIDE
MAYOR   BUT   SOW
     PAL   MUSS
RAM   BIS   BLOOM
INIMICAL    OLLA
SOLIDIFY    OVER
ENDS   TEE   PEAK
```

PUZZLE 11

```
CHAT     SLY   APES
LABOR   PEAR  LIMA
AZURE   RANI  OXEN
PETER   INKS  NINE
     URGE  EDGED
PHONE    SPRY
WEAK  ANTE  ELATE
ASTRIDE   RADICAL
STEAM  TAMP  FILM
     PAST  SWEDE
BURST    HOER
LANE   TALL  OFFER
AKIN   IRED  TRADE
METE   CITE  EARED
BREW    DEN   TENS
```

PUZZLE 12

1. Bath, 2. Boy, 3. Place, 4. Drop, 5. Hop, 6. Sugar, 7. Way, 8. Shell, 9. Blue, 10. Skin.

PUZZLE 4

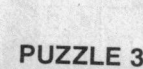

```
BAG   CASH   DAMS
EVA   OHIO   UTAH
TOP   RANG   MANY
SNEER    GASP
    LAP   NEEDED
WAFFLES    ADAGE
ALE    WON    RAN
VALVE   SECONDS
ENTIRE    TAN
    SALT   BEAST
ANDI   DOLL   COO
GOUT   ERIE   TIN
OWES   REED   SLY
```

PUZZLE 8

```
JOE    DARK   SHAW
IRA    OJAI   PINE
MARIOANDRETTI
     ORR    UNSER
TOOLS    SLID
ALVA   SPONSORS
REU  ROOTS   BOA
SAMHANKS    MESA
     OISE   MEYER
ANGUS    CAM
PARNELLIJONES
ENID   AUTO   ARA
RAPS   OMER   PAT
```

PUZZLE 13

```
RADISH     BIGAMIST
E  O    O    R  S  G  R
TOWELS    DISPENSE
A  N   E  Q  S  S  O  N
IMPS   PUSHY   PROD
N  O  A   A  S  A  E  S
EQUESTRIENNE
R   R   S   T   G  A  C
RELENTLESSLY
T  I  T   R  E  R  S  L
OWNS    SHORE   MAGI
P  F  S  O  S  P    I  N
PAINTERS    MULLED
E    R  U  S   M  E  E
REMINDER    SPIDER
```

PUZZLE 14

```
BEG  CHAP  THAT
ERE  RODE  HALO
IRE  YESTERDAY
NOSES    EGO
GREATER  GAILY
    RADAR  TREE
PEG  LIKED  KEN
OVAL  TEARS
PESOS  SLEETED
    CAB  STORE
ANNAPOLIS  TOP
BOAT  GENE  ADO
EDGE  SONS  LET
```

PUZZLE 18

```
DARE  FITS  OWE
ALAN  IRAN  WON
TEST  RECALLED
ASPIC    ORE
    BRAG  SENSE
KNEELED  THAW
EAR  FEARS  USE
GIRL  YIELDED
    LYING  GLAD
    NOR  FRESH
TIRESOME  ERIE
ACE  EVES  DELI
BED  YEWS  ODOR
```

PUZZLE 22

```
PEG  ALPS  SHOW
ERA  TAIL  HAVE
PER  TREASURED
    LIED  METERS
LEARN  AMES
OWNED  PEN  OLE
RED  FAD  POD
ESS  ERR  FLOOD
    PLOT  RISKY
BROOKS  KIDS
LIMESTONE  URN
EDIT  EDEN  MOO
WETS  DEED  SET
```

PUZZLE 15

```
MASH  YAMS  STY
ECHO  ALEC  ERA
TEEN  NARROWER
    OAK  CEASED
COARSE  YES
OAF  HEM  NIPPY
STAB  SAD  SOLE
THREW  DAB  LAW
    GOB  WAGONS
APPALL  DYE
RAINFALL  EARS
KIT  ERIE  SNAP
SLY  DEED  EDGY
```

PUZZLE 19

```
FUR  SLAT  CLAY
APE  EACH  RIDE
CONFETTI  ODDS
ENOUGH  COO
    SEE  KANSAS
DEFER  HER  IRE
ORES  PAN  FLEE
OIL  SAT  CLOAK
METHOD  TOE
    OLD  HASSLE
THAN  OVERHEAD
AUTO  CARS  ACE
DEER  KNEE  TEN
```

PUZZLE 23

```
PRY  FROG  TRAY
EYE  IOWA  ROLE
GENERALS  IOTA
    WED  ACTOR
SKIES  HAWK
ENDS  CARESSED
LEE  TURKS  OLE
FEATHERS  NOSE
    EASY  PETER
PECAN  WAX
ADOS  WHITTLED
IDLE  HUNT  IRE
DYED  OBEY  PEN
```

PUZZLE 16

```
POP  ALAS  BOLD
EMU  RODE  IDEA
AIR  OPEN  NEED
STEAM  STAG
    CAB  COBRA
FEAR  IDLE  ROD
AXLE  RUE  COLD
DIE  ADOS  AWES
STEEL  SAP
    ALSO  DEBTS
SAGS  ALTO  URN
EPEE  LEER  LEA
TELL  TONE  BEG
```

PUZZLE 20

```
LEG  PRO  ABLE
URN  TOOL  REAP
GRUESOME  CAME
    GALE  THREE
ACTORS  OWE
CUES  ADORNED
IRE  FUNDS  IVY
DENTIST  GLEE
    ALE  FRIEND
ANGLE  REAR
MILE  BEWILDER
ICON  EDEN  ORE
DEBT  NOR  GAD
```

PUZZLE 24

```
BAG  SHA  GALA
URN  BIAS  ENID
STUDENTS  ATEE
    RAGE  WRENS
FAMOUS  LEE
ATOP  GANDER
NOR  COAST  DOG
    MELONS  CEDE
    APE  BRUNET
SPADE  TOUR
ARID  BORDERED
FADE  ANNE  AWE
EYER  DEE  PEN
```

PUZZLE 17

```
BLEW  YAWN  SHE
RAVE  AWRY  KEY
ICED  MEALTIME
MENDS    POE
    ETCH  NAKED
POWDERED  SAVE
ABE  MORAL  TIN
SEEN  POLITELY
TYPES  NEAR
    COP  RISER
BOOKWORM  PERU
IDA  ERIE  LARD
BET  DEBT  ELSE
```

PUZZLE 21

```
    FIR        CAB
  SALON      SAVOR
  CUCKOO     CRANES
 HIT  TEA   CAT  DEW
 SIT  WELD  ANON  FAR
LAC PER IMP  NAB  LEI
ANKLET  EAR  PEELER
STEEP  QUAIL  AROSE
AND  EMU    ILE  EWE
     ROE    KEY
OFF  APE    ENE  DOT
ELLEN  ROBIN  LOREN
ALINED  GYM  DOCILE
TIC WIT LEA  DIN  OLD
EKE  MORE  GOOD  SLY
EVE  MAD   ERN  SEE
REDCAP      EAGLES
RIOTS       STOOD
TOO          EBB
```

PUZZLE 25

```
GAS  BLEW  AWAY
ICE  RAVE  LOGO
NEW  IDEA  TEEN
    SNOB  ROE
    FEAR  PRICE
BOAT  WARE  RAY
OAR  BEGUN  APE
ATE  IDES  ONES
SHAFT  STEW
    RED  MEAT
RATE  ARAB  RUE
OBOE  RODE  INN
TEND  EWER  DAD
```

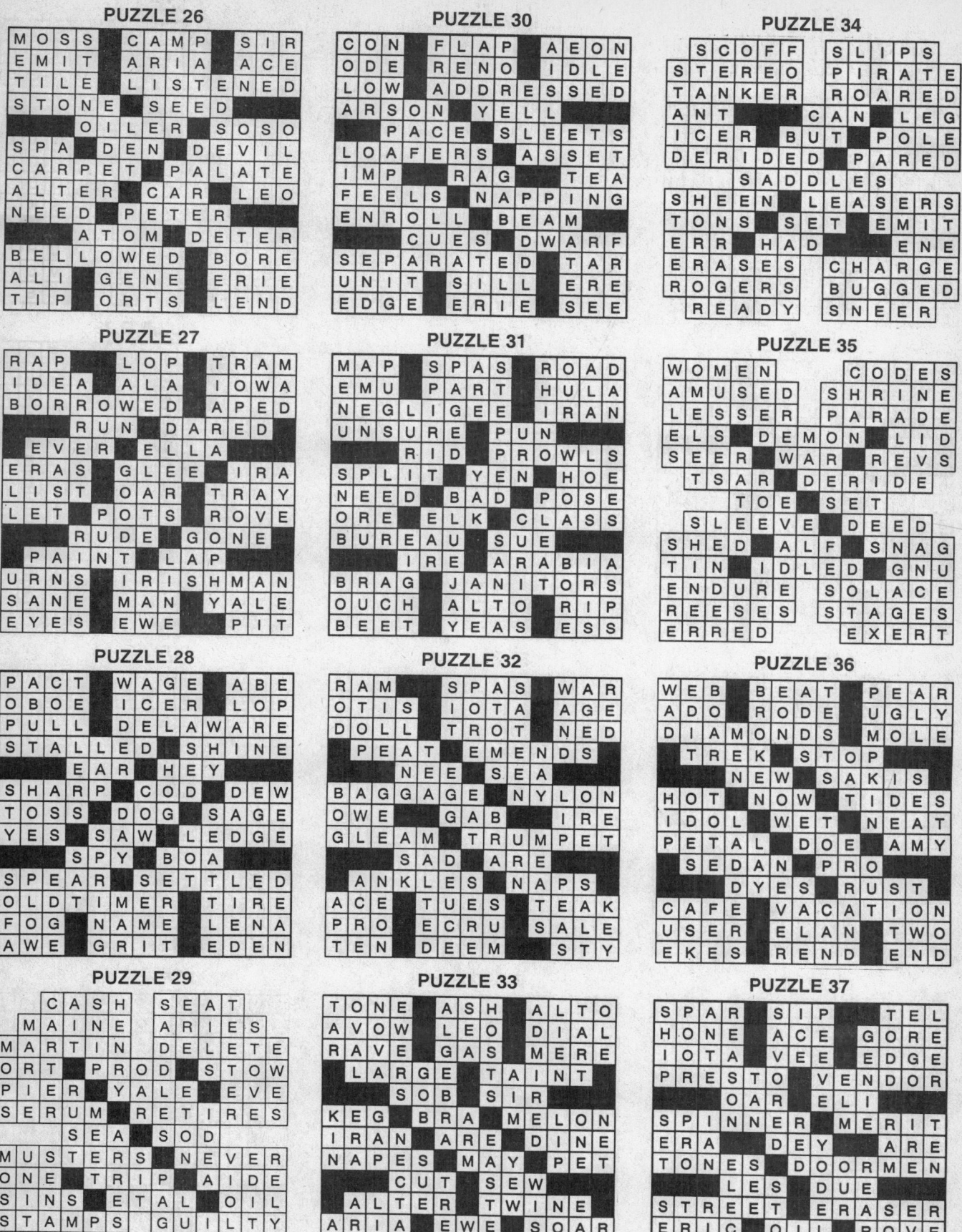

PUZZLE 26

```
MOSS CAMP  SIR
EMIT ARIA  ACE
TILE LISTENED
STONE  SEED
   OILER  SOSO
SPA DEN  DEVIL
CARPET  PALATE
ALTER  CAR  LEO
NEED  PETER
   ATOM  DETER
BELLOWED  BORE
ALI  GENE  ERIE
TIP  ORTS  LEND
```

PUZZLE 30

```
CON  FLAP  AEON
ODE  RENO  IDLE
LOW  ADDRESSED
ARSON  YELL
 PACE  SLEETS
LOAFERS  ASSET
IMP  RAG   TEA
FEELS  NAPPING
ENROLL  BEAM
  CUES  DWARF
SEPARATED  TAR
UNIT  SILL  ERE
EDGE  ERIE  SEE
```

PUZZLE 34

```
 SCOFF  SLIPS
STEREO  PIRATE
TANKER  ROARED
ANT   CAN   LEG
ICER  BUT  POLE
DERIDED  PARED
  SADDLES
SHEEN  LEASERS
TONS  SET  EMIT
ERR  HAD   ENE
ERASES  CHARGE
ROGERS  BUGGED
READY   SNEER
```

PUZZLE 27

```
RAP   LOP  TRAM
IDEA  ALA  IOWA
BORROWED  APED
  RUN  DARED
 EVER  ELLA
ERAS  GLEE  IRA
LIST  OAR  TRAY
LET  POTS  ROVE
  RUDE  GONE
 PAINT  LAP
URNS  IRISHMAN
SANE  MAN  YALE
EYES  EWE   PIT
```

PUZZLE 31

```
MAP  SPAS  ROAD
EMU  PART  HULA
NEGLIGEE  IRAN
UNSURE  PUN
  RID  PROWLS
SPLIT  YEN  HOE
NEED  BAD  POSE
ORE  ELK  CLASS
BUREAU  SUE
  IRE  ARABIA
BRAG  JANITORS
OUCH  ALTO  RIP
BEET  YEAS  ESS
```

PUZZLE 35

```
WOMEN     CODES
AMUSED  SHRINE
LESSER  PARADE
ELS  DEMON  LID
SEER  WAR  REVS
 TSAR  DERIDE
   TOE  SET
 SLEEVE  DEED
SHED  ALF  SNAG
TIN  IDLED  GNU
ENDURE  SOLACE
REESES  STAGES
ERRED   EXERT
```

PUZZLE 28

```
PACT  WAGE  ABE
OBOE  ICER  LOP
PULL  DELAWARE
STALLED  SHINE
  EAR  HEY
SHARP  COD  DEW
TOSS  DOG  SAGE
YES  SAW  LEDGE
  SPY  BOA
SPEAR  SETTLED
OLDTIMER  TIRE
FOG  NAME  LENA
AWE  GRIT  EDEN
```

PUZZLE 32

```
RAM  SPAS   WAR
OTIS  IOTA  AGE
DOLL  TROT  NED
 PEAT  EMENDS
  NEE  SEA
BAGGAGE  NYLON
OWE  GAB   IRE
GLEAM  TRUMPET
  SAD  ARE
 ANKLES  NAPS
ACE  TUES  TEAK
PRO  ECRU  SALE
TEN  DEEM   STY
```

PUZZLE 36

```
WEB  BEAT  PEAR
ADO  RODE  UGLY
DIAMONDS  MOLE
 TREK  STOP
  NEW  SAKIS
HOT  NOW  TIDES
IDOL  WET  NEAT
PETAL  DOE  AMY
 SEDAN  PRO
  DYES  RUST
CAFE  VACATION
USER  ELAN  TWO
EKES  REND  END
```

PUZZLE 29

```
 CASH   SEAT
 MAINE  ARIES
MARTIN  DELETE
ORT  PROD  STOW
PIER  YALE  EVE
SERUM  RETIRES
  SEA  SOD
MUSTERS  NEVER
ONE  TRIP  AIDE
SINS  ETAL  OIL
STAMPS  GUILTY
 STOUT  ERNES
 EGGS   SENT
```

PUZZLE 33

```
TONE  ASH  ALTO
AVOW  LEO  DIAL
RAVE  GAS  MERE
 LARGE  TAINT
  SOB  SIR
KEG  BRA  MELON
IRAN  ARE  DINE
NAPES  MAY  PET
  CUT  SEW
 ALTER  TWINE
ARIA  EWE  SOAR
SEER  NOR  PESO
PADS  DON  SLED
```

PUZZLE 37

```
SPAR   SIP   TEL
HONE  ACE  GORE
IOTA  VEE  EDGE
PRESTO  VENDOR
  OAR  ELI
SPINNER  MERIT
ERA  DEY   ARE
TONES  DOORMEN
  LES  DUE
STREET  ERASER
ERIC  OIL  ROVE
AUNT  UKE  ERIE
LEG   TED  DELL
```

PUZZLE 38

```
CAPE  BIDS   RIFLE
URAL  ALOE   ERROL
RIDE  NILE   TOILS
BERMUDATRIANGLE
SLEETED    DISH
    NED DELL  TNT
WHETS  LIVES  EUR
HANS  ROVER  ENDO
ELD  REGAN  INSET
YOU   EBON   ART
    RACE  ALARMED
TRAFALGARSQUARE
HINTS  ALGA  SCAN
ASCOT  BLOC  TOSS
TEENS  SANE  SNEE
```

PUZZLE 42

```
MASTS  WEAR  CRAB
ASTRO  HAVE  RALE
THEINVISIBLEMAN
TERN  ETTA  YEAST
    ATEE  RASP
HALLE  TOYS  IOTA
ARI  MAIR  TINTIN
DISAPPEARINGACT
OSTLER  TERR  RAE
NEST  IRED  ELULS
    ERLE  LAME
OHARE  LAIR  GRAS
VANISHINGCREAMS
IRON  INCH  UNSET
DING  MEET  EDENS
```

PUZZLE 46

```
BALL  PERIS  SHAM
AMIE  ENORM  POSE
NOLA  LOCKSMITHS
GRIDLOCK   INEES
    ETH  PANELS
MARINA   DEBIT
ARIZ  TURBO  ACE
UNDERLOCKANDKEY
LEE  EASTS  AIDE
    ACHES  BONNES
BEWARE   LAW
ARNAS   FETLOCKS
LOCKERROOM  TRIP
MARE  AVENA  TETE
EDEN  ESSEN  OWED
```

PUZZLE 39

```
LAST  NIHIL  STAR
AMAH  ENACT  HYPO
MINE  ACRES  EROS
BETTE  APR  ABODE
SOILURE    ATE
EASER   MOLINE
BASS  SOV  SPINEL
OMIT  FAT  ETAL
BATHES  LEI  VOLE
STEADY   LATHE
TIN  EMERSON
NIOBE  TYS  HIRER
ASTI  COPTS  NINE
PEON  ANTES  MEET
SEED  NEARS  ELSE
```

PUZZLE 43

```
BEES   SSTS  POSE
OATH  TULIP  OPAL
ARNO  HEIDI  WELL
LADDERPERFECT
DORS    AIR
STYRO  NELLFILE
CIO  MADAM  LUMET
ANTS  DENIM  LENO
SEATS  ECLAT  ANN
AWLREADY  NANNY
OTT   ANTE
ALLABOUTEAVES
EVIL  ERROR  ARAB
WINE  SCANS  DIRE
EDER  TALE  ACID
```

PUZZLE 47

```
BIB   IMP   METE
ARID  CARA  ATONE
BONE  IDOL  YARDS
ANDITCAMETOPASS
ELM   ORE
SABINE  EEK  MRS
AROSE  ANTA  EEL
GREATISTHYMERCY
EAR  SEES  ELITE
SSS  TAR  CASTOR
SEL  MEN
ANDIWENTUNTOTHE
MAIZE  REST  FOOD
TIMER  ANTE  FROG
LESS   SYR   EKE
```

PUZZLE 40

```
CAFE  SAIL  SPAS  ILES
ICES  OLLA  CENT  SATE
THESONGOFBERNADETTE
EEL  VIA  IONE  OREAD
SIC  ETRE  CLUE
SAPID  TATI  BEAS  PAM
LEAN  RICE  LARGE  AWL
ARS  FOCH  SEMIS  BREL
VOSGES  BOMBS  ARIDE
PATESDEFOIEGRAS
AMORE  URBAN  RODINS
MERE  CRIES  SLEW  AIT
ANT  CHEFS  CLAY  ONCE
DDS  LETT  MUIR  OASES
FARE  MAST  CPS
RADII  SERT  ALE  AZO
THEFRENCHCONNECTION
EIRE  BEAT  MONA  ARLO
STER  BETA  STIR  ISAR
```

PUZZLE 44

```
DAMS  TARS   DIET
ATOM  ALOE  CIRCE
TORE  CLAN  ROARS
APOLLOANDNEREUS
TIM   SAT
AME  NABS  MELOS
NITRE  ROSE  ALAR
ATHENAANDSELENE
TRET  LEDA  BOOTY
ELEMI  EKES  SOS
OBI   DEN
OLYMPIAANDNEMEA
FUSEE  MCII  NORD
FREED  BENE  ENID
SERT  EROS  SASS
```

PUZZLE 48

```
SNAG  BAKE  SHAM
HOLE  EVERT  TIDE
ADAM  RELAY  ODDS
HER  WARP  CARESS
SMARTS  SOLE
LIE  COASTAL
VISIT  EARNS  ALE
ABUT  ALIAS  BLOT
SEE  PSALM  FREES
EXTRACT   TEA
EPEE  READER
BARMAN  SEAR  AIM
AREA  DATES  OGLE
TIED  STAVE  PLEA
SALE  EYES  TEST
```

PUZZLE 41

```
ASKS  COMES  DARE
SLIP  ALAMO  AMID
POLO  RERUN  KONG
GORGEOUSGEORGE
TEES   SAT
VISION  DETRACTS
ESTER  SURE  LIP
GEORGECMARSHALL
ARA  LAPS  LINDA
SETTLERS  NUGGET
YAM   BASH
GEORGEGERSHWIN
LAVA  NADIA  ACES
IVAN  TRIAL  YORE
BELT  SEERS  SNOW
```

PUZZLE 45

```
PAL  SEPIA  IMP
SAGA  AGENT  DOOR
TOTEM  MARSHMALLOW
IDE  PLOD  PEA  DIME
SANGRIA  PINTS  CAP
LED  CARS  ANENT
SPRAY  LACE  PLUS
LOAD  LAKE  FLATTOP
ALP  COTE  GOOD  AVE
MESSAGE  HOOT  STAR
CURE  HAND  WHELK
SHAME  MAZE  BOO
CAL  THERE  PURPOSE
OILS  ADD  DUSK  COR
TRIALLAWYER  MOTOR
SOME  LOESS  EDEN
NEE  SNAKE  NET
```

PUZZLE 49

```
AMAS  GABOR  BARB
GOSH  ALONE  ARIA
ELEE  TOAST  RELY
DEARDEER  IDEALS
PEGS   GLIB
CASABA  ERLEEARL
HOT  TITLE  MARIA
ERAL  TAMER  ROCK
ATREE  CEDES  SEE
PAREPAIR  ANGERS
REST   BLEU
STOLES  TARETEAR
PALE  EROSE  TARA
ALDA  TANTE  EVEN
SEER  STEEL  DESK
```

PUZZLE 50

```
GUSTO  PRONE  FRETS
ALLOW  RABID  RAYON
STATE  ALIBI  OMEGA
PRY  DANE  SCOW  SAP
SASS  SKIP  TUNE
  TAP  GAD  REMISS
AMEN  SHREW  DITTO
CRYPTIC  KNOT  THAW
AGO  SMOG  TREE  AVE
TYPE  PORT  REDUCED
CLING  PURSY  ERAS
HEADED  BIT  INN
  SNOB  MILL  SALT
WAG  EGAD  RAKE  LEA
RULER  SOARS  CHEAP
ARENA  INPUT  HORSE
PANEL  SEEPS  OTTER
```

One way to make dreams come true is to wake up.

PUZZLE 51

```
ARAB  RATIO  SPAT
BOIL  ELAND  TRIO
ECRU  ATONE  RODE
ESSENCE  LOPES
  ATRANDOM
STRAPS  MOOT  LET
CRIME  CEDE  BEAR
RAVE  PARES  RAGE
ACES  URIS  DIVES
PER  EPIC  TIMERS
  ALABAMAN
RAMPS  OPERATE
ALOE  ROUSE  ENID
PARR  EATER  TONG
TRES  DRESS  SNEE
```

PUZZLE 52

1. School, 2. Tail, 3. Club, 4. Book, 5. Shoe, 6. Shot, 7. Glass, 8. Pole.

PUZZLE 53

```
PLUM  GAFFE  COO
AONE  ALLEN  CHAR
SPIN  ROUND  REST
SET  WANE  UBOATS
  PAGE  DRYUP
RENEGE  CREEPERS
ABELE  BOERS  NOT
NEAT  SODAS  DINO
ERR  TONED  PANDA
ETAGERES  CARGOS
  TENET  WELT
ATHENS  GRAS  AVE
BRAS  POLES  IRED
BONE  OBESE  MING
ADD  TINTS  PATE
```

PUZZLE 54

1. Inflation, 2. Contingent, 3. Abandon, 4. Uppercut, 5. Toreador, 6. Perforate, 7. Bulkhead, 8. Artistic.

PUZZLE 55

```
SPAT  ICONS  BLEW
EASE  NAVAL  RIPE
TRIM  TRACE  OPEN
STAPLES  REVISED
  EER  REVEL
NONSENSE  ENERGY
OMIT  ALAS  DRONE
MEN  GLIDERS  VOL
AGORA  MERE  HEMP
DANISH  RESTORES
  PEARS  PAL
FINESSE  MODISTE
ANON  SPAIN  DAWN
DIVE  LEANS  AMID
STAR  ELATE  YENS
```

PUZZLE 56

A-2, B-6, C-3, D-1, E-8, F-7, G-5, H-4, I-9.

PUZZLE 57

```
SPED  ALA  TSAR
TODO  ROC  EERO
URAL  EAR  SEEN
DEMEAN  OPTS
  FLAMBOYANT
AWFUL  OAT  WOE
NOEL  OUT  FETA
TRA  IFS  RIDER
INTERFERED
  UTAH  AFGHAN
PERU  APT  EAVE
AGED  NIT  TROT
NOSE  DAY  YENS
```

PUZZLE 58

```
LEAF  SEW  SOB
CARGO  ALE  ERA
ANNOY  LIBERAL
BEE  EPIC  VALE
  PROVIDE
ROAR  DATE  NOT
IDIOM  NAIVE
BED  OBOE  PLAN
  COURAGE
ALSO  RATE  SUP
BETWEEN  NOISE
LEA  NAG  UNDER
ERR  DUE  SEED
```

PUZZLE 59

```
SCAR  UFO  CLAP
PACE  PAN  RAVE
AIRS  PRODUCER
SNOOPER  INERT
  SLED  MAC
ALTER  GOPHERS
TAI  CREPE  VIA
EXCLAIM  RUING
  OLD  FEND
SINCE  TIDIEST
TREASURE  SNOW
EMIT  GIN  OCTO
MANE  HOD  NESS
```

PUZZLE 60

```
LAIC  COPE  HOD
ALDA  APEX  AVA
BEAR  BRACELET
  HOLY  EXTRA
EUROPE  ALI
CRAPS  BISTROS
RIG  TUT  APO
USELESS  FLYER
  ACE  CLIENT
SWIRL  TRUE
COCKATOO  LADY
ORE  IOTA  OBOE
WED  REEK  WETS
```

PUZZLE 61

```
TIP  APT  FLAME
ADO  RAHS  CLOVER
BASSINET  ROTATE
SETS  ORDERS
  EEL  AREA  DIP
POP  OWNED  LINE
SAL  LORDS  FALSE
ANIMATE  STABLER
DIVES  SHEEN  ERS
ICED  STARE  ART
ESS  TELL  NAB
  RIVETS  REDS
GARAGE  ENVELOPE
AWAKEN  RUIN  WRY
PETER  BEA  NYE
```

PUZZLE 62

SP/LAS/HY

PUZZLE 63

```
COVER  TOTE  BATS
ALIKE  APEX  OBOE
LINES  REAP  SURE
FOE  CORN  LASTED
  FURY  ROPY
DEGREE  HARE  MAR
RARER  SAVES  ERA
AGUE  EMBER  WAIT
MEN  AVAIL  MANSE
ART  SECT  NURSED
  PERK  BODY
BETRAY  HERD  GOB
ACRE  OVER  LARGE
THIS  NINE  EXILE
HOPS  EAST  DETER
```

PUZZLE 64

1. Tennis, 2. Soccer, 3. Fencing, 4. Hockey, 5. Boxing, 6. Rowing.
BONUS: Skiing

PUZZLE 65

```
BEGIN  C  ASE
RA  NDO MDR  IP
PART  NE R  IRE
OP  ERA  CO A RSE
W R  IN KLEW O
L  AC ET A R  T
SAL  ADR EM O TE
E Y  EOI  L WAN
MU  TT  ERSEN D
AD  DERUNITLIT
ROB  US TA C E D
N E TAI  SL  E
  ABSOL  VEER R
STRI P CE  ASE
HO  TE LK E  EN
```

519

PUZZLE 66

```
IMPALE YACHT AREA
COUSIN AROAR REDS
ERRANT MANNA CLIP
SEE CEN SKIP ATE
   FOREST STANTON
BASAL TWIG LEERS
LATIN ANA TAD
ARAL MAP SHOT ACT
SON POD ODE BAR
END LOOP WED ROBE
   DAD AGE DAVIS
SABOT ROAD OVENS
ELECTED BROGUE
WAC ERAS ERG EEL
ARAB AMISS ALUMNI
RILE SARAH NATION
DAME ENEMY TSETSE
```

PUZZLE 70

```
NEWT KID PAS SLED
OPAH ROVE CAST TARO
LONI ERAS ALSO EXIT
ASTRIDE ILL ERIE
STRANGEINTERLUDE
MATEO ONICE SEELEY
BAS ASST SONG RENE
ARIL EWER ERIC STD
ALAE ARABY AVAL
LONGDAYSJOURNEYINTO
SARI ARMED ROOM
PRO BING ASEA ANTE
LOBE GOAL TEMP EIN
EMERGE TRACE ARETE
BEYONDTHEHORIZON
DUDE ORA COMRADE
MIMI IDOL TWIN OVID
ADEN EDNA EONS LOVE
TANG DYE DOG SWAN
```

PUZZLE 74

```
TAB OLD
CHIEF TRAIL
FEUDAL RAGGED
ADD MOTEL NAY
DESI ARE FINE
DUTY ARTS
FAR TOY
JOHN WOES
HERO PAD THAN
EWE BUDDY AGO
MEMBER LEERED
LAYER YARDS
NET RAY
```

PUZZLE 67

```
SPORT PAGE
TABOO TALON
ENEMY ALLOT
MESA LEASE
SENATE HER
BIN
LAW SETTER
ALICE ORES
SIREN ATOLL
EVENT RADIO
REST ELECT
```

PUZZLE 71

```
CAN BRAT LARK
AGO ROLE ALAN
TERRIBLE PETE
OBEY JESSE
BASTE EEL
URNS BEARSKIN
LEO BLACK IRA
BABERUTH ATOM
LEE SCENE
THROW POPE
HEAP CAMISOLE
ERIE OVEN DON
MOLD GENE DUD
```

PUZZLE 75

```
LAS AFAR GLOW
ASK CUTE EASE
WHISTLED NILE
PEEL HOTROD
TAPED SEAL
HUES PARENTS
ERR WORDS ORE
MASCARA SMUT
ANDY SPIES
MINUTE SWAN
ADOS RECITALS
ROSE ERAS TEA
SLED DENS EGG
```

PUZZLE 68

```
MAC BRAT SCAM
ALA RAID ARTE
PIGTAILS LEER
STEAKS JAW
LEE MADCAP
SAGES MOM USA
TORS JOB STIR
ANA SAP CASAS
GEYSER SAD
HAT TRADES
TEAS FLATTOPS
OTIS LAKE LET
MARY APER LES
```

PUZZLE 72

```
ROSES GROSS MEETS
OLIVE RELET ALLIE
ALTER ANEAR OMEGA
MIA MAST SUR NET
ERRORS TOTO MARS
ONE EON CPA
HAWN IVE ATLAS
ELIA ACES CAPTAIN
MIN IDOL POLA IDO
ADDISON NORA KNEW
NASAL INN NESS
GET SLY BEE
FARO ARTE HELENA
IGO PIE MONA ORB
RAMON NEVER ILONA
ETAPE GLASS NOSIR
SENTA SENSE EMEER
```

PUZZLE 76

```
DAB JADE FRO
ODE EXIT FLAN
DIE RENO EASE
OTTER NORTH
RYE ANT
APER LAST EGO
SIN LARKS RED
PET ANTI DYED
RAT PER
RACER QUITE
ZONE OAHU DIP
EATS ALAI OLE
ENS RAMP LEE
```

PUZZLE 69

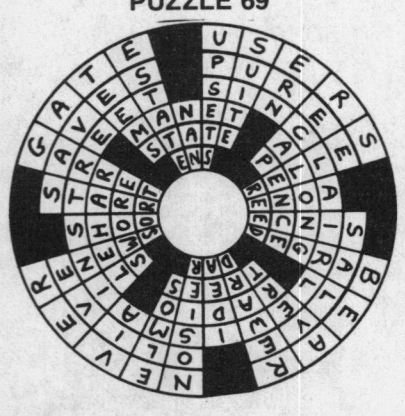

PUZZLE 73

```
TEE AWES AWAY
URN RAGE PORE
RID ODOR ANTS
NESTS SEAR
RED STRAW
SATE RAMS USE
HIRE AGO ALES
ADO OWED NEAT
METER EAT
VEST DENTS
ACRE LIED OAT
ROAR IDLE TIE
COPY MELD ELM
```

PUZZLE 77

```
FOG SHOP SPY
RARE PAGE TOE
ORAL AILS ART
SMOG RETORT
POP DEN
ALGEBRA REVEL
DOE ODD ARE
SWEET DELETES
LAM WAG
BALLOT BRAG
RAP EVIL EVER
ABE NILE TONE
YES TEED WED
```

PUZZLE 78

```
HARP ACT      DRAB
AREA RARE    QUIRE
ZEAL CRIB    UNDID
END      EMBRACED
   ASPIRE    ARE
   LOIN  ANT FEW
SPRUNG  WHIZ AXE
TEAM    VIA  QUID
ORT SLAG  JAUNTS
ATE HOT   MAGI
   CAP   EMOTES
   TRAVELED  RIM
LEAVE EDDY  GONE
ELVES GALE  ASKS
ALES      MET LESS
```

1-Z, 2-I, 3-D, 4-P, 5-S, 6-Q, 7-W, 8-T, 9-V, 10-E, 11-A, 12-H, 13-B, 14-Y, 15-C, 16-N, 17-U, 18-J, 19-G, 20-R, 21-M, 22-L, 23-O, 24-K, 25-F, 26-X.

PUZZLE 82

```
SNUB AORTA NEW ALAS
LOLA CRUEL OVA PALP
OVAL REMAP PANDOWDY
BANZAI    ABE   ULNA
   ADD ORCA  REEL
BOCCE BROAD ACTORS
AHA BULB OCHS  ACE
NIB BADE CAMEO CZAR
GOATEE AIMER FLORA
   LINZ ARGON BLUR
POLED BLEAR RABBET
EYED BRIAR ARAB ANY
DER FEAT  ABUT COP
ZODIAC IBSEN ANKLE
   RODE DAHL  VIA
   BOAR OAF ALBANY
WINGDING FLAIL BRIE
OTTO CAR LOIRE ETNA
ETON ETE EGRET DYER
```

PUZZLE 86

```
SANG   DOT     BAD
ODOR   ERAS    IVY
DETERGENT      TIE
   EAR      GORED
CHANCE       ONE
LEG KEY      YACHT
AREA SEW     POOR
PERCH TAB    POE
   MOD     RECEDE
   SPEAR    MAR
HOE      REFERENCE
ODE DAIS     SOON
GAL   MET    TROD
```

PUZZLE 79

```
HOSS EATS TASK MANE
ADAH SLAM ECHO ARES
LOVE PALO TRAP REST
FREDERICKLOEWE VASE
   DIN ION   LEI
GADGET ANT PLANTER
ALIEN GIG SHE RHONE
RENO OAT STARS ARON
REGRETS EWER ALMOST
   GOT TREAT LIL
CHEESE ORAL RATIONS
HANG RIGOR LAD SLOE
ASNER SAL SOW SCENE
PHARAOH TCU SCHOOL
   SPA CIA   EMU
SETH RICHARDRODGERS
CROW ISLE LIMO RAIN
ASTI NEAL ERAT ASTA
NEON GENA TESH DEEP
```

PUZZLE 83

```
CALF  MAPLE      BALM
ARIES OSIERS  SPECIE
TAKENTOHEART  ARDENT
ONE  OISE  RENO  SEE
   ROBES   FOILED
   BOOZE GOADS SHEAF
HAULER MOORE   ALGA
ANTE MITTS  SHERBET
LAOS SENAT  STEREO
ELF UPTOTHEEARS WHO
   HATERS EVILS ARID
EMANATE ABONE  TONE
TENN SPIKE  ALLOTS
ANDES LISLE  ROAMS
   ENAMEL   PROWS
VAT VIDI   OUSE  MCI
ELEVEN LOSEONESHEAD
SALINE ELAINE TORSO
TILE   ETNAS   PEEL
```

PUZZLE 87

```
ALAS BOAST WHIZ SHAM
ROLE ARNIE MOIRA MULE
CASABLANCA COPENHAGEN
NOTABLE ICES  ZEROED
   TWOS  HOOD  DIRT
SCYLLA STONY EBB AAH
TREES THAWS COMAS LEA
AIM  HIM  ODOR  DIGS
REE BREMERHAVEN WAIT
SNORERS HOMES DRESSY
   KALE  SOLAR  COOL
ROMANY TUNES SENATES
UREY DARESSALAAM TAB
MILS HOPE   TIS   HUE
BOB METER CREPE AGENT
ANA OLE  SHINS CALLAS
   LOSS  SOAP  AURA
SOMALI WAFT  EXPOSED
ALEXANDRIA WELLINGTON
RARE KEELS ARMED ONCE
AVER INNS  DROSS WAKE
```

PUZZLE 80

```
OKRA ABBE BALI BASS
REEL DEEP ALAN OLLA
CRAG DALI REND ODIN
ARRAU CACAO DICTATE
   ENVOY END  GAL
UMP PAN ARIA ODESSA
ROLLIN ASIAN  GOAL
GLEAN VITAL WAD FRA
EDAM CAROL RABELAIS
   BURGER BAKERY
BEDSTEAD CADET SAIL
ABE EEL AARON GOUDA
LOSE  IBSEN CALLER
ENIGMA TSAR POI DAD
   GAB SIB  BADLY
BAGHDAD NAVEL YACHT
AGEE CAST ARAB HOAR
TUNA UTAH INCA ORLE
SEED SAGE NEER OMSK
```

PUZZLE 84

```
ELG  MASS  SAM  GET
SIR  ADIT  FAME YAR
STALLONE AGAR  PSI
MAL  GESTE  MOSES
MAMIE LAST   ALY
OVER EDEN  ANDREW
DAR ALE DERN   OVA
   AMEN LEN  ASER
DESPAIR  SPENCER
RANK NRA   ETAT
ORT  OONA   ATT
KEELER  BITE  SARA
   RON MAUD HINES
PITTS ASTIN   ASA
UMA IMRE OURVINES
MII GALA TICE  ACE
ANN NEO  STAN  SON
```

PUZZLE 88

```
ETCH  SEW  BOLD
GALE  IRA  ERIE
GREATSALTLAKE
STATES  TELLER
   RELY  ONO
SWIRL  ENTWINE
PIN  PSS   NEA
ANGLERS  RATER
   EVE  ROBE
ENAMEL  EARNED
NATURALBRIDGE
OVER  TIE  DEAN
SEES  EEL  EDDY
```

PUZZLE 81

```
FROM SWAB IBIS COAL
LAVA HOER METE OLGA
AJAR YOGA PEEN NEAR
MALIC FINAL MILFORD
   ARLES AID  LAI
AHA EAR ECCE EUROPE
DURHAM SAHIB  MULL
DREAM COVET PAT SIM
SLAV HELEN SOCRATES
   OSIRIS SCENIC
CHUCKLED CLOSE RAND
DER ITS SOOTY TIBIA
NEAP  RABAT DEDUCT
ELLIOT HAWN TAN TEE
   ADO ORE  MANOR
STANDBY IBSEN NAIAD
LOCI AEON ALDA IDLE
ARTS GAVE IBEX SEAL
GNAT ORAN LAME ESNE
```

PUZZLE 85

```
ALES SADIE SETA APPAL
LINT AMEND INON DIANA
ETTA TANTE NORI ANTIC
CHERRYSTONECLAM GEESE
SORTERS PES  ALIASES
   EDS BABE  ALOOP
SKIDS BOBLEMON ASPENS
AIT KOALA INCH  LOIN
BLUEBERRYHILL ESSENCE
ENPLANED GAY RCT SEE
   ASTAS SEN  BEARD
ALB SOL APT ACREAGES
TORTONI GRAPESOFWRATH
OLIO SERA EXAMS  LEA
PAMPER MAYAPPLE TRASH
   BRADS MOOT  BEE
LALANNE TAO  SLACKEN
ATONE CLOCKWORKORANGE
IRMAS AERO ALIEN NERO
RIANT LAIR RAGED TEEN
DANAS SKIN SNITS SSTS
```

PUZZLE 89

```
REST  LAD  CABS
LAHR  ALA  OBOE
STAIRWAY  RENE
   RTE SLANTED
GAPED     ICE
RUE  WAGERING
ARNO ASH  STAR
BASSINET   EVE
   POD  SHREW
LEARNER   PEA
ONCE RECANTED
DORY EAR  NEST
EWES DRY  ADES
```

PUZZLE 90

```
EDISON KNOLL      LANE
BOCCIE EUROPE    SIREN
BROADWAYBOUND    WEIRD
SENT  EMS     IFE  DOS
         SETS BIBLE
HEIR  TROP INLET   DUE
ECLAT INA   BLEACHERS
ROUGHAGE PEAS   HABIT
ONS  EGO HOLY    ANTS
     FOE PESOS ARK
AMID   REST  TRI  RYA
AWARD VILE   LITTLEST
DETECTIVE LAP   YODEL
ASA OATER EMTS   SORI
      UNITS UPON
TWO  PGA     PEI AIRE
REPEL THEGOODDOCTOR
ELATE EASELS   EDICTS
ELLA    SPLAT  REDHOT
```

PUZZLE 95

```
         TOUR
      VOLGA     PACA
      ATILT     SLAV
       GRAVY   LAINE
       ANILE  CALVES
       HORAE  CHIME
       OVERDO DEER
ABACUS    SHELF
BEGUM    STEAL    JAM
LEES  BORER    LAMA
END   GEOID   HAVOC
       BLANC DEMARK
       DIET HEGIRA
       ASIAN BAKER
COSMOS    BIBLE
ALTER    SYRIA
PLEA     COLON
PARR     ORANG
         DEWY
```

PUZZLE 99

```
         OMAR
         FAME     ALA
FLIMFLAM         RONA
LAVA  TSAR       TUTU
OMAN   SNAG     STATS
PEN    DRAG      OCA
       ERRS    ANON
       ROC  ALONE
  SHAD METRONOME
  POWEROFATTORNEY
  PARAMETER  ODEA
MANET  ATE
ATOM   SELF
SIR   DEEM       LOS
OASTS    REAM   LATH
MOOT    TROT    ASTA
ALTO    ROADSHOW
DOW     ORLE
        WELL
```

PUZZLE 91

```
 OFT      CLUE
ALIEN   MOOSE
MILNE   INFER
EVE  WIG   TRY
   EDS  CHESS
     ELITE
   TITAN  LAG
DOM UGH    SEA
AWARD   UTTER
VEGAS   MOIST
EDEN     PRE
```

PUZZLE 92

```
 OAK       BITE
PURE      AREA
WITTY     BOAS
EEL      DENSE
BRAG    HAS
   WAS CAN
   SCRATCH
   RAP EAR
   VAT    MARK
STEAM      CUE
COAL      BEING
ANTE      OWNS
REST       BEG
```

PUZZLE 93

```
MOLT
IDIOM      CAR
COMEON   THROB
ERA  DISHITOUT
    EXTOL  FROG
 PAS AUD   YALE
MIST        TOY
WEAK       CURE
ELS        JURY
BOTH  NAP   URN
NEED  ASIAN
RAINCHECK  ANT
LEERY  TELLER
TEE     TASTE
         DOSE
```

PUZZLE 94
1. Smothering, 2. Pocket-fuls, 3. Bush jacket.

PUZZLE 96

By clue 3 the dental office is located at the NE corner and Diane's workplace is located at the SW corner. The gas station is further north than Joe's workplace (clue 1), so the gas station is located at the NW corner and Joe works at the SE corner. Since Gus's workplace is further east than the bookstore (clue 2), he works at the NE corner and the bookstore is located at the SW corner. Consequently the remaining workplace, the grocery, is located at the SE corner and Terry works at the gas station.

In summary:
Diane, bookstore, SW
Gus, dental office, NE
Joe, grocery, SE
Terry, gas station, NW

PUZZLE 97

```
 ETA      OVA
 LOG      FIN
MARE      TAT
ASP       ELS
CUTE     OPAL
AVID PIN NAPE
DECORATE EGRET
   ARSENAL
SHARP  DELICATE
HULA  SEA  ACES
YEAR       BANS
 SET        ADD
 ERA       ORES
 RUN       HEM
 MET       STY
```

PUZZLE 98

S	SISTER	TIRES	REST	I
P	SPIDER	RIDES	DIRE	S
R	HEARTS	HASTE	SEAT	H
I	AISLES	SEALS	LASS	E
N	RIPENS	SPIRE	PIES	R
G	GRAPES	PEARS	RASP	E

PUZZLE 100

Pinocchio's nose was 2 inches long after the first lie, then 4 inches, 8, 16, 32, 64, 128, 256, 512, and finally 1024 inches long.

PUZZLE 101

```
            BED
 RIM        ARE
 AND        NEW
TRAINS    SEND
RUIN       AGO
ELM        LOO
SEE     BEE NOR
TOP     VIA PAW
IRA   SAINT EVE
PAR    USE  RED
LEA   AMP   TEA
SIR         TIE
TOT        CURL
FANS     TRIBES
NIL        WIT
ORE        ODE
TEE
```

PUZZLE 102
1. Back, Bark, Bard, Yard.
2. Post, Pose, Pole, Hole.
3. Peat, Meat, Moat, Most, Moss.
4. Land, Lane, Line, Fine, File, Fill.

PUZZLE 103

```
    NAGS
    OGRE      SAD
FED DEAR      TRY
ACE DIVE     FIRE
IRATE NEW  LUNAR
RULER     ENERGY
 AGO FROG
   BEAST
  GOLD  EEL
 AGREED  RIFLE
BROOM ELF RELAY
LORD  RAID  EVE
USE   PERT  DAD
RED    SLUE
       EDGE
```

PUZZLE 104
```
  5 2 1
x     6
-------
3 1 2 6
```

522

PUZZLE 105

PUZZLE 110

```
CORAL SAID SHAH
ADORE TUNE HOBO
RODEO ANNE ALES
ERE PART PADDLE
    BARE HERE
ASSORT HONE SIT
AHEAD SATES PRO
ROWS SAVED LEAN
ORE LIBEL SALTY
NED EDEN APPLES
   DEER FLOP
RAZORS GRIT BAD
IVES HALO THOSE
PERE OPEN EERIE
EROS WENT DREAD
```

PUZZLE 115

```
LESS SPY TINA
ORAL TOE WREN
TALE ADS EAST
  STEER LENT
   VAT POT
WATER LESSONS
ELI DEN LEE
ELECTED CADET
   HEW SAD
  ALEE TROTS
FREE SPA REAL
REAR ORR ELLA
YAPS WOE SLED
```

PUZZLE 106

```
ELSA MEDAL CASE
DAIS ADORE AVOW
INTHENICKOFTIME
TEE TUCK UNDER
   CHAT OKRA
BUSHEL RUN PAGE
ALTAR MANE WON
STEP DANCE PART
IRE URGE BARGE
CARP ARE PONDER
   ONLY SOOT
CANOE LEST ADO
LIEDOWNONTHEJOB
ORAL HOUSE FAME
TYPE ORDER TREY
```

PUZZLE 111

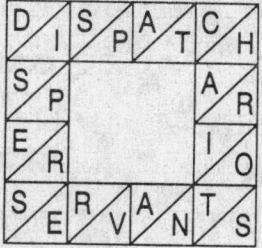

PUZZLE 116

```
TEE GAP UTE
AID SARA SPOT
BREAKSUP TAME
SENTA TETON
  OTT REACT
BEUPSET ASHES
AMP DAM ONO
RICKY UPWARDS
TONER SAM
  MOPES TOADS
WAIT STICKSUP
ERNS EACH IDA
BEG TRI NET
```

PUZZLE 117

```
GAB LAD MULL
ERR COME ASIA
TOY ALIS DALY
 CARRADINE
KNIT ITEMS
 PETERLORRE
ART WOE ATE
MARCSINGER
OHARA MUSS
 ELIZABETH
ALES GAPE RAM
MITT ONER IRE
YVES RED PIG
```

PUZZLE 107

1.
```
LAB
OPE
VEN
EXT
```

2.
```
CHIN
LOCO
IRON
PANE
```

3.
```
PLAN
RAVE
ONES
PERT
```

PUZZLE 112

```
POMP PASTE BLOB
ARIA USHER EIRE
CELLOPHANE STAT
ALLAN EGO SIENA
   COP RISER
OPERATE NEGATE
APES RIVES ETAL
RID ALIST ULM
ONES DELTA IRES
NESTLE SENATES
  TRESS TVA
AERIE COO OLDIE
FLIP COMPANIONS
ALAE ONEAL AMIS
REND BERLE NOTE
```

PUZZLE 113

```
SELDOM  S  MODEL  O  MELD
CAMPER  P  CREAM  M  RACE
REASON  A  SNORE  E  RONS
CANDLE  N  DECAL  L  ACED
BUSIER  I  REBUS  E  RUBS
CHASTE  S  CHEAT  T  ACHE
PHRASE  H  SPEAR  S  REAP
```

PUZZLE 118

```
LOSS BIRD AWE
ONCE OLIO LAW
GEAR SLOWPOKE
 LUSH SUPER
BLAME TIER
LOW CHIT LAMB
AGA TIMER FEE
BEGS DIME TAN
 APED AMEND
STAGE SPUR
LIBERACE LAUD
ADE IRON ELSE
WED LENT SLEW
```

PUZZLE 108

```
SHOP ALLAH GATE
EERO GAUGE EMIR
CRYPTOGRAM EARN
TAXER SET ESTEE
   SID SETTEE
CAB TAG SIC USE
AWAKENED CHORES
RARE CLOAK DINT
ARGYLE CREVASSE
TEA ARC TRA HER
  IRISES SUB
CANON NIB NECKS
AVID ITERATIONS
GENE REGAL GRIT
ERGO ARENA EATS
```

PUZZLE 114

```
DEF ADS CAP
ERR SOL APE
ALE TEA TAN
FENCE TSARS
 SCORE TNT
 HANDLED
PTS SEEMS
SLOTS DROOP
LOA TAG UNO
OWS ADE SGT
EST NOR ESS
```

PUZZLE 109

must have taken a lot of courage to
scover that frog legs are edible.

Veggies, 2. Offshoot, 3. Beckett, 4.
aduate, 5. Elliott, 6. Railroad, 7.
me run, 8. Caveats.

PUZZLE 119

```
ERRS MAP DAB
DIET ELLA OLE
SODA ALAS CAN
 BILLYTHEKID
SHARES TEN
PURSE FENDERS
EGO BAR SEE
DENOTED TACIT
 FEE ORGANS
BUFFALOBILL
ONE SIDE EARS
WIT ENOS ATIP
STA ERE MEGA
```

PUZZLE 120

```
RIPE  SOLVE   BLAB
ACID  UNION   LAMA
GONG  NESTS   OVER
ENTERS   PELICANS
      EEL  ARK
ARRESTED    VISION
GUILT  GASES   DUO
RINK   ART    PENS
END   RULER  PEACE
ESSAYS   RELEASES
       GEE  WON
COLESLAW   STALKS
AKIN  ELOPE  CONE
PANT  SEVER  TREE
EYES  SEERS  SEWN
```

PUZZLE 121

1. Sprint, Print, Pint, Pit, It, I.
2. Scarce, Scare, Care, Are, Re.
3. Trapping, Tapping, Taping, Aping, Ping, Pin, In, I.
4. Breast, Beast, Beat, Bat, At, A.
5. Stinger, Singer, Singe, Sing, Sin, In, I.
6. Statute, Statue, State, Sate, Sat, At, A.
7. Tapper, Taper, Aper, Per, Er.
8. Bramble, Ramble, Amble, Able, Ale.
9. Arrow, Arow, Row, Ow, O.
10. Manse, Mane, Man, An, A.

PUZZLE 122

```
MISS  MEDOC   WEDS
EDIT  ARENA   OXEN
SORE  DECOR   VANE
ALERT  ASP   ELSE
    NEWSY  ENTER
PAW  EAT  SEW
ECHO  RATTLETRAP
ARID  DREAD  ROBE
REGENERATE   YALE
   ANY  ESP  DEN
SHEEP   ASTER
TEAR  GAL  WINCE
ALSO  ABOVE  GOOD
SLED  GENIE  IDLE
HOLE  STEAL  DEAN
```

PUZZLE 123

1. Braggart, Grab; 2. Revolver, Over; 3. Infernal, Fair; 4. Decrepit, Iced; 5. Glossary, Slay; 6. Ethereal, Hare.
FIRST LETTERS: Bridge, Go Fish.

PUZZLE 124

```
SKIP  SOLOS   EWER
AIDE  TWINE   NODE
GLEN  ELDER   JOGS
STANZAS   VIOLET
     EEL  ENEMY
BEADS  IRE  PELTS
LAG  TOMATO  DARE
ERR  YAP  TWO  TEE
STEP  RECENT  END
SHELF  DAD  HERDS
     ALTER  VEX
SACQUE    FARTHER
ECRU  NOTES  ROLE
TREE  DRONE  APSE
SEWS  SENDS  SEEK
```

1-S, 2-H, 3-R, 4-N, 5-Y, 6-B, 7-Q, 8-E, 9-U, 10-V, 11-G, 12-P, 13-X, 14-L, 15-I, 16-A, 17-Z, 18-K, 19-T, 20-C, 21-W, 22-M, 23-D, 24-F, 25-O, 26-J.

PUZZLE 125

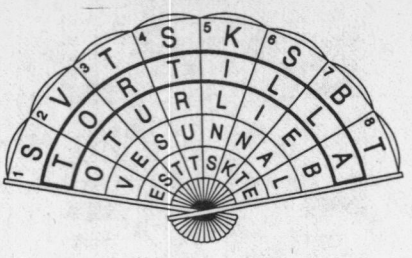

PUZZLE 126

```
SLAP  AESOP   DARE
TAME  VIOLA   IGOR
ANON  ARLES   LIAR
FAN  GLEE  TALONS
FIGARO    STOLE
    PINS  ARMREST
ROPED  HELAS   LEO
AVID  LAPEL  PARE
GAP  BASIN  BONES
ELEMENT    TORE
    OSCAR  TAMPER
HECATE  EFTS  OVA
EDEN  LADLE  VOID
AIDE  OSIER  ALTA
DEED  TIDES  TSAR
```

PUZZLE 127

```
FALA  CLUB  TIER  ACHE
OTIS  AARE  ASTI  SHAD
REDHANDED  BLACKHAND
DESTROY  SALE  ENERGY
    RAE  WINE  SCAN
ABAT  TODO  SOAP  BRA
LILY  GREENBACKS  LED
IDA  SUES  LIKE  TUNE
BECAUSE  SPANS  POETS
KNIT  SHIRT  LAMB
UNFIT  SIEGE  DISSECT
POOL  PERE  SAMS  ARA
ISO  GREENTHUMB  BREW
NET  OURS  HALE  MADE
RODS  RANK  CON
AMOUSE  REND  FRAGILE
GOLDENEYE  BLUEBLOOD
ERLE  CEES  AILS  ETTE
DEAR  ERSE  GELS  SAIN
```

PUZZLE 128

```
PAST  TALE  SNUB  SPAN
OBOE  ADEN  HOSE  TRUE
OLDMANOFTHESEA  YORE
LEAPT  TEAK  RUB  CAD
   EELS  RYES  SAME
THORNIER  SLOT  RADAR
OOLA  ERIE  SOWS  DUNE
MEET  DELIS  TIP  ARKS
ESSES  EGOS  NUTMEAT
    HEADHUNTERS
PEPPERS  TROY  KEVIN
AREA  MIG  SURER  YALE
PART  ADAM  TODO  ELLA
ASCOT  ENID  LITTLEST
   ONES  GNAT  TARA
YUL  DAN  IDEA  ISSUE
ARAB  GERMANSHEPHERD
KATE  ESAU  TIED  ELSA
SLED  STEM  SAWS  SLAM
```

PUZZLE 129

```
FUN  MARS  SLAP  MODE
ANON  OMNI  COHO  IVES
RAGE  RISE  ORAL  FANS
MUSCLE  SANDBARFLY
   TBAR  TIE  RYE
ATLAS  OSAR  ARCADES
NEAR  FOES  SLOAN  APT
TEMPLATE  CLOMP  SAO
IMPIOUS  SEINE  SPENT
   TON  WILDE  ELI
TRYST  BUGLE  STELLAR
LEO  DORMS  HEADLINE
CAW  TULSA  BOAT  OMIT
PLUMMET  MATT  SWALE
   NAB  SON  OHED
RAINBOWTIE  UTOPIA
GAGS  EMIR  FAIR  WADI
ECHO  LETO  UNDO  NULL
LEAN  LISP  LYON  LES
```

PUZZLE 130

```
CAST  KALE  GARLIC  ANEW
HILO  AWOL  APOLLO  MILE
ADAM  YAPS  TIDDLYWINKS
PATACAKE  HEADS  IDEST
   TAKE  DOWRY  WACS
ARSON  MORAY  FOLKTALE
BOLES  KENNY  PUREE  RIM
AMES  SIDES  CATSCRADLE
SEE  ANTI  DIVOT  BEAR
HOPSCOTCH  ATEN  AGENCY
   MIRY  UTTER  ALIT
PARADE  CREE  SIMONSAYS
OPAL  SHOED  RAHS  NOT
SPILLIKINS  GRETA  PIKA
ELL  ADITS  TRINI  HOTEL
RESIDUES  SWALE  ERASE
   DINS  PEEVE  TARP
WIELD  ALLAY  REDROVER
HIDEANDSEEK  CONE  IOTA
OWES  BUTANE  ATOP  SLOG
MINT  ABIDED  PERT  ETNA
```

PUZZLE 131

```
APACE  TAPED  COTTA
CAVILS  SAVAGES  PEAHEN
CREDIT  THELOSTWEEKEND
EIN  ARAID  TRET  CAR
NAG  GUSTO  ARABS  TONE
THESUNSHINEBOYS  POUTS
   AVAS  NAYS  LAWN
OBLATES  ATTS  HULOTS
PIRATE  ATREE  COMPORTS
ILOSE  SMEAR  MORE  YEA
ELA  ROBERTDONAT  GLS
RED  YUAN  ARAGE  HAILS
SAWGRASS  DIANA  DELRAY
KALINE  BUNT  SERIALS
   YENS  CAME  RIDS
LAMED  BARBRASTREISAND
ORES  SARTO  SERES  DOE
DEL  YUAN  HEEDS  MIT
GOODBYEMRCHIPS  ELOISE
ELDERS  SERENES  NEARER
SAYSO  DOMED  DRESS
```

PUZZLE 132

```
ASHE  RASH  BALE  THESE
STAN  ERIE  DEMAS  WADED
KANT  DIVA  RAITT  IRATE
EGGS  HEADLESSHORSEMAN
DEY  GEL  BOATS  NETS
   OBAN  GOADS  LINE  YEA
CRUET  BRANS  HEADDRESS
LORDS  LARS  BONN  ALTO
ACHE  FOND  VIDA  MAHLER
SHE  PEND  GALA  COLAS
HEADANDSHOULDERSABOVE
DOLCE  ILLY  LEER  NIL
ECORSE  DRAT  HOES  NERI
RAVI  MIEN  VEIL  HOSEA
SPEARHEAD  LEANS  ATHOS
EER  OILS  CORDS  FREE
   OSLO  SONGS  LOT  ATE
LAYHEADSTOGETHER  ADAF
ASEAT  ITAKE  AONE  ROMA
HEART  EATER  RUTS  IFAT
RAREE  STER  TROT  AFRC
```

PUZZLE 133

```
KAO   ESAET   DEEF
SIHT  TELNI   ENOL
URCE  SDAEH   TILA
RAEHRAEH  HANNAH
   CIHC  HCRA
SRETAC  OTNIRAET
SETA   SIRI  GNUR
EVAH  SELIP  REVA
REVE  SSOM   OREH
DLOHTOOF  YTFARC
   TARD  STAE
ETOYOC  EMITKRAM
MAER  DETON  AERA
ANLU  ENOTA  TEID
SGOB  ROVAS   LLA
```

PUZZLE 134
AUSTRIA

Austria is known for its Viennese coffee houses, cultural figures such as Mozart, and the Danube River. Actually, Strauss's "Beautiful Blue Danube" was and is murky brown!

PUZZLE 135

```
PUSH  TRAPS  SPAN
ANTI  RAVEL  AIDE
LIAR  EMOTE  PLOW
STREWS  NEED   ORE
   SITS  SPATTER
RED  SLAB   SIR
AVA  HELEN  SIDES
NETS  SALES  MARE
GREAT  DOVES  TIE
   MAN  WENT  AND
REVERES  RAIL
ERA  PAPA  TRAMPS
MANY  RINGO  GALE
ISEE  ENTER  EDEN
TESS  DEEMS  READ
```

DIAGRAMLESS STARTING BOXES

PUZZLE 136

1. Stanza, 2. Amazon, 3. Wigwam, 4. Gifted, 5. Crafty, 6. Orchid, 7. Tuxedo, 8. Luxury, 9. Comely, 10. Mexico, 11. Excuse, 12. Catsup.

PUZZLE 137

```
PHIL   SOAP   HOT
RORYS  EVIL  SAVE
YEARN  WERE  TREE
  SNEAKER  ALIENS
     RID  PSALMS
EVADED  ROUTE
LIMES  TERRE  ANA
SLEW  SINCE  DROP
EEN  BIRTH  POISE
   CODES  WANDER
  PLANES  SAL
SHINES  PARADES
POND  HEAL  CRATE
ANDY  OKLA  EASEL
TEA  WELD   GEMS
```

PUZZLE 138

```
F O R E S T A L L
SHOE L A ACES S
MAST E R R I N G
EV ER T MORE D E
COUNT E R DE D E
COMMA N DEE R
PROS T RATE
```

PUZZLE 139

```
SHED  COAL  APT
EAVES  IPSO  AMOR
THEFOURTHOFJULY
HAS  LACS   RARE
   PERU  FAIR
PEALS  STAVE  ART
ARNO   ETON   TOR
REDWHITEANDBLUE
ACE  IDEM   RATS
STS  CEASE  BASES
   ICES  STEN
  AINU  ATEN  IRE
INDEPENDENCEDAY
STES  SEER  HALVE
MES   TESS   TEES
```

PUZZLE 140

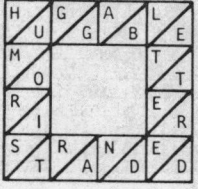

PUZZLE 141

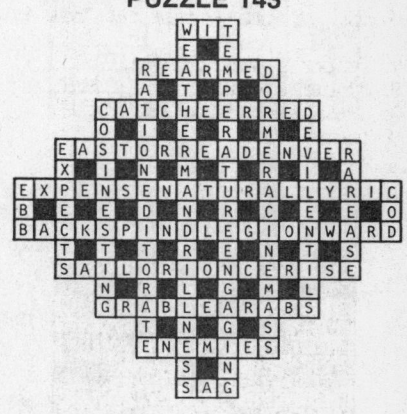

```
    HELICOPTER  GALLEON
  FALTER    LANCES
 BATTLE  IRONS    TOT
ITCHY   BERING   CAPS
 SING  DABS    REMUS
     TERRA  REAPER
    CREAM   PALMS   BROW
CANTOR   LADS   STAIN
LEE  MOTIONS   HARDING
ANODE     STARTLES
MORSELS   AGENTS
```

PUZZLE 142
PERFECTION

PUZZLE 143

```
        WIT
        EE
      REARMED
      AT P O
    CATCHEERRED
    O I ERM E
  EASTORREADENVER
  X IN MTRIA
EXPENSENATURALLYRIC
BE ED N R CE E O
BACKSPINDLEGIONWARD
T T T RENTS
SAILORIONCERISE
N R L GM L
GRABLEARABS
TN GS
ENEMIES
  SN
  SAG
```

PUZZLE 144

```
DOME  CLASP  RIMS
OMAR  RANEE  EDIE
TIME  ENDED  VEER
STACKED  PAGEANT
   TIP  MELON
RAVEN  BAD  AGNES
OWED  HIT  SLEEVE
BAN  DITCHES  WEE
ORDERS  HOW  TEND
TESTY  MET  PORTS
   HEROD  PER
ATTIRED  HEARTEN
LAIC  SEVEN  ERIE
ELLA  TRIED  NERO
SELL  SNAPS  TEEN
```

PUZZLE 145

As the sun colors flowers so does art color life.

1. Introduce, 2. Cosset, 3. Floors, 4. Shore, 5. Falls, 6. Sear, 7. Wool.

525

PUZZLE 146

```
POP . GASP
LAIRS OPERA
ALLOT LEVEL
VEE OFF EEL
ARRIVE ANN
    CENTS
SHE CAPERS
LIE HEM MAE
ALAMO PROVE
DORIS SITES
STAT DEN
```

PUZZLE 147

```
COPS GRAB AGE
ABET AONE TAN
ROAR MONGOOSE
RETIRES SUM
  NESTS RIFT
SONGS SAM ZOO
PHASES DETERS
AIM TAR LARKS
TOES LATER
  SIS PEERING
FRANKLIN IDOL
OAK AIDE ELLA
EYE TEST DEAD
```

PUZZLE 148

```
FIN ROME JEST
ARE AFAR ARIA
CAW STIR LARK
ENTICED POSSE
  CAN PEP
STEEL PLAYPEN
AIM BUY ALE
NEUTRON RINSE
  HEY RAM
ROWED QUIPPED
ORES SUBS ERE
BALI HALE RIB
ELLS EYED MET
```

PUZZLE 149

```
FLEW BAJA TOE
LATH APEX ELL
ANNA GARLANDS
PEARL TREE
  FISHY SHOE
HAS BAY NOISY
ARISEN TOPPLE
LEGAL GET SOD
OAHU REACT
  DEAN HURON
ACTIVITY TUNE
VOW ISLE ODES
EGO LEES REST
```

PUZZLE 150

```
WALL GAP OLD
ARIA SILO WOO
STEP PRETENSE
  SAIL TESTS
MODEST MEL
AWASH PERSONS
YES MAT NOT
ADHERED ARENA
  RAN CLOSER
WHEAT POLO
HAMSTERS MAPS
ALI LOOT EVIL
TOT END DENY
```

PUZZLE 151

```
TABS PAPA FRO
IDEA EWES LAW
MOTHBALLS ICE
ESSAY TAPPED
  READ YAP
TOGA HAG DATA
IDA ORE NOR
EELS YEA STEM
  LAB DRIP
GROPED RIVER
LIP RIGMAROLE
OLE TREE ALMS
WED HEEL LEST
```

PUZZLE 152

```
SLED RED COIF
HALO EAR HARE
OMEN PREPARED
PEP DENSER
  HAIL SAMPLE
ERASE PER ROW
RANK GAR HOPE
ART SET TIMER
LESSON CAPE
  PREFER NOD
APPEARED BALE
FARE ATE IDLE
TROD LED NEAR
```

PUZZLE 153

```
LODI OVER TIP
AMUN LIRE HOE
VAST DANG RUG
ARTEL EASE
  CREST LIETO
LEONATUS DYAD
ARM DUNES ETE
MAMA DEBONAIR
BLACK RADAR
  NEAT ASSET
HAD URAL SOLE
ILE AONE ALIA
SIR IDEA UDAL
```

PUZZLE 154

```
FARO LAST SALTS
EDIT ETTE ADEAL
MANHATTAN PEACE
GEL NEAP RTE
AVERSE TRY NIP
MARS TENSE TELE
STS NATO EIDER
  INTERIORS
BORNE SERE FAD
ARES OPERA STAR
NET ARI LLAMAS
AGO BORE ESE
NATTY ANNIEHALL
ANAIS TGIF EDIE
SOLES ERNS SEED
```

PUZZLE 155

1. Every dog has its day.
2. Haste makes waste.
3. People who live in glass houses shouldn't throw stones.
4. All that glistens (glitters; glisters) is not gold.
5. Don't count your chickens before they're hatched.

PUZZLE 156

```
BELT ARE STOP
OLIO PER PINE
ALTO ELEGANCE
  ELM ICE EEL
MAR EASTER
OVA ASH ASP
PETALS TUMULT
  RED AIL PEA
  DEADEN EAR
TOO RUM AIR
ORGANDIE DIAL
GALL IRK LODE
ALEE TEE ERST
```

PUZZLE 157

```
MAP LAME BITE
IRE OPEN ACHE
SET YELL SOUL
SAUNA TIDINGS
  LULL GUN
TOAD ECHO SAT
ERNE GOT RUDE
NET SITE AIDE
  BUS NEST
STEEPLE PHASE
LAVA ALOE BED
IRIS TALE LEG
PELT ENDS EKE
```

PUZZLE 158

```
ALPS REDO SNAP
TIRE ERODE TELE
OMIT TREED ARIA
MEN SEER IDIOTS
  COULD STAR
SNIVEL SPONSORS
TOPAZ STARE VIA
ROLL POETS LENT
ONE ROLES TERSE
PESTERED BATHES
  RATS WORSE
STRIDE TANS ADO
CRIB ROUGE ATOP
AIDE SANER PETE
TOES REDS EDEN
```

PUZZLE 159

Crocodiles and alligators eat stones, and the stones remain inside their stomachs. Scientists think they might do this to help them dive, or to help grind up their food, or to keep them from feeling hungry.

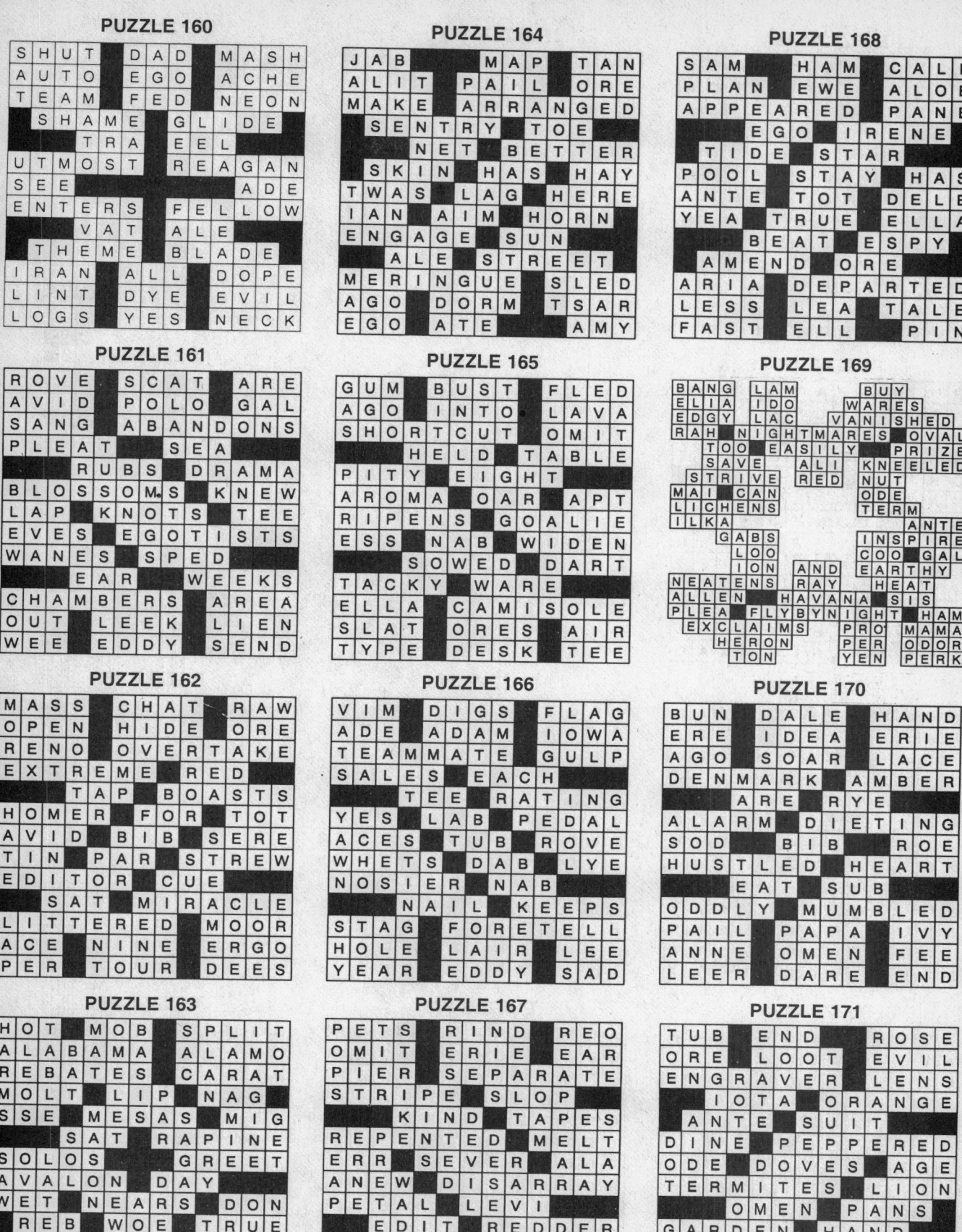

PUZZLE 172

```
BANGS  ERE   SOD
ALERT  BOX   POE
RATIO  BAPTIZE
   PRO  MARKED
DILEMMA  NEEDS
ICED  ABIDE
DYE  SHOTS  SEA
   SLAVE  OPEN
TABLE  EMERALD
AMOUNT  SAP
KINGDOM  SHAFT
EGG  ERA  EAGER
NOS  RED  SNOWY
```

PUZZLE 176

```
EARL  JOIN   LAB
TRUE  AWRY   ERE
NABS  MEALTIME
ABYSS  SNOW
   OLE   NOBEL
TORNADOS  SAGA
USE  TIRED  LOT
CLAY  TELEVISE
KOREA   LEE
   LETS  PROWS
JUMPSUIT  SKIP
AGO  ONTO  EASE
WHO  PEST  DYED
```

PUZZLE 180

```
FRY  ARAB  ARCH
ROE  CAGE  DELI
OBSERVED  ODOR
   BEEN  ABODE
CRAB  STOLE
OILED  SUB  ODE
SPADED  TUNNEL
TEN  AYE  MITES
   DREAM  CODE
FAKES  GENE
INNS  ALTERING
REEK  GEAR  DOE
EWES  OSLO  ADE
```

PUZZLE 173

```
RUT  SPAR  CHOW
AGO  KALE  RAVE
WHODUNIT  ORES
   ONE  ACCENT
CRACK  BILK
HACK  COLA  YAM
ARE  ZONED  OBI
RED  EVER  MULL
   BRED  DARED
INDOOR  HEM
SOUR  ISOLATED
LONE  NEWT  IRA
EKED  GALA  MAD
```

PUZZLE 177

```
 WHIG   RATS
 PEALE  ERNES
NETTLE  LITTLE
EAT  SEA  TAX
ACE  MEATS  ENE
TERSE  REPORTS
  ANS  SIN
SCHOOLS  CAROL
CAA  TEASE  ABE
APR  NCO  TOA
NETTED  LITTER
 REESE  ORALS
 SEER  SAGE
```

PUZZLE 181

```
TAPED  NAP  RAM
ABOVE  ACE  ALE
RESET  IMP  TIE
  TREBLE  VENT
PEA  ROE  AIDES
URGE  ADOPT
TEETER  PEANUT
  HEDGE  LORE
RAVEL  ARE  ONE
ODOR  FLAMED
BOW  PAL  BALES
ORE  ADO  EVERT
TED  TEN  RESAY
```

PUZZLE 174

```
BODE  TAR  SHAG
RAIL  ROE  TUBE
AFRICANVIOLET
SST  ODE  DRAT
  ABE  FLY
BOIL  ARE  PRO
ALLIGATORPEAR
ADE  RIA  RAGE
  ROD  PLY
 GLOW  COO  PAT
DOUBLEHEADERS
INTO  RAM  ASEA
MEET  ERS  BOAR
```

PUZZLE 178

```
LOST  OPAL  BOW
ARIA  URGE  ABE
DALMATIAN  RIB
SLOPS  VISIT
  ALDEN  MESA
GEM  EAT  APRON
AWAKED  WISEST
RECAP  RED  DOE
BRAT  AUDIT
  REEFS  NERVE
BOO  DISAGREED
OWN  IRIS  SANG
ALI  TEAK  EDDY
```

PUZZLE 182

```
ALMS  ASS  AONE
LOOT  NAP  TROY
BONAFIDE  HERE
OPERA  AGO
  YELL  REMISS
LAB  LIP  MELEE
IRA  TAR  LEA
ANGLE  ROB  ARM
RESORT  TACT
  CAR  CREST
SOFA  INTHEAIR
EVIL  COO  ESNE
WANE  EWE  LEST
```

PUZZLE 175

```
LOPS  ADD  SLAB
AVOW  WOO  LODE
MERE  AGO  OOZE
ANTLER  MAGNET
  LED  SPA
MEASLES  ENTER
ARM  DAB  WOE
DEPTH  DIAMOND
  EAR  DRY
CHASTE  DISMAL
HOST  BEE  TOLE
ALEE  ERR  IVAN
READ  LAS  CENT
```

PUZZLE 179

```
ACED  HARP  SOB
DUDE  OLEO  ORO
DRUM  LAVENDER
  CORE  TEASE
CRANE  DOSE
LET  BLOT  DEMS
ADOS  ANT  SNAP
NORA  TOOT  VIE
  BRER  AMEND
WHALE  ORAL
REVEREND  NOTE
ERE  AGED  OPEN
NOR  NODS  REED
```

PUZZLE 183

```
COLA  LOP  PULL
ORAL  OAR  ARIA
DEDICATE  INKS
  BAD  SUNSET
ADLIB  RUNT
FOES  FAMISHED
ALA  FACET  ELI
REFERRED  SALE
  DEED  CARAT
REVIEW  HOG
ERAS  ELATEDLY
SILO  LET  LUAU
TEEN  LIE  YOWL
```

PUZZLE 184

```
BRAN CACAO APSE
ROTE AVOWS SLEW
ALTO NAILS TELE
GEE EVIL IDEALS
    NAVAL AFAR
LADIES ACIDNESS
ADAMS RITES ATE
TONS FADED TREE
CRT CRIED BATED
HESSIANS RICHLY
   CANS GORKI
UNHOOK TOAD NAG
TOUR ERROR SERE
EDGE REUSE ASIA
SEER SPEED TSAR
```

PUZZLE 185

```
  2 2 3
x     5
───────
1 1 1 5
```

PUZZLE 186

```
STEP RASP EGG
PAPA ALAI CAP
ERIN STYLISTS
DECAMP SORT
  MAUL TIARA
PILASTER STAR
IDA HIVES INC
NOVA NEGLECTS
SLAMS LIAR
  LOUD MYSELF
FAIRGAME AREA
OWE ALAN TITI
PER RENT ZEAL
```

PUZZLE 187

```
ADD ABA PRATE
DOE NAG RESIN
ENTENTE OASES
PEER ENDURE
TERRA DAD RIP
  ALTAR ETRE
LITTLE TEASER
IDEA POSES
PAR SIN LIEGE
  TRADES EVER
ORIEL WEARING
RIATA ARM COO
BALED YET TAT
```

PUZZLE 188

```
BEEP USMC MAHAL
RATE NOAH AROMA
ACTA RANI REWED
CHARGER CAVALRY
  LASH MEL
MENTAL ABEL ADA
ALOUD INRE AXEL
CLOSEORDERDRILL
RISK HAIR EMOTE
OSE WANE LAYMAN
    OAR RAIL
SORTIES ATTACKS
ABETS TARA COAL
TENET UPON EDNA
EYERS DENY DEEM
```

PUZZLE 189

1. Cart/Chariot, 2. Fail/Fragile, 3. Ward/
Awkward, 4. Pure/Pasture, 5. Ring/
Warning, 6. Else/Eclipse, 7. Dial/Admiral,
8. Reed/Freedom, 9. Ally/Wallaby, 10. Peep/
precept.

PUZZLE 190

```
UNIT RAGED EMIT
SARI ATONE LOSE
EMIR BONDS POLE
RESEMBLE PLANES
   SAIL BIAS
ACTORS BASSOONS
DRUMS RESET ROM
DONE FEATS GAVE
ENE BLARE METAL
REDWOODS SANEST
   ADOS PAST
STAGED RUTHLESS
ERGO IVORY EVIL
LEAN NITER SERA
LESS GASES TREY
```

PUZZLE 191

Canvas, Studio, Sketch, Mosaic,
Crayon, Shadow, Pastel, Fresco,
Pencil, Design.

PUZZLE 192

```
LOSER PRAM KNOW
ABOVE LURE NINE
MODEL ASKS ICES
PEA EACH SAFEST
  HARE CAFE
REPAST SAGA SOS
OLIVE LATER PAL
WANE CAGES RISE
ATE VOTER DARED
NED IRIS RECESS
   ICON LUTE
DARREN DINE LOT
OLEO EDEN CHIVE
LEAN TIME TOMES
TEDS SPIN START
```

PUZZLE 193

1. Louis Armstrong, 2. Glenn Miller, 3.
Dave Brubeck, 4. Count Basie, 5. Benny
Goodman, 6. Wynton Marsalis.

PUZZLE 194

```
SQUID STEW AJAR
OUNCE TARA RENO
DATES APARTMENT
ADO SAGE AIRES
  PETE LAME
ASPIRE SALESMAN
SLANT WAGER OLE
TALE LIVES SLOE
EVE PAPER STAND
RESERVED ENERGY
   SEAR CLOT
SPOTS OHIO HOE
TELESCOPE POUND
ISEE ADES ERRED
ROOM BENT DELAY
```

PUZZLE 195

FRIEND

PUZZLE 196

```
SEAS PARES SAPS
LILT ACORN ELAN
AREA SHANE TAPA
WEST TENSE TRAP
   ICE ZOE
SCHOOLS METEORS
TAINT APART LAP
AMPS EVANS SATE
REP AYERS SONIA
SLOTTED ECUADOR
   AAL HEP
DART IRATE STOW
RIOT NOTES URGE
IDLE EVENT DIRE
PEER REEDS SPED
```

PUZZLE 197

Interdenominational, Radioactivity, Re-
capitulation, Parallelogram, Supertank-
er, Feasible, Mortar, Den.

PUZZLE 198

```
BAJA FAD ALA
ELATE ITEM SPUR
LOCAL RULE TARE
LEK LUMBERJACKS
  FLAT LUGES
CERISE BAIL
ODOR SALINE JAB
MISER RED SLATE
OTT INCASE ICED
  LIST SPOKES
  ASSET TANS
JACKDEMPSEY NAB
AREA RARA EDILE
DONT SLOT RIPEN
ENE EWE NEED
```

PUZZLE 199

A. 1. Least, 2. Surge, 3. Gloss, 4. Swept,
5. Pride, 6. Drift, 7. Finch, 8. Cable.
B. 1. East, 2. Urge, 3. Loss, 4. Wept, 5.
Ride, 6. Rift, 7. Inch, 8. Able.

PUZZLE 200

```
TALC SHAM SOLO PADS
ELIA HOPI AVID ALOE
LAMP ALES VALENTINE
LIBRARY FOOL ASTER
   ICE LIAR BABY
ELECT MUTT JARS PIE
RACE SAMS PERK PINT
ASH SLIP GRAB TANGO
STOPPED BRINE ESSEN
   RIDE LAG RANT
BASIC NEEDS SWEATER
ENEMY HOSE CHAT AXE
TONE BANS TROY BOIL
AND DAIS DROP RUSTY
   DEAR CREW DUN
HEMEN BAYS JUGGLER
OVERSHOES SOUP LARA
SERB ABET ELSE EMIT
TREY TIRE SETS DANE
```

529

PUZZLE 201

```
        AGILE
ALA    CARAT    SHE
COCKERSPANIEL
TORE            ITAL
ARF PEN REB  BELA
RIO    DAMES    SPAT
LOX  CHIHUAHUA  OWE
OTT   AID  APT  MEN
  ELATE      SENSE
  RID          EAR
  REESE      GRETA
ALI  ART  PIE  NAT
SEE  GREATDANE ICE
HERB  AVIAN    ANN
AGED  END  IDA NED
  LOVE        RILE
  SAINTBERNARDS
  ALL  ROSIE  TOP
      AGENT
```

PUZZLE 202

```
SEW  AMID  CLAW
AGE  SANE  ROME
DOLPHINS   ACES
  CUED   EFFORT
ODORS  FRET
POME  WAVE  TAP
APE  CARET  RUE
LED  AIMS  CURT
  ARTS  COMAS
ANSWER   WARP
BOLA  EVILNESS
EVER  SILL  TIE
LADD  SETS  SPA
```

PUZZLE 203

```
ALA    ESS   PORT
TINE   RAT  ALOE
ENTREATY    REND
  TEAR    EWE
    SNOB  AROMA
PORE   ARMY  LAG
APE   TEE    ICE
PAN  CHAR  DOER
ALONE  DELI
    YEA   ONCE
CALL  MASTERED
OLEO  EVE  RARE
BEEN  NET   BYE
```

PUZZLE 204

```
TEA   SPA   CHUM
ARC  CAPE   HOSE
MATTERED   ABET
  ONE  IGNORE
  TART   STAG
BASE   HOVERED
IMP  SCORE   AGE
DESSERT   SIGN
  PROS   GUNS
SCREEN    GAR
IRON  ELEMENTS
TOLD  SANE  AWL
EWES   YES   BOY
```

PUZZLE 205

```
SPARK    BLOAT
ARDENT  PLEASE
NODDER  EASTER
    EAVES    SAM
MURAL   ART
IRAS    TEE  ADS
MAYHEM  DRIVEL
ELS  NOW  RILE
    TOO  REDID
WAS  ERODE
ENCORE  AMORAL
STARED  DILATE
TINED    TEPEE
```

PUZZLE 206

```
DOTE   IDA  MASH
ABEL   RED  ANNE
SOAK  INVENTOR
HEM  ASTER  EBB
   MADE   RIB
SPARES   BEAGLE
KATE        SOIL
IDEALS  OLIVES
   SAT  PACE
ODE  VASES  RAG
PENTAGON   INDY
ALDA  ELL  ROAM
LIST  SOY  ARMS
```

PUZZLE 207

```
PAW  SCAT  BRIM
EGO  COLE  LODE
PEN  ARIA  OWLS
  DARN  CLOSES
SCENE   THEM
WARN  BRIG  SEA
AREA  RUN  STAN
TED  BING  PAST
   PINK  WINES
STRONG   SAND
ORAL  SEAT  ADD
LINE  URGE  RIO
DOTS  PEER  DEN
```

PUZZLE 208

```
SHY   FOE   LAST
PEER  LIE   ONTO
ANTI  ALL  GNAW
   FOX    VEER
  NOTE   EWE
RAN  RELAX  JAB
AIL   PER   ALI
PLY  SIGNS  DAD
   ICY  AMEN
  KNOT   AWE
PAIR  BOX  NEON
ELLA  OWL  UNDO
PEEL  WEE   DEW
```

PUZZLE 209

```
EVEN  ADAM  BUD
GAME  LANE  EGO
ALPS  EYESIGHT
DELTA       WAD
   OSCAR  SOFAS
RAY  MIEN  LOLL
EKE  EMBED  USE
DIRE  SERE  ROD
ONSET  LOADS
   LAB    NICER
CONSULTS   GORE
ABE  NAIL  IRAN
BID  THEY  TEST
```

PUZZLE 210

```
BATS   ART  CART
ALEE  CUE  AREA
LOST  ONE  LINK
LETTER    PLATE
   LANCER
METER  RAY  BAY
OVER  HAT  PORE
PAN  BAN  AROMA
       EMERGE
STAGE    HOPPED
ERGO  ADO  ALVA
LIEN  NOD  REED
LODE  DEE  EASE
```

PUZZLE 211

```
ACT  CHAP  STEM
DUO  LOVE  TOTO
STREAMER   IDOL
  ELDER   ALONE
ORAL   STATE
LADEN  SIS  BEN
ATONER  RESALE
FAR   SOD  ATLAS
   STEEP  ALMS
PARIS  ALAMO
IRAN  FLAGPOLE
PING  RENE  NOR
SAGE  ARES  SUN
```

PUZZLE 212

```
ALT  HAIG  PROPS  BAL
NEH  ABBA  AUDIT  UTA
THECREOLESTATE   CLI
APART  LASH  STOKER
EVERY  MERES   FESS
ORAD  NOON   PANTY
SEC  AEON  HERO  ELA
  HAVEN  SHOWME   ON
MASSED  STEREOS  ANE
ALTOS  THINNER  TREN
GEAR  ORANGES  PREST
OCT   BADGER  FOIST
OKEH  IDES  HOLM  AR
  OATES  CERE   GRO
OLIOS   ECLAT  PAST
POSSESS  GOAT  DELTA
TITI  THEGOPHERSTAT
ERLE  ROGET  ERAT  TE
DEER  STORY  RAGS  ED
```

PUZZLE 213

```
ZIP FEW PIT
ONE AGE ODE
NAT COB SIR
ENACT BISON
SELL  TENETS
   ABODE
BALSAM  REST
AMISS   STATE
SON SOP GEN
IRK ERA LEO
LES TEN ERR
```

PUZZLE 214

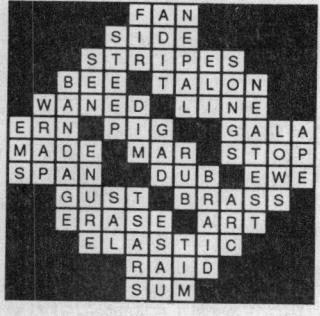

```
     FAN
     SIDE
   STRIPES
 BEE   TALON
WANED   LINE
ERN PIG GALA
MADE MAR STOP
SPAN DUB EWE
GUST   BRASS
ERASE   ART
  ELASTIC
    RAID
    SUM
```

PUZZLE 215

```
  RIBS
  AREA    PISA
 TEEMS    ARIL
CID  FOUL CITE
AROMA    ADOPTS
SALADS    DOES
ENTREE   NEST
   RHINE
  EVIL  NATIVE
  FAIR  SCALES
PARCEL  TOKEN
ECRU ERIE   ARE
LOOS   SOLAR
KEPT   NAME
       SNIP
```

PUZZLE 216

Binoculars, 2. Blue orchid, 3. ecathlons.

PUZZLE 217

```
 CROW
 HOPE        FAR
 CASED      BORES
SIREN    GEORGIA
INT   WORRY  ONTOP
LE   TOWARD   UVE
LMO  HOLDS   BRIG
SANDED      LANDS
  SAY        FUR
REED       JAGGED
ENT   STOUT  EVEN
AR    STAIRS  ILE
ROPE  EARLY  SNOW
LEADERS     EPICS
LASER       STOLE
REB          ROLL
             ONLY
```

PUZZLE 218

Half, Hale, Tale, Tame, Time. Hard, Herd, Held, Hell, Sell. Wind, Mind, Mint, Mist, Gist, Gust. Fish, Fist, Mist, Mast, Mask, Task, Tank.

PUZZLE 219

```
    HUB      PORK
    HOPIS    ALOE
   ROASTED   MITE
   SOUR   TEASPOON
  CHAR   PEDDLE
AHEM  VERY    ORB
TEL  SEAN   SWEEP
TALKIES   CHEDDAR
PALMS   BOAR  LIE
COP   FUND   PANE
   NEGATE   DIME
HANDRAIL   BEES
ALAI    SNEERER
RISK     TREAD
KITE      SLY
```

PUZZLE 220

1. Candy store, 2. Subjection, 3. Poker hands.

PUZZLE 221

```
   HUB      OFF
   MORAL    ALI
  LAUGHAT  KISS
ELSE   CAP  THAT
GEE   KNOB  SLY
       KIT  TIP
  NAP  LETALONE
CELL  MAR   SIRE
GIVEAWAY    KEY
ATE   NAG
SIR   RIND   ARM
HEMP  CAR   OBOE
SILL   BIGSHOT
NAY    PILOT
DYE     NOR
```

PUZZLE 222

1. Well, Dell, Doll, Dole, Done.
2. Fore, Fork, Cork, Cock, Lock.
3. Good, Wood, Word, Worn, Torn, Turn.
4. Last, Cast, Cart, Wart, Ward, Word.

PUZZLE 223

```
 APT       ALP
 DROP     DART
AROMA    DREAD
LIBERAL   SPRY
APE  LES   ATE
LOFT MODE CARS
 TENTATIVE
 RISE  FINE
DIPS  FRO   ERA
EON   ERRATIC
GOGH   ELUDE
ORLON   DUDE
SEMI     MER
TOP
```

PUZZLE 224

1. Tumble-down, 2. Transfixed, 3. Hypnotizes.

PUZZLE 225

```
    THY
   SHEET
  EQUATOR
 BLUNT  EAT
 SALAD  DIN
CAR BED RAPID
DOUGH REFER BEG
CONCEAL FOG MOP
ANTE MINERAL PEAR
NOR BUN LIBERTY
ROB TENSE PARIS
LEVEL END SIT
TAN   DEVIL
TOP   TONIC
   REVERSE
    RINSE
     ADE
```

PUZZLE 226

1. Card, Care, Came, Game.
2. Half, Hale, Tale, Tame, Time.
3. Foot, Boot, Bolt, Boll, Ball.
4. Blue, Slue, Slum, Slim, Slip, Ship, Chip.

PUZZLE 227

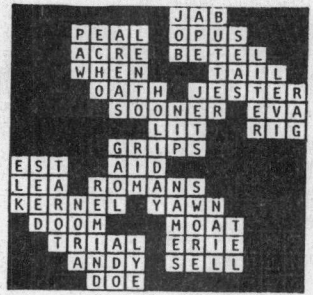

```
        JAB
   PEAL OPUS
   ACRE BETEL
   WHEN  TAIL
   OATH JESTER
   SOONER  EVA
     LIT   RIG
     GRIPS
EST   AID
LEA  ROMANS
KERNEL  YAWN
DOOM    MOAT
TRIAL   ERIE
ANDY    SELL
DOE
```

PUZZLE 228

1. Flying aces, 2. Air pockets, 3. Afterglows.

PUZZLE 229

```
          RAPT
   LIP    ODOR
  JOKE    DEPOT
 RAVEN    COOK
 MAZE     COPPER
DAZZLE CUR  INA
IDO YAM THEN COT
PER  COCOA
   HOLDOFF
    EASEL    EFT
ANT STAY WAN SEA
SOU HEN  TOSSUP
HANGON   GOAD
HERO     STORY
SATAN    HOOT
SALE     END
STEW
```

PUZZLE 230

1. Back, Beck, Beak, Beat, Seat.
2. Junk, Bunk, Bank, Bark, Bard, Yard.
3. Head, Lead, Lend, Land, Lane, Line.
4. Life, Lift, Loft, Loot, Boot, Boat.

PUZZLE 231

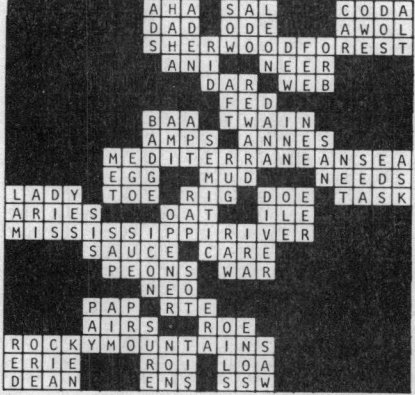

```
   AHA  SAL    CODA
   DAD  ODE    AWOL
  SHERWOODFOREST
   ANI    NEER
      DAR  WEB
       FED
  BAA  TWAIN
  AMPS ANNES
 MEDITERRANEANSEA
  EGG  MUD  NEEDS
LADY TOE RIG DOE TASK
ARIES  OAT   ILE
 MISSISSIPPIRIVER
  SAUCE  CARE
  PEONS  WAR
   NEO
  PAP   RTE
  AIRS  ROE
 ROCKYMOUNTAINS
ERIE  ROI   LOA
DEAN  ENS   SSW
```

PUZZLE 232

```
PAST   ARIS    PAL
ACTI  AMINO   SANE
THECOMMANDMENTS
HEM  TAOS    AVES
     SOS    BAKE
 DATES   PARENTS
WADE   BRIAR  RAT
ANDTHELORDSPAKE
GEL  OLEAN   AMEN
 SETTLES  BLISS
    REED    RID
 AWOL   SOAR  HEN
ORELSEHOWCANONE
WELL  BORNE  AMOS
EAT   BITS   BOSS
```

PUZZLE 236

```
CALL   ASONE  EASY
AREA   ELFIN  NILE
BATTLEOFBULLRUN
STATUTES   RAISES
    ICES   HESS
SPECKS  BEDSTEAD
ALLEE  SLAT  SOPH
BAL  DINEROS  SEA
ETAL  NEST  UMIAK
RESERVES  SPANKS
   GOER  PIER
STEAKS  RATRACES
WALLSTREETBULLS
ARAL  OBESE  DIET
PONY  RIDER  SIMS
```

PUZZLE 240

```
LADS   MAID  PAWN
ATOP  HELLO  ALEE
MOVE  ORION  PALE
AMEN  AIT  AMEND
  DART  STAR
  PESTS  STENCIL
BAR  EERIE  URAL
TINS  RADAR  PATE
UNIT  MELON  TED
 TEACUPS  SOBER
  LASS  ETNA
RALPH ODE  LAIR
DELI  ELDER  LURE
NATO  RAINS  ETON
AMON  SONS   TONE
```

PUZZLE 233

```
OPTED   AMOS  EASE
CHORE   SORE  APOS
HIMALLHISANGELS
OSE  TIE    OLDE
   LAIR   AMIE
MODES   SINISTER
ETON   CONE   NAE
NOWTHEKINGSATIN
DES  OVEN   MESO
 SETTINGS  CARES
   RELS   TORT
 SAIL   ARE  FEE
ANDASMANYASWALK
DEAL  ALEE  TITLE
DEMS  TEED  STEED
```

PUZZLE 237

```
MEG   AIRIER  ASIF
OVA   CRUSOE  GORE
NEZ  HELLSCANYON
ARAB  NEE  VIAND
   OWED   COE
TORIES  RED  AGAG
ALALA  AEROSPACE
RIVEROFNORETURN
OVERSHOES  ANGIE
TESS  IRE  GREEDS
   WOE  SASS
SAMBA  SKI  SULK
COEURDALENE  SUN
ALAN  EVENED  EGO
REDD  WADERS  SET
```

PUZZLE 241

```
BELT  CHER  MOA  SAP
ARIA  HALE  ARM  PANES
HARRYANDTONTO LINES
 TATERS  AVES  CANINE
ANT  IKES  BETTE
PLANS  BRER  CAN  SHAD
IANS  ERAS  SILT  AGE
AMI  SPIN  LODES  CLUE
PLATEN  SIDE  PALED
 SUEGOTMARRIED
PECAN  TIES  ERASER
HELP  HATES  YAKS  RAN
IRE  AMES  CAMS  ALTO
LOOM  FOR  HEMS  SNEER
  PORTS  HERS  BIG
BLADES  FIRE  SENORS
EATEN  ZORBATHEGREEK
LORRE  OLE  LOOT  ASTA
SAN  ODD  SEES  STAY
```

PUZZLE 234

```
LAIC  EMMA  BRIE  SLAB
AERO  AIDE  ROLL  POME
COMMISSIONEDOFFICER
ENABLES  LINE  ICING
  ILL  PINT  FARE
ALONE  ALAE  FADE  PRE
TELE  ADEN  FACED  HEP
ETE  ASEA  GRITS  SAME
 ARIL  RIOT  ELSIE
 ADMIRALOFTHEFLEET
BROOD  LOTH  LEAD
LANK  SCOTS  PLAN  COD
ABO  BUOYS  SEER  CODE
TYR  LEWD  STEN  MONEY
  MURS  SEEN  MAN
SIREN  OPAL  EARNEST
COASTARTILLERYCORPS
OTIS  ROTL  AGIO  RARA
WANY  AWOL  ROAR  STYR
```

PUZZLE 238

```
MAAM   ACTOF  PILE
INRE   MEUSE  ORAL
SYNCOPATEDCLOCK
SASHLESS  ERINYS
  AARE   CRAT
JOANNE  LOITERED
ALTI  DUNCE  ADO
CLOCKWORKORANGE
OIL  ERNES  PIER
BELFRIES  SPENDS
  ANNE  ALAR
PEGLEG  SNORTING
THECLOCKSTRUCKI
ARNO  URIAH  ROVE
SEEN  TOMES  ENDS
```

PUZZLE 235

```
DUAL   SPREE  CPAS
OSLO   OLIVE  LASH
MEATLOAFER  ENTE
 RETINUES  BAHIA
  ONES   TARA
NAP  TRIM  OLAND
ADAD   BARTENDER
RATE  ALOES  CLIO
CHISELERS  EEGS
 SEPTA  ITSA  RNA
  NETS   ALGA
VOTRE  CAROUSEL
IRMA  GAMEWARDEN
NEAT  AREAL  EDDO
ESNE  BOSSY  DYAD
```

PUZZLE 239

```
EGGS   ALTAR  EAVE
LOOK   LOOSE  AMID
MYWILDIRISHROSE
SAN  AER  NIELSEN
  LINED   DAY
TOPICS  EVER  RAN
AVER   BANS   ILO
MADAMEBUTTERFLY
PTA  UNES   ALOE
SEL  RTES  TAPERS
  ARR  YEARS
AFFRAYS  MIO  PIE
MERRYWIDOWWALTZ
ITEA  ANITA  PEER
SEES  YEMEN  RASA
```

PUZZLE 243

```
LEO  PLOP  MORAL  SLOB
ARC  LEAR  OCALA  IAGO
CRUZEIRO  CHILD  GILA
 LABS  LIKED  YONDER
TWINE  LOVER  ABBA
WISE  PAGED  GUILDER
AFT  MENUS  SINGS  ADE
SESTERCE  ACRES  BLIP
  SAKE  SARIS  GRETA
SWEATY  CORES  TRASHY
LORRY  BELOW  SHAW
EONS  WIDEN  DOUBLOON
ELI  GENES  TENDS  PIA
PFENNIG  WINGS  PULP
  EARS  WANTS  TULSA
SHREWD  PATTI  EYRE
LIED  ERODE  SIXPENCE
URAL  SANER  TREE  COW
GERE  TEDDY  SASS  EYE
```

PUZZLE 244

```
GORP ASPS TACIT WOK
ELEE CLAP ALONE HIE
NEVERHADACHANCE INN
TOSLEEP REO SAT TKO
    EDS TENET NENE
ASTRO VEST RETRACTS
BAHS PAST WERE THRU
ERE MESS CHARDS RED
SAPIENT LOADS PLIES
    IRAN RANTS FEES
RACED CEDES BREATHS
ONT EDUCED HEAD MAO
STUN IRAS GATS CALL
AIRBOATS AURA LASSO
    EARL TOTEM TOT
TIS ITA LES MIDEAST
RAH GODBLESSAMERICA
AGO INDIA EASE EDAM
MOW NESTS DOSS DAME
```

PUZZLE 248

```
EIDER    ASP    CKW
CANDIDA APPEAL SHARIF
ANTARES PURANA AERATE
RYE EEL ACTS INVITE
DARKLADYOFTHESONNETS
   NAB EMO DELTA
MAJORBARBARA RAJ STAT
ARABIAN LEI OTIOSE
COBB CID SODAS AIRMAN
AMOY YMA SENTENCE
WAT ALA TOA KAA
   CYCLAMEN ARP EONS
FLORAL TOROS SLO NAGS
RETAKE SAT AURALEE
AGOG OAT THEAPPLECART
   SPIEL ERE ITT
MRSWARRENSPROFESSION
TOOHOT EVOE ANO ORO
INDOOR TENDON ONEIDAS
SIENNA ELEGIT DESTINY
COE    SEL    SERAC
```

PUZZLE 252

```
WIFE   CAP    TOM
IDLE   ODE   BIDE
SEAR   NET   ADOS
PATIOS    ADDERS
      ERE LOG
STY   END   GEESE
HOE   TIC    GAY
YEAST POT    OWE
      AIM MAR
VALLEY    PROPER
ALEE   TEA   LORE
TONS   HEN   LOIN
SET    SLY   SLED
```

PUZZLE 245

```
PAVE POLE GAFF TUBE
OBIS ADEN RILE ELLA
SEEK NEWS EMIR ENOS
EDDIED DUET PRIMATE
   MAAM IRAQ ERE
MAJOR EDNA UPTODATE
EGOS CRAG GOREN LOG
AUK LAID PLIED DANA
DEEPEST SOOTY SHIED
   EAT CURBS BOO
CLARK BLAKE DRAWBAR
LACK GRAVY TEAK AXE
ONE GEESE HAFT GALA
DESSERTS SURE JULEP
   LAO YOUR RAIL
CAVERNS WEDS EMCEES
USED ICON LAPS HALE
SING MOLE ECHO EVIL
PATE OWED SKIP SEAL
```

PUZZLE 249

```
GRUB CHAP DELI JEST
SNARE LASH LUMEN ALTO
WOMAN ALOE ICONS USES
AMBLE STRAYCATS GNAWS
MEL FUSS SUITE SAT
ICILY CARTS MARINAS
CNOTE RUNT CONFETTI
LOGOS PERT WISP USHER
EYRE FOBS KITT TNT
WOODPILE GENE AOK TAB
ITS ELECTRICRANGE RBI
SEE NED MATE STALWART
PAD DASH PIES EMUS
PEARL EONS ALAS HAPPY
ANNOTATE ELAN VERST
REDWINE ITALY FEAST
LEA SNORE HIED ESP
NARCS ROVINGEYE IDAHO
AGHA YODEL OPEN NAMES
PEER AMASS REND GREAT
SEAS PEST YEAS SERF
```

PUZZLE 253

```
SHARP   SET    HAL
TOWEL   AVOCADO
ATALE   FEMALES
GER  AFAR   NIL
SLENDER     BIB
   EERIE  TUNE
CANADA  ABATED
ODOR   LEGAL
NUT    DEFECTS
   LID SURF HAT
PACIFIC  LEASE
ITEMIZE  ELITE
TED  XED  DINER
```

PUZZLE 246

```
SELF MACH HUBBUB WALL
OMAR EDIE EMERGE ALEE
LIMA LOTS FIREHYDRANT
ORANGERY STALL ADITS
   KLEE SPIKE FAKE
STELE SORES BELONGS
LORIN PIPER ALEUT AHA
ORAN MOSHE DALMATIAN
SST LANAI ARABS HUNT
HOOKANDLADDER CRISES
   ROES EON MOUE
ACCOST ASBESTOSSUITS
PLAN AERIE CELTS NEW
SAFETYNET GESTS ACME
ERE SAILS CANTS DRAPE
ASCENTS PASTY ASSET
   ATKA LANES SOHO
ADAMS MESAS DULLNESS
RUBBERBOOTS BONE ISLE
IDLE HORNET ANNO SPAR
DEER ODESSA DAYS TYPE
```

PUZZLE 250

```
PASSION SHAMAN MATS
ASTARTE CALORIE ACHES
THEGOODHUMORMAN CHELA
HELEN ALIEN GAGE GEL
STARS MILTS GATOR OCT
   PERSE VIREO LOTS
ALF MOOD TINA DEED
GOODYTWOSHOES ADDEDTO
ERRANTS LATS BRAF IAN
REGMAS SASH FLAY MERE
ONS INTHEGOOD BOY
EGOS GRAY GENT GENOAS
LED COAG MOLD EARDUST
MENTION GOODANDPLENTY
ENID WARD AGEE GAL
BEST FLARE TOMES
LAS FOILS IONAS SLOPE
ARS ARED ANNAT CADIS
SNARL GOODNIGHTLADIES
TEKEL ERUDITE VALENCE
DEBS FRASER AMASSED
```

PUZZLE 254

```
STAR   RAM    THEM
HALE   ELI    RARE
OXEN   FIN    EDEN
DISTRIBUTE
      UNITE  AWL
POLITE    ENDURE
ODOR       AREA
REPAIR  DEMAND
ESS  CEDAR
   DECORATION
SURE   INK   HOME
ASIA   POE   AWES
NEON   ERR   WANT
```

PUZZLE 247

```
LATH FACT SCALE SALT
ALEA AFAR ERROL TRAIT
DETROITREDWINGS LOIRE
SEEDER EKE NIS TOURED
   WRY SAGE SOUS
DORA SPRITE TINIEST
APERS PEARL HIDES EOS
ELEE ATSEA UTE CONTE
RE AGREE NESTS ABNER
AT TOT TYKE TREADS
STEAK MAE READY
ERILS NAIF LXI RAP
LITE TIBIA APAIN OPA
SSES OVA LMNOP ATLAS
IE ESTES CITES LEERS
ESTATES BORATE ROSE
   AHEM MINI AAR
NITAS PAT ART TIARAS
ENEW BALTIMOREORIOLE
LERK OTTER TILL NOON
LESS OHARE OPAL STET
```

PUZZLE 251

```
BENDS GRIN BRAG HEMP
ONION LEDA SAUTE IGOR
ALBEE ODER OSSEO DALE
SABRA BYAWHISKER EDDY
TIL KLEE HALES GAY
EDITS WAIST MISHAPS
ROARED BOLL ORATORIO
ANWAR SEWS KITS ALIEN
SWAG SKIS WATT FIE
PAYS PEG HIRE JAR SET
ERA QUIETASAMOUSE QUA
DDT URN ABET DIT BUCO
SEN MUIR ROCS LEHI
PLUME BATT MIRE SOARS
DESERTED HIPS WICKET
QUELLED SCENE PERKY
LYE BOARS TODO CST
LAMA TAILGATERS CELLO
AGAR ERNIE RYES CLEAT
PUMA REEDS ERSE OKAPI
PEAT SASS LESS SENSE
```

PUZZLE 255

```
CHAP   FED    TRAP
HALL   ORE    RARE
AREA   RAG    ACTS
RESCUE    ROCKET
      ESS EWE
BASSET    ENDEAR
EYE        OWE
TEAPOT    DARNED
      RUE EVE
SPRITE    TAPPED
PAID   MOE   ERIE
ANTE   ENS   LORE
TEES   DOT   SPED
```

PUZZLE 256

```
STEM  HAWK  PRY
LAVA  ALAN  RUE
OXEN  RESIDENT
PIRATE    TAP
    GAMES  MASH
RAKES  EAT  ROE
ICE  TARDY  ERR
TEE  ELI  PASTE
ASPS  LEVER
    SUB  ESCAPE
DIAMONDS  ARID
IRK  ROOT  DEED
MAE  EWES  EASY
```

PUZZLE 260

```
AHA  CATS  CHAT
REP  ALEE  LEVI
IRE  MEAN  AXES
DODGE  STAR
  ALS  WASTE
SHOT  HAVE  EEL
WAVE  ODE  TEES
ILE  OPEN  ANNA
MORAL  TAR
  PELT  VANES
ALDA  ERIE  EAT
LEER  NEAR  AVA
PENT  TENT  LEG
```

PUZZLE 264

```
WAGS  ATLAS  CHAP
AMEN  NOOSE  HERO
DINE  GROPE  OREO
  DEEPEST  DISBAR
    ZERO  SITE
SPIES    TEENAGE
THANK  SPASM  GAY
RANG  CHART  LATE
AVE  CHATS  ROPES
PEDALED  MINES
  LADY  TOPE
DEMAND  LEVELER
OVER  ALINE  ICON
SIAM  RARER  ERIE
ELLS  SPATS  RULE
```

PUZZLE 257

```
SULK  OAK  PAGE
ASIA  PIN  ANNE
LEER  ORIENTAL
ESSAYS  TWEET
    TOSS  ELL
HOMERUN  SODA
UFO  EMILY  POD
ETCH  FAUCETS
  COB  FULL
LATIN  GEORGE
ROSEBUSH  SEAL
EVIL  DOE  EATS
DENS  END  TREE
```

PUZZLE 261

```
LASH  DOE  PACE
ELLA  IDA  IRON
EDEN  VET  LEAD
SADDLE  SEATS
    BARREL
SALAD  HEY  WAR
TWIG  OIL  WACO
YET  RAN  AIDED
    AROUND
CHIMP  STEREO
AURA  ASH  NEAR
PLAN  LIE  ELSE
SANE  ERR  DYES
```

PUZZLE 265

```
RAFT  ECHO  ALAS
ACRE  LAIR  ELOPE
PIER  AREA  RIPEN
DEMOTE  LARGEST
    LIE  HEN
BEN  DONATED  GAS
OXYGEN  VIM  SOFT
OILER  PEP  ROUTE
SLOT  SIR  SINGER
TEN  MEETING  ERN
    HOE  MOO
REBOUND  PORTAL
ALERT  ATOP  USED
SLASH  WISE  BEAR
HATE  NEED  EASY
```

PUZZLE 258

```
PUN    ALA    COG
ONE    RIG    USE
DIM  KITE  FELT
STOVES    PESOS
    EYEBROW
CARTS  LOW  LAY
ODES  TOE  DOSE
NOD  WON  EIGHT
    GANDERS
FUMES    ARCHES
ITEM  DOGS  ORE
TAR  ELL  GIN
SHE  WEE  SET
```

PUZZLE 262

```
DALE  CLEFT  STEM
IRON  EERIE  EAVE
MINT  NERVE  APES
EDGERS  SETTLERS
  ROOF  SHE
  DESIRED  ERRAND
SEA  LEMON  MELEE
PAGE  DUNES  DOWN
ALLAY  ROWER  NET
STEREO  REMODEL
  ACT  REAR
IMMORTAL  SNARES
TEAL  ALERT  MODE
ERIE  VENUE  ALEE
MEMO  ESTER  SEND
```

PUZZLE 266

```
AMP  SNAP  SLAB
LEE  TORE  PIMA
ESS  REEL  AMOS
CHOCOLATECAKE
  OKS  IRE
SHINE  INA  WIT
PURE  FOG  LOCO
ARK  GIN  MONEY
  PAR  SAN
CHEESEBURGERS
HALT  BARK  DOE
ELSE  URGE  ALA
WEAR  GEED  MET
```

PUZZLE 259

```
  ENOS  STAR
  SARI  ARIA
COPPERSMITH
OKRA  ASP      HUG
LOS ALI NAP ONE USE
IRA LATHERS DOG SAT
PAGES  EWE    TOOT
LANTERN    ALEE
  DOME    LOCKETS
ANT VIP    APR RAP
CORSETS    VEIN
TREE      MANNERS
  AWED POI  OBOES
ADD YET PARASOL PAP
GEL ELI ART AMI ERA
OWE    MEL ELAN
  COBBLESTONE
  OLEO  ARNO
  TERN  ROAN
```

PUZZLE 263

```
BRAD  SALAD  FEAT
LOLA  AMATI  URGE
EVER  VINES  LION
DECKHAND  TALENT
  RAGE  FACE
OPPOSE  MUSHROOM
TROOP  FONTS  RIA
HARM  ERODE  BALI
EDT  AVERS  FATED
ROOMMATE  MILERS
  EONS  CALL
SPARSE  TOLERATE
HILT  STILL  OBIT
INTO  CANOE  OLLA
PEON  EXERT  MEET
```

PUZZLE 267

```
FADE  LOS  BLOW
IRON  ANT  ROBE
RIOT  PEA  ALOE
MARRY  NAILED
  BYES  DID
FOE  SHY  REFER
AWLS  EON  DARE
DELAY  NEW  SAP
  DEW  TEST
SUNDAE  THESE
TREE  DIM  ANTE
EGOS  GNU  DEAL
WENT  END  ERRS
```

534

PUZZLE 268

```
BAD AURA   GET
ONE PROP  AERO
OAF INTO  BOIL
STERN   SEEMED
  NAG STATE
BEST WELT   TIE
EEE SHIES   RAW
ALL PINS  PINE
  ERASE ARC
ASSIST   LEAST
ROSS LATE   LEA
IDLE EVER   LAM
DAY  RENT   YRS
```

PUZZLE 269

```
HAM SET  SALVE
ALABAMA  PREEN
SENATOR  AIDED
   TITTERS
ENCORE  STEEPS
LOANED  TANGLE
IMP        RAW
TARIFF  GAMETE
EDITOR  ORATOR
   HOOSIER
GAMAL  ANNEALS
APACE  STASHES
STRAD SOS  ATE
```

PUZZLE 270

```
HAM PETE  GLIB
ALE ALAN  LOCO
DISTRICT  ORES
  SITS RIVERS
PLANS   BASE
RAGE PANE  CAN
ONE DANCE  ADE
DES AIDE  TRIM
  INNS SETTO
BASSET  CLEO
ORAL  ILLINOIS
NILE NEAT  NOS
ODES GEMS  SUE
```

PUZZLE 271

```
BAN TARA  ROBE
RUE EDIT  AWOL
ARC NOCTURNAL
GATOS   EASE
 AWED   ERRED
MORE AVID  EVA
AMID TIN  OPEN
RAN FEET  DONE
CREME   OVER
 ERIN  ASTER
ESSENTIAL  EMU
BEET ECRU  RID
BATS METE  STE
```

PUZZLE 272

```
BING ACT  CHAR
AREA WOE  AUTO
GIRL APE  SLOT
SOLAR  PSALM
  OLD EEL
SCENES  EASILY
EAR        NEE
ENROLL  BONNET
  PIE ARE
 GREEN  BEACH
LOAN GOO  ROOF
ANTE TWO  BLUE
DEER HEN  YARD
```

PUZZLE 273

```
PARK IRON  SIP
OXEN MINE  ERA
DELI POSE  MAN
 AFAR  EDGING
TUXEDO   TEA
ELI EVE  DEPOT
ANNA EGG  LAVA
MAGIC OLD  RIM
  ROB ARCADE
LAWYER  DYED
ALE READ  DING
MAR CAGE  ASEA
PIE EDEN  REEL
```

PUZZLE 274

```
HALT  SOFA  DATE
ALEE TOLLS  EGAD
GENE AREAS  CORE
CONESTOGAWAGON
  ITS   URN
SPARE  RELATION
ALICE DITTY  RAE
MAKE BIDES  PETS
ONE AIRES  MONET
STRANGER  CATER
  BAH   BAR
SHORTORDERCOOK
LAVA ROAST  GRAY
AVID NOTES  RARE
MEDE SKAT  ELLA
```

PUZZLE 275

Harrisburg, Pennsylvania

Harrisburg is the capital of Pennsylvania. The city lies on the Susquehanna River and began as a trading post established by John Harris. Products of Harrisburg include building materials and airplane parts.

PUZZLE 276

```
CORN      SUN
ALIAS   NASAL
RIDGE   AMUSE
EVE EBB   ATE
 ERODE   FLY
   ASIDE
SAT   NEEDS
OWL AGE   ROB
RELIC   DRILL
ELECT   SIEVE
LYE      BREW
```

PUZZLE 277

```
ADAM RAVE  HIT
TAPE EVEN  ORE
OMEN VENTURED
MEDDLE  TEST
  EARN REEDS
SUNRISE  SNEE
ATE NEWTS  SAW
LEAF  ERASERS
ESTES   RENT
 NEAP  AGATES
CRESCENT  VILE
HAS KANE  ELSA
INS SLED  SEER
```

PUZZLE 278

```
CALM  SPA  TALL
OLIO EWERS  ERIE
PIER SONIC  RIND
ADO TOT  ARMADA
  SPAN ALAI
GREAT  PLANTERS
DIE REMIT  TENET
AVES SINEW  SALA
MESAS MERIT  CAR
PRELATES  NASTY
  EVES ANNA
REDSEA OLE  LAP
ADAM RUMOR  VIAL
MIRE STANS  EDGE
STEN ERE  REED
```

PUZZLE 279

```
PATE RUN  OPT
ALLOR EKE  BEA
WAGON LASHING
STAT   LISTE
 HEAVE  MOLD
STE GRE  MANIA
HYBRID SANDAL
ORRIS CUT  ERE
WOOL  CHEAT
 ELIAS  RENO
VENDORS  PETER
AVA OCT  AVANT
TEN SEE  SITE
```

PUZZLE 280

1. Dime, Dame, Dare; 2. Rear, Reap, Harp; 3. This, That, Tart; 4. Ruse, Rust, User; 5. Note, None, Gate; 6. Earl, Tale, Tree.

PUZZLE 281

```
STEW WRAP  SCARE
NODE HERA  TIMID
OGEE OPAL   LACE
BANKROLL  FLEDGE
  EASY PEER
PLINTH CONSOMME
HINDS ELECT  OAT
YVES BLAME  MOTH
LER BOORS  FORTE
ANTELOPE CLOSER
  TOTE ULAN
EIGHTH SNOWBALL
DONAT LACY  ERIE
INANE ISLE  AGAS
ESTER SHED  MORE
```

PUZZLE 282

1. Nothing lowers the level of conversation more than raising the voice. 2. A speaker who does not strike oil in ten minutes should stop boring.

PUZZLE 283

```
CRAW BIRD VAL  ASTAR
LOTI ONER SODA BROWSE
AMAT OTTO ELEM RARITY
MELT TAIL CAPP AMATI
POLITICALCARTOONIST
 CHET NONE OLDS ERS
DARIUS LEST ENDS PREP
AMISS BIST GLEE SLICE
DOOM ALAS BRAD STANCE
ANT STAN SLOT TWINGED
 ACOMEDYOFERRORS
INFLAME OSTE EARS WAG
MOLARS JOTS SPIN TIME
BRINE CONS ANON PINON
EMPS BOLE WRIT CATERS
DAP FOIL SHAG MOLT
AFUNNYTHINGHAPPENED
ANISE GRAM EARP RIDE
OSTLER OILS RITE ITEM
RILLES OKEY EKER NEMO
BAYES DES  DUNS GRAB
```

PUZZLE 284

```
CHAP ASTAS SAGA
LANE THEGO PIES
ALTO MANIC INAS
POINTOFNORETURN
      RST   AGE
TOMCAT CATO ATE
OPIUM DELI ARIL
WESTPOINTCADETS
ERSE VETS SINAI
RAY WETS OCTANE
   DAR SPA
COMESTOTHEPOINT
RUIN UNION IDEA
ASST RENTE LEAR
BETS ESTER YORE
```

PUZZLE 285

```
LASSO SCAM PUPA
ABATE TADS ONYX
METERMAIDS NILE
PLEA AIR ACTOR
   MAIDOFATHENS
CAVERN ELMO
AVERT KILO SPAN
FEN SPICIER ORO
ERIS ARES UNLIT
   AGIO SNEEZE
MAIDENVOYAGE
AROSE DOG DRAG
NINA MAIDENLADY
ODIC ELLE BEGUN
RECK GAEL ASSET
```

PUZZLE 286

```
MASS CASTE MAUL
ERIA AVIAN IDLE
SMELLSARAT NINA
TEN OISE RENTAL
ADAMANT BARI
   ITO DECREASE
MARCH DRAT MILE
IRAK AROSE OMAR
LINE DINT MUSTY
LADYLOVE BOS
   MARE DONEFOR
ANGORA CELT ORA
PERU BELLTHECAT
EROS LEAVE LATE
DOGE ENDED FLED
```

PUZZLE 287

```
ADAM SCORE ITIS
SINE EATIN TENT
TENDERFOOT ANDA
ANAIL ESSA KNOT
REMAKE IDEE
   TENDRILS SPA
CATO OREL OASIS
OMER SALON TELA
MANSE WINE TEEN
ENA TENTACLE
   COAL KINDER
ALIA APSE ATONE
HOOS TENDERIZED
ABUT ETUDE VERD
BESS SEGAL EROS
```

PUZZLE 288

```
PRAM PETER DART
LULU ALINE EGER
ATOP RENTE ROSE
THEPRICEISRIGHT
   EAST REED
PARTS STE PETAL
ERASED ELL DINE
ADD DELAYED BEA
LEIF WAS ORBITS
SNOUT BEN YEAST
   NOSE ETAL
THENEWLYWEDGAME
RANI ELATE IRES
OTOE DELON UTES
TESS EDENS METE
```

PUZZLE 289

```
SHUT BASIS SAM
LUSH PETITE ATE
ALEE ASHCAN TOT
MARC TOO OPINE
   OWE UNPRUNED
ACUMEN SOLAN
RUPERT ANY CREW
ABODE ANE CHIDE
MANI AND FLANGE
   ASPIC LANDED
TOWNHALL END
ERASE ODD JEAN
NAG BIGWIG URGE
ETE ATONCE DIRE
TED TEASE YEAR
```

PUZZLE 290

```
TIFF SPAT HELP
AMOI CUBIT ALIE
MACE ARENA SATE
MINERSDAUGHTER
   DOPE LEERS
DAVIS NOPAR
ALAS BAITED LOS
FATHERKNOWSBEST
TIS LAINES RATE
   SUNNY BINET
CASED AIRS
UNCLETOMSCABIN
RIAL OVATE ADIT
ELLE PIKER NONE
SEAR DORS ELEE
```

PUZZLE 291

```
PASTA ATOP OVER
ACORN RIGA VINE
NOMAD TERN ELIE
   RECOVERED REDD
EVA SASH
ISM ELSA STERNS
OPA REALM ARIEL
TIRO SLOAN ELLA
ALIVE TENOR ELK
STEEPS SETA SSE
   RICO ATA
GIST OVERTHERE
ATTU NEVE ERODE
ONOR ERIN RITAS
LOPE STLO SEEMS
```

PUZZLE 292

```
MUTT TATAS STAR
ERIE ARENA PALO
SANANTONIOTEXAS
SLY EAST ANISE
   PARE PELT
AWAITS CELL SAD
SAGS HOBO PEA
SYRACUSENEWYORK
ENE ANTS ARIA
TEE PIES GARTER
   LETT WREN
AMEER PAIR TIP
SARASOTAFLORIDA
ODIN PANEL ILLS
RENT TIERS BEET
```

PUZZLE 293

```
ABC SLAP PRIM
LALA COVE DIODE
ASAN ONER INSET
SISTERGREETTHEE
SHINE SET
   TRAP ROMPER
STAR VAGI ANSA
AWISESONHEARETH
SITS INEE PLUS
SMITES SETA
   LAS ACRES
ANDALLTHEPEOPLE
LEAVE ROVE PEAR
LACES APER YETI
ARES PENS SEE
```

PUZZLE 294

```
SPAT CREEL ECHO
AONE EAGRE AREA
SPEAKSFORITSELF
SEW EATS REEDS
   EARS TOED
COARSE HERB MAN
OMNI PANEL ORO
SIGNEDANDSEALED
TTU NARDS LATE
ASS ILES SPARES
   AGES ATOR
DATUM ACRE SAP
OPENANDSHUTCASE
MEET ADEEM ALPS
ODDS BEADS NEST
```

PUZZLE 295

```
BELL CEDAR PILL
ATOI ALATE ANOA
ETON RULED SCOT
RENEGADE ROTATE
   CAFE HIDE
SARAPE REVOLVER
CREME PALER ONE
REAP RAZOR MINE
OTC CARET GALES
DEHORNED CAVEAT
   PAGE LORE
RENEGE SOMBRERO
AVON WEAVE IRAN
MENE ARMED CIRC
PROD REEDY KNEE
```

PUZZLE 296

```
DADE IMAGE ORAL
OVEN NICER BALE
REDD DECORATION
PSI SENT LUNTS
  CITE  DAIS
TRACED CONCERTS
RATES DANTE ERA
ENID TURNS SVEN
AGO BEERY STEAD
TENDERLY CHILDS
  ARMS  LARA
LOIRE FLOG TAB
IRRITATION MILL
SCAN MORSE ROTE
TANG PRESS SNOW
```

PUZZLE 297

```
SPEECH  PAINTS
POTSHOT ACCUSED
IRATELY THEBEAR
EGG FER IER TWO
LIED DOVER RUIN
SERUM LEN TENSE
SEDAN SCROOGES
   BESPEAK
JEANETTE TEXAS
ANGEL RRS NYMPH
SCAB BESTS ZERO
POI AUS EAR RUM
ERNESTS AVARICE
RESTATE MENACER
STONED  STEADS
```

PUZZLE 298

```
WALT IMAGE CBS
ALEA MARIN HALO
REDPEPPERS ISAR
DEARTO ALLOCATE
OAST SALOL
REPOTTED VISTAS
ITEMS NUMEN WIE
GAPS PORED GAME
OPP SANER SIRED
REESES RICHTERS
RINSE TORT
HAMSTERS ZUIDER
ALIT SALTIGRADE
WINE USUAL ELIE
STR PERRY DEED
```

PUZZLE 299

```
FROG PERIL SLAP
LIVE ALICE TOLE
OPEN RAVED ELIA
GENERATE VALET
ODE BAIL
REMOTE DIGESTED
ERODE CITED ELI
CARD BREED PAIN
ASS FEATS BASTE
PEERLESS CAREER
AIRS FAN
STRIP LINGERED
ORES FROND DATE
RITE RIVAL ICON
TOES ADELE TENT
```

PUZZLE 300

```
ADLIB SCOT SLIT
BROKE THAW PONY
LAPEL OUTOFLUCK
EYE LOOM LATHE
SHIP PLUS
SCHOOL FOOTHOLD
CLAMP SLIDE ZOO
OOZE CHASE BOWL
USE SHAME PANEL
TELLTALE CELERY
EARL BOND
CREST LOON BAD
RAISECAIN ABATE
OGRE ACME MASON
PEER PEAR ENEMY
```

PUZZLE 301

```
CLUB SCAR TRAM
LORE CARE RULER
OVAL OMIT UNITE
TELLER ZONE BAN
ONE ORE SILT
CROWD ENTRAP
ROT SEA VIOLET
ABIGAIL BEDTIME
BECALM HAS FUN
SAILOR CREST
RAMP LET FOE
ADO PEAS ATTACK
MOTTO REEK IRON
SPOIL NAVE RIPE
TREE STAR EASE
```

PUZZLE 302

```
PASS MIDAS WILT
ADIT ADAPT ERIE
NATIONALPASTIME
ERECT ELIA SEN
KIND ENID
TOR SEEP SNARL
AMID ATOM TROOP
DIVA RELAY EVOE
STEMS RETE SENT
STEAM SELL RYE
SLOB SPAS
DIP ALEE SPACE
ASOLDASTHEHILLS
SLOE RENEW RIOT
HELD STARE ETTE
```

PUZZLE 303

```
VITAL CASE CLUB
AVISO YVES HONE
SECONDRATE RAIL
ESK GAULS DITTO
BASS CASHEW
SLOUGH FAINT
TONTO FORT ORAL
ABUT PRIME POKY
ROSE EASY CHOIR
RHETT GRETNA
SINFUL ROAR
POULT THIRD ARM
ANTI TRAVELOGUE
SITE HULA EAUDE
MAYS YELL SKEET
```

PUZZLE 304

```
HELP DARES VAIN
AREA ANISE ELSA
TIER UTTER STAG
SCRAMBLE VISORS
DOSE EIRE
GELID REPTILIAN
AMUSES DEUS RUE
LICE TRIED CAGE
ALI ORAL ELATED
SEDATIVES APERS
PIKE TAMS
PRAISE VAMPIRES
ROBE OPERA ZULU
ALEC URGES ESSE
METE TOADS DEED
```

PUZZLE 305

```
CRAB WASP DANE
OEIL ALOOP AGED
MENU HONOR ROTI
BLUESINTHENIGHT
NINE VON
CARIBE BLUEGUMS
ABELS ARIEL NEE
RENE GLASS BIDU
OLD ARMET SLOES
BLUESEAS SAUNAS
NCC CANE
REDWHITEANDBLUE
OMAR AERIE IOTA
DIVA NEINS RTES
STEP MEET DIST
```

PUZZLE 306

```
MONA PEAR CORPS
ENOL LAVA OBOES
SAND ARAN WEDGE
NICELYNICELY
ERENOW LEA TIE
GIG RUNYON
ITEM TRUE LORNA
MRNATHANDETROIT
POTSY BEAN ALAE
ELATER MAD
LLD ASF CUBITS
SKYMASTERSON
DAMON ASTI ETTE
ITALO SHUN ALEE
GENET HANG MESS
```

PUZZLE 307

```
CUBS BETA SAME
OLLA OARED EGOS
GNAW RHINOCEROS
SAC CAIN ERASE
KOALA HARE
CABINS AIREDALE
ADELE MULES ROS
RIAS SANTA AMIS
OER PELTS STARE
MUSKRATS ANODES
EONS OKAPI
RAVEN TWIG LAP
ORANGUTANS ELBE
OGLE GORES MOLE
DOER HOOD USER
```

PUZZLE 308

```
BLED SPY CURL
ROTA LEA AREA
ICON ELM BANG
MONGREL TALES
LATERAL
POKED TON SIR
RAISIN CATTLE
OFT COO GAYLY
RATTLER
TIDAL HARNESS
UNIT TED IVAN
SERE ERE SORA
KEEL ASS HEAP
```

PUZZLE 309

```
PUSS SHALE CANT
OLIO TOMES OLOR
LADY IRONS WINE
ONE INSIDETRACK
BINGE NOISES
POUNCE IRENE
RARE RESIST FLO
ASNER REF ORLON
MTS ECARTE EIRE
STOLE NIPPER
AVALON STOPS
SIDEWINDERS IKE
IRID FORTE ODER
AGOG ELATE REND
NOSE ROTOS OSSA
```

PUZZLE 310

```
S E R A C   O R A D   D A T A
A R U B A   P O S E   E R A L
F I N E T O O T H E D C O M B
E S E   T Y R E   P O I S E S
      P I E T   M E L D E D
A F I N E R O M A N C E
L A B O R   A L E E   B O B
I T E M   A C R I D   T A B U
T E X   S W A T   S O L A R
    T H E F I N E P R I N T
  C U R I A E   E E L S
S O N A N T   S E R A   M A R
A F I N E H O W D O Y O U D O
C R O C   E P E E   E L I A S
R E N E   R E D D   D E R M A
```

PUZZLE 311

```
J A M B   C H A D   S E D A N
I D E A   L E N A   T R I B E
V E S T M E N T S   A R A B S
E N S   E A R S H O T   L O T
    E B O N Y   B U R S T S
  G N A W S   T H E S E
S I G N S   F R A Y   F R E E
P L E A   S E A L S   R E D O
Y A R N   C E D E   S A T I N
    A B O D E   S H I R T
D A M S E L   A T O N E
O L E   A D M I R E R   A G A
T I L E S   I N S P E C T O R
E V E N T   S T O P   H E A T
D E E D S   T O N E   I D L E
```

PUZZLE 312

```
S C A N   M A L L   D Y E
E R M A   A V I A N   T E A L
T O A D   D E R M A   I N K S
  C H I N A C A B I N E T S
    N O M   L O T
P A C E R   I C E   W A S H
A C H   S E D A T E   C H A T
C H I N E S E C H E C K E R S
T E N O   P A T I N A   E T A
  D O G S   S I C   P E T E R
    G O B   E E L
  C H I N A S Y N D R O M E
G L E N   S H O E S   P O M E
E A R S   H O R N E   E V I L
E Y E   P E E L   D E L L
```

PUZZLE 313

```
C H I C   D O V E   S O A P   R A H S
L I R A   E M I R   H I V E   E L I A
A R A R   C A M I S O L E S   S A S S
M E N T I O N   N O W   R O G U I S H
    E L D   L E S   S U M
N I L   K E N   C O R P S   Y E L P S
O D E S   S A L O N   L A C   S E A L
R E F E R   V A N   S I G H S   F R A
M A T T E R E D   D O T   I N S T E P
  G I B E S   S A Y   E R A T O
P R U N E S   C A M   R E P R O V A L
R I A   L E G A L   P O R   E L E G Y
A G R A   W A R   R A B I C   E R I E
M A D L Y   D E C O R   E R G   S O S
    L O S   T A B   I O N
D E C A N T S   C O S   I N T O N E S
A W A Y   R I G H T W I N G   B A R K
M E T E   A L E E   A C R E   L Y R E
P R O D   P O E T   T E E S   E S S E
```

PUZZLE 314

```
A M A T   O O F   S P A R   S T A Y S
M A R E   U N O   T O R E   L U M E T
I S I N   Z E N   O U C H   A D A M S
T H E S W O R D I N T H E S T O N E
Y A L T A   S A T E S   A M E R I N D
    O N T   N E O   T R I S   T I E
S C A N T E S T   F R O S T   P A T E
E R L E   N E S S   A Y E   D O S E D
L E I   A D A   T A C O   S O O
L E F T N O S T O N E U N T U R N E D
  I N N   A N A M   O A R   A L E
A D A M E   F I E   E D O M   C R I B
L A T E   F O N D A   O N E D A Y A T
A T A   M O R T   S A M   N A P
N E L S O N S   S T R I P   I S L A M
  L A I D T H E C O R N E R S T O N E
H I N D I   A V O N   A C E   O V E R
A N T E S   M E N E   N A N   N E A L
L E A S H   E N E S   T N T   E R R S
```

PUZZLE 315

```
M A L L   B U L B   J A K E   G A P E
U V E A   A S E A   A I N T   O L A F
T E N N   N E I L S I M O N   N E W T
E R O D E D   A H A   W A R D E N S
    A K A   S A L E   S R O
S E Q U E N C E   G A D S   S L U B S
C R U   N A B S   I O N S   A N O A
U N I   A B B O T   O A F   D O C
M E Z Z O   S E A N   W I E N E R S
  Z A G S   D R O I D   D E A R
S T I P E N D   T A I L   D E L A Y
H I C   E A R   E M M E R   I C E
E D A M   G I L D   B E D E   N E A
S E L A H   P E R T   S A M E N E S S
    S A D   V E R B   A A A
S H O T P U T   S O U   R U C H E S
M A M E   A W E S T R U C K   H A I L
O V E R   D I R E   S L O E   O K R A
G E N S   S T A R   A U L D   S E E M
```

PUZZLE 316

```
L A M B   D R A B   D A L E S   A N E A R
A R I L   E I R E   E B E R T   R U M B A
S C R A M B L E D   S U N N Y S I D E U P
  D I A L   O S S A   P A G E T
A S S E N T   A G E E   M I N E R S
S H E   D E B A S E R   S T A G S
S A G E   A S S E T   T R I O   S A R D
A M A N   A N N E   A I N T   E L E E
Y E L L O W J E S S A M I N E S   A L A N
  A L L O W   A L O N E   O N I C E
I M P R E S S   T U T U S   S T R E E T S
C A R G O   E A T E R   S T I N T
E L I E   W E S T E R N O M E L E T T E S
N E A R   A N T E   D I N E   L I L T
I S M S   S T E R   S E E T O   E R I E
  C H E S S   A T T E S T S   E T E
A R C H E R   P L U S   R A I S E D
  S H E E R   T A L I   J O I N
W H I T E S P R U C E   S H E L L G A M E
V E N U S   R E L E T   H E A L   L O O N
A N O S E   O M E R S   Y E N S   E K E D
```

PUZZLE 317

```
R A W   C L A P   W A K E
A G O   L O D E   A R I A
M E N   E N D S   T E N T
    D R A G   T R E A D S
S H E E R   P E A R
L O R E   P O R T   P A L
A P E D   A R E   T R I O
W E D   L I E D   H E N S
    T O N S   P A S T E
R E S I S T   F A T E
I R O N   E D E N   N O T
P I L E   R O L E   T A R
S E E S   S E L L   S K Y
```

PUZZLE 318

```
A D O . S P Y . . P U G
J A M . T E E . . O N E
A L I . P U T T . E D I T
R E T U R N . . T E S T S
. . . P I G T A I L . .
G R O O M . R I M . H A D
E A R N . W A D . A U R A
E W E . H A M . U R G E D
. . A I R P O R T . . .
M A I D S . . I N S E C T
E L M S . A W L S . L O U
A S P . . L I E . . L A B
N O S . . A N D . . A L E
```

PUZZLE 319

```
T A P . A B L E . A N T E
I R E . N E O N . D O O R
L I G H T E S T . O D O R
E D S E L . T E A R . .
. . N E W . R I N S E D
J O G . R E D . L E E R Y
A M E N . D O T . D A L E
W I N E S . G A S . L E S
S T E A K S . N I P . .
. R I O T . G A V E L .
S A M E . N O O N T I M E
E R A S . G O R E . S U N
T E N T . S L E D . E S S
```

PUZZLE 320

```
E D E N . B O A . C A B
L U R E . C A P S . L I E
M O R T G A G E S . O D E
. . S I R . R E D D E N
L O W . R E L A T E . .
A V E . L E E . A D D S
C A L F . R A T . R E E L
E L L A . S I P . A L I
. M A T T E R . L I T
W A T E R Y . P I P . .
A C E . O P T I M I S T S
I R E . M E A N . S E A L
T E N . A S P . A W R Y
```

PUZZLE 321

```
G U Y . B A L D . B R A
A R E A . O L E O . R I B
S N A G . M E O W . A C E
. E B B S . E D G E D .
B R I D E . S L Y . .
R O T . G A M E . E V E S
D E S . M A R . S A V E
M E M O . I D E A . L I E
. F E D . F I E L D .
P A S T A . M A T S .
O R E . R E A R . L O U D
F I N . T R I M . E A S E
S A D . H A N S . F E W
```

PUZZLE 322

```
L A N E . S A P . C U B E
I C E D . T I E . A R I D
P R O D . A D E . S N A G
S E N I O R . P R I S S Y
. . E A R . S A N . .
L O B S T E R . M O O D Y
E L I . D A B . R O E
T E N D S . G A D G E T S
. O A F . C U R . .
D E C I D E . K E E P E R
I R A N . A L I . A L D A
R I N G . S O N . S E E N
T E E S . T U G . Y A N K
```

PUZZLE 323

```
K E G S . S A P S . Y E A S
S E I N E . P U R E . A C R E
U N D U E . A R E A . W H A T
R Y E . M A D A M . S N O B
F A R R . D E S I S T S . .
. E L S . E K E . F E W
D I A N A . S C R I P T U R E
I N N E R . O R E . P E R I L
S T O W A W A Y S . E A S E D
C O N . M A P . E S S . .
. R I C O T T A . E D G E
O B O E . P A R T Y . R I D
C H O P . D E L I . O L I V E
A I D E . A R L O . R A V E N
B O Y S . B A Y S . E W E R
```

PUZZLE 324

```
H O M E . H O S E S . J U N E
U P O N . A D U L T . A S I A
L A R D . B O I S E . L E N T
A L A . D I R T . A B O D E S
. S L E E T S . F L A P . .
. . Y E S . T R I C Y C L E
A D D E D . P R A N K . E A R
B E A D . S L A N G . A N N A
E L M . S T A C K . B I T E S
L I P S T I C K . C A D . .
. . N I C E . M U S E U M .
R E M A R K . C A T S . N A P
O V E R . E L O P E . A C R E
M I N E . R O L L S . P L E A
P L U S . S W E E T . T E S T
```

PUZZLE 325

```
F U L L . R O O M . R O A R
E R I E . O N I O N . E L L A
E G O S . B E L L E . F L I T
S E N S E . S E P A R A T E
. O A K . A D E . . .
C O U N T E D . S L O S H E S
I M P S . P E E L . S H O R N
N A P . T R A Y S . P R O
C H E E P . B R E W . M E O W
H A R S H L Y . R A P I D L Y
. T I E . M A N . . .
B O N E L E S S . D E L A Y
A L E E . R I L E D . R I P E
R E A M . S P A R E . A M E N
B O P S . S T E W . L A D S
```

PUZZLE 326

```
S W A M P . T I E S . C U B
N E P A L . A T O P . P O N E
A I S L E . M A N E . A R I A
G R E T A . E L S E . R A T S
. . S A R I . C H A L E T
B A N T E R . A S H E S . .
L I E U . T E N T . W I L T S
A D O R N E D . U P S T A R T
H E N N A . G E N E . E R I E
. . S I R E N . W I S D O M
N E S T L E . H I S S . .
A L A I . A F A R . L I V I D
D O L L . L A N K . E R O D E
E P E E . M I C E . T A L E S
R E S . S L E D . S N E A K
```

PUZZLE 327

```
T A R P . C H A T . B O G S
A R E A . A I D E S . E L I A
L I A R . S T O M P . T E R M
C A R R O T S . P O T H O L E
. . Y U L . O R A L . .
Y E T . R E E L . E N E R G Y
O A R S . S L A P S . H A R E
U T A H . S I R . E V E S
R E D O . R A R E R . M E T E
S N E E Z E . S P E W . L A S
. L I M A . F A N . .
S C R A P E D . A U D I T O R
A L E C . D I A N E . C A N E
V A N E . Y O D E L . K I T S
E N D S . S E W S . S L O T
```

PUZZLE 328

```
L A R G E . C H E R . A M E S
O C E A N . L I V E . M O P E
P R I N T . O P A L . A R I A
S E N D I N G . D I S S E C T
. . E R E . B E E P S . .
W H E R E V E R . F R E T S
O I L S . E X I T . I D A H O
O D E . G R A T I N G . K I N
D E C A L . M I L E . H E R E
. S T R A W . S E R V A N T S
. T R A S H . V E T . .
N O S I E S T . P E R C H E S
A D O S . T A P E . S H A R E
P O U T . E R A S . E E R I E
E R R S . D E N T . S T E E P
```

PUZZLE 329

```
D R I P . A D O B E . C O K E
R A R E . R E P E L . H A N D
A J A R . C L E R K . A R I D
B A N I S H I N G . M I S T Y
. . D U E . T A N . .
. C O B R A . W A T E R E D
W A R T S . S E E M . D O L E
A T E . S T Y L E . U S E
N O E L . H E E L . T I G E R
E M P E R O R . S C E N E
. . O U T . H A S . .
S W E P T . O P P O S I T E S
L A V A . S H E I K . S A L T
O V E R . A I S L E . T I L E
T E N D . N O T E S . S L A M
```

PUZZLE 330

```
ROSES   ELLA
APACE   ROAN
NETHERLANDS
 NEO OILED
      GAS        ASEA
TADS
HIRE REMBRANDT   SPAR
EDAM ONES   IOU  PERT
YEW  TON    BEL  ESS
   BRATS     ICED
   RAGE      PITS
   IGOR    ABACK
BID  DAD    EWE    ADS
LOGS ALE   FLED   ATOP
UTES MILKMAIDS    CEDE
EASE       AIR    TROD
     STATE  SSW
  WOODENSHOES
  OLGA     EARTH
  NOSY     THESE
```

PUZZLE 331

```
HORN  UFO  SIGN
IDEA  ROW  IDLE
ROMP  GENEROUS
ERA  WISER  LET
   IRAN  RIB
AWNING  SEALED
DEEP     TIRE
ODDEST CHOSEN
   NOR  RANT
STY WOOED  EAT
TREASURE  ANNE
OILY  TAP  PETE
POLE  SLY  EDEN
```

PUZZLE 332

```
LOAD  IDA  RUBY
ABLE  REV  ASIA
SEAPLANE  WELL
TYCOON  NEEDLE
  ASP  BUDS
HERE   REDTAPE
OAT  DAISY  DAN
PRETEND   SOLD
  HATE  FIR
DESIRE  BOGART
ODOR  NEIGHBOR
EGOS  NET  ELLA
SENT  ALE  DEEP
```

PUZZLE 333

```
AXE  CHIC  ENID
FIN  RUDE  VALE
TIC  ALAN  EPIC
   HUSK  STREAK
SLASH   SOOT
TONE  FORESEEN
APT  HALES  COO
GESTURED  PONS
   ANTS  MANSE
SLEIGH   HALO
HOWL  ELAN  MAD
AGEE  SANG  ICE
WORD  TODO  CEE
```

PUZZLE 334

```
RUB  CHAD  PREY
AGO  ZUNI  EASE
WHO  ENOS  OPAL
  SACK  CONSUL
VETCH   QUAY
OMIT  TUSK  COT
TINS  HIE  SHOE
ERG  EWES  PENN
   BEAT  DREAD
LAMARR   KEYS
ACID  TAIL  IAN
TELL  ELLA  EVA
EDDY  DENY  REB
```

PUZZLE 335

```
TAMP  NERD  CUD
IDEA  ALAI  EKE
COLLAPSES   NEW
   AREA  BETSY
SMOCK   ALI
EAVE  WINNIPEG
RYE  SALAD  ERA
FORMERLY  ADIT
   JAR  SCENE
AGORA   BRIE
FAY  PALESTINE
APE  ETON  IRIS
RED  SECT  CAPP
```

PUZZLE 336

```
OHM  CHAT  COLA
WAY  REDO  LIAR
LIT  AREA  ELSE
  RHINO   SPA
  ONE  ETERNAL
BILK  PLEA  AGO
ADO  MOORS  TEN
LEG  ASPS  RISE
LAYETTE   BOO
  TSP  LAWNS
BATH  ORAL  AUK
ALOE  NAME  LEE
DEER  EWES  STY
```

PUZZLE 337

```
COLA   TAP  THY
ADAM  ARIA  RAE
TEMPORARY  ALA
  LAC   MANOR
TAMER   PEEPS
AGO   FRANTIC
GEM  ALERT  ERR
DEPRESS    NEE
  NOTES  CITED
MOTEL    PAD
ERA  EPHEMERAL
TAR  SEAN  AIDA
SLY  SAG  LOOP
```

PUZZLE 338

```
NAPE  TOPS  PEW
ALAS  ADIT  IRA
BENT  PETERPAN
  CAPER   REES
SKATED    SEN
TAKEN  CHOOSES
ITE   POE   ATE
RESUMED  ROUTE
  NAG  DANCED
  LOIS  GENIE
PANTHERS  OPAL
ARC  ERIK  NAME
MAE  DENS  SNAG
```

PUZZLE 339

A

```
STEM      AFT
NOMAD    CROW
AGILE   TIRES
RAREE    DODO
ESS   PICASSO
    HENRY
DAVINCI   STA
AMIN    NAPES
DELTA   GRANT
SLED    ENTER
 ARE     ESTO
```

B

```
PACT      USA
ERROL    STEP
AMINO   SIRES
ROBES    NINE
YRS   SARGENT
    CEDES
MATISSE   ASH
ERIN    LENTO
LINDA   ELDER
 AGER   DARES
 ERR     MERE
```

PUZZLE 340

```
WATCH  BAA  MAP
ALOHA  ELS  ERA
RIPER  EMPOWER
  MESS  SERENE
PROPHET  CEDAR
LOSS   DARTS
YET  TACOS  AGE
  RANKS  SNUG
SMEAR  YELPING
PASTRY   SEAM
RUSSIAN  GRASP
AVE  ELI  ASTIR
YES  SEA  LEERY
```

PUZZLE 341

```
 STAVE   FEAST
CLIMAX  UTTERS
HELENA  SCENIC
EELS  MASH  SPA
EVE  TIDY  FELL
PERSONS  EASED
   ONE   SOW
DOWRY  RUNNERS
ACRE  MOBS  TUT
NEE  FEED  SOFA
CANCEL  UPLIFT
ENCORE  ECOLES
 SHONE   STEED
```

PUZZLE 342

```
PAPA    SAMS
EGOS   TRAPS
TURKEYTROT
SET  ALE  RID
    ERE  STER
TETES  MESSY
OPAL   TEA
AIR  EON  ORE
COLDTURKEY
STONE   AIDE
SPAS    WEDS
```

540

PUZZLE 343

```
SKY    FLO
TIE    RAN
RENT  SLOPE
PEW    SEA
LOP    OAT
ALE  BALLET
SONG ARE RATE
 TRACKS  NAG
  ADO    GIG
  CAN    ILL
TOTEM  WADE
ERA    OIL
EBB    ORE
```

PUZZLE 348

```
APE      HEN
LAX      ADO
ELAN    AVER
 SCAN  AMEN
  TIE  PUN
ATE   LEAPS
LETUP  CLEAR
LEASE IRE WORSE
ERODE  LEAKS
 PESTS   TIS
  LEA OLE
 EARL PEGS
ARIA  DRAW
SIR    EVE
HES    TED
```

PUZZLE 353

1. Phantom, Hamper, Charm, Math; 2. Central, Letter, Title, Tile; 3. Conceit, Beyond, Tenor, Neon; 4. Gesture, Bought, Tough, Gust.

PUZZLE 344

```
       TRAP
AWL    RACE
RAY    ERIE
EYED  NEEDLE
 ECHO   DAM
 COED  PICA
 OWNS  ICED
       WETS
SPUR   NOVA
ALAS   ERAS
GIVE   SENT
ODE DECENT ELAN
 GALA   EWE
 GRIP   DEW
 SEAS
```

PUZZLE 345

. Chin, Niche, Nice, Since, Sine, Stein;
. Diet, Tried, Ride, Pride, Pier; 3.
sle, Flies, File, Elfin, Fine, Fiend; 4.
eel, Sleek, Eels, Sleet, Lest, Stole; 5.
ief, Field, Lied, Liked, Dike, Hiked; 6.
eal, Lamer, Real, Abler, Bear, Break;
. Nape, Plane, Pale, Pleat, Tale, Least.

PUZZLE 350

```
          TESS
          ARIA
         SCORN
       CLOSECALL
      SHAM   TREE
     GUAVA   IRAN
    KNIFE  CROAKS
    ENATE  SHINY
   CRETE   DUETS
   SEALS   CURSE
APPALL    POPES
HORS      SAVER
ALEE      APED
BEEFEATER
   IDLER
   RISE
   ETON
```

PUZZLE 354

```
             PLOT
DEEM         ROBE
ENDOR       MONEY    DEW
MINUET     LINDY    RAGE
DANCES SANTO    HINGE
TARKINGTON    BUCK
PRIMA        RUSH
APER         WALK
STEINBECK
   NEEDY
  CARTELS
   MOLAR
  HAWTHORNE
   JAIL  IANS
   CULL  DRUMS
PURL FITZGERALD
WEARY AGREE ELAINE
ARID PINED LINEAR
YEN ALLOY NERVE
    DEER  DOES
    DADE
```

PUZZLE 349

1. Impudently, 2. Police vans, 3. Grouchiest.

PUZZLE 355

```
               FLO
               RAW
               INN
       BABE
ALB   ABEL  SLEDS
BLEED NUTS  LANA
THEPITANDTHEPENDULUM
ROI  AREA  OWE  ANO
EONS   INGOTS  AMIR
EDGARALLANPOE  PETS
STALE  UTE  SPREE
VEE          STE
MUSIC  SEE  HEATS
ORAN  MYSTERYWRITER
TINE  ESSENE  ARNE
EAT TAM  TILE  EIN
THECASKOFAMONTILLADO
ALAI  ELAM  DREAM
STERN LAMB  EOS
HER   TEES
ORT
OSS
```

PUZZLE 351

1. Live, Dive, Dove, Dole, Hole.
2. Lost, Loot, Boot, Bort, Born.
3. Live, Love, Lore, Lord, Load.
4. Lost, Host, Hose, Home, Tome, Time.

PUZZLE 346

```
ARM      HER
PEAT    DOMES
SHARE  BECOME
ACCIDENTAL  TOTE
REED   DAREDEVIL
TEN    TETE  END
ELF    ADEPT
SEES   STAS
 TRASH   HIT
AGE ALTO  ALA
REVOLVERS  STOP
ANET EVANGELIST
ENTIRE  ANTIC
STEMS   PATE
SRA     WAR
```

PUZZLE 352

```
ICED    APT    ALB
DOVE   ALSO   PIE
OGEE DWELLINGS END
 OAT    APART
 ZERO   LOW
 TOO    GATE
DODO   SORE   STY
PALE   OPAL   TEA
WAND   LIT   SEEM
AID    GONE  ATEN
SLY    USES  AGED
  ALAN       COW
  CAP   PEAT
  CREME ANT
ALI  EXPRESSED
DAM  RAYS   OVEN
OWE  ONE    TIRE
            SEAT
```

PUZZLE 356

```
        AMP
IRS     MAL
RAT     OLE
AGES   SLAV
  MAG        APT
  RAP       ALOE
  AVA       ROLES
SAT TOTS CRO PAS
ODES ORIEL  YARN
LEXINGTONANDCONCORD
AREA   SORER  HOUR
SET RPM DARK  PRY
SHALE   PIT
IVAN    ESO
PEN     EWE
 TRAY   NAPE
 ARE    SIR
 TIA    TEN
 EAR
```

PUZZLE 347

" we profited by our mistakes we would
l be millionaires.

Powwow, 2. Illinois, 3. Baffles, 4. Tur-
ey, 5. Rumble, 6. Radio, 7. Limited, 8.
ase.

PUZZLE 357

```
FAT   TAB
SERE  ACE PAY
CINEMA SCHEDULE
ACID  HIE ARIA
BED  BAIT BIBS
 ENGULF   FIT
 ONSET BUY
 VAT   FEN
 SAW SALAD
SAP   TREMOR
ARID  PACE OAF
BORE KEG RUSE
EMINENCE SEETHE
RAT LEA OGLE
  MEN BOY
```

PUZZLE 361

```
WIDE FLED TAMES
EDEN RAGE OLIVE
SEEDLINGS METER
TAP ELK EYE ENE
 EVIL IRE ARTS
BONES ENTAIL
EDIT MAT SNARED
TON PARENTS AVA
ARGUED RAY OVER
 STRONG LAINE
BASE APE BETS
OVA PSI TAN HIE
WANDA NARRATION
LITER ERIE ANTI
SLANT DAMS EGAD
```

PUZZLE 366

```
SWIM FABLE CRAB GOO
LILY OILER HURL RAD
IRKS OMEGA INCUBATE
DESERT WASNT SEEN
 LABS LEECH SEDAN
UNAFRAID REHEM RENO
LAC ALDEN DALES UKE
TIRE LEMON TEMPORAL
RAIDS SOWED NOON
ADDING NAPES STEPPE
 TALC YACHT SALAD
MONSIEUR LARRY LUNG
IKE LAGER LUAUS TEE
NABS MACAW BILLFOLD
TYROL TONES LEAR
 ALIT IDAHO TWANGS
BASEBALL VIKKI MAIL
ELK ERIE ERRED ERLE
TEA LADD STAGE SCADA
```

PUZZLE 358

Don't work up a head of steam before you find out what's cooking.

1. Donations, 2. Doughnut, 3. Kooky, 4. Coffee, 5. Famous, 6. Powder, 7. Wreath, 8. Bait.

PUZZLE 362

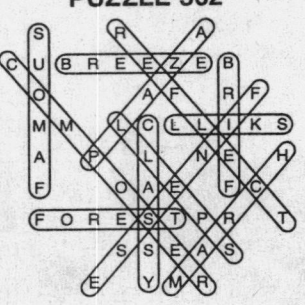

PUZZLE 359

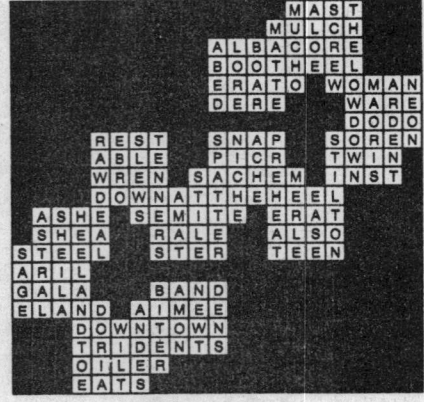

PUZZLE 363

```
CRIB LANAI PONG
LOLA ADAMS UREA
OTIC RATIO RARE
PEAK EGO PHENOL
 AIDE CREE
STUCCO AREA PAD
PITHY BLAND ELI
LATE CEASE PAIN
IRE MYRRH PARKA
TAR ITEM KELLER
 SCOT SEAL
ACTUAL STY IAMB
BABE OATEN AGEE
BRAD GLARE TAME
EYRE YARNS EROS
```

PUZZLE 364

A. 24 (+9 -4 +9 -4 +9 -4 +9 -4)
B. 19 (+4 +5 -6 -7 +8 +9 -10 -11)
C. 36 (x3 x3 ÷6 x3 x3 ÷6 x3 x3)
D. 46 (+7 +7 +7 +7 +7 +7 +7 +7)
E. 44 (-5 x4 -5 x4 -5 x4 -5 x4)
F. 54 (-9 ÷3 -9 ÷3 -9 ÷3 -9 ÷3)
G. 20 (+4 ÷4 -4 x4 +4 ÷4 -4 x4)

PUZZLE 367

A

```
FAST   STOW
REPAIR SPACES
ENIGMA TATTLE
ADE ERROR ADA
PECK EEL OVER
REAL TENDER
 REFINED
TEETER WEST
WARN LED ROWS
ARM MIDAS RIA
DRIVEN RECESS
SENATE TRUSTS
DENS   BETS
```

B

```
SLOW   TOPS
READER VETOED
INSANE INTONE
ADS TAROT DIN
LEIF MEL ALOE
REEL GENDER
 RELATED
THROAT DENT
TRAY STY REAR
RAM PHASE EMU
ADMIRE EVADED
PEERED REVERE
DRAY   LADS
```

PUZZLE 360

```
ROME BAH COD MONA
AMEN ALVA BOLO EVEN
TARE BEEN OLEO LEAN
AREMYLUCKYSTAR ERRS
 IRE EOS TET
LACES HERNANDOS HAY
OCHS MARS ARNE EVA
ARI CODA BESET PRIM
DEMEAN SPORTS ROADS
 CARTS INS SWAMI
BAHTS TEPEES EVENTS
ALIS ROVER EINE BOP
NOM LEVI PART PORE
DEC EDELWEISS TOWED
 HAT AWN FIR
EVEL WHITECHRISTMAS
DARE HONE HAIR EERO
ONER AMOR ETON RAND
MEET TEN DET STOA
```

PUZZLE 365

```
PASS STEW CRAB LOIN
RITT TARA HANA IAGO
EDIE ROIL ENDS THOU
PARADISELOST SATURN
 LAP ALT SOIL
HUT VENICE HOMERUN
ECOLE EVE THAN BORE
ALSO JOE FRAN OLGA
PASSION SLAVE TYLER
 TRY ETUDE HAL
MARIS ORATE COLONEL
AMEN PIKE NOD SOLO
TONY GENE BIL STRAM
TROOPER HANDLE ANA
 NANA PIT ARM
TACKLE LOSTANDFOUND
ACHE ROOK EGAD OPIE
TEAR ANNE RETE SONE
SSTS LEER YSER ENOS
```

PUZZLE 368

```
FLAT CUSP CASH IRPS
LASH OKLA ARNO ROSE
AMIE NEAT REAR MOLE
BEARIT THERAINMAKER
 ARES SRI LEE
DEFIANT REF DARREN
ERIN TAWS RIM NAIVE
FIFI SNOWS BOG IDES
TEENS DROOP MANNERS
 SUM DORIS BAR
CLIPPER PANIC TACER
HORA LOW STARE IRA
AVOID NOR AMEN NAVE
PENNED EAT PLUGGED
 LAS GOT TITO
APRILSHOWERS SEALE
READ HOME ALIT WALL
TELL ERNE MULE ALAS
SPEE REID PEKE YAN
```

PUZZLE 369

```
FAD  CASH  ATOM
AGO  OBOE  MAMA
RECKLESS  ORAL
   TEAL  IGNORE
OGRES   STAG
TRIP  BOAT  AMP
TIN  SAUTE  CAR
ODE  ACRE  AQUA
   RAHS  TRULY
ADMIRE   CIII
MAID  LEONARDO
ONCE  OGLE  END
SEES  RODS  DAD
```

PUZZLE 370

```
COD  ICED  SARA
AWE  NONE  OPAL
RELOCATE  LEGS
  ERASE  RODEO
SAGA  TREES
ABATE  SAP  MAT
METERS  REBATE
SEE  ROD  LASER
  BONER  STEM
TENOR  CASTE
OLEO  BITTERLY
PEAK  IDEA  EYE
SETS  BERG  DEN
```

PUZZLE 371

```
CARD  SPAD  AMI
ALOE  PALE  RON
RIOGRANDE  KEN
RETRO  ORCA
  EAT  ERNES
ICEMAN  OSSA
AMO  SPORE  ATM
CALE  DEPOSE
EMOTE  FOR
  RENT  DIETS
BOA  TENNESSEE
AND  ELAN  ONER
TOO  RETE  NENE
```

PUZZLE 372

```
WELL  HOOP  JIM
AREA  ERNE  ODE
GRANTWOOD  HER
  CON  DENSE
OFFER  ISLAM
PAR  STEERAGE
TRA  STEWS  RET
SENATORS  INN
  SLAPS  MANTA
OTHER  SIN
MIA  RAOULDUFY
ALL  EVER  EKED
RES  DARE  SEES
```

PUZZLE 373

```
ELSA  PEALE  RIDS
NEAT  REGAL  ABEL
DAFT  ERODE  DINE
SPEEDS  EMBASSY
  SATE  REAR
MENTION  NASALS
ALOES  NERTS  DIT
REND  AUTOS  HONE
EVE  SPICY  GARDE
SETSUP  CONCEAL
  PELT  ETUI
TAMARAO  TSETSE
ITER  URASE  NIPS
LIDS  SUPER  DEAN
EPEE  ESTES  ARTE
```

PUZZLE 374

FRUGAL

PUZZLE 375

```
PISA  LIFT  ELITE
ADEN  ERIE  DEVIL
LONG  SALT  ITEMS
ELDERS  LOST  SEE
  LIES  NOON
FEW  ONCE  DRIFT
OVAL  SANTA  NERO
RATE  RAH  ELIA
EDEN  DECOR  SOBS
ERICA  TREE  NET
  NOTE  NAGS
CAT  VEST  SOMBER
ALONE  TARO  EAVE
MINER  ELAN  AREA
STEWS  SETS  REND
```

PUZZLE 376

Chisel, Hammer, Pliers, Sander, Shears, Shovel, Sickle, Square, Trowel, Wrench.

PUZZLE 377

```
HAM  MATE  ATOP
ALA  ALAD  NANA
HITTHEJACKPOT
ASTER  MALE
  PEAR  CESAR
APSE  MESH  TRE
QUEENOFHEARTS
URN  ASIA  NYET
ALONG  TYRO
  ROAD  EUBIE
HAILTOTHEKING
ASTA  LOOS  TKO
THAN  LOPE  ESS
```

PUZZLE 378

```
PALO  BIB  SCAB
AMEN  ONE  TONE
CONTRAST  ONTO
ASSAY  HUNTER
  PERU  PER
FACE  UNDO  IMP
EGO  SITIN  TEE
WON  ANIL  BELT
  CHI  ELSA
MORALE  ARROW
AVER  CONTRIVE
RATE  RUE  EVEN
CLEM  UTE  LEND
```

PUZZLE 379

```
APT     OAT
SEAT  OLIO
PANHANDLE
   ANT
   PANDORA
ESP   MARK  ABE   PAD
BOA  POLE  PULP  ALE
BIN  AWE   TEA   NOW
LOAN        ENATE
RIA          CRY
MARCH        ACHE
DIM EEL    ASK  OWL
ALA  ALEE  ERIE  SEA
YES   PAR  AVID  ERG
   PANELED
     ELI
PANAMAHAT
OVER  SINE
PET    DYE
```

PUZZLE 380

```
GASH  BATED  PLAT
ANTI  EVOKE  AILS
SNAG  HELEN  DATA
PATH  IRE  TERROR
  RANT  FIRE
SECOND  DISASTER
PLEAD  CENTS  UNO
RIND  KHANS  DRAB
ADS  FEELS  PRICE
TEENIEST  AGENTS
  ALPS  SCAN
CRATES  TIC  CLUB
LIEU  ASIDE  HARE
ODOR  KEELS  EDGE
GENE  EASES  DYER
```

PUZZLE 381

The darkest hour is just before you're overdrawn.

1. Bruise, 2. Avert, 3. Duets, 4. Endorse, 5. Rake, 6. Hoof, 7. Jury, 8. Worth.

PUZZLE 382

```
TUBAS  SCAR  ROPE
ORATE  TARE  ERIE
AGREEMENTS  DELL
DEN  TARS  PASSES
  SHIN  MODE
BOLTED  FANDANGO
ALOES  BETS  ERA
LISP  PLATE  LAOS
EVE  ROSE  CARVE
SERGEANT  POSSES
  ARID  BIAS
SPARER  FITS  TAU
WARN  IMITATIONS
ALEE  EASE  ACUTE
BEAT  SETS  LYRES
```

PUZZLE 383

1. Acme, 2. Urge, 3. Banjo, 4. Askew, 5. After, 6. Vacuum, 7. Luxury, 8. Stucco, 9. Circus, 10. Anybody.

PUZZLE 384

```
ACT  ABBY  SWAY
ROE  TREE  LOBE
CONSTANT  ELLA
     CAD  SEVER
ODORS  EAVE
GREW  ALGERIA
OAF  CASKS  ICY
BLEMISH  KNEE
  NETS  BONED
PADDY  RIO
EVIL  SAILBOAT
TINE  ANNE  ALI
EDGY  DYED  RAM
```

PUZZLE 385

```
OBESE  DOSES
SCORIA  EXILED
LEVELS  CERISE
ELI  TETON  CAN
DONE  LAD  TIME
STEAM  REFUTES
  GAD  SOB
SOBERER  GASPS
OMAR  BAY  SARI
WEN  MATES  TAN
ELATES  LOPING
DENOTE  PRINCE
TAPED  SENSE
```

PUZZLE 386

```
SOAK  PROBE  CLOG
IDLE  RADAR  HOME
MOOT  OPERA  EVIL
PRETEXT  SWEETS
  LAY  BLEAT
QUEER  BEE  RAVES
USE  NOUGAT  HIRE
OUR  SPY  GAD  TOE
TRIP  TENURE  ADD
EPEES  RUE  BALES
  ROAST  JUG
CRAFTS  WATERED
LORE  HAZED  NAVY
EPIC  ELOPE  TREE
FELT  SPOTS  SEND
```

1-F, 2-V, 3-W, 4-M, 5-T, 6-H,
7-I, 8-U, 9-Z, 10-R, 11-C,
12-N, 13-P, 14-Y, 15-J, 16-K,
17-B, 18-G, 19-O, 20-A,
21-E, 22-X, 23-L, 24-S,
25-Q, 26-D.

PUZZLE 387

1. Robin, Falcon, Finch, Martin,
Drake, Osprey.
2. Visa, Hotel, Bags, Tourist, Train,
Postcard, Junket.
3. Pancakes, Fruit, Toast, Butter,
Ham, Jelly, Cereal.

PUZZLE 388

```
ATTA  CHOIR  SPAS
SHOT  LADLE  CALL
HITTHEROAD  ASIA
ENE  AVER  WARSAW
  STEM  COMET
LECHER  WHOOSHED
ETHOS  GOODY  ELI
ANEW  ARK  CHIN
SAW  PAUSE  GLADE
ESTRANGE  BOOTED
  HORNE  MOOT
CREATE  FITS  VAL
OAFS  TOETHELINE
BRAT  THERE  ASTA
SETS  ESTER  WEEP
```

PUZZLE 389

```
Q  SQUEAK  UKASE  UKES  A
U  CURARE  RACER  CARE  R
I  PIRATE  TAPER  PEAT  R
V  SOLVED  DOLES  SLED  O
E  SWEDEN  WENDS  DENS  W
R  PHRASE  SHAPE  HEAP  S
```

PUZZLE 390

```
CHOP  APT  LEER
LURE  WEE  OGRE
ALAS  LASTWORD
WALTZ  STAG
  SOW  MERIT
BOA  NEST  AIDA
APPLEPIEORDER
RASE  TRAP  EAT
BLEAK  MET
  FIRE  NOTCH
WELLTODO  POLO
ERIE  BED  IRON
BEET  END  CEDE
```

PUZZLE 391

```
PAL  PLAN  CALL
ELI  LONE  ASIA
PEN  EATS  REED
  GLAD  TREADS
STEEDS  LID
TURNS  BED  HAD
ONES  PAD  ROLE
WED  GET  FALSE
  PER  SAILOR
DREAMS  TILE
EARN  ORAL  RAP
ACRE  NILE  EGO
LESS  SPED  DOT
```

PUZZLE 392

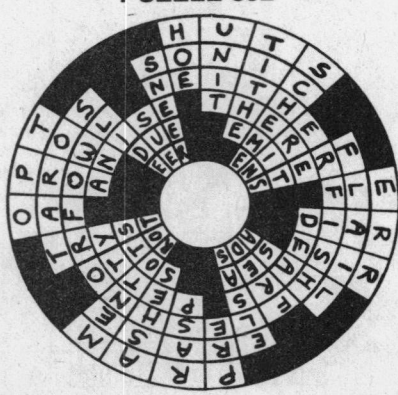

PUZZLE 393

```
LAPP  SPARE  TURF
EVER  PERON  ASIA
NERO  ELIDE  MEND
TRUMPET  EMBARGO
  OLD  ROYAL
EMPTY  LAS  TEACH
VOLE  SOW  BISCAY
AGA  SKYHOOK  HIE
NUCLEI  IRA  TORN
SLEEP  ADE  KRONA
  TITLE  LEO
UPSTART  DUGOUTS
LIEU  AARON  PLEA
ALEC  CRANE  ENDS
NENE  ESTES  RASH
```

PUZZLE 394

1. Being modest is the art of not bragging
right away.
2. Snap judgment has a way of becoming
unfastened.
3. Trying to squash a rumor is like trying
to unring a bell.

PUZZLE 395

```
DAMS  SLOOP  IPSO
ALIT  LODGE  MULL
ZULU  EIDER  PLOD
EMENDER  ESCAPEE
  NAPES  OUR
MITERS  IGNITION
ERODE  EDNA  SORE
MAN  DIP  ALS  TAW
OTIS  NEAT  PLATE
SECONDED  WEASEL
  LEO  OCEAN
SPRAWLS  LARGESS
LAIC  ELTON  URAL
ANNE  NURSE  OLGA
WEDS  TREED  REAP
```

PUZZLE 396

Maggie Seaver, June Cleaver, Carol
Brady, Jill Taylor.

PUZZLE 397

```
RED  BAWL  PEA
ORE  ABIE  SURF
CRESCENT  ASIA
  TOTE  ETHER
REDAN  GEE
AMOR  DWELLERS
SMOG  RAN  LION
PARADISE  IRMA
  ZIP  STEEP
RAVEN  FLEE
OVER  PLEASURE
SONS  AINT  SEA
ANT  SPAS  EFT
```

PUZZLE 398

```
CHAR  SEE  MESS
RIDE  PAR  ANTI
EDEN  ARRANGED
WESTERN  SNIPE
  INK  CHAN
SPEND  BOY  EAT
PANG  PAT  SEGO
AND  CAT  STREW
  ORAL  CHA
STRAP  PEERESS
LISTENED  TRIO
ALEE  IRA  LILT
BEDS  PER  EELS
```

PUZZLE 399

```
RASP ACES EYER SERB
USER SORE MERE TRUE
TELEPHONE CASSEROLE
SALVOES PIES IRISES
    ANN BADE CDEF
VALID PAGE SAUCEPAN
EVIL BUREAUCRAT ELI
TOM SERA MALL OPEN
SWEATER PABLO LAPSE
STAT VEXED SATE
CATER LASER ENTHRAL
UFOS WONT NOAH OLE
FAN SHOESTRING ANOA
FREENESS EELS SPIEL
    RAYE CANE TEA
PILAFF BORE BRECCIA
UNUSUALLY GREENHORN
PLIE COIL EINE ERAT
SASS ESPY DOTS SESS
```

PUZZLE 403

1. Gamble, 2. Sooner, 3. Doctor, 4. Acorns, 5. Strong, 6. Polite, 7. Export, 8. Dinner.
Historical principle: Monroe Doctrine.

PUZZLE 404

```
VIVID HIP WEB
ARENA ADO OLE
NOTED LITERAL
NOR WOO DENT
    TAR MUG
ILL SAP NERVE
COO SPEED OIL
EXTRA AVE EEL
    AYE ERA
HOCK RAN ROW
ILLEGAL FORAY
LEA USE IMAGE
TOY NEE TALES
```

PUZZLE 408

```
BOMB SOTS TWAS CEBA
OLIO ROGET RAREE RAIL
BASS OPERA ILIAD ORNA
STEPHENFOSTERSSONGS
ONE FATES EAN
ANTIS VOTER ALLEN
ELL NEWER MRS REED
REARS DANDY ROI SIRE
SAMOA ANT OHIOANS LIB
TROMBONE BUYS SEA SST
PER DRUMMER EFT
ELS ADS ORAN ANDERSON
LIT NOCTURN RIO SEATO
SERB ONT STUNT TESTS
ASIA ART ESSES SOY
PRICE SMILE DAISY
IST SIEVE ICE
BEETHOVENSYMPHONIES
INTO RINGS ALERT MAME
LOON STOLE NESTS EGAD
ESNE ARES NASH DENS
```

PUZZLE 409

```
ABOR PTAS MACH LAPFUL
DELIRIOUS OSHA ORELSE
OLDMILNESTREAM BRAYED
NIS PAIR REARS OASIS
ANTHERS PINOT YEN
IDEAL HALEOFANOTE GPS
SARPY CAD ORAD CLU
WAIT HASTEN AHUM
AMT WILDEOATES CLAMP
LAICIZES SCHMO CROUP
ARRIVES SIKES PLAICES
SEVEN SERIN DEEPNESS
DUDES CRIESWOLFE RTE
APAT CARESS ITES
FIN AARE SEA MAAMS
TAD STEELEMILLS ANTON
ATT INAND TARTARE
HIHOS ANTIC IASI NOA
BAKERY PAINEINTHENECK
THESIS OGRE FREELANCE
UNNEAT DEER SONS ODOR
```

PUZZLE 400

```
CANTATA METS STRIP
AVOIDED AMOK SEWAGE
DODGERS REMI ORISON
NEE ROBIN MARINERS
REARENDS ITES
CLASS BRA PARIS SEC
AID THEE PASSE UNAU
REDS ADANA PIS SERB
EDITOR ETHIC GUANS
CANDLESTICKPARK
ASTRO EXTOL ESPIES
GAIT CEP NOOSE SETH
ENOS IRONS LENT SUE
DEN ANISE GAN OSTIA
ABEL WAINSCOT
BLUEJAYS RADIO ETA
RANGES OPEN BREWERS
INDICT RANT LOMENTA
EGEST ALAS ETERNAL
```

PUZZLE 405

```
CHIC SEW ORB
SAUNA OVA DUE
ORGAN LENIENT
PEEN BONER
    EGO OFF
ROW AGOG NAIL
AGE BURRO SLY
GLAD SEED TEE
EKE ADO
    LIGHT PEST
RAVIOLI VILLA
ICE TEN ONSET
PET ANT WEED
```

PUZZLE 401

```
TEAS SWAP PAUL BAER
RASP TILE AGRA AERO
ECHO ONTO LOGS BOIL
THEKINGANDI ESSENCE
ACE RYES OCS
EARNEST RATA RILES
TRUER SOUNDOF INURE
NIL STALL ENA MARIE
ALEC ARENA REPRESS
ORC SARAH ISM
HORNETS CLAIR SAIL
DRANT EMS ERNES TRA
BANER PACIFIC ACTOR
SLICE TROT ASTOUND
TAP OCTA TEN
RECITAL THEBOYSFROM
OPEC NOTE SELL IONA
MENU EVER TALE DICK
SETT LETS AMAS ELEE
```

PUZZLE 406

```
ALVA CAL OTTO
ROAR AGE POOR
KANGAROO OGRE
UMP PERON
PAGES TART
ALAS PARROTS
SAN BARDS ALE
IGUANAS FROM
NITS LANES
SOUTH DOT
BARS ELEPHANT
ALAE RAN ELEE
TEND SPY RIDE
```

PUZZLE 407

```
ANTS LAP BELL
PERU AIR ERIE
SLEIGHTOFHAND
ELATER TOAST
SOL PEAL
SPUR FLIMFLAM
OAR ION ELA
PRETENDS TBAR
WADS LEA
PIERS PINNED
DECEPTIVENESS
USED ONT ISTO
NODS OKS SEES
```

PUZZLE 402

```
LO N DES REA S ON  P RI ZE
T O PER  D OVE S  O V AL
S NE AD  ER R  SCA ND AL OUS
    O UT  EI DE R
RIER ENS I GN S  TRE N D
DE S PO IL S  PIS C AT OR IAL
S T INT  TH RE ES OME  SE ED
    A MUS ED  T AFT
RE SE A RCH  U SE  ER RAN D
UR NS  LO CA LE  WAR D ENS
S EWER  DE TE CT  D OM E
```

PUZZLE 410

```
ARAM CHILI DEANS ALAD
BALI HONOR ADLAI PIMA
BILLHICKOK MATTDILLON
ELA ARKS STARE ENOSIS
HIPS JOHNS FARM
ARDORS TAMES BERIBBON
REAPS BEDEW ALEM UNA
BANS SORE IMBED DFAS
ODI STUNS LOESS BEFIT
REENTERS ADATS HARAR
LORAN NEWTS BETEL
ABEAM LARIS BLACKOUT
SCOLD PERIL BROTH BPS
COOS INKED RATS LISA
URN NETS WEANS BALER
PNEUMATO BECKS VAULTS
NOVA AISLE BEND
SIENNA AMATI SERT LEO
CASEYJONES PAULBUNYAN
AGAS OPINE SEPIA ERSE
BOUT SALTS EASEL PEER
```

PUZZLE 411

```
SHARP TEAM ERAS PESOS
CANOE OLLA RARE ARENA
OTTOSEAALDERGENTLEMER
TEETER NEED EASE IRA
STIR EMIR SERER
SAG ACID OTIS STOKES
PURISAMARISPARNEAPOLI
ARIL SELES SHEA SERGE
CASES ETES LETT DEAN
ESTATES ILLS VIES ARA
CATAMALUTHEVETE
TOM YOHO EERO EMERGES
AVON NAVE DART TRAIT
PILOT READ IDEAS OLGA
INDMARARTESGENTCOLLEG
RESALE SETH SERB SRS
DEEPS METS SEER
SHE SONS RENO ELATED
MEXIPELICANDOMINIVATI
ERASE ADAR GRID SEPAL
WOMAN RENT ETTA KNELL
```

PUZZLE 412

```
IDLE ZEE  SAFE  ICES
REEL EROS TILL  NOTE
ELSE BANE IDOL  VITA
DISCARD EINE  INANE
   TRAINING  OPAL
ACES CONE  AUSPICES
GLAD RANG ESSE  DARE
EEL  DOTE WANTS ALIE
MCI  ATE  BARES STEED
   BONE TRIER THEN
BARBS CHILD ERA  DAM
ORAL RAIDS CLAW  AMA
ANTI ERNE SLIM  PRAY
SEETHING  TEAM  BASH
   EASE GERMINAL
FARMS MADE  NEGATES
LIMA UNIT SLAW  VALE
ADIT EERO TATE  ELLE
DOSE DEER PER   REAM
```

PUZZLE 416

```
DATA  SPRAY   HAWK
IRIS  PIECE   ACHE
SEEP  EASES   TRAY
HASH  ANT   BEETS
   AFRO  GLAD
SKILL  SALAD  TEE
MENTAL  DOG   HAD
INN  WIDOWER  EGG
LYE  MAR  RAFFLE
EAR  WIDEN  GATES
   BITS  EVER
SHRUG  PEA   ACID
TOAD  BEADS  WORE
AMID  AGILE  ALAS
RELY  TONES  YANK
```

PUZZLE 420

```
ABLE BANC SERE  SNIP
LEES EACH MAYA  TODO
BRAKESHOE OVERHAULS
STRIDES RACE MAGNET
   MAT HUNK PURE
SODOM BABA SOFTSHOE
ALES COTS COIFS  OAK
SEN  PODS FINNS MOTE
HOTSHOE DAVIT PATHS
   HEN RELIC MOP
ELBOW SHELL GUMSHOE
FOOD ACIDS HIDE  UMP
TAN  ICONS PALS GLEE
SNOWSHOE ALMA CRANE
   ALIT OPUS POE
PROPEL ANTS GELATIN
LIMITLESS HORSESHOE
ADIT ERIE EDIT EATS
YETI SEAT REDO SWAT
```

PUZZLE 413

```
LAMP  EBBS   MOM
EVIL  LEAN   IRA
TARA  MAROONED
   ATEST  RAISE
RACER  SET
ALL  RASE  EDD
EDEN  BOA  REED
ASA  ELLS  RAY
   MAT  ALINE
ASPEN  TIMED
SPARKLED  AIRS
EAR  LINE  SNIT
ATE  ELSA  EGGS
```

PUZZLE 417

```
SERB FRET AMES  YSER
OLIO REAR ROVE  VALE
OKAY AFRO OPEC  OLLA
NELSON SUMMERRENTAL
   OAKS BEA  ERN
SHAFT WALT  STEEPLE
IONS WARE CATES  AIL
TUTU ILK  PANE  SINK
EREMITE SEDAN MULES
   MAT FACET ARM
SEVEN PILOT DESMOND
AVER ARES ORR   EMIR
KIT  ARIES OBEY RANA
SLOBBER TRIS ABRAM
   RBI  SOD  STIR
INDIANSUMMER OREGON
NEED ETRE RAIN  ELMO
GANG ROSA LYLE  ZEAL
ERTE SPAR YEAR  ENNA
```

PUZZLE 421

```
SPA  TIES LESS  ALES
PARS ECRU LAWN  MAMA
EVES NEAR ASIA  EVIL
RESULTS POMEGRANATE
   IRIS GALA  LID
CADET ELSE TRIM  FEE
ONES TEAS THINS  IDA
INN  BOLD PRONG SLIT
LETTERS BEARD TILTS
   HEN DRAIN OUT
STRAP LEARN SOBERLY
IRAN COSTS DAZE  AYE
NUN  DOCKS TUNE GIRL
KEG  INKS SONG PANEL
   ANT  REDS FIRM
GINGERBREAD MANMADE
ODOR ALAN LIAR  EKES
WERE CURT ERIE  NEWS
NAME TEES DENS  TRY
```

PUZZLE 414

```
PAL   CAT   SHE
OXEN  ATOP  PAY
OLEO  PETE  IRE
HERO      ERNE
   KEY  SKY
LIE  LOON  EKED
ANT  LURES  IMA
SKEW  TEAL  DUN
   ASH  DYE
PARK      DANG
TAM  IRON  GLEE
RIO  NILE  ETON
ARK  DEW   ONE
```

PUZZLE 418

```
ACT  TAG  PULP  FADE
BAHS ARIA AREA  EMIL
BRET MORNINGGLORIES
ASSUMED NODE  ARETE
   UNAS LENA ETTE
CENTS META  SWEETER
PASS LEAS CHEER  RAG
ARE  DEAN BOERS CANE
STRAND SOLE  MATTE
   AFTERNOONTEAS
SHIRT  EARN  STEEDS
RODE BANKS BATS  AIL
ILL  BASTE TARA BYTE
DEBATES ROWS  CEDED
   ESTA SOUL BAER
ARRAS STAR  SETTEES
HEATOFTHENIGHT LARA
ADIT ARUM SOUS  EMIT
BODY DANS TOT   SEE
```

PUZZLE 422

```
AGED AWLS DATA  SOLD
SAME REIN OMIT  AHOY
ISIS SPEARMINT SIDE
APRICOT RUED ECHOES
   GUN MISS GNU
SCENE GENE  MEDDLING
LAVA DRAG AIRS  IRON
UNIT EEL  CLAM  PISA
RELEASE ROOM  ASSET
   PINCUSHIONS
PAINT  RITA  ZIPPERS
LIVE BANS TAN   ALEC
ODES FIBS DARE  PLEA
WESTERNS NICK  DEALT
   RED MOAT MAR
MATURE KING  RANCHES
ACES WONDERFUL LIKE
MINE AREA ARTE  IDEA
ADDS YEWS MOSS  PEST
```

PUZZLE 415

```
HANG  SPA   ESAU
ALOE  WAS   AWLS
RATTLERS  SALE
TIE  OAK   PEN
   MAR  BULLET
SPIED  GIN  ARE
TINT  PAD   SKIN
ANT  OIL  SHEET
BEETLE   STY
   RID  BOA  MOB
SEEM  MARRIAGE
APSE  AIR   DIRE
TATS  PLY   ODES
```

PUZZLE 419

```
RAFT  DAM  TABBED BILE
EBON TILE ORIOLE  EDIE
CARTWHEEL PADDLEWHEEL
OFT HUGE WIRES  PAEAN
NTH  EGO PICAS  PEGS
RIA  DEFAT MUSETTES
FIFTHWHEEL MARTS ERE
HOGS IRON OOZE  ANNA
MPH ANEW POTTERSWHEEL
SST  INNS LUTES POETS
   KOIS BEZEL BALM
SCALE SOBER DORF WEB
FERRISWHEELS ERRS IVE
IDOL HERS OLEO  ODIN
LAW FAIRS WATERWHEEL
ENSCONCE TAXIS  ERS
HIGH NUDES SKA  PHD
TWILL WINDS GAIT RUE
CHEESEWHEEL BIGWHEELS
PELF RESCUE ALAI TALK
ANTS STEEPS GAS  ADOS
```

PUZZLE 423

```
SWAB  THEME   AQUA
WALL  AURAS   CURB
IDLE  REEDS   CAGE
GEYSERS  RECEDED
   SLY  RISEN
RUSES  FED  ATLAS
ANTS  PEA  ASSAIL
FLY  BONDAGE  IDA
TILLED  EGO  TREK
STEER  ARE  JESSE
   BEADS  SIR
SCRATCH  MIGRATE
CAIN  TEPID  IRAN
UNTO  ERASE  FIND
MEAN  DENTS  YAKS
```

PUZZLE 424

```
CAT SON   MAP
ABE OUI  SAGE
PEANUTBUTTER
  TRY   NEED
    DEN DIP      BAR
GAB SUR OLIO     USE
EMU PRO MANNER TIN TAD
LIT RIP EYE ROW  TAD
  TAI       ADORE
  EVE         OAR
  RESTS       DYE
DAM  TIE RAP FAR DAD
ARI MALICE IWO  UPI
LIL  ANTE  DEW  PEN
YAK   ADD  KEG
     TELL  GEE
   BUTTERSCOTCH
   INTO EAU ERE
   TEA  DOT DUN
```

PUZZLE 428

```
LAND  LEAP  SEA
ODOR  ARLO  ARM
SORE  PRETENSE
    AGES  ALDEN
POMMEL  STS
AVAST  PHOENIX
PEG  GEE    OAR
ARIZONA  MANNA
   IOU  HERESY
OLAND  LATE
SINCLAIR  NEAT
LET  ERNE  ALTO
ONE  STEM  SLEW
```

PUZZLE 433

```
WISH  ROAD  TAM
ECHO  ERLE  ONE
BEET  AGITATOR
    BODY  ATONE
COMEDY  RIO
ABIDE  HELMING
GEM  FAD    BAR
EYEBALL  SUITE
    EMU  WINDOW
SQUAB  HARK
NURTURED  IFFY
ION  SURE  NORA
TDS  HEED  DOOM
```

PUZZLE 425

```
WHETS   TIMID
REMIT   ADORE
ALONE   NATAL
POT  PAD  ETE
  TEA  BELLE
    GNOME
  STEER  TAM
AMA  UTE  GOT
PICOT   GRADE
ELIDE   GIVEN
DETER   SMELT
```

PUZZLE 429

```
RUT      PER
INERT  ARID
MINER  WAVER
  TOTE  ALE
  ERASE SLED
    ISLET
GOWN   FIRST
OVA     DOTE
BEGET  EVENS
NOVA   REPEL
  NET    STY
```

PUZZLE 430

```
ROAD  CASK  ALL
URGE  ELAN  PIE
BEEP  DATE  EVE
    EDEN  ADDER
ALINED  ODE
LADDS  RESPECT
ASEA  HER  LIAR
STABBED  HORSE
  LAW  TERETE
WIDEN  MAMA
ADO  NEAP  BLOT
ILL  ERNE  LANE
LET  RAYS  EPEE
```

PUZZLE 434

```
PAPA  AIMS  AWL
ALAN  ITEM  NEE
REST  LANE  NET
RETIRE  DATE
    CARE  REALM
CAR  POLO  ALOE
ARE  SNIPE  EVA
NEAR  STEP  DEN
EASED  ERIE
    ODES  ACUMEN
BAN  CAST  LORE
ADE  OLEO  ELIA
ROD  REAR  RENT
```

PUZZLE 426

```
EVA  DAUB  PEON
WAD  RISE  LEVI
ENDEARED  ALAN
  IMPS   AISLE
ARTIE    END
MEIR  HANDSOME
ADO  LEROY  MAD
HONEYDEW  PICA
  TRY    TOTEM
GRACE   SENT
RASH  STEADIES
ACHE  OWES  NAP
DEED  DOME  GUY
```

PUZZLE 431

```
  TIDE    ODE
  MINOR  RANT
PATTER  ANTI
ISLE    ULCER
THERMOS  ERE
    NEWER
SAG  ENDURED
ADULT   MAXI
IDEA  NAPKIN
DESK  OWLET
RTE   WEED
```

PUZZLE 435

```
PASS  ALL  ROWS
ALIT  DOE  EVIL
DETONATE  GENE
    RAM   PARED
SWEEP  TSAR
TOAD  REINDEER
ERR  RANGE  ARE
PENTAGON  ASIA
    USER  STEEP
SHARP    TAT
TORN  GARDENER
ALEE  ONE  SERE
READ  BYE  TEND
```

PUZZLE 427

```
MALE     PLATE
ALARM    EASEL
ZORRO    SPINE
ENG  TOT  DOC
  GENES  PERT
    ULCER
WARN    ADOPT
ADO  TRI  EAR
SOBER   TRACE
PRIDE   SOCKS
SENSE    TEST
```

PUZZLE 432

```
SPAR  ABE  OTTO
POLO  PEN  FROM
AUTO  PAD  TAME
TROTTER   SEVEN
    SEA  ONE
SOB  ARROW  LAW
IRA  EAR   EVE
PER  EDGAR  RED
  GAS    TUB
SCANS  MINUTES
LAID  LEO  TORE
ANNE  INN  TALE
MESS  BUS  EDEN
```

PUZZLE 436

```
ALP  ABLE  ROSE
WOE  DRAW  EVER
ESTIMATE  FEAR
  DIVE  PORTS
DELETE  FAR
AREAS  TORMENT
TIE  FIX   DOE
AEROBIC  DUETS
  RAN  HORNET
ASIAN   PEON
CLOT  HELMSMAN
TOTE  ISLE  OLE
SEAS  MOOD  WET
```

547

PUZZLE 437

```
ERAS  LASS  CLOY
LOCHS ALTO  LEAD
MARAT DIAL  EATS
 DEMONSTRATORS
  SERE    SRO
    EWES    PERIL
   DESERT   PICA
OPAL REAPS ITEM
HUTS    NOTICE
SNEAD    SEEN
    EGO   ECHO
 CALLIGRAPHERS
PAGE ALOT  ELBOW
ERRS NEMO  SPIRE
NEAT TRAM  STET
```

PUZZLE 438

```
DIN   FOUR  MATES
EDIT  EASE  INERT
ALEE  STEP  STAGE
RECENT DEBT  MOW
 RETAIL NOES
   HIVE TARNISH
TAT  VENT   ARIA
ABOVE SAP  APORT
GLEE    POTS  NEE
SEDATES COIL
  LARK ORDEAL
PIC PEAT REASON
ADORE TIME  SITE
SOLAR EDEN  HATS
SLAMS SENT   NOT
```

PUZZLE 439

```
BAT  EVITA  STY
AGA  GINAS  LEE
DONTROCKTHEBOAT
   KAY     TOO
ALS ENE LOO ALP WEE
WATERS  BARBS ASTERN
LYRE   TOWBOAT  AIRS
  ILL RAN EMU EGG
ILK IDA   GIG  HIT
RAE NEW   BAR  ADO
ADS ELL   ONE  NOT
  APR ERA LEA TIC
FAIR ROWBOAT  THUS
ABLEST YEAST CHOOSE
DES TOE DYE DUO RAW
    END    ARI
 ONESSHIPCOMESIN
WAR   ANEAR   TOY
LES   SNARE   SUE
```

PUZZLE 440

```
     MISS  PACE
     AMOK  ELAN
     CANISTERS
       NIA
     CANDLES
      VERY  SATE   COD
DOC   PILE  TART   APE
ISH   ELL   RIO    NAN
ELI   DOCILE  CUDDLY
DOCILE  ARI    COY
 MENACE       PASCAL
 AVE ARK  BAN  AHA
 MER NORA LENS NOM
 ANY SIGH SEAT EYE
     SOUPCAN
       BEE
     BUCCANEER
     ASIA  TREE
     REAP  SELL
```

PUZZLE 441

```
QUEST    CHARISMA   MEDEA
ACTOR    STEER      ATOM
 KERN  EL    IMMATURITY
    IC ON   BASS
HERM ITAGE    H  HOBBLE
DUO    ERRATIC    TAUNT
GENTLEMAN   SKINFLINTS
      SIMON   GAP
REACTIONS    PERSISTENT
BURN    TROUT    DEALER
TESTED  OUSTED   LED
```

PUZZLE 442

1. Speak the truth and shame the devil.
2. Figures won't lie, but liars will figure.

PUZZLE 443

```
MINORS   DIGEST
ASTEROID  LIVELIEST
HER   LISTENERS  PAM
SLAG   CERES  SERPENT
CEREMONIAL  LIVERY
  ERRING  PUMICE
  RESTS  CHANGEABLE
MUTED  WASTE  LEAST
TAU  PRETENSE  THEE
TRANSFER  TAPER
STILLER    REARED
```

PUZZLE 444

Distance is a great promoter of admiration. (Denis Diderot)

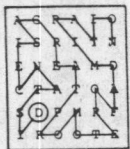

PUZZLE 445

```
SOW   CON
EPIC  ALOFT
RASH  BEDLAM
FLEE    SURE
   AREA  TON
  INTERPRET
ADO  DATA
NIBS   VAMP
DOLLAR EVIL
TEENY  LOCO
  DYE    WET
```

PUZZLE 446

```
TIM  PAPA  ARMS
WOE  AGES  BEAK
OUTBREAK  SEMI
   LINK  SEDAN
ADJUST  VAN
GEAR  CASTING
ELM  BOOTH  TEA
DISHRAG  PEAS
   EAR  WARMTH
SWEAT  TRIO
TEAR  WOODSHED
EAST  ANTE  AGO
PREY  SEES  GOT
```

PUZZLE 447

```
MAST  CAL  BASH
ALEE  ARE  ACHE
PEAL  PRO  LION
  LATIN ADES
HOD  TAVERN
ADO  TIE  ACTED
ROTTEN  SPEEDY
PREEN  FOP  AGE
  ADVICE  RED
ALEC  ELIDE
WASH ILE  MERE
ETTE LET  ITEM
DEER STY  TABU
```

PUZZLE 448

```
LARD  ZAP  CAME
OBOE  ELI  ARIA
ALAS  STEEPLES
MEMENTO  ATONE
   RAY  PRO
WITTY  SUNRISE
ORE   WON  MEL
WADDLES  REPAY
   AID  COT
BRINE  ARCHERS
LANGUAGE  IDOL
URGE  COD  CITE
REAR  EGO  STEW
```

PUZZLE 449

```
PAIR  ISLAM  MODE
OBOE  MEALY  AVID
PETS  PIPER  NEED
STATIONS  THIRTY
  ELSE  FLEA
BANDIT  AREACODE
ADO  EERIE  DAZED
DOME  ROLES  LOCI
GRANT  BERTH  NOT
ENDORSED  EIDERS
  READ  CEDE
WARMED  MOLESTED
OREO  DRIVE  ERGO
LIEU  LINER  RIOT
FADS  EMITS  TOSS
```

PUZZLE 450

```
1. LEAP  2. STEM  3. SALE
EDGE     TAME     AVID
AGES     EMIT     LIME
PEST     METE     EDEN
```

PUZZLE 451

```
G A S . L A S . C R I S P
A D E . A F T . H O M E R
L O P . B A Y . E M P T Y
E S T H E R . E R A . . .
. . E E L . P A I N T E D
. A M Y . T A R S . R A Y
H U B . T R U T H . A R E
I R E . H U S H . A D S .
S A R D I N E . A L I . .
. . I R K . S K A T E S .
P A P A S . N O R . I R A
E V E N T . U F O . O I L
R E P A Y . T A N . N E T
```

```
P O M P . R A C A . P A N
I D E A . A R O D . R I O
S E A L . V A G A B O N D
A S H A M E D . G E M . .
. . C A N . M E L I T A .
M O N E Y . H A S . S I N
O N E S . G I N . L E N T
A C T . S A T . B A S E S
B E W R A Y . W A R . . .
. O A R . F I N G E R S .
B A R N A B A S . E L A H
A R K . H E R E . S O R E
Y E S . S E E R . T I E D
```

```
L I D . B E E R . A B E T
I R E . U R G E . G O N E
F I N . T R O D . R O D E
E S T A T E . U S E . . .
. . R O D . C H E A T S .
A L I E N . B E E . T O E
C O L A . R I D . B O N E
I N K . O A T . N A M E D
D E S E R T . D E N . . .
. . L E T . R E D E E M .
A V I D . L E A D . A R E
D I C E . E V I L . S I N
D E E R . S A N E . T E D
```

```
E K E S . M I L D . B A L L . S E A L
B U L L . A D O R E . O L E O . A R L O
B R I E F C A S E S . P O L O P O N I E S
S T E E L . S T A I R . N E A T E S T
. V A N . S H I P . B A S T E .
R E N E G E D . E R I C A . H E F T S
A L I . G A R T E R S N A K E . I R A
F I G S . R E A L . G R E W . T A U
T A H O E . W R I S T . S E T S . T I C
. T U R N . S O L I D . R A T . O N E
. S P R I T . T A M E S . S C R U B
R A H . O N O . Y E N T A . K A T E
E L I . L A N G . S T A R K . W A T E R
A L F . I L L S . M E N U . H I D E
L I T . C O A T O F P A I N T . E G O
M E S A S . A G O R A . T I R A D E S
. L E A S T . O A R S . T U T .
A L A B A M A . I G L O O . S L O S H
P A J A M A G A M E . U N S U I T A B L E
E V A N . T A R E . T A U N T . S E A R
S E X Y . I N I T . R B I S . T Y P O
```

```
M O P S . A L E C . N O T
A R E A . L A V A . E W E
N E W S P A P E R . V I A
. . H A S . O M E N S . .
B R E E D . E N L A R G E
O A R S . C R E E D . . .
A P E . R A R E R . B O Y
. A I M E D . F A D E .
T R U D G E D . B I N D S
H A R S H . H U G . . .
E G G . T R E A S U R E R
S E E . L O L L . R E N O
E S S . Y E L L . E D D Y
```

```
. Y E S . S H U T . A S I A . M A S T
P A R E . T A K E . C U R L . A C H E
A L M A M A T E R . T R E A S U R E S
T E A B A G . R E E F . P L E A T
. E R E . P O N D . F O E S .
G O L D . C H A R D . W A R N . D I P
A D O . N O E L . S L I C E D . Y O U
F O G . E A R L S . E V E S . S E W N
F R O L I C S . P O S E D . S O D A S
. U G H . G L A S S . G E M .
C A T C H . C A I R O . M I N E R A L
O B E Y . M A T T . N O O N S . O B I
A L E . W I D E S T . U R G E . L E E
T E N . A C E S . A G R E E . V E L D
. D I E T . I C E S . R Y E .
S H O R T . I R O N . S E R E N E
L I V E S T O C K . I D E N T I C A L
A R E A . A L O E . A U R A . T R I M
P E R M . M E N D . L E A P . Y U L
```

```
B O L D . P R O M . S E D A N
A R I A . R A V E . C R I M E
R A N T . E W E R . R A C E S
S N E E R S . N I L E . E S S
. S A S H . T E A R . . .
H O P . M E E T . A M I C E
A P I A . D R I N K . V O L T
L E V I . O N E . E R I E
E R O S . A N G E L . R A T S
. A T L A S . E D A M . L E T
. E M I T . S U I T . .
T O R . P A I L . N A I L E D
O B E S E . G O L D . T A L E
M I N E R . E P E E . A K I N
S T O N E . R E A R . N E A T
```

```
I T E M . D I S C . M O W
M O L E . A R E A . A B E
P O L A R B E A R . M E T
. G A S . O K A Y S .
W O M E N . H A L E . .
O D O R . C A Y E N N E
N E T . L A C E D . O A F
. S H R I N K S . F U S E
. I C E S . M I N E D
T R A D E . H E N . .
H A D . N O M I N A T E D
E G O . S L U R . L A V A
Y E S . E D G E . S P E D
```

PUZZLE 460

O	W	N		C	O	L	D			G	A	B	S
W	O	O		H	A	I	R			L	I	E	U
L	O	S		A	R	E	A			A	M	E	N
	D	E	A	R			W	A	R				
		S	T	I	R			P	E	T	E	R	
R	A	S	H		D	A	T	E		O	N	E	
A	B	E		W	E	I	R	D		A	I	D	
I	L	L		E	A	S	E		O	D	D	S	
D	E	L	L	S		E	Y	E	D				
			A	T	E			N	E	S	T		
P	A	I	D		V	O	I	D		A	I	L	
I	D	O	L		E	I	R	E		N	E	E	
T	O	N	E		S	L	E	D		E	R	A	

PUZZLE 464

M	O	P		B	A	S	H		A	V	I	D
E	V	A		O	S	L	O		P	I	L	E
L	E	N	G	T	H	E	N		P	A	L	E
T	R	E	A	T		D	O	L	L			
			P	L	Y		R	E	A	S	O	N
R	U	B		E	A	T		G	U	I	D	E
E	R	R	S		P	O	P		D	R	E	W
A	G	A	I	N		Y	E	T		E	S	S
D	E	N	T	A	L		T	E	E			
			U	N	I	T		E	V	I	L	S
A	S	I	A		C	O	S	M	E	T	I	C
S	E	N	T		K	N	E	E		E	R	A
S	A	K	E		S	E	E	D		M	A	R

PUZZLE 468

J	O	E		M	E	S	H		H	U	S	H
A	L	L		I	D	E	A		A	S	I	A
R	E	M	I	N	D	E	R		V	E	N	T
			R	O	Y		B	R	I	D	G	E
O	S	C	A	R		N	O	U	N			
B	E	A	N		O	R	E	G	A	N	O	
O	A	R		G	R	O	S	S		P	E	N
E	M	P	T	I	E	S			M	E	A	L
			O	N	C	E		T	A	S	T	Y
O	P	P	O	S	E		T	I	M			
S	L	O	T		I	M	I	T	A	T	E	D
L	O	S	E		P	O	L	L		E	L	I
O	W	E	D		T	O	T	E		A	S	P

PUZZLE 461

B	O	N	E		A	C	I	D		R	I	D
A	R	I	D		L	O	N	E		E	R	E
R	E	L	I	G	I	O	N	S		N	O	N
			T	E	A			E	B	O	N	Y
D	E	P	O	T	S		E	R	R			
O	V	E	R		C	A	T	A	L	O	G	
L	E	T		T	A	R		E	G	O		
T	R	E	A	S	O	N		H	E	R	O	
			C	U	E		A	D	O	R	E	D
T	A	S	T	E		G	A	R				
R	U	E		D	E	F	E	N	S	I	V	E
A	R	E		E	V	E	N		E	R	I	N
P	A	R		S	E	N	T		S	E	E	D

PUZZLE 465

O	D	E		G	A	L	E		M	U	L	E
V	E	X		O	N	E	S		O	P	A	L
A	L	I		A	G	E	S		D	O	G	S
L	I	T	T	L	E	R		S	E	N	S	E
			O	I	L		P	E	R			
B	E	T	T	E		P	R	A	N	C	E	R
I	R	A		H	A	Y		A	L	A		
D	A	B	B	L	E	D		S	A	D	L	Y
			E	A	R		V	E	T			
B	O	W	L	S		D	I	L	E	M	M	A
E	V	I	L		P	A	C	E		A	I	M
N	E	R	O		A	L	E	C		I	C	E
D	R	E	W		N	E	S	T		D	E	N

PUZZLE 469

O	L	D		A	D	D	S		A	N	T	E
R	U	E		R	U	I	N		V	I	E	W
B	R	A		M	E	M	O		E	P	E	E
S	E	R	V	E			B	I	N			
			I	D	O	L		D	U	N	C	E
C	A	F	E		A	L		L	E	A	R	N
A	X	E		S	T	A	G	E		M	O	D
S	L	E	E	T		M	E		R	E	P	S
H	E	D	G	E			A	L	E	E		
			O	W	E			A	D	D	E	R
M	I	N	I		D	R	A	G		E	V	E
A	C	E	S		G	A	P	E		E	E	L
N	E	W	T		E	W	E	R		D	R	Y

PUZZLE 462

	D	I	P	S			S	O	N	S	
	M	E	L	E	E		U	N	I	T	S
P	O	P	L	A	R		R	E	C	A	N	T
O	R	E		T	U	R	F		E	R	O	S
S	A	N	D		M	E	E	T		E	R	A
E	L	D	E	R		D	R	E	S	S	E	R
			E	A	R		S	E	T			
S	T	A	R	T	E	D		M	A	L	E	S
A	R	C		E	T	O	N		B	E	A	T
V	A	T	S		I	T	E	M		A	V	A
E	D	I	T	O	R		S	O	L	D	E	R
	E	V	A	D	E		T	R	I	E	S	
	E	Y	E	D			S	E	E	R		

PUZZLE 466

A	D	D			S	U	E			S	P	A
R	U	E		C	A	R	T		S	K	I	P
T	E	N		A	N	N	E		A	U	N	T
			T	A	N	K		R	I	F	L	E
S	M	I	L	E			N	O	E	L		
W	I	S	E		C	A	N	S		A	D	
A	N	T		C	O	A	L	S		O	N	E
M	E		L	O	R	D			F	A	T	E
			B	I	R	D		C	A	T	E	R
	P	L	A	N	E		W	A	R	M		
W	E	A	R		A	P	E	S		E	R	R
H	E	N	S		L	I	N	E		A	Y	E
O	L	D			S	E	T			L	E	D

PUZZLE 470

A	C	T	S		A	P	E		A	R	E	A
N	O	A	H		G	A	L		L	I	A	R
T	O	U	R		R	Y	E		A	C	R	E
		S	T	A	G	E		V	A	S	E	S
			N	E	E		E	L	K			
H	O	N	K	E	D		N	E	A	R	B	Y
E	W	E								E	Y	E
P	E	T	A	L	S		B	R	I	D	E	S
			R	A	M		A	I	M			
	C	A	R	G	O		I	D	A	H	O	
M	O	D	E		O	W	L		G	A	V	E
O	D	D	S		T	E	E		E	V	E	N
B	E	S	T		H	E	Y		S	E	N	D

PUZZLE 463

C	A	P		B	E	D	S		C	I	T	E
O	D	E		A	L	O	E		I	D	E	A
N	E	W	S	C	A	S	T		N	E	S	T
			T	O	T	E		V	E	S	T	S
F	A	M	I	N	E		A	I	M			
L	I	A	R		A	R	C	A	D	E	S	
E	R	R		W	A	S	T	E		A	L	E
E	Y	E	W	A	S	H		F	R	E	E	
			A	R	K		B	R	A	K	E	S
A	D	O	R	N		H	E	A	R			
B	E	N	D		B	E	L	I	E	V	E	D
L	A	C	E		E	E	L	S		A	R	E
E	D	E	N		G	L	E	E		T	E	N

PUZZLE 467

C	O	A	T		P	O	D		G	R	A	B
U	R	G	E		L	I	E		R	I	C	E
T	E	E	M		A	L	L		A	D	E	S
			P	A	Y		E	L	D	E	S	T
B	A	G	E	L	S		T	O	E			
A	F	I	R	E		P	E	W		M	E	T
L	A	B	S		C	A	D		S	O	A	R
E	R	E		I	L	L		S	T	O	R	E
			E	R	A		H	O	A	R	S	E
B	A	R	G	E	S		E	B	B			
L	I	A	R		S	A	D		L	A	M	P
E	D	G	E		E	G	G		E	P	E	E
W	E	S	T		D	O	E		S	E	N	T

PUZZLE 471

W	A	I	T		H	A	T	S		A	D	O
A	W	R	Y		E	D	E	N		L	E	D
R	E	A	P		A	S	S	O	R	T	E	D
			E	R	R		T	R	O	O	P	S
B	L	A	D	E	S		S	T	Y			
O	A	R		D	A	B		S	A	C	K	S
A	M	E	S		Y	A	K		L	A	N	E
S	P	A	I	N		N	E	T		L	E	T
			D	I	G		E	A	G	L	E	S
A	P	I	E	C	E		P	R	O			
N	O	N	S	E	N	S	E		N	E	R	O
T	O	N		L	I	A	R		G	R	E	W
E	L	S		Y	E	W	S		S	A	V	E

PUZZLE 472

```
HAM  SHE  AWFUL
OLE  PAL  RAISE
ROMPERS  EDGED
SHOOED  END
EASED  ITALIAN
     TEACH  ERIE
SPA  DRIED  ART
EELS  BERET
TRACTOR  SALTS
     OAR  PIGEON
HOBOS  FORSAKE
ERUPT  ERE  RYE
MESSY  WED  NOR
```

PUZZLE 476

```
SACK  ALDA  GUY
LION  DARN  ORE
IDLE  OPINIONS
METER  EVEN
     LADLE  DABS
OFF  WAS  BERET
BOILED  TUXEDO
OUTER  SOY  ASP
ELSE  SLYER
     ROPE  ROWED
MEASURED  MIRE
OLD  RAVE  ALAN
OLE  STEW  NEST
```

PUZZLE 480

```
SLAM  SWAN  STAR  TEST
MAMA  HOBO  TORE  HAIR
OMEN  OVERLOOKS  OSLO
GENUINE  MILK  PARTLY
     ACE  GALE  SEWN
HILLY  COLA  ANCESTOR
ODES  HAD  CADETS  ERA
OLE  LASSO  BIAS  MEAT
FERTILE  BROOK  AISLE
     UFO  PLODS  WIN
ADOBE  RHODE  FARTHER
SAKE  COON  SCALY  ADE
IRA  CHANGE  OIL  URGE
ANYWHERE  VEAL  STEEL
     AIMS  SELL  FIT
BIKINI  TUNE  FIREMAN
EDIT  SWEETCORN  ROBE
TOTE  TOAD  TREE  ELLA
SLED  SOME  SEED  DEER
```

PUZZLE 473

```
SEA  MOVE  ORAL
ARM  EVIL  MAMA
DAYDREAM  ACES
     URN  CHEST
HEFTY  SARAH
AWRY  FADE  OLD
LEO  ALLOW  ROE
ESS  DOES  ASPS
     TRAPS  GREEK
ALBUM  PIT
RAID  PARASITE
ANTE  IRON  MEN
BEER  NEST  PAD
```

PUZZLE 477

```
COGS  ADAM  BED
OPEN  PURE  ERE
MANE  TERM  LIE
BLEED  LOBSTER
     ZOO  WEE
VINEGAR  READY
ADO  FOE  WOE
TASTE  NESTLES
     URN  LEO
OUTGREW  TONGS
SPY  AWES  TALE
LOP  NERO  EVEN
ONE  DREW  DYED
```

PUZZLE 481

```
ASH  RACK  PERU
LIE  OBOE  IRIS
ELL  SING  LACE
COMRADE  POSED
     ARE  GET
WITTY  CAPSIZE
ADO  FRY  NOR
DAYLILY  MANOR
     AMY  CAD
CHIRP  WHISPER
HOOD  MAUL  ELI
ANTE  ACRE  ASP
TEAR  POND  TEE
```

PUZZLE 474

```
HAT  RANT  APES
IRE  OLEO  CAVE
STALLION  OPEN
     ELAN  BRAND
CARESS  TIN
OVER  PEASANT
WON  EPEES  LIE
SWOLLEN  FACE
     ASP  LOOSEN
TRIBE  PAIR
HARE  CAULDRON
EVIL  ACRE  AWE
MESS  BEAD  WET
```

PUZZLE 478

```
LAW  BELA  STOP
ONO  AGES  CONE
STRENGTH  OPEN
SEDAN  SELL
     SET  SEDATE
CATERED  ASPEN
LIE  LEE  SAD
IDEAS  ERASERS
PESTER  ATE
     HEIR  TABLE
POSE  DECISION
ARON  ENOL  ANI
WEDS  SODA  SID
```

PUZZLE 482

```
SHOW  CAD  RITE
LAVA  ODE  EDEN
OVER  ROB  VEND
TENDON  TREADS
     ELF  SIR
AMENDED  BEACH
NOR  DID  BAA
TOAST  PESTERS
     WAS  FOR
POTATO  ENACTS
ADAM  FUN  MOAT
CORP  ASS  PACE
TRAY  SEE  STOW
```

PUZZLE 475

```
CARD  DAISY  TAGS
ALEE  UNCLE  RILE
SLAB  STEEL  AMEN
TYRANTS  ELAPSED
     TOP  POLE
GENERALS  WIZARD
HEED  NAIL  TEPEE
ORE  SPLIT  ACE
SIDES  SLOE  SCUM
TESTED  SNEAKERS
     EARS  TIE
SCARLET  REDTAPE
TORN  ARBOR  CLAW
IDEA  MAYBE  HOPE
REAL  SPEED  YEAR
```

PUZZLE 479

```
ASA  AIDE  HEROD
STD  GNATS  IRONY
HOLLANDAISESAUCE
RIO  DOG  TED
HAMBURGER  SORE
ERIC  EELER  ALTOS
BORE  ENGLISHMUFFINS
BEE  SAO  TOUT  GEE
     STUD  DENSE
TEE  EAR
REMUS  VERY
OBI  GOAD  AGO  FEW
FRENCHDRESSING  OLEO
TOSCA  ELECT  RARE
OREL  IRISHSTEW
ALI  REP  ALA
HUNGARIANGOULASH
ALTER  TOOLS  ITE
BLOTS  RODE  NEW
```

PUZZLE 483

```
FEED  COP  HATE
ELSE  AWE  AWRY
DISC  DEN  BLUE
     IRE  ARISES
CREDIT  LOT
RODEO  STY  RUT
APED  HAY  CURE
MEN  POP  RANGE
     ART  HORSES
BALLOT  YEA
ORAL  ERE  VETO
WERE  SUN  AGED
LADY  TEA  NONE
```

551

PUZZLE 484

```
DAMES   SHALE
RECALL  TALONS
RESERVE RIPPLES
APE TEETERS ILO
PERK STRAY EVER
SAVED YAM ELECT
LENIN PENDANTS
NAIL RAGS
ASSERTER PATED
BILLY AIR RIMED
IDES AFTER CERO
DIN ISLAMIC RID
ENDORSE AVOCADO
GENIES TEMPLE
RESTS SNEAD
```

PUZZLE 485

```
GRAFT RATES ELSAS
RETIE APART SATIATE
ADANA BORROWTROUBLE
DESIRABLE PIER LAD
EATS NIL PRO TESS
SLA BOSOM SEEGER
SNOOD ISIS ARABIA
DRYER TAN ENAMELS
MISTS ABET TATS SET
ANTS CAREERS AIDE
IDI SPED ERIE OLDER
MILLARD ANN SINGE
SALINE OISE MEATS
ESTERS SLAPS HIM
BOAS OVA OLE DELE
AAR RANT BALLGAMES
STEPPINGSTONE AMASS
SENORAS ARDEN MARIE
ORATE REEDS ANKAS
```

PUZZLE 486

```
PAVE APPLE VAST
IBEX COLON IDEA
SUSPICIOUS ADAM
ATTIRE PIUS IRE
RING ERUPT
DIVESTED ELOISE
UNI HEARS KNOLL
MUCH DROOP ENID
ARTEL SPRAT ACE
SNORES STROLLER
RESTS SARA
ANI TOPI PUTTEE
NOOK REFRESHERS
ETUI MANET ERIS
WEST SKITS SNEE
```

PUZZLE 487

```
MASS SHE CABAL
ESTIMATOR EDILE
THEBARREL MONET
ZEN LOA EMERGES
WASP ENE
POPEYE PORTSAID
IVIES BUNGS TRE
LINK FARCE HOOP
ONE SERGE TENNO
TESTCASE SOREST
EHS STUB
GANNETS TAP SUP
ABEAM CORRELATE
BERNE OVEREAGER
SLOTS TAW COST
```

PUZZLE 488

```
SUB SHE BOAS
ORE AURA ABLE
SNEAKERS ROOT
HES SPREES
BOOS SURE
AIRY ENROLLED
GAB KNEES ADO
ESSENCES TWIG
REAR BUST
STRAWS SUN
PIES ENTRENCH
ALEE DEAR ARE
REDS EGO GYM
```

PUZZLE 489

```
LOB CELL PAPA
IRE AREA EDEN
KEG NANNYGOAT
ESSAY DOG
PODS NEWER
FOOTNOTE DARE
ADS SLAVE ROD
SOLE EVENNESS
TROLL ERGO
AID ATLAS
BARTERING ALE
ARTE ALEE ROE
DEED BLED DEN
```

PUZZLE 490

```
UNIT BIT STEW
SORE LOW HIDE
EWER ONE AMID
RAN EGRETS
DEMAND ZAP
AGAIN LEG PAD
TORN JAR CORE
ASS DEW PREEN
JAW QUOTAS
ARCADE UPS
GOOD LEE SAGA
ELSE RYE EWES
SETS YEN SEEP
```

PUZZLE 491

```
FLAP WAY ACED
EARL ONE WORE
LIEU UNSHAVEN
TRAMPLE EKE
BAD WIENER
EATEN NOR ADO
PLOD MEN SNIP
IDA ROE BETTE
CASHEW COT
TOE ELATION
SPITFIRE EDGE
PEEL VIA ELLA
AWRY YEN SEER
```

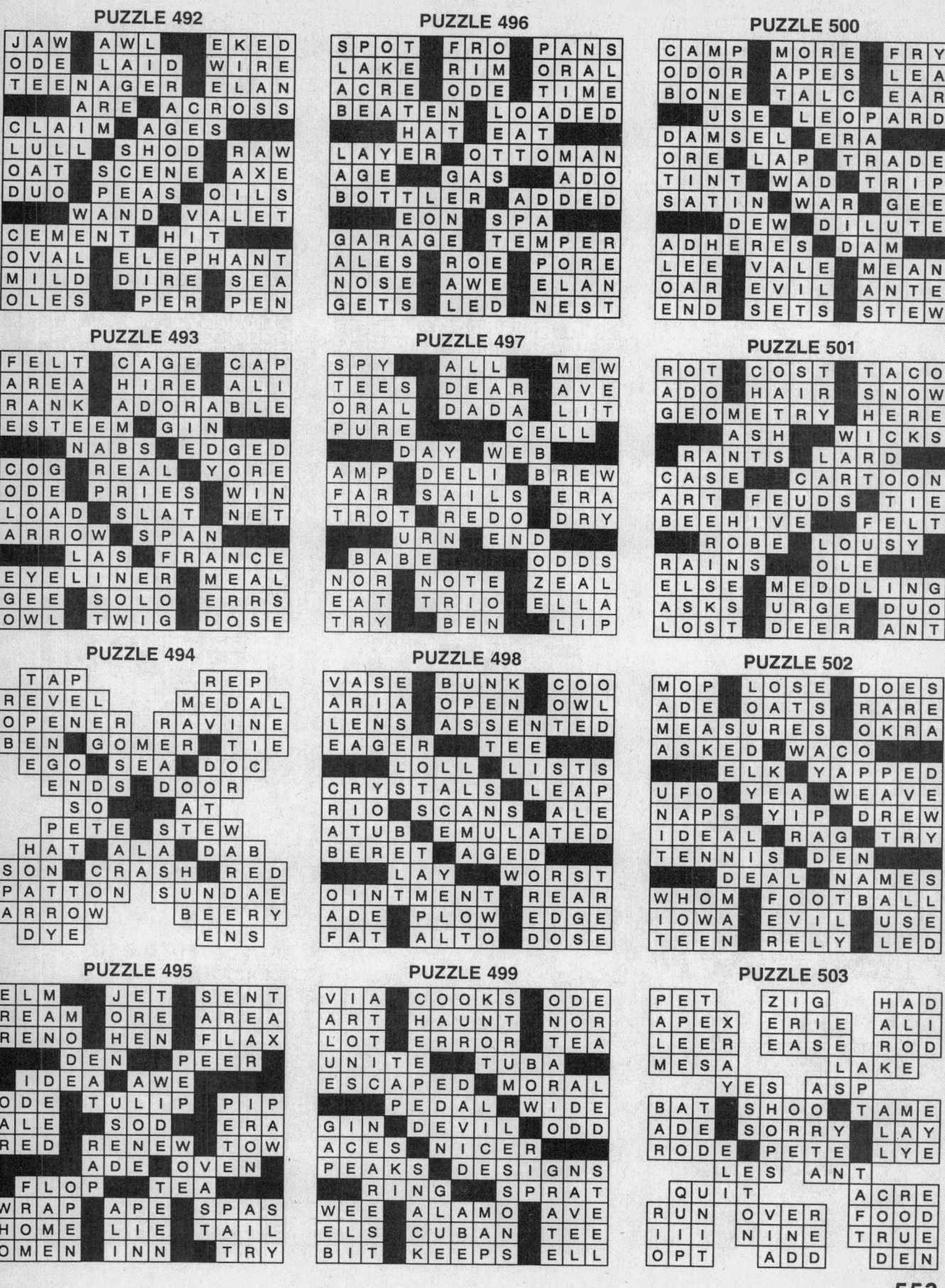

PUZZLE 492

J	A	W		A	W	L			E	K	E	D
O	D	E		L	A	I	D		W	I	R	E
T	E	E	N	A	G	E	R		E	L	A	N
		A	R	E		A	C	R	O	S	S	
C	L	A	I	M		A	G	E	S			
L	U	L	L		S	H	O	D		R	A	W
O	A	T		S	C	E	N	E		A	X	E
D	U	O		P	E	A	S		O	I	L	S
		W	A	N	D		V	A	L	E	T	
C	E	M	E	N	T		H	I	T			
O	V	A	L		E	L	E	P	H	A	N	T
M	I	L	D		D	I	R	E		S	E	A
O	L	E	S		P	E	R		P	E	N	

PUZZLE 496

S	P	O	T		F	R	O		P	A	N	S
L	A	K	E		R	I	M		O	R	A	L
A	C	R	E		O	D	E		T	I	M	E
B	E	A	T	E	N		L	O	A	D	E	D
		H	A	T		E	A	T				
L	A	Y	E	R		O	T	T	O	M	A	N
A	G	E		G	A	S			A	D	O	
B	O	T	T	L	E	R		A	D	D	E	D
		E	O	N		S	P	A				
G	A	R	A	G	E		T	E	M	P	E	R
A	L	E	S		R	O	E		P	O	R	E
N	O	S	E		A	W	E		E	L	A	N
G	E	T	S		L	E	D		N	E	S	T

PUZZLE 500

C	A	M	P		M	O	R	E		F	R	Y
O	D	O	R		A	P	E	S		L	E	A
B	O	N	E		T	A	L	C		E	A	R
		U	S	E		L	E	O	P	A	R	D
D	A	M	S	E	L		E	R	A			
O	R	E		L	A	P		T	R	A	D	E
T	I	N	T		W	A	D		T	R	I	P
S	A	T	I	N		W	A	R		G	E	E
			D	E	W		D	I	L	U	T	E
A	D	H	E	R	E	S		D	A	M		
L	E	E		V	A	L	E		M	E	A	N
O	A	R		E	V	I	L		A	N	T	E
E	N	D		S	E	T	S		S	T	E	W

PUZZLE 493

F	E	L	T		C	A	G	E		C	A	P
A	R	E	A		H	I	R	E		A	L	I
R	A	N	K		A	D	O	R	A	B	L	E
E	S	T	E	E	M		G	I	N			
		N	A	B	S		E	D	G	E	D	
C	O	G		R	E	A	L		Y	O	R	E
O	D	E		P	R	I	E	S		W	I	N
L	O	A	D		S	L	A	T		N	E	T
A	R	R	O	W		S	P	A	N			
		L	A	S		F	R	A	N	C	E	
E	Y	E	L	I	N	E	R		M	E	A	L
G	E	E		S	O	L	O		E	R	R	S
O	W	L		T	W	I	G		D	O	S	E

PUZZLE 497

S	P	Y		A	L	L		M	E	W
T	E	E	S		D	E	A	R		A	V	E
O	R	A	L		D	A	D	A		L	I	T
P	U	R	E			C	E	L	L			
			D	A	Y		W	E	B			
A	M	P		D	E	L	I		B	R	E	W
F	A	R		S	A	I	L	S		E	R	A
T	R	O	T		R	E	D	O		D	R	Y
			U	R	N		E	N	D			
		B	A	B	E			O	D	D	S	
N	O	R		N	O	T	E		Z	E	A	L
E	A	T		T	R	I	O		E	L	L	A
T	R	Y		B	E	N		L	I	P		

PUZZLE 501

R	O	T		C	O	S	T		T	A	C	O
A	D	O		H	A	I	R		S	N	O	W
G	E	O	M	E	T	R	Y		H	E	R	E
			A	S	H		W	I	C	K	S	
	R	A	N	T	S		L	A	R	D		
C	A	S	E			C	A	R	T	O	O	N
A	R	T		F	E	U	D	S		T	I	E
B	E	E	H	I	V	E			F	E	L	T
		R	O	B	E		L	O	U	S	Y	
R	A	I	N	S		O	L	E				
E	L	S	E		M	E	D	D	L	I	N	G
A	S	K	S		U	R	G	E		D	U	O
L	O	S	T		D	E	E	R		A	N	T

PUZZLE 494

T	A	P						R	E	P	
R	E	V	E	L			M	E	D	A	L
O	P	E	N	E	R		R	A	V	I	N	E
B	E	N		G	O	M	E	R		T	I	E
	E	G	O		S	E	A		D	O	C
	E	N	D	S		D	O	O	R		
		S	O				A	T			
	P	E	T	E		S	T	E	W	
H	A	T		A	L	A		D	A	B
S	O	N		C	R	A	S	H		R	E	D
P	A	T	T	O	N		S	U	N	D	A	E
A	R	R	O	W			B	E	E	R	Y
D	Y	E						E	N	S	

PUZZLE 498

V	A	S	E		B	U	N	K		C	O	O
A	R	I	A		O	P	E	N		O	W	L
L	E	N	S		A	S	S	E	N	T	E	D
E	A	G	E	R		T	E	E				
		L	O	L	L		L	I	S	T	S	
C	R	Y	S	T	A	L	S		L	E	A	P
R	I	O		S	C	A	N	S		A	L	E
A	T	U	B		E	M	U	L	A	T	E	D
B	E	R	E	T		A	G	E	D			
		L	A	Y		W	O	R	S	T		
O	I	N	T	M	E	N	T		R	E	A	R
A	D	E		P	L	O	W		E	D	G	E
F	A	T		A	L	T	O		D	O	S	E

PUZZLE 502

M	O	P		L	O	S	E		D	O	E	S
A	D	E		O	A	T	S		R	A	R	E
M	E	A	S	U	R	E	S		O	K	R	A
A	S	K	E	D		W	A	C	O			
		E	L	K		Y	A	P	P	E	D	
U	F	O		Y	E	A		W	E	A	V	E
N	A	P	S		Y	I	P		D	R	E	W
I	D	E	A	L		R	A	G		T	R	Y
T	E	N	N	I	S		D	E	N			
		D	E	A	L		N	A	M	E	S	
W	H	O	M		F	O	O	T	B	A	L	L
I	O	W	A		E	V	I	L		U	S	E
T	E	E	N		R	E	L	Y		L	E	D

PUZZLE 495

E	L	M		J	E	T		S	E	N	T
R	E	A	M		O	R	E		A	R	E	A
R	E	N	O		H	E	N		F	L	A	X
		D	E	N			P	E	E	R	
	I	D	E	A		A	W	E			
O	D	E		T	U	L	I	P		P	I	P
A	L	E		S	O	D		E	R	A	
R	E	D		R	E	N	E	W		T	O	W
	A	D	E		O	V	E	N			
	F	L	O	P		T	E	A			
W	R	A	P		A	P	E		S	P	A	S
H	O	M	E		L	I	E		T	A	I	L
O	M	E	N		I	N	N		T	R	Y	

PUZZLE 499

V	I	A		C	O	O	K	S		O	D	E
A	R	T		H	A	U	N	T		N	O	R
L	O	T		E	R	R	O	R		T	E	A
U	N	I	T	E		T	U	B	A			
E	S	C	A	P	E	D		M	O	R	A	L
			P	E	D	A	L		W	I	D	E
G	I	N		D	E	V	I	L		O	D	D
A	C	E	S		N	I	C	E	R			
P	E	A	K	S		D	E	S	I	G	N	S
		R	I	N	G			S	P	R	A	T
W	E	E		A	L	A	M	O		A	V	E
E	L	S		C	U	B	A	N		T	E	E
B	I	T		K	E	E	P	S		E	L	L

PUZZLE 503

P	E	T			Z	I	G			H	A	D
A	P	E	X		E	R	I	E		A	L	I
L	E	E	R		E	A	S	E		R	O	D
M	E	S	A			L	A	K	E			
		Y	E	S		A	S	P			
B	A	T		S	H	O	O		T	A	M	E
A	D	E		S	O	R	R	Y		L	A	Y
R	O	D	E		P	E	T	E		L	Y	E
		L	E	S		A	N	T			
Q	U	I	T					A	C	R	E	
R	U	N		O	V	E	R		F	O	O	D
I	I	I		N	I	N	E		T	R	U	E
O	P	T		A	D	D			D	E	N	

553

PUZZLE 504

```
S I P   A B I E   L A C E
I D A   S O O N   O V A L
N O R   H O U S E W O R K
    D I E T     N E W S
O D O R S   S T A R
R I N K   E P I C   R A P
A R E   S T A R T   E R E
L E D   H O N E   A S E A
    R A N K   V I T A L
  S C A R   S I L L
C H A M P I O N S   E N D
P O M P   R I O T   S I R
A P E S   E L B A   S P Y
```

PUZZLE 508

```
    0 1 2 3 4 5 6 7 8 9
1.  I M P O R T A N C E
2.  U N P O L I S H E D
3.  C H I V A L R O U S
```

PUZZLE 509

```
B A R O N   B E I N G   E A S E S
A W A R E   A R S O N   C L A R E
S A V O I R F A I R E   R E L A X
I R E   L I F T S   I O U   E S E
E D N A   F L O   A S P   U S E S
    F A T E   D I S T I L L
W R I T E S   T I L   I G U A N A
O U T E R   S H A M P O O   D E S
O N E R   F I R   E O N   S I R S
D I M   C O C O O N S   S T E V E
S C I P I O   N U T   T H E S E S
    Z E S T I E R   D I E M
C O A T   E M S   B U R   S O R T
H U T   F R A   T O N E S   W O E
A G I L E   G R O U N D L I N G S
S H O E D   E A G R E   A L E U T
E T N A S   S T A N D   P O R E S
```

One great use of words is to hide our thoughts. (Voltaire)

PUZZLE 510

```
W R A P   C R A B   B U S Y
E A S E   P L A N E   A N N A
S K I S   A U N T S   S T O W
T E A K   V E G E T A T I O N
    I D E S     Y E L P S
A G R E E D   V O L E S
L O E S S   H E R E   S A D
B A L T I M O R E O R I O L E
S L Y   E B B S   U N I O N
    S O L O S   T I T L E S
E M B E D   G E N E
R O U N D T A B L E   G A B S
R O D S   H U R O N   E R I E
E D G E   A R A B S   R E N T
D Y E D   W A D E   S A G S
```

PUZZLE 511

1. The best thing we can give a person is one more chance.
2. Civilization is just a slow process of learning to be kind.

PUZZLE 505

```
H O M E   M A T   G I N
A P E X   C O D E   A R E
T A R T   R O M E   S E T
S L E E V E   I N T O
    N E W E R   E L S E
T I L T S   L E A D I N G
A D E   T R E S S   N A G
C L A S S I C   P E E P S
T Y P E   S T E I N
    F A L K   A C T I V E
N O R   A I M S   R O I L
A D O   S E A T   A T O M
B E G   T R Y   P A L S
```

PUZZLE 506

```
T I P   A B A   P A P
A D I T   D E L T A   S E T A
L O N I   O L D E R   P A I R
C L A N   B L A C K H I L L S
    F O E S   A R E T E
S T O O L S   B E T T E
A E R I E   A I D E   D E S
Y E L L O W S T O N E P A R K
S S E   A H E M   V O L G A
    R A G E S   F I N E S T
C O R A L   S A L T
O R A N G E B O W L   O T T O
L A N G   V A L E T   O R A L
A T E E   A S I D E   N I L E
S E E   O E R   P E G
```

PUZZLE 507

```
I B I D   S T A G   S C U B A
D E N Y   H O M E   E L T O N
A L D E B A R A N   Q U E S T
H O U R O F T H E G U N
O W E   L E E   R E G A L E
P E R   A V A L   M E L
A B H O R   O P E N   V I V A
Y E A R O F T H E D R A G O N
R A V E   O T I S   O L A N D
E L O   E R O S   A C E
S E C A N T   A S K   B Y E
    D A Y O F T H E D E A D
A T E A M   R O T O T I L L S
M A R G E   A G A R   B I T E
A N G E L   L Y R E   S E A L
```

PUZZLE 512

```
A P T   A B E T   F A D S
R O E   F A R E   U R A L
M I N S T R E L   R I L E
    L E E   E R O D E D
S O B E R   A V E R
A V O W   S P I N   A D A
F E N   F I R S T   R E E
E N D   A L O E   B E E R
    M I E N   S E A M Y
A S T E R N   A T E
R O O T   C O L O N I Z E
A F A R   E V I L   V E T
B A D E   D A T E   Y E A
```

PUZZLE 513

```
H O P S   C A R   S L O B
O M I T   L I E   H O L E
G E N E   A D S   I N E E
S N E A K S   T A N G O S
    L I S S O M E
C H A S M   P R I S O N S
O A R   O R E   D O T
P L A C A T E   R U D D Y
    I N H E R I T
B R O N T E   A D M I R E
L U R E   L E G   O N E S
A D A M   L E E   S C A T
B E L A   O L D   T A L E
```

PUZZLE 514

```
N A M E S   C A R O M   R E A   B E G
E M O T E   A L I V E   E N L A R G E
B A T H E   M A D E T O M E A S U R E
T H Y R O I D   R E M O   E S N E S
F E E L   R O D E   S I R E   E T T E
O U R   B E N I T O   T S A R S
P R O B E S   N A U T   E R A S U R E
F O R T E   S T O A   P R O P E L
E M P A N E L S   O L L A   A R T A L
L Y E   S K I N F L I N T   O D A
D R A P E   O P A H   A N I M A T E S
E N R O L S   S P A S   A B A S H
R A L L I E D   E N O S   E S K E R S
    T A R E S   D R A F T S   M O A
P U R R   S P E D   A P I A   G I S T
O L I O S   O A R S   P E N D E N T
S E T O N E S M I N D O N   I N U R E
E M A N A T E   B E A R D   S I T U S
D A S   P O D   S E G O S   T E E M S
```

PUZZLE 515

```
R A J A   B L A S E   P A T
I T A L   R E S E T   E N I D
G O N E W I T H T H E W I N D
A P E   R A G E   A T L A S
    N I R O   W I R E
K N O T S   E N T R I E S
C L O N E   L E I G H   N R A
A U T O   T O N G A   S C A N
S T U   P O O C H   S E U S S
H E P B U R N   S T A R E
    A R T S   T H A T
D I E T S   P R O F   G A S
O N T H E W A T E R F R O N T
T R E E   A V A N T   D A N E
E S S   R E S T S   S L A M
```

PUZZLE 516

A metaphysician is a person who goes into a dark cellar at midnight without a light looking for a black cat that isn't there.

PUZZLE 517

```
L O B O   S P A R E   C L I P
E D A M   T A P E R   R I D E
N O N E   A S T E R   E L L A
T R E L L I S   L O C A T E S
    E I D E R   R A T
A D I T S   S O Y   T E P I D
B U R S T S   T A P   D A R E
A D O   S P E A K E R   P E N
T E N D   A R T   R E S E N T
E S S E S   N O R   P A R E S
    C A P   R A G E D
A W A I T E D   C O L D E S T
C O R D   T O W E R   L I N E
T R E E   A D O R E   E R I S
S E A S   L O E S S   S E T S
```

PUZZLE 518

```
CHOP RAGES SLAV
ROLL ECOLE TAPA
OBIE WOODCARVER
WOODWARD  DAIRY
     ERN STOKES
PASTED SAONE
ANNA SANTA  TRE
WOODLANDDEITIES
LAW ITALY  ALAS
 STORY  MANTLE
  DAPHNE POI
TORII  SOURWOOD
WOODCHUCKS ALMA
ANSE ALOES  SLED
SEER METRE  HARE
```

PUZZLE 519

From top to bottom: Beetle, Grasshopper, Butterfly, Moth, Spider, Mosquito, Cricket.
7-letter word: TERMITE.

PUZZLE 520

```
FLAT CROAK  SCAB
LAVA HELLO  ARIA
AMEN ADDER  FADS
KERNEL  ADAGES
   ELK LONER
EWERS JAM  PIECE
TEN TUXEDO  MAN
HAT GAM LIT ONE
EVE EMBLEM  TOM
RERUN LET TEENY
 PIPED  SOL
STEREO OPAQUE
TIRE RAZOR  PURL
ULNA ELOPE  SAGA
BEER SLOTS  EDEN
```

1-L, 2-J, 3-Q, 4-C, 5-W, 6-D, 7-F, 8-Y, 9-T, 10-U, 11-V, 12-R, 13-I, 14-G, 15-Z, 16-B, 17-E, 18-K, 19-A, 20-S, 21-H, 22-M, 23-X, 24-O, 25-N, 26-P.

PUZZLE 521

```
LOW  SEA  BOA
EPIC SCANT WOOL
GUSH EARTH HAZE
SHIVER  ADORE
  LED NEWEL
QUIT SOX  LEER
SUN FEDORA  JET
HAD SOW DAY EVE
EKE TEACUP  CUE
ERNE GAS  MATE
 ORDER  JAB
PHONO  GENIAL
IRIS MAPLE DROP
LAKE ERROR EASE
LYE  MOB  BET
```

1-L, 2-G, 3-D, 4-E, 5-S, 6-H, 7-W, 8-Q, 9-O, 10-M, 11-F, 12-U, 13-Z, 14-R, 15-P, 16-N, 17-B, 18-C, 19-T, 20-Y, 21-A, 22-X, 23-K, 24-I, 25-V, 26-J.

PUZZLE 522

```
SLOW ASSET  HASH
LAVA CHORE  ECHO
AMERICANINPARIS
PEN VERGE  ADEPT
  LANK  PRY
RECENT AVID  GAP
ALAN ALAMO  AWE
JAPANESESANDMAN
ATE AVERT  AURA
HER PEAT CARTEL
   CON GANT
APPAL OVERT  GUN
REUNIONINVIENNA
IRMA FLARE  VAIN
DUAL TYLER  ETTA
```

PUZZLE 523

1. Plate, 2. Manes, 3. Stain, 4. Regal, 5. Parse, 6. Crate, 7. Times, 8. Resin. 8-LETTER WORD: ANAGRAMS.

PUZZLE 524

```
STOW GRAF ASWAN
MALI RILL PHONE
ERIN ACTI PEONS
WOODENHORSE DOT
 OLD STEADY
BETWEEN  TRIALS
ALI CEASE  SALON
RINK SPEAR  SLOE
DOWEL SATED  ESE
STORES SPINNER
ORATES  AVE
PHD NATALIEWOOD
REMIT HOUR  ELMO
ERATO ONCE  SLOG
PONES SEED  TAOS
```

PUZZLE 525

AUTOMOBILE

PUZZLE 526

```
RAISE  CHEWS
CORDON HURRAH
HOMEOFTHEBRAVES
ERAS TEEM  SPIRE
ANN FERRIC  SNOW
PECTIN SCAB  GEN
STAIN FEARLESS
TRAIL  LLAMA
SHELLACS MICRA
ATE SETH MERCER
REDO STORED  OBI
EARNS ERIN  DUAL
ALASKARESIDENTS
SLEEVE KARATE
STEED SLURS
```

PUZZLE 527

1.

2.

PUZZLE 528

```
GRACE CAPS  REEL
RACES OMIT  ALOE
EVENT RILE  NINE
WESTERN  LEAK
ERE MOPS  ART
FIR FLAW TOWER
DAM PIER SERAPE
IMPARTS STROKES
VIOLAS SPUN  ENS
ESSAY LEAP  TNT
SHE ERIE  POE
 BRAT ERRATIC
FACE ITAL OPERA
EVEN SEWS POLAR
NEED ERNE STONE
```

PUZZLE 529

FAMILY

PUZZLE 530

```
SHOT STALE  CRAB
LAME CURES  RULE
ALAN ABIDE  ASIA
BORDERED  OTHER
 PER MOVE
CLOSES BEVERAGE
AERIE WATER  ROD
TAGS WAKEN  FROG
EVA DIVES  PROSE
RENDERED SLOWER
 ICED RIO
SPARK BANDAGES
WIPE SLING  BALE
ALEC TINGE  ELSA
TEST ADDED  DEEM
```

PUZZLE 531

1. Clef, 2. Fuel, 3. Long, 4. Guam, 5. Main, 6. Next, 7. Trip, 8. Path, 9. Hook, 10. Kiev, 11. Verb, 12. Brad, 13. Dais, 14. Saga, 15. Alto, 16. Oath. 7-LETTER WORD: Foghorn.

PUZZLE 532

```
MAR SLAP  ACRE
ALE MACE  LAID
TIS ICER  ANTI
 TILE  ASSET
TORTE  MARK
ALAS RESTATES
LEI WALKS  EVA
CONVERTS PREP
 ORES BURNS
SPITE  CUBA
HAVE POOR  CON
AVER AIMS  ERA
MESS SLAT  SAT
```

PUZZLE 533

```
BEET TAM  CLOY
ARNI IDA  HIDE
LITTLESTROKES
DEALER  CERES
 NEA SHEA
EGGS SPILLANE
SAL SHINS  CIL
ELECTING UCLA
 HIVE ONO
AFINE DALLAS
FELLGREATOAKS
ORAL ERN  ADIT
BOGS DEE  DENS
```

PUZZLE 534

```
MISS  SEER  PEAKS
EDIT  OSSA  ALPES
DOLOMITES  TAPER
ELOPERS  PORTALS
     GEE  CIEL
DECADES  CHORALE
REAPS  CARET  CEM
ORRS  BONER  SHAM
SIP  TRUES  FAIRY
SEAMIER  TURBANS
TANA       BIO
SCHISMS  TOMTOMS
ELITE  HIMALAYAN
PEARL  ETAT  GERE
TONES  DENS  ESTE
```

PUZZLE 539

1. Top Hat, 2. Shall We Dance, 3. Ziegfeld Follies, 4. Royal Wedding, 5. Funny Face, 6. Blue Skies.

PUZZLE 540

```
HAIR  AMPS  AMI
OGLE  MART  LET
GOLDAMEIR  ONE
IAGO  MUSEUM
DANCE  PEDA
RIOT  DEVELOPS
ARI  DECAL  VIA
MYSTICAL  LENS
OPEN  PYRES
BECALM  NARC
AXE  OBNOXIOUS
BID  MEET  CASH
ATE  AREA  STAY
```

PUZZLE 535

To be trusted is a greater compliment than to be loved.

1. Overstated, 2. Challenged, 3. Better, 4. Promote, 5. Mist, 6. Unit, 7. Boa.

PUZZLE 544

```
WON  CRY  PAY  RAB
ABE  HUE  AWE  AIR
NOS  ABS  RAT  IMA
DETAIL  WAR  ELSE
   PRESIDENT
WAGE  ODE  AORTA
ALE  RARE  DINERS
RLS  EDT  CUL  GAI
MOTIVE  BROS  ADD
SWEDE  ARA  FLEE
   ELIZABETH
SAPS  NUT  NEATER
OLE  FAR  ITS  RAO
ATE  ONE  NET  ISM
KOR  RES  DRY  PTA
```

PUZZLE 545

```
PIA        CAW
TENDER  OLEO
RESOLE  RARE
AVE  SPINNER
MER     ONE
STBERNARD
OAT        EER
SQUARES  MAE
AUNT  REMOLD
WIDE  STAVES
POD        PER
```

PUZZLE 536

```
BRIG    SLASH
CRAVAT  PORTAL
RECEDE  ROTATE
AMI  STRAP  TEA
BENT  HAY  TURK
NEATER  CRESS
   CARIOLE
CABIN  TRIALS
ARAT  JAG  DELL
RAN  BANAL  VIE
ERASED  NOTICE
DANITE  SPITES
TATAS    SEED
```

PUZZLE 541

```
AVER  ALEC  ASK
MENU  DUAL  LEA
YEAS  ARTIFACT
HUGE  CASTE
CHEESE  SHY
LEVEE  SPEEDER
URI  GUY  AXE
BELLHOP  PERIL
OAT  DAINTY
AMASS  CURT
FOOTSTEP  HUGH
ANN  LODE  ESAU
RAE  EYED  RAPT
```

PUZZLE 546

```
ALP  KAYAK  SPA
PER  OLIVE  TAD
EGO  RIPER  ERE
SHE  SNEAK
APPEARS  ELMS
TEEM  ATOLL
EAR  AREAS  REO
SLEPT  CALF
ARAB  SHERIFF
COMET  SYN
ROB  ROBOT  BAT
ORE  TRADE  OWE
ENS  ANGER  WED
```

PUZZLE 537

```
BABA  ALP  ABAS
ALAS  RAH  TACO
RAISEANOUTCRY
TNT  ABANC  KEA
   TSE  ELKS
ATOUTS  RANOUT
GAUL       OURS
OUTLAW  OUTTIP
   DEMI  LBS
FRA  ETUDE  ILE
OUTERHEBRIDES
ANEW  ILO  TEAS
MEDE  NEY  SAKE
```

PUZZLE 542

```
SAL  BLAH  BALES
ALOP  RITA  EMOTE
IAGO  ODOR  MADAM
CROSSWORDPUZZLE
GENES  COSI
TARRED  SILENCES
ELISE  DADE  GALA
NIP  SMILERS  BAN
OCHS  AVER  ORATE
RESTATES  COALER
ONER  PATTI
CRYPTOGRAPHISTS
LOUPE  EERO  OTIC
ABLER  NAST  NITA
PTERO  TREE  CON
```

PUZZLE 547

```
METE  GAP  MAR
AKIN  DIVA  ORE
TEND  OVER  AIL
URGE  CANDY
COBRA  KEG
ALIEN  BELOVED
SIN  GAY  OWE
TODDLER  OFTEN
EAT  ALERT
FAINT  DATA
LID  ELAN  NABS
ADO  NEWT  GNAT
GEL  TEN  EDDY
```

PUZZLE 538

```
SKIM  ASTER  GABS
AIDA  FLAKE  AMEN
FEEL  LIMES  RILE
EVALUATE  TODDLE
ARMS  POLE
CHARGE  SERENADE
HORDE  SITES  WAD
AVES  SORES  PANG
FEN  OILER  FARCE
FRANKLIN  SANDED
IRED  UNIT
CANCAN  STARRING
ERIE  CHAIR  IDOL
DIPS  EAGLE  ELSA
EAST  STEED  SEED
```

PUZZLE 543

Anaconda, Anagram, Analgesic, Analytically, Angel, Answer, Antelope, Antique, Anybody.

PUZZLE 548

```
EDAM  AND  SABU
GILA  RIO  EROS
GLEN  ELL  VILE
LEARN  PLEAT
TEACHER
STEED  HIT  LAG
PURE  SIN  BITE
AGE  TEL  HOVEL
SWALLOW
SPOOL  OTHER
SLAB  IRA  ERIN
HONE  OUT  ALTO
EWER  NTH  DEED
```

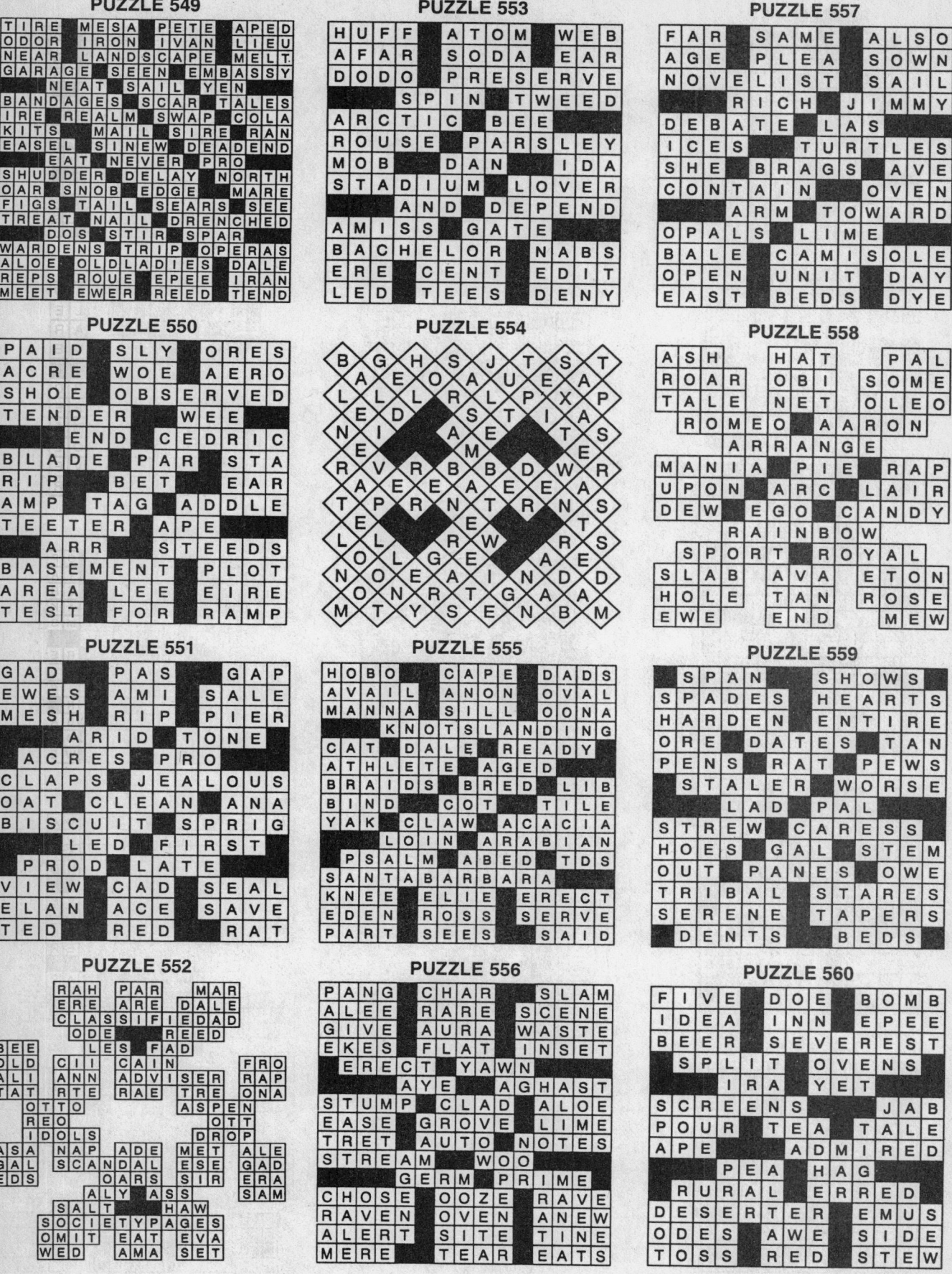

PUZZLE 549

```
TIRE  MESA  PETE  APED
ODOR  IRON  IVAN  LIEU
NEAR  LANDSCAPE  MELT
GARAGE  SEEN  EMBASSY
    NEAT  SAIL  YEN
BANDAGES  SCAR  TALES
IRE  REALM  SWAP  COLA
KITS  MAIL  SIRE  RAN
EASEL  SINEW  DEADEND
    EAT  NEVER  PRO
SHUDDER  DELAY  NORTH
OAR  SNOB  EDGE  MARE
FIGS  TAIL  SEARS  SEE
TREAT  NAIL  DRENCHED
    DOS  STIR  SPAR
WARDENS  TRIP  OPERAS
ALOE  OLDLADIES  DALE
REPS  ROUE  EPEE  IRAN
MEET  EWER  REED  TEND
```

PUZZLE 553

```
HUFF  ATOM    WEB
AFAR  SODA    EAR
DODO  PRESERVE
      SPIN  TWEED
ARCTIC  BEE
ROUSE  PARSLEY
MOB   DAN    IDA
STADIUM  LOVER
   AND  DEPEND
AMISS  GATE
BACHELOR  NABS
ERE  CENT  EDIT
LED  TEES  DENY
```

PUZZLE 557

```
FAR  SAME  ALSO
AGE  PLEA  SOWN
NOVELIST  SAIL
     RICH  JIMMY
DEBATE  LAS
ICES  TURTLES
SHE  BRAGS  AVE
CONTAIN  OVEN
    ARM  TOWARD
OPALS  LIME
BALE  CAMISOLE
OPEN  UNIT  DAY
EAST  BEDS  DYE
```

PUZZLE 550

```
PAID  SLY  ORES
ACRE  WOE  AERO
SHOE  OBSERVED
TENDER  WEE
    END  CEDRIC
BLADE  PAR  STA
RIP  BET  EAR
AMP  TAG  ADDLE
TEETER  APE
   ARR  STEEDS
BASEMENT  PLOT
AREA  LEE  EIRE
TEST  FOR  RAMP
```

PUZZLE 554

```
B G H S J T S T
A E O A U E X A
L L L R L P X P
E D I S T I T E
N I A E M I T S
E A M R A S
R V R B B D W R
A E E A E E N A
T P R N T R N S
E N E W R E S T
L L R E W R S
O L O G E I A E
N O E A N A D D
O N R T G A A M
M T Y S E N B M
```

PUZZLE 558

```
ASH   HAT       PAL
ROAR  OBI      SOME
TALE  NET      OLEO
ROMEO  AARON
   ARRANGE
MANIA  PIE    RAP
UPON  ARC   LAIR
DEW  EGO  CANDY
   RAINBOW
SPORT  ROYAL
SLAB  AVA  ETON
HOLE  TAN  ROSE
EWE   END   MEW
```

PUZZLE 551

```
GAD   PAS    GAP
EWES  AMI   SALE
MESH  RIP   PIER
   ARID  TONE
ACRES  PRO
CLAPS  JEALOUS
OAT  CLEAN  ANA
BISCUIT  SPRIG
   LED  FIRST
PROD  LATE
VIEW  CAD  SEAL
ELAN  ACE  SAVE
TED   RED   RAT
```

PUZZLE 555

```
HOBO   CAPE  DADS
AVAIL  ANON  OVAL
MANNA  SILL  OONA
   KNOTSLANDING
CAT  DALE  READY
ATHLETE  AGED
BRAIDS  BRED  LIB
BIND  COT  TILE
YAK  CLAW  ACACIA
   LOIN  ARABIAN
PSALM  ABED  TDS
SANTABARBARA
KNEE  ELIE  ERECT
EDEN  ROSS  SERVE
PART  SEES  SAID
```

PUZZLE 559

```
SPAN   SHOWS
SPADES  HEARTS
HARDEN  ENTIRE
ORE  DATES  TAN
PENS  RAT  PEWS
STALER  WORSE
   LAD  PAL
STREW  CARESS
HOES  GAL  STEM
OUT  PANES  OWE
TRIBAL  STARES
SERENE  TAPERS
DENTS  BEDS
```

PUZZLE 552

```
   RAH  PAR  MAR
   ERE  ARE  DALE
   CLASSIFIEDAD
     ODE   REED
     LES  FAD
BEE  CII  CAIN  FRO
OLD  ANN  ADVISER  RAP
ALI  RTE  RAE  TRE  ONA
TAT  OTTO  ASPEN
OTTO      OTT
REO       DROP
IDOLS
ASA  NAP  ADE  MET  ALE
3AL  SCANDAL  ESE  GAD
EDS  OARS  SIR  ERA
   ALY  ASS  SAM
   SALT  HAW
   SOCIETYPAGES
   OMIT  EAT  EVA
   WED  AMA  SET
```

PUZZLE 556

```
PANG   CHAR   SLAM
ALEE   RARE   SCENE
GIVE   AURA   WASTE
EKES   FLAT   INSET
   ERECT  YAWN
   AYE   AGHAST
STUMP  CLAD  ALOE
EASE  GROVE  LIME
TRET  AUTO  NOTES
STREAM   WOO
   GERM  PRIME
CHOSE  OOZE  RAVE
RAVEN  OVEN  ANEW
ALERT  SITE  TINE
MERE   TEAR  EATS
```

PUZZLE 560

```
FIVE    DOE   BOMB
IDEA    INN   EPEE
BEER   SEVEREST
SPLIT  OVENS
IRA    YET
SCREENS      JAB
POUR  TEA  TALE
APE   ADMIRED
   PEA   HAG
RURAL   ERRED
DESERTER  EMUS
ODES  AWE  SIDE
TOSS  RED  STEW
```

PUZZLE 561

```
CLAW STAIR PECK
RIFE PONCE AREA
ANTE RAGED LILT
TEE SIDE ORACLE
ERRANT LILAC
LIED DEPENDS
SCRAP EVENT ARC
LOON STOAT TRIO
OPT SPELL SWEPT
TEETERS SAKI
EMITS CITRUS
OBTAIN TACT ALL
KRIS KNAVE INTO
RIME LURED NERO
AGED ENTRE NEAP
```

PUZZLE 562

```
OTIS SPA UNIT
FACE EAR NODE
FREQUENT COLA
URN IRONER
RADII AFAR
OXEN BLACKTOP
OLE CROCK ONO
MERCHANT TACO
LINE CUTER
ISLAND JON
ROAM INUNDATE
ALTO SEA RIOT
NEER HEN AREA
```

PUZZLE 563

```
PLAY ATOM PAD
LODE ROSA HIE
YUMA GNAT INN
ORLY GUILTY
TUNNEL ERR
ARI GEL EASEL
RISK SEA NERO
ASHES DUD DIG
ETA DOMINO
MAGNUM ITEM
ORR ROOT DEAN
ALI DRNO INGA
TOT YEAR ATOP
```

PUZZLE 564

```
CABIN IRK
OLIVE ERIE
PLATES LONG
ELS STRINGS
PIKE SOD
EARS BEST
RAP DEWY
PARADES TEE
OVEN SKATES
LEAD TIRED
ERR STIES
```

PUZZLE 565

```
TOE FLEW RAMP
URN RAVE ERIE
BELIEVES SILT
AREA TRIALS
BARKS HEAD
RIGS GARMENTS
ADE BARNS ERE
GESTURES HEEL
ENDS MODEL
CREATE GIRL
OILS NEATNESS
IDLE ELSE SIP
LEAD RIPS STY
```

PUZZLE 566

```
LIP HAT TOLL
AVA HIGH OLEO
KANGAROO WETS
ENTIRE USE
LED GARDEN
CURL SHY ADO
ONO WAITS NET
TIM ERR PANE
STEVEN PTA
IDO AORTAS
POST LICORICE
AREA DIET ERA
DEAL SID SET
```

PUZZLE 567

```
AMOR SAD EWER
DELEGATE FACE
ELEVATED FIRE
EDE USEFUL
STARS SCAT
ESNE RETREAT
TAT RAVED LET
REFUTED SORE
ODIN SCENE
STEREO ALE
HOLE NOMINATE
ERAS ADOPTION
DENT LES SLED
```

PUZZLE 568

```
JIGS TSPS SHOP
ORATE ATEE PICO
SONAR GIRL ALEE
ENGINE CODETTAS
PRIG KNOT SNY
ALL EAST MOM
LIAR DOOM NOBEL
MONEY AYE STORE
ANKLE POSH HAMS
YAW USER RAE
AMI ROAR LEAD
SINGSONG MERGES
KNOW LOUT DIANE
MENE EDNA SAMOA
EDEN NEST SEWN
```

PUZZLE 569

Move 2 southwest, 3 northeast, 4 south, 2 northwest.

PUZZLE 570

```
ASTO ASPS ROMP
CHOU FSTOP AMIE
TATTLETALE TART
SHE EROS ENTREE
BONN IDOL
ROMANS SLIVERS
ELATE GALL BOOM
FELT CAGEY RUBE
SILL OVER CASES
NEEDLES BRIERS
ROLL MEAN
MOROSE SALT PTA
OBEY CATTLECARS
TINA TRITE ATEE
HEEL SIRE BETA
```

PUZZLE 571

PAT/IENT/LY

PUZZLE 572

```
AFTER TRASH STEMS
TAILOR ACHES SADAT
RILED ASTOR STARE
ERECT PEPPER EDIE
EMIT ALTERS AMEND
SADE PARTON PINES
TRADE GEESE INTRA
ASS TREX REED TATI
RARE EREFER ARDEN
TRITE ANALOG OAST
LAPEL LOLLER ASTA
ABES STOKER ASTIN
DIANE OLIVE STONE
DARIN SALE SPENDS
SNAPS SNORT ARGOT
```

PUZZLE 573

```
CALF DABS UNTO
LIAR ELATE ROOD
EDDY LADYBEGOOD
FEY PACE BRINKS
FRANK STAN
FRIEND SHINGLE
RINDS STADT AMP
IAGO SPUME EDIE
ONE ATONE STYLE
TREMORS LINGER
SAKE MACAO
CHASTE HOWE DEB
MYFAIRLADY FIVE
ILAY SEGUE IVES
VARS USSR RANT
```

PUZZLE 574

There once was a young man named
Gale,
Who cherished the thought of a sail.
He boarded a yacht,
But remained on his cot,
Except when he hung o'er the rail.

PUZZLE 575

```
SALAD STOAT MIG
ALONE SPARSE SOON
IODIN NORTHDAKOTA
DEE SHAKES LUNAR
UKES CHIN
ALI AMEN CHUCKLED
SERAPIS CRANE AVE
PEERED COURT STAY
LAD BURST FEE
MOAB CARAT SOARED
ANN BASEL CARTAGO
REDDENED CALK NOG
ANTS CAPE
SCARE CAROMS DIP
PLANTAGENET HOUSE
OURS SEDATE ABELE
TEE KEELS MILER
```

PUZZLE 576

```
GNAT NESTS TRADE
ATLAS IDEAS SOARED
THEBELLSARERINGING
LEE ILE ATE
MATE DUMBBELLS
ALI SATIRE BAN
TAN CRUDEST EVA
ASKED ASH LAY
ERIN STILL
RACES SADAT
BLEAT REDO
ADE SPA REWET
GEL GREATLY ERR
ELL EERIER RIO
BELLICOSE USED
EVE ARE GOP
BELLBOTTOMTROUSERS
RELIES ALIEN RELIT
OPALS TEXAS TIDY
```

PUZZLE 577

```
ALTO THAT  JAPAN
QUIP RACE  EXILE
UNDEFINED  RENEW
AGE RAG  ILK  GET
     GAL SUE
TARRY WOMAN  VIM
OBOE SAD  DOMINO
POVERTY  FEDERAL
AVENUE BAN  TUNA
ZED  BRAID LASER
     END PAL
SPA JOT  FEZ  HAS
LARGE HOLLYHOCK
ALIAS EDIT  ANTI
BEAST METS  TEST
```

PUZZLE 578

1. As, Case, Chases, Shackles; 2. Be, Bode, Combed, Combined; 3. Do, Road, Adores, Assorted; 4. Is, Stir, Sprint, Pointers; 5. Do, Mood, Domino, Demotion; 6. No, Noon, Onions, Snoozing; 7. Of, Fort, Softer, Fortunes; 8. Pa, Plea, Sample, Tramples.

PUZZLE 579

```
SLAV  FADE  GALAS
NISI  ALIM  OLIGO
AMIR  LOVERSLEAP
PASA  LEANTO  NTP
     GAS DEMPSEY
BARONIAL  SEE
ELI ALLAH  WRATH
SPLITLEVELHOUSE
TEETH  MAKIE  BAR
     CES RETRIERS
KASHMIR  TES
ONT ALINER  LAME
ANASTOMOSE  AMOS
LEROI  APTS  NILS
ATTIC  LEES  DELE
```

PUZZLE 580

1. Lionel Richie, 2. Frank Sinatra, 3. Andy Williams, 4. Barry Manilow, 5. Neil Sedaka, 6. Elvis Presley, 7. Glen Campbell, 8. Michael Jackson.

PUZZLE 581

```
ATE    GAL    JAB
HERB TAROT  SALE
ANNE ARENA  TREE
 DEFERS  EXPOSE
   OVA TRIAL
DARE  ERS  CEDE
AIDE AVA  SESAME
LEO SNAPPER  TOW
STREET POE  PETE
SERE  RED  POSE
   ADDER FOR
 PASSED  WRITES
PARE EERIE  EVIL
ALES SEINE  RETE
LEA    MOO    NEE
```

PUZZLE 582

1. Clover, 2. Celery, 3. Orange, 4. Carrot, 5. Orchid, 6. Radish, 7. Turnip, 8. Barley, 9. Nettle, 10. Catnip.

PUZZLE 583

```
LIP  PRIM   RITE
ORE  IOTA   AMOS
RES  AMERICANS
ESSEN       STE
    IRONS ADORE
CAME ETAL   LON
ALI  PERRY  EDO
LES  EDAM  MASS
METER  PYLON
     LOB ANDES
MARINATED   ELL
ANET  SEAL  RIA
TIDE  SATE  SAY
```

PUZZLE 584

```
ERAS  NET   HOST
LAST  ARE   ALEE
SNEAKPREVIEWS
AGAIN      IRONS
     REF SAC
AND  ELAN   UTAH
DOUBLEFEATURE
ODOR  ETAL   BIN
     ANT DAS
STOWE      RAWER
WORLDPREMIERE
ANNE  EON   NAIL
BEER  ADD   TREY
```

PUZZLE 585

```
TAPE   POTS   SODA
ORAL  CANOE  AVER
TOSS  OPENS  LENT
ASTERN  SEASONS
LEE  ITS   MEN
   PEP DEW ERA
EACH  NAME  NOVEL
ACHE  TRAMP DEEM
START  EPEE  ENDS
ESP  HIS   ARE
   AID NIB GAS
 WITNESS  OBTAIN
GIRL  AWARD RUSE
ARIA  LANES OGLE
LESS  SPED  DEER
```

PUZZLE 586

P	STRIPE	RITES	TIRE	S
R	TRIALS	TAILS	SLAT	I
E	GREASE	RAGES	EARS	G
T	MOTHER	HOMER	MORE	H
T	RATTLE	LATER	REAL	T
Y	YEARNS	SNARE	NEAR	S

PUZZLE 587

```
SLAP  SAC   TROT
CAPE  ILL   RODE
ATOP  ALE   ETON
BEDLAM   ALBERT
     UTE  TIL
CALMEST   DEPOT
ADO   EAT   ERE
LAYER   GRIMACE
     LOB  ANA
ONSIDE   UNITES
VOID  VIM   DASH
ETTE  ERA   ELSE
REED  LAS   NEED
```

PUZZLE 588

```
ARIA  RIM   PASS
LENS  ELA   IDEA
ONTHESLY    READ
ETHER      ODA
    ESNE ROTATE
DEW  ELF   MELON
URI  LAD    LOT
MINES  TAN  ATE
BEDLAM   MOAT
     PIE ALOHA
SOFA  CASHINON
ARES  CIA   ACRE
TODO  ARC   SENT
```

PUZZLE 589

```
RAKE   FLAT  TYRO
AREA  GRATE  REED
PIES  AORTA  ALEE
TAPERS  DISTILL
    LOTS  REAL
CAB ART ESP  TOT
AGRARIAN   SCOPE
PIER  CRISP OPEN
ELECT  PERSPIRE
RED ADS TOW  CAT
    GREW  SCAN
CRYSTAL   EMOTES
DEEP  ETUDE VIAL
IDES  SHRED ALSO
DEFY  TEEN  STEW
```

PUZZLE 590

1. Lolita, 2. Lassie, 3. Juliet, 4. Judith, 5. Martha, 6. Amelia, 7. Rachel, 8. Gracie, 9. Jennie, 10. Elaine, 11. Miriam, 12. Emilie.

PUZZLE 591

```
CHAR  COMMA  GRAB
LOBE  AREAS  ROLE
ALEC  RASPS  OPAL
DELI   ETA URGENT
    PALE  ARE
SERENE   PRESENTS
TEA  TSARS TRAIL
ARIA  SLOOP EIRE
LISLE  INNER  VEE
KEEPSAKE   NICEST
     PIE  RIPE
ALLAYS   GOT  ACRE
LOAM  LEAVE SAIL
ANTI  ELLEN EROS
SEED  SMART SATE
```

559

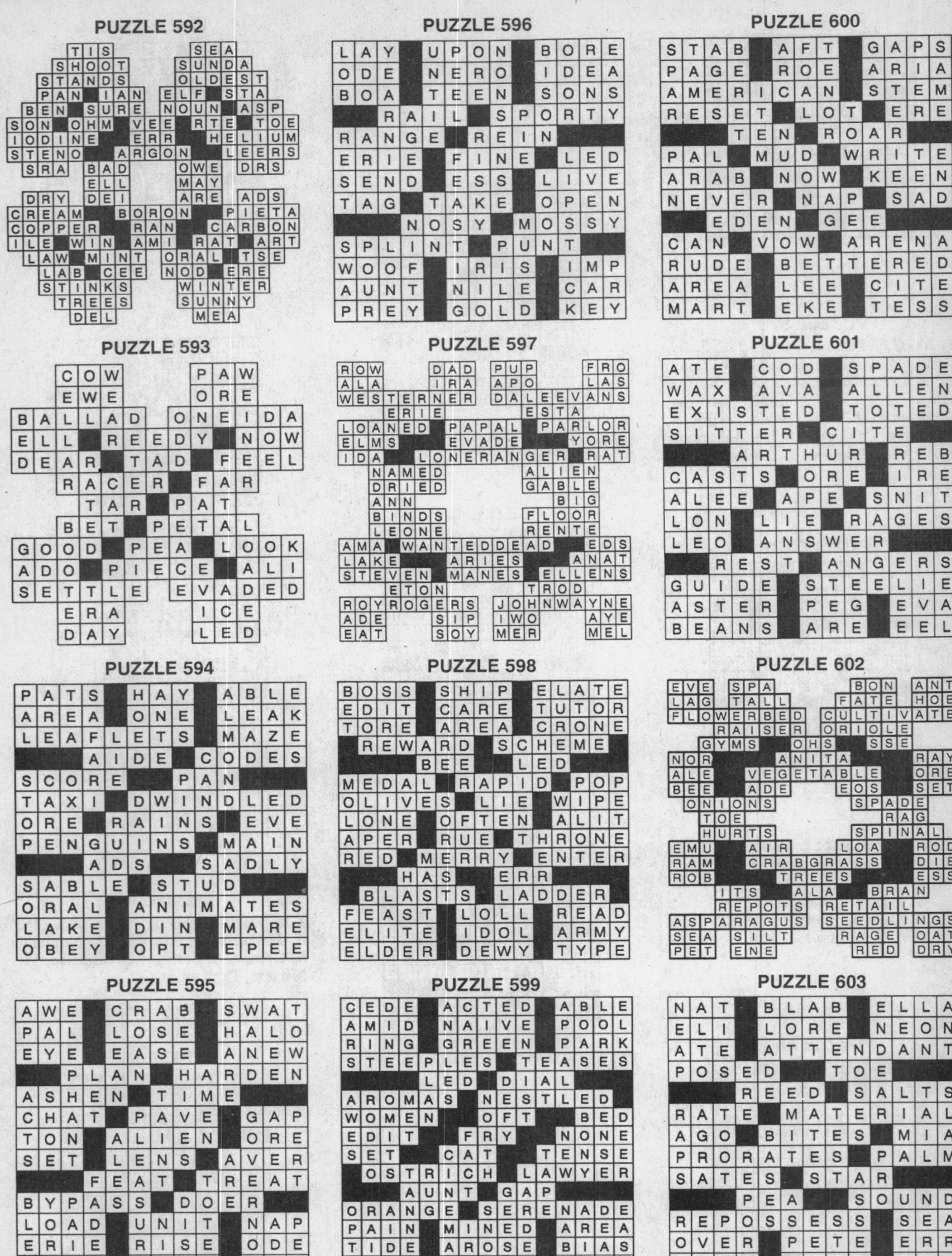

PUZZLE 604

```
OWES   ACTS   ATE
ARCH   POOL   IRK
FARO   PLEA   RUE
SPURNED   TAPES
   TOT   ELL
NIL   DIME   LAST
ARE   STONE   NEE
BEAD   EDDY   EWE
   FOG   EEL
PALER   CASINOS
ADE   AFAR   MANE
POT   NOSE   BITE
ASS   DEED   SLOP
```

PUZZLE 605

```
FROG   LOG   RACE
LIVE   OUR   OVAL
ITEM   SNOOPERS
PER   RECOVERS
   TIE   EVER
CLUMP   SER   CAP
PURPLE   STOOGE
AVE   APE   IDIOT
   ACID   MEN
   SAFESIDE   CUB
ANTIDOTE   HIRE
BAER   DOE   EDGE
EPEE   ERR   MEET
```

PUZZLE 606

```
   RATE   PASS
   OXEN   ALEE
RECENT   NEEDLE
ARK   ELI   AID
TIE   ROC   TAG
SETTO   WHERE
   IN   HO
SHAPE   YEAST
TOP   TNT   MOO
ALP   ROB   ALL
BEETLE   OPENED
   ARIA   NERD
   RAPT   ETNA
```

PUZZLE 607

```
FUN   FITS   PROS
EGO   IDOL   ROLL
ELM   DAME   ANDY
LYING   ELI
   NEED   POSSUM
SCATTER   GEESE
TOT   WAG   PER
ELECT   MANMADE
WASHED   SOAR
   ONE   OPALS
MOPS   ERAS   TAP
ERIE   DALE   EVE
TEEN   SPAS   DAD
```

PUZZLE 608

```
SAD   EAR   SPA
ORES   SLOP   TEN
NEAT   SAME   RAY
GALES   SELLER
   WOO   TEA
CONSUMED   EMIT
ADO   RARER   ERA
NERD   RELOADED
   SUN   LAD
   REDONE   MOTOR
MOM   OATH   RIPE
ATE   KITE   EDEN
DEN   LAX   END
```

PUZZLE 609

```
FAZE  SLAP  GAFF  DAMP
IRON  TUTU  ELIA  EPEE
LEOS  AGES  TANS  WERE
MAKINGS  HOUSEHOLDER
  EGOS  GULP  IDA
OPENS  TAPE  WOODPILE
NIPS  DIGS  EARNS  LED
CEE  SAPS  MAIDS  EKED
ERRANDS  GESSO  BOSSY
  BAA  CADET  PIN
STOUP  PUMAS  CLASPED
TOUT  MOTEL  PIUS  RNA
ITS  ZONES  BUNG  PEON
RETAINER  WILE  PASSE
  BOO  HARP  GAPE
SAVINGGRACE  ANDORRA
OVID  ROOT  TACO  OVER
SOLE  ABLE  TRIM  SEAM
OWED  MILD  AIDE  ESPY
```

PUZZLE 610

```
READ   FISH   DUB
ACHE   ERIE   ORE
CHOP   DILIGENT
YOYOS   SODA
   SIT   IGLOO
INTEREST   SING
COW   EXERT   EEL
EPIC   TEAHOUSE
DENIM   PAR
   TONE   NAVEL
CHEERILY   NERO
OUR   ACME   GIRD
PEA   LEST   ELSE
```

PUZZLE 611

```
BED   TENS   REDO
ORE   ATIP   AVID
BASEBALL   VEND
   ALS   APER
MASSE   STINGER
ANTE   ROTE   RAE
SIR   CEDES   EVE
OLE   LIAR   DEES
NEATENS   TENSE
   MOOD   AIL
DIET   EARNINGS
ACRE   ERIE   OOP
MESS   REDS   TOY
```

PUZZLE 612

```
T I N   A R E A   W I N K
W O E   D E A N   I R A N
O U T S M A R T   R O B E
    L I D S   R I N S E
I D I O T   M A N
C E N T   D R U G G I S T
E L K   B R U T E   S E A
D I S C O U N T   F L A G
    E L M   R E E L S
A D U L T   S C A R
L U R E   C U L I N A R Y
D E A R   O R A L   L Y E
A L L Y   G E M S   L E T
```

PUZZLE 613

```
D I R K   P L Y   E D G Y
I R A N   R O E   R O L E
G E N E R O U S   E D E N
    G E E   D E A C O N S
T W I L L S   S I T
O R E   Y A M   M E D A L
N E S T   T A B   D E L I
E N T E R   Y I P   V A N
    A Y E   B E G O N E
T I M B E R S   A R T
A R E A   U P S T A I R S
L O N G   P U P   P O E T
E N D S   T R Y   E N V Y
```

PUZZLE 614

```
  M A C   F L O   R E A P
L I S A   T R A P   S A L L E
A S I S   R E S T   T R E A T
R E D H E A D S   G R E E N E
A R E   V I A   L I E
    A L S   E L E A N O R
A P E R   E T A S   T R A D E
L A T E   R A I L S   O M E N
A R T I E   I D I E   W E S T
S T A N D E R   E R E
    D O E   C P A   G A L
M A D E I N   H A I R Y A P E
A D E L E   M A R C   E Y R E
K A R L S   O M O O   A L I S
E M M A   D A N   R E L
```

PUZZLE 615

```
E A C H   M A L E   A L I T
R A R E   S O L O N   B E D E
I R O N   C O A S T   O N E S
S E W   H O R S E R A D I S H
    S T A R E   A N E N T
C A N I N E   B A N N S
A M E N D   D A N C E   S T A
P E S T   D A N T E   S C A B
A N T   S E R G E   F L A M E
    C A S E S   S O A P E D
    S L A V E   B A R G E
B E A V E R B O A R D   G O T
E A V E   V E R S E   S O L E
S T E R   E L A T E   S A L E
T O R N   D A N E   S T A N
```

PUZZLE 616

```
M A L T   C A T   B E A D
A L O E   H U E   U G L Y
M A I N   A N E C D O T E
A N T   D I T T O   S O D
    E M U S   H I P
S C R I B E   E L E C T S
P O E M   R O O K
A D D I N G   G U I L T Y
    C A R   I S L E
S U E   G A U G E   S A D
O P P O S I N G   E L S E
S O I L   N I L   R A I N
O N C E   S T Y   A W A Y
```

PUZZLE 617

```
E O N   S H A H   F A I L
A L A   M A C E   E C R U
R E T A I L E R   W H I R
    I D L E   G E E S E
E R O D E   M R S
P E N S   T R E A T I N G
I D A   G R I M Y   L O U
C O L O R A D O   P L U S
    B O Y   D A U N T
S C R E W   S I R S
A H O Y   N O O N T I D E
W I D E   A B L E   O U R
S P E D   P I E D   N E E
```

PUZZLE 618

```
W I D E   A H E M   A L A
I D E A   S O L O   M A R
T A B S   H E I R L O O M
    T O E D   M E S S Y
S H R E W S   V O N
L E A R N   B A N D I T S
U R N   D O T   O R E
R E G A L I A   M O T O R
    N A G   V A C A T E
S O B E R   A I D E
C H E W I E S T   L O B E
A I R   A R E A   O B E Y
B O G   T E A L   T I D E
```

PUZZLE 619

```
S H O T     H E L P
S T O W E D   S E R I E S
C O R N E R   T R A N C E
R O N   M A N E D   N A T
A G E D   B E E   T E N S
P E T A L   S L E E T S
    R E S T E R S
M A N D E L   S T A R T
M A R S   V E E   S L E W
A R C   L E D G E   L E E
T R A D E R   G R I E V E
S E D A T E   S I N G E D
D E B S     E K E S
```